P9-DZO-119

SAIL PERFORMANCE

TECHNIQUES TO MAXIMIZE SAIL POWER

SAIL PERFORMANCE

TECHNIQUES TO MAXIMIZE SAIL POWER

C A MARCHAJ

INTERNATIONAL MARINE
Camden, Maine

Published by International Marine,
a division of The McGraw-Hill Companies

10 9 8 7 6 5 4 3 2 1

Published in 1996 in Great Britain by Adlard Coles Nautical,
an imprint of A & C Black (Publishers) Ltd., London.
This edition based on *Sailing Theory and Practice* by C. A. Marchaj,
first published by Adlard Coles in 1964.

Copyright © 1990 C. A. Marchaj

A CIP catalog record for this book is available from the Library of Congress.

ISBN 0-07-040250-7

Typeset in 10 on 13pt Baskerville by Falcon Oast Graphic Art, Wallington, Surrey
Printed and bound in Great Britain by Butler and Tanner Ltd, Frome, Somerset

CONTENTS

PREFACE

More than thirty years have passed since I wrote *Sailing Theory and Practice* in which the aerodynamic performance of sails was discussed in some detail. The continuing demand for a book of this nature has been most encouraging and the present volume is a response to this request.

In the interim, much water has flowed under the bottoms of sailing boats, and there have been many advances and developments in the field of sail aerodynamics. These developments enlarged our understanding of a number of issues and also factors which determine how much power a given sail configuration can extract from the wind.

One may enjoy sailing without understanding what forces or physical phenomena are involved. On the other hand, there are people – perhaps the majority – who want to know how and why a sailing boat moves. After all, the efficient operation of any sailing craft, or designing an efficient rig for a given purpose, largely depends on understanding the 'how' and 'why' of sail aerodynamics. Besides, sailors with an inquiring mind may enjoy additional pleasure when they can exercise their brains as well. To quote Darwin: '... I discovered, unconsciously at first, that the pleasures of observing and reasoning were much higher ones than those of ... sport.'

My primary aim in writing this book was mainly to satisfy the second category of sailing people, and to set down the principles of sail aerodynamics as clearly as I could, incorporating the most important recent developments. The book is aimed specifically at the reader who is familiar with elementary mathematics but has no knowledge of aerodynamics. Almost all quantitative statements are given in the form of simple graphs rather than mathematical formulae. Graphs can usually demonstrate a given property more clearly than by other means. This is why most people prefer visual impressions to abstract words. The text leans heavily towards the intuitive approach, and illustrations are used to explain the meanings of terms or concepts used whenever possible.

Some readers, whilst turning over the pages of this book, may notice the omission of topics which they might consider to be of importance, such as, for example, the computational sail shape design. However, this type of book is not intended for specialists but for practical sailors who have no desire to become professional sailmakers.

The views expressed in this book should never be regarded as dogmatic. Sailing theory, like any other theory or interpretation of physical facts observed in nature is not self-terminating but to use P W Bridgman's words: '... it can always be pushed indefinitely with continually accumulating refinements.' Moreover, any science contains not only truth, but also half truths and plain errors – *Hominis est errare*!

R Feyman put this matter admirably in his famous *Lectures on Physics*: 'In fact, everything we know is only some kind of approximation, because *we know that we do not know all the laws* as yet. Therefore, things must be learned only to be unlearned again or, more likely, to be corrected' ... '*The test of all knowledge is experiment*. Experiment is the *sole judge* of scientific "truth".'

Features of this book include the comparative wind tunnel tests on fourteen different rigs. What may surprise some readers is that the ubiquitous Bermudian rig of sailing boats is not necessarily the fastest. A number of traditional rigs, used nowadays mainly by small fishing vessels, are potentially more powerful. Even when sailing close-hauled the sprit and gaff rigs proved to be superior. Despite being of higher aspect ratio and requiring a significantly higher mast, the Bermudian rig tested may in some conditions prove to be 40 per cent less efficient in terms of driving force than the rectangular sprit rig. These results are likely to stir a controversial discussion of something that '... has been a regular subject of conversation among boatmen since the first cave-men climbed on to a log for a ride downstream'. A conversation in which an irrational, emotional opinion – such as the following: 'Yes, it may not be the handiest of rigs, but I love it, and I use it, because it is so beautiful' – may clash with a rational argument based on numbers derived from impartial wind tunnel tests. 'Of only one thing do I feel sure' observed D Desouter in one of his articles in *Practical Boat Owner* 'that there is no "best" rig. There is only the rig that any particular owner likes the best.'

In bringing this book up to date, an important addition has been made in Part 3. This deals with the rather extraordinary behaviour of foils in unsteady, non-uniform wind – the so called Katzmayer effect. For too long, unsteady flow aerodynamics dealing with foils operating in non-uniform wind, ie unsteady in velocity and/or direction, has been seen as a subject for specialists and of limited application. However, sailing boats operate, as a rule, in unsteady flow conditions. And, in a sense, it is just *steady*, uniform flow aerodynamics that are peculiar, and an almost unattainable ideal. It is known that the true wind (V_T), and so the apparent wind (V_A), is never steady. The same applies to the hull appendages: keel and rudder. The motion of a sailing boat is essentially unsteady. The disturbance velocities due to wind gustiness and wave action (rolling, yawing) are frequently not insignificant relative to the characteristic velocity of the boat. Thus, the hull appendages, like sails, are also subject to unsteady flow.

The fact is that a non-uniform flow has more kinetic energy than a steady, uniform flow with the same average velocity. And it was experimentally demonstrated that due to the effect of periodic oscillations in the airstream, the drag can considerably be reduced, and even at times change from a positive to a negative value. What it actually means is that energy is, in some way, being drawn from the pulsating wind to do the work of propelling the foil against the wind direction. This seems at first to suggest perpetual motion, but this effect is already exploited in nature by some fish and birds. Whether such an advantage can or will be utilized by sailors, only time will tell. However, one thing appears to be certain: the sail efficiency, (expressed, say, in terms of L/D ratio) measured in a conventional wind tunnel, tends to be underestimated compared with real sail efficiency manifested in natural sailing conditions. In other words, a model test of sails in the conventional wind tunnel with uniform wind almost always violates the important requirement of dynamic similarity.

Every effort has been made to annotate the book with well-chosen references, so that readers requiring more information than is given here may go directly to available literature on the subject.

C A Marchaj

ACKNOWLEDGEMENTS

A book of this nature could not have been written without the help and co-operation of many individuals and some organisations. I especially thank Jeremy Howard-Williams for his unfailing help in the wind tunnel work when we carried out tests on a number of traditional sailing rigs. These tests could never have been done without co-operation with MacAlister Elliott and Partners Ltd who on behalf of the Overseas Development Administration of the British Government carried out the research programme. With gratitude I would further mention the ever-benevolent interest of Ian Hannay who occasionally came to my assistance in the wind tunnel, and who read the manuscript and gave many hours of his time to discussion of the problems of presentation in the book. I want also to thank Mike Brettle and Mike Molyneux of the Meteorological Office Research Unit, RAF Cardington, who generously let me have the data and graphs pertaining to the coastal winds. This part of my preface can not be closed without expressing my heartfelt appreciation to Janet Murphy, Editor of Adlard Coles Nautical, who held me firmly to the commitment and waited with extraordinary tact and patience for a result.

My final acknowledgement to the authors of the references must be of a rather different sort. Much of this book is derived from their work and I should like to express my gratitude to them, but without saddling them with any responsibility for the views the book now contains.

LIST OF SYMBOLS

$AR = \dfrac{b^2}{S_A}$ = aspect ratio

b = height of the sail (span)

c = chord of the sail section

C_D = aerodynamic drag coefficient

C_{fr} = friction coefficient

C_H = aerodynamic heeling force coefficient

C_L = aerodynamic lift force coefficient

C_R = aerodynamic driving force coefficient

C_T = aerodynamic total force coefficient

CB = centre of buoyancy

CG = centre of gravity

CE = centre of effort

CLR = centre of lateral resistance

D = aerodynamic drag

D_i = induced drag

DWL = designed waterline

E_n = entry angle (air)

f = depth of the sail camber

F_H = heeling force (normal to the course sailed)

F_{lat} = horizontal component of the heeling force

F_R = driving force (along the course sailed)

F_s = hull side force

F_T = total aerodynamic force

F_V = vertical (downward) component of the sail force

F_x = driving force acting along the hull centreline

F_Y = heeling force normal to the hull centreline

g = acceleration due to gravity 32.2 ft/sec^2

I = height of the fore–triangle

J = base of the fore–triangle

L = length of the hull and also lift force

L_w = length of the wave (sea wave)

LOA = length overall

LWL = load waterline

M_H = heeling moment

M_R = righting moment

p = static pressure

q = dynamic pressure = $\rho\dfrac{V^2}{2}$

R = total hydrodynamic resistance of the hull

Re = Reynolds Number

R_T = total hydrodynamic force on a hull

S_A = sail area

S_J = jib streamlines

S_t = stagnation point

V_A = apparent wind velocity

V_{mg} = speed made good to windward

V_S = boat's velocity

V_T = true wind velocity

W = weight of the yacht

$\triangle$ = displacement in long tons or pounds

$\triangledown$ = immersed volume in cu ft corresponding to the displacement

α (alpha) = angle of incidence of the sail

α_F = angle of incidence of the foresail

α_M = angle of incidence of the main sail

β (beta) = apparent course

$(\beta - \lambda)$ = heading

γ (gamma) = true course

δ_F (delta) = angle of trim of the foresail

δ_M = angle of trim of the mainsail

ε_A (epsilon) = aerodynamic drag angle

ε_H = hydrodynamic drag angle

θ (theta) = angle of heel

λ (lambda) = angle of leeway

ν (nu) = kinematic viscosity:
air $\quad 1.57 \times 10^{-4}$ ft^2/sec
water $\;1.23 \times 10^{-5}$ ft^2/sec

ρ_A (rho) = mass density of air: 0.00238 lb sec^2/ft^4

ρ_W = mass density of water:
fresh 1.94 lb sec^2/ft^4
salt $\;$ 1.99 lb sec^2/ft^4

PART 1

YACHT EVOLUTION, RATING FORMULAE AND SPEED PERFORMANCE

1 • SPEED AND SIZE

'It is hard to say whether it is or is not in the best interest of the sport of yachting that sailing craft should be such very unpredictable creatures. Scientifically, they present a problem so complex that a complete solution is quite out of the question... Above all, good reader, beware of him who claims knowledge of yacht design, for we know only about the rudiments – the rest is conjecture.'

J Laurent Giles

Sailing has grown enormously in popularity as a means of sport and recreation in the last three decades. Most recent major developments, resulting in a large variety of types of contemporary sailing craft, have been inspired by a desire for greater speed. It appears that the fascination with speed for speed's sake has more of a hold today than ever before. 'Unthinkable' futuristic shapes – some resembling aeroplanes more than boats – and the speed records achieved have captured the public attention and attracted almost unlimited financial sponsorship, without which such creations could not have appeared and proliferated so rapidly.

Speed fever, which has descended recently on a large part of the sailing population is well reflected in the cartoons by Chris Wood (Figs 1a and 1b) and rather differently in Fig 2 by an exponential curve. Fig 2 and Table 1 illustrate the increase in speed recorded by a variety of sailing craft during their west–east transatlantic passages over the last 130 years or so (1.1)*.

*Numbers in brackets refer to the References and Notes at the end of the book.

Fig 1a

Speed fever!
In one of the scientific papers on future wind driven ships we read: '...to be credible the novel design must differ from all previous commercial ships and from all yachts except small catamarans and specially built record breakers.'

All sorts of novelties, all geared towards higher speed, are being worked out in scientific establishments or in designers' fertile imaginations. And, of course, the advertising sponsor dictates that spectator interest be created and catered to.
Courtesy: Chris Wood

Table 1

Relative speeds Vs/√LWL achieved by some outstanding mono and multihulls when sailing across the Atlantic west–east.

YEAR	NAME OF YACHT	TYPE	LWL FT	BDR MILES	$V_s/\sqrt{LWL}$	REMARKS
1851	*America*	mono	90	284	1.25	Speed V_s for
1866	*Henrietta*	"	84	280	1.27	all boats is that
1866	*Alice*	"	48	207	1.24	of the best day's
1869	*Sappho*	"	121	315	1.19	run (BDR)
1887	*Coronet*	"	124	291	1.09	
1905	*Atlantic*	"	135	342	1.23	– record 12 d 4 hrs
1928	*Elena*	"	96	282	1.20	
1931	*Dorade*	"	37	210	1.44	
1935	*Vamarie*	"	54	222	1.26	
1952	*Caribbee*	"	44	212	1.33	
1977	*But*	"	70	298	1.48	– ex Ondine III
1980	*Desperado*	ULDB	47	245	1.49	
1981	*Kriter VIII*	"	62	304	1.61	
1983	*La Vie Claire*	"	213	447	1.28	– ex Club Mediterranée
1988	*Phocea*	"	213	490	1.42	– record 8 d 3 hrs 29 min
1979	*Kriter IV*	tri	66	340	1.74	
1980	*Paul Ricard*	tri	46	357	2.19	– record E Tabarly 10 d 5 hrs 14 min 20 sec
1981	*Elf Aquitaine*	cat	62	370	1.96	
1981	*Sidinox*	proa	52	350	2.02	ex *Funambule*
1981	*FMV*	cat	60	361	1.94	ex *Sea Falcon*
1981	*Le Turnesol*	tri	46	312	1.92	ex *VSD II*
1981	*Fleury Michon IV*	cat	42	301	1.94	
1981	*Dict Robert*	tri	50	301	1.77	ex *Cap 33*
1981	*Gautier II*	tri	43	250	1.59	
1981	*Brittany Ferries*	tri	60	400	2.15	
1982	*Gauliosis IV*	tri	42	325	2.09	
1984	*Jet Services II*	cat	60	433	2.33	– record P Morvan 8 d 16 hrs 36 min
1984	*Formula Tag*	cat	74	420	2.03	
1984	*William Saurin*	tri	80	447	2.08	
1986	*Royale II*	cat	80	468	2.18	– record 7 d 21 hrs 5 min
1987	*Fleury Michon*	tri	75			7 d 12 hrs 50 min
1988	*Jet Services V*	cat	75	454	2.18	7 d 6 hrs 30 min
1990	*Jet Services V*	cat	75			record S Madec 6 d 13 hrs 3 min

ULDB stands for ultra light displacement boat

By January 1995 the record passage achieved by Serge Madec and his crew, sailing *Jet Services V*, still holds. No doubt further improvement in speed for this type of craft will be increasingly more difficult.

Fig 1b Speed fever! *Fantastique!* How daring they are! Without the handicap of rating restrictions, wingmasts, hydrofoils, water ballast, winglets and so on are now being experimented with in earnest. *Courtesy: Chris Wood*

The increase in speed plotted against time (Fig 2) is expressed in terms of 'relative speed', that is speed/length ratio $V_s/\sqrt{LWL}$. These terms refer to the fact (well known since William Froude's findings and publications at the end of the 19th century) that simply increasing the size of the vessel, with no change in basic design philosophy, will increase its sailing speed roughly in proportion to the square root of the increase in the waterline length of the hull. Thus, for instance, if the size of the hull is increased twofold, all other things being equal, its potential speed should increase roughly in proportion to $\sqrt{2} = 1.41$ ie about 40 per cent. Therefore when comparing the speeds of different types of sailing craft 'size for size', it is not speed alone that should be used as a yardstick of the design excellence or the crew achievement, but speed in relation to the length of the craft ie the relative speed $V_s/\sqrt{LWL}$. In other words, in order to compare objectively the speed potential of boats of different length, one must reduce them to the same '*corrected*' length.

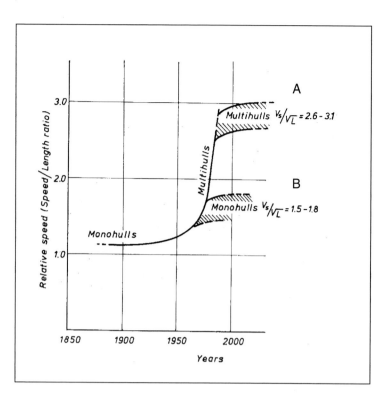

Fig 2 The sailing speed of the best day's run (BDR) achieved by mono and multi-hulls, expressed in terms of their speed/length ratios and plotted against the year of the relevant west-east transatlantic passage (Ref 1.1). If one examines the speed controlling factors such as, for example, displacement/length ratios or sail area/displacement ratios, one must conclude that none of them is likely to exceed some ultimate limit. Nothing can grow or increase indefinitely, and all growth curves (including those relevant to speed records) eventually flatten off.

2 • THE TRADITIONAL CRUISING YACHT CONCEPT

'Both men and ships live in an unstable element, are subject to subtle and powerful influences, and want to have their merits understood rather than their faults found out.'

J Conrad, The Mirror of the Sea

It was Dr Davidson, the pioneering researcher on boat performance, who wrote around 1950 that 'Modern cruising and racing yachts [monohulls] are descendants of the large square rigged ships of a hundred years ago rather than of the small log canoes of antiquity. They reflect much the same philosophy as the ships, *in the balance struck between speed and other qualities*' (the italics are mine), other qualities being their cargo-carrying capacity and sea-keeping ability (Ref 1.2). In other words, the desire for speed had to be tempered in varying degrees to produce thoroughly reliable sailing vessels which were able to keep the seas in *all* reasonable weather all year round. During this period, until early 1960, and despite some spasmodic, shortlived heresies, the prevailing belief was that the basic quality needed in sailing boats designed for deep water (fishing vessels, pilot cutters and yachts alike) was the ability to survive, *not speed alone* (Ref 1.3). The famous *Jolie Brise* shown in Fig 3 can be regarded as the epitome of such a philosophy. E G Martin, at one time her owner, and founder of the Royal Ocean Racing Club, expressed this philosophy briefly: 'Provided she is weatherly, and absolutely dependable in all conditions of wind and sea, it seems to me to be *far more important* that she should be steady and comfortable in rough water, than that she should sail very fast.'

Fig 3 *Jolie Brise*, LOA 56 ft, LWL 48 ft, draft 10.2 ft, sail area 2400 sq ft, was one of the most successful and consistent boats to race in the early Fastnets, winning in 1925, 1929 and 1930, and coming 2nd in 1928. Built in 1913 as a Le Havre pilot cutter, *Jolie Brise* is now owned by Dauntsey's school and is run in conjunction with the Exeter Maritime Museum.

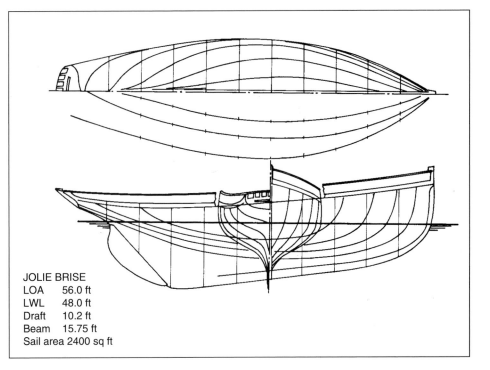

JOLIE BRISE
LOA   56.0 ft
LWL   48.0 ft
Draft   10.2 ft
Beam   15.75 ft
Sail area 2400 sq ft

This definite view can be found incorporated into the fundamental objectives of both the Royal Ocean Racing Club (RORC) in Great Britain and those of the Cruising Club of America (CCA): 'to make it possible for yachtsmen to race seaworthy, cruising boats of various design, types and construction on a fair and equitable basis.' In a report on the aims of the CCA the following views were expressed: 'The Cruising Club of America, as its name proclaims and its constitution declares, is organized to promote cruising... The cruiser chooses his rig, the type of hull, and fixes upon all the details with an eye single to the comforts, convenience and safety of cruising. After all these ends have been accomplished, he will add all features contributing to speed that are not inconsistent with the demand of his ideal cruiser. The real fact must always remain that *the cruising boat cannot be a racer*!' (the italics are mine).

Figures 4–9 illustrate some of the well-known yachts of the past which were designed according to the conventional wisdom of the dominant group of yachtsmen of that time and were acceptable to them (Ref 1.4).

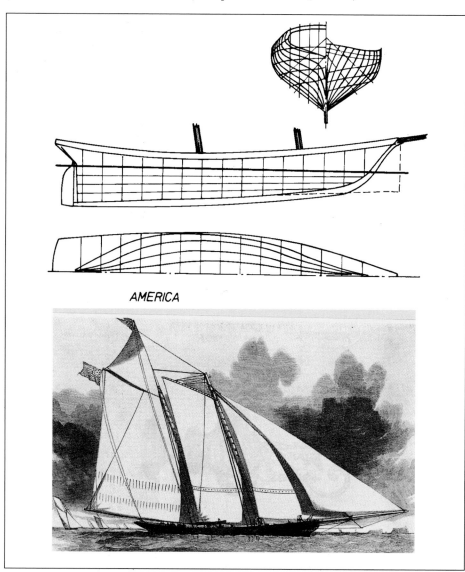

AMERICA

Fig 4 *America*, designed by G Steers, well known for his pilot cutter designs, was launched on 1 May 1851. She was probably the only yacht in history to be guaranteed by her builder, Mr W H Brown, who had undertaken to deliver the schooner on the following conditions: '...if the umpire decides that she is faster than any vessel in the United States, you are to have the right, instead of accepting her at that time, to send her to England, match her against anything built there, which in your judgement gives her a fair chance in a trial of speed and, if beaten, reject her altogether...' Who would take a similar risk today?

America was sent to England. She proceeded under sail from Sandy Hook, New Jersey, to reach Le Havre, France in 19 days and 23 hours. Her North Atlantic passage of 3095 nautical miles indicated that a well designed yacht could safely venture beyond coastal waters. Thus *America* set the stage as the first transoceanic yacht race in what is now known as the America's Cup (Ref 1.1).

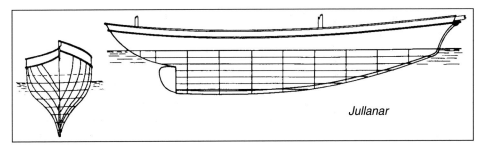

Jullanar

Fig 5 *Jullanar* LOA 110.5 ft, LWL 99 ft, draft 13.5 ft, displacement 126 tons. Designed by E H Bentall in 1875 in cooperation with J Harvey, boat builder, she may be regarded as an example of the influence of Froude's theory of resistance on yacht design. An attempt was made to drastically reduce the wetted surface of the hull by a cut in the fore-foot, although the salient traditional features of fishing and pilot boats of that time were long straight keels and short or no overhangs.

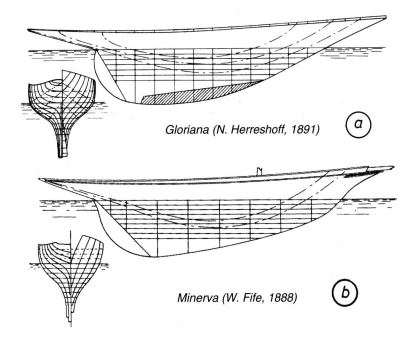

Gloriana (N. Herreshoff, 1891) (a)

Minerva (W. Fife, 1888) (b)

Fig 6a *Gloriana* LOA 70 ft, LWL 40.25 ft, beam 13 ft, draft 10.25 ft, sail area 4100 sq ft. This notable yacht, designed by Nat Herreshoff, is less radical than she appeared to be on her sensational debut in 1891. The popular belief at that time was that she length-ened her sailing lines as she heeled. In fact, in common with many other yachts of the day, she actually lost as much forward as she gained aft. The knuckle of the forefoot, just under the forward end of the waterline (as also seen in *Minerva* below) was cut away to give even longer overhang. The measured length of the hull thus saved gave some rating gain, which could be traded off for more sail area.

Fig 6b *Minerva* LOA 54 ft, LWL 40 ft, draft 9 ft, sail area 2724 sq ft. Designed by W Fife in 1888, she was one of the most successful yachts of her time. Contemporary opinion was that suggested by rulemakers tax on draft would have been a doubtful policy, bear-ing in mind that '...draft gives grip and power to windward, and seaworthiness.' This belief is well reflected in *Minerva*'s lines (compare with those of *America* in Fig 4).

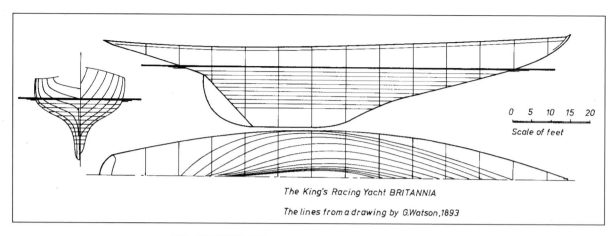

The King's Racing Yacht BRITANNIA

The lines from a drawing by G.Watson,1893

In 1882 well before Watson, a celebrated British designer, produced *Britannia* (Fig 7), he expressed the following prophetic remarks so relevant to future developments in yacht design and aeronautics: 'Some yachting authorities assert that you have only to make the boats long enough to beat all existing racing craft, and it seems strange that with this knowledge in their possession they should not only have

had sufficient self-denial to resist the building of certain successes, but have even gone to the lengths of turning out duffers of normal dimensions... We have not exhausted the possibilities of *form* yet, and really know very little more about it than Salomon did, when he confessed his inability to understand "the way of a ship in the sea", and when we do arrive at perfection in shape we can set to, then, to look out for better material. The frames and beams, then, in my ideal ship shall be of aluminium, the plating below the water of manganese bronze, and the top sides of aluminium; which I think it will be well to deck her, too, with that lightest of metals, as good yellow pine will soon only be seen in museums. For ballast, of course, we should have nothing but platinum, unless the owner grudged the expense, when we might put the top tier of gold. By that date, however, I hope we won't care for sailing in such a sluggish element as water. I firmly believe that some day the air will become as easily traversed as the earth or ocean.' (Ref 1.5)

Forty-six years later, the year in which the picture of *Britannia* shown in Fig 7b was taken (with an aeroplane), a great era of pioneering long-distance flights culminated in the 34 hour non-stop transatlantic flight by Charles Lindbergh from New York to Paris.

Fig 7a (above) *Britannia* LOA 122 ft, LWL 87 ft, beam 23 ft, draft 15 ft, displacement 153 tons, sail area 10,800 sq ft (gaff). Designed by G L Watson in 1893. One of the critics of the period said that with an immense lead keel, she was covered with a cloud of more or less inefficient sails (see Fig 7b). Nevertheless, in a career lasting more than 40 years, she sailed 635 races and won no fewer than 231 of them (gaining a further 129 second and third flags).

Fig 7b (above left) The photograph depicts *Britannia* in close-hauled attitude as she appeared in the year 1927, after a number of modifications to the sail plan and mast.

Although platinum ballast has not so far been used, all sorts of other new and very expensive materials and techniques have been introduced by yacht designers as a direct commercial spin-off from military, aviation and space technology. Thus, for instance, to make a deck covering lighter in an attempt to produce still lighter and faster boats, deck panels are constructed from a honeycomb core sandwiched between two layers of thin composition, a technique which was developed in the space industry.

However, in one respect, Watson was wrong. In spite of the fact that people now 'traverse' the air easily, and at speeds well above the velocity of sound, the desire to achieve high speeds under sail, 'in such a sluggish element as water', has not diminished. On the contrary, the feeling of exhilaration that comes from sailing at speed continues to stir many people's imagination.

The interesting thing about the 'hull form' Watson referred to, and which was demonstrated in *Britannia* (and in Herreshoff's *Gloriana*, Fig 6a), is that as the years have progressed and other possible forms of sea-going hull have been intensively investigated and tested, it appears that a better compromise has been very difficult to find between the basic performance factors and characteristics of a reasonable ocean-going cruiser/racer. These are:

1 Resistance due to form (slenderness and configuration of hull underbody)
2 Frictional resistance (wetted surface area)
3 Stability (power to carry sails effectively)
4 Steering effectiveness (ease of steering and controllability)
5 Course-keeping ability (self-steering)
6 Seakindliness (easy motion in rough sea)
7 Seaworthiness (good survival characteristics and behaviour in extreme weather conditions)
8 Habitability (more than just space for living quarters with good headroom, it is affected significantly by characteristics 4–7)

The type of sailing cruiser/racer (Figs 6 to 9) which we usually refer to as *classic* or *traditional*, has obviously nearly reached the limits of its evolution with the production of a design of lasting value. In fact, the canoe-body of the hull proper, as distinct from its keel (appendages), has not changed much since the time of *Gloriana* or *Brittania*. Any changes to the design were mainly superficial; periodical variations in hull shape to suit particular measurement rules or simply vagaries of fashion.

Fig 8 *Dorade* LOA 52 ft, LWL 37.26 ft, beam 10.25 ft, draft 8 ft, displacement 14.75 tons, sail area 1100 sq ft. Designed by Olin Stephens in 1929. An interpretation along the lines set earlier by the five yachts shown in Figs 4–7. In 1931 *Dorade* won the transatlantic and Fastnet races; in 1933 she cruised across the Atlantic and won another Fastnet.

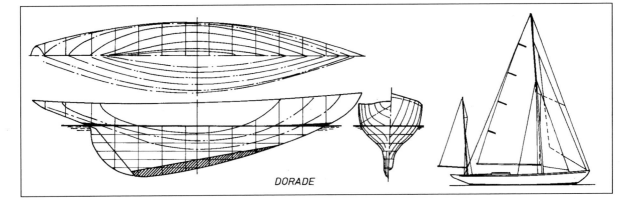

DORADE

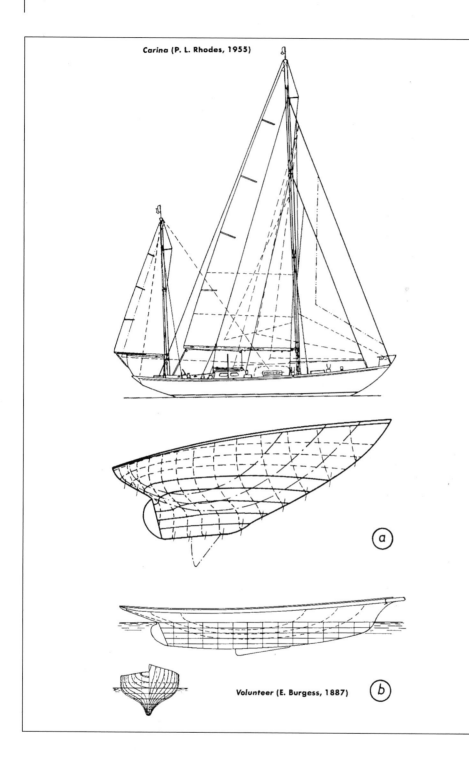

Carina (P. L. Rhodes, 1955)

(a)

Volunteer (E. Burgess, 1887) (b)

Fig 9a *Carina* LOA 53 ft 6 in, LWL 36 ft 6 in, beam 13 ft, draft 6 ft, displacement 14 tons, sail area 1194 sq ft. Designed by P L Rhodes in 1955, *Carina* was described by Uffa Fox as, 'One of the bravest boats to sail the Seven Seas.' With a splendid racing record, having twice won the trans-atlantic race in 1955 and 1957, *Carina* has been considered one of the most successful genuine cruiser/racers ever built. The concept of the keel/centreboard hull is similar to that applied by E Burgess in *Volunteer*, shown below, and in his other America's Cup defenders *Puritan* and *Mayflower*, which won the fifth, sixth and seventh series of races.

Fig 9b *Volunteer*, designed by E Burgess in 1887.

However, designers are always keen to experiment, and inevitably, attempts were made by yacht designers to investigate the possibilities of many widely divergent and unconventional shapes, some going to great extremes and producing 'wild freaks and strange sailing machines unworthy to be called yachts' (Ref 1.5). Chief amongst the more radical designs were boats capable of surface skimming, with hulls of a dish-like shape producing little displacement and a

3 • REACTION AGAINST FAST BOATS

Typical of this type of boat was *Wenonah*, Fig 10. Designed by Nat Herreshoff in 1892, she possessed the characteristics both of a light displacement dinghy and a ballasted yacht.

Fig 10 Some short-lived hull forms invented by the end of the 19th century. The main features of these hulls are: light displacement, small wetted area, separated keel-rudder configuration and unseaworthiness. These boats can be regarded as the ancestors of modern ultra light displacement boats (ULDB) built today. Yacht racing fads come and go; some last longer than others.

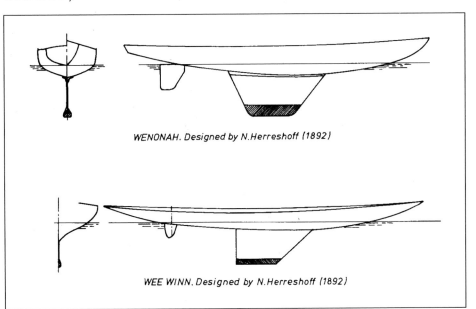

WENONAH. Designed by N.Herreshoff (1892)

WEE WINN. Designed by N.Herreshoff (1892)

Fin-keel yachts with bulb ballast were unmatched in speed but only over short, inshore courses. This type of yacht had been considered as entirely unsuited to the open sea. With the advent of the bulb keel, a large degree of stability was achieved not by sheer displacement of the hull, but by means of a concentrated mass of profiled lead fixed at the bottom of a deep steel fin. In the pursuit of speed, the weight of the hull was drastically reduced, the superstructure removed, the freeboard lowered, thin planking used, etc. So developed the *skimming dish*, which was light and fast, but open to the elements and dangerous to sail except in mild weather conditions.

Such an alternative design philosophy was disapproved of by many yachtsmen, who vigorously opposed these unhealthy tendencies. In 1896 action was taken by R E Froude (son of the famous William Froude, and a hydrodynamicist himself), who proposed that a good yacht design should combine comfort, habitability, speed and seaworthiness. Consequently, a new 'Linear Rule' for rating the speed potential of racing yachts was accepted. The formula had the following form (Ref 1.3):

$$\text{Rating} = \frac{L + B + 0.75\,G + 0.5\,\sqrt{S_A}}{2} \qquad \text{Eq 1}$$

where
L = length at waterline
B = maximum beam
G = skin girth at midship section (Fig 11a)
S_A = sail area

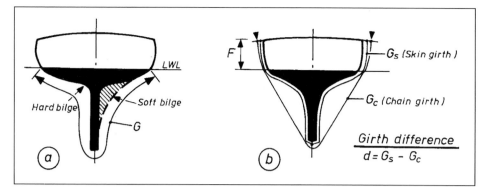

Fig 11a
Measurement of skin girth, G, at midship section of the hull.

Fig 11b
Measurement of d factor, which ultimately discouraged yacht designers from taking advantage of a dish-like hull shape with hard bilges for the sake of speed.

It was hoped that the measurement of girth (G), which would be larger for a shallow hull with hard bilge and bulb keel than for the conventional hull with soft bilge, would prevent the proliferation of these unhealthy flat-bottomed yachts. It will be seen in the rating formula 1 that the factor G, considered as a speed producing factor (like length L and sail area S_A) increases the rating of shallow-hulled yachts, placing them in a faster category.

However, the 'girth rule' in its original form failed to deter designers, who succeeded in introducing modifications to circumvent the formula. Consequently the rating rule was amended and adopted in 1901 in the form:

$$\text{Rating} = \frac{L + B + 0.75G + 4d + 0.5\sqrt{S_A}}{2.1} \qquad \text{Eq 2}$$

where $G = G_c - 2F$, which is the chain girth deck to deck, minus twice the freeboard F (Fig 11b)

The new factor, d, was the tax which had to be 'paid' by the skimming dish hull forms. This was a strong enough penalty to eliminate the skimming dish from competition. It can easily be seen from Fig 11 and straightforward analysis of formula 2 that, the length of the hull L and sail area S_A being equal, boats having soft bilges and fuller, more habitable sections (and thus a smaller value of d, which is multiplied by four in the formula) would have a more advantageous, lower rating in comparison with flat-bottomed bulb-keel yachts.

After a number of modifications the girth rule survived until recently. In the form:

$$\text{Rating} = \frac{L + 2d + \sqrt{S_A} - F}{2.37} \qquad \text{Eq 3}$$

it is used (with the d factor reduced to 2) as the rule which controls the shape of the 12 Metre yachts which participated in the America's Cup contests. Strangely enough, the traditional shape of working and pilot boats, safeguarded by the d factor in the girth formulae, still persists through its incorporation in the 12 Metre class formula, even though the reason for the shape of these boats has long since lost its purpose. Certainly, modern 12 Metre boats cannot be called cruisers.

On the other hand, the International Offshore Rule (IOR) and its replacement, the International Measurement System (IMS) tries to encourage the design and building of dual-purpose sailing yachts: cruiser/racers in which speed and seaworthiness are combined. However, neither the d factor nor any other contrivance which might safeguard seaworthiness has been included in the IOR or IMS formulae. The philosophy or reasons which led to the girth formulae and the lessons learned in the past have been forgotten. In such circumstances uncontrolled preference for speed and racer fashions of the *Wenonah* type (Fig 10) had full sway.

In principle, the basic idea behind the IOR (as well as all previous rating rules) is straightforward: to assess the speed-producing and speed- reducing factors such as the sail area, length of hull, beam, stability, displacement, and so on, in order to calculate the boat's *rating*, which is supposed to be proportional to her speed potential.

When yachts began to form a distinct class of their own, having hitherto been used simply as pleasure craft, they raced regardless of size or other features. Regattas at that time were organised without handicaps for size or time allowances, so that the first yacht to cross the finishing line was the winner. However, it was soon discovered that the larger and longer yachts sailed faster than the smaller and shorter. There was therefore a marked tendency towards building larger yachts in order to compete more effectively. The rating rules that grew out of such conditions considered that the hull length, not the sail power, should be the principal dimension to be taxed (Ref 1.3). The rating is therefore expressed in units of length (feet or metres), the length being close to the LWL of the boat.

After more than a century of numerous changes and new developments, the rating and measurement formulae now in use are rather complicated as a result of their two conflicting aims, which reflect those of the rule-makers and the designers:

1 On the one hand to produce a mathematical formula, based on knowledge and experience, which would indicate accurately enough the speed potential of a given yacht, and to encourage the development of seaworthy cruiser/racers.

2 On the other hand to design faster boats than the measurement rule might intend, by detecting weak points in the measurements or formulae and evading them even at the cost of unhealthy or even dangerous design features.

4 • THE FLAT-OUT RACER CONCEPT

'One cannot find solid ground on which to stand, or an objective standard of evaluation, without... the correlation of recent events with the more distant past and the perennial qualities of human nature underlying both.'

H J Morgenthau

As we shall see, speed performance is affected by three primary hull design factors: *displacement* for given a length of hull, *wetted surface* of the hull underbody, and *stability* – that is, the hull's ability to carry sails effectively. If, therefore, in a radical design, the wetted surface of the hull (friction drag) and displacement (wave drag) can be reduced, one might expect that higher speed will result. Such a doctrine was promulgated by Uffa Fox. As he argued, 'with their light displacement they climb almost every sea instead of smashing their way through them... weight being useful only in a steamroller.'

'These were eccentric views to hold in the mid-thirties', commented Phillips-Birt (Ref 1.6), 'and they must be taken with a pinch of salt even today.' Nevertheless, Uffa Fox made a fairly determined attempt to prove his point by designing the Flying series: Flying Fifteen, Flying Twenty Five and Flying Thirty. It will be seen in Fig 12 that the Flying Fifteen, a typical representative of the family, has its wetted surface reduced to a minimum. She is light, and in basic concept not too different from early skimming dishes of the late 19th century such as *Wenonah* and the like. Speed achieved by the Flying series is not open to question: they were faster than any other boat of comparable size (length). It has been claimed that the Flying Fifteens reach a speed of 12 knots! Its speed/length ratio:

$$V_s/\sqrt{LWL} = 12/\sqrt{15} = 3.1$$

is very high indeed.

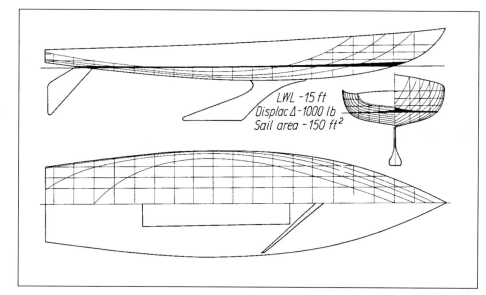

LWL - 15 ft
Displac Δ - 1000 lb
Sail area - 150 ft²

Fig 12 The radical Flying Fifteen designed by Uffa Fox. In principle, the basic design philosophy which produced this peculiar shape is not new. It is just a repetition of the pattern developed by the end of the 19th century (see *Wenonah* in Fig 10 and more examples in Ref 1.3).

A useful criterion for comparing the ability of boats to attain high sailing speeds is the displacement/length ratio:

$$\triangle/(.01L)^3$$

where $\triangle$ is the displacement in tons (1 ton = 2240 lbs)

L is the waterline length of the hull in ft.

When using this ratio one should bear in mind that whereas displacement, $\triangle$, can be regarded as a speed-reducing factor, the length, L, is the speed-producing factor. In other words, the displacement/length ratio may be defined as a measure of a load put on a given length L. If the displacement $\triangle$, that is the immersed volume of the hull (corresponding to a displaced mass of water which the hull in motion must push away), for a given length L is reduced, the resistance will also decrease, and so the maximum attainable speed will increase.

Returning to the Flying Fifteen (Fig 12) her displacement/length ratio:

$$\triangle/(.01L)^3 = \frac{.447}{(.15)^3} = 132$$

has not been carried to the extreme, although compared with traditional cruiser/

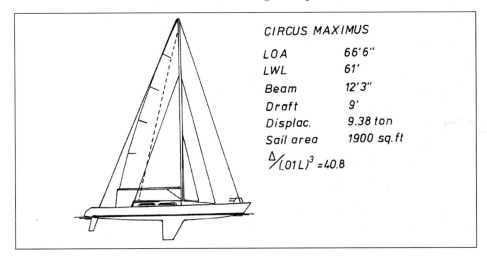

CIRCUS MAXIMUS

LOA	66'6"
LWL	61'
Beam	12'3"
Draft	9'
Displac.	9.38 ton
Sail area	1900 sq. ft

$$\triangle/(.01L)^3 = 40.8$$

Fig 13 *Circus Maximus* Designed by Ives-Marie Tanton. It was believed that this boat would have a good windward performance in addition to her obvious potential for sliding downwind. However, as reported by Bob Payne at the Survivors' Ocean Racing Conference: 'she turned out to be a downwind flyer that could go only downwind. Despite the relatively deep keel, the light displacement boat went to windward like a dog. Somebody was trying to drag to the pound... her downwind speed approached 14 knots but as soon as *Circus Maximus* turned the corner and started punching back into the seas, it dropped to almost a third of that.'*

It might appear that a lighter boat with a slimmer, more easily driven hull would produce more speed. But in the search for speed, stability should not be overlooked. Less displacement generally means less stability, which varies at much the same rate as displacement. Stability, in turn, is the characteristic upon which the driving power (which may be delivered by sails) depends, except in downwind condition. *Circus Maximus*'s failure appears to indicate that it does not pay to reduce displacement/length ratio of a monohull racer below 100, if sail carrying power is lost.

SAIL magazine, 1978.

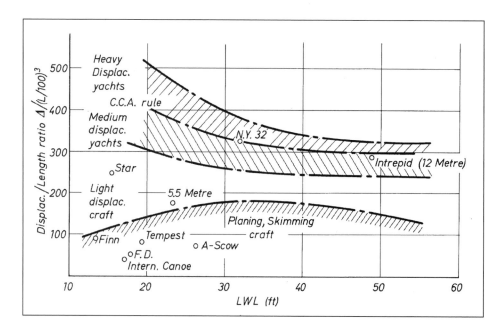

Fig 14 The plausible division of sailing craft of increasing length in terms of displacement/length ratio:

1 Heavy displacement yachts of the older, ocean-going type.

2 Medium-displacement cruiser-racers, built to the International Measurement Rule.

3 Modern light displacement cruiser-racers, fin-keel day sailers.

4 Planing and skimming craft of exceptionally low displacement/length ratio.

Note that the length of the hull determines to some degree to which division a craft belongs. For example, the boat with 20 ft LWL hull is classified as heavy displacement craft if her displacement/length ratio is between 500 and 400; for 40 ft LWL hull this ratio is reduced to 350–300. Heavy boats are easier to sail in a wider spectrum of weather than light, flat bottomed dinghy-like types. They are also more reliable, seakindly and seaworthy.

racers of the time its value is low; of about the same order as that of modern 'maxi-raters'. Their designers' avid interest in 'first to finish' honours have produced amongst the lowest displacement-to-length ratio in the ocean-going fleets. Some designers of those light displacement big boats (60–80 ft in LOA) even went so far as to reduce the displacement/length ratio to about 45, ie less than that of an Olympic dinghy Flying Dutchman! However, because of the limitations of the rating rules, they had little racing success (Fig 13). See also Fig 14 which may be revealing in this respect.

The displacement/length ratio for the last two decades had been rapidly reducing. A rather abrupt break with tradition, implicit in the combination of light displacement with separated fin-keel and rudder, is demonstrated in Fig 15. 'At one time, a sea-going cruiser of 26 ft on the waterline', Phillips-Birt recollects, 'could not have displaced less than about 8 tons without appearing to be as dashing as her contemporary Rosie Boote on the stage' (Ref 1.6). This means that the displacement/length ratio of those cruisers was about 450 (Fig 14). More recently, some thirty years later, this ratio of a respectable *ocean-going yacht*, shown in sketch d of Fig 15, has been reduced to ⅓. Hulls have become much lighter, because the new materials that Watson dreamt about, and new building techniques – albeit more complex and much more costly – have become available.

Thus, over the century two different types of sea-going yachts evolved: one following the fashion of working boats of the past, of which *Gloriana* (Fig 6a), *Britannia* (Fig 7), *Dorade* (Fig 8) and *Carina* (Fig 9a) are examples; and the other following the concept of the flat-out racers like *Wenonah* (Fig 10) and Uffa Fox's *Flying* family (Fig 12).

'The best ocean racer is the best ocean cruiser', maintained Uffa Fox around 1934. Perhaps this was true some sixty years ago. Is it possible today to develop a dual-purpose cruiser/racer yacht which could satisfy those sailors, both cruising and racing, who are searching for the ultimate? Or is that kind of ideal just a dream?

Fig 15 Recent development in hull design since about 1960 is characterized by: **1** Lighter displacement; **2** Greater beam and flat bottom of the hull; **3** Reduced wetted surface of the hull underbody (separated fin-keel and rudder); **4** Higher centre of gravity of the boat This figure demonstrates the noticeable changes in the displacement/length ratio ($\triangle/(.01L)^3$) and shape of midship sections which are largely responsible for the gradual decrease of ultimate stability and seakindliness in yachts.

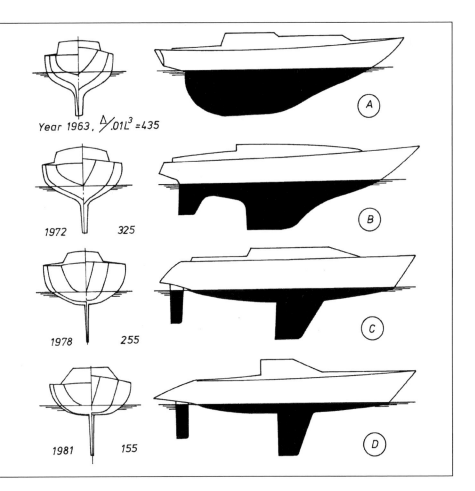

Boats have evolved directly from fishing and pilot vessels. In Laurent Giles's opinion, 'these early yachts were essentially balanced hulls, for the evil influences later to be introduced [rating rules] had not then appeared. They represented a culmination of development untrammelled by any requirement leading away from the natural and rational trend. A balanced type was therefore to be expected, since no other distractions beyond the seaman's demand for good manners become paramount.'

Every sailing vessel can be looked upon as a compromise between many different elements, each of which if carried to its extreme would be incompatible with another. In the quest for the ultimate performance in one direction, sacrifices must be made; yet often the undesirable consequences of these pursuits are only reluctantly taken into account or ignored altogether.

The evolution of sailing boats has been greatly influenced by the progress made in ships, science and aerodynamics. Knowledge gained in these areas is inevitably in advance of every current measurement rule, and this has frequently encouraged designers to find loopholes in the rule in order to construct a faster boat within a certain rating, often to the detriment of her seagoing abilities. The history of the last hundred years of yacht design is to a great extent the history of the unending quest to develop a measurement formula to establish *justly* the potential speed performance of racing yachts.

D Phillips-Birt, in his excellent book, *An Eye for a Yacht*, says that 'a system of measurements has more profound effect on the shape of yachts than the sea in all its moods... The yacht is an artificial product, and an eye for a yacht, like an eye for the finer points of a painting, depends on a knowledge of the circumstances which produced it.'

So far, all attempts to devise an equitable rule which could produce a sound, dual-purpose cruiser/racer have ended, like the search for the Holy Grail, in failure.

5 • SEAKINDLINESS AND SEAWORTHINESS

'Those will survive whose functions happen to be most nearly in equilibrium with the modified aggregate of external forces.'

Herbert Spencer (1820-1903) Principles of Biology

One more point deserves to be briefly mentioned in connection with the controversy over heavy versus light displacement boats. Although the word 'cruising' means many different things to different people, we may all agree 'that cruising first of all means *living*'; it is a way of life rather than a sport. We may also agree that the most desirable quality in a cruising boat is *seakindliness*. In broad terms, this means that quality in a boat which enables her to receive the forces of a violent sea and render them kindly, giving easy motion through the seaway. Seakindliness is therefore linked with habitability; providing an environment that permits the crew to function to the best of their mental and physical abilities without being hampered by excessive rolling, pitching, heaving and yawing of the boat (Fig 16).

It is a matter of common experience (and accords with Newton's second law) that the boat in a seaway, subjected to sudden action of wave or wind forces, will experience accelerations. These are more or less rapid changes in boat motion and might manifest themselves in the form of rolling, pitching, heaving or yaw-

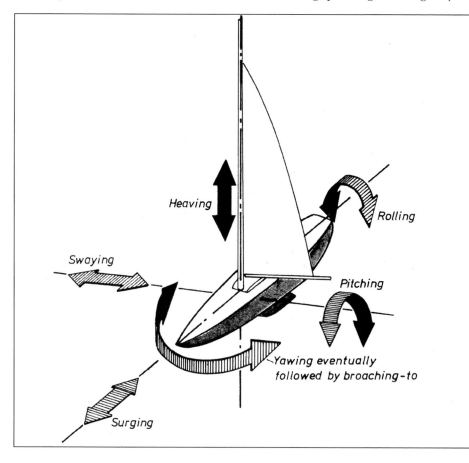

Fig 16 Basic components of boat motion which, if violent, may incapacitate the crew to the point that some crew members may become unable to perform any work on the deck. Their proficiency level depends on the magnitude of accelerations experienced and the adaptation period which is different for different people. Quite apart from the effect of these motions on the crew, combinations of the two motions, such as rolling and heaving, greatly affect the ultimate stability of the boat in waves. That is, stability in dynamic conditions can be drastically reduced to a fraction of that in calm seas (Ref 1.3).

ing. These movements can be fatiguing and exhausting to the point that some or all crew members may become totally incapacitated. In general, the magnitude and frequency of accelerations will depend on the boat's inertia – broadly speaking, her displacement. Thus, two boats – one of heavy and another of light displacement – when acted upon by the same sea forces, will experience different accelerations. One may rightly expect the heavier boat to be more seakindly to her crew than the lighter one. And if one boat is, say, twice as heavy as another, the accelerations will be about half those affecting a lighter yacht.

The magnitude of accelerations will also depend on the ratio of the area and volume of the hull above the waterline to that below. Light and beamy modern boats with superstructure that is much further above the water (Fig 15) are particularly vulnerable in rough seas, both in terms of seakindliness and seaworthiness.

Figures 17a and b show the effects on crew capability of the rolling motion (angle of roll) and acceleration when pitching and heaving. These results can only be regarded as preliminary. Studies of the relationship between the incidence of motion sickness and acceleration, rolling motion, or a combination of two or more motions (such as rolling and heaving or rolling and pitching and so on) are, so far, sparse. But the problem is partly offset by the fact that the few studies already carried out in this field had relatively consistent findings.

An interesting point is that only under natural conditions of self-propelled locomotion do the human senses, which convey to the brain information about the body's position in space, function in harmony. But when the human being is transported passively, and the senses (and in particular the vestibular system) subjected to rapid motion and accelerations, these senses may cease to be

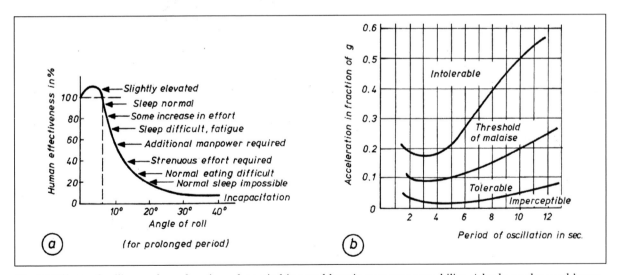

Fig 17 Effects of rolling and acceleration when pitching and heaving on crew capability. A body on the earth's surface is pressed towards the centre of the earth by the pull of gravity force (force = mass × gravity acceleration, g; g = 32.2 ft/sec^2 = 9.8 m/sec^2). It has been established that the maximum acceleration for fishing vessels in heavy seas is in the neighbourhood of one g below or above the acceleration due to gravity. This acceleration is thus about ten times larger than the value of g at which seasickness occurs (graph b). This gives some idea of the stresses to which fishermen and yacht crews are exposed in the pursuit of their occupation. It has been frequently observed that it is not the boat which wins races, it is the people who sail her. If boat motion becomes unbearable the crew won't sail her to her best advantage; they won't win races and, if the worst comes to the worst, chances of survival can be seriously impaired. Habitability is more than the available space below deck.

reliable. The delicate harmony is artificially disturbed by the *dynamic* sequence of events, thus producing a mismatch between what is currently being signalled and expectations based on previous experiences with a basically *static* environment.

These introductory remarks may seem to be written in support or defence of traditional types of yacht like *Dorade*, but that is not the intention. They are rather intended to emphasize the extent of the differences between the cruiser and the more recently developed 'grand-prix' racer. In considering whether it is possible to design an effective dual-purpose cruiser/racer, another question might be posed. Is it possible to produce a successful hybrid-car in which the best features of a motor-caravan and racing car could be incorporated to the full satisfaction of the different kinds of user? Or can a racehorse be used successfully as a carriage horse between races or vice versa?

To close this brief deliberation about cruisers and racing boats, it may be appropriate to quote the two experts on this subject. The prominent designer, Laurent Giles, considers that, 'Your sailing yacht can never be better than a skilful compromise between conflicting considerations. An open and enquiring mind, the widest possible experience of yachts of every conceivable type, above all sound judgement and the mentality of a psychiatrist are the personal attributes upon which good design rests; for good design implies satisfied clients, and a satisfied client must have derived maximum enjoyment from what he has been given.' Dr K Davidson, the scientist who first developed the method of predicting sailing yacht performance based on small model testing in the towing tank, says, 'It would be idle to attempt to argue the relative merits of heavy displacement boats against those of the particular light displacement craft... It is simply a matter of how much one chooses to emphasize maximum speed for its own sake and how much one cares to sacrifice in the way of seakeeping, and so on, in order to get it!'

One more point should be made here. Modern yacht design is the art of modelling new materials (exotic), which are not wholly understood, into shapes which frequently are not or cannot be precisely analysed, in order to withstand forces which cannot be properly assessed. To cope with these uncertainties, designers employ the so-called 'factor of safety' sometimes referred to as a 'factor of ignorance'. The concept of a factor of safety is often misunderstood by those outside the profession of structural designers to imply some large safety margin on a predictable design, which it is not.

For a factor of safety to be effective, the reason for failure must be known, and the cause of the failure determinable by experiments. In fact, both the reason and the cause of failure are frequently not known or determinable. This explains why the ultralight displacement boats (ULDB) have chronic difficulty (or so it seems) in keeping their keels firmly attached to the hull, and also why rudder and/or blade failures are not uncommon nowadays. It has been argued that IOR boats normally rated poorly if they were stern heavy, and often it was the structural integrity of the separated rudder which suffered when trying to achieve lighter boats for the sake of speed. Conservative design tends to be less fast, which means that there is always pressure to reduce factors of safety. Moreover, cutting safety margins to reduce costs is common today in all engineering disciplines.

6 • SPEED PERFORMANCE FACTORS

Fig 18 The weatherliness of various sailing vessels as measured by the course, γ, relative to the true wind V_T. As the objective in much close-hauled work is the speed that a sailing boat can make good directly against the true wind, V_T, we shall be particularly interested in her speed component represented by an arrow labelled potential V_{mg}. This is called the *speed made good to windward*.

V_{mg} is frequently used as the yardstick upon which a boat's overall sailing efficiency is measured and compared with that of other vessels. The reason for using the V_{mg} yardstick is found in a simple problem of averages. An average speed of a boat sailing against the wind is lower than her average speed in any other direction. Thus, over a series of races, her upwind performance (time-consuming), becomes the dominating single factor determining her chances of winning. The average speed of yachts – about twice as high as that of square-rigged vessels of comparable size – could not possibly be attained without good progress being made in heawinds.

Returning to Fig 2, which illustrates speed achieved by various sailing craft, it will be seen that the relative speed performance $V_s/\sqrt{LWL}$ seems to be increasing at a faster and faster rate. This is simply exponential growth. We are familiar with such curves nowadays, whether we are considering the gross national product or world population increase or the number of scientific publications which presumably indicate the growth of knowledge. The two questions to be answered in relation to the exponential curve in Fig 2 are:

1 Can we carry on expecting sailing speeds to increase indefinitely?
2 Why did the curve suddenly bend upwards around 1965?

If sailing speed increase had gone on indefinitely in an exponential growth fashion, the curve in Fig 2 would have remained J-shaped. With a little imagination and without great risk we may predict that this will never happen in the real world. Eventually, the rate of increase will begin to slacken, the curve will rise less steeply and ultimately it will become flat, almost S-shaped.

Almost all the technicological systems we deal with (and a sailing craft can be looked upon as a system) have natural limits, since as they grow they are bound to generate certain setbacks which will slow further development.

What can we learn in this context from the past achievements? Table 2, based on Davidson (Ref 1.2), illustrates the point. The data sampled in column 5 give the relative average speed for a number of different sailing craft, expressed in terms of speed/length ratio $V_s/\sqrt{L}$, where L is the *overall length* of the hull. This facilitates the comparison of sailing performance of craft of such widely different lengths on a 'size for size' basis.

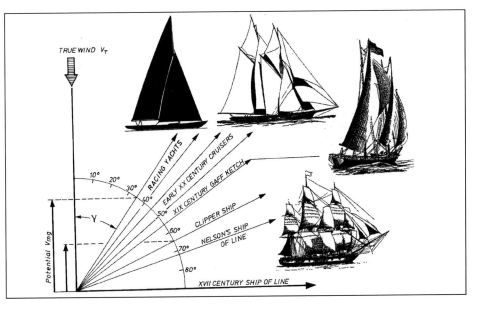

Table 2   Sailing Speeds

Note: the speed/length ratios are calculated taking LOA instead of LWL. If LWL were taken, which are shorter usually by 15–20%, the $V_s/\sqrt{L}$ given below should be increased by about 10%

1 DATE	2 VESSEL	3 AVERAGE ACTUAL SPEED V_s KN	4 LENGTH OVERALL L FT	5 AVERAGE RELATIVE SPEED $V_s/\sqrt{L}$	6 REMARKS	
1492	Santa Maria Columbus	3.5	70	0.45	Good passage	
1837	Sumner's ship*	6.5	200	0.44	Good passage	Square-rigged ships
1850	Clipper ship	6	250	0.38†	Mean figure	
1902	Preussen‡	7	410	0.35	Mean figure	
1932	Parma	7.5	330	0.41	Mean figure	
1932	Parma	9.0	330	0.49	Best passage	
1935	Stormy Weather	6	53	0.90	Good passage	
1935	6 Metre boats	5.75	36	0.97	Mean figure	Fore-and-aft rigged yachts
1935	J-class boats	9.75	135	0.84	Mean figure	
1950	} Bolero participating		73	0.99 }	Mean figure	
1954	in the Bermuda races			0.68	0.83	

*Thomas H Sumner was the American ship's captain who devised the Position Line method now used in astronomical navigation.
†According to an analysis of 420 voyages of the wool clippers (Amateur Yacht Research Society) the average speed of those ships sailing from Australia to England was 6.5 knots. This gives an average relative speed of $V_s/\sqrt{L} = 0.41$. The clipper *Champion of the Seas* held the record for the longest day's run until the 1984 Transat TAG race (Table 1). In 1854 *Champion* sailed 462.04 nm in 23.28 hours to average 19.85 knots. Another clipper, *Lightning*, built in 1854 for the Australia–Great Britain route, made a record day's run on her maiden voyage of 436 miles in 24 hours with average speed just over 18 knots. With LWL of 226 ft this gives a relative speed $V_s/\sqrt{LWL}$ of 1.2.
‡The largest sailing ship ever built (1902) belonged to the famous 'P-line' of Bremen, Germany (*Passat, Priwall, Pamir, Parma, Peking, Padua, Preussen*).

A glance at Table 2 reveals first that there is a striking uniformity of relative speed actually achieved for square-rigged ships and fore-and-aft rigged yachts respectively. Secondly, the mean value of speed/length ratio for yachts is roughly *twice* as big as that for ships. From Fig 18 it can be inferred that the key to this superiority of fore-and-aft rigged yachts lies in their ability to sail closer to the wind, a quality never attained by sailing craft in the days of commercial sail. Because of the great windage and slack rigging it was difficult to persuade square-rigged vessels to go to windward. Thus, for instance, the difference between the windward pointing ability of a modern racer and of the clipper is in the order of 30 degrees; which means that the *speed made good to windward*, labelled V_{mg}, of a 12 Metre class yacht is about twice as big as that of the clipper. This is a great step forward.

However, further spectacular improvement along the same line of development, ie the point of sailing and relative speed, should not be expected. The evolution of monohulled sailing craft of *inherently limited stability* has already reached its limit. There is evidence that the exceptionally high speed performance figures recorded by some of the modern racers have been achieved at the expense of the sea-keeping abilities that were prized by past generations (Ref 1.3).

If in the future, sailing craft return as an alternative to power-driven merchant vessels, the sailing yacht may well serve as a pointer to the development of wind-driven ships. The relative speeds of cargo ships in service today range from 0.6 to 1.0 $V_s/\sqrt{L}$. They are therefore slower, size for size, than modern sailing yachts.

In Table 2 we find that the clippers, when compared size for size, were no faster than Columbus's *Santa Maria*, which sailed some 350 years earlier (Fig 19a). The data in Table 2 also suggests that there was not much real improvement in relative performance between a sailing ship of Columbus's time and the biggest sailing ships ever built, four centuries later, represented by *Preussen*.

A surprising comparison is that of the performance achievement of *Stormy Weather*, a 53 ft cruiser-racer, with that of the clipper five times longer and *Preussen* eight times longer (Fig 19b). Their average speeds are roughly the same, in spite of the fact that in the most favourable reaching conditions the much larger clipper could attain 15.5 knots (16.5 knots were also claimed).

From Fig 18 one may infer that the progressive improvement in the windward ability of sailing craft can be attributed mainly to the remarkable developments in rigs and the underwater part of the hull (see also Fig 20). This led to much higher sail and hull efficiency on which, as we shall see, the potential performance of any sailing craft directly depends.

The relatively low average speeds of the square-riggers were largely due to the low aerodynamic efficiency of their sails which, although good in reaching and downwind sailing conditions, were hopelessly poor in the close-hauled attitude when compared with fore-and-aft rigs. It seems that the main difficulty

Fig 19a (right) Columbus's *Santa Maria* (1492). She was slower than the other two vessels *Nina* and *Pinta*, and Columbus never liked her. In 1893 a replica of the *Santa Maria*, built as nearly as possible (with the data available) to the exact dimensions of the original vessel, was used to cross Atlantic on the course followed by Columbus. The elapse time was thirty-six days, and the maximum speed about 6.5 knots. More recently one built for Gerard Depardieu's film is now in Bristol Docks.

Fig 19b (above) *Preussen* (1902). This enormous vessel, over 400 ft (122 m) long, with five masts, a deadweight capacity of 8000 tons, carried 59,000 sq ft (5500 sq m) of canvas. In 1910 *Preussen* was involved in a collision off Dover and was beached in St Margaret's Bay, eventually becoming a total wreck.

was that their leading edges, set to windward work, could not hold hard enough to avoid sagging off badly. Not being attached to spars, as in the fore-and-aft rig, the square sail had a tendency to come aback as soon as the ship's head was brought to about 65–70 degrees relative to the wind. Thus, the square rig was unsuited to close windward work. It is fair to say that of all changes that contributed to the substantial improvement of windward ability of sailing craft, the most important was the shift from square to the fore-and-aft rig; and thereafter the aerodynamic 'cleaning' (reducing drag) of the whole rig, and modification of the underwater parts of the hull.

Fig 20 illustrates the trend toward higher aspect ratio sails and keel planform observed since 1883, which is particularly noticeable in racer designs. It appears that the publication by the celebrated French engineer Gustave Eiffel of some of his wind tunnel results on aerofoils in 1910 stimulated yacht designers. According to A E Reynolds Brown (Ref 1.7), 'there was no doubt that something happened to sail plans in 1912. Mr Charles Nicolson brought out *Istria* with a taller sail plan than anything before; also a topmast long enough to make a topsail yard unnecessary, the topsail luff setting on a track like a modern Bermudian rig. The mast was thought to look like a wireless mast, and in derision it was called the 'Marconi' rig. But it stood through the windiest summer in memory, and she collected 35 prizes in 36 starts, 25 of them first.' Indeed *Istria*'s mast was cleaner aerodynamically than most contemporary rigs: the airflow around the most sensitive leading edge of the mainsail was no longer disturbed, as it was in the presence of the topsail yard and topmast junction. Besides, a reduction of the weight of the spars aloft certainly contributed towards greater stability and a reduction of pitching in rough seas.

These, however, were not the only developments which led to higher speed in yachts compared with past merchant vessels driven by sails. Progressive improvements in the rig were followed by progressive changes in the hull; now the overall configuration and proportions have become radically different.

Fig 20 Evolution of sail plans and underwater profiles of hulls towards higher aspect ratio foils. These go-faster shapes are not, however, without some undesirable characteristics on courses other than close-hauled. The yachts are not drawn to the same scale.

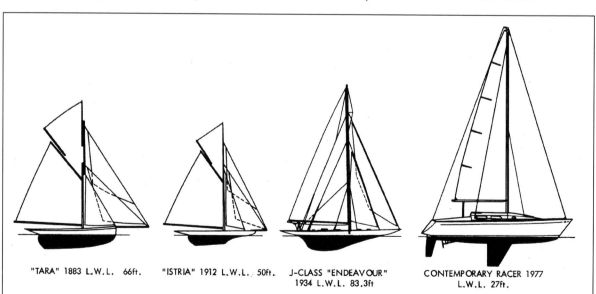

"TARA" 1883 L.W.L. 66ft.   "ISTRIA" 1912 L.W.L. 50ft.   J-CLASS "ENDEAVOUR" 1934 L.W.L. 83.3ft   CONTEMPORARY RACER 1977 L.W.L. 27ft.

7 • How Fast is Fast?

In Fig 21 and Table 3, based on Davidson (Ref 1.2), a large and a small racing yacht are compared with a typical square-rigged merchant ship of about 1860. Different proportions are evident and so are the ratios S_A/A, $S_A/\triangle$ and $\triangle/(.01LWL)^3$ given at the end of Table 3. Yachts are seen to be slim compared with the full-bodied hulls of merchant vessels. Their displacement on a nominal overall length has been greatly reduced (is three to four times less) without a corresponding loss of lateral stability. An ingenious concept – heavy ballast suspended low down and a full mid-section of the hull above the waterline – gives a much greater ability to carry sails effectively when on the wind. As a result, yachts have proportionally much more sail area for a displacement, $S_A/\triangle$; *from ten to twenty-five times more* than that of a merchant vessel. And the ratios of sail area to wetted surface of the hull, S_A/A, are over twice as large as those of the old sailing vessels. Also, as shown in Figs 20 and 21, the immersed lateral plane area of the hull became gradually more concentrated towards the mid-length. This provides a better aspect ratio for the keel which, as we shall see, contributes to higher efficiency of the hull in close-hauled work. By about 1850 yachts had become remarkably good sea-boats.

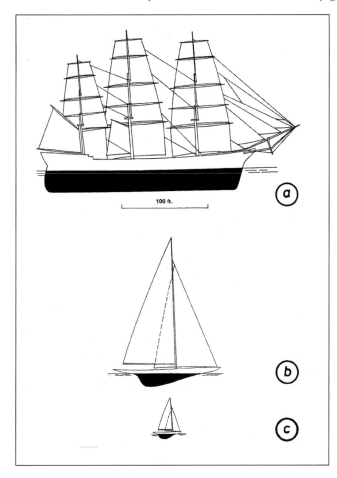

100 ft.

Fig 21 Comparison of a square-rigged merchant vessel with two racing yachts:
a) sailing ship (1860)
b) J-Class yacht (beginning of 20th century)
c) 6 Metre class yacht

All craft are depicted on the same scale. A larger sail area/displacement ratio, $S_A/\triangle$, for a smaller racing yacht of 6 Metre class – as compared with that of J-class which is geometrically similar (geosim) – is to be expected on account of the square-cube relationship involved. Thus, for example, if a boat has been geometrically expanded twofold so that the length L of big boat = 2L of small boat, ie, the scale ratio SR = 2, then the sail area of the bigger boat will increase in proportion SR^2, that is fourfold. However, the displacement of the bigger boat will increase in proportion SR^3, ie, it will have 8 times the displacement of the smaller boat. This means that the $S_A/\triangle$ ratio of the big boat will be reduced by a factor of 2. In other words, the larger boat will be undercanvassed or the smaller one overcanvassed. Of course, such vessels, although belonging to the *geosim family*, will have unequal sensitivity to the wind, particularly when close-hauled. Elaborate treatment of the scaling problem of sailing yachts can be found in a splendid paper by H Barkla (Ref 1.8).

Table 3
Comparison of the actual dimensions of a square-rigged ship with racing yachts (see Fig 21)

	SHIP (1860)	J-CLASS YACHT	6 METRE CLASS YACHT
Length overall LOA (ft)	242	135	36
Load waterline length LWL (ft)	221	87	23.5
Beam of the hull B (ft)	45	25	6.5
Draft of the hull Dr (ft)	23	15	5.4
Sail area S_A (ft^2)	22500	10000	600
Wetted surface of hull A (ft^2)	15200	2200	192
Displacement $\triangle$ (tons)	4100	166	4.1
S_A/A	1.5	4.5	3.1
$S_A/\triangle$	5.5	60	146
$\triangle/(.01\ LWL)^3$	380	252	316
Displacement on a nominal overall length of 100 ft (tons)	290	68	88

The speed performance which has been attained by some old and more modern monohull yachts is given in Table 4, which supplements Tables 1 and 2. *America* (Fig 4) was the winner of the Royal Yacht Squadron Cup that was to become known as the America's Cup; on her passage across the Atlantic in 1851 to reach the Isle of Wight and participate in the race which won her this prize, she recorded the speeds shown. Her maximum relative speed $V_s/\sqrt{LWL}$, based on her best day's run, was 1.25 but the average relative speed also given in Table 4 was only 0.7.

Table 4
Characteristiscs of some W–E transatlantic traditional monohull winners (elapsed time, no handicap correction)

1 YEAR	2 YACHT	3 LOA FT	4 LWL FT	5 DISPLACED $\triangle$TON	6 SAIL AREA S_A FT^2	7 DISTANCE N MILES	8 ELAPSED TIME D HR M	9 BDR N MILES	10 AVER SPEED KN	11 MAX $V_s/\sqrt{LWL}$	12 AVER $V_s/\sqrt{LWL}$
1851	*America*	102	90	147.3	5263	3095	19,23,00	284	6.65	1.25	0.70
1866	*Henrietta*	107	84	205.4	8850	3070	13,21,45	280	9.57	1.27	1.00
1905	*Atlantic*	185	135	446.4	18500	3013	12,04,01	342	10.4	1.23	0.90
1931	*Dorade*	52	37	14.8	1100	2838	17,01,16	210	6.95	1.44	1.14
1955	*Carina*	54	36.5	14.0	1194	3450	20,09,17		7.13		1.18

Note: BDR best day's run
V_s boat speed in knots
LWL load waterline length in feet
LOA length overall in feet

In 1866, the New York Yacht Club organized the first trans-oceanic yacht race. The 84 feet LWL *Henrietta* won with a time of 13 days 21 hours and 45 minutes, thus reducing the passage time by more than 6 days compared with *America*. Another Atlantic passage record, attained by the 135 feet LWL *Atlantic* (Fig 22a) almost forty years later, with crossing time of 12 days 4 hours 1 minute 19 seconds, was to stand for 75 years until finally broken by Eric

Fig 22a The three-masted schooner *Atlantic*, built in 1871 (LWL = 135 ft 41.15 m), whose speed record for the Atlantic crossing west to east stood unbroken from 1905 until 1988 (Fig 23b).

Tabarly in 1980. He was sailing a very different kind of craft: a 46 feet LWL hydrofoiled trimaran *Paul Ricard* (Fig 22b), which made the crossing in 10 days 5 hours 14 minutes 20 seconds.

The fast passage of the monohull *Atlantic* in terms of elapsed time may appear impressive. If, however, her achievement is compared with other yachts on the more objective basis of 'size for size', that is, in terms of relative speed $V_s/\sqrt{LWL}$ (where the boat's speed V_s is that of the boat's best day's run), it will be seen in Tables 1 or 4 that her performance was by no means outstanding. A half-century earlier yachts had sailed as fast as *Atlantic*. Her record crossing time, kept for so long, was attained by virtue of her sheer size, and not because of her extraordinary design features. This is rather evident if *Atlantic* is compared in size to *America* or *Henrietta* in Fig 22b. As a matter of fact, *Henrietta*'s speed performance, in terms of maximum and average $V_s/\sqrt{LWL}$ ratios, was

Fig 22b Profile views of three old west–east transatlantic record-holding yachts: schooners *Atlantic*[1], *Henrietta*[2] and *America*[3]. Yachts are drawn to the same scale and arranged in relation to the scale below which gives their crossing times (Ref 1.1). For comparison, profiles of two record holding catamarans are also shown. *Jet Services II*[4], *Elf Aquitaine*[5], and the hydrofoiled trimaran, *Paul Ricard*[6].

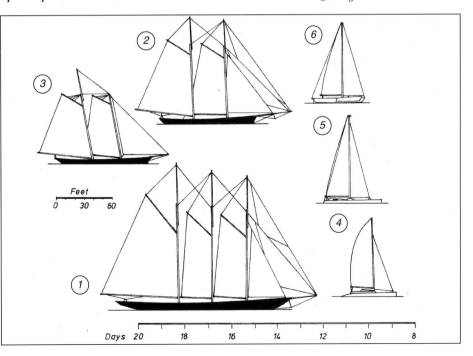

better than that of *Atlantic*, and achieved forty years earlier. What Fig 22b reveals is the direct correspondence between the size of the vessel and its speed performance, though this sober observation should not detract from the remarkable technological advances that have been made.

Deliberate attempts have been made more recently to use the supreme merits of hull length as a dominant speed-producing factor. The giant 236 feet LOA *Club Méditerranée* shown in Fig 23a may serve as an example. This four-masted schooner, designed to win the *Ostar* race to Newport Rhode Island in 1976, failed disastrously. Her maximum speed capability, estimated at about 22 knots (based on hull length alone ie 1.5√LWL assuming favourable winds) did not materialize. The prevailing weather conditions did not match the designer's expectation. Her average speed was only about 5.2 knots, which in terms of speed/length ratio gives $V_s/\sqrt{LWL} = 0.36$! *Club Méditerranée* belonged to the category of so-called ultra-light displacement boats (ULDB). With her displacement/length ratio, $\triangle/(.01LWL)^3$, about 30, and sail area/displacement ratio, $S_A/\triangle$, about 43, she was understandably undercanvassed, being designed for single-handed sailing. Under her new name *La Vie Claire*, this giant attained in 1983 a speed/length ratio (based on the best day's run, Table 1) of about 1.28, not much improvement over that attained 120 years earlier by *Henrietta* (Table 1). This adds corroboration to the author's opinion, expressed earlier, that no remarkable design advance in terms of the speed potential of monohulls has been made during the last hundred years or so.

A modified four masted schooner *Club Méditerranée* (Fig 23b) carrying new

Fig 23a (left) The giant *Club Méditerranée*, built for a specific purpose according to the 'no holds barred' rule. Her name was subsequently changed to *La Vie Claire* and thereafter *Phocea* (Fig 23b).

Fig 23b (right) The four-masted schooner *Phocea*, LWL 213 ft (65 m), set a new transatlantic monohull speed record in 1988 of 8 days, 3 hours, 29 minutes. Sailing speed record-keeper Richard Boehmer points out that the Atlantic record was first broken by a ULDB monohull in 1981 when *Kriter VIII* completed a west–east French race in 12 days, 3 hours, 41 minutes and 3 seconds.

name *Phocea* established in 1988 a new West-East transatlantic speed record for a monohull. She sailed 2 810 miles from Ambrose Light (near New York City) to the Lizard (near Falmouth, England) in 8 days 3 hours and 29 minutes; the average speed was 14.37 knots which gives *average* speed length ratio $V_s/\sqrt{L}$ just about 1.0. The greatest distance sailed in one day ie the best days run (BDR) was claimed as 490 miles which results in *maximum* speed length ratio $V_s/\sqrt{L} = 1.4$. This is about 14 per cent higher than that achieved by *Atlantic* some 80 years ago.

Phocea's sail area was increased from about 1000 m^2 (10700 ft^2) originally carried by *Club Méditerranée* (designed for single handed racing) to about 1600 m^2 (17 120 ft^2).

No doubt, much cleaner aerodynamically, the rig of *Phocea* as compared to that of *Atlantic* (Fig 22a) was one of her assets. The other was a tactical advantage offered by up-to-date weather forecasts (including TV satellite pictures of the current changes of the weather in the given area), available nowadays through all sorts of weather fascimile machines. These gadgets help to eliminate a combination of 'bad luck and poor judgement in choosing the best route – taking into account prevailing currents and winds. With no size limit for boats and no handi-capping, such a tactical advantage will tend to favour larger boats which, by sailing at their best speed, can keep company with fast frontal passages and thus be capable of exploiting consistently stronger winds. The old addage that 'a good big 'un will always beat a good little 'un' has been amply borne out at transatlantic races.

The speed/length ratios already reached by outstanding monohulls and given in Table 1 are instructive in their implication for the future. They indicate that average relative speeds have now been brought so close to the *maximum* relative speed, set by the heavy wave making resistance barrier (which will be discussed in following chapters) that further improvement along the same lines of development must of necessity be extremely limited. The possibility of further speed increase, already explored by the ULDB such as, for example, *Kriter VIII* or *Desperado*, which attained speed/length ratios of about 1.6 and 1.49 respectively, will always attract ardent believers in their speed virtues, just as they have done in the past. The ULDB are, however, very capricious creatures in terms of performance. They may deliver the goods, provided there is just a right kind of wind and from the right direction to sail 'full and by'. And since weather is also capricious, the ULDB and weather seldom suit each other. 'Light- displacement craft,' Davidson remarked, 'are not new in principle' (1.2). For many centuries there have been canoes, proas and the like in the South Pacific and other places, with similar displacement in proportion to the sail area and hull length. Racing dinghies, or dinghy-like modern offshore racers, so common today, are typical examples of the same principle. In all instances the combination of the major design features: displacement, sail area, length and stability ie power to carry sails effectively, is radically different from the combination found in the traditional seaworthy and wholesome yachts.

8 • WEATHER FACTORS

Fig 24a Atlantic routes as seen by a meteorologist. The wind patterns reflect average conditions which are, of course, modified by the actual weather systems – cyclones and anticyclones – moving across the oceans at the speed of 12–18 knots (see charts in Fig 24b). The unaided mariner does not see these overall pictures, so trends must be deduced from listening to weather forecasts, and watching the barometer and the sky. The favourable and unfavourable winds indicated refer to westbound passages.

'We cannot raise the winds. But each of us can put up a sail, so that when the wind comes, we can catch it.'

E F Schumacher, Small is Beautiful

Trade winds and ocean currents are obviously crucial factors in the quest for a speedy passage across large oceans. Natural forces have played havoc with many ambitions and projects, as for example *Club Méditerranée*, but have also occasionally rewarded others in the guise of luck, in which case the poor performance of the boat or crew, or both, might be more than compensated for by helpful contributions from the elementary forces of nature.

Fig 24a which illustrates the average wind and currents of the Atlantic Ocean, gives some idea of the extent to which the favourable and unfavourable winds and currents might affect the crossing time and so the speed performance of any kind of sailing vessel (Ref 1.9). Nothing knocks down average speed more quickly than a couple of days in the windless Horse Latitudes.

The long-distance Transat en Double race, which starts and finishes at Lorient, France, with the one mark being a buoy off St George, Bermuda (for a total great circle distance of approximately 5800 nautical miles) has been monitored by the *Argos* satelite system since 1979 (Ref 1.11). An interesting feature of the Transat en Double race is that the first leg is into the wind whereas the second leg is a downwind run.

One generalization concerning the dominating effects of wind and currents on the crossing time became evident; for most of the yachts in the 1979 race

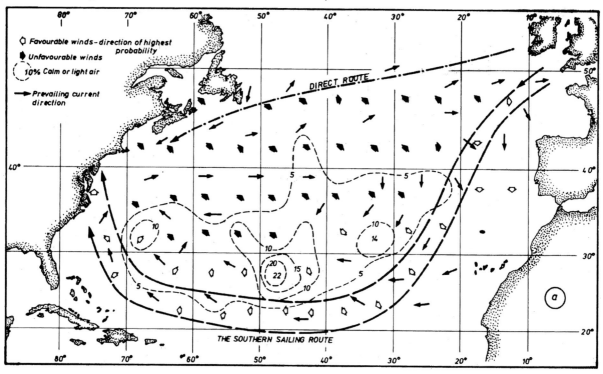

and for the first five finishers in the 1983 race, the sailing time back to Lorient from Bermuda takes about 75 per cent of the time taken to sail from Lorient to Bermuda. In terms of speed performance, this means that the yachts sailed 33 per cent faster in favourable and prevailing downwinds than in upwinds. As a matter of fact, only with the wind more or less abeam is greatly increased speed possible. Another observation based on race results is that there is not much difference between the monohulls and the multihulls as to their relative speed performance (size for size) to windward. When their relative speeds off the wind are compared, however, multihulls are much faster. Interestingly enough, the difference between the windward and downwind performance of a sailing yacht becomes more pronounced as the race duration increases (Ref 1.10). Since ocean- racing monohulls are outclassed in terms of relative speed by ocean-racing multihulls (Fig 2), it is nonsensical to organize races in which both types of craft are supposed to compete on equal terms. If for one reason or another monohull participation is desirable, something must be done to promote their interest, such as having different monohull and multihull classes competing separately.

Of course, the wind pattern depicted in Fig 24a reflects average conditions. Inevitably, some modifications are superimposed by the weather systems (cyclones and anticyclones) moving at random across the Atlantic at speeds of 12 to 18 knots. Large monohull yachts, and particularly multihulls sailing fast, with a speed approaching the movement of those weather systems, can potentially choose to a certain extent the weather configuration for tactical advantage. This ability again raises the question of the need for equitable rating rules and associated handicap methods to compensate for the disadvantages suffered by slower, small craft sailing against faster big ones. One thing is certain: there never has been and never will be a perfect handicap system. Even if the rating rule could measure to a high degree of accuracy the speed potential of a fleet diversified in size, which is doubtful in the first place, true equity would be difficult to achieve.

The principal reason for this is just the simple fact that, inshore or offshore, the weather conditions are variable and changing constantly. Tides, currents and winds are variables that can and frequently do make a mockery of fair play handicap racing. Yachts which are different in size or type (mono or multihulls) and therefore sailing at different speeds, might or might not be in the right place at the right moment to take advantage of favourable weather conditions. Thus the element of chance plays an important part.

Technological advances taking place in yacht navigation and weather routing for trans-oceanic racing may, to some degree, reduce that part of luck which can be attributed to the elusive meteorological factors. The increase and rapid exchange of weather information from both satelite photographs and weather stations, can now be combined with relatively low power-consumption, compact computers. The weather information input is linked to the speed performance characteristics of a given boat (speed polar curves) so that changes to course steered can be made with sensibly accurate predictions of both the speeds and distances covered, thus decreasing the voyage time in the prevailing weather conditions by leading the boat into the right place to take advantage of the next predicted weather change (Ref 1.12).

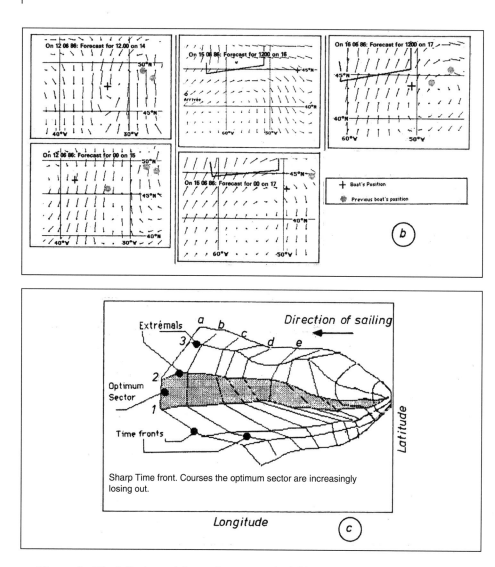

Fig 24b Ever-changing weather systems and the associated wind distribution may radically alter the actual speed performance of any vessel, depending on the chosen course relative to the destination. The shortest route may not be the most favourable.

Five charts for a specific area (given by the latitude and longitude) show the wind distribution encountered during the Two-star Race in June 1985.

Fig 24c An example of the most efficient course to steer offered by the weather routing programme instruction. The boat must sail in a fairly narrow 'optimum sector' to expect good speed performance, and there are obvious gains to be made here. The knowledge imparted by such maps is essential when racing against highly trained professionals pushing their superbly prepared racing machines to the limits. A deviation from the optimum course of only a few degrees is enough to miss the weather-train and so the chance of winning.

Charts in Fig 24b, issued from the numerical files of the *Meteorologie Nationale* (France) for a number of days during the Carlsberg Two-Star race, June 1985, illustrate what kind of weather information can be conveyed to on-board computers. Also included are the actual and previous boat's positions. Fig 24c gives an example of a long range optimization routing for a particular boat ie, the best route to steer.

Inputs are: weather predictions
oceanographic data (waves, tides, currents, etc)
boat's speed performance for various wind strengths and sea states
Outputs are: the course to steer, with expected speeds and meteorological comments indicating a good tactical opportunity
For example: 'Go to the Nova Scotia coast in SW winds, next tack in NW wind set by the cold front of a low expected over Canada.'

Roughly concentric curves a, b, c, d, e, in Fig 24c are 'time fronts', spaced every 6 hours. These time fronts, which are nearly perpendicular to the courses, indicate at any time the set of points which can be reached by a given boat while sailing *at her best*. Transverse lines 1, 2, 3, etc, called extremals, show the best courses to steer to any point of the time front. The diagram also shows the most efficient sharp time front sector; southern and northern routes are losers. Thus, for instance, a departure of 10° from the optimum course within the efficient sector may result in 10 hours' loss in 3 days (14%).

The concept of electronic navigation/weather routing for trans-oceanic racing may ultimately lead to entirely automatic navigation. The course to steer can be transmitted to an auto-pilot which will take into account speed, heel angle, sea state etc (Fig 25). Handling facilities for shorthanded sailing are also envisaged, instructing the auto-pilot, for example, to steer close-hauled, tack, or bear away for speed and come back close-hauled on the new tack. All without touching the tiller, but still hopefully with an emergency release (Ref 1.12). It appears that the possibilities of a powerful navigational microcomputer is limited only by the user's and the designer's imagination and, of course, the financial resources available.

The strong effects of meteorological and oceanographic factors on the actual attained speed of any sailing vessel must be kept in mind if the merits or achievements of yachts are compared in terms of recorded maximum speed/length ratio or ocean crossing time, as given in Table 4 and Tables 5 and 6. Exceptionally favourable sequences of weather changes met in the race might well conceal the otherwise mediocre performance characteristics of the boat in question.

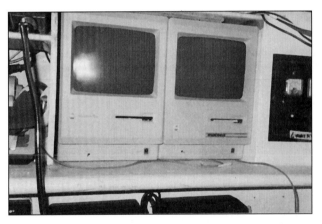

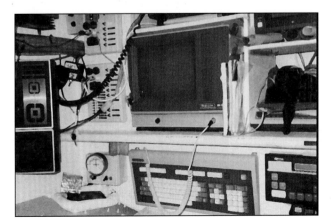

Fig 25 Part of the electronic equipment on one of the boats participating in the BOC Challenge in 1986–87. Top: twin Apple Macintosh for Macsea routing programme. Bottom: Magnavox satellite communication system and Robertson autopilot.

Table 5
Characteristics of 12 sailing craft which surpassed the 400 mile-per-day mark

1 NAME OF CRAFT	2 NAUTICAL MILES	3 TIME HRS.*	4 AVER SPEED KNOTS	5 TYPE OF CRAFT	6 LOA FT	7 LWL FT
Formula Tag	512.55	23.70	21.63	cat	80	74
Credit Agricole II	508.60	24.00	21.19	cat	69	66
Royale II	506.22	25.03	20.22	cat	81	80
Charente Maritime II	457.68	23.85	19.19	cat	85	81
La Vie Claire/Cl.Med.	447.00	23.83	18.76	mono	236	213
William Saurin	447.00	24.00	18.63	tri	85	80
Fleury Michon VII	429.80	23.58	18.23	cat	85	79
Jet Services II	433.38	23.80	18.21	cat	60	57
Elf Aquitaine II	418.26	23.62	17.71	cat	66	60
Elf Equitaine	440.07	25.23	17.44	cat	66	65
Brittany Ferries GB	414.00	24.00	17.25	tri	66	59
Charente Maritime	400.08	23.87	16.76	cat	60	61

*Runs are not exactly 24 hours because the ARGOS tracking satelite does not fly over boats at 24 hour intervals. Only a very few runs have been exactly 24 hours in duration; they are based upon noon-to-noon positions. As any vessel moves west to east, the time between noon readings becomes three minutes shorter for each degree of longitude travelled (longer when sailing east to west).

Table 5 (a)
Characteristics of 12 sailing craft which surpassed the 400 mile-per-day mark

8 BEAM FT	9 SAIL AREA S_A FT^2	10 DISPL. $\triangle$TON	11 $\triangle/(.01LWL)^3$	12 $S_A/\triangle$	13 AVERAGE $V_S/\sqrt{LWL}$	14 DATE
42	2500	8.66	21.4	288.7	2.51	Aug 1984
39	2420	7.37	25.6	328.3	2.61	Aug 1984
40	3350	7.86	15.4	426.2	2.26	Aug 1984
44	3000	9.9	18.6	303.0	2.16	Aug 1984
36	12960	275.6	28.5	47.0	1.28	Feb 1983
49	3300	9.82	19.2	336.0	2.08	May 1984
43	3000	9.64	19.6	311.2	2.05	Aug 1984
32	1920	5.58	30.2	344.1	2.41	Apr 1983
43	1970	5.13	23.8	384.0	2.28	Aug 1984
36	1880	7.86	28.6	239.2	2.16	June 1982
39	1780	6.7	32.7	265.7	2.24	July 1981
34	1820	5.13	22.6	354.8	2.14	June 1983

Note: Some dimensions given in this table may be slightly inaccurate, but this does not affect the trends that this table aims to indicate.

Table 6

Design characteristics of some outstanding fast yachts – mono and multihull – speed record holders or potential record holders, W–E Atlantic crossing.

1 NAME OF YACHT	2 LOA FT	3 LWL FT	4 BOA FT	5 S_AFT^2	6 DISPL △TON	7 MATERIAL	8 △/(01LWL)3	9 SA/△	10 REMARKS
America	102	90	23	5263	147.3	wood	202.0	35.7	mono
Henrietta	107	84	22	8850	205.4	wood	346.5	43.1	mono
Atlantic	185	135	29	18500	446.4	steel	181.5	41.4	mono
Dorade	52	37	10.3	1100	14.8		292.5	74.3	mono
Carina	54	36.5	13	1194	14.0		288.0	85.3	mono
Phocea	236	213	36	12960	276.0		28.5	47.0	mono
Paul Ricard	54	46	56	1830	6.92	alum.	71.1	264.5	tri+hydrof.
Elf Aquitaine	66	62	36	1880	7.14	alum.	30.0	263.3	cat
Jet Services II	60	60	33	1920	5.08	comp*	23.5	378.0	cat
William Saurin	85	80	49	3300	8.93	comp	17.4	369.5	tri
Charles Heidsieck VI	85	79	85	3100	10.85	comp	22.0	285.7	tri+ hydrof
Charente Maritime II	85	81	44	3000	9.9	comp	18.6	303.0	cat
Fleury Michon VII	85	79	43	3000	9.64	comp	19.6	311.2	cat
Royale II	81	80	40	3350	7.86	comp	15.4	426.2	cat
Formula Tag	80	74	42	2500	8.66	comp	21.4	288.7	cat

* comp. stands for composite structure.

Note: Some dimensions given in this table may be slightly inaccurate but this does not affect the trends this table aims to indicate.

9 • THE DRIVE TOWARDS ULTIMATE SPEED

'What we call "progress" is the exchange of one nuisance for another nuisance'

Havelock Ellis

The maximum relative speeds, $V_s/\sqrt{LWL}$, attained by monohulls are presented graphically in Fig 2, and the horizontal branch marked A indicates limits of $Vs/\sqrt{LWL} = 1.5 - 1.8$, which can be attained by ULDB type of yachts in most favourable weather conditions. This includes the extra speed added by surging the fronts of following seas. But if that is disregarded, the figure $V_{smax}/\sqrt{LWL} = 1.4$ appears to be roughly representative of traditional monohull cruising boats of displacement/length ratio: $\triangle/(.01LWL)^3 \simeq 300$.

The next horizontal branch marked B in Fig 2 indicates the limits of relative speed attainable by all sorts of so-called 'offshore' multihulls, including those equipped with hydrofoils which produce hydrodynamic lift that may either augment stability, or lift the hulls partly or totally out of water to reduce wave drag. Figures 26, 27 and 28 illustrate some of the better known multihulls – actual or potential speed record holders. The design characteristics of 12 sailing craft which surpassed the 400 mile-per-day mark, together with their average relative speeds, $V_s/\sqrt{LWL}$, are given in Table 5. It will be evident from Fig 2 and Tables 1 and 5 that the relative speeds attained by multihulls in favourable weather conditions, and based on their best day's run (BDR), are up to 60 per cent higher than that of monohulls sailing in similar conditions.

It will be shown that, in order to achieve such a speed increase, it is necessary

Fig 26 Futuristic dreams made into reality. The French hydrofoil assisted trimaran *Charles Heidsieck IV*, 85 foot long by 85 foot wide, designed by G Vaton, built in 1985 for a Round the World Race. The hull incorporates a variety of aerodynamic ideas, all in an attempt to lift a substantial part of the hull out of the water. Sustained speeds of well over 20 knots without difficulty have been claimed. *Photo: C Fevrier*

Fig 27 (left) The French catamaran *Royale II* which established a speed record in 1986 when sailing across the Atlantic west–east in 7 days 21 hours and 0.5 minutes (see Tables 1 and 6). *Royale* carried 6 crew, not counting the computer routing specialist, Jean-Yves Bernot. Day's mileages from the start on the third of July were 322, 329, 381, 468, 425, 422, 335 and 181, giving a total distance sailed of 3061 nautical miles at an average speed of 16.29 knots. *Photo: C Fevrier*

Fig 28 (right) One of the fastest French multihulls belonging to the *Fleury Michon* family of multihulls sailed by F Poupon, who is/was regarded as the world's premier single-handed ocean racer. In 1987 he established a speed record crossing the Atlantic west–east in 7 days 12 hours and 50 minutes sailing another trimaran *Fleury Michon VIII* (see Table 1). *Photo: C Fevrier*

first to circumvent the sharp upturn of the curve of hull resistances with speed, mainly the wave drag component. One way to accomplish this is to reduce the hull fullness (displacement) drastically, sacrificing space within the hull and a measure of the sea-keeping ability of the *normal yacht* (Ref 1.2).

The second problem is then to provide lateral stability in some way that does not require heavy ballast (and large displacement), so that the sail area can at least be retained or increased, otherwise the net gain might be small. Thus the requirements for higher speed are fairly straightforward. Catamarans comprising two long, narrow and very light hulls abreast of each other with a connecting framework (Figs 26 and 27) satisfy both those high speed requirements. The same applies to multihulls, whether assisted with hydrofoils or not (Fig 26).

The degree to which these requirements have been met by modern fast multihulls compared with traditional monohulls can be judged from Tables 5 and 6. The two ratios are relevant: the displacement/length, $\triangle/(.01LWL)^3$, and the sail area/displacement $S_A/\triangle$ ratio. The first has been reduced from 15 to 20 times! Compare, for instance, *Royale II* with *Dorade* or *Carina* in Table 6. Modern multihulls are extremely light, and so their wave drag must be much lower than that of traditional monohulls. Such a reduction in displacement (weight) of the craft could only be achieved by introduction of fibre reinforced composite materials. They offer a range of strength and stiffness characteristics, combined with lightness, which conventional materials such as wood or aluminium cannot match. However, as yet no 'wonder fibre' with superior characteristics to all others has been invented; and in all probability it never will be. Each fibre and resin has a range of properties which are promising in some respects and inferior in others. Finding the optimum balance between weight saving, strength, stiffness, weathering characteristics and cost is central to the successful design of high speed craft. So far, the road to perfection has been paved with good intentions, and failures. Bearing in mind the destructive power of the sea, it is difficult to assume that any great weight reduction in the boat's structure can be realized without sacrificing reliability and longevity.

Referring to the second high-speed parameter, the sail area/displacement ratio $S_A/\triangle$, it can be seen in Table 6 that contemporary multihulls carry from 5 to 10 times more sail area per given displacement than traditional monohulls! Multihulls are therefore bound to be fast; but remember the proverb: you can't get something for nothing. Multihulls as well as experimental hydrofoils are, by the standard of traditional, deep-keel, heavy displacement monohulls, basically unseaworthy. And the single reason is that, once they have capsized, these craft are more stable upside down than right side up (Ref 1.3). There are all sorts of sailing craft between the two, characterized in Table 6, embodying quite a range of compromises between speed and other desirable attributes such as seakindliness, seaworthiness, handiness and so on. It would be idle to attempt to argue the relative merits of one type of boat against another: one can take one's choice.

Currently observed and rapidly growing interest in fast sailing machines, and the proliferation of all kinds of transatlantic and round the world racing, with raised expectations of earth shattering speeds, would be unthinkable without commercial sponsorship and mass-media coverage. But this has its price. Obsessed by the winning-is-all syndrome, the professionals appear to dominate the contemporary sailing stage. As one crew member who sailed the speed record breaking *Formula Tag* (see Table 5) aptly described it: 'In the world of sponsored racing, if you can't finish first you might as well capsize or break a record; there's no other way anyone wants to know about you.' As boats become more and more overpowered in terms of sail area for a given displacement, lighter and more sophisticated, and at the same time the competition intensifies, less and less room is left for genuine amateurs. Fair competition between professionals and amateurs becomes an illusion.

The entry on stage of the professional at the expense of the true Corinthian is seen by many as a lamentable development. Nostalgic voices are frequently raised in defence of the dear, dead days of an era in which the international rating rules, it is believed, gave not-so-wealthy a chance to compete on equal terms with wealthy. An era of racing in which paid skippers and crews were not allowed, and relatively small cruiser-racers were helmed and crewed exclusively by amateurs. As long as common sense prevails, though, one thing is certain: the proliferation of multihulls and professionalism, advertising and sponsorship – the latter being the main concern at the International Yacht Racing Union (IYRU) meetings – will not eradicate the traditional monohull yachts and the ancient spirit epitomized by the so-called 'Corinthian' sailing clubs.

In the context of Corinthian sailing one thing, however, bothers the author. Corinth, a town in Ancient Greece was famous for two reasons: first, widely recognized activities of efficient and energetic merchants and shopkeepers, and secondly, well trained ladies of easy-virtue, otherwise known as Daughters of Corinth. Why is it that genuinely amateur sailing has become associated with Corinthian virtues the author and his readers will probably never know (Ref 1.13).

PART 2

AERODYNAMICS OF SAILS

1 • INTRODUCTION

'Common sense, do what it will, cannot avoid being surprised occasionally. The object of science is to spare it this emotion and create mental habits which shall be in such close accord with the habits of the world as to secure that nothing shall be unexpected.'

Bertrand Russell, The Analysis of Matter

In a given wind strength, the speed that a boat can attain along any course relative to wind direction is determined by the combination of forces of different origins: aerodynamic, hydrodynamic, buoyancy and gravitational (pull due to gravity). These, in turn, depend on the wind strength, the shape of sails, type of rig and control gadgets, the size and shape of the hull (in particular the configuration of the immersed part of the hull including keel and rudder), displacement of the boat and distribution of weight (inertia and centre of gravity), sea conditions and the crew's level of expertise.

Initially we will look at *steady* sailing conditions in which, it is assumed, the wind velocity and its direction do not change and the water is relatively calm. The effects of unsteady wind and waves are thereby omitted. This limitation is clearly drastic. We all know that whilst under sail the aerodynamic forces and consequently the boat speed constantly changes due to wind variation, and that the hydrodynamic force also alters. As a result, the boat may in some conditions behave in an apparently incomprehensible manner; for instance, rolling or broaching may occur. In order to understand these rather bizarre phenomena, which will be discussed later, it is easiest to first look at steady sailing conditions.

The basic principle of a yacht's motion through air and water can be grasped easily by considering the aerodynamic and hydrodynamic forces separately; and then studying the reciprocal action of these two kind of forces by adding their effect together. The most helpful approach to the analysis of boat performance is to regard her *primarily* as a combination of an aerofoil (sail) and a hydrofoil (hull plus its appendages). Success in racing as well as in designing a high performance boat is most likely to be the result of combining a particularly aerodynamically efficient sail plan and/or hydrodynamically efficient hull appendages. This is not to say that the hull proper is unimportant. Its function from the view of speed performance is to provide stability to carry sails effectively (at possibly low cost in terms of water resistance) and, thereafter, adequate buoyancy, accommodation, and an efficient working platform for the crew.

In the following chapter we shall consider how a sail can utilize wind energy and turn it into the propulsive force which drives the boat.

2 • How and Why An Aerodynamic* Force is Produced

'Common sense is not so common.' **Voltaire, Dictionnaire Philosophique**

In many cases the effects of wind, or water flow for that matter, are fairly easy to understand and predict. Nevertheless, there are times when our intuition may deceive us. For example, Fig 29a illustrates a wind blowing over two types of roofs. Try to guess which type is more likely to be blown off. Common sense would say that the steep, high roof is the more likely to be damaged, but in reality it is usually the lower pitched roof which gets lifted off in heavy winds. A second example can be seen in Fig 29b. The wind here blows over two sails of the same camber (curvature). One is set at an angle of incidence of 20° to the wind direction, the other at 90°. Which sail will develop the larger force? Contrary to expectation, it will not be the one at right-angles which does so, but the first one.

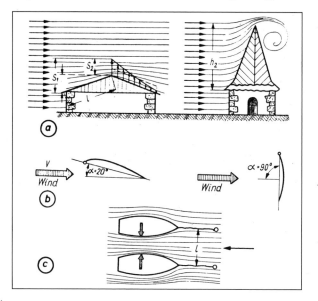

Fig 29 The effects of high-speed winds on buildings, roofs in particular, are not easy to predict. However, as forecast by wind tunnel tests, and corroborated by the statistical data, low-pitched roofs usually suffer worse damage than high-pitched ones in the same areas subjected to the same wind. Due to large suctions caused by the wind being funnelled over rooftop edges, tiles may be lifted and swept away.

Another example of forces acting contrary to expectation, and one which could have unpleasant consequences, is shown in Fig 29c. Two boats are moored in a strong current. What would happen if these boats were moored near one another? Many would expect that the water flowing between them would push them apart, and that, the smaller the gap between them, the greater would be the repelling force. In fact the opposite is true: the two boats will tend to move closer to each other, and this tendency will increase as the gap between them becomes smaller. Non-observance of this apparently incomprehensible phenomenon has been the cause of many serious accidents at sea, and the law nowadays expressly forbids two ships to pass close to each other on nearby parallel courses at high speed to avoid broadside collisions. The reasons for the phenomena illustrated in Fig 29 will be discussed later.

* The term aerodynamic comes from the Greek *aer* (air) and *dynamikos* (power).

EARLY ATTEMPTS TO ESTIMATE AERODYNAMIC FORCE

A sailing yacht moves on the boundary between air and water, being partly immersed in each. In the study of flow pattern past sails and hulls, and resulting forces exerted by air and water – called respectively aerodynamics and hydrodynamics – both air and water are generally referred to as *fluids*, as distinct from *solids*. The differences between air and water are relative rather than fundamental. Thus, for both fluids, one important characteristic is their weight density ie weight per unit volume, say cubic foot, usually designated by the Greek letter *gamma* γ*. For sea water γ_W = 64 lb/cu ft. The corresponding figure for air at sea level is γ_A = 0.0765 lb/cu ft. The density of sea water is therefore about 835 times the density of air.

The wind is only a special case of air in motion, and when considering its effects in terms of forces one must – according to the laws of Newton – know the *mass density* of air. This can be found from the familiar relationship:

Mass = Weight/Acceleration due to gravity

If we introduce the weight density of air, γ_A, into this equation, we find the mass density of air. It is usually designated by another Greek letter, *rho* δ_A ie

$$\rho_A = \gamma_{A/g} = \frac{0.0765}{32.2} = 0.00238 \text{ lb/sec}^2/\text{ft}^4$$

where g is the symbol for the acceleration due to gravity, which is taken to be 32.2 feet per second per second (ft/sec^2). Conversion tables to the International System of Units (SI) are given at the end of the book.

The wind (air in motion) having both mass and velocity possesses *kinetic energy*, the energy due to motion. This energy expressed in customary way

$$(\text{kinetic energy} = \frac{\text{mass x velocity}^2}{2})$$

is usually called the dynamic pressure q (the force per unit area) and is given by the formula:

$$q = \frac{\rho_A \times V^2}{2} = \frac{0.00238\ V^2}{2} = 0.00119\ V^2 \text{ (lb/sq ft)} \qquad \text{Eq 4}$$

where V = velocity of the wind (speed of known magnitude and direction in ft/sec).

The *rational* attempt to estimate quantitatively the force felt by a flat surface (a foil) of a given area set at certain angle relative to the flow direction, be it air or water, can be found in the famous Newton's *Principle* (1687). Scientific interest in fluid mechanics was greatly stimulated at that time by the naval architects of the day. They had already encountered difficulties in designing fast and manoeuvrable vessels which would suit the newly invented doctrine that those who wish to rule the world must first rule the waves. Fast sailing craft were an essential ingredient of this concept of political power.

*By introducing some letters from the Greek alphabet and some simple mathematical expressions, the author has no intention of intimidating the reader, but a few Greek letters have standardized meanings. The advantage of introducing such a shorthand notation, which should not be regarded as scientific jargon, becomes evident with frequent use.

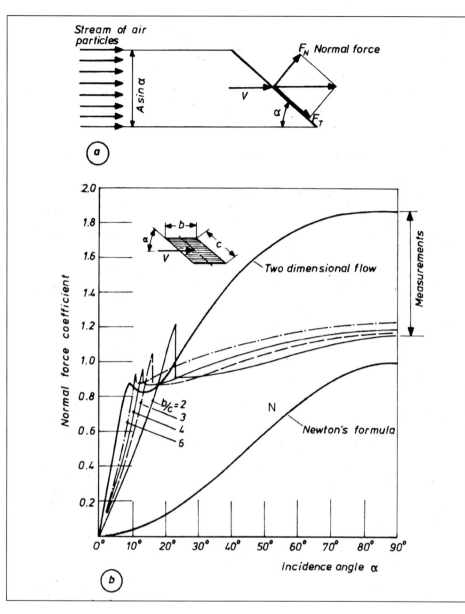

Fig 30 Normal force F_N on flat plates versus angle of incidence α. Forces F_N are expressed in nondimensional units called force coefficients, C_N. These are obtained (see Part 2, Chapter 2) by dividing the force actually measured by the relevant dynamic pressure, q (Eq 4), and the area of the plate, ie,

$$C_N = \frac{F_N}{q \cdot A}$$

Newton's idea relevant to air flow is presented in Fig 30a. It was assumed that the windward side of a flat plate inclined at an angle of incidence, α, to the flow direction is bombarded by a stream of air particles moving in straight parallel paths with speed V. Due to collision with the windward side of the plate of area A, a part of the momentum of air particles, normal to the surface which is A sin α, is transferred to the plate. It manifests itself as a force F_N. It was further assumed that the tangenial component of the momentum indicated by an arrow marked F_T has no effect on the plate. In short, Newton's formula for the force F_N is:

$$F_N \sim \rho_A\, V^2 A \sin^2\alpha \qquad\qquad\qquad \text{Eq 5}$$

where $\sim$ means: proportional to
       A   :   area of the plate

(for further explanation see References and Notes, 2.1). It will be seen that this force will depend on fluid density ρ; and in water it will be about 835 greater for a given velocity V than it will be in the air. This force will also vary with the square of the relative velocity V with which the air moves against the windward side of the plate (relative means that the plate may move towards the air too). F_N force will depend on the area of the plate: it is evident that a postcard will not experience the same force as, say, a barn door, other things being equal. Finally, the force exerted upon the plate will depend on the sine squared of the incidence angle α.

A thick curve marked N in Fig 30b, which gives the variation of force F_N in nondimensional units with incidence angle α, is calculated according to Newton's formula. Above, for comparison, there is a set of three broken line curves obtained much later experimentally. These show changes in F_N force actually measured on plates of three different aspect ratio, at incidence angle α increasing from 0 to 90 degrees (see Table 7). A small sketch above these curves illustrates the meaning of aspect ratio ie b/c ratio. All curves give F_N forces relevant to plates of the same area. Evidently, Newton's formula as reflected by the thick curve is at variance with experimental facts. The measured forces F_N are much higher than those predicted by Eq 5.

Table 7
Approximate relationship between wind speed and force developed on one square foot of a flat area set perpendicular to wind direction

WIND SPEED		APPROX	FEELING OF THE WIND FORCE
LAND MPH	FT/SEC	FORCE IN LB	
1	1.47	0.05	Hardly perceptible
2	2.93	0.02	
3	4.40	0.04	Just perceptible
4	5.87	0.08	
5	7.33	0.12	Gentle pleasant wind
10	14.67	0.50	
15	20.00	1.11	Pleasant brisk gale
20	29.34	1.97	
25	36.67	3.07	Very brisk
30	44.00	4.43	
35	51.34	6.03	High wind
40	58.68	7.82	
45	66.00	9.96	Very high
50	73.35	12.30	Storm or tempest
60	88.00	17.72	Great storm
80	117.36	31.49	Hurricane
100	146.70	49.20	Hurricane that tears up trees, destroys buildings, etc

Scientific theories must allow sufficiently accurate predictions to be made. At an angle of incidence α = 10° Newton's formula gives a value of F_N, which is about 30 times smaller than that actually measured! For α = 90° the formula holds relatively good, giving an F_N value of about 80 per cent of that measured experimentally. Although demonstrably false, Newton's formula was widely used in naval architecture for many years.

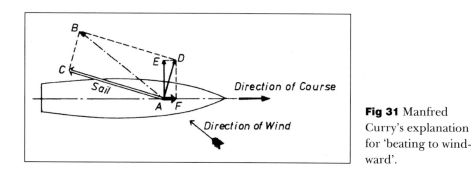

Fig 31 Manfred Curry's explanation for 'beating to windward'.

In more recent times (1949), this theory was repeated by Manfred Curry in his famous *Yacht Racing – The Aerodynamics of Sails* in which he made an attempt to explain how sail forces are produced – probably unaware of who was the originator of the idea. We read how 'it is possible for a boat to beat to windward – let the following brief explanation of this remarkable phenomenon be offered: The annexed diagram Fig 31 [faithfully redrawn from Curry's book] represents a boat on the wind on the starboard tack. The direction and strength of the wind are represented graphically by the line AB. According to the parallelogram of forces, this resultant force may be resolved into two component forces: the larger one, AC, which acts parallel to and along the sail, without producing any other effect than a certain amount of surface friction, and may thus be neglected, and the smaller one AD, acting at right angles to it...'

It should be said in defence of Manfred Curry belabouring the obvious error that he wrote his book as a young medical student and was not trained in aerodynamics.

Why then did Newton – the master in dealing with *solid* heavenly bodies – fail in this particular branch of fluid mechanics? We have to admit that his formula is within the realms of logical possibility, but scientific knowledge cannot be justified or validated by logic alone. All the theories that we consciously or unconsciously hold are based on certain implicit or explicit assumptions; if our assumptions are wrong, then so are the theories.

Newton's basic assumptions are incompatible with what one can observe in the case of fluid action on inclined surfaces. His first assumption was that the fluid flow approaching and finally striking the inclined surface can be pictured as a uniform stream of particles moving along straight parallel lines (rectilinear as shown in Fig 30a). Today, supported by photographic evidence (Fig 34a) we know that the trajectories of air particles close to a sail, or any foil, including a flat plate, are not rectilinear. Instead, the air particles follow curvy lines called *streamlines*; decelerating in one place and accelerating in another. Sometimes the flow is quite irregular and random, ie turbulent. Newton did not have such evidence at hand (how could he?).

His second assumption was that the force F_N (normal to the plate) is a result of the material impact of air particles on the windward side of the plate only. Today we know that this component is relatively minor when compared with the *suction* force operating on the leeward side of the sail, particularly when the sail is set at a small incidence angle, ie below the angle of stall.

Some two hundred years had to elapse until another Englishman F N Lanchester (1868–1946), together with others including M W Kutta (1867-

1944), N Joukowski (1847–1921) and L Prandtl (1875-1953), put the record straight and explained the nature of forces produced by the deceptive flow of air or water. Thus the aerodynamic forces generated on a sail due to wind action depend almost entirely on the pressure differential, called *suction* for short, which pushes the sail from the high pressure region prevailing on the windward side towards the low pressure region dominating over the leeward side of the sail.

PRESSURE DIFFERENCES – THE RIGHT WAY TO EXPLAIN SAIL FORCES

There is no better way to learn about aerodynamic and hydrodynamic forces operating on a sailing boat than to know more about those pressures – how they come into existence and how they can be measured. Consider a glass tube, of the shape shown in Fig 32a, filled with water to the level L–L and then placed in an airstream, Fig 32b. Inlet No 1 of the tube is perpendicular and inlet No 2 is parallel to the wind direction. We would find that the difference in water level in the two tubes will be greater for the higher wind speed V. What does our simple manometer measure? So long as there is no wind acting on the manometer, Fig 32a, the water level in both tubes is the same, since through both open tubes there is the same static pressure, p_{st}, acting, that of atmospheric pressure, P_{atm}. At sea level, which is the bottom of our atmosphere, this pressure on average is assumed to be 2116 lb/sq ft (14.7 lb sq inch), and is balanced in a glass barometer by a column of mercury 29.92 inches in height. If the barometer were filled with water, the height of the column would be 33.9 ft. From this we can calculate that a water column of 1 inch height is equivalent to a pressure of about 5.2 lb/sq ft.

If our manometer is placed in an air stream as shown in Fig 32b, the static pressure acting on the water in both tubes would be the same, and equal to atmospheric pressure ie the prevailing pressure, P_{st}, in the immediate surroundings. However, tube 1, pointing into the flow, would receive, in addition

Fig 32 A method of measuring directly the dynamic pressure, q, and indirectly the flow velocity, V, by means of U-tube manometer. The so-called 'Pitot tube' is based on the above principle.

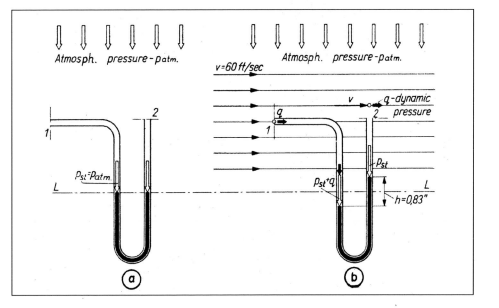

to the static pressure P_{st}, the dynamic pressure, q, of the wind ie that local increase in pressure which arises when the stream of air is brought to rest. Tube 2 will not receive the dynamic pressure, since its inlet, being parallel to the wind direction, offers no impediment to the flow.

The sum of static pressure, P_{st}, plus the dynamic pressure q, is called the total head pressure or the stagnation pressure:

$$P_{tot} = P_{st} + q \qquad\qquad \text{Eq 6}$$

As an example; if the wind velocity V = 60 ft/sec, then the dynamic pressure q would, according to equation 4, be:

$$q = 0.00119 \times 60^2 = 4.3 \text{ lb/sq ft}$$

and this value would be indicated on our manometer by a difference in water levels of h = 0.83 in. The height of the water column in the manometer can therefore be used to measure the dynamic pressure of the wind

$$q = \triangle p = P_{tot} - P_{st} \qquad\qquad \text{Eq 7}$$

where $\triangle p$ means the difference in pressure between the two inlets of the same manometer.

The so called Pitot static tube – the standard instrument suitable for measuring wind or water speed – is based on the principle shown in Fig 31b (Ref 2.2). If connected to a pressure gauge of the aneroid barometer type, the scale can be calibrated directly in miles per hour, and it is used in this form on aircraft. Such instruments can be reasonably accurate (to within 1 per cent) over a wide range of speeds down to about 4 ft/sec; and the error due to inclination of 10° to the direction of the stream can be less than 3 per cent.

The relationship between the speed V (ft/sec) and the difference in water levels h (inches) is given by the formula:

$$V = 66.8 \sqrt{h} \text{ ft/sec} \qquad\qquad \text{Eq 8}$$

Let us carry out another experiment which can be verified in laboratory conditions. Between and around the two plates – one straight and another convex, shown in Fig 33 – flows an air stream passing the stations S_1, S_2, S_3, S_4. At these four points are attached U-tube manometers filled with water to the common level L-L, and having their inlets in, and parallel to, the air stream between the plates. So long as there is no air flowing through the duct, all manometers will indicate the same level. When, however, air flows through, we would see that the water levels in manometers B and C alter, thus clearly indicating reduced pressure (suction) at points 2 and 3 respectively – the greatest change in level occurring at station S_3, where the cross section is minimum.

What is the reason for the different levels on the manometers? Why did the pressure fall at the stations 2 and 3, relative to the surrounding static pressure P_{st}? Evidently, these changes must be caused by the varying velocity of the air as it flows through sections S_1, S_2, S_3, S_4. Manometers A and D will not indicate any difference in levels because sections S_1 and S_4 have the same cross-sectional area and thus both are affected by the same flow velocity V_1 (for the sake of simplicity we ignore small losses in air speed due to friction against the plates). However, the air must flow faster through the smaller sections S_2 and

Fig 33 Simplified picture of the flow through a duct (the Venturi principle). Note that at station S_3 the airstream is converging and as a result the flow velocity, V_3, is increased twofold as compared with velocity V_1 at station S_1. It should not be assumed (although it might be a tempting idea) that the overlapping head-sails operate on the Venturi principle.

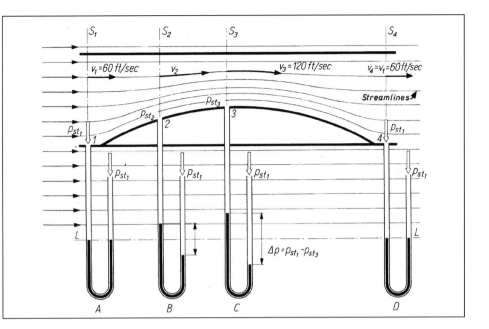

S_3 than through S_1 and S_4 if the quantity of air passing all sections in a given time interval is to be the same. This quantity of airflow is given by the product of the relevant section area and the flow velocity; we can therefore write:

$$S_1 \times V_1 = S_3 \times V_3$$

or

$$\frac{S_1}{S_3} = \frac{V_3}{V_1}$$

Thus, if at station S_1 the air speed is, say, $V_1 = 60$ ft/sec, and the sectional area S_3 is half that of S_1, then the flow speed at S_3 must be doubled ie $V_3 = 120$ ft/sec. Consequently, the dynamic pressures at S_1 and S_3 will, according to formula 4, be:

$$q_1 = 0.00119 \times 60^2 = 4.3 \text{ lb/sq ft}$$
$$q_3 = 0.00119 \times 120^2 = 17.2 \text{ lb/sq ft}$$

This means that the kinetic energy of the air at station S_3 increased fourfold over that at S_1, which is the square of the ratio of the relevant speeds. As shown in Fig 33, this *increase* in dynamic pressure, q_3, at station 3 was followed by a *decrease* in local static pressure, p_{st}, there. Evidently, some kind of interplay between these two forms of pressure takes place.

It is well known that energy cannot be created from nothing, but it can be converted from one form to another. In 1738 Daniel Bernoulli established a simple relationship between the dynamic and static pressures in the same airstream, namely, that the sum of these two pressures measured at the same point is constant along a given streamline (six such curvilinear streamlines are drawn within the duct in Fig 33). This can be written as:

$$p_{st} + q = p_{st1} + q_1 = p_{tot} \text{ (constant)} \qquad \text{Eq 9}$$

ie   static pressure + dynamic pressure = total pressure (constant).

In other words, as the speed increases, the local static pressure decreases and vice versa. This is essentially what occurs with a sail in a close-hauled position, or with a lifting aeroplane wing or with a keel operating at certain leeway angle. In honour of its discoverer, this relation is known as the *'Bernoulli equation'*.

We are now able to calculate the local static pressures at the various stations (Fig 33) taking, say, p_{st1} as equal to the standard atmospheric pressure 2116 lb/sq ft. At station S_1, the total head:

$$p_{tot} = p_{st1} + q_1 = 2116 + 4.3 = 2120.3 \text{ lb/sq ft}$$

In order to satisfy Bernoulli's equation, the total pressure at station S_3 must be the same, and we already know from earlier calculations that $q_3 = 17.2$ lb/sq ft.

Therefore: $P_{tot} = 2120.3 = 17.2 + p_{st3}$
Hence: $P_{st3} = 2120.3 - 17.2 = 2103.1 \text{ lb/sq ft}$

Thus the difference $\triangle p$ between p_{st3} and atmospheric pressure p_{st1} will be:

$$\triangle P = P_{st1} - P_{st3} = 2116 - 2103.1 = 12.9 \text{ lb/sq ft}$$

and this difference will be indicated on manometer C by the column of water equal to:

$$\frac{12.9}{5.2} = 2.48 \text{ inches}$$

Manometer B will indicate a value between A and C, since the section area and thus the velocity V_2 are intermediate.

We are now in a position to explain one of the examples quoted earlier. The low pitched roof of Fig 29a is somewhat similar to the previous example of air-flow through the duct. The wind, as it passes over the ridge, will create suction forces tending to lift the roof, the pressure inside the building being equal to the atmospheric pressure. If at the apex of the roof the section area, S_2, for the wind to flow through is half that at the eaves, S_1, and the wind speed $V = 60$ ft/sec, then the lifting suction over the roof ridge would be about 13.0 lb/sq ft. In winds of hurricane strength, say about 100 mph (ie about 150 ft/sec), the suction forces would increase in proportion to the ratio of relevant wind speeds squared, ie:

$$\left(\frac{150}{60} \right)^2 = 6.25.$$

That is, the forces tending to lift the low pitched roof might increase from about 13 lb per sq ft to 81 lb per sq ft. Severe wind-induced damage has been reported on this type of roof, where structural strength has been inadequate to resist high suction forces. The force is particularly damaging at the apex of the roof, where the airstream goes through a sort of throat, accelerates (the Venturi effect) and may reach very high local speed.

In the case of a steeply pitched roof of the same length, $h_2 = 1$ (half the width of the low roof), the flow over the lee side is turbulent. A consequence of this is that large suction forces are not developed over the rear half of the roof, and thus the total drag force is much less than that for the low pitched roof.

FLOW VISUALIZATION AND OTHER MEANS OF EXEMPLIFYING THE THEORY OF FOIL ACTION

At this point it is appropriate to say a few words about the visual presentation of the flow of air or water. The steady motion of the air in a stream is shown graphically in Fig 33 by means of imaginary smooth lines called *streamlines*. These are the paths taken by the air particles which can be made optically distinct from the surrounding flow by an injection of a filament of smoke upstream of the model. Flow visualization is easier in water than in air as the range of available techniques is greater. Thus, water can be used with advantage to simulate aerodynamic flows (Ref 2.3).

Photographic records play an important part in understanding the nature of aerodynamic or hydrodynamic flow pattern which, in turn, determines the forces. 'Seeing is believing'; a good picture may be worth a thousand words. Some examples of such pictures are given in Fig 34a, b, c. Interpretation of the flow pattern shown in Fig 34a is fairly straightforward. In such a steady flow, air particles will follow the same trajectory (streamline). Since a streamline is everywhere tangential to the local velocity, it is possible to calculate these local flow velocities and hence the relevant pressures. As a rule: where the spacing between neighbouring streamlines is narrowing (see the flow pattern over the leeward surface of the airfoil in Fig 34a), the flow velocities there *increase*. Conversely, where the spacing between streamlines widens, as seen over the windward surface of the same airfoil, the local velocities there *decrease*.

Fig 34a (right) A photograph of a simple flow past a foil (it might be rudder or wingsail). Kerosene smoke introduced at equidistant points in front of the model indicates so called *streamlines*. Note a crowding of streamlines above the nose (the leading edge of the foil). Such a converging of the streamlines, similar to that above section S_3 in Fig 33, is associated with an increase in the local velocity of the flow between the streamlines. Conversely, the diverging of the streamlines depicted below the leading edge of the foil is associated with a decrease in the local velocity. It will be seen that the fluid particles can 'feel' the presence of an obstruction before it is reached, and will never touch the obstruction but follow it at a distance.

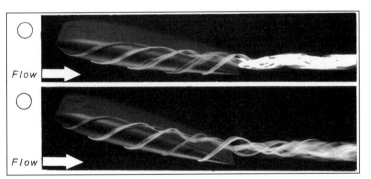

Fig 34b (above left) Flow round the tip of a foil set at two different angles of incidence: 10 degrees (upper picture) and 15 degrees (lower picture).

Fig 34c (above right) Flow pattern on a hull showing separated flow region (the dark area just ahead of the propeller). One of the techniques widely used in aeronautics to reveal the flow character is to paint the model with a mixture of Kerosene and French chalk.

However, there are cases when the flow is *unsteady* or separated. Interpretation of the results of visualization is not so easy in these cases, and the flow pictures might be open to misinterpretation. Attention is drawn to Photo c in Fig 34 which demonstrates a 'frozen' flow pattern in which the surface streamlines along the hull afterbody were made visible by coating the model with a mixture of white pigment in mineral oil. This picture reveals that, in the region of the stern, the steady flow breaks down (dark area) and separates from the surface of the hull just ahead of the rudder and propeller. Such a flow pattern indicates that, without modification of the stern shape, or application of other means preventing separation (such as vortex generators), neither the propeller nor the rudder would be fully effective.

Consider in turn the air flow around a sail (Fig 35a). The air stream divides into two parts: that traversing the lee side, and that on the weather side of the sail. We can see from the diagram that the flow on the lee side is constricted, from a section S ahead of the sail to the section S_L. The wind speed, V_L, in this region must therefore be greater than the free stream speed V ahead of the sail. According to Bernoulli's equation, an increase in speed is associated with a corresponding decrease in static pressure, p_L, on the lee side. The greatest change in speed, and hence suction, must occur near the luff of the sail, provided that the incidence angle α is not increased to such an extent that the airflow breaks away and separates from the sail surface, whereby the kinetic energy of the wind is dissipated in a disorderly fashion.

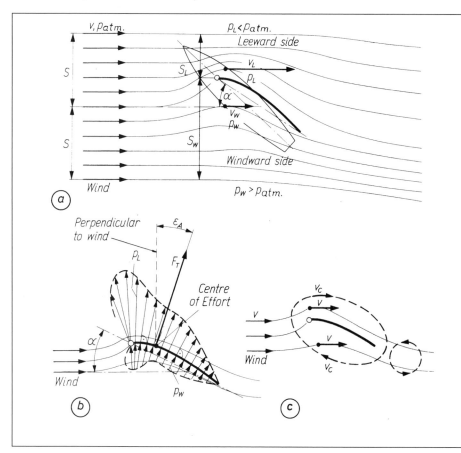

Fig 35 Distribution of local wind velocities and local pressures around a sail in close-hauled attitude. Perhaps the most striking feature which can be detected by measuring instruments such as the Pitot tube is that the velocity, V_L, of the wind flow along the front part of the leeward side of the sail is much higher than V_w to windward. The ratio of those local wind flow velocities, V_L/V_w, can be more than two, and might be as high as three.

A similar analysis of the weather side shows that the local wind speed, V_W, falls as compared with V ahead of the sail. Consequently, the static pressure, p_W, rises as the kinetic energy of air is decreased. As a result, on the windward side we have pressures *greater* than atmospheric, and on the lee side they are *less* than atmospheric. These local pressures, indicated in Fig 35b by a number of thin arrows marked p_L (leeward pressures) and p_W (windward pressures) can be combined to give a single resultant force F_T, acting at an angle ε_A (epsilon) to the perpendicular to wind direction. The line of action of F_T, which will be in the fore part of the sail, passes through a point called the centre of effort.

Some sailors believe that on the windward side of a sail the air is being compressed ('squeezed'); ie that its density is increased. This view is erroneous, as air compression due to motion only becomes significant at speeds near and above that of sound. The aerodynamic forces we are dealing with depend primarily on the conversion of the kinetic energy of the wind into unequal pressures distributed over the sail, and this process takes place at a constant air density.

The generation of aerodynamic forces can be explained in yet another way, compatible with Bernoulli's equation. One can assume that the resultant flow round the sail is composed of two superimposed parts (Fig 35c). First, there is a component of the wind velocity, V, as measured ahead of the sail, but in addition there is a circulating flow, Vc, round the sail. Resolution of these two components will lead to a reduction in the actual velocity on the weather side, and to an increase on the lee side, and hence increases and decreases respectively the local pressures.

It is interesting that this concept, apparently contradictory to common sense, can be confirmed by experiments (Ref 2.4). For instance, if one takes a strip of corrugated cardboard and pivots it on a pin as shown in Fig 36a, and then moves a piece of curved cardboard underneath it in the direction V, one will find that the corrugated strip will move in the direction Vc, opposite to V. The curved piece of cardboard, like a sail, induces a circulation around it in the direction previously described. If there were no circulation, the corrugated strip would move in the same direction as the cardboard, under the action of air friction.

Fig 36 Experimental examples corroborating the theory of sail action. These experiments should not be regarded (as an ignorant critic described in a different context) as a mode of cooking the discernible facts for the sake of exemplifying the physical law.

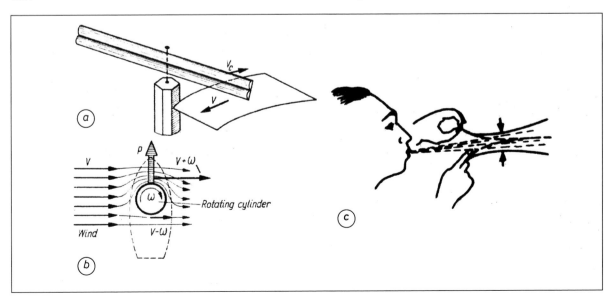

This theory of circulation can also be illustrated by the experiments first carried out by Magnus (1852). He demonstrated that if a wind of velocity, V, blows relative to a circular cylinder rotating with an angular velocity, ω, a force P, perpendicular to the wind direction, will appear, as shown in Fig 36b. This phenomenon, whereby an aerodynamic force is generated, is called the 'Magnus effect'. On this principle, A Flettner constructed in the 1920s two vessels, *Buckau* and *Barbara*, which were driven not by sails or propellers but by vertically mounted rotors. With the wind abeam, the driving force was directly forward. Although the idea worked in practice, it was not commercially successful due to its limited application and low fuel prices at the time. More recently, attention has been paid again to the Flettner rotor as an alternative to conventional sails (Ref 2.5).

Sketch (c) in Fig 36 demonstrates the action of accelerated flow between two pieces of corrugated cardboard. Since the air velocity between two pieces is higher than that outside, the pressure differential will tend to move the cards closer together, as indicated by the two broken lines. The more intense the blast of air, the stronger the action of the pressure forces. This example of Bernoulli's principle is relevant to the behaviour of two boats moored in strong current shown earlier in Fig 29c.

3 • DISTRIBUTION OF PRESSURE OVER SAILS

'Learning is the kind of ignorance distinguishing the studious. I don't want to downgrade studiousness, but I don't think knowledge should be an obstacle to understanding.'

M A Biot

The pressure forces distributed over the lee and windward sides of the sail can be measured using manometers, either on sail models in wind tunnels, or on the full-sized sails of a moving yacht. Such pressure measurements on both sides of the sails of the American yacht *Papoose* were made in close-hauled, light weather conditions (Ref 2.6). Figure 37 shows the location of the three lines of measurement points on the mainsail, and one line on the jib. Small holes in the sails were connected by rubber tubing to a battery of manometers on the deck. The readings on the manometers were recorded simultaneously by photography. The principle of the measurements is illustrated in Fig 38 which, for the sake of clarity, shows only one manometer connected to the lee side of the sail. By changing the tack, the researchers were able to obtain measurements from either the windward or leeward side.

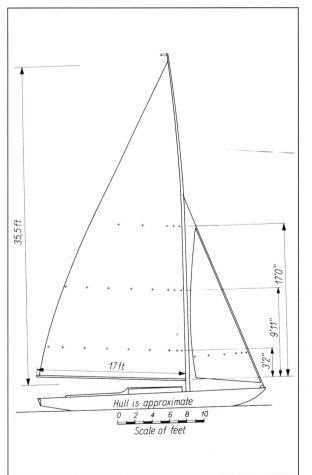

Fig 37 (left) The sail plan of the Marconi rigged yacht *Papoose*, which was used by Warner and Ober in full scale experiments conducted in 1923. The yacht was fitted with cotton racing sails, the leech being made as flat as possible.

Fig 38 (below) The principle of measuring the suction on the leeside of a sail. The object of research on the pressure distribution over sails is to obtain information relevant to sail design and sail trimming. The term p_L designates the static pressure at a given point on the leeside surface of the sail.

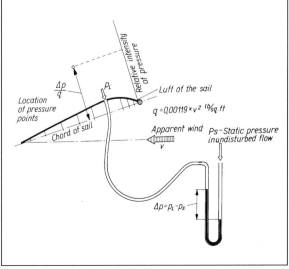

The manometers indicated the differences, △p, between the actual static pressure on the sail and the static atmospheric pressure, ps, at the deck. To obtain results in a convenient nondimensional form, and to eliminate the effect of the different wind speeds at which the tests were done, the static pressure differences, △p = pL – ps, were divided by the appropriate values of the wind dynamic pressure q. Results were presented in graphic form as in Fig 39, which shows the pressure distribution for one row of points on the mainsail (Fig 37). The horizontal scale gives the ratios (in per cent) of the distance from the luff to the length of the sail chord. The vertical scale gives values of the ratio △p/q, adopting the convention that positive values are relevant to measured pressure *above* the atmospheric, and negative values (suction) indicate the pressure *below* atmospheric. It should be noted that negative values appear above the origin O, and positive values below. From such a graph we can estimate both the pressures and suctions at different points on the sail. Thus, if the wind speed is 30 ft/sec, its corresponding dynamic pressure will be q = 0.00119 × 30² = 1.07 lb/sq ft; then, for example, at the point on the sail where △p/q = – 2 we shall have a suction:

$$△p = – 2 × 1.07 = – 2.14 \text{ lb/sq ft}$$

ie below the atmospheric pressure.

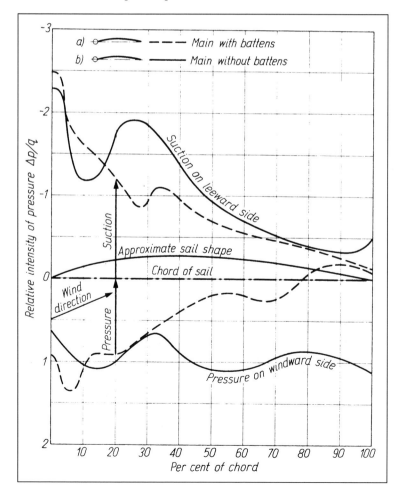

Fig 39 Pressure distribution over mainsails, with and without battens, set in close-hauled attitudes. Measurements were taken along the middle row of points (see Fig 37) running across the sail from luff to leech and parallel to the boom. The term 'suction' is just a quick way of designating the pressure difference across the sailcloth, which tends to push the sail from the higher pressure region (windward side of the sail) towards the lower pressure region (leeside of the sail). Undesirable pressure distribution obtained on Sail B (without battens) can also be found when the stiffness of battens is not sufficient in relation to the wind strength. This condition is usually met when the position of maximum camber of the sail moves aft toward the leech with increasing wind speed.

The only mechanisms whereby a force can be communicated to a sail are the pressure difference and friction (sheer stress) distributed over the sail surface; the latter being relatively small.

An explanation should be given as to the value of the relative intensity of pressure, $\triangle p/q$, recorded on the windward side of the sail in Figs 39 and 41: it should never be greater than 1. Values equal to 1 can only be recorded when the maximum energy available from the airstream, as given by q, is totally converted into the maximum pressure exerted at the point on the sail where the air is brought to rest, ie *stagnates*. In such a case $\triangle p = q$ and so $\triangle p/q = 1$. The fact that an intensity of pressure, $\triangle p/q$, greater than 1 has been recorded suggests some inaccuracies in the measurements taken on *Papoose*. In fact, the research team admitted that they had met some difficulties in measuring the pressure on the full-scale sail in natural conditions. For instance, the shape of the sail, and therefore the pressure distribution at given angle of incidence, must change with the wind speed and with the angle of heel, as well as with the vertical wind gradient at the instant, and some other meteorological factors which can hardly be defined quantitatively will also affect the measurements. However, their results as presented may serve in a qualitative sense.

UNEQUAL CONTRIBUTION OF PRESSURES TO THE DRIVING FORCE

Three striking features of the pressure curves in Fig 39 will be noted and particularly relevant to the lee side of the sail: *first* is the concentration of high suction near the luff (leading edge) of the sail. In other words, all pressure intensities increase towards the luff. On the other hand, away from the luff the suction decreases quite rapidly, approaching zero at the leech.

This first significant conclusion is in accordance with what would have been expected from tests on aeroplane wings, for it is a fact familiar to all students of aerodynamics that the maximum suction on any wing or inclined surface occurs near to the leading edge. Another glance at Figs 34a and 35a should be of some help in understanding the reason for this typical pattern of pressure distribution. These figures reveal densely spaced streamlines just above the leading edge of both foils, showing high local flow velocities. Consequently, we can state that the most intensive suction should occur where the streamlines converge, thus indicating that the local flow velocity gradually increases. Inevitably, as shown in Fig 39, a corresponding drop in suction forces must follow when the streamlines diverge, in accordance with Bernoulli's equation (Eq 9).

The importance of this concentration of suction near the luff becomes apparent when considering in some details the mechanics of the process whereby the pressure developed on a sail drives a boat to windward. At any one point along the sail section (Figs 39, 40a) the suction on the lee side and the pressure on the windward side can be added, and represented by vectors, indicating the direction and magnitude of the resulting pressure, as for example P1, P2, P3 in Fig 40a. These always act normal to the sail curvature at any given point. Resultant pressure can be resolved into two components: one parallel to the course sailed, the other perpendicular. Obviously only the former, marked Pᴅ, has a direct effect on the driving force. It is evident that the greatest contribution to the driving force comes from the pressures developed on the fore part of the sail, by virtue of both their magnitude and their direction. Further from the luff, pressure contribution towards the driving component decreases quite rapidly, and may in some cases – on sails which exhibit a 'hard leech' (hooking to windward

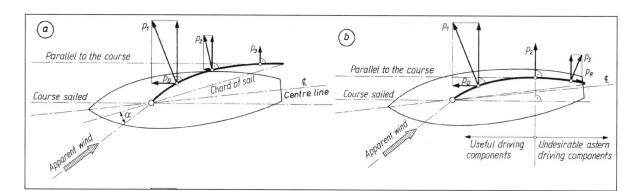

for example) – become negative, ie produce the retarding component marked pR in Fig 40b. Such a pressure distribution is characteristic of sails without battens, or of sails with battens which are not stiff enough near the trailing edge.

Two sets of pressure distributions for a mainsail are shown in Fig 39. In one case (a) the sail had the roach stiffened with battens. In the other case (b) the sail was tested without battens, and excessive curling to windward of the roach occurred. By comparing the pressure distributions for these two cases, we can appreciate why the use of battens with proper stiffness, particularly on a sail with a large roach, is so advantageous. The leech of a sail, like the trailing edge of an airplane wing, acts to guide the airflow away from the forward part, and so to improve the efficiency of the foil as a whole (Ref 2.6).

Any doubt in this respect may be dispelled by considering Fig 40b. If we draw a tangent to the sail, parallel to the course sailed relative to the wind, then the pressures on the windward side and suctions on the lee side will give a forward- driving component p_D if they act ahead of the tangent point (see arrow marked p_2). Aft of this point, both the pressures and suctions are harmful. They contribute only to the side force (heeling force), which should be kept small so that both the leeway and heeling angles will not be excessive, and so that reefing in heavier winds may be (as far as possible) delayed or avoided. If the sail is hauled in too far (Fig 40b), the driving force component may be reduced and the side force component increased.

The *second* striking characteristic of the pressure distribution on a sail (Fig 39, mainsail with battens) is the considerable difference between the magnitude of the pressures on the leeward side and those on the windward side. Comparing the suctions and pressures in the fore part of the sail section, we can estimate that the leeward side contributes 60–75 per cent of the total aerodynamic pressure. To obtain a large driving force, every attempt should therefore be made to employ the suction side as much as possible. This can be done by using two interacting sails – a mainsail and a headsail, be that a genoa or just a small jib.

WHICH SAIL CONTRIBUTES MORE TO THE DRIVING FORCE: MAINSAIL OR HEADSAIL?

It will be observed in Fig 41 that the curve of suction on the lee side of the jib lies far above the mainsail curve, providing more than *twice* as much force in relation to its area as does the mainsail. How can the relatively high performance of the headsail be explained? In view of the close proximity of the two sails in a sloop-type rig, it is hardly surprising to find that the region of suction

Fig 40 Resolution of local pressures p_1, p_2 and p_3 for three measurement points on a typical cross section of a sail set in close-hauled attitude. Note that practically all the driving force is developed in the immediate vicinity of the luff, where the forward component is relatively large. Another component of pressure, perpendicular to the driving component, is undesirable but unavoidable. It should be kept down in order that both the leeway and the angle of heel may not be excessive.

over the leeside of the main will be close to the region of increased pressure over the windward side of the headsail. Inevitably, these two regions, with different pressures (indicated by a circle in Fig 43), will tend to neutralize each other, the suction intensity over the mainsail being partially reduced. The extent of this interference was investigated on the yacht *Papoose*, and

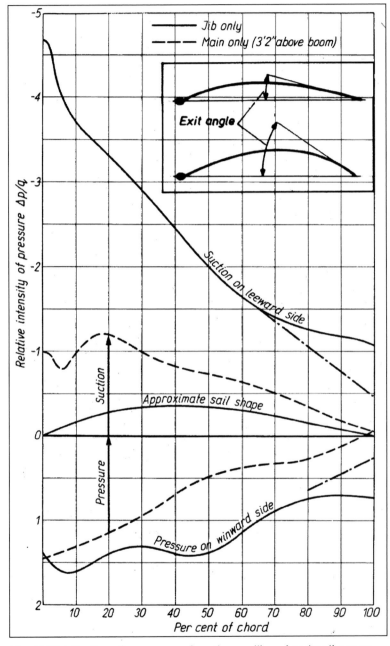

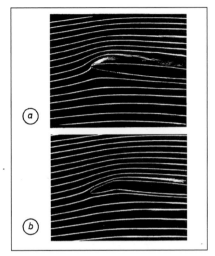

Fig 42 An abrupt separation of the flow at the nose as shown in photo (a), (followed by a sudden loss of foil efficiency in terms of favourable distribution of suction near the luff) largely depends on the leading edge radius – in the case of a sail, the shape of the mast or the headfoil. Larger nose radii delay the probability of leading edge separation of the flow. Such a separation, which readily occurs at the nose of thin airfoils – and soft sails belong to this category – can be mitigated or delayed by a change in the foil curvature right behind the leading edge. This effect is shown in photo b. In general, the curvature of the sail entry is *the most important* feature of sail's geometry apart from the sail camber. If the flow is not to meet the nose abruptly, as it does in photo (a), the front part of the sail should curve in some fashion to meet the oncoming air flow gently – similar to that depicted in photo (b). In other words, in order to avoid premature separation, the curvature of sail entry must correspond to the incidence angle of the local oncoming flow, and be different for different sail trim.

Fig 41 Distribution of pressure and suction on jib and mainsail operating together. Measurements were taken on full scale yacht *Papoose* along the sail section parallel to and 3′ 2″ above the boom (Fig 37). The form of distribution of suction over the surface of a sail is of utmost importance for the driving force, and for an isolated sail (or foil) much depends on the shape of entry. Figure 42 demonstrates the point.

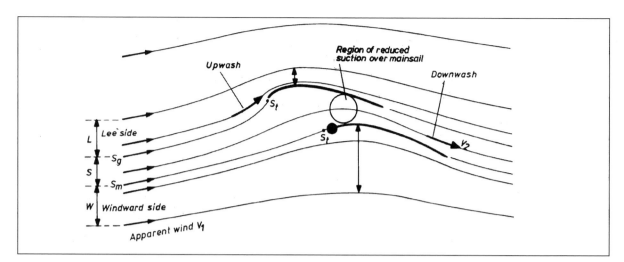

Fig 43 This airflow diagram explains the slot effect. The realistic streamlines for both the jib and the main cannot be determined by guesswork, but they can be correctly established by means of the analog field plotter (Ref 2.7).

The space marked S between the stagnation streamlines S_g and S_m, which strike the leading edges of the genoa and mainsail respectively, indicates the amount of air which will pass through the slot. We can see that the flow diverges within the slot area shown by the circle, and this indicates that the flow velocity there decelerates – hence the static pressure in this area must inevitably increase. This increase may be (and usually is, depending on the headsail trim) large enough to cause 'backwinding' of the mainsail, which clearly demonstrates that the pressure on the leeward side of the mainsail is higher than on the windward side.

The spaces marked L and W indicate the amount of air which will subsequently pass and accelerate over the leeside of the genoa, and decelerate in the vicinity of the windward side of the main. Note that, due to interaction with the mainsail and the resulting *upwash*, the headsail is actually operating at higher effective incidence angle. This is one of the reasons why the genoa develops much more suction when it is operating in the flow field modified by the presence of the mainsail. The other reason for the higher efficiency of the headsail is that the presence of the main induces considerably higher velocities, and so more intense suction over the leeside of the headsail as compared with those developed on an isolated sail (Ref 2.7).

results are presented in Fig 44. To determine in detail the nature and magnitude of such effect, the pressures on the mainsail were measured with and without the jib. The crossed area indicates quite a substantial loss of suction over the mainsail due to the 'slot effect'.

Another feature of the suction distribution when the mainsail and jib are used is the absence of the distinct peak of high suction normally observed when single sails or foils are tested without an interacting companion (Fig 45). It will be observed that when the incidence angle increases, the suction peak becomes more pronounced. However, at a certain angle of incidence, which largely depends on the foil camber, the stall takes place. This is due to the flow failing to follow the curvature of the leeside surface of the foil, and separating from the surface along the line marked S. After stall, the suction distribution is characterized by greatly reduced intensity, and absence of a suction peak near the leading edge of the foil. As a rule, the higher the suction peak, the more susceptible the foil to stalling. The stall may therefore be delayed by assisting the flow to remain attached. That is precisely what a headsail does in relation to a mainsail, as does a small, highly cambered, auxiliary aerofoil (slat) positioned just above the upper nose of an aircraft wing.

Fig 44 The effect of an interacting jib on the suction distribution over the mainsail. Measurements were taken on the *Papoose*, Fig 37.

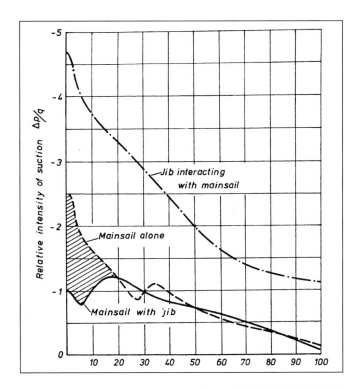

Fig 45 Changes in pressure distribution (particularly conspicuous in suction) on a foil with angle of incidence α. Such graphs make it possible to establish:

- The location of the suction peak and its relative intensity
- The position of the centre of pressure
- The beginning and type of stall
- The relative contribution of the suction and pressure to the total force developed by the foil at given angle of incidence.

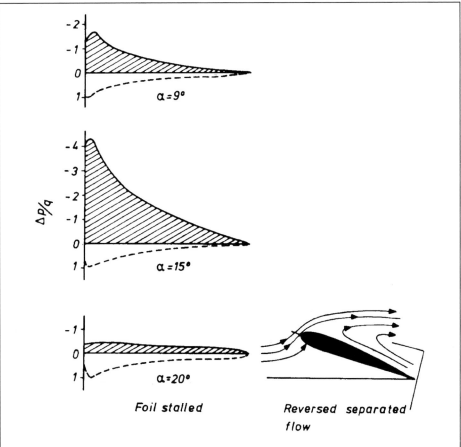

THE SLOT EFFECT CONTROVERSY

Interaction between jib and mainsail has long been one of the most controversial issues in sailing theory discussions. The conventional wisdom is that, due to the presence of the headsail, airflow over the leeward surface of the mainsail must be speeded up due to the Venturi effect. This view is motivated by the many misconceptions incorporated in almost every textbook on aerodynamics. The whole idea of jib action, similar in principle to the slot effect on a wing, can be traced at least as far back as L Prandtl (1875–1953), the world authority on theoretical and experimental aerodynamics.

According to Prandtl's followers, 'the air flowing through the slot is accelerated and moves toward the rear of the airfoil section, before slowing down and separating from the surface. One prominent effect is the energizing of the retarded flow in the boundary layer, by the venturi action of the channel between the auxiliary airfoil (slat) and the main airfoil.'

As a matter of fact, the slot does *not* operate as a large venturi with the air speeding up in the space where jib and mainsail overlap. And the distinct drop in suction measured in early tests on *Papoose*, as shown in Fig 44, clearly indicates that in this region the airflow cannot possibly be increased. That would be against the Bernoulli's law (Eq 9).

A useful and very interesting study of the jib–mainsail interaction has been made by A E Gentry. By using the electrical analogy technique (analog field plotter), he explained correctly for the first time the slot effect (Ref 2.7). As shown in Fig 43, the air particles approaching the slot between the two sails actually slow down, and only start to accelerate just before reaching the leech of the jib. This process of deceleration and acceleration of the airflow can, perhaps, be more easily understood by comparing the distribution of streamlines and, in particular, the spacing between the two streamlines marked Sg and Sm approaching the jib and main respectively. These separate the quantity of air which will flow through the slot. Widening space between these two streamlines indicates deceleration of airflow and, conversely, narrowing distance between them points to the acceleration of the flow. Consequently,

Fig 46a Streamlines about jib and mainsail showing local flow velocities and relevant angles. Although the flow field created by the interacting jib–mainsail is different in a quantitative sense from that generated by a single foil, it is, in a qualitative sense, similar. One has to go several boat lengths upstream and downstream before a free stream velocity $V_o = 10$ knots would be reached. The dotted lines show the streamlines. The pairs of numbers along the lines indicate the local wind velocity (upper number), and the variation in local flow angle (lower number) at a given point. The above figure is included herein by kind permission of Arvel Gentry (Ref 2.7).

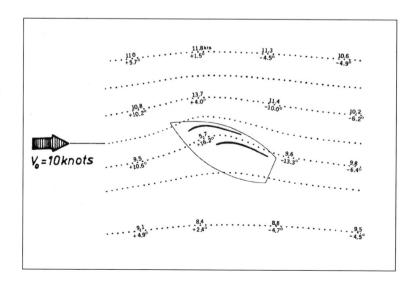

Fig 46b Visual flow studies around the model rig of a 12 Metre made by the author in the 1960s in the Southampton University wind tunnel. Note the upwash in front of the genoa, similar to that in Fig 43 and above. One of the principal components in sail performance is the flow field developed by interacting sails. By the term 'flow field' it is understood the actual non-uniform local wind velocities and directions affecting directly the sail forces. These are different from uniform wind well ahead of the rig tested.

if the streamlines are crowded together, the flow velocity is increased and the pressure is reduced, and when the streamlines diverge, flow velocity is reduced and the pressure increased.

As a result of interference between the two sails, pressure distribution on the mainsail is modified in such a way that the suction peak is reduced; so the flow separation is delayed, or even prevented, depending on the slot geometry. At the same time, the air velocity over the entire lee surface of the jib is greatly increased (Fig 46), and this, together with an *upwash* shown in Fig 43, contributes to the much higher efficiency of the jib, and of the jib–mainsail combination, with the headsail carrying a heavier load per unit area than the mainsail. And although the mainsail suffers some loss in suction, as depicted in Fig 44, the gain in suction over the leeside of the jib more than compensates for this deficiency.

Interactions between headsail and mainsail, and the practical implications of the slot effect, have been discussed in some detail in the author's book *Aerohydrodynamics of Sailing*, so there is no need to repeat all the arguments. However, one general remark may be appropriate. It appears that too many scientists give too much credence to their own theories; quite erroneous views can thus become firmly established as scientific knowledge. Subsequently a whole generation of experts may become so heavily indoctrinated that they find it difficult, whatever the evidence, to face the possibility that a 'time-honoured' and cherished theory might be false. If we analyse the meaning of suction decrease over the front part of the interacting mainsail in Fig 44, we must come to the conclusion that the local flow velocity in this region *must be lower* than when the mainsail is operating without an interacting jib. This inference should be sufficient to reject the Venturi analogy espoused by Prandtl's followers, or at least to encourage critical consideration of its validity. Yet apparently the Venturi analogy followed by Prandtl's interpretation – in which more attention was paid to the main wing and the slot effect on its boundary layer than to the slot itself – was so compelling that the premises were extrapolated into a theoretical dogma. And it has been argued ever since that the main wing (or mainsail) bears the burden of the total aerodynamic force increase, whereas the experiments performed some 60 years ago unmistakably indicate that the slat (or jib) does (Ref 2.8). So we must face up to the fact that even the 'hard' sciences are fallible; it may take years to unlearn an uncritically absorbed view.

And one more point. Why should we pay so much attention to the airflow approaching sails, and going round and through the slot, and to the streamlines as depicted in Figs 42, 43 and 46? Because these prove that the conventional explanation of sail interaction is useless for the further advancement of sailing theory and practice. The more realistic explanation should lead directly to a number of constructive suggestions for further research and to more fruitful 'trial and error' experiments in rig development. Some of these will be discussed in later chapters.

THE EFFECT OF THE MAST ON PRESSURE DISTRIBUTION

The flow around a thin sail section without a mast is more complicated than the flow around, say, a much thicker wingsail.

The presence of the mast, attached to the leading edge of sail, makes the flow and resulting pressure distribution even more complex. One of the reasons, but not the only one, is that the pressure distribution around the mast itself (and the associated flow pattern) does affect, in particular, the suction distribution behind the mast. An examination of the suction curves in Fig 39 shows a characteristic drop soon after the mast – the result of the strong modifying effect of the mast on the pressure distribution in its vicinity. Reference to Fig 47, which shows the pressure distribution round the mast *without* the presence of a sail, demonstrates the point. The maximum suction is developed when the local flow velocity relative to the mast is greatest. Just behind this point the flow separates, the local flow velocity decreases, and so does the suction intensity. Dead air, deposited in the wake of the mast, inevitably incurs some losses in the pressure distribution both on the lee and windward sides of the sail.

Obviously, depending on the shape of the mast, or the headfoil (headstay foil, luff-groove system) in the case of a streamlined forestay, the pressure distribution around the whole sail will be different. Also, the tolerance of the jib or genoa, set behind the headfoil to varying angles of incidence, will likewise be different from that of a knife edge, bare sail with hanks. The tolerance in this context means the sail's ability to maintain attached flow right to its trailing edge, despite variation in the angle of incidence. Normally, any sail with a sharp leading edge is sensitive to the change of the airflow direction at its leading edge. And, if the angle of incidence is not just right, a considerable flow separation may occur on the lee of the luff, followed by a decrease in suction intensity. The *ideal* angle of incidence is defined in aerodynamic science as that at which the airflow enters the leading edge of sail smoothly, ie without separation on either the lee or windward side. With a round-nosed, well designed streamlined headfoil, the airflow attachment can be retained over a larger deviation from the ideal angle of incidence. The use of a thicker headfoil section also permits the incident airflow to approach from a considerable range of angles without risk of imminent flow separation (Ref 2.4).

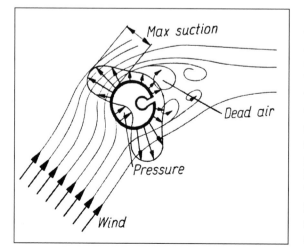

Fig 47 Pressure distribution around a circular mast without the presence of a sail. The mast as the leading edge of a mainsail is an important factor determining the pressure distribution over the forward leeside of the sail behind. Part of the mast contributes significantly to the total forward thrust developed by the mast–sail combination. When searching for possible improvements in the mast shape it should not be forgotten that the flow around the mast–mainsail combination and the resulting pressure distribution over the leeside will be strongly influenced by the presence of the jib. It means that the 'gain' corroborated by measurements obtained on an isolated mast–mainsail may be misleading if a headsail is added. Fig 48 explains further the flow pattern round a circular mast.

A thick, streamlined leading edge is thus equivalent to an adjustable nose, demonstrated in Fig 42. It might be expected that the sail set at the ideal angle of incidence ie without any initial flow disturbance at its luff, operates optimally in terms of the driving force. But, as we soon learn, it is not so. Although we must give as little occasion as possible for the occurrence of flow disturbances near the front edge of the sail, there are also other considerations which must be given proper attention.

Since mast contributes to the total pressure distribution and disturbs the airflow over the mainsail, an intense search has been made for possible improvements in the mast-sail interaction. The prime objective has been to improve the airflow pattern and thus to *maximize the pressure differences* between the windward and leeward sides of the mast-mainsail combination near the luff.

Consider first the airflow around a circular mast shown in Fig 48. In the absence of friction due to air viscosity, the flow would travel smoothly round the mast in the manner predicted by Bernoulli's equation. From point 1 (sketch 48a) it would gradually accelerate to V_1 and finally, its maximum velocity V_2, and hence maximum kinetic energy at point 2. As the velocity increased, the static pressure would fall to a minimum at point 2. It would then progress to point 4 in an exact reverse of the process carried out in going from 1 to 2.

Due to viscosity and friction, however, the air particles adjacent to the mast suffer an extra retardation as they travel around (sketch 48b). Consequently, the flow velocity at 2 is less than it would be in the absence of viscosity, and this implies that its kinetic energy is less than it should be. Now, to travel on the path 2–3–4 would require the expenditure of the full amount of kinetic energy, and since this is not now available, the air particles are unable to adhere to the mast contour. Instead they separate from the mast, and flow downstream in an

Fig 48 Flow pattern and pressure distribution around a circular mast.
a) Flow without friction (nonviscous flow)
b) Flow with friction. The flow velocity gradient (increase in velocity from the mast surface upwards) above points 1 and 2 is greatly exaggerated for the sake of demonstration of the friction effect.
c) Pressure distribution and wake (dead air) left behind the circular mast. Note that due to friction the maximum suction occurs somewhere between point 1 and 2, and not at point 2.

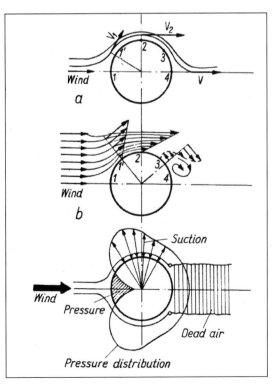

eddy-making reversed manner. The extent of the dead air wake left behind the mast, as depicted in sketch 48c, is an indirect indication of the level of *form drag* of the mast.

For present purpose it does not matter what the mechanism is whereby the friction forces due to air viscosity (Ref 2.9) – apparently very small – determine the flow pattern, the size of the wake and related forces. However, by way of a small digression, you might be surprised to learn that without air viscosity sails could not possibly develop their driving force. Nor could aeroplanes fly. In other words, if air were nonviscous, no airfoil, no matter what shape, would be capable of producing either drag or lift, that is forces parallel or normal to the airflow direction (wind). The flow pattern round a flat plate shown in Fig 49 demonstrates that in 'ideal', frictionless air, the streamlines would be the same on both sides of the plate. Consequently, the pressure distribution and hence the forces on both sides would be identical, and would therefore balance each other regardless of how we turned the plate. So although air viscosity creates friction and drag, these are the very elements that produce lift too.

Returning to our previous discussion; numerous experiments carried out on many different sections have demonstrated that the deciding factor influencing both the form drag and mast–sail interaction is the shape of the mast. The more abruptly curved the contour, particularly over the rear portions, the more readily the air flow ceases to follow the contour, and separates. It might follow, then, that for a low form drag and hence a small wake, the mast section should be streamlined in the familiar pear shape, and should present a small frontal area to the flow. But such an inference would be premature.

In Fig 50a, drag coefficients for various mast sections are given. They range from 1.0 to 0.15. We can see from these diagrams how much streamlining can reduce the drag and wake from that of the basic circular mast. However, if we bear in mind that a yacht never sails closer to the apparent wind than about 20°, and mostly sails at a greater angle than this, we must conclude that a streamlined mast may not be better than a circular one, unless the former rotates with the sail.

In the fifteenth America's Cup race, the defender *Rainbow* employed a profiled mast which nevertheless was found to be inferior to that of the challenger *Endeavour*. The disadvantages of *Rainbow*'s mast were particularly apparent on a broad-reaching course, when it was found that the greater portion of the leeward side of the sail was adversely affected by large wake from the mast (Fig 50b).

To obtain a complete picture of the pressure distribution over the whole of a sail, it is necessary to carry out measurements along many sections at different heights, as indicated in Fig 51, which shows the results of such measurements for a Bermudian sail. These were taken along sail sections marked 0–8, ie the lines roughly parallel to the flow direction. The results are plotted in the form

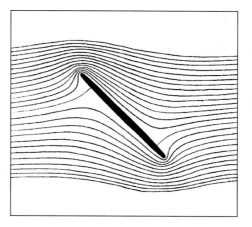

Fig 49 In ideal 'perfect' air without viscosity and friction, the effective drag of the above plate, subjected to so-called potential flow, would be zero; a result which is obviously counterfactual. Without reference to air viscosity and the boundary layer concept, neither the circulation (see Fig 36) nor lift could be produced (Ref 2.4).

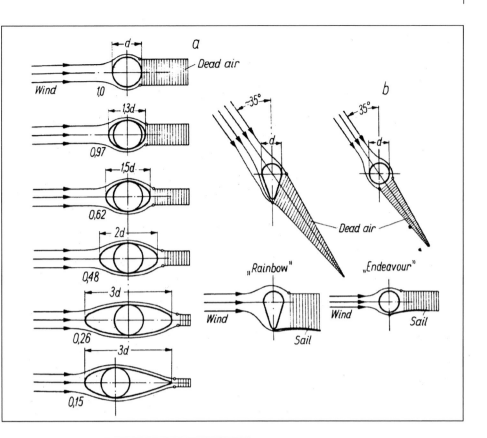

Fig 50 Drag of different mast sections. Attention should be called to the fact that the source of drag is not to be found in what happens at the front of the mast, but in the wake which forms behind. If the aft-part of the mast tapers so gently that the streamlines follow its contour, the drag experienced is mainly due to surface friction only. On the other hand, if the aft-part of the mast tapers quickly, the streamlines separate early and the mast carries behind a wake made up of a complex system of eddies whose formation requires a continuous dissipation of the flow energy 'felt' by the mast as a drag.

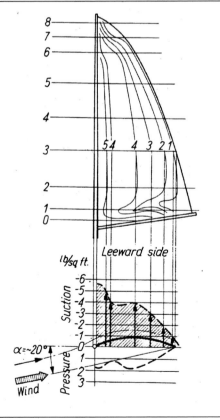

Fig 51 Approximate distribution of pressures over the sail section and leeward surface of a Bermuda type of sail.

of contour lines (isobars) joining points of equal pressure (suction) on the leeward side of the sail set at an angle of incidence of 20° to the wind. It will be noticed that the contour lines follow a regular pattern in the middle of the sail, but near the head and boom they have certain irregularities, indicating that the flow changes at the extremes of the sail close to sections 0–1 at the boom and sections 7–8 near the head.

We shall return again to the effect of mast on sail performance when discussing the results of wind tunnel testing, the object of which was to measure the forces, not the pressures, developed on the mast – sail combination.

Let's consider in some details the basic pattern of the flow over the sail alone, and also over the mast-sail section.

THE BASIC FLOW PATTERN AROUND THE SAIL SECTION

When steering the best course to windward, and off the wind too, it is crucial to keep the sails at the correct angle of incidence relative to the apparent wind. After all, the character of the flow on both sides of the sail, and hence the pressure distributions and, ultimately, the sail efficiency in terms of driving force, are all mutually interrelated and primarily depend on the angle of incidence. Neither the pressure distribution nor the driving force can be seen directly by the crew. But the character of the flow can be identified by means of wind indicators: streamers, telltales or yarns. Visual study of the flow pattern using these types of indicators is frequently used in aeronautical experiments, and has now become quite common in yachting. They give the helmsman useful visual clues as to what is really going on up on the sails, but it is important to know what to watch for and how to interpret their movement.

Observations made by the author in the wind tunnel, of tufts attached to a cambered rigid sail (at first without mast) showed that smooth, attached flow along the whole leeward side occurs only at one unique angle of incidence, mentioned earlier; the *ideal angle of incidence*. Only at that one angle did the wool streamers fly steadily straight aft, on both sides of the sail entrance, as indicated in Fig 52 by the streamlines marked l (leeward) and w (windward). In this flow condition, the sail is on the verge of *luffing*, and any decrease in the incidence angle may lead to flapping of the sail at the luff; preceded by the fluttering of the windward telltales attached not far from the leading edge of the sail (Refs 2.10, 2.11).

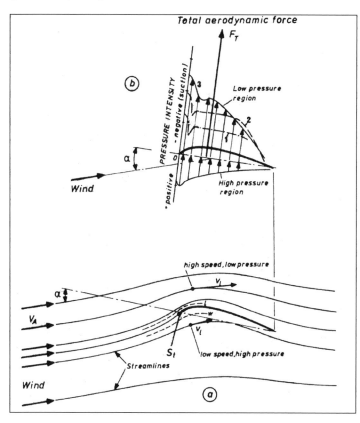

Fig 52a Flow pattern around a single sail (without mast) set at an ideal angle of incidence. Such a flow can be observed somewhere in the middle part of the sail where the flow is not affected by so-called tip vortices (see Fig 51).

V_A is the apparent wind velocity measured some distance ahead of sail. V_l is local flow velocities (different from V_A) due to the influence of the sail.

Fig 52b An approximate distribution of pressures over the windward and leeward sides of the sail. The increasing suction intensity shown by curves 2 and 3 is due to an increase in the incidence angle. More precise distributions of suction over the sail with increasing angle of incidence are presented in Fig 57.

Sailing close to luffing is only justified in strong wind conditions, in which the wind power that might be absorbed by the sails is restricted by the available boat stability. That is, the helmsman's desire to extract as much driving power from the wind as possible must be mitigated in order to keep the boat at a reasonable angle of heel (no more than 30°), beyond which her performance deteriorates for aerodynamic as well as hydrodynamic reasons. In such a sailing condition the area of suction over the leeside of sail might roughly be represented by the curve marked 1 in Fig 52b. The size of this area is of particular interest, as it is this that contributes most to the driving force. As soon as the wind strength is eased, and the boat stability becomes of secondary importance, the suction area can gradually be enlarged by increasing the angle of incidence, α, either by sheeting the sail closer to the boat centreline, or by bearing off slightly, depending on the circumstances. The effect is schematically depicted by the curves marked 2 and 3 in Fig 52b. Noteworthy are two trends: when the angle of incidence increases (curve 3), the suction peak becomes higher; at the same time the area of more intense suction shifts towards the front part of the sail. Both trends are favourable, bearing in mind what has been inferred when discussing the practical meaning of the measurements shown in Figs 40 and 41. Unfortunately, such a gradual increase in sail driving power cannot go on indefinitely. It must come to an end, and is usually followed by more or less rapid deterioration in sail power. The cause is, as might be expected, the airflow separation from the lee surface of the sail (ie stall – failing to keep going), which takes place when the incidence angle becomes too large.

This far, a sail can operate at two extreme trim conditions: the luffing and the stall, neither of them efficient in terms of the speed performance of the boat. Taking for example an una-rig of the Finn type, there are about 10–15 degrees of heading angle between these two extreme conditions. And there is also a smaller range of several degrees of efficient, or say *optimum* angles of sail incidence within these extremes, at which the sails operate most efficiently. The actual optimum angle depends primarily on the course sailed (windward or reaching), wind strength and sail camber (camber ratio and camber distribution).

As soon as the incidence angle is increased above the luffing condition, the airflow separates from the leading edge, LE. Figure 53a illustrates in exaggerated form, what is then happening over the leeward side of the sail. It will be seen that the stagnation point marked St moves from the LE (compare with Fig 52a) to the windward side. As a result, the air particles have to make sharp turn around the LE and then follow along the sail entry towards the trailing edge. This causes high local flow velocities near the LE (and we all know that the faster we go round a corner in a car, the greater is the centrifugal force which tends to push the car away from the inside of the bend).

The air particles within the laminar boundary layer, BL, that is the layer of air immediately adjacent to the sail surface (Fig 53a), are in no better a situation. Unable to withstand that sort of rapid change in direction they go into a 'skid', ie they are forced to separate tangentially from the sail surface. Subsequently, the separated BL is driven downstream by the faster flow outside, which is not affected by the friction forces operating within the BL only.

Such an abrupt change in flow direction in the LE vicinity is usually, but not always, accompanied by a local reversed flow vortex, rotating inside a bubble

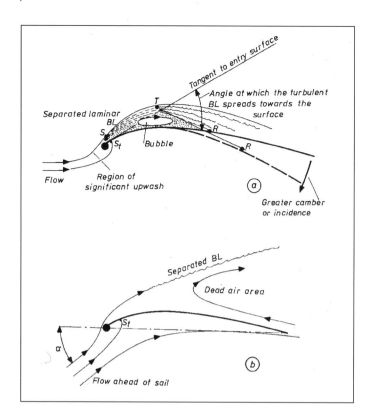

Fig 53 Two types of flow separation:
a) Separated flow with reattachment of turbulent boundary layer
b) Separated flow without reattachment (laminar separation). S_t indicates the so-called stagnation point, where the flow is brought to rest.

It appears that, by building up the bubble, a kind of artificial thickness at the leading edge LE, nature makes the flow round a sharp LE easier. Without a bubble the flow would separate and never reattach itself to the foil surface, sketch (b). Rapid deterioration of the foil efficiency (drastic reduction of suction intensity on the leeside) is just a consequence of that kind of separation. Thus, the bubble may be regarded as an agent which prevents or delays the laminar separation. For definition pictures of laminar separation and turbulent boundary layer, see Fig 54.

underneath the separated BL. Observation of tufts attached to the leeward side of the sail indicated that the airflow reattached itself to the sail surface some distance behind the bubble, and then followed the surface closely. As the angle of incidence was further increased, the separation *bubble* grew in both thickness and streamwise extent, until it covered the entire surface of the sail model. At that moment, the flow over the whole leeward side of the sail was totally separated in the manner shown schematically in Fig 53b. This was full stall, with the reversed flow operating beneath the separated BL.

Observations of flow pattern were then made on the same cambered sail model, but with a streamline head-foil attached to its LE. Attention is now drawn to the wool tufts in the photographs, Fig 54. The picture of recorded flow patterns was similar to that in Fig 53a, the significant difference being that separation of BL at the leading edge occurred less readily when the incidence angle was increased. In other words, due to the presence of the head-foil, the flow at the LE became somewhat less sensitive to the variation in the incidence angle.

The peculiar behaviour of the wool-tufts 1 and 2 in photo a of Fig 54 (see also explanatory sketch below) clearly reveals the presence of a circulatory motion within the bubble. This is one of the factors which apparently helps to entrain the separated BL, so that it reattaches to the sail surface, as revealed by tufts 3 to 7 which can be seen streaming smoothly towards the sail leech.

Fig 54b illustrates a distinctly different flow pattern, also revealed by tufts. This is the stall. Here the flow over the whole leeward side is dominated by large scale reversed flow, shown schematically in Fig 53. Such a flow drives the tufts towards the leading edge of the sail, ie, in the opposite direction to the

Fig 54 Two types of flow over the leeside of a sail, discussed earlier with reference to Fig 53a and b, but this time detected by wool tufts. Photograph (a) demonstrates visually what was graphically illustrated in Fig 53a, while photograph (b) shows the full separation flow pattern depicted in Fig 53b. Hopefully, these complementary figures 53 and 54 are of some help in understanding the 'language' of telltales.

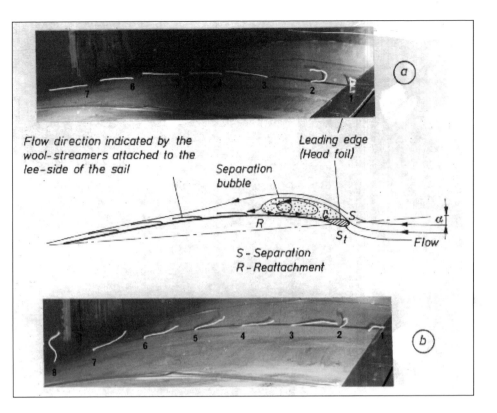

airflow outside the separated BL. Noteworthy is the behaviour of the wool tuft no 8 in Fig 54b, which is attached to the leech. It tends to go out of sight of the helmsman with discerning eyes, thus sending him a clear message that the sail begins to operate well below its potential capability.

Whether or not the airflow will smoothly negotiate the LE without separation, and then follow the leeward surface up to the trailing edge, depends on:

- The incidence angle at which the sail is set relative to the wind.
- The curvature of the sail entry, ie the sail shape right behind the LE.
- Apparent wind speed.

The influence of the first two factors has, for the present purpose, been sufficiently discussed when referring to Figs 52–54. The effect of the third factor should be examined in view of the traditional thinking that one should have full (well-cambered) sails in light air, and flat sails in heavy winds, to match stability of the boat. This common sense argument is based on the assumption that the driving power which can be delivered by the sails is related to the sail camber (draft), that is, the more camber, the greater the driving force. Such a premise is correct, but only up to a point. When the apparent wind becomes light, around 4 knots or so, the flow pattern at the sail entry may change radically as compared to that depicted in Figs 53a and 54a; then the rule – the lighter the wind, the more camber – is not borne out in practice. Why?

Let's look again at Fig 53a, first at the leading edge. The airflow here, and so too the laminar boundary layer, tends to move along in a direction tangential to the sail surface. Due to unavoidable friction over the sail surface, the BL suffers a continual, though small, drain on its kinetic energy. For those two reasons it is increasingly difficult to keep the BL attached to the sail surface, and as a result the laminar BL separates from the surface at some point on the leeward side. Subsequently, the BL may or may not reattach, depending on the flow velocity and the shape of the sail entry.

If the flow velocity (apparent wind) is above a certain critical value, a bubble is formed as indicated in Fig 53a, and transition of the laminar BL into more robust and turbulent BL occurs at maximum bubble height. The resulting turbulence spreads and entrains the 'healthy' flow streaming above the BL, so that it reattaches at some point, R, downstream. A circulatory motion within the bubble also *helps to entrain* the separated but now turbulent BL.

Test results have indicated that there exists a critical flow velocity (Reynolds Number) below which bubble formation is not possible, so that the laminar BL, once separated, never reattaches itself to the foil surface. This is shown in Fig 53b; consequently, on account of the large wake left behind, and the associated drag, the sail efficiency is low. It appears that another role of the bubble is to *facilitate transition*, and to make the BL turbulent. It has also been found that, after transition, the turbulent BL seemed to spread towards the surface at an angle – marked A in Fig 53a – relative to a tangent to the surface at the point of transition, T (Ref 2.12). This spread of turbulence meets the surface at the point of reattachment, R. Its exact downstream position will depend, all other things being equal, on the sail camber and/or its incidence. The two camber lines (one broken) with an arrow indicating 'greater camber or incidence might be of some help in foreseeing the effect of sail shape and its incidence on reattachment. With 'less camber' the reattachment point marked R tends to move towards the LE – a desirable tendency. On the contrary, with 'more camber', the turbulent BL may never reattach.

This observation accords with practical experience: that a less cambered sail is more resistant to the laminar BL separation, and therefore more efficient in drifting conditions in which this type of separation is most likely to occur. In other words, a flat sail with reattachment (Fig 53a) is better than a fuller sail with no reattachment (Fig 53b).

The loss in suction over the leeward side of an airfoil operating in the critical range of speeds at which reattachment did not occur can be estimated from Fig 55 (Ref 2.13). The large crossed area between the two pressure distribution curves indicates how inferior the performance of the airfoil is, because of laminar separation without subsequent reattachment. Its suction distribution is

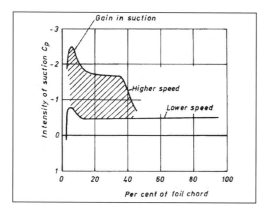

Fig 55 Suction distribution over a foil (Gottingen 801) set at the same angle of incidence, 18 degrees, but at two different wind speeds (Reynolds Numbers Re = 4.2×10^4 – lower speed, and Re = 7.5×10^4 – higher speed.) The significance of the Reynolds Number is explained in Appendix 2.

At subcritical flow condition (lower wind speed), the laminar separation without reattachment took place; consequently the lift was low and the drag high. At supercritical flow condition (higher speed) a bubble was formed, resulting in higher lift and lower drag. Although the above graph is valid only for a particular foil, the demonstrated trend is universal.

radically different from that relevant to the flow with reattachment; the much-needed large suction area near the LE is not achieved. Instead, a suction distribution of a greatly reduced, flat level extends along almost the entire leeside – a characteristic of most separated flow (Fig 53b).

Finally, Fig 56a and b illustrates the pressure distributions over a rigid mast–sail combination (Ref 2.14): a) gives the pressure distribution around mast and both sail surfaces at the incidence angle, 5 degrees, while b) presents, in the form of 3- dimensional plots, the evolution of suction with changing incidence angle from 2.5 to 10 degrees. Although the character and type of air flow around the mast and sail appears to be highly complex, the resulting form of the pressure distributions was found to be remarkably ordered, and generally its basic pattern was similar in qualitative sense in all cases tested. Fig 57 demonstrates this characteristic pressure pattern and nine associated air flow types. These are readily identifiable by using wool tufts or other visual means as a guide.

A useful development would be special sensors – possibly incorporated into sail fabric – which might identify and detect the streamwise extent of these different flow regimes listed in Fig 57. Such instantaneous information might eventually be compared to pre-recorded data relevant to efficient sail settings tested earlier, thus assisting the crew in tuning sails to the best advantage.

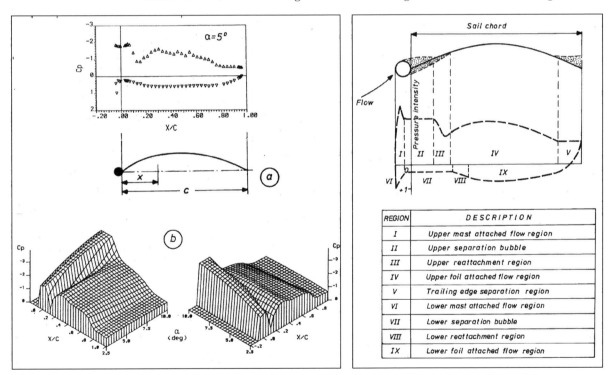

Fig 56a (left: top) Distribution of pressures over the mast–sail combination at incidence angle $\alpha = 5$ degrees.
Fig 56b (left: bottom) Evolution of suction distribution over the leeward side of a sail with changing incidence angle from 2.5 to 10.0 degrees. The camber ratio of the sail was 12.5 per cent of the sail chord. The ratio of the mast diameter to the sail chord was about 4.0 per cent. The intensity of suction expressed by the pressure coefficient C_p is equivalent to $\triangle p/q$ (used earlier in Figs 39, 41 and 44). Ratio x/c gives the distance of the pressure tapping x in relation to the sail chord c. The test data are taken from Ref 2.14.
Fig 57 (right) Characteristic pattern of pressure distribution and flow types around a thin sail supported by circular mast (Ref 2.14).

4 • THE EFFECTS OF AERODYNAMIC FORCES

'...without the higher powers of imagination and reason, no eminent success can be gained in many subjects.'

Charles Darwin, The Descent of Man

The total resultant aerodynamic force F_T generated by sails can be resolved into two components in a plane passing through the centre of effort CE, as shown in Fig 58a and b. These components are:

- A driving force F_R acting along the direction of the course sailed.
- A heeling force F_H acting perpendicular to both the course and the mast.

The force F_H can be further resolved into two components, whose magnitudes will depend on the angle of heel, Θ, thus:

$$\text{Horizontal, or lateral force} \quad F_{lat} = F_H \cos \Theta$$
$$\text{vertical force} \quad F_{vert} = F_H \sin \Theta$$

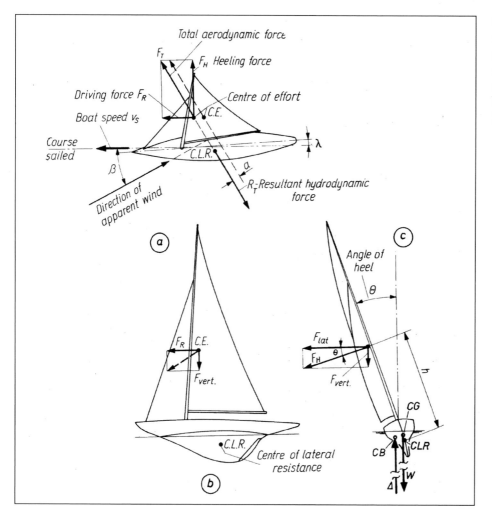

Fig 58 The geometry and definition of aerodynamic forces developed on a yacht sailing close-hauled at a certain angle of heel.

Consider in general terms, the effects of these force components on a yacht's behaviour:

1 The yacht will move along a course with a velocity V_s. The magnitude of V_s depends on the driving force F_R, and will increase if F_R increases.

2 The drift of a yacht can be described by a leeway angle λ, measured between the course sailed and the centreline of the hull. As F_{lat} increases, so does λ.

3 The heel of the yacht is given by the angle Θ. This will depend on the magnitude of the heeling moment $M_H = F_H \times h$, where h is the distance measured along the mast, between the 'centre of effort' (CE) of the total aerodynamic force, F_T, and the 'centre of lateral resistance' (CLR), through which point passes the corresponding resultant hull force R_T (Fig 58a). Increases of F_H or h both lead to increases in the heel of the yacht.

4 The directional balance of the yacht can be measured by the amount of helm needed to maintain a given course. Balance is obtained when the total aerodynamic force, F_T, and the resultant hydrodynamic force, R_T, act along the same straight line, in the plan view (Fig 58a). Large lee helm will be carried if the CE is forward of the CLR by, relatively, a large distance 'a', and if it is aft a distance 'a' of the CLR, then the yacht will carry weather helm. In all cases, increases of F_H will lead to more imbalance.

5 Trim of the hull. The force F_{vert}, together with F_R (Fig 58b, c), tends to change the hull trim in relation to the designed LWL, in particular the longitudinal trim, as shown in Fig 59. It depresses the bow and raises the stern.

Fig 59 Here we have a classic dinghy with keel boat additions changing drastically her longitudinal trim with angle of heel. Crossbreeding of the ocean-going yacht with a sailing dinghy does not appear to be promising from the viewpoint of seaworthiness. Unseaworthy behaviour in heavier wind is more the rule than the exception with boats built to the IOR or IMS rules. It is not only the strong, active crews of racing yachts who bear the brunt of current design trends – it is also the cruising folk who are directly influenced by the racing fashion. Although the great builders and designers of the past had an intuitive feel as to how to build seaworthy craft (now in danger of extinction), the concept of balancing speed against safety and seaworthiness appears to be losing ground.

The various effects described in 2, 3, 4 and 5 may be – usually are, in fact – detrimental to the yacht's performance, since they may increase to a greater or lesser extent the hydrodynamic resistance of the hull and hence reduce the speed.

From the point of view of a good helmsman (whether cruising or racing), one of the primary objectives is to achieve a large driving force, F_R, and simultaneously to alleviate as much as possible, by proper tuning and sail trim, the harmful effects indicated in points 4 and 5.

To be able to predict the effects of the aerodynamic force, F_T, we must know its three characteristics:

- Magnitude
- Direction
- Point of application (here termed the centre of effort, CE)

'Art' wrote Sir Richard Fairey, the pioneer of sail testing in wind tunnels, 'deals with pleasing the senses, an imponderable quantity, since the sense impressions registered are not necessarily alike in any two people. Science deals with measurements, and the forces acting on yacht hulls and sails are manifestly subject to measurement and comparison.'

Since it is obviously the action of aerodynamic forces which makes a boat move and/or changes the hull trim, we shall investigate the relevant factors which affect the air forces developed on sails, and hence yacht performance. These will be discussed in the following chapters, written in the hope that the art of yacht design and the art of sailing might benefit.

5 • MEASUREMENT OF AERODYNAMIC FORCES

'I have seen so much danger arising from presenting results or rules involving variable coefficients in the form of algebraic formulas which the hurried or careless worker may use far beyond the limit of the experimental determination, that I present the results mainly in the form of plotted curves.'

J R Freeman, Experiments upon the Flow of Water

From experiments carried out on yachts, in wind tunnels and also from aerodynamic theory, it was established that the three characteristics of an aerodynamic force – its magnitude, direction and centre of effort, CE – depend on:

- The dynamic pressure $q = 0.00119 \times V_A^2$ of the apparent wind V_A in ft/sec (see Eq 4)
- The sail area S_A (sq ft)
- The angular position of the sail, or sails, relative to the apparent wind, known as the angle of incidence α
- The geometry of the sail, its planform, camber, etc
- The sail cloth's porosity, smoothness, stiffness, etc

In considering the sail geometry, an important quantity is its aspect ratio, AR, given by the ratio of the sail height (span) to its mean width (mean chord).

For a rectangular sail (Fig 60a) the aspect ratio is simply

$$A R = \frac{b}{c}$$

where b is the height (span) of the sail
and c is the length of the sail chord.

For planforms other than a rectangle (Fig 60b and c), the aspect ratio is obtained somewhat differently. If the sail area, S_A, is defined as the product of the height b and a mean chord c (Fig 60b), the mean chord is obtained by dividing S_A by b. Hence:

$$A R = b \div \frac{S_A}{b} = \frac{b^2}{S_A}$$

Fig 60 The meaning and definitions of camber and aspect ratio:

$$\text{camber} = \frac{f}{c}$$

aspect ratio

$$AR = \frac{b}{c}$$

for a rectangular sail, or

$$AR = \frac{b^2}{S_A}$$

for any other planform

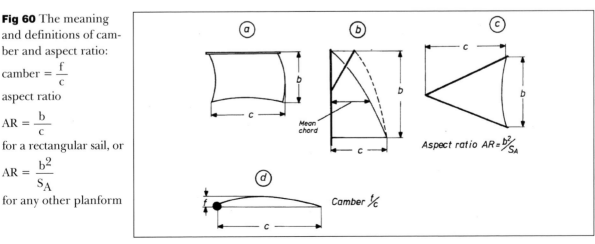

The camber of a sail is usually expressed as the ratio of the bow f of the sail section to its chord c (Fig 60d):

$$\text{Camber} = \frac{f}{c}$$

With certain reservations we may combine the factors mentioned previously as determining the forces on a sail into a mathematical formula. The formula implies that if we have two sails of the same geometrical shape set at the same incidence angle but of different areas (ie sails that are geometrically similar), working in winds of different dynamic pressures, then the forces developed will be proportional to their respective areas and dynamic pressures:

$$F = q \times S_A \times C$$
$$= 0.00119 \times V_A^2 \times S_A \times C \qquad \text{Eq 10}$$

where
- F is the aerodynamic force in lb.
- V_A is the velocity of the apparent wind in ft/sec
- S_A is the sail area in sq ft
- C is the aerodynamic force coefficient or shape factor

It is usually more convenient to discuss the properties of a sail in the coefficient form since, in doing so, we are not tied down to actual size and wind speed. If a model sail satisfies all the geometric conditions for similarity with a full-scale sail, then it should have the same coefficient.

The aerodynamic coefficients can be derived experimentally by measuring forces on a model sail in a wind tunnel, or on full-sized sails tested in natural conditions (for example the yacht *Papoose* described earlier, see Fig 37). The geometric factors, such as aspect ratio, planform, camber and angle of incidence can be varied, and the dependence of the coefficients established. Experiments in the wind tunnel have their limitations, as it is hardly possible to simulate the natural wind encountered in practice. Although measurements made on models are not strictly representative of true sailing conditions, they do assist in understanding the aerodynamic forces developed on sails, and it is possible to establish the influence of many different factors such as camber, angle of incidence, twist of the sail, mast, etc, under closely controlled conditions. To understand fully the aerodynamic phenomena of sailing, one must study full-scale yachts *and* perform experiments on models. Each complements the other; either one by itself is inadequate.

The significance of wind tunnel experiments will be better appreciated if the method of measuring the aerodynamic forces is explained, and the results presented graphically. Figures 61, 62 and 63 show the principle of the measurements of the forces on a model sail. The sail (or sails in presence of the hull) under investigation is placed in a controlled wind stream and is connected to a suitable weighing system, called a balance, to measure the forces. For reason of convenience it is usual to construct the balance so that instead of measuring the total force, F_T, it measures two components:

1 The cross-wind force, ie lift, L, perpendicular to the wind direction. Lift is so called because the most familiar example of a similar force is the upward component acting on an aircraft wing. Despite its name, however,

Fig 61a A schematic diagram of the wind tunnel (working section for sail testing) at Southampton University.

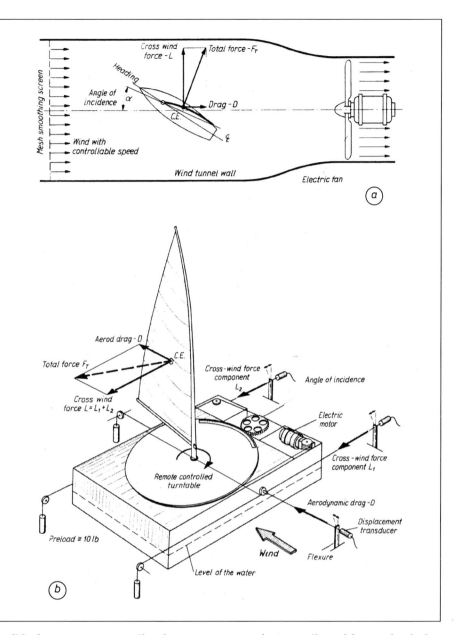

Fig 61b Balance arrangement in the wind tunnel section shown in a. This balance, designed by the author in 1961, was used to measure sail characteristics, that is the cross-wind force (lift), drag, vertical and longitudinal position of the centre of effort, CE, and also heeling moment. More details are given in Ref 2.15.

lift does not necessarily always act upwards (on sail, rudder or keel, for instance)

2 The drag force, D, along the wind direction

The balance in the wind tunnel at Southampton University, shown in Figs 61, 63b and c, was designed bearing in mind past experience and conclusions based on the analyses of early sail tests carried out during the last 30 years in various wind tunnels. From many of the lessons learned in previous experiments, it became obvious that to make it possible to determine the influence of important factors on sail efficiency with a reasonable degree of accuracy and reliability, it was necessary to experiment with fabric ('soft') sails on a sufficiently large scale. With one exception (the Sir Richard Fairey Wind Tunnel (GB) test of a big square section, 12 × 12 ft (Figs 62 and 63a), where the primary aim of

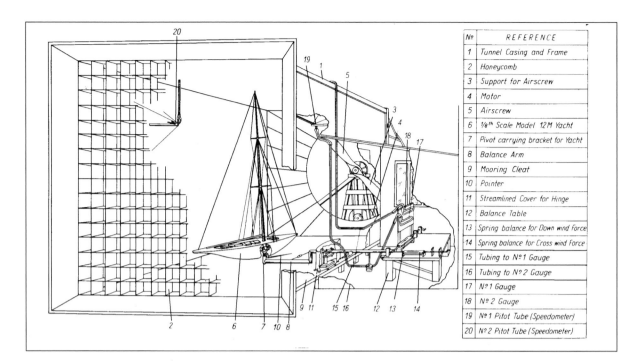

№	REFERENCE
1	Tunnel Casing and Frame
2	Honeycomb
3	Support for Airscrew
4	Motor
5	Airscrew
6	⅛th Scale Model 12M Yacht
7	Pivot carrying bracket for Yacht
8	Balance Arm
9	Mooring Cleat
10	Pointer
11	Streamlined Cover for Hinge
12	Balance Table
13	Spring balance for Down wind force
14	Spring balance for Cross wind Force
15	Tubing to Nº 1 Gauge
16	Tubing to Nº 2 Gauge
17	Nº 1 Gauge
18	Nº 2 Gauge
19	Nº 1 Pitot Tube (Speedometer)
20	Nº 2 Pitot Tube (Speedometer)

Fig 62 Experimental wind tunnel for research on model sails (Sir Richard Fairey, England), mainly used for the development of rigs for America's Cup challengers.

the tests was to tune up and improve the performance of J class yacht), all other experiments have been performed in relatively small working sections, using conventional tunnel balances not suited to these purposes.

This necessarily limited experimenters to using small, in most cases, rigid sheet metal sails. Tests on solid sails cannot be completely successful, as they do not simulate fabric sails, although they are very convenient tools for predicting general trends and also for obtaining qualitative information.

According to the opinion of leading sailmakers, the length of the luff should be not less than about 7 feet to overcome problems of manufacturing a proper model of the sail. On this scale the camber of the sail could reasonably be predetermined; the similarity between model and full-size sail (with regard to the method of cutting, elasticity and structural details) could also be maintained.

It is desirable to simulate the working condition of sails as closely as possible. It is therefore necessary:

- To simulate the sea surface
- To heel the sail and hull relative to the sea surface
- To modify the tension in and directions of sheets and other tuning devices to change the relative position of interacting sails.

The arrangement of the balance is shown in Figs 61 and 63b and c.

The sail is attached to a mast and boom connected to a pontoon floating in a water tank which is recessed into the floor of the wind tunnel. The pontoon is made large and buoyant enough (with motion damping devices) to minimize pitching and rolling motion, so that it remains virtually horizontal and without vibration. Its motion along and across the wind direction is controlled by three flexures, the deflections of which are proportional to the force components L_1, L_2 and D. Deflection in the range 0–0.025 inches is measured electrically using inductive displacement transducers. A remote controlled turntable enables the

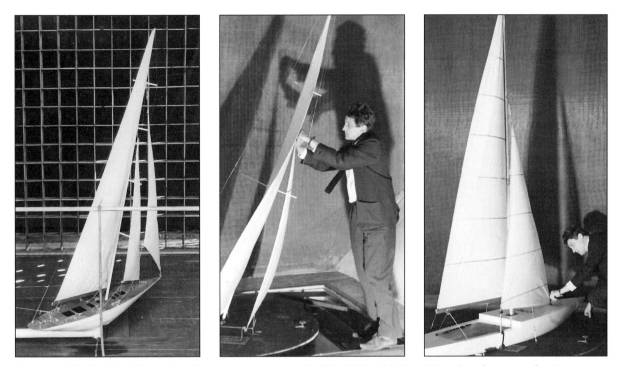

Fig 63a (left) Model of the yacht *Flica* in the wind tunnel of Sir Richard Fairey. Note that the sea surface is not simulated, and the whole model, including the underwater part of its hull is tested in the air.

Fig 63b (centre) A model of the sail of a X-One-Design class yacht in the wind tunnel at Southampton University. The size of the rig, which can be tested with or without hull, can be up to 7.5 ft (2.3 m) in height.

Fig 63c (right) Model of a $^1/_4$ scale Dragon class yacht undergoing tests in upright position. In order to enable the twist and camber of the sails to be recorded under various test conditions, the black lines were painted on the sails one foot (30 cm) apart and parallel to the boom. The model was then photographed using a camera in the roof of the tunnel.

rig to be rotated to simulate a change of heading angle of the yacht relative to the wind, or to simulate a change of angle of incidence of the sail. Special fittings on the turntable allow the sheeting of the sails to be varied. In other words, the vertical and horizontal position of the boom can be altered. In this way, not only can the effect of the sheeting base be investigated, but also the effect of the sea, ie the gap between the boom and deck and also between the sails and the sea surface, which seem to be significant factors.

For various angles of incidence, α, from the minimum angle at which the sail flutter ends up to 90°, the corresponding values of L and D are measured, say, in increments of 2.5 degrees; other factors such as wind speed remain equal. The test results can be presented in form of a table as that to the left of Fig 64a but, as we will soon learn, it is more convenient to depict the result graphically.

The magnitude of the lift force is marked along the vertical axis, the drag force, D, on the horizontal axis. When the model sail is set at an angle of 27.5 degrees, for example, the measured lift and drag are given along the vertical and horizontal axes respectively and, from a parallelogram of forces, we find the resultant force, F_T, which is represented in both magnitude and direction. In a similar way, we mark the values of L and D for $\alpha = 5°$, 10°, 15° and so on (from Table a) and then draw a curve which conveys at a glance how the magnitude and direction of the resultant force vary with incidence. Such a curve,

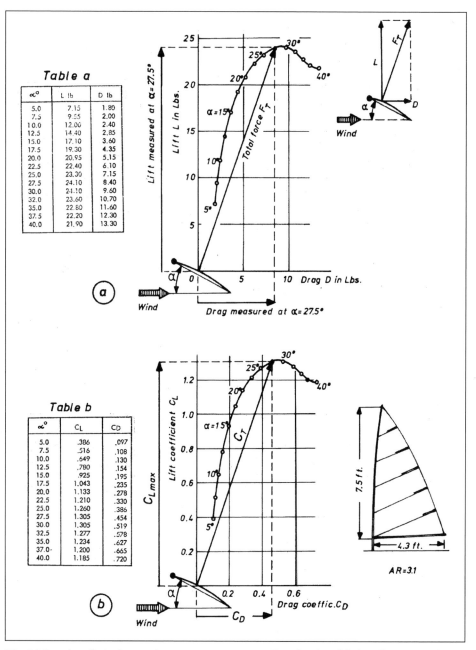

Table a

$\alpha°$	L lb	D lb
5.0	7.15	1.80
7.5	9.55	2.00
10.0	12.00	2.40
12.5	14.40	2.85
15.0	17.10	3.60
17.5	19.30	4.35
20.0	20.95	5.15
22.5	22.40	6.10
25.0	23.30	7.15
27.5	24.10	8.40
30.0	24.10	9.60
32.0	23.60	10.70
35.0	22.80	11.60
37.5	22.20	12.30
40.0	21.90	13.30

Table b

$\alpha°$	C_L	C_D
5.0	.386	.097
7.5	.516	.108
10.0	.649	.130
12.5	.780	.154
15.0	.925	.195
17.5	1.043	.235
20.0	1.133	.278
22.5	1.210	.330
25.0	1.260	.386
27.5	1.305	.454
30.0	1.305	.519
32.5	1.277	.578
35.0	1.234	.627
37.0	1.200	.665
40.0	1.185	.720

Fig 64 Results of wind tunnel measurements on a 2/5 scale Finn fabric sail presented in form of polar diagrams of forces (a) and also coefficients (b). The sail was tested without hull over angles of incidence from 5 to 40 degrees in increments of $2\frac{1}{2}°$, its area $S_A = 18.1$ sq ft (1.68 sq m), height b = 7.5 ft (2.29 m) and aspect ratio $AR = \frac{b^2}{S_A} = 3.1$. Measurements were taken at wind speed $V_A = 29.3$ ft/sec (17.5 knots) which corresponds to force 5 on the Beaufort Scale (fresh breeze) with the model unheeled. Lift and drag coefficients C_L and C_D respectively were obtained by dividing the relevant values of lift and drag given in Table a by the sail area $S_A = 18.1$ sq ft and the dynamic pressure of the actual wind at which the model was tested, ie $q = 0.00119\, V_A{}^2$, thus

$$C_L \text{ or } C_D = \frac{L \text{ or } D}{S_A \times 0.00119\, V_A{}^2} = \frac{L \text{ or } D}{18.55}$$

Table b gives the result of calculations in terms of sail coefficient.

known as a 'polar diagram' (with incidence angles inscribed along the curve) is valid only for one particular sail of a certain area S_A planform, and for the distribution of camber and twist along the sail height as shown in Fig 65, tested at one particular wind speed, V_A. It provides a ready means for determining the forces on given sail, but lacks generality.

To make the results from tests on a model sail generally applicable to other, similar sails, but of different area and operating in different winds, and to allow comparison of one sail with another, we express the results in terms of coefficients by dividing the measured forces by the dynamic pressure of the airstream in the wind tunnel and by the model sail area:

$$\frac{L, D, F_T}{SA \times 0.00119\, V_A{}^2} = C_L, C_D, C_T \text{ respectively} \qquad \text{Eq 11}$$

If at any time we want the actual forces which would be developed on, say, a similar full-size sail, we multiply the coefficients by the full-size sail area and the dynamic pressure of the wind in which we are interested, thus the total force:

$$F_T\text{F.S.} = C_T \times 0.00119\, V_A{}^2{}_{\text{F.S.}} \times S_{A\text{F.S.}}$$

where the subsuffix F.S. refers to 'full-size'.

By plotting the coefficients in polar diagram form, we can readily compare results of tests on a variety of sails and establish the relative merits of different sail configurations. Fig 64b shows the polar diagram of the coefficients of the sail forces presented in Fig 64a; the latter reflects faithfully all the characteristics of the former, indicating the correct line of action and magnitudes proportional to those of the original forces.

In subsequent discussions on aerodynamic properties and sail efficiencies we will frequently, for the above reasons, consider them in their coefficient form.

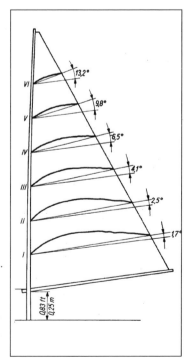

Fig 65 Distribution of camber and twist along the height of a 2/5 scale Finn sail recorded using a camera mounted on the tunnel roof directly above the masthead and photographing downward. The sail was tested at a wind speed V_A = 29.3 ft/sec (17.5 knots). The test results presented in Fig 64 are relevant only to this particular sail supported by a bendy mast. At different wind speeds, the camber and twist combinations adopted by the sail will be different and so will its aerodynamic characteristics and their effect on boat performance. These matters are discussed in Refs 2.4 and 2.16.

Distribution of camber recorded at the incidence angle α = 25 degrees

Section	I	II	III	IV	V	VI
Camber (%)	10.7	11.6	11.0	9.2	7.8	6.7

INTRODUCTORY INTERPRETATION OF WIND TUNNEL TEST RESULTS

Referring to the polar diagram in Fig 64b, it will be noticed that after stalling, which occurs at the incidence angle about 27.5 degrees, there is no abrupt decrease in the lift coefficient if the incidence angle α is increased beyond the stall. The reason is that twisted, triangular sail does not stall simultaneously all along its height. As we shall see later, some parts of the sail stall earlier than others still operating well below the C_L maximum. Inevitably, some penalty must be paid in terms of maximum attainable lift for that sort of uneven distribution of effective angle of incidence along the sail height. Associated loss in attainable lift can to some degree be assessed by comparing the polar diagram in Fig 64b with that shown in Fig 66 and obtained from measurements made at the Göttingen Institute on sheet metal rectangular foils without masts (Ref 2.17).

Curve I refers to a flat foil and Curve II refers to a foil having a camber of 1/10. The areas in both cases were the same and AR = 5. It will be seen that both camber and angle of incidence have a large effect on the magnitude and direction of the force coefficients C_L and C_D and thus on the total force. It can also be seen that the maximum lift coefficient C_L = 1.3 for the soft triangular sail (Fig 64b) occurs at an angle of incidence α = 27.5 whilst C_L max = 1.54 of the foil of comparable camber (Fig 66) occurs at α = 15°. Maximum lift coefficient of untwisted, rectangular foil is about 18 per cent higher than that of the twisted, triangular planform!

It is interesting to compare, from Fig 66, the values of coefficients for the two

Fig 66 Polar diagrams for two rectangular, rigid, untwisted foils – one cambered and one flat – of aspect ratio AR = 5. Two sketches on the right indicate the potential driving force which can be developed by these two foils in reaching conditions. When the apparent wind V_A is at 90° to the hull centreline, the driving force corresponds to the lift force L measured directly in the wind tunnel. The maximum lift coefficient of a given sail can therefore be regarded as one criterion of its efficiency.

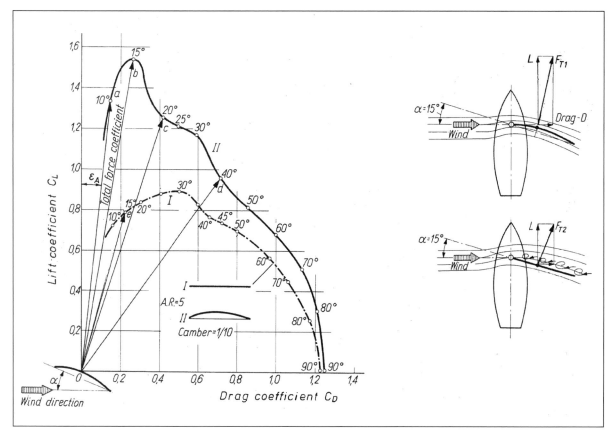

Fig 67 The potential driving forces developed by a rectangular foil (of aerodynamic characteristics given in Fig 66) in reaching conditions at different angles of incidence, α (trim angles of the sail). In this case, the driving force F_R is equivalent to lift L. It should be stressed that the above figures are relevant to this particular, untwisted sail of rectangular planform. We shall soon learn that sail efficiency depends much on its planform, and the Bermuda type of sail is by no means the best configuration in terms of driving power.

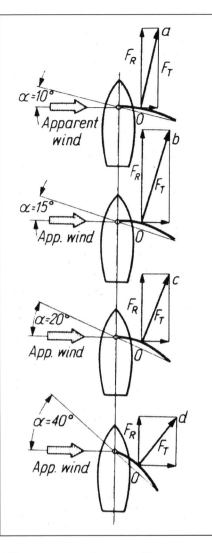

foils, one flat and one cambered. Particularly at the smaller angles of incidence, the differences are very marked, both in magnitude and direction. For instance, at an angle of incidence α = 15°, the total force FT2 of the flat aerofoil is about half that of F_{T1} of the cambered aerofoil (see small sketches to the right of the polar diagrams). This same information is conveyed in a more concise manner in Fig 66 by the two lines Ob and Oe.

Conspicuous differences between Curves I and II are attributed to the different flows over the leeward sides, as a result of the foil curvature. With the perfectly flat foil, the flow finds it impossible to go smoothly round the leading edge, and so separates, covering the lee side of the foil with eddies. As already mentioned earlier, one effect of camber is to introduce the leading edge more gently into the flow, so the flow will not separate readily. Instead, it passes smoothly round the lee side, accelerating as it is constricted, giving rise to a large suction. At greater angles of incidence, when the flow separates over most of the cambered foil as well, the differences between the two foils tend to disappear. At an angle of incidence, α = 90°, corresponding to sailing on a run, the difference is so slight as to be negligible. At this high angle of incidence, the total sail force depends much less on the lee side suction forces than at the relatively small angles of incidence. The foregoing remarks explain why a perfectly flat sail is inefficient. Later the disadvantages of too large a camber will also be discussed.

Consider now the total force coefficients Oa, Ob, Oc and Od for cambered foil in Fig 66 at the respective angles of incidence α = 10°, 15°, 20° and 40°. If these results are translated in terms of actual sailing on a reach, as in Fig 67, we can clearly see how important is the angle of incidence for the yacht's motion. Depending on the trim of the mainsail, the driving forces will vary significantly. If the sail is pulled in too hard, to an angle of incidence beyond stall, the driving component F_R may drastically decrease, with corresponding reduction in the speed of the boat.

6 • AERODYNAMIC DRAG OF THE SAIL

'It is the purpose of a scientific hypothesis to stick out its neck, that is to be vulnerable.'
Herman Bondi, Professor of Applied Mathematics

When beating against the wind (Fig 68a) we should like to have the maximum possible driving force, F_R, and simultaneously a minimum heeling force, F_H, so that we may sail at high speed with negligible heel and drift. It will be seen from the following trigonometrical relations that the magnitudes of F_R and F_H depend on the angle ß between the course and the apparent wind, and on the lift, L, and drag, D.

$$F_R = L \times \sin ß - D \times \cos ß$$
$$F_H = L \times ß \cos ß + D \times \sin ß \qquad \text{Eq 12a}$$

or in coefficient form:

$$C_R = C_L \times \sin ß - C_D \times \cos ß$$
$$C_H = C_L \times \cos ß + C_D \times \sin ß \qquad \text{Eq 12b}$$

It is evident from either pair of these equations that the drag not only decreases the driving force, F_R, but also increases the harmful heeling force, F_H.

The action of aerodynamic drag is particularly harmful when sailing close-hauled, for reasons best understood by referring to Fig 68b. By gradually luffing into wind, it is possible to reach a condition where the yacht loses forward motion and only drifts to leeward. This will occur when the total sail force, F_{T1}, acts perpendicular to the direction of the yacht's course, and so the forward

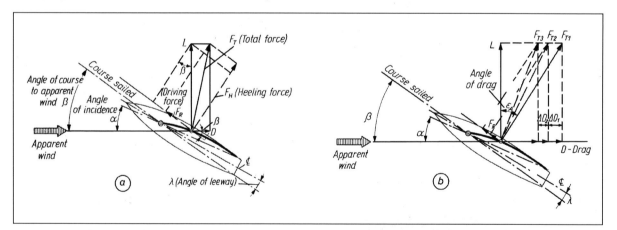

Fig 68a The geometry of aerodynamic forces when close-hauled. Once the total force F_T is known (from measurements of L and D in the wind tunnel), it can be re-resolved into two alternative components. These are the driving force F_R and heeling force F_H. Equations 12a and b give the relationship between measured L and D, course sailed ß and F_R, F_H forces.

Fig 68b The effect of a reduction of aerodynamic drag D on the magnitude of the driving force F_R. It can be argued that, if at a particular course sailed to windward, ß, an alteration in sail shape, ie, planform, AR, twist and camber distribution, results in a decrease in drag and hence an increase in driving force F_R (or driving coefficient C_R) without a corresponding increase in heeling force, the performance to windward should improve. In other words, the rig efficiency is higher. With some reservation, this is tantamount to saying that the aerodynamic comparison between different rigs should be made at the same lift coefficient, the better rig will be the one with lower drag.

force component, F_R, disappears. This then represents a limiting value of ß for beating to windward. If we could reduce the aerodynamic drag, D, by say, an amount $\triangle D_1$, we could alter the direction of the total force to F_{T2} and the yacht would regain forward motion due to the appearance of a driving component F_R. For a further reduction of the drag by $\triangle D_2$, we could obtain a further increase in speed to windward. In other words, the smaller the drag D for given lift L, the larger the driving force.

From the foregoing argument we may infer that the windward performance of a sailing boat depends to a large extent on the L/D ratio. This ratio can also be expressed by the *drag angle*, ε_A, between F_T and lift L, ie cot ε_A = L/D. The smaller the ε_A, the better the rig for close-hauled work.

The question now arises as to whether the drag D could possibly be reduced, and how? Theory and experiment indicate that the drag D of a given rig is made up of three components:

a) Induced drag
b) Friction drag
c) Form drag or pressure drag

Their individual contributions to the total drag D depend on the sail aspect ratio, planform, incidence angles, speed of the wind, sail-cloth properties etc.

INDUCED DRAG

The physical process involved in the development of the induced drag is too complex to be discussed in detail. It is comprehensively summarised in the author's book, *Aero-Hydrodynamics of Sailing* (Ref 2.4). Sufficient for our immediate purpose is to say that this drag component is a measure of the wind energy inseparably expended in obtaining a lift force. Every lift-generating device, be it airplane wing, sail, keel or rudder, spins the airflow near its tip into a kind of small tornado called a tip vortex or trailing vortex. The origin of these vortices is the flow of air or water from the higher pressure to the lower pressure (suction) side around the 'ends' of the lift-producing foil. Consequently, the pressure difference between two sides of the foil gradually become smaller and smaller towards the tip, so that the lift changes along the foil span and finally disappears at the very end of the foil, 'replaced' by the tip vortex. The existence of such vortices has been amply confirmed by photographs; some of them are presented in Fig 69.

Fig 69a The pattern of trailing vortex system developed at both tips of the foil. Reference line X–X can be considered to be the bottom of a hull.

Fig 69b, c Another view of the flow round the tip of the foil set at two different angles of incidence 10 and 15 degrees. The intensity of the trailing vortex depends on the magnitude of lift, ie, the pressure difference between the two sides of the foil. The larger the lift, the more intense the trailing vortex, as reflected by the greater angle between the centreline of the tip and coiled streaklines (photo c). The sideways displacement of the tip vortex axis also depends on lift or, in other words, the angle of incidence.

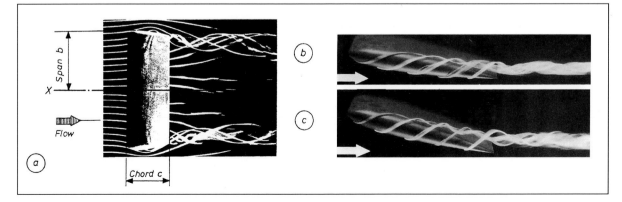

Since these vortices are continually generated as long as there exists a pressure difference between two sides of the foil, a quantity of wind kinetic energy is continually dissipated, ie lost to the foil, but it is trailed behind the sail in the form of a rotating mass of air (or water in the case of a keel). Expended flow energy which is 'felt' by the foil as drag is imaginatively called either the *trailing vortex drag* or *induced drag*. The second term is, in some ways, more descriptive, since it reflects an

important consequence of the trailing vortex action: its influence on the induced deflection of the flow in the vicinity of the sail, in the opposite direction to the lift, and called *downwash*. This is shown in Fig 70 behind the lower part of the sail only. As a result of this flow modification – which in turn depends on vortex intensity and the planform of the sail – the *effective* angle of incidence at each station along the sail height is different from the *geometric* angle of incidence apparent from mere visual observation of wind indicators, attached, say, to the masthead.

Thus the effective angle of incidence at which each sail section actually operates, and the geometric angle of incidence of the apparent wind, measured by instruments some distance ahead of sails, are two different things. These angles must be clearly distinguished between if reliable measurement of a yacht's performance is to be obtained. That was why the sensors indicating apparent wind speed and direction, which were installed on the experimental Dragon class yacht depicted in Fig 71, were kept some distance ahead of sails.

It can be proved that the magnitude of the induced drag can be estimated from the formula:

$$D_i = k \, \frac{L^2}{\pi \, AR} \; = k \; \frac{L^2}{3.14 \, AR} \qquad\qquad Eq \; 13$$

where k is a constant depending mainly on sail planform.

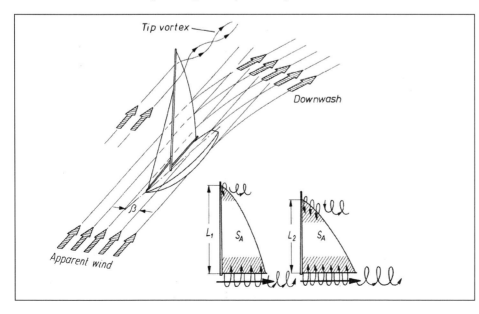

Fig 70 The upper drawing shows schematically how the flow around the sail head rolls up, from the windward to leeward side, into a spiral vortex. Such a vortex travels downwind and gradually disintegrates in random turbulence stretching some distance behind the rig. This drawing demonstrates also the principle behind one of the racing tactics. Not only is the astern boat unable to point high because of downwash, but she also sails in dirty air due to a disintegrating vortex left by the leading boat.

Fig 71 An experimental yacht of the Dragon class used by the Southampton University team for measuring its windward performance. The boat was equipped with 'fully gimballed wind sensors' – kept ahead of the sails at a height close to the anticipated centre of effort, CE, of the sails. It should perhaps be added that the apparent wind speed and its direction are also affected by wind gradient, that is the variation of wind speed with height above the sea surface. The effect of this factor was not, however, investigated.

Fig 72 *Enterprise*'s Park Avenue boom aimed to reduce induced drag. This invention is based on Lanchester's concept of the endplate effect discussed in his book *Aerodynamics* written in 1907 (see 2.4).

The above formula bears out an intuitive feeling – assuming that intuition in science designates clear understanding and interpretative ability. Lift force depends on the pressure differences between the windward and leeward side of the sail, and on these depends the amount of flow around the boom and head, and so the induced drag. It is relatively easy to recognize why the aspect ratio, together with the sail planform, also determines the magnitude of the induced drag (Fig 70, bottom sketches). The higher the aspect ratio, the smaller the pressure loss (pressure 'leak') round shorter foot and head in comparison with the rest of the sail area.

In an attempt to decrease the induced drag, some designers introduced wide booms, whose function was to prevent the flow around the sail foot. An example of such a device was the Park Avenue boom, used on the *Enterprise* – winner of the 14th America's Cup in 1930 (Fig 72). An additional benefit, it was believed, to be gained from this idea, was the smooth continuation of the sail shape right down, since the foot was attached to the boom on transverse runners.

Other possibilities for reducing induced drag arose with advances in mast construction and the discovery of the new, synthetic glues which enabled light, hollow, tall masts to be made. These allowed sail plans of high aspect ratio to be used. A good example of this can be found in the 30 Square Metre depicted in Fig 73a. This exceptionally high rig was a result of the class rule which placed few limitations on the hull, but limited the sail area. Hence the sail area could be disposed in the efficient, windward-going manner to give a low induced drag. The large amount of stability required to balance the tall rig was obtained from

the relatively large, heavy hull.

It seems that the practical upper limit to aspect ratio for boats built to current rating rules is about 4–4.5. Beyond this, the necessary increases in hull size and ballast, to avoid excessive heeling, make the gains in speed performance problematic, to say the least.

Induced drag may, for some triangular, twisted planforms, be the greatest component of the total drag of the rig. Because of that, there is a large scope for improvement in sail efficiency, which has been overlooked by sailing people and theoreticians alike.

The development of *Lionheart*'s rig by the author may serve as an example. The new rig of the British challenger for the 1980 America's Cup shown in Fig 73b was aimed at drastically reducing the induced drag component alone. According to the opinion expressed by the American expert N Hoyt, '*Lionheart*'s extraordinary bendy topmast rig is the greatest performance breakthrough in 12 Meter design'. While most yachting journalists might agree with Hoyt's view, they seem divided in their opinion of what this British 'plastic-topped, walking-stick mast' really provided. Did it permit more unmeasured sail area with associated extra driving power? Or perhaps there was something else involved which made *Lionheart*'s rig more powerful than any other conventional 12 Metre rig used so far. If so, where did the secret lie? Was there a way of knowing in advance just how much extra power this type of rig would in practice produce? (Ref 2.18).

Some 65 years ago, Max Munk, a German scientist, who later emigrated to the USA to work for the National Advisory Committee for Aeronautics (NACA) proved mathematically that, for a single wing, *minimum induced drag* occurs when the airstreams are deflected with the same downwash velocity all along the trailing edge. The elliptic wing of the famous Spitfire aircraft (Fig 74) has exactly

Fig 73a (far left) 30 Square Metre boat. The class rules do not resistrct the aspect ratio of the rig.
Fig 73b (left) *Lionheart*'s rig. The British 1980 Challenger for the America's Cup. Rigid class rules restrict the length of the battens. Thus it was virtually impossible to substantially improve the aerodynamic effectiveness of the upper part of the mainsail without bending the mast above hounds within its elastic limits, whereby the chord length at the sail head could be increased.

Fig 74 (right) The Supermarine Spitfire first flew in 1936. Some of its Second World War success was due to its elliptic wing form.
Fig 75 (far right) The mainsail luff can be reduced up to about 15 per cent at the head, practically without effect on sail performance when close-hauled.

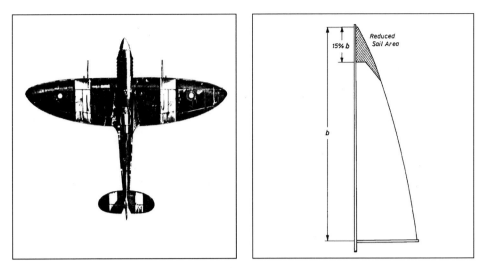

this property, and in this sense might be considered as an ideal planform. All other planforms, except one to which we shall refer later, are to different degrees worse in this respect; but the worse imaginable planform which the aerodynamicist could possibly invent is the triangular one. And that is because the triangular planform manifests a strong tendency towards premature stall of its upper part (see Fig 212). This propensity, not directly visible but detectable by telltales, is typical of any triangular, untwisted planform. The more pointed the head of the sail, the more liable it is to develop an early stall in that region, to the detriment of sail efficiency in close-hauled conditions. For that reason, rectangular or trapezoidal planforms are potentially more efficient in terms of sail power than Bermudan or lateen rigs, particularly those with a large sweepback angle, which accelerates incipient breakdown of airflow near the head. As suspected, the wind tunnel tests indicated that up to 15% of the Bermudan mainsail length might be cut out from the top and have practically no effect on sail performance, even with the penalty of the now-vacant topmast left in place (Fig 75).

The significance of premature stall cannot be overemphasized. It is the hidden enemy, although not the only villain responsible for the lower efficiency of a conventional triangular Bermudan sail as compared with that of low speed aircraft wings – for which the triangular planform has never been adopted (the delta aircraft configuration is linked to high speed flight). Nature also appears to know about deficiency of the triangular planform, since birds, particularly those renowned for their soaring ability, do not favour this particular shape.

Premature stall on triangular planforms occurs because the upper part of the sail, with its small chord, is more heavily loaded than the part of the sail close to the foot, where the chord length is much greater. In general, flow breaks down more easily over heavily loaded areas unless sail twist, ie the reduction of the effective angle of incidence is deliberately used as a dodge, but such a remedy incurs an aerodynamic penalty as well (2.4). The most efficient way to alleviate this undesirable tendency is to increase the streamwise dimension of the planform in places where the stall develops first, that is to increase the chord length at the sail head, as demonstrated in Fig 76. Such a modification may, however, be difficult to realize, bearing in mind limitations imposed by the measurement rules, not to mention tradition. The penalty exacted, for example, by most sail

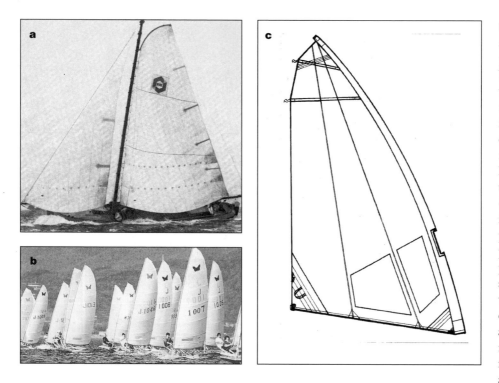

Fig 76 More efficient
shapes of the upper
part of mainsail can
be developed, pro-
vided the measure-
ment rules do not
interfere with aero-
dynamic require-
ments. Even relative-
ly small modifications
to the sail shape
(even a small 'blunt-
ing' of the sharp
pointed triangular
planform, for exam-
ple), may bring sub-
stantial gains in dri-
ving force. The rapid
development towards
aerodynamically
more efficient sails
for windsurfers (**c**) is
admirable. In this
respect, sailing peo-
ple can learn more
from developments
made in small classes
than from ridicu-
ously expensive
'developments' made,
say, in the America's
Cup type of rigs. The
old Dutch compro-
mise of a small
curved gaff (**a**) or an
extra-wide head-
board may well
improve sail effective-
ness.

measurement systems on excess width of the headboard of a mainsail, or too
long a top batten, is so high that it virtually precludes any attempt to improve
the aerodynamic effectiveness of the modern tall rigs.

Since the 12 Metre rule does not allow a permanently bent mast, nor a wider
headboard, and the batten length is strictly controlled, the only way whereby
the mainsail planform could approach the desirable elliptic form, is to bend the
upper part of the mast within its elastic limits, and independently of any 'normal' mast bend which may be used to control sail camber.

Results of wind tunnel tests on *Lionheart*'s 1/12 scale model rig shown in Figs
77 and 78 fully confirmed the theoretical premises. It is seen that the whole
polar curve for the elliptical mainsail is bodily shifted to the left, towards lower
drag. And, for example, at the heading angle $(ß – λ) = 20$ degrees, the rig with
elliptical mainsail produces about 30% more driving force, F_R, than the conventional rig; the actual force magnitude depends on the course sailed and range
of lift at which the boat operates, that is the true wind speed. It was estimated
that such a difference in the rig power would, in close-hauled conditions and
average wind $V_T = 12$ knots, improve the challenger's performance by about
0.25 knots, ie 4 per cent in terms of speed made good to windward, V_{mg}. This
gives an enormous edge over the boat driven by a conventional rig, bearing in
mind the fact that the speed margin by which the American contenders usually
win in elimination trials is about 0.03 knots – less than $^1/_2$ per cent of the speed
recorded around the whole race course.

Another question to be answered is: did *Lionheart*'s 'bendy' mast permit more
unmeasured sail area, with associated extra driving power, as compared with a
conventional rig? A glance at two sketches of those rigs shown in Fig 78 is
enough to say yes. However, the 'tax free' area is not the primary factor determining the superiority of a rig with an elliptical mainsail. The performance

Fig 77 (left and above) A 1/12 size scale model of *Lionheart*'s rig in the wind tunnel of Southampton University. Various combinations of mast bend and sail models to match the bend were tried in the search for a better performance. Although the IYRU decided to take action against the bent-topped masts, the underlying theory should be an object lesson not only for future contenders but also other classes driven by the Bermudan type of rig.

Fig 78 (right) Test results on the conventional mainsail rig and the 'elliptical' mainsail rig fully confirmed the theory and expectations. Due to a drastic reduction in induced drag, the whole polar curve for the elliptical sail is shifted bodily to the left of the graph. At the same heading angle, therefore, the driving force F_R is much greater. All tests were performed on a 1/12 size scale model heeled to 20 degrees at a constant wind speed $V_A = 25$ ft/sec which corresponds to force 4 on the Beaufort scale.

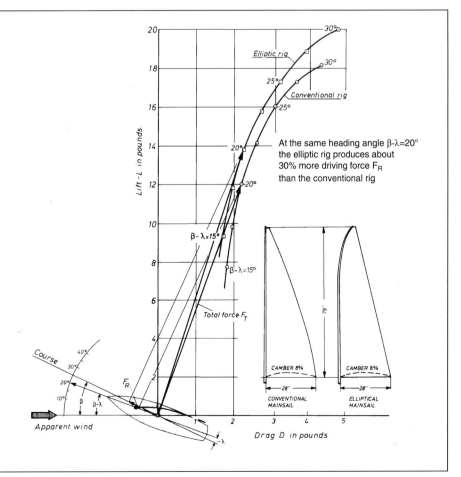

At the same heading angle β-λ=20° the elliptic rig produces about 30% more driving force F_R than the conventional rig

advantages of this rig lie in the very nature of the aerodynamic phenomena involved and associated with induced drag.

Figure 79 demonstrates the test results which clarify the issue. The continuous line curve in the upper part of the graph shows the polar diagram of the rig with a conventional mainsail, while the broken line curve relates to the rig with the elliptical mainsail, but with its main sail area reduced by 14.3 per cent.

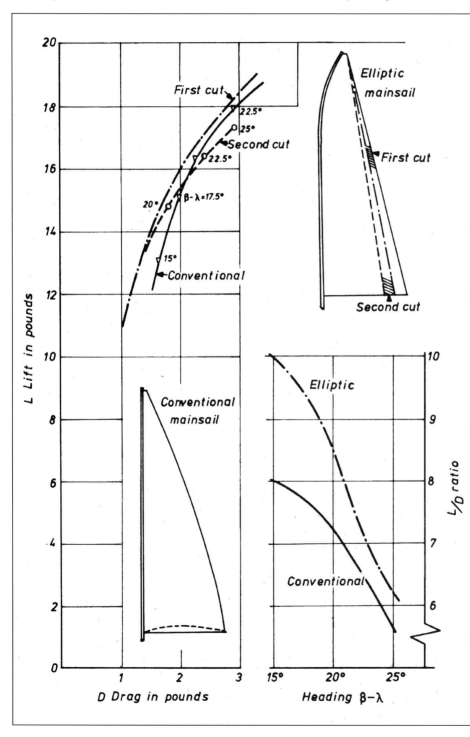

Fig 79 The results of tests on two Bermudan rigs, one with a conventional mainsail and another one with an elliptical one. Rigs were tested in the presence of the same genoa. The camber of both mainsails was similar, about 8 per cent. Forces L and D were measured at heading angles $(\beta - \lambda)$ from 15 to 25 degrees in increments of $2\frac{1}{2}$ degrees. The basic rated area of the elliptical mainsails, $S_A = 7.68$ sq ft – nominally the same as the conventional mainsail – was reduced first by 14.3 per cent and thereafter by 28.6 per cent by cutting strips of material along the leach as indicated.

Tests were performed with the model heeled to 20 degrees and at the wind speed V_A = 25 ft/sec (14.8 knots).

Comparison of the L against D curves of both types of rig reveals the dramatic superiority of the elliptical mainsail configuration over the conventional one, despite the much reduced area of the former. The whole curve representing its aerodynamic characteristics is bodily shifted to the left, towards lower drag (relative to the conventional rig). The differences are more pronounced in the lower range of heading angles. Resulting gain can be assessed in a different way by comparing the variation of Lift/Drag ratios of both configurations shown by two curves plotted to the right of Fig 79. This ratio, which can be regarded as a criterion of rig efficiency in close-hauled sailing, increases advantageously for the elliptical rig when the heading angle decreases.

Even with the mainsail area of the elliptical rig curtailed by 28.6 per cent (second cut), its performance is comparable to the conventional rig carrying intact canvas. Thus, a considerable reduction in induced drag can be obtained by reshaping the sail with the object of making its upper part less and lower part more heavily loaded. Evidently what matters most is not sheer sail area, but how that area is invested, ie distributed along the mast; in other words, the sail planform. No question can arise in the test case illustrated in Fig 79 of gaining extra sail area. The wind tunnel proved beyond any doubt that the sail with the wider head is *more efficient, area for area.*

One more point. The author called the rig developed for *Lionheart* the *elliptic rig*, as a convenient verbal shorthand, and he is aware that meticulous aerodynamicists might easily criticize him for using the term. This is because the elliptic planform is not the most efficient when the sail operates in a *non-uniform* flow, ie when, due to wind gradient, the apparent wind is twisted in direction and non-uniform in velocity along the mast. All he can say in defence is that this particular 'elliptic' planform can be regarded as a first approximation. In real sailing conditions (in the presence of non-uniform wind), which were not simulated in the wind tunnel, the minimum induced drag might be achieved when the induced *downwash angle*, not downwash velocity, is constant all along the sail height.

FRICTION DRAG

Air possesses a certain viscous property, similar to, but less than water or oil. Although air viscosity gives rise to a relatively small friction drag, its effect on the flow pattern developing around any lift-producing foil is not insignificant. When a stream of air flows past a sail or any foil, the air particles immediately adjacent to the surface are brought to rest. These particles do not 'slip' along the surface with the main flow, but instead they stick to the surface, and subsequently exert a braking action on their immediate neighbours, which are thus slowed somewhat. These, in turn, reduce the speed of the next layer of particles, and this process is repeated so that it is only at some distance from the surface that the air flow reaches its 'full' speed. The region between the surface and the main stream within which this braking action takes place is termed the *boundary layer*. The perfect example to demonstrate the existence of such a layer can be taken from the way dust remains settled on motor vehicles even when they are driven at high speeds; irrespective of the speed of the car, the wind velocity at its surface must be zero since the dust remains.

The concept of the boundary layer, BL, introduced by L Prandtl in 1904, is based on the above well-substantiated observation that the flow around any foil can be subdivided into two distinct regions:

1 The thin layer in the immediate vicinity of the foil surface, where the viscosity of the fluid (be it air or water) exerts its influence. Within this BL the speed changes from zero at the surface to a velocity unimpeded by viscous forces at the outside edge of BL, as shown in Fig 80.

2 The main flow outside BL, in which the influence of viscosity may be disregarded altogether.

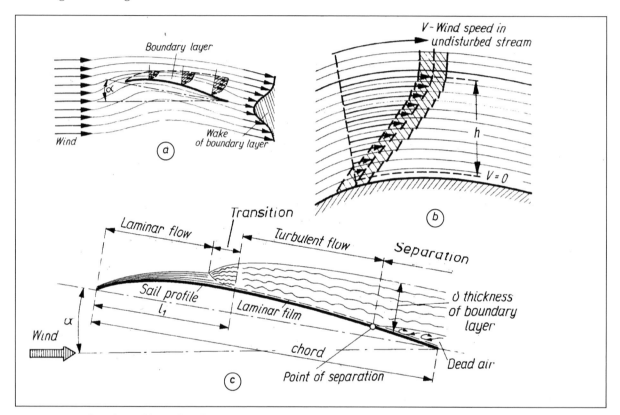

Fig 80 A greatly enlarged boundary layer, BL (for the sake of clarity), over the suction side of sail (see photographs in Fig 81).

a)   Since the air particles are slowed down within the BL due to the action of viscosity, they lose kinetic energy. This loss is indicated as a shaded area – called 'wake of boundary layer' which can be measured behind the trailing edge of sail

b)   Laminae of air particles within the laminar BL of thickness h. Each lamina slides over the next (without mixing) with increasing velocity, beginning from V = O at the surface to 'full' velocity, close to the undisturbed wind speed.

c)   For a low Reynolds Number (see Appendix 2), ie, low wind speed, the thickness of the BL beginning at the LE of sail is relatively small, reaching a maximum of about 0.5 per cent of the sail chord. If the Re exceeds a certain critical value, the flow within the BL undergoes transition. The air particles no longer flow smoothly, in parallel lines, but instead start to oscillate in a random fashion, perpendicular to the general flow. This type of BL, called turbulent, grows at higher rate, and its thickness can reach about 2 per cent of the sail chord. Very close to the surface there exists a thin *laminar film* or laminar sublayer which has one useful effect: it makes the sail texture effectively more smooth than it actually is. The small size imperfections of the texture are simply covered by this laminar film.

Fig 81 Three types of flow over the suction side of an airfoil. The photographs were obtained using very fine smoke filaments to indicate flow.

a) Laminar flow in two different views: a profile view and a view from above the foil.

b) Transition of the initially *laminar* flow into the *turbulent*, BL, from the two different views as in (a).

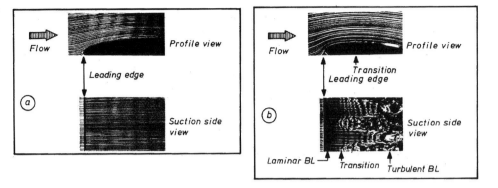

The BL, though thin, plays a crucial part in flow studies. The experimentally measured friction drag in attached flow, and the occurrence of separation and resulting wake drag could not be understood without taking into account the influence of BL and the type of flow within it.

The BL starts on both sides of the stagnation point at the LE of a foil as a *laminar* BL. This type of BL may be pictured as a smooth, orderly motion of air or water particles along distinct lines parallel to the surface, and separate lines or laminae without any crossflow mixing, as shown in pictures (b) and (c) of Fig 80 and in 81a, relevant to the suction side of the foil. The photographs in Fig 81b illustrate the same foil as in 81a, but set an an incidence angle of 10 degrees. It is seen that, initially, laminar BL undergoes *transition,* beginning at some downstream position and extending over a relatively short distance, and then continues as *turbulent* BL.

The location of transition region (Fig 80c), which is highly erratic, depends on the suction distribution and normally begins at a small distance downstream of the point of suction peak. Turbulent BL, as distinct from laminar BL, is characterized by the motion in which local flow velocities and direction fluctuate irregularly in a random fashion; so the flow lines are no longer parallel, but a crossflow mixing takes place which varies from place to place. As the turbulent BL spreads downstream, it entrains the faster main flow outside BL, so that it acquires some additional energy which makes the turbulent BL more resistant to separation. In this respect, the laminar BL is different, being more susceptible to separation; it contains less kinetic energy and leaves the surface earlier, mainly because its kinetic energy is dissipated by viscosity.

The problem of skin friction was of primary interest for ship-builders well before it became of paramount interest for aircraft designers.

Ultimately, it was established that since the thinner laminar BL absorbs less energy from the external flow than the thicker turbulent BL (Fig 80c), the friction drag of foils (and hulls too) subjected to laminar flow is lower than that experienced when the BL is turbulent. Figure 82 presents a plot of skin friction coefficients, C_{fr}, as a function of the Reynolds Number for a flat plate of length L. The broken line A shows the friction coefficients for the turbulent BL, while the continuous line B is relevant to the coefficients of laminar friction. Another curve called 'laminar/turbulent' is also included. This fits neither the laminar nor the turbulent line, and corresponds to the case where the BL begins in laminar state, then undergoes transition at a certain point to become turbulent thereafter. The critical Reynolds Number at which this transition occurs

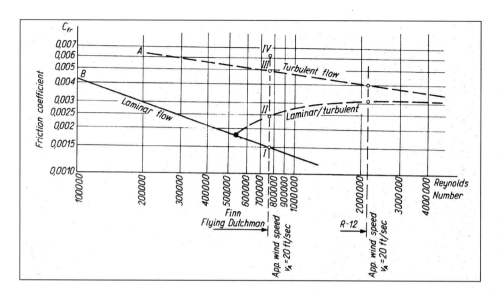

Fig 82 The approximate skin-friction coefficients C_{fr} for smooth, flat plates, as a function of Reynolds Number. These coefficients can be used to roughly estimate the friction of foils operating in air or water.

Roughness on the front part of the foil may cause premature transition to turbulence. But when the Re is below a certain limit, the irregularities of the surface do not produce additional turbulence in the main flow of air or water; the laminar sublayer may simply exceed the height of the protruding surface imperfections. However, with increasing Re, the laminar sublayer (film) becomes thinner and thinner, so that the protruding elements gradually emerge and begin to influence the flow character of the main stream.

depends mainly on the surface roughness and disturbances within the oncoming flow. That is, this critical point may 'shift' to the left along the laminar flow line towards a lower Re if the surface is rough and/or the oncoming flow is already in a turbulent state.

The Reynolds Number for a triangular sail varies from almost zero at the head to about five million at the foot of a 12 Metre class yacht, depending on the apparent wind speed. Let us calculate the Reynolds Numbers for some sails in order to estimate roughly relevant friction coefficients, assuming:

Apparent wind speed V_A = 20 ft/sec (11.8 kn)
Average chord length of the sail at half-mast height
for Finn or Flying Dutchman   L = 6 ft
for 12 Metre   L = 17 ft

Reynolds Number for airflow can be expressed (see Appendix 2) as follows:

$$Re = 6370 \times VA \times L \qquad\qquad \text{Eq 14}$$

hence for Finn and FD
$$Re = 6370 \times 20 \times 6 = 765.000$$
and for 12 Metre
$$Re = 6370 \times 20 \times 17 = 2.166.000$$

From Fig 82 we find that if sails of Finn or FD were sufficiently smooth, the BL might, in some favourable circumstances (though it's rather unlikely), be entirely laminar, giving a low friction coefficient C_{fr} = 0.0015. The greater likelihood is that on the forward part of the sail the BL will be laminar, and over the rest it will be turbulent, as in Fig 80c. This condition arises at point II on Fig 82, giving C_{fr} = 0.0023, ie about 70 per cent more than at I. Point III corresponds to conditions when the turbulent BL is initiated right at the leading edge and extends over the whole sail profile.

The coefficient of friction, C_{fr}, depends not only on the Reynolds Number but also on the smoothness of the sail surface. Line A on Fig 82 gives values of C_{fr} applicable to a smooth surface, the texture of which does not exceed a certain *admissible roughness* calculated from the following formula:

$$k_{adm} = \frac{0.188}{V_A} \qquad\qquad Eq\ 15$$

where k_{adm} = height of surface roughness in inches

     V_A = apparent wind speed in ft/sec

Hence, for the apparent wind velocity V_A = 20/ftsec, admissible roughness of the sail surface should not exceed:

$$k_{adm} = \frac{0.188}{20} = 0.0094\ in = 0.24\ mm$$

Fig 83 The effects of roughness degree (a) and roughness distribution (b) on lift and drag coefficients. It is seen in b that, depending on the location of roughness, the total force for the given incidence angles marked C_{TI}, C_{TII} and C_{TIII} tends to be inclined toward higher drag. The location of roughness near the leading edge is particularly harmful.

This roughness height will be covered by the laminar film underneath the turbulent layer. If it is exceeded, the friction coefficient will increase to that, say, indicated by point IV, but its actual value depends on the form or texture of sailcloth. Sail together with the stitching, tablings, batten pockets, wrinkles and other surface imperfections, when it is made up, has an effective roughness exceeding 0.0094 in (0.24 mm). For this reason, smaller friction coefficients than those indicated on Curve A (that for a fully turbulent boundary layer) are practically unobtainable. It might be added that a conglomeration of things, including a certain amount of ignorance, is generally lumped under the heading *roughness*.

 The roughness of the sail surface influences also the magnitude of the lift coefficient, C_L; more so, in fact, than it affects the friction coefficient C_{fr}. Experiments carried out on aerofoils with different degrees of roughness on the leeward side have shown that both the height of roughness and its location relative to the leading edge are of great importance in determining the lift. The experiments were performed in such a way that the effect of induced drag was eliminated by fitting large endplates on the aerofoils to prevent the pressure-equalizing flow round the ends. The roughness of the leeward side was varied by sprinkling sand, graded for size, on to the freshly varnished surface. With the varnish dry, lift L and drag D were measured.

 The polar diagrams of Fig 83a show how the coefficients C_L and C_D were affected by gradually increasing roughness, from Curve O for the smooth aerofoil, to C, the most rough. The polar diagrams of Fig 83b were obtained on a basically smooth aerofoil, having localized rough regions. The position of these regions is shown on the sketch of the foil section by I, II, and III. From a comparison of the curves it is seen that the magnitude and direction of the resultant aerodynamic force is much

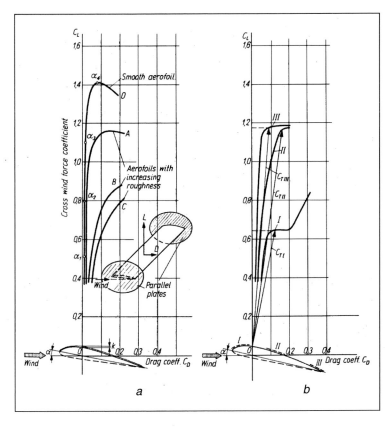

a   *b*

more detrimentally affected by roughness near the leading edge than by roughness near the trailing edge.

When Dacron/Terylene was introduced to replace cotton sailcloth, it became noticeable, as shown in the Portsmouth Yardstick Table (Table 8) that the performance of small centreboard classes driven by new synthetic sails improved by up to 7 per cent. The figures for Terylene/Dacron sails are shown in brackets. Such a gain can only be explained by the effect of the smoothness of the new sailcloth; apparently, the actual roughness of sails made of Dacron was close to the admissible roughness given by equation 15. The following comparative coefficients of friction were obtained at the Göttingen Institute:

average smooth fabric	83
similar fabric with protruding fibres singed off	50
similar fabric, doped three times	47

Table 8
Portsmouth Yardstick table (an example – not a complete table)

PRIMARY YARDSTICKS

National 14ft Merlin Rocket	(91)	96
Royal Dart 16 ½ ft OD		96
Teign Corinthian 16 ½ ft OD		96
Teign Corinthian 16ft		97
X Class OD		100
Essex OD		100
Thames Estuary OD		100
National Redwing 14ft Dinghy	(98)	101
National 12ft Dinghy	(98)	103
National Enterprise (racing rig)	(98)	103
National Firefly 12ft OD	(100)	103
Wildcat		103
Benfleet OD		107
14ft Jewel OD	(111)	113
RN 14ft Dinghy		115
Hamble Star OD	(112)	115

Started in 1951, the Portsmouth Scheme is not a handicap system, but is the means whereby any boat that has been given a handicap under one system can be given an equivalent handicap under any other system when it sails in a regatta. The scheme is based on the Portsmouth Standard Yardstick Table, which is a list of one-design and restricted classes rated in terms of Portsmouth Association Numbers defined as 'times over a common but unspecified distance'. As an example, the Portsmouth Number of X Class OD is 100 and that for the RN 14 ft Dinghy is 115, because it has been established that, on average, an X Class OD will take 100 minutes to cover a distance which can be covered over the same course and in the same race in 115 minutes by a RN 14 ft Dinghy.

Fig 84 The effect of masts of different diameters on the aerodynamic characteristics of a rectangular, rigid model sail (aspect ratio AR ≃ 5.0 and camber ratio 1/10). Approximate sail dimensions: height 1 m (3.28 ft), chord 0.2 m (0.66 ft). No hull present.

Tests were carried out in the Göttingen wind tunnel and reported in Ref 2.19. All models were tested at a wind speed of 30 m/sec (98.4 ft/sec) which gives the Reynolds Number Re = 411 000 = 4.11×10^5.

FORM DRAG

Although the physical source of form drag is intimately connected with friction drag (in the sense that in the absence of viscosity and therefore of friction there would be no form drag), it is convenient to consider the two separately.

Form drag arises from the separated flow which always exists over some part of a foil or a body in an air stream, as demonstrated in Fig 50. It is called form drag because it is largely a consequence of the shape of a body and the extent of wake left behind.

An example illustrating the effect of wake on drag is the cloud of dust which rises up behind a bus on a country road. A large vehicle raises a large wake, whilst the aerodynamically smooth lines of a smaller car cause little disturbance in relation to its size; in other words, the car has a much lower form drag coefficient.

The speed performance of a boat might be improved a great deal if we could succeed in reducing the adverse effect of the mast on the flow round the sail. As we have already mentioned (in Chapter 3), the presence of the mast at the leading edge of the sail is of some importance in determining the nature of the airflow around the sail. Its effect is particularly harmful in terms of the development of high suction on the leeward side. As a result, the boat is unable to point as high up into wind as it would if the adverse influence of the mast were eliminated.

We already know that the maximum speed of a yacht and its ability to sail close-hauled depend upon the magnitude and direction of action of the total aerodynamic sail force, F_T. The diagram in Fig 84 gives the values of the coefficients C_T of this force for some model sails designed to establish the effect of the mast on the aerodynamic performance of given sail planform. The sail of the rectangular planform had a camber of 1/10 of the chord, and aspect ratio AR = 5. From the graphs one can find the maximum values of the coefficient C_T and the corresponding drag angles.

From Figs 84 and 85a and b – the latter demonstrating the effect of the mast on the driving force in close-hauled (a) and reaching (b) conditions – the reader will be able to see that in the close-hauled attitude (Fig 85a), the angle of drag (ε) is of primary importance in determining the yacht's speed; conversely, as the boat comes off the wind, the drag angle becomes less important, its place being taken by the magnitude of the maximum lift force or its coefficient C_L (Fig 85b).

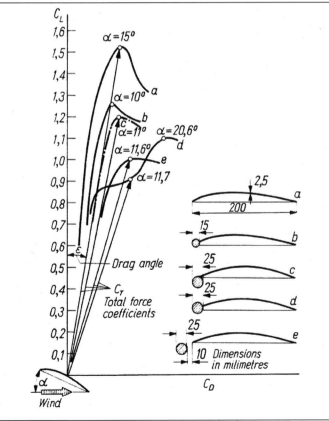

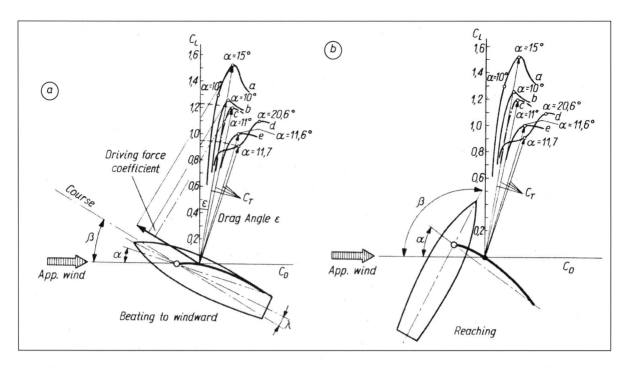

Taking model a (Fig 84), without mast, as a datum, it can be seen that the addition of a circular mast of diameter 7.5 per cent of the sail chord (model b) causes a fall of about 17 per cent in the value of the maximum lift coefficient C_L. A further increase of the mast diameter to 12.5 per cent of the sail chord (model d) produces a further reduction in the sail force. At the same angle of incidence, $\alpha = 11.7°$, the loss in C_L coefficient is about 40 per cent, and furthermore the direction of action of the total force, as reflected by its coefficient C_T, is altered for the worse, particularly when considering a close-hauled course.

The position of the mast in relation to the sail is also important. If the mast is offset to windward, as for model c (Fig 84), the sail lift coefficient is much improved. Roughly comparing $\alpha = 11.7°$ for model d, with a centrally positioned mast, with $\alpha = 11°$ for model c, we see that the latter gives an increase of about 30 per cent of C_L over the former, and an added bonus is that its drag angle ε is less, ie, the total force is directed favourably more forward for model c. The differences between these two models can be explained if we bear in mind that the flow on the leeward side of the sail is particularly susceptible to disturbance. If, on this side, the sail is connected smoothly to the mast, the flow is less likely to separate.

If the sail is attached to the mast with a gap between, as when hoops are used or the sail is hoisted on slides (model c), a particularly poor sail performance may result. This is due to the gap permitting pressure equalization between the two sides of the sail, which reduces the most useful suction peak. Figure 86 demonstrates the effect of such a gap on lift and drag. The tests were carried out by the author in connection with a 12 Metre rig development in 1962. Older 12 Metre boats had their mainsails hoisted on slides, and the gap between the rear part of the mast and the luff rope of the mainsail was about 1.5 in (3.8 cm). The estimated effect of closing this gap (by introducing the mainsail into a mast groove) on speed made good to windward, Vmg, was in the order of 2 per

Fig 85a The effect of the different mast–sail combinations shown in Fig 84 on the driving force when beating to windward.

Fig 85b When reaching the maximum lift coefficient becomes of primary importance. It is tacitly assumed that if the sail camber and twist remain constant, the aerodynamic characteristics of sails, as given in this figure and Fig 84, will not radically change when a hull is added and the course sailed relative to wind is altered. It will be shown in following chapters that such an assumption on which many performance calculations are based is wrong.

cent. Thus, over 50 per cent of *Sceptre*'s inferiority in relation to the American defender *Columbia* could be explained by this factor alone.

We can conclude from the tests that the adverse effect of a mast can be reduced by careful positioning and profiling, particularly on the leeward side. Since, however, it must work under a wide variety of conditions, it should revolve, always to point into the wind. In practice, the easiest means for alleviating detrimental effects is to site the mast to windward of the sail (as in model c, Fig 84), to eliminate any gap between the mast and sail, and reduce – to the minimum compatible with strength – the diameter of the mast.

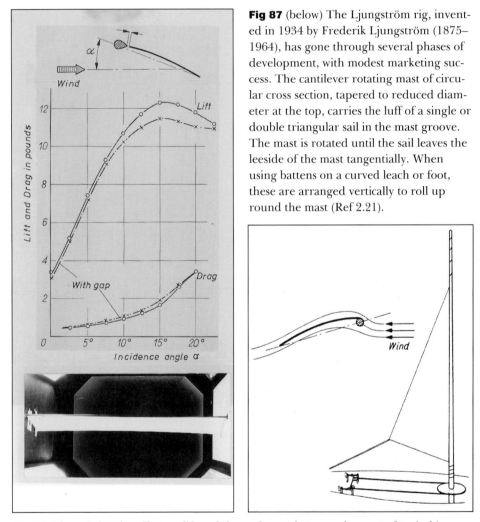

Fig 87 (below) The Ljungström rig, invented in 1934 by Frederik Ljungström (1875–1964), has gone through several phases of development, with modest marketing success. The cantilever rotating mast of circular cross section, tapered to reduced diameter at the top, carries the luff of a single or double triangular sail in the mast groove. The mast is rotated until the sail leaves the leeside of the mast tangentially. When using battens on a curved leach or foot, these are arranged vertically to roll up round the mast (Ref 2.21).

Fig 86 (above left) The effect on lift and drag of a gap between the mast of typical 'pear-shaped' section and a rectangular soft sail. As shown in the photograph, the model was tested in 'two-dimensional' condition, ie, both tips of the model sail were so close to the wind tunnel walls that the 'pressure leak' around its tips and so the induced drag was practically eliminated. The tests were designed to be comparative, so no particular attention was made to controlling or measuring the spanwise variation in camber and twist. The ratio of the mast thickness to the sail chord was 4.7 per cent, and the ratio of the gap to the mast thickness was about 6 per cent. The model was tested at a wind speed of 25 ft/sec, Re = 230 000.

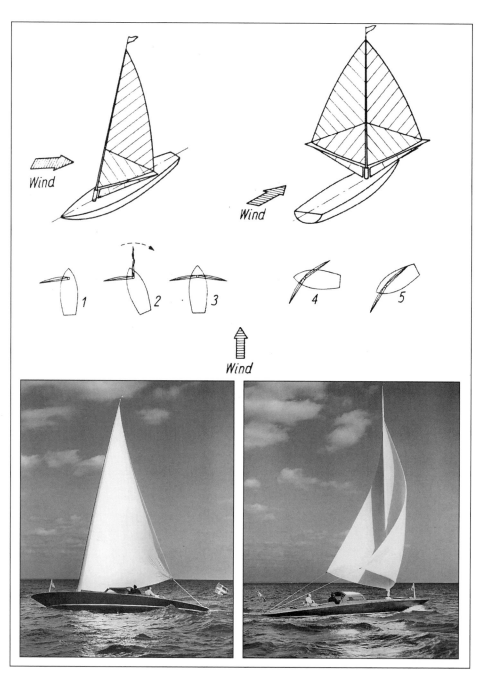

Fig 88 The Ljungström rig operating at different courses relative to the wind. Two photographs depict a 40 footer driven by this rig when close-hauled and running. In this rig a headsail cannot be used, and it thereby loses more than it gains.

One possible solution to the problem of smoothly connecting the sail to the mast can be found in the Ljungström sail (Fig 87), which was later developed by Vosper–Hasler (Fig 88), and which satisfies the requirements of model c, Fig 84. A free-standing flexible mast is used, with a rigid boom. To these are attached twin sails, which pass round the mast. When going to windward, the two sails lie together and act as one double-weight Bermudian sail. When sailing off the wind, the two sails are separated and goose-winged (Fig 88) giving double the close-hauled area. Reefing is effected by rotating the mast and thus rolling both sails on to it. The camber of the sail can be adjusted by regulating the tension at the clew.

In comparison with classic rigs, those of the Ljungström type have certain advantages, more important for cruising than for racing:

- Reefing is greatly simplified, and the rather dangerous business of the crew working in the bows when changing headsails in heavy weather is eliminated.
- When sailing before the wind, a Ljungström-rigged yacht can quickly and easily double its sail area, thus eliminating the more or less troublesome change of headsails.

Another solution to the problem of supporting the sail is found on the yacht *Jester,* which was sailed by H G Hasler in the Singlehanded Transatlantic Race of 1960. The rig was adapted from the Chinese junk, in which the front part of sail projects well forward of the mast (Fig 89) and thus is not disturbed by it right at the leading edge. The rigging, although apparently complicated, is reputedly easy to handle and reef. It has been claimed that in the original Chinese version, the camber of the sail could be adjusted within wide limits.

Numerous attempts have been made to eliminate the harmful effects of the mast by using semi-rigid sails. A typical example is shown in Fig 90 in which a streamlined 'yard' is supported on a somewhat short mast. A halyard running

Fig 89 (right) *Jester,* sailed by H G (Blondie) Hasler, at the start of the single-handed transatlantic race in 1964. Hasler experimented with a Chinese junk rig and played a leading part in originating the first single–handed transatlantic race in 1960, and the Round Britain race in 1966. In his Folkboat, *Jester* (25 ft, 7.6 m) he was second in the 1960 and fifth in the 1964 single-handed transatlantic races. The reefing system is demonstrated in the drawing. The photograph is shown here courtesy of *Yachting World*.

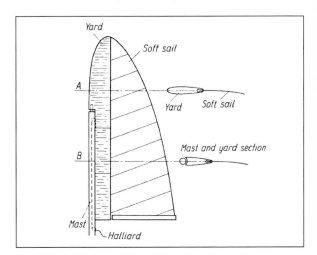

Fig 90 (above left) Some years ago, certain yachting journalists prophesied that the Bermuda sloop rig was destined to be displaced by the airfoil. This figure illustrates one of the many attempts to develop a more aerodynamically efficient propulsion system by integrating the circular mast into a streamlined fairing. So far, futuristic concepts (which in- variably picture a single airfoil as the ultimate sail) have not materialized, except for very special craft (Fig 92). Is it because too many sailors are more romantic than rational, or perhaps because soft fabric, conventional sails have cer- tain virtues which rigid, high lift/drag ratio aerofoils lack? Answers will be found in the following chapters.

through the hollow mast allows the yard to be hoisted on to its bearing. The sail runs in a groove in the yard as on a normal mast.

Fig 91 shows, for example, the successful wing sail for *Lady Helmsman*, which dominated the C-class catamarans for some years and won the International Catamaran Trophy – better known as the Little America's Cup – for Britain. This Una-rig was designed by Austin Farrar following experimental work first carried out by General J Parham; a quarter scale model was tested in the wind tunnel at Southampton University. To remove the mast interference, a deep, stream-lined, build-up mast, which provided the front third of the sail, was extensively investigated (Ref 2.4).

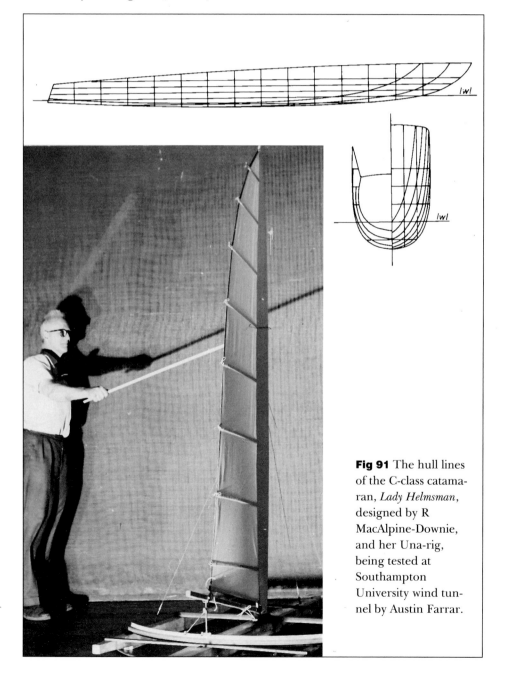

Fig 91 The hull lines of the C-class catamaran, *Lady Helmsman*, designed by R MacAlpine-Downie, and her Una-rig, being tested at Southampton University wind tunnel by Austin Farrar.

Fig 93 (below) One of many solutions to the mast–sail inter-ference problem. Gone is the separated flow and uselessly swirling dead air right behind the mast shown in the photo-graph below. However, losses associated with the presence of a mast may be a lesser evil than the parasitic drag pro-duced by the sails supporting structure erected behind.

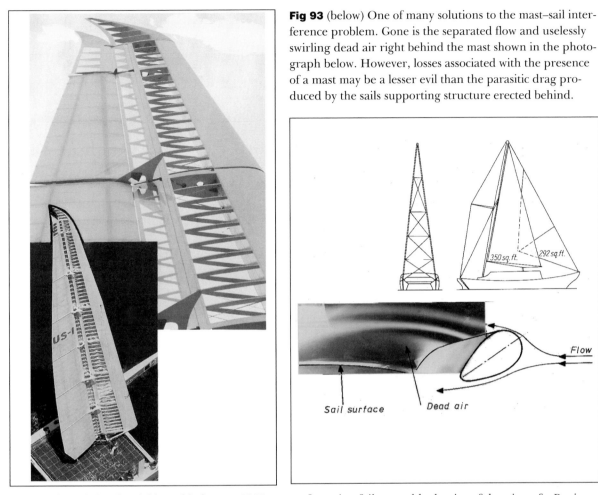

Fig 92 (above left) The rigid, multi-element 1300 square foot wing foil – roughly the size of the wing of a Boeing 757 – which drove *Stars and Stripes*, the American defender of the America's Cup, in 1988. As expected, this giant catamaran of LOA 60 feet, displacement/length ratio $\triangle/(.01\ LWL)^3 = 16$ and sail area/displacement ratio $S_A/\triangle = 476$ (see for comparison Table 5) easily defended the cup against the mega monohull *New Zealand* of LOA 123 feet, carrying 6000 sq ft of soft sails. This unorthodox defence – not in fact prohibited by the America's Cup Deed of Gift – caught the public eye: apparently there was a widely shared feeling that this XXVII America's Cup match – called by some journalists 'the tortoise and the hare mismatch' – pitted the respected principles of fair sports-manship and tradition 'against the greed, commercialism and zealotry that threaten to vulgarize the sport'.

Latterly, wing sails have reached a form wherein mast and sail are combined either into a *single airfoil* which, in its general shape, resembles those of gliders and sailplanes, or a *multielement airfoil* such as that developed for the 1988 America's Cup defender, 60-foot catamaran *Stars and Stripes* (Fig 92). Development of wing sails has been relatively rapid, largely because much of the great store of general fluid dynamics knowledge can be drawn upon when designing them (Ref 2.20).

Yet another solution to the mast interference problem was demonstrated by C O Walker on the catamaran *Marara* (Fig 93). The mast, a braced lattice struc-ture in the shape of the capital letter A, is mounted aft of the leech of the main-sail and hence does not disturb the flow around the sail.

ADDITIONAL AERODYNAMIC DRAG

In our consideration of the aerodynamic drag of the sail, and the way it affects the magnitude and direction of the resultant aerodynamic force, we did not include the forces generated by the wind on the hull, rigging, crew etc. The influence of these on the resultant force F_T can be considerable, and cannot be ignored in the overall estimation of the yacht's performance. Any sailor can feel the effect of drag created by the mast and standing rigging: when driving a boat by engine directly into a strong wind, for example, or when hauling the boat up to her anchor, or when a heavy wind is on the beam in a marina berth. How great the aerodynamic drag of the rigging can be is evidenced by the many centreboard boats which have capsized on their moorings in strong winds.

The total area of whatever is above the waterline and exposed to the action of the wind can be divided into two parts:

1 Effective sail area S_A
2 Parasitic area S_p, of everything except the sail area, S_A.

The wind forces arising from the parasitic area, S_p, act along the apparent wind direction, and can therefore be added to the drag of the sails. The effect of this additional drag will depend on the ratio of the areas S_p to S_A, and on the angle between the yacht's course and the wind direction. When sailing off the wind, the drag component will act forward, and thus be beneficial to the total driving force. As the yacht comes on to the wind, the parasitic drag will act more against the direction of motion and hence reduce the speed.

On balance, the advantages obtained from the parasitic drag when sailing off the wind do not equal the losses suffered when sailing to windward, and hence the parasitic area is undesirable. In short, it pays to reduce to the minimum the ratio S_p/S_A.

Consider a course on the wind, as in Fig 94, the resultant sail force, F_{Tsail}, is at a drag angle ε_s. The driving force, F_{R1}, is given by the vector OA. The total sail force, F_{Tsail}, is made up of two components: a lift force, L, and a drag, D_s. To represent the forces acting on the complete yacht, we must include the parasitic drag, Dp. On the polar diagram of Fig 94, this is shown by the additional drag vector CD. The total aerodynamic force, $F_{T(yacht)}$, of the yacht is now given by the two components: the lift force L of the sail, and the combined drag of the sail and hull, etc. By the usual parallelogram of forces construction we can see that the $F_{T(yacht)}$ is inclined more to the stern, and thus its driving force component, F_{R2}, shown as OB, is smaller than F_{R1}, represented by OA.

Simplifying the problem, one can now draw the polar diagram for the whole yacht (see broken curve in Fig 94) by shifting the sail polar diagram bodily to the right, by the amount of the parasitic drag, D_p.

The complete elimination of unwanted drag is impossible, but some of its components can be reduced by suitable design of the superstructure and standing rigging, by appropriate positioning of the crew, and by tidying up the running rigging. It is also possible to reduce drag due to the hull, by taking into consideration the hull's position between the boom and the water's surface, particularly in close-hauled sailing.

An exhaustive series of tests on Dragon sails *and other rigs* at various angles of

Fig 94 An approximate effect of the parasitic drag on the combined aerodynamic characteristics of the sail plus hull. Polar curve relevant to sail forces alone is shifted to the right, toward higher drag if parasitic drag is added. This harmful effect is mitigated when close-hauled due to the favourable interaction between the flow above the hull and the flow over the lower part of the sail.

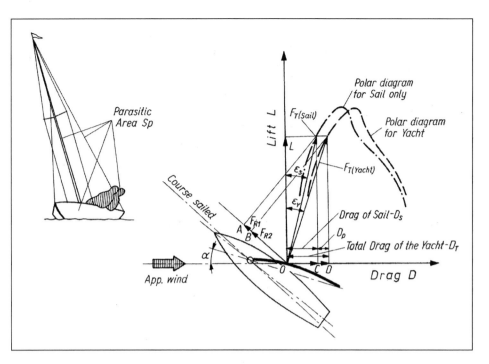

heading, both with and without hulls, were carried out in the wind tunnel at Southampton University. The results showed that the gap between the foot of the sails and the water's surface plays an important role. Under certain conditions – depending on both the course of the yacht and the reduction of the gap between the boom and the water's surface due to the hull presence – it was found that the hull does not spoil the aerodynamic efficiency of the sails; on the contrary, it improves their overall efficiency when close-hauled.

This beneficial influence of the hull, which apparently affects somewhat the flow of air around the lower part of the sail, becomes smaller and smaller when bearing away. In close-reaching conditions, when the boom is far off the centre-line of the hull, the drag angle ε_Y for the whole yacht becomes great in comparison with the drag angle ε_S for the sails alone. We shall return to this issue again in Chapter 12.

It is apparent from these observations that it is certainly worth while reducing to a minimum the distance between the foot of the headsails and the deck; similarly, it generally pays to keep the boom as low as possible over the hull.

According to Rod Stephens, the headsails of *Constellation,* the America's Cup defender 'were tacked below the deck, and the foot of the genoa was so close to the deck that it was hardly possible to get a hand under it.'

7 • APPARENT WIND STRUCTURE

'A fool sees not the same tree that a wise man sees'
William Blake, The Marriage of Heaven and Hell

The aerodynamic forces produced by the wind vary as the square of the apparent wind velocity. In other words, a twofold increase in the velocity of the apparent wind will produce a fourfold increase in the aerodynamic force on the sail. The apparent wind over the sails is not uniform in magnitude and direction, but depends on the following factors:

1 The angle between the yacht's course and the true wind direction, γ
2 The speed of the yacht, V_s
3 Variations in the true wind velocity, V_T, at different heights above the sea
4 Rolling of the yacht
5 Pitching of the yacht

The apparent wind felt by the crew on board a moving yacht is the resultant wind composed of the vectors of the true wind velocity and the yacht's velocity. As an example, we will consider a true wind speed of $V_T = 10$ knots and a yacht speed of $V_s = 5$ knots. For various points of sailing, we can construct the appropriate velocity triangles as in Fig 95.

It is seen that in the range of angles between the course sailed relative to the true wind from γ_1 to γ_2, ie, from close-hauled to close-reaching, the velocity of the apparent wind, V_A, is greater than that of the true wind, V_T. From the angle γ_2 onward, as the boat comes more and more off the wind, the apparent wind velocity, V_A, decreases and reaches a minimum when running dead before the wind. In our case, the apparent wind speed has varied between 14.5 knots and 5 knots, a ratio of nearly three to one. Thus, the aerodynamic forces, all other factors remaining constant, may vary by up to nine times the minimum value, depending entirely on the course sailed.

Changes in the apparent wind speed are of considerable practical importance, especially when the question of reefing sails occurs. The degree of reefing will depend on the course being sailed. Much more canvas can be carried if the leg is before the wind than if the boat is beating to windward. This state of affairs is sometimes a trap for the unwary, particularly when sailing before the wind in a freshening breeze or in restricted sea room. When the time comes to reef or alter course, it may be too late to change the sails safely.

The speed of the true wind increases with the height above the sea. At the surface of the sea the motion of the air is retarded by friction, and this process is continued upward through successive layers, in a similar (though on a larger scale) manner to the formation of the boundary layers described in previous chapters. From meteorological measurements it is known that the rate of increase of the wind speed, ie, the wind gradient, depends on the weather conditions and the state of the sea. Figure 96 shows a typical wind gradient curve for average sea conditions over open water. Near land, or on inland waters, the shape of the curve may be different.

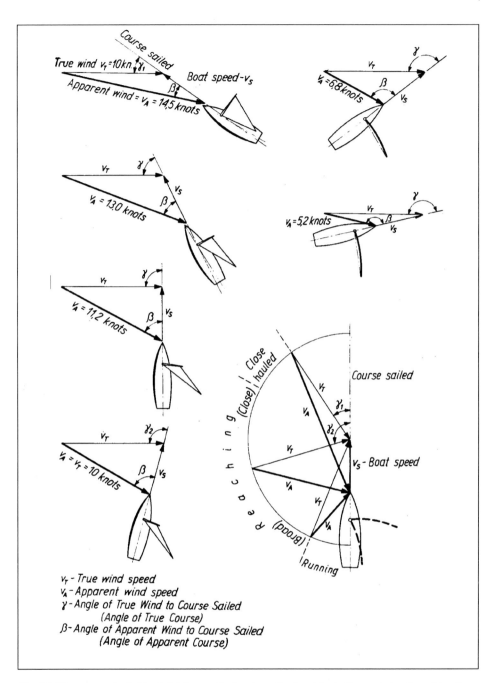

Fig 95 The true wind, V_T (which one feels when the boat is stationary), is altered by the boat's motion V_s. The resulting *apparent wind* V_A is different in strength and direction compared with V_T. Wind indicators on the moving boat measure the apparent wind only. Any change in either the boat heading or her speed affects the apparent wind. Similarly, any change in either the true wind speed or its direction also causes changes in the apparent wind. Aerodynamic forces developed on sails depend *entirely* on the apparent wind, V_A. An easy way to find the apparent wind is to draw to the same scale a velocity triangle as demonstrated, ie, using the vectors of the true wind speed, V_T, and the boat speed, V_s, as the sides of the triangle. Vectors V_s and V_T intersect each other at γ angle. The apparent wind speed V_A is given by the thick line vector (see Appendix I, The parallelogram of forces and velocities).

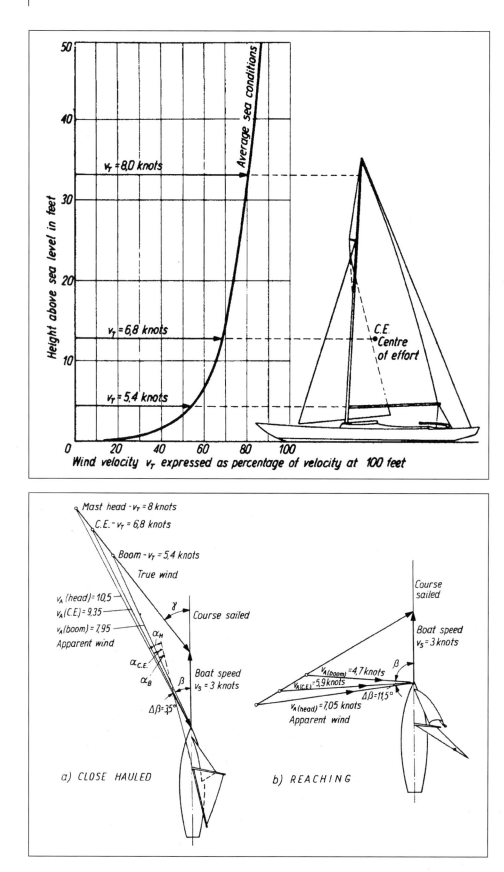

Fig 96 Does the wind blow with the same velocity at sea level as it does, say, 10, 20 and 30 feet above the water surface? This question of the 'wind velocity gradient' (wind sheer) and its effects on sail power have been debated for years by sailing people anxious to know how much sail twist is justified (Fig 97). The subject of wind gradient is also discussed in some details in Part 3.

Fig 97 The effect of the true wind gradient on the angle of incidence of the apparent wind at the foot and head of a Dragon class mainsail (shown in Fig 96) when close-hauled and reaching. The wind gradient, ie, the wind velocity increase from the sea surface upward, is a function of the water roughness (waves), presence of the hull, air temperature, and the true wind turbulence. In general, the presence of a yacht's hull deflects the wind over it, speeding it up, so the true wind gradient is somewhat reduced over the lower part of the rig. When pointing high into the wind a sail should have a very small, almost imperceptible twist.

Supposing that, at a height of 100 ft, $V_T = 10$ knots, then from the curve which shows a Dragon class yacht to scale, the true wind at the head of its mainsail will be only 80 per cent of this value, ie, $V_T = 8$ knots, while at the centre of effort of the sails it will be 6.8 knots. The variation of true wind speed, V_T, with height will affect the apparent wind velocity in magnitude and direction for each sail section. This is illustrated in Fig 97 which reveals the velocity triangles for a Dragon sailing at a speed $V_s = 3$ knots. Thus, for a close–hauled course, the apparent wind at the masthead is 32 per cent stronger than that at the height of the boom, and in addition, its direction, given by the angle $ß + \triangle ß$, is 3.5° greater than at the boom height.

Similarly, on a reach (Fig 97b), we find that the upper wind velocity will be about 50 per cent greater than the lower one, and the twist in the apparent wind direction will be 11.5°.

In light winds, when we are not limited by stability considerations, it is profitable to hoist additional sails (such as spinnaker) as high up as possible to exploit greater wind strength at a more advantageous angle than that lower down, and hence generate a greater aerodynamic force.

Figure 97 shows how the direction of the apparent wind is twisted up the height of the mast. This is relevant to the problem of deliberate twisting of the sails, which often provokes strong discussion among sailing folk: there are those who think that untwisted sails are better, and those who prefer them twisted. To settle the matter, we may reasonably assume that each section of the sail – from foot to head – should operate at the same effective angle of incidence relative to the apparent wind. For close–hauled sailing it is clear from Fig 97a that if the sail had no twist, its upper section would operate at a larger effective incidence angle than the sections near the boom. In order to maintain the same effective incidence angle for all sail sections, the sail should be twisted about 3.5° because the apparent wind twist, $\triangle ß$, is 3.5°. On the reaching course shown for the *Dragon* in Fig 97b, the apparent wind twist is larger and $\triangle ß = 11.5°$, hence greater sail twist is demanded. Such a correction in sail twist, taking into account the apparent wind behaviour alone, would not however be sufficient: sail twist must be larger than that imposed by the apparent wind variation due to wind gradient. Why? The reason is that the upper part of a triangular sail has a tendency to stall prematurely, as indicated in Fig 212.

The lighter the wind, ie, the higher the angle of incidence at which a sail is set to produce a large lift coefficient, the greater must be the amount of twist in order to prevent or alleviate an early stall of the upper part of the sail. In other words, the optimum twist in close–hauled conditions must gradually be reduced as the wind becomes stronger, since the sail is operating at a smaller and smaller lift coefficient. When bearing away, the amount of twist allowed should gradually be increased. In short, the higher the lift, the larger the required twist for optimum sail efficiency. So although some degree of sail twist, to match the twist in the apparent wind (and for other reasons) is desirable, it should never be as much as that shown in Fig 98.

Rolling and pitching can also influence the apparent wind strength and direction, because of the associated movements of the mast and sails (Fig 99). The effect is greatest toward the top of the mast, where the motion is most violent. Looking at the rolling case, Fig 99a, it can be seen that as the top of the

Fig 98 The course sailed γ relative to the true wind (Fig 97) has an effect on the change △ß in the apparent wind angle; this requires more sail twist in reaching conditions than when close-hauled, but never as much as 50 degrees or more, as shown in the photo (left)!

Wind gradient changes from place to place, depending on the prevailing weather pattern and local shore configurations. For example, San Diego is a place of strong wind gradient and wind sheer. Paul Cayard, the *Il Moro* America's Cup challenger skipper, reported that sometimes the wind direction recorded at the masthead was 5 degrees to the right or left of the wind hitting the bottom quarter of the genoa, and often with two knots more wind at the mast head than at deck level (Ref 2.22).

Since catamarans sail faster than ordinary monohulls, their sail twist should be slightly larger than that for monohulls. The photo (right) demonstrates the twist applied to the upper part of the multielement solid rigid wing-foil of the successful Australian defender of the little America's Cup (C-class catamaran). The top half of the No 3 element is partly open, thus effectively twisting off the upper leech of the rig.

mast oscillates between the positions 1 and 2, it can reach a velocity w_1 as it rolls (say) to leeward, and a velocity w_2 as it recovers. The effect can be considered in terms of velocity triangles drawn in the second sketch, which show the resulting changes in the apparent wind.

The angle of incidence of the upper portions of the sail can vary within wide limits, and can be appreciable when rolling is violent. As a result of the dynamic fluctuations in the apparent wind, periodic changes both in the magnitude and direction of the aerodynamic force may occur, similar to the process of 'pumping'. This will be discussed later. Particularly on a reaching course, the periodic changes of incidence will produce an effect similar to that obtained by making rapid and repeated changes in the mainsheet position. In a similar analysis of Fig 99b, one finds that the pitching motion of a yacht also induces alterations in the apparent wind.

Relatively large variations in the magnitude of aerodynamic forces developed on sails, due to rapid changes in the apparent wind direction – as distinct from forces developed in steady wind – will be discussed in Chapter 8, Part 3. These variations in forces do not arise in light winds and a rough sea, when the sail finds it difficult to fill in its usual shape, but is deformed through frequent shaking, so the flow round the sail becomes disrupted.

Fig 99 Due to rolling and pitching, the effective angles of incidence at which the sail operates decrease and increase periodically and at different rates, depending on the height of the sail section above the deck.

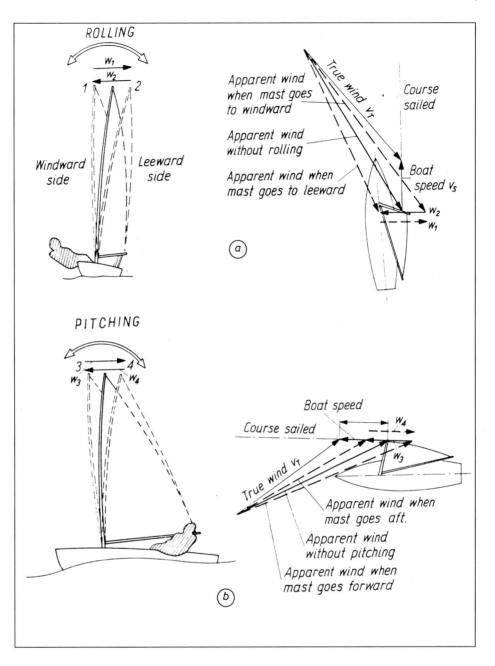

8 • THE DEPENDENCE OF THE OPTIMUM ANGLE OF SAIL INCIDENCE UPON HEADING ANGLE AND WIND STRENGTH

'The case – said Sherlock Holmes, as we chatted over our cigars that night in our rooms at Baker Street – is one where... we have been compelled to reason backwards from effect to causes.'

Sir Arthur Conan Doyle

Why does one boat sail faster than another? How close to windward can a given boat sail? To inquire meaningfully into questions like these, it is necessary to consider first the effect of the incidence angle (or sheeting angle) on a boat's performance, beginning from the simple case of a boat sailing at a reaching heading relative to the apparent wind.

REACHING CONDITIONS (WIND ABEAM)

Consider two cat-rigged boats having identical sails of 100 sq ft area, and sailing on the same course, as in Fig 100a. Let us assume that the aerodynamic characteristics of their sails are as those given in Fig 100b, the average apparent wind is V_A = 10 knots (16.9 ft/sec) and both sails are twisted so that each maintains its chosen angle of incidence over the whole sail. If helmsman A keeps his sail at the angle $\alpha_A = 27°$ to the apparent wind, then the corresponding coefficient of the total aerodynamic force will be C_T = 1.38. On the other hand, if helmsman B sheets his sail harder to an angle of incidence $\alpha_B = 37°$, the corresponding coefficient will be C_T = 1.28.

Fig 100 The effect of incidence angle on the driving and heeling components of the total sail force developed on a Bermuda type of mainsail (of aspect ratio AR = $\frac{b^2}{S_A}$ = 4.2) in reaching conditions, wind abeam.

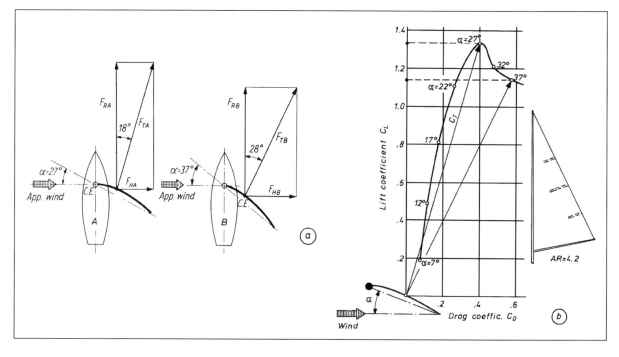

Hence we can calculate the total forces:

boat A: $F_{TA} = 0.00119 \times V_A{}^2 \times S_A \times C_T$
$= 0.00119 \times 16.9^2 \times 100 \times 1.38$
$= 46.8 \text{ lb}$

boat B: $F_{TB} = 0.00119 \times 16.9^2 \times 100 \times 1.28$
$= 43.5 \text{ lb}$

From Fig 100b we can also obtain the directions of these forces and thus resolve them to obtain corresponding driving forces F_{RA} and F_{RB}.

$F_{RA} = F_{TA} \times \cos 18° = 46.8 \times 0.951 = 44.5 \text{ lb}$
$F_{RB} = F_{TB} \times \cos 28° = 43.5 \times 0.883 = 38.4 \text{ lb}$

This example demonstrates the importance of correctly trimming the sail. A reduction in driving force of about 14 per cent is the result of sheeting the sail too far inboard; in addition, the undesirable side force, F_{HB}, is greater. At the other extreme, if the sail is set at too small an incidence, again it will not be working at its full efficiency. The maintenance of the correct angle of incidence of the sail as the wind varies is of importance if we wish to maintain optimum sailing speed at all times. This is particularly so in light winds, when even small changes in driving force affect the speed performance considerably.

As shown in Fig 100b, the maximum sail force is obtained only in a limited range of angle of incidence, at about 27°. This optimum angle applies to a sail with negligible twist, a camber of about 1/10 and aspect ratio AR = 4.2. For sails of characteristics other than these, this angle will be different.

If a sail is twisted, its upper part may flutter (this indicates that the sail is working at too small an incidence) while the lower parts are stalled ie, at too high an incidence (see Fig 98). Inevitably, the sail will not be as efficient as it could be if all its section along the mast height were working at the same optimum angle of incidence.

The curves of Fig 101 show to what extent the maximum value of the aerodynamic force is reduced by excessive sail twist. Not only is there a decrease in the maximum force, but also the drag angle is larger, which will result in the boat with the twisted sail not going so well to windward. The loss of sail power due to twist, in terms of maximum lift, can be best judged quantitatively on an experimental basis. Figure 102 presents a number of polar curves (C_L versus C_D) for the same rectangular sail of AR = 1.6, but gradually twisted from 0 to 31.5 degrees (measured between the chords of the lower and upper edge of the sail). As shown in the photograph, the sail

Fig 101 The qualitative effect of sail twist on the maximum lift, and the drag angles (ε_1 and ε_2) which determine the boat's ability to sail close to the wind (see Fig 102). The boom–vang increases the sail forces at every angle of incidence.

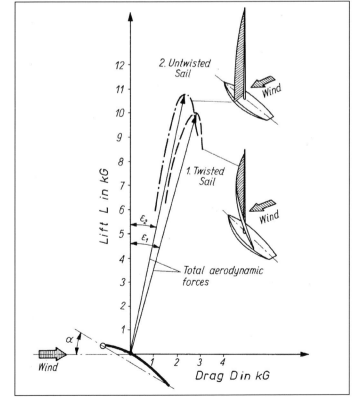

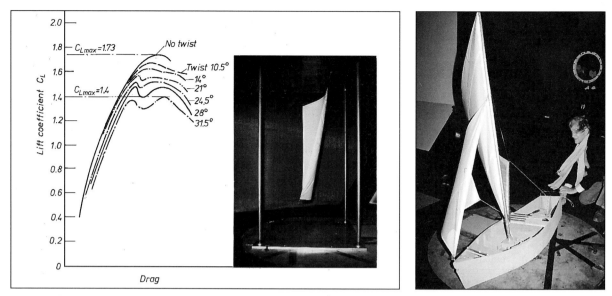

Fig 102 (left) Results of tests on a mastless, rectangular sail of AR = 1.6, set with different amounts of twist, ranging from 0 to 31.5 degrees, measured between the upper and lower sail section. The twist shown in the photograph was 24.5 degrees (Ref 2.23).

Fig 103 (right) The twist of a Bermudan mainsail on a boat with a simple sheeting system (ie, without an effective kicking strap (boom-vang), such as are used on sophisticated racing boats), may be as much as 70 degrees. The photograph shows one of the rigs tested by the author within a programme funded by the Natural Resources and Environment Department of the Overseas Development Administration of the British Government (Ref 2.24).

had no mast, but was supported by wires kept under high tension to minimize spanwise variation of its camber.

It will be seen that the sail which was twisted 31.5 degrees developed only about 80 per cent of the C_{Lmax} obtained in the untwisted condition. The rate at which sail efficiency deteriorates appears to increase as twist increases. That is, from 0 to about 10 degrees of twist, its deleterious effect on L/D ratio is negligible; thereafter the bad effect becomes more and more pronounced, both on L/D and C_{Lmax} as well (Fig 103).

Sails are particularly susceptible to twisting when sailing on a reach, or broad reach, when the tendency of the boom to lift is not counteracted effectively by the tension in the mainsheet (Fig 104a). The working condition of such a sail can be greatly improved by the use of a kicking strap, which pulls the boom downwards. Ideally it should secure uniform effective incidence for all sections of the sail. The kicking strap tension should produce such a twist that the apparent wind sheer is accounted for. Reasonable proof of a well–adjusted kicking strap tension will be the instantaneous flutter of the whole length of the luff of the sail when the sheets are eased or the boat luffed slightly. If the tension is not correct, either the upper or lower part will flutter first, indicating uneven working conditions at the different heights of the sail. It is possible that in spite of correctly tensioning the kicking strap, all parts of the sail do not flutter together. If this is so, the sail cut may be at fault and should be rectified.

A well-designed kicking strap should effectively counteract the tendency of the boom to rise, so leaving the mainsheet free to perform its main function of controlling sail incidence only. Leading the mainsheet to the centreline of the

Fig 104 Ineffective (a) and effective (b) means of preventing and controlling too large a twist of sail.

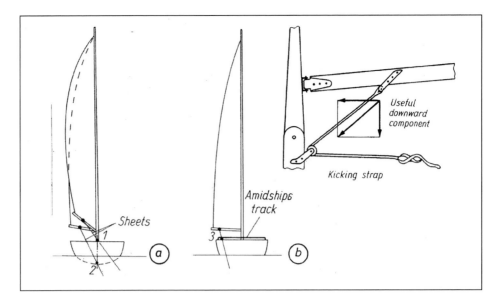

Fig 105 The effect of the angle of incidence at which the sail is set relative to the apparent wind on the driving and heeling components of the total aerodynamic force. A polar diagram of this particular sail is given in Fig 100.

hull at deck level (point 1 in Fig 104a) should be avoided; position 2, although slightly better, is also inefficient, as it does not prevent the boom from rising up, and thus inflicts large twist. One of the best ways to reduce the twist of the sail is to use a mainsheet track mounted amidships (Fig 104b). This allows a near vertical action of the mainsheet, and consequently a large component of the tension is available to pull the boom down, and so control the twist. The only snag is that sheets operate now as a kicking strap, and so the angle of incidence of the sail must essentially be controlled by changing the position of the mainsheet traveller along the athwartship track.

CLOSE-HAULED, CLOSE-REACHING

From the example of Fig 100, we can derive the conclusion that the maximum driving force, F_R, is attained when the sail is set at or close to the angle of maximum lift. The question now arises, is this angle the optimum angle for

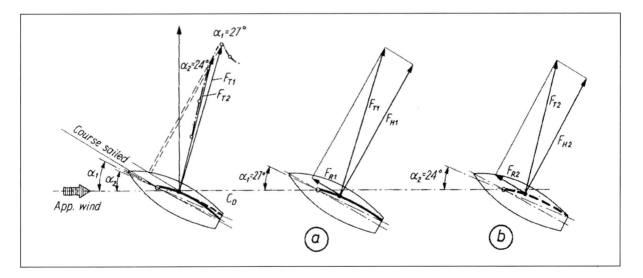

setting the sail relative to the apparent wind for all points of sailing? The example shown in Fig 105 will prove that this is not the case.

In Fig 105a, a boat is sailing on the wind. The sail is set at an angle of incidence $\alpha_1 = 27°$ at which this particular sail generates the maximum aerodynamic force, F_{T1} (maximum lift). The driving component of this force acting in the direction of motion is shown by the vector F_{R1} (sketch a).

Figure 105b depicts the same boat but with the sail set at smaller angle of incidence $\alpha_2 = 24°$. The aerodynamic force, F_{T2}, is now less, but when resolved into a driving force component F_{R2}, and a heeling force F_{H2}, causing drift, it is seen that the former is larger, and the latter smaller, than the corresponding components for boat a. Hence boat b should sail faster and make less leeway than boat a. In addition, the force F_{H1}, larger than F_{H2}, will cause boat a to heel more than boat b. This again reduces her speed performance, since the extra heel causes more hull resistance.

The above example demonstrates that to attain the maximum speed for a boat on any selected course, the angle of incidence of the sail must be so adjusted that *not only the magnitude* of the resultant aerodynamic force, *but also the direction* in which it acts, are taken into account.

Conclusions derived so far may serve as a first approximation only. The reason is that the correct sheeting angle of any sail, ie, its angle of incidence relative to the apparent wind depends also on the hydrodynamic characteristics of the hull, and in addition, the strength of the wind.

Some important general principles in this respect can be extrapolated if the sail and hull characteristics are known. Typical curves representing aerodynamic properties of the single sail have been given previously in Figs 64 and 100. Now the reader will have to accept as valid some simplified assumptions concerning hydrodynamic characteristics of the hull, which are based on information to be found in later chapters of this book.

Although the hull appendages may not look as conspicuous as the sails, it does not mean that their shapes and related action are less important (Fig 59). There is little difference in the principle of operation between a sail and a keel; when it comes to sailing to windward, keel action is as vital as that of the sails.

An examination of the geometry of forces in Fig 106 will demonstrate that the effective driving force, F_R, produced by the sail, is equal to the total aerodynamic force, F_H, multiplied by the sine of the *drag angle*, ϵ_H of the hull:

$$F_R = F_S \times \sin \epsilon_H \qquad\qquad \text{Eq 16}$$

This hydrodynamic drag angle, ϵ_H, considered as a measure of hydrodynamic efficiency of the hull plus keel, is directly related to the side force/resistance ratio F_S/R of the underwater part of the hull; and as such it gives an idea of how much is paid in terms of hull resistance, R, in order to generate the side force, F_s, necessary to resist the aerodynamic heeling (side) force, F_H.

Equation 16 may seem a little surprising at first, as one might imagine that the effectiveness of the wind forces in driving the boat depends directly on the quality of sails and their trim. This is so, but the aerodynamic and hydrodynamic forces are mutually interconnected. The trim of sails relative to the hull determines the leeway angle, and this in turn affects the hull drag angle at which the hull operates.

Fig 106 In steady sailing conditions, ie, with constant boat speed, the aerodynamic sail forces are balanced by similar hydrodynamic forces generated on the underwater part of the hull plus its appendages. Thus:

$$F_R = R$$
$$F_H = F_s$$
and $F_R =$
$$F_s \times \sin \varepsilon_H$$

The hydrodynamic drag angle ε_H – similar to the aerodynamic drag angle ε_A (Figs 68b, 94) – is an important parameter which determines (together with ε_A) how close to the wind a given boat may sail.

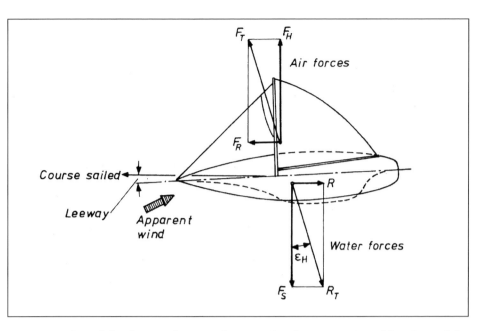

As mentioned in the caption to Fig 106, the forces produced by the sail in steady motion are exactly balanced by similar forces on the hull. This is illustrated in Fig 107a, which shows the polar diagram of forces for a sail developed at a certain apparent wind speed and heading angle, β_A. Opposing the sail polar diagram, there is a resultant hull force, R_T, which can be balanced at only one point on the sail curve, at point A. Thus, with the configuration shown, it is possible to sail with the sail set at one incidence, α_A, ie, sheeted in one particular position, δ_A. If α_A is altered to, say, α_B by hardening the sheets to δ_B, conditions elsewhere must of necessity, alter too (sketch b). Two such quantities which alter are the speed of the boat, V_s, and the leeway angle, λ, between the course and the hull centreline.

The two quantities just mentioned control, to a large extent, the hydrodynamic force developed on the hull. In Fig 107a the outlines are shown of some hull sections, or waterlines, of a fixed-keel yacht sailing to windward at a certain angle of heel and leeway angle, λ. Under the asymmetric flow conditions, the underwater part of the hull acts as a hydrofoil and develops a side force, F_s, and a resistance, R, by a process similar to that of the sail. As the leeway angle, λ (angle of incidence of hydrofoil) increases, so will both the side force F_s and resistance R.

In addition to the variation of the leeway angle, the hull forces also vary with boat speed, V_s. The side force, F_s, will change in proportion to V_s squared, as do the aerodynamic forces in proportion to V_A squared, but the resistance will increase with V_s at a greater rate. Thus, at a fixed leeway angle, the total hull force R_T will vary in a manner shown in Fig 108, which presents results of tests obtained on a hull model of the *Pirate* centreboard dinghy (Ref 2.25).

At a low boat speed, V_{s1}, the ratio side force/resistance $F_s/R = 4.5$. As the speed increases, this ratio gradually falls to 1.8 at the speed V_{s4}, with a corresponding increase in the hydrodynamic drag angle ε_H. In this respect the ratio of aerodynamic forces F_H/F_R does not vary with wind speed, provided the incidence angle α remains constant. Generally, a fixed-keel hull demonstrates

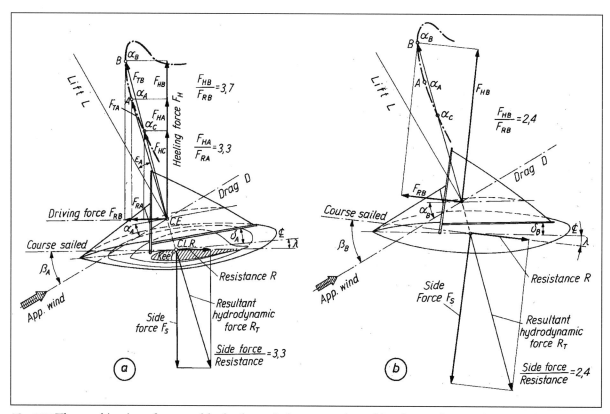

Fig 107 The combination of aero and hydrodynamic forces together with relevant drag angles ε_A and ε_H indicate that these two main performance determinants and depending ß angle are closely linked. The process of attaining the equilibrium of aero-hydrodynamic forces depends partly on the helmsman's action through sheeting (changing the sail incidence) and rudder application, and is partly automatic. In other words, the constant speed and the balance of forces is not achieved until the driving force F_R equals the hull resistance R, and the heeling force F_H equals the side force F_s – a balance which occurs when all self-adjusting and interrelated variables such as leeway angle λ, course sailed, ß, sail incidence, heeling angle, wind speed, etc, allow that sort of equilibrium to occur. Usually, because both the wind velocity and its direction are seldom steady, the boat continually accelerates and decelerates to a greater or lesser extent, all the time seeking for this elusive equilibrium.

characteristics similar to those of a centreboard dinghy. Of course, the hydrodynamic ratio F_s/R will depend on the shape of hull and its appendages – keel, fin-keel, centreboard, rudder; these substantially affect the boat's ability to produce a large side force at possibly small expense in terms of resistance, R, for given boat speed, V_s.

In the example shown in Fig 107a, the ratio $F_s/R = 3.3$ is relevant to a 6 Metre class yacht sailing at speed $V_s = 5.9$ knots, on the wind, whose true velocity is $V_T = 12$ knots. The yacht is sailing at a steady angle, $ß_A$, between the course and the apparent wind direction, so the hydrodynamic forces are in equilibrium with the aerodynamic forces when the sail is set at the angle of incidence, α_A.

The question now arises as to what may happen if the helmsman decides to increase the driving force from the sail by hardening the sheet without touching the rudder. Since the angle of incidence of the sail increases to α_B, the total aerodynamic force will increase to F_{TB}, changing its direction at the same time.

The aerodynamic ratio, F_{HB}/F_{RB}, increases now to 3.7, which must be matched by the hydrodynamic ratio of F_s/R to balance the forces. The boat will do it automatically by bearing off the wind, and so increasing the angle ß until a new equilibrium of forces is reached. In this process the aerodynamic ratio of F_{HB}/F_{RB} will decrease, since the heeling force/driving force coordinate system will rotate relative to the apparent wind. The final state of equilibrium, when $F_{HB}/F_{RB} = F_s/R = 2.4$ is shown in Fig 107b, where it can be found that the angle $ß_B$ equals 36.5°, an increase of 6.5° over β_A, and that the leeway angle, λ, has also altered.

On the other hand, the helmsman may ease the sheet, reducing the sail incidence from α_A to α_C; then the resultant aerodynamic force will fall to about 70 per cent of F_{TA}. If, as shown in Fig 107a, the new force, F_{TC}, acts along the same line as F_{TB}, then the corresponding ratio of the forces, F_H/F_R, will be 3.7. As a result of the smaller driving force, F_{RC}, the yacht speed V_S must decrease. Reference to Fig 108 suggests that the same ratio required of the hull forces may be met solely by the reduction in V_S.

The above plausible deductions are based on the assumption that the heel did not alter. As a matter of fact, increasing the angle of heel adversely affects both the aerodynamic efficiency of the sail, ε_A, and the hydrodynamic efficiency of the hull, ε_H, in a similar manner, so that the ß angle tends to increase. The influence of rudder angle on the leeway angle is also important.

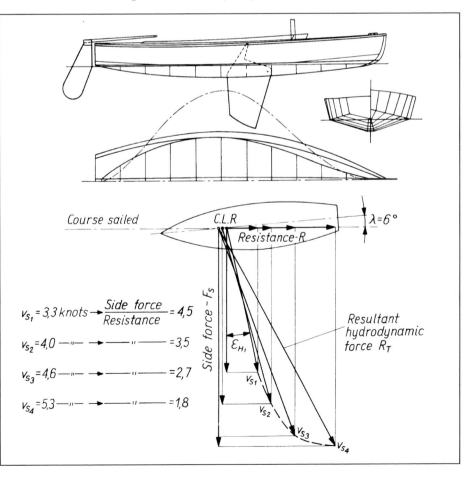

Fig 108 Side force F_s and Resistance R developed on a centreboard dinghy at a constant leeway angle $\lambda = 6°$, and four different boat speeds. As shown, the boat resistance increases at a much higher rate with speed V_s than the side force. Consequently, the relevant hydrodynamic drag angle, ε_H, increases with speed.

Course sailed   *C.L.R* $\lambda = 6°$

Resistance-R

$v_{S_1} = 3.3\ knots \rightarrow \dfrac{Side\ force}{Resistance} = 4.5$

$v_{S_2} = 4.0\ —''— \rightarrow —''— = 3.5$

$v_{S_3} = 4.6\ —''— \rightarrow —''— = 2.7$

$v_{S_4} = 5.3\ —''— \rightarrow —''— = 1.8$

Side force - F_s

Resultant hydrodynamic force R_T

COURSE THEOREM (LANCHESTER'S PRINCIPLE)

Let us consider the geometrical relationships between the apparent course, ß, and the aerodynamic and hydrodynamic forces. Fig 109 gives the relative angular positions of the sail and hull forces on a boat sailing on the wind at ß = 30°. The boat is sailing upright at a constant speed and the centre of effort (CE) of the sail and the centre of lateral resistance (CLR) of the submerged hull are coincident at the point O. These simplifications do not affect the geometrical relationships we shall derive. The line of action of the resultant aerodynamic force, F_T, is defined by the aerodynamic drag angle, ε_A. Its magnitude can be calculated from the relationship between the lift L and the drag D, so that cot ε_A = L/D. Similarly the hydrodynamic drag angle, ε_H, is found from cot ε_H = F_s/R.

Under steady sailing conditions, when V_s is constant, the resultant air and water forces, F_T and R, are of the same magnitude and act along the same line. From Fig 109 we find:

$$\varepsilon_A = <c \ o \ d \ \text{(where < designates angle)}$$
$$\text{and} \qquad \varepsilon_H = <d \ o \ e$$
$$\text{and hence} \quad \varepsilon_A + \varepsilon_H = <coe$$
$$\text{but} \qquad <coe = <aob = \beta$$
$$\text{thus} \qquad ß = \varepsilon_A + \varepsilon_H \qquad\qquad \text{Eq 17}$$

ie, the sailing angle to the apparent wind or, in other words, the *apparent course ß is the sum of the aerodynamic and hydrodynamic angles of drag ε_A and ε_H*. This simple geometrical relationship was first identified by W F Lanchester in 1907

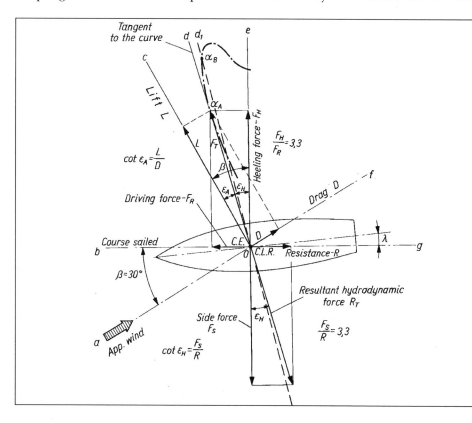

Fig 109 Beating to windward. The ß angle is determined by the sum of two drag angles ε_A + ε_H. A decrease in boat speed V_s, and hence ε_H, due to the decrease in wind speed V_A, requires an increase in ε_A (higher angle of sail incidence) to keep the ß angle constant. In other words since, for an unchanged course, ε_A is inversely proportional to ε_H, any modification of one results in an equal and opposite modification of the other; it is impossible to minimize these two interdependent variables at the same time.

(Ref 2.26) and is of fundamental importance in understanding principles which control the performance of any sailing boat. We can derive from it a number of practical conclusions which are particularly important for competitive sailing.

In order to maintain ß constant, any increase or decrease in ε_A must be accompanied by the same amount of decrease or increase in ε_H. Bearing in mind that there is a correspondence between apparent wind speed V_A and yacht speed V_s, increases in the former leading to an increase in the latter, we can also take the hull characteristic from Fig 109, with the leeway angle, $\lambda = 6°$ remaining constant. Then, as the boat speed V_s varies, provided that the apparent wind strength V_A is sufficient, so must the hydrodynamic angle ε_H vary as follows:

$$V_{s1} = 3.3 \text{ knots} \qquad \cot \varepsilon_{H1} = 4.5 \qquad \varepsilon_{H1} = 12.5°$$
$$V_{s2} = 4.0 \text{ knots} \qquad \cot \varepsilon_{H2} = 3.5 \qquad \varepsilon_{H2} = 16.0°$$
$$V_{s3} = 4.6 \text{ knots} \qquad \cot \varepsilon_{H3} = 2.7 \qquad \varepsilon_{H3} = 20.3°$$
$$V_{s4} = 5.3 \text{ knots} \qquad \cot \varepsilon_{H4} = 1.8 \qquad \varepsilon_{H4} = 29.0°$$

If ß = 30° is to be maintained, the corresponding values of the aerodynamic drag angle ε_A can be obtained from Eq 17.

Thus: $\varepsilon_A = ß - \varepsilon_H$

Hence for:
$$V_{s1} = 3.3 \text{ knots} \qquad \varepsilon_{A1} = 30° - 12.5° = 17.5°$$
$$V_{s2} = 4.0 \text{ knots} \qquad \varepsilon_{A2} = 30° - 16.0° = 14°$$
$$V_{s3} = 4.6 \text{ knots} \qquad \varepsilon_{A3} = 30° - 20.3° = 9.7°$$
$$V_{s4} = 5.3 \text{ knots} \qquad \varepsilon_{A4} = 30° - 29.0° = 1°$$

Unfortunately not all required values of ε_A are available. Looking at the sail polar diagram in Fig 109 it is clear that a minimum possible drag angle, ε_A, is obtained at the point where a line from O is a tangent to the curve. This point, shown as α_A, yields a value $\varepsilon_A = 12.5°$. By interpolation of the data in the above table, we estimate that the maximum speed, V_s, under the conditions chosen, is about 4.3 knots.

The arguments we have so far used are not completely sound, since the leeway angle λ would not have remained constant under different sailing conditions, and it was tacitly assumed that the wind strength was such that a balance of forces as well as their ratios could be obtained. Nevertheless, an important point emerged: the significance of the minimum attainable angle of aerodynamic drag, ε_A. This is particularly true when considering racing One-Design classes, such as the Finn, Flying Dutchman, Star and Dragon, when all hulls are nominally identical, and hopefully have the same hydrodynamic characteristics. In this case, the boat speed, V_s, will depend almost entirely on the rigging, trim and set of the sails, since these control the angle of aerodynamic drag, ε_A.

The new generation of semi-professional or professional sailors have greatly perfected the technique of tuning and trimming sails to best performance, and frequently mediocre boats, sailed by outstanding crew, are capable of scoring spectacular successes in regattas just by virtue of the crews' expertise in adapting the boats to the actual sailing conditions.

Let us consider now the effect of reduction of wind strength. Assuming the course ß = 30° is maintained, we know the boat speed, V_s, must fall, and consequently the hydrodynamic angle of drag, ε_H, will decrease (Fig 108).

Therefore, the aerodynamic drag angle ε_A should increase by the same amount, sheeting the sail to the incidence α_B (Fig 109). This complementary interaction between ε_A and ε_H is shown by the broken line marked d_1, Fig 109, going through the origin O of the coordinate system and intersecting the polar diagram at α_B. Thus, while sailing on the wind, the sails operate over the whole range of incidence angles, beginning from a small angle close to sail flutter to the angle just below the C_L maximum.

It should be stressed that the ß angle, ie, the course angle relative to the apparent wind, cannot be regarded as a direct index of the boat's potential ability to achieve best V_{mg} (speed made good to windward), as demonstrated in Fig 18. Noteworthy is the simple mathematical formula:

$$V_{mg} = V_s \times \cos \gamma$$

which indicates that V_{mg} is a composite product of the boat speed V_s and the course sailed, γ, relative to the *true wind*, V_T. It will, however, be shown elsewhere in the book that the ß angle as determined by ε_A and ε_H (Eq 17) has a crucial effect on attainable V_{mg}.

THE RELATIVE IMPORTANCE OF SAILS AND HULL IN BOAT PERFORMANCE

Some practical question can be answered with the help of Fig 110; for instance, which is more important from the viewpoint of yacht performance, sails or hull? The answer is that both parts are important because the sailing craft must be considered as a *complex system consisting of two interdependent parts* – aerodynamic and hydrodynamic. Each part is therefore the cause and effect of the other, so there is no reason to assume or believe that one of the parts is more important than the other. The only difference from, say, the crew's point of view, is that the *sail efficiency is somewhat more accessible to intervention*, through the tuning or adjusting process, whereas the hydrodynamic properties of the hull, once determined on the designer's drawing board, are dependent very little on the crew's efforts – except, perhaps, in that they can keep the hull surface smooth!

Another question which can be answered from Fig 110 is: if a development or modification of a given boat is considered, which is more likely to give more conspicuous gain in terms of windward performance, the sails or the hull? The answer is: the part that is poorer aerodynamically or hydrodynamically deserves more attention, ie, the part that in average sailing condition produces a lower L/D or F_s/R ratio. In other words, there is relatively little to be gained by improving the efficiency of an already good rig which is driving an inefficient hull.

Let us consider this problem numerically, assuming that the underwater part of the hull (the shape labelled 'original design' in Fig 111), develops in average conditions the F_s/R ratio in the order of 2.9. The boat is driven by a sloop type rig, producing an L/D ratio in the order of 6.0, which is an average value applicable to this type of rig. If these numbers are entered on the graph in Fig 100, we can see that the minimum pointing angle ß would be about 29 degrees. An improvement of rig efficiency, say from L/D = 6 to 7 (not necessarily easy to achieve), would result in a reduction of the ß angle from 29 to 28, one degree only. In contrast, improving the keel efficiency by the same step from 2.9 to 3.9 will result in a ß reduction from 29 to 24 degrees, ie, five degrees.

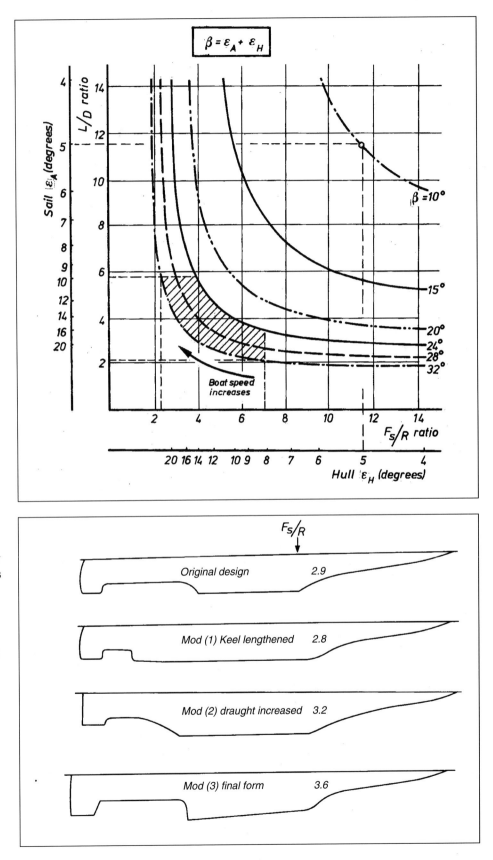

Fig 110 The effect of a change in the L/D ratio (or ε_A) of a sail and the F_s/R ratio (ε_H) of a hull on the windward ability of any sailing craft.

Fig 111 Keel development guided by towing-tank tests may yield substantial gains in terms of ε_H. The planforms of the underwater part of the hull are relevant to the vessel depicted in Fig 112. The results are published here by kind permission of Laurent Giles and Partners Ltd, Lymington, and Southampton University.

A difference of one degree in windward pointing ability means 90 to 180 feet (27 to 55 m) more made good to windward for every nautical mile sailed. The smaller gain value is applicable to already sophisticated racers such as 12 Metres; the larger benefit could be expected by improving vessels of less efficient aerohydrodynamic forms, such as those presented in Fig 112. Thus, 5 degrees reduction in ß angle could mean about 900 feet (270 m) more made good to windward per nautical mile sailed.

In the context of Fig 111 it should be noticed that shallow draught does not entirely preclude the possibility of reasonably efficient side force generation. Modification of the initial design, leading to a slightly swept bottom of the keel, demonstrates that relatively small changes in keel planform may greatly improve the windward ability of the vessel in question.

These examples, together with the results implicit in Fig 110, show that spectacular improvements in windward ability can only be achieved if the craft in question is inefficient in terms of the L/D and/or F_s/R ratios. But when these ratios are already high, as in the case of modern racing yachts, further progress toward higher performance becomes painfully slow, and no dramatic breakthrough can possibly be expected in these or similar racing machines.

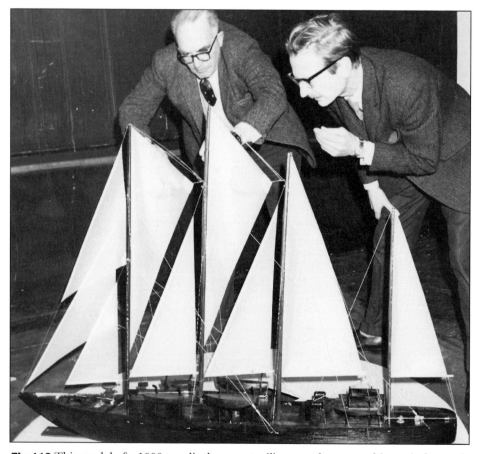

Fig 112 This model of a 1000 ton displacement sailing vessel was tested in a wind tunnel and a towing tank. The question asked was: is the rig efficient enough to drive the vessel at a predetermined speed and a given wind velocity? *Photo by the author.*

THE EFFECTS OF WIND STRENGTH ON SAIL PERFORMANCE IN CLOSE-HAULED CONDITIONS

As the boat heels beyond some critical heel angle, which may or may not be upright, both drag angles ε_A and ε_H, increase at first slowly, then more rapidly, and so the boat performance deteriorates. One may rightly infer that in stronger winds, in which the highest speeds may be attained, stability becomes the supreme merit of any kind of boat. Experience with dinghies supports this inference, for it is known that at a given wind speed the boat can be sailed closer to the wind or faster the more upright she is kept. Moreover, it is also known that a keel boat performs to windward at its best if the heeling angle is not allowed to exceed some critical angle of 20–25 degrees.

The aerodynamic heeling moment arising from the action of the heeling force, F_H, which may be tolerated in stronger winds without penalty in windward performance, can only be resisted by an equal and opposite righting moment. This is usually largely provided either by heavy ballast at the bottom of the hull or, as in the case of a light dinghy, by shifting the crew to windward. The crew acts then as 'live ballast'.

Figure 113 shows some results of experiments carried out by the author on a rigid sail of aspect ratio AR = 4.6 and camber 1/25 of the chord. Comparing the two polar diagrams for heel angles $\theta = 0°$ and $30°$, we can see that the latter curve has moved to the right (to higher drag), incurring obvious disadvantages. The minimum drag angle, $\varepsilon_A\theta$, for the heeled yacht is greater than ε_A for the upright one. The reason for the difference between the two is twofold: firstly, when the sail is heeled, its effective incidence, α, becomes less for geometrical reasons, and

Fig 113 The effect of heel angle θ on the aerodynamic characteristics of a triangular sail. Up to about 20 degrees, the effect of heel on sail efficiency is negligible, but thereafter the deterioration in terms of the drag angle ε_A and maximum C_L becomes more and more pronounced.

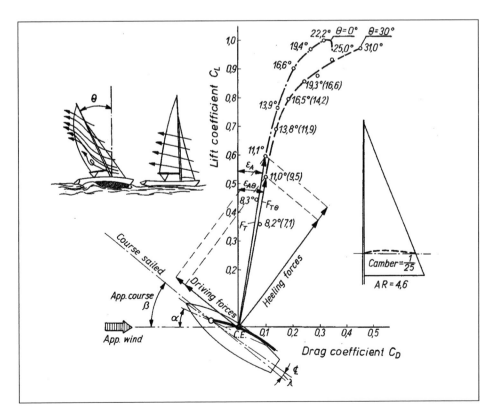

secondly, the sea surface influences the flow around the sail more when the boat is heeled. These effects can sometimes be seen when a boat is heeled to a very large angle, usually on the verge of capsizing, then the sail may get the wind on the lee side. The polar diagram for $\theta = 30°$ (Fig 113) gives in brackets the reduced angles of incidence due to heeling, and the accompanying sketch roughly indicates how the air flow over the sail may change for the worse as the boat heels.

Since the angle of sail incidence is gradually reduced when the boat heels, a sail which has been already working at a low incidence, as it should be in strong winds, may begin to flutter at the luff. Thus the automatic reduction of the incidence angle operates as a kind of safety valve, mitigating the effect of gusty wind. The flapping parts of a sail contribute little to the driving force but much to the drag, and so the crew who cannot keep their boat upright carry a penalty in terms of windward performance. Other ways to avoid excessive heel are to reduce the incidence angle, to flatten, ie , decrease the sail camber or reef the sail.

The angle of heel at which the sail incidence becomes zero (and hence no driving and heeling force can be produced) is a function of both the heading angle $(\beta - \lambda)$ and the angle of sail trim δ (Fig 107). This critical heel angle $\theta(\alpha = 0)$ can be estimated from the formula:

$$\cos \theta(\alpha = 0) = \frac{\tan \delta}{\tan (\beta - \lambda)} \qquad \text{Eq 18}$$

Anyone who has ever capsized a dinghy when sailing to windward might have noticed (before being plunged into the water!), that the sails are backwinded from leeward. As a result, the capsize is quite a gentle event. In fact, the boat capsize is not entirely due to the action of the aerodynamic heeling force, which only initiates the large heeling angle, but due to the action of negative righting moment once the boat reaches the point of vanishing stability (Ref 2.27).

The fact that the aerodynamic forces are approaching zero (and may even change from + to –) when the heel angle becomes sufficiently large, is reflected in the '*Gimcrack* sail coefficients' devised by K S M Davidson (Ref 2.28) (Fig 114). If the C_R and C_H lines are extended till they intersect the horizontal axis, this critical angle of heel $\theta(\alpha = 0)$ is found to be about 50 degrees.

It is also seen from Fig 114 that more recently derived '*Baybea* sail coefficients' are greater than those of the *Gimcrack* set (Ref 2.29). The authors of this MIT project explained the difference, assuming 'that the sail camber ratio is much bigger on modern boats than on the yachts designed in the thirties'. A straightforward and more convincing explanation is offered by paying more attention to the rig planforms of both boats shown in Fig 114. The *Gimcrack* had a $^3/_4$ non-overlapping rig and the reference sail area was the actual area; whereas, in the case of *Baybea*, the rig is a masthead genoa sloop with large overlap which was not measured as a reference area; only its rated IOR area was noted. This is the primary contributing factor to the difference between these two sets of sail coefficients. Besides, the *Gimcrack* sails were made of cotton, whereas sails used by modern boats are made of Terylene (Dacron); this also contributes to the higher efficiency of contemporary rigs.

We can see that the scatter of results marked by triangles (Fig 114), relevant to *Baybea* sail coefficients, is such that almost any line can be drawn to give the average values of the driving and heeling coefficients. Apparently, to facilitate

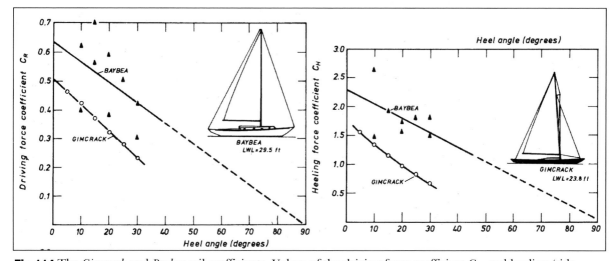

Fig 114 The *Gimcrack* and *Baybea* sail coefficients. Values of the driving force coefficient C_R and heeling (side force) coefficient C_H in horizontal plane (Fig 58) are unique and linear functions of heel angle only. Coefficients are relevant to a close-hauled course – for *Gimcrack* the ß angle was in the range 26–31 degrees; for *Baybea* the apparent course ß, given by the masthead indicator and uncorrected for the sail interference, was 27 degrees. Neither of these set coefficients can reliably be used to accurately predict the performance of boats driven by rigs different from those of either *Gimcrack* or *Baybea*, no matter how these coefficients are subsequently modified. Manipulating an increasing number of unrealistic or wrong data does not lead to right answers. As originally envisaged by Davidson, a standard set of sail coefficients can be of some help for towing tanks dealing with the simulated windward performance of various hull designs in order to establish their relative order of merits.

the plotting of C_R and C_H lines, it was arbitrarily assumed that when the heeling angle becomes 90 degrees, the aerodynamic forces become zero – which is at variance with Eq 18. Bearing in mind that the validity of the *Gimcrack* sail coefficients was questioned by many, including Davidson himself, one may perhaps be forgiven for feeling some doubt as to whether the *Baybea* set of coefficients will result in better, more realistic prediction of speed performances of contemporary boats driven by diverse types of rig, and·on heading angles other than close-hauled. This conclusion will be corroborated by the test data presented in later chapters.

The unwanted heeling force, which is the price we pay to obtain a driving force, is not a problem when sailing on a reach. Referring again to Fig 100, it is seen that the heeling force is considerably less than the driving force as the apparent course relative to wind (ß) is increased. The hull is then called upon to produce less side force to balance the sail heeling force. It therefore pays to trim the sail near to its maximum driving force (maximum lift), almost irrespective of the wind speed. However, in close-hauled sailing, the requirements are different depending on wind strength; the heeling force may become of primary importance. Progressive deterioration of sail performance when the boat heels is not the only problem to contend with. The hull resistance increases and the side force diminishes, and the hydrodynamic drag angle, ε_H, therefore becomes larger. It follows that the sailing angle ß does so too, ie the yacht does not point so high as when upright. In other words, for each boat there is a certain tolerable heeling force, F_H, and resulting heel angle, $\theta = 20$–25 degrees, which should not be exceeded.

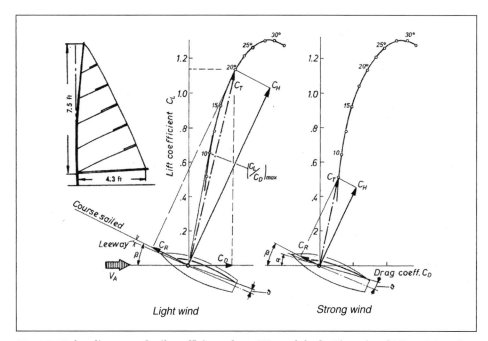

Fig 115 Polar diagram of sail coefficients for a 2/5 model of a Finn rig of AR = 3.1 and sail area S_A = 18.1 sq ft (1.68 m²) obtained through wind tunnel testing. This particular polar diagram is relevant to the sail shape (camber and twist) recorded in Fig 116 and marked VI. For other distribution of camber and twist (controlled by the kicking strap tension), the polar diagram will be different. Two sketches labelled 'Light wind' and 'Strong wind' indicate sail coefficients employed in different wind conditions when sailing close-hauled.

Tests were carried out with the sail model unheeled, without hull, and the wind speed applied was 29.3 ft/sec (17.3 knots).

One of the ways to prevent excessive heeling is to adjust the incidence angle of the sail in such a way that the tolerable heeling force coefficient, C_H, is gradually decreased according to wind strength. To illustrate the problem and make the presentation simple, let's analyse the case of a Finn dinghy driven to windward by a single sail of area S_A = 107.6 sq ft. The tolerable heeling force F_H and its coefficient C_H will depend, apart from the wind strength, on the helmsman's weight (wet sweatshirts inclusive) and his ability to operate outside the gunwale as 'live ballast'. To a reasonable degree of accuracy, the tolerable heeling force for a 180 lb (82 kg) helmsman will be about 76 lbs. If the wind strength, V_A = 13.5 knots (22.8 ft/sec, V_T = about 9.6 knots – gentle breeze), the maximum heeling force coefficient, C_H, approximately equal to C_L, can be calculated indirectly from Eq 10:

$$C_H = C_L = \frac{F_H}{0.00119 \times V_A{}^2 \times S_A} = \frac{76}{0.00119 \times 22.8^2 \times 107.6} = 1.14$$

This coefficient can be obtained when the sail incidence α = 20 degrees, as shown in the sketch labelled 'light wind' in Fig 115.

If the wind blows harder, say, V_A = 20.5 knots (34.6 ft/sec V_T = about 15 knots – moderate breeze) the helmsman has to ease sheets in order to reduce the heeling force, so the boat can be sailed upright or nearly upright. The C_H should now be:

$$C_H = \frac{F_H}{0.00119 \times V_A{}^2 \times S_A} = \frac{76}{0.00119 \times 34.6^2 \times 107.6} = 0.5$$

which can be obtained by reducing the sail incidence angle α to about 7.5 degrees. The sail is then operating on the verge of flutter. This situation is shown in the sketch labelled 'strong wind' in Fig 115.

The polar diagram in Fig 115, derived from the wind tunnel testing on a 2/5 scale Finn sail, is relevant to one particular sail setting, marked VI and shown in Fig 116, where the geometrical characteristics such as camber and its distribution, together with sail twist (recorded photographically), are given for one kicking– strap position only (Refs 2.4, 2.16).

Fig 116 Planform of nominally one-design Finn sail with different distributions of camber and twist depending largely on the kicking strap tension. These different sail shapes, marked VI and VII will produce different polar diagrams and so different speed performances (Refs 2.4, 2.16). The geometrical features of the sail were recorded photographically by the author.

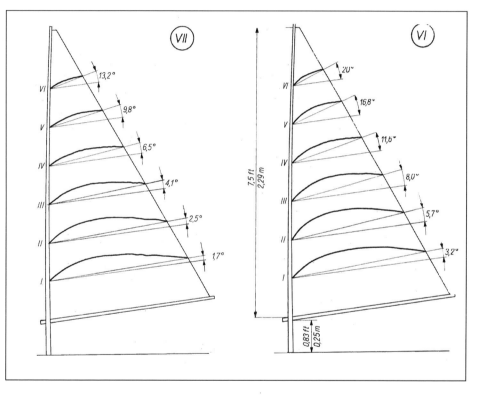

Let us now tentatively assume that all those characteristics do not change within the range of wind speeds considered in the above calculations. In Fig 117, the curves marked VI give the values of incidence angle, α, and sail trim angle, δ, which are the optimum ones for given true wind speed, V_T, to achieve the best speed made good, V_{mg}, in sailing to windward.

Thus in lighter winds the sail must be set at a high incidence angle α, ie trimmed close to the centreline, to obtain maximum driving coefficient C_R (Fig 115). With increasing V_T, the maintenance of tolerable heeling force requires that the sail is trimmed at larger angle, δ, ie, at a lower angle of incidence, α.

Another set of curves, marked VII in Fig 117, are applicable to the same sail, but here the kicking-strap tension has been increased, which results in modification of the sail camber and twist, as depicted in Fig 116 (sail marked VII). It is

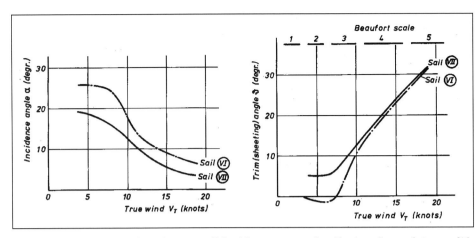

Fig 117 Optimum incidence (left) and trim angles (right) for the same Finn sail of planform shown in Fig 115, but different distribution of camber and twist as depicted in Fig 116. To obtain best V_{mg} when sailing to windward, the sail incidence and trim angle must be selected according to the wind speed, available stability, sail shape, etc. There is no general prescription giving the correct trim angles, sail type regardless, even when using one particular sail planform (Refs 2.4, 2.16).

seen that the required optimum sail incidence, α, and sail trim, δ, angles are different now.

And, as might be expected, the optimum speed performance of two identical hulls driven by nominally a 'One-Design' sail will be different, depending entirely on the applied kicking-strap tension.

Since the amount of sail that can be carried without suffering a large heel is strictly determined by the hull stability, this hull property can rightly be called *the power to carry sail effectively*. Taking stability into account, the performance equation may crudely be written as follows:

Performance to windward = hull efficiency (ε_H) + sail efficiency (ε_A)+ stability.

To summarize our discussion we can say that, with the aid of some specific sail and hull characteristics, we have established certain broad principles that will help us obtain the best performance from a yacht. Although for other hulls and sails of different aspect ratio and camber, the relevant coefficients and drag angles will be different, the principles will remain unaltered.

The chief point to emerge is that the well-known rule for trimming the sail, *to free it until the luff is just about to flutter*, is inadequate. Instead, a range of optimum sail incidence is found, which depends on the wind strength, the available stability, and the point of sailing. Two limits to this range were found:

1 The sail incidence at which the ratio of heeling force, F_H, to driving force, F_R or C_H/C_R, is possibly minimum, being applicable when sailing close-hauled in strong winds with a restriction imposed by the F_H maximum. This incidence corresponds roughly with the incidence given by the 'near-fluttering-luff' rule

2 The sail incidence at which the maximum driving force, F_R, or equivalent, CR_{max}, is obtained, being applicable when sailing close–hauled in light winds, without an F_H restriction, and when reaching in any wind strength

Bearing in mind the previous discussion on sail twist, it is worth noting that, in the present context, the sails should be trimmed close to the centreline when sailing close-hauled in light airs, but as the wind strength increases, the trim angle, δ, should gradually be increased to a point on the lee side of the hull.

So far, we have established two fundamental criteria: the minimum ratio of C_H/C_R and the maximum value of C_R, by which the merits of sails can be assessed.

9 • THE IMPORTANCE OF SAIL CAMBER

'Indeed, it is not our task to carry out construction of concepts... which are as complicated as can be, but rather to discover simple but powerful intuitions.'

Andreas Spiser, Swiss mathematician

The magnitude and direction of action of the aerodynamic forces depend to a large extent on the sail camber – its magnitude and fore-and-aft distribution. Class rules, in some form or another, place restrictions on the choice of sail area, planform, and how it is disposed. There are no such limitations on the amount of camber in a sail, and crews are therefore able to set sails of different camber according to their needs.

Views on the importance and necessary degree of camber have varied considerably throughout the history of yachting. Up to the middle of the last century, sails with large camber were universally used. This was to some extent a consequence of their being made of flax. In those days yachts could not sail closer to the wind than 55 to 60 degrees. The traditional conviction that a 'bellying sail' was best underwent a radical change after the racing victories of the schooner *America* (Fig 4). This yacht, which in comparison with her rivals had very flat sails made of well-woven cotton, demonstrated a marked superiority when going to windward, being able to sail about 6° closer to the wind than her opponents, driven by more porous sails made of flax. Designers imitating *America* soon confirmed that her victories could be attributed to her sails, and so the full sail went out of fashion.

With the progress made in aerodynamics, and through racing experience, the position has again reversed, and sails of considerable camber are again in favour. The old controversy has been revived: is camber a good or bad thing? The fact is that both flat and cambered sails have their advantages and disadvantages, and the choice of a suitable sail must be made with regard to the prevailing racing conditions, the course, and the wind strength. There is no such thing as a universal sail. What may be an excellent sail under certain conditions may, as a result of incorrect camber, be hopelessly bad in some other conditions.

SELECTING THE OPTIMUM CAMBER

In Fig 118 are plotted polar diagrams for three rigid, untwisted rectangular aerofoils, having cambers of 1/7, 1/10, and 1/20 respectively, with a common aspect ratio AR = 5. Although the results represent the properties of aerofoils without masts, they illustrate the influence of camber for most sails, though the effect would be modified if a mast were fitted or a sail were twisted. There are profound differences among these polar diagrams. Take for instance the maximum value of the total aerodynamic force coefficient, C_T. For an aerofoil with 1/7 camber, C_T is about 1.7, for one with 1/10 camber it is 1.55, while for the one with 1/20 camber it is only 1.1.

Let us arrange these three diagrams in the manner of Fig 119 to assess the relative merits of sails for the apparent courses ß = 30 and ß = 90 degrees. On

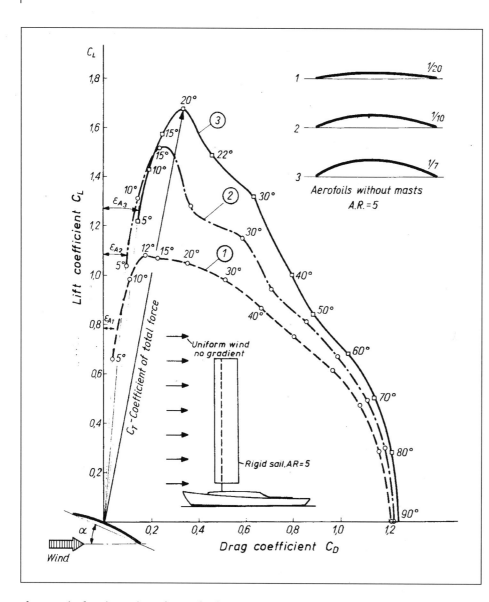

Fig 118 This set of sail coefficients (applicable to a rigid rectangular sail of AR = 5, operating in a uniform wind), should be regarded as for reference only. Coefficients of sails of different planforms, twisted and operating in a non-uniform wind (with vertical gradient) will be different and, as a rule, worse than those presented here; however, the basic trend reflected in the shape of these curves will be similar.

the vertical axis, going through the centre of effort of the sail, a scale for the heeling force, F_H, is marked, for a sail area $S_A = 100$ sq ft and wind strengths of $V_A = 10$ knots (gentle breeze) and $V_A = 20$ knots (fresh breeze). On the horizontal axis is marked a relevant scale for the driving force, F_R. Coefficients C_H and C_R are also indicated. Consider first the case ß = 90°, ie the apparent wind abeam. If three boats are similar in all respects except for the camber of their sails, it is easy to predict that the yacht with sail 3, of 1/7 camber, will be the fastest. Comparing the values of the maximum driving force for $V_A = 10$ knots, we have:

> for sail 3 – 57 lb
> for sail 2 – 52 lb
> for sail 1 – 37 lb

Such a large difference between sail 1 and the others (Sails 3 and 2 have a 57 per cent and a 40 per cent greater driving force respectively) is unlikely to be

Fig 119 The relative merits of three different sail cambers 1/20, 1/10 and 1/7 in windward work and reaching. The driving and heeling forces indicated along the vertical and horizontal axes are calculated for apparent wind speeds 10 and 20 knots. The polar diagrams plotted close to the horizontal axis are applicable to wind abeam attitude ß = 90 degrees, whereas the polar diagrams orientated close to the vertical axis are relevant to the windward course ß = 30 degrees.

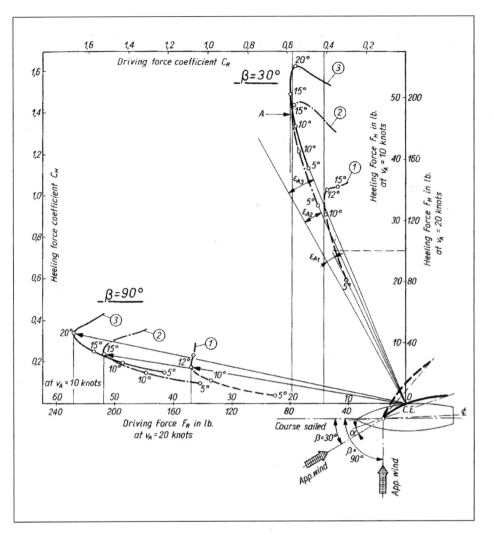

compensated by any amount of sailing skill or tactics. We are assuming here that all three helmsmen are able to trim their sails to the appropriate angles of incidence for maximum driving force. It should be noted that these angles are different for each sail, being 20, 15 and 12 degrees for sails of camber 1/7, 1/10, and 1/20 respectively.

It is evident from this example that, when sailing off the wind, a sail with a large camber is desirable, particularly when sailing a light displacement craft in gentle winds, when the boat speed, V_S, increases almost proportionately to the driving force. In strong winds, when rapidly increasing hull resistance sets a limit on a boat's speed (rather a sharp barrier for heavy displacement vessels), the advantage to be gained by increasing driving force will be less conspicuous.

Compare now the merits of these sails when beating to windward at ß = 30°. In light winds, when considerations of stability (F_{Hmax}) and hull hydrodynamic efficiency (ε_H) do not impose limitations on the driving force from the sails, our criterion for comparison is the maximum driving force coefficient, C_{Rmax}. For the virtually flat sail, with 1/20 camber, the value of C_{Rmax} is approximately 0.4 and the corresponding driving force is 13 lb for a wind speed $V_A = 10$ knots. For the sails of 1/10 and 1/7 camber, their maximum C_R coefficients are just under 0.6, giving driving forces of 20 lb. In this case also, sail 1 is inferior to 2 and 3 but the differences between 2 and 3 are negligible. For incidences below the intersection of these last two polar diagrams (point A) sail 2 offers a slight advantage, since at the same driving force as 3, it has a little less heeling force. This is another way of saying that the angle of drag, ε_{A2}, for sail 2 is less than ε_{A3} for sail 3.

A somewhat different pattern emerges if the wind strength increases to 20 knots, ie, the aerodynamic forces increase fourfold over those at 10 knots. As was mentioned earlier, a good criterion for comparison in this case is the minimum ratio C_H/C_R, ie, the minimum drag angle, ε_A. On this basis, from Figs 118 and 119, it appears that sail 1 will now be better than 2 and 3, since it has the least minimum ε_A. If, for example, one assumes that a heeling force $F_H = 100$ lb is the maximum that can be tolerated without causing excessive heel, and that an incidence angle of 5° is the minimum at which all three sails are set, then sail 1 will develop a heeling force of 80 lb at this incidence. Sail 2, on the other hand, will develop a heeling force of about 130 lb, and although it will also produce a larger driving force than sail 1, it will not be able to take advantage of it, because of the excessive drift and heel.

The desirable amount of camber on a sail for windward courses will therefore depend on the strength of the wind. Beginning in light winds, when a camber of 1/10 is needed, this should be successively reduced with increasing wind strength to a practical minimum of about 1/25 to 1/30. A sail camber should be adjusted so as not to heel the boat more than 20–25 degrees, so that she can be sailed as nearly upright as possible without 'spilling wind' from the sail.

Figure 120 shows how the driving force coefficient, C_R, (vertical axis), varies, depending on the point of sailing and sail camber (indicated on the horizontal axis). Thus, when sailing close-hauled in light winds, the required maximum camber is 1/10, whilst when sailing right off the wind a camber of 1/8 and even more is required, since the curves VI and VIII are still rising at this point.

Fig 120 Sail cambers needed for different headings relative to the apparent wind, and associated approximate driving force coefficients C_R.

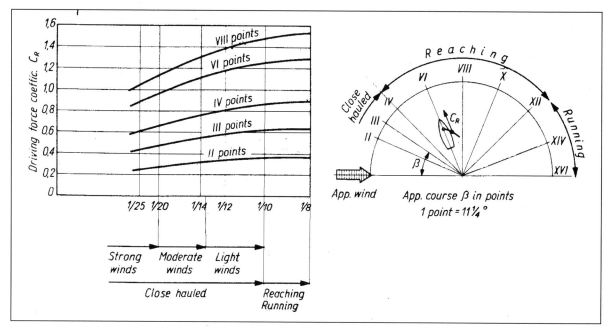

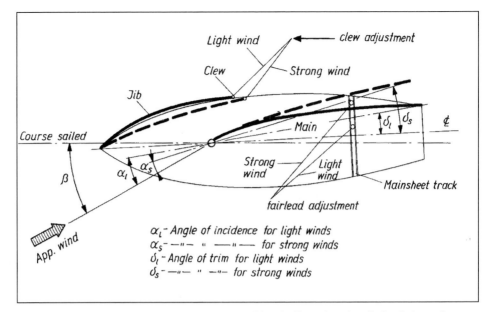

Fig 121 Basic principles for the adjustment of headsails and mainsails for light and strong winds. The greater the wind speed, the larger the trim angle, δ, of the mainsail. In light winds the trim angle, measured between the boom and the centreline of the hull, may approach zero degrees or even become negative, depending on the sail camber, twist, hydrodynamic characteristics of the hull, wind gradient, etc. Alterations in the incidence angle of the mainsail are accomplished through mainsheet and traveller controls, whereas fine adjustments of camber for variable winds are carried out through the kicking-strap tension, mast flexibility and Cunningham hole.

The sail camber can to some extent be adjusted by the crew, and Fig 121 shows how this can be done. In light winds, when the sail is working at a large angle of incidence, the jib fairlead and mainsheet block should be shifted well inboard. With increasing wind speed, the genoa incidence is reduced by paying out the sheets; then, to avoid excessive twist and to flatten the sails, the leads should be further outboard, and if possible, further aft. The advantages of a wide mainsheet horse for the mainsail are particularly apparent when sailing on a close reach in strong wind. Without it, the necessary easing of the sheets allows the boom to lift, and the sail to belly, resulting in an inefficient sail setting (Fig 122a). The ideal solution to this problem would be to have the facility whereby a continuous and automatic adjustment of the sail camber to varying wind and course conditions is feasible. This is partly possible in such classes as Star, Finn, Flying Dutchman and on sailboards, with the use of a flexible mast and sometimes boom (Fig 122b). The bending of these flexible spars, together with other tuning devices, serves to adjust the sail camber and its fore-and-aft distribution.

Although it is possible to reef heavily cambered sails, or to allow partial flutter when the wind is too strong, these practices are disadvantageous compared to setting a sail with the correct camber. Predicting the weather conditions likely to prevail throughout a race, and then determining the selection of the set of sails with the correct camber, sailcloth weight and area, should mean that reefing is not necessary, though forecasting conditions may not always be easy.

Fig 122a (left) An inefficient sail setting in a strong wind. The upper part of the sail is allowed to flutter, presumably in an attempt to reduce the heeling force caused by too large a camber. Apparently, the crew was overwhelmed by a strong and shifting wind.

Fig 122b (right) A variety of control gadgets can be applied to tune sails to the wind strength and course sailed. The flattening of the mainsail by a judicious bending of the mast is one of the ways to effectively cope with strong, gusty winds.

The Star class pioneered adjustable mast bent whilst sailing. Still others, such as the Finn, employ cantilevered, rotating, flexible masts which automatically bend in accordance with the wind strength and the corresponding pull of the kicking strap.

Carrying full rather than reefed sails confers advantages in addition to those obtained on the windward leg. A reefed boat will have to shake out the reefs when coming off the wind, when lateral stability is not so important a factor, and later may have to reef again, wasting precious time.

If the wind strength is such that even the use of the flattest possible sails will not prevent excessive heel, then the sail must be reefed to such an area that the yacht can be sailed without spilling wind from the sails. This will also guard against the unconscious but wrong tendency to luff too much in gusts, ie, pinching the boat, which ultimately results in a deterioration of her performance. This effect is illustrated in Fig 123. The helmsman of pinching boat (b), carrying too much canvas or sails with excessive camber for the given wind speed, may enjoy a false impression, observing his bearing, that he will easily clear the mark, albeit rather slowly. In reality, boat (a), sailing faster, with less canvas or preferably flatter sails, will sail closer to the wind and should safely reach the mark before boat (b).

The advantages of carrying full sail are well borne out in practice. In modern small racing dinghies it does not pay to reef, except in a gale. Generally speaking, a reefed boat will not win, unless all those who carry full sail fail to complete the course. The majority of racing helmsmen have now realized this fact, and consequently race with whole sail, adjusting its camber and twist according to the changes in wind strength. If the wind is strong, the performance of the sail depends on the drag angle, ε_A, ie, mainly on the sail camber and nothing

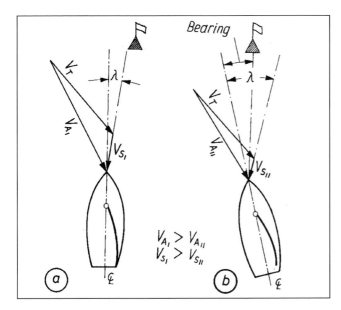

Fig 123 Pinching boat (b) could easily miss the mark, despite the helmsman's belief that he is watching the bearing angle carefully.

else. In other words, when the lift which can be used is limited by available stability to resist heeling, the driving force that can be delivered by the sail depends almost entirely on the drag angle, ε_A.

Finn and Star classes and sailboards, are good examples of how much the sail performance can be manipulated by adjusting its camber by means of the fore-and-aft bend of the mast, and other control devices such as Cunningham holes, the kicking strap, the clew outhaul, etc. By flattening the full sail area, the helmsman can advantageously reduce both the drag angle ε_A, and the heeling moment, whereas by reefing, the drag angle tends to increase, due to the distortion of the initially good shape of the sail.

And one more point: the sail which at times will be set on a straight as well as a curved mast, must be cut, and afterward trimmed, with a specific purpose in mind. In practice, one finds that sails, while setting well on one particular point of sailing, may on another course exhibit an uneven camber distribution at various heights up the mast.

THE EFFECT OF THE POSITION OF MAXIMUM CAMBER

A commonly shared view by sailors is that the position of the maximum camber should be about 1/3 of the local sail chord aft of the mast. This position is supposed to be the most favourable aerodynamically. It originated from analogizing sails and birds' wings, and noting the usual position of maximum thickness of aeroplane wings. Nevertheless, experiments on sails have shown that this traditional view cannot be accepted without reservation.

Figure 124 presents the results of measurements made on three rectangular plates of AR = 6, with the same camber of 1/13.5 but with three different maximum positions. These tests made by Eiffel (Ref 2.30) many years ago are indicative of a trend which should not be ignored when considering sail performance. Model I has the maximum camber position at 1/3 of the chord length from the leading edge, sail II in the middle and sail III at 2/3 of the chord. The differences between their resultant total aerodynamic force coefficients C_T at similar incidences are rather small and do not exceed 4 per cent, yet the models considered as sails are not alike, and their merits will depend on the course sailed relative to the wind.

On windward courses sail II with its maximum camber in the middle and flat after is the best, since it has an aerodynamic drag angle, ε_A, about 2 degrees less than its rivals. When reaching, sail III shows some superiority of driving force F_R. Sail I is everywhere inferior to both sail II and III. It is most important to emphasize that these remarks are only applicable to a single sail without a mast. If two or more sails are working together, other considerations apply (see Chapter 14 on sail interaction).

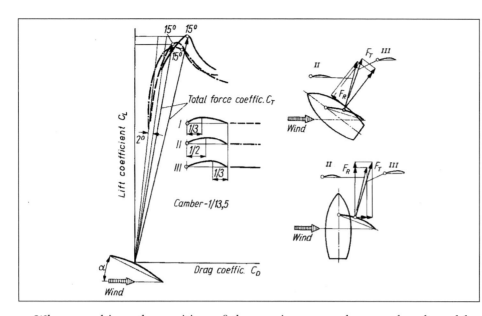

When reaching, the position of the maximum camber can be altered by means of the leech-line; increasing tension moves the camber aft. From the performance point of view, the amount rather than the position of the maximum camber appears to be more important. Changes in the former affect the aerodynamic forces by amounts which are large as compared with those obtained from the latter. Nevertheless, even a small gain should not be neglected if one is attempting to tune the rig for greatest efficiency.

The magnitude of the sail force can also be influenced by the use of a flexible boom. if a sail is fitted on a straight, stiff boom, its camber must necessarily fall to zero at the boom, which may result in a loss of efficiency of the sail as a whole. Experiments conducted in the Junkers Aerodynamic Institute showed that a sail with an elastic boom which took up the curvature of the sail, gave about 8 per cent more driving force than when fitted on a rigid boom. This gain was greatest for reaching courses and least when close-hauled or running.

Ideally, the elasticity of the boom should be such that for all wind strengths its curvature is the same as that of the sail, but this cannot easily be achieved. The amount of bending of the boom will depend on the attachment point of the mainsheet. If this point is at the aft end of the boom, the curvature will be a maximum and may follow that of the sail. if, however, the attachment point is further forward, the bending will be less and may even be reflex. The latter might be used in strong winds when a relatively flat sail is required.

One method of obtaining the advantages of both a rigid and flexible boom was used on *Enterprise* (Fig 72). Here the foot of the sail was attached to the wide, flat boom by means of slides running athwartships. This allowed the desired sail shape at the foot to be set regardless of the course or conditions, but at the cost of some complication.

Another solution to the problem is to employ a loose footed sail or one only attached to the boom at its tack and clew. By suitable adjustment of the line of the sheets in the first instance, and of the clew outhaul in the second, the sail camber can to some extent be controlled (see for example the rigs in Fig 76 and Fig 88).

Let us consult Fig 124 again. The test results suggest that the location of the maximum camber (draft) for close-hauled work should be somewhere in the middle of the sail chord. However, one argument may be used against this advice, namely: sail camber has a natural tendency to move aft with increasing wind, ie, with an increasing pressure difference developing over the windward and leeward sides of the sail. And it must be brought forward again mechanically, by means of a luff–tensioning device such as the Cunningham hole.

A sketch marked I above the planform of a Finn sail in Fig 125a illustrates the sail section along X–X line with its camber dragged aft by the wind pressure – a harmful tendency, particularly if the sail is cut from insufficiently stable cloth. To combat this tendency, and to be on the safe side, it is better to design the sail in such a way that the location of the maximum camber is approximately 40 per cent aft from the leading edge. Now, if a strong wind tends to distort the sail and shift the maximum camber towards the leech, the Cunningham hole can be employed to bring the draft closer to the luff again, as shown in sketch II. Figure 125b illustrates this concept. Through a Cunningham hole (A) a line is rove, which may or may not be attached to some sort of purchase, and provides a means of increasing the tension on the luff rope. Tightening the Cunningham hole has the effect of preventing, or at least minimizing, the tendency of the maximum camber to travel towards the leech, while at the same time flattening the upper part of the sail. This is what is wanted for windward work in windy conditions. It is also simple to ease off the tension when camber is required aft when reaching.

Sometimes a second cringle (B in Fig 125b) is fitted to the foot of the sail and this reduces the sail fullness near the boom. It appears that this additional complication is hardly worth the bother unless the sail is extremely baggy in the foot. Such a shape does not seem to add much to sail efficiency and needs at best expert recutting, but it was fashionable for a while.

Figure 125c demonstrates an arrangement for a sliding-luff jib (or genoa). As in the case of the mainsail, increased tension on the tack cringle brings the maximum camber closer to the luff.

Fig 125a, b
Arrangement for adjustment of the Cunningham hole for Finn class or other dinghies. Pulling down on the Cunningham hole transfers the maximum camber back toward the mast as the wind gets up to force 4 or 5.

Fig 125c The Cunningham hole can also be used for tuning headsails by shifting the maximum camber towards the luff where it is wanted for windward work in windy conditions. The advantage offered by a controllable position and amount of camber can only be obtained by using sufficiently soft cloth. Sails made of a hard-finish cloth, sometimes known as 'tinplate', may hardly be stretched enough to get any advantage from an additional load put through the Cunningham device.

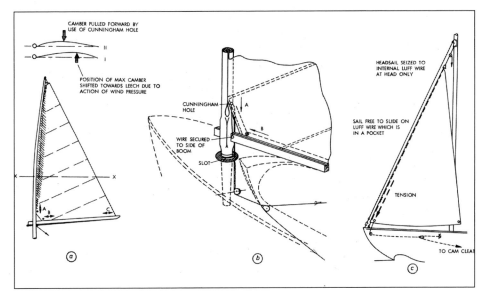

10 · THE IMPORTANCE OF SAIL PLANFORM

'Many concepts in current use are really personal views of the matter, put forward by some individual scientist or some school of scientists or engineers and then more generally adopted (and quite often mistakenly treated by some as though they were "laws of Nature" which permit exact solution to be obtained...)'

D Küchenmann, The Aerodynamic Design of Aircraft (1978)

The early days of yachting were characterized by yachts carrying enormous sail area (Figs 4 and 126). It was commonly assumed that *the speed of a yacht was directly proportional to the size of the sails* (Ref 2.31). For reasons of stability, the sail area had to be distributed close to the waterline, and consequently the length of the hull was exploited to the full, and even extended by means of a bowsprit. The many different types of sails used were, as a rule, of small aspect ratio.

With the growth of knowledge of aerodynamics, greater attention was paid to the planform and the mutual interaction between sails (eg, results of wind tunnel tests published in 1910 by Eiffel (Ref 2.30)). Since man naturally seems to delight in competition, it became desirable to increase the driving force available from a given sail area and, at the same time, to make yachts sail closer to the wind. These improvements were effected by increasing the aspect ratio of sails, reducing the harmful effects of the mast and rigging, perfecting the sails interaction, and introducing new types of sails for specific purposes (for example, the spinnaker).

Experiments carried out on both model sails and aerofoils have shown that the planform of a sail and its AR have a large effect on its aerodynamic force

Fig 126 A nostalgic picture of the 154-ton schooner *Suzanne*, sailing in the Solent, and representative of the 'brute' type of yacht which dominated in the 19th century. Big yachts are inherently stable, ie, they have more stability than the scaled-down replicas, and a 'cloud of sails' was essential to show these at their best (Ref 2.4).

Fig 127 The qualitative effect of aspect ratio on the aerodynamic properties of sails. The polar curves drawn are based on Eiffel's measurements on rigid plates of camber ratio 1/13.5 (Ref 2.30).

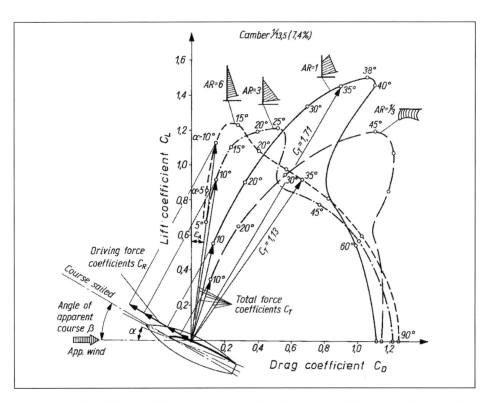

characteristics. Figure 127 shows the polar diagrams of force coefficients for four aerofoils having the same camber 1/13.5 (7.4 per cent) of the chord but different planforms and aspect ratios AR = 6, 3, 1, and 1/3. Results are qualitatively applicable to sails.

From a comparison of curves we can see that for small angles of incidence, up to 10°, relevant to close-hauled work, the sails can be placed in order of merit corresponding to their aspect ratios, AR = 6 being the best. This planform, the characteristic Bermudian sail, can develop larger driving forces at smaller drag angles ε_A. This is a consequence of it having a low induced drag (see Chapter 6).

Consider now the sails' merits in a different way. The angles of incidence at which they achieve maximum total aerodynamic force, are α = 15°, 25°, 38°, 45°, for AR = 6, 3, 1, 1/3 respectively, ie, the lower aspect ratios require the largest angles to develop maximum force. It should be noted that the lower aspect ratios also develop the largest total forces, C_T, AR = 1 being outstanding; thus the values of C_T = 1.13, 1.71 for AR = 6 and AR = 1 respectively.

TESTS ON SINGLE SAILS

Similar results were found in tests on rigid sail models at Southampton University. Some of these results for three models A, B, C are shown in Fig 128. All models had untapered masts of the same diameter and sails of 1/25 (4 per cent) camber. In each case the position of maximum camber was at 15 per cent of the local chord behind the mast.

At first sight these results are not entirely consistent with those of Fig 127. As expected, the angles for maximum force increase with decreasing aspect ratio.

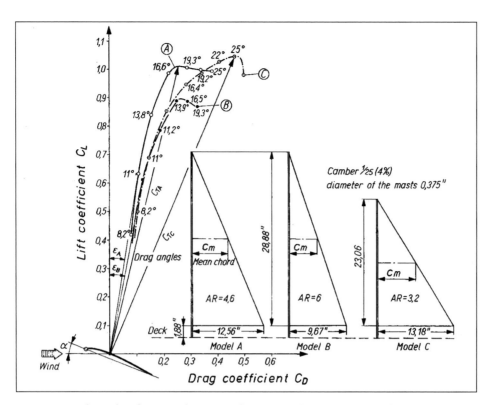

However, when the drag angles at moderate incidence are considered, model B does not occupy the position of merit we expect it to by virtue of having the largest aspect ratio. In fact, when sailing to windward, model B would be less efficient than A. This can be attributed to the effect of the mast, which adversely affects the flow round the sail. In each case the mast diameter is the same. Thus the ratio of this diameter to the average or mean chord, C_m, will be larger for model B, which is of higher aspect ratio than model A, and its adverse effect will be correspondingly greater.

An example of how the mast diameter can upset theoretical expectation of an efficient sail plan can be found in the 6 Metre *Atrocia* (Fig 129) on which Sherman Hoyt tried, without success, an unusual distribution of sail area between main and foresail. The area of the mainsail was reduced, its aspect ratio increased, and a large foresail used. Although the main reason why this set-up was inefficient is to do with the problem of interaction between sails (which will be discussed later), undoubtedly, too, a large proportion of the relatively small mainsail was inoperative, working as it was behind a mast of relatively large a diameter.

Fig 129 The 6 Metre class yacht *Atrocia* with an unsuccessful distribution of sail area between the mainsail and headsail.

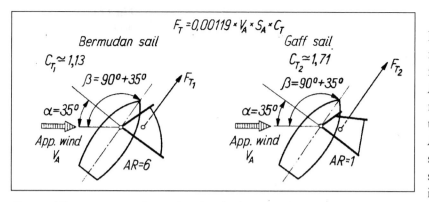

Fig 130 The potential driving force coefficients developed by a Bermudan and gaff sail in reaching conditions.

Referring again to Fig 127, let us examine the relative magnitudes of total aerodynamic force coefficient for different AR; the coefficient C_T for the model of AR = 1 is greater than those for sails of higher AR, ie, AR = 6 and 3. Consequently, the superiority of sails with high AR when sailing close to the wind will not be maintained when off the wind. Comparing a Bermudan sail of AR = 6 and a gaff sail of AR = 1, consider their aerodynamic forces on a broad reach, sailing at ß = 125° to the apparent wind (Fig 130). If both sails are working at an angle of incidence α = 35° and have the same area, the driving forces should be proportional to the coefficients, C_{T1}, C_{T2}, ie, 1.13 and 1.71 respectively (from Fig 127). In other words, the gaff sail will develop about 50 per cent more driving force than the Bermudan sail, and hence on a broad reach the boat driven by the gaff sail will be faster.

There is no ideal type of sail that is superior on all points of sailing. The curves of Fig 131 show how the driving force varies for sails of different AR on all points of sailing. Sails of high AR are superior from close-hauled to close-reaching courses when the apparent course angle, ß, is less than about 70°.

Fig 131 The potential driving force coefficients developed by single sails of aspect ratios 9, 6, 3, 1 and 1/3, on courses ranging from close-hauled to running.

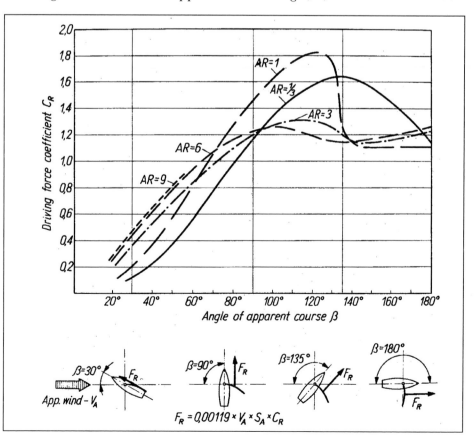

When further off the wind than this, lower AR sails deliver more driving force, in particular those with AR $\simeq$ 1. On full courses, from a broad reach to a run, the square rig appears to be superior. This explains why the square-rigged clippers were unchallenged on a broad reach, but yielded to gaff schooners when close-reaching.

To assess the advantages of one rig over another, it is therefore necessary to consider the sailing course. On races over a triangular course, were windward ability is of prime importance, the Bermudan rig is pre-eminent. In passage and offshore races, on the other hand, where beating may not prevail, the lower aspect ratio gaff-rigged yacht may well prove superior.

TESTS ON SLOOPS; BERMUDAN RIGS

Similar qualitative trends have been observed in the case of sloop-rigged models of 3 different AR shown in Fig 132 and tested in the wind tunnel (Ref 2.32). Again, no one rig was superior over the whole range of heading angles ($\beta - \lambda$) from 15 to 30 degrees, but there were appreciable differences in their performances. The tests were run over ranges of mainsail and genoa trim angles, and heading angles to cover close-hauled conditions.

For a quantitative assessment of sail efficiency, there can only be one approach; namely, a complete calculation of a yacht's performance using known hull data. This however, is not always convenient, since one may wish to consider sail performance, in approximative but nevertheless plausible terms, without reference to a particular hull. The question arises as to what criterion should be adopted when comparing different rigs?

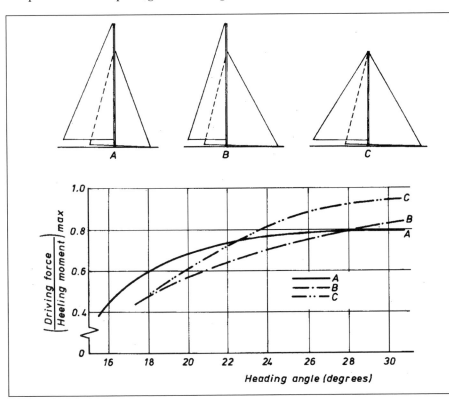

Fig 132 The relative merits of three sloop Bermudan rigs with different distributions of sail area between the main and genoa, all sailing close-hauled. Tests were done on rigid, unheeled models at a wind speed of 50 ft/sec (29.6 knots) which corresponds to a Re number based on a mean chord of 3.2×10^5.

For this particular test it was considered not unreasonable to use the maximum ratio of driving force coefficient to heeling moment (driving force/heeling moment)$_{max}$ as a criterion. The underlying assumption was that if at the same heading angle ($ß - \lambda$) a rig develops a larger driving force and an equal or preferably smaller heeling moment than another rig, then it can be considered superior.

Results plotted in Fig 132 were obtained in such a way that at a given heading angle, both sails were trimmed for maximum driving force, and for this value the driving force/heeling moment ratio was calculated. Thus, up to ($ß - \lambda$) = 22^1/$_2$ degrees the sail plan A is clearly better than B or C, and eminently suitable for close-hauled work in racing 'round the buoys'. But, beyond 22^1/$_2$ degrees heading angle, the sailplans B and C gradually improve their performance until they are superior to A at ($ß - \lambda$) = 27^1/$_2$ degrees.

An attempt was also made to assess the relative merits of sailplan A, using three different positions of maximum camber on the mainsail but the same genoa. The tests revealed that the maximum camber should be forward of the trailing edge of the foresail for maximum advantage to be obtained from the sloop rig.

In the absence of more comprehensive test data, one might guess that the main effect of the foresail on the mainsail is to delay separation of the flow from the leeward side of the main. This assumption is corroborated by the results of other tests that will be discussed later in the book (Ref 2.33). With no foresail, this delay in separation is most likely to occur at, or aft of, the position of maximum camber. If the trailing edge (leech) of the foresail is forward of this position, it is doubtful whether it will have a big effect in delaying separation. If, on the other hand, it extends beyond the maximum camber position of the mainsail, it could substantially delay separation.

As we shall see later, this plausible and logical explanation is not entirely correct. Logical inferences are necessary in developing reliable and creative hypothesis and theories, but not sufficient in themselves. There are no unquestionably true results and no infallible, logically derived statements.

11 • THE SAIL POWER OF VARIOUS RIGS

'It is always a silly thing to give advice, but to give good advice is absolutely fatal.'
Oscar Wilde

While much is known about high performance sailing rigs for racing – mainly the Bermudan rig – little or no systematic research has been carried out into other traditional sail configurations. So it is difficult, if not impossible, when selecting a sail plan for a boat, to determine with certainty whether one proposed rig is more efficient for a given sail area than another (either anticipated or already existing). Anyway, there is considerable difference of opinion as to the merits of the Bermuda type of rig to begin with.

Most people believe that this rig, which dominates the contemporary sailing scene both for racing and cruising, must be the best rig available; to quote: *'Everyone knows the Bermuda rig is more efficient than the gaff, sprit, or whatever. It can be scientifically proven: comparative curves of lift vs drag etc would put the triangular sail with its longer leading edge way ahead.'* (Ref 2.34). After all, yachts competing for the America's Cup – the epitome of achievement in the field of high performance boats – are driven by this type of rig.

To gain recognition, any competing sail configuration should at least match the Bermudan sail power and, preferably, surpass it on some points of sailing. However, the current rating and measurement rules have practically precluded development of any other sail configuration. Even when unorthodox sails are not explicitly prohibited, the wording of the measurement system is such that experiments with unusual rigs are effectively discouraged. So it is that people regretfully abandon any hope of developing other types of rig under current rules.

One may rightly ask the question: what is the basis for the assumed superiority of the Bermudan rig; can it be scientifically proven that this triangular sail is indeed more efficient than 'whatever'?

Recently, the author carried out wind tunnel tests on the potential power of a number of rigs: Bermudan, lateen, sprit, gunter, dipping lug and crab claw – some with modifications, as shown in Fig 133, and used to drive small fishing vessels (Ref 2.35). Hopefully, this research, based on analysis of wind tunnel results, will enable the advantages and disadvantages of various sail configurations to be better understood and more accurately predicted. It will also indicate areas for improvement in traditional rigs, whilst giving guidance on the selection of appropriate sail configurations in all sorts of sailing boats, including fishing and working craft. A comparative assessment of the merits and demerits of various rigs is also made, and explanation is given as to why certain rigs are superior. Also, an attempt is made to find a correlation between the potential driving power of the rigs in question and the speed performance of a given standard hull driven by these different rigs.

Sails were initially adjusted to each predetermined heading angle relative to the wind, so that the set seemed good to the practical sailor's eye. Subsequently, lift and drag measurements were taken over a selected range of headings in

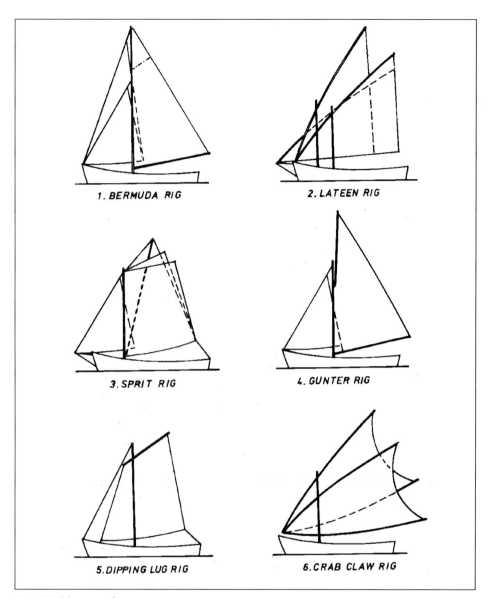

Fig 133 Rigs tested:
1   Bermuda rig (with and without large and small jibs; this also shows how much of the head of the mainsail was removed)
2   Lateen rig (three different shapes of sail)
3   Sprit rig (three different aspect ratios)
4   Gunter rig
5   Dipping lug rig
6   Crab-claw rig (sail set at varying sweepback angles)

Altogether six basic rigs were tested, some with one or more modifications, giving a total of fourteen different configurations. All rigs were tested in presence of a representative fishing boat hull (shown in Figs 103 and 134), consisting of that part normally above the water, and at the same angle of heel $\theta = 10$ degrees. Measurements of forces were taken at a constant wind speed 29.3 ft/sec (15.7 knots, 8 m/sec). Only some of a wide choice of sail planforms were investigated. These have evolved independently in different parts of the world, due to varying influences such as prevailing winds, availability of materials, operating conditions and tradition.

such a way that the 'best' polar diagram for a given rig could be established (2.36). Since fishermen in developing countries do not normally use sophisticated gadgets or devices to tune the sails to give their best performance, so, in this research, sheets only were used to adjust sail incidence angles relative to the wind direction. This restriction implies that, if tuning devices were allowed, better performances might be obtained.

CRITERIA OF SAIL POWER ADOPTED

Close-hauled The essential requirement of a sail is to generate a large driving force component, F_R. But, except on a 'dead run', it cannot do that without producing at the same time a heeling force, F_H. The driving force attained is proportional to the heeling force, and in the close-hauled condition (ß about 30°) the F_R is roughly one-fourth to one-third of the F_H, or even less depending on the hull. In other words, every pound (or kilogram) of driving force generated on the sail is accompanied by three to four pounds (or kilograms) heeling force that the boat must withstand by virtue of her stability. By analogy, the heeling force and associated heel is like the throttle of a motor boat: it puts a limit on the sail driving power which can be extracted from the wind.

Let us start with two lateen rig configurations, 1 and 3, shown in Fig 134. Figure 135 presents the polar diagrams of these two rigs. It is seen that on the same heading angle (ß–λ) = 33°, the driving force coefficient C_x1 of the lateen sail configuration Nb 1 is about 0.47, while that of configuration Nb 3 is about 0.31. (Read the caption to Fig 135 and consult Fig 136).

In this typical close-hauled condition, at a heading angle of 33 degrees, both rigs develop the same lift coefficients, C_L = 1.36, but rig 3 produces higher drag. As a result, the drag angle of rig 3 is much greater; consequently, its driving component is about 37% less than that of rig 1. Since the differences in the heeling (side) force components are relatively small (about 8%), one might expect that rig 1 would be more efficient to windward than rig 3. Evidently, the ratio of driving force to heeling force, C_x/C_y, is higher and therefore more favourable for rig 1 than for rig 3. Thus, the hull will be less heavily burdened

Fig 134 The lateen rig and its modifications. The photograph shows sail number 1 in the close-hauled attitude. Sail areas and spar lengths are indicated. Deliberately, no modern gadgets such as a kicking strap (vang), mainsheet traveller, outhaul, Cunningham hole, etc, were applied in these tests. Although quite effective, these devices are not normally used by fishing crews in developing countries.

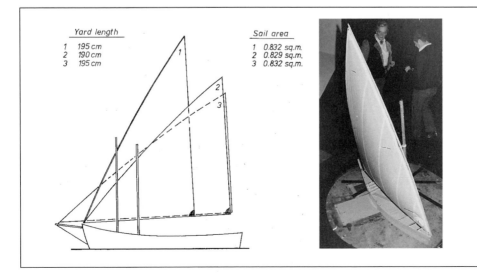

Yard length
1   195 cm
2   190 cm
3   195 cm

Sail area
1   0.832 sq.m.
2   0.829 sq.m.
3   0.832 sq.m.

Fig 135 Polar diagrams of two lateen rigs numbers 1 and 3 demonstrate the principle of windward performance interpretation. The arrows drawn from the origin of the Lift axis and the Drag axis (marked O) to the points marked 32.9° and 33.0° along the curves relevant to Rig 1 and Rig 3 show the line of action and magnitudes proportional to those of the original total aerodynamic forces. These can subsequently be resolved in the manner indicated. It gives two component coefficients: the driving force coefficient C_X and the heeling force coefficient C_Y, which like C_L and C_D are in fact empirical shape factors of given sail configuration. For a further explanation see Fig 136.

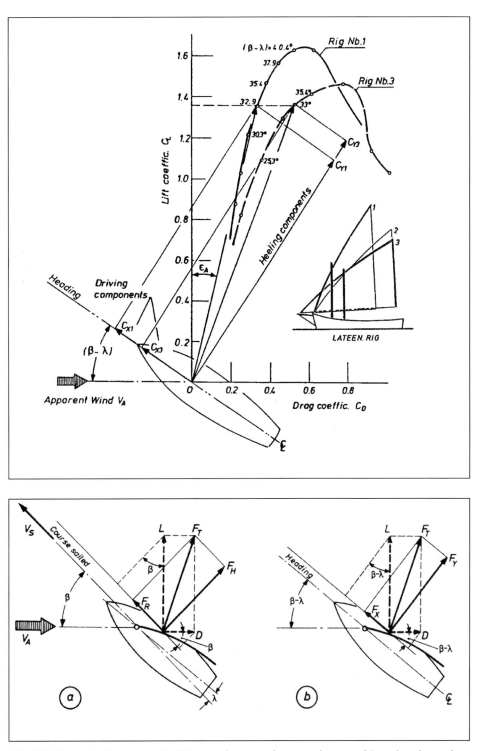

Fig 136 Since the leeway angle (λ) is not the same for every boat, and its value depends not only on hull shape but also on the course sailed (ß) and boat speed (V_s), it became common to present wind tunnel results in a slightly different way to that shown in sketch (a). This is illustrated in sketch (b), where the two components (F_X, F_Y) of the total force (F_T), are parallel and perpendicular to the hull centreline, ie, the boat's heading (ß – λ) instead of related to the course sailed (ß).

in balancing undesirable heeling (side) force – an action which always incurs hydrodynamic penalties in terms of increased resistance, and therefore slows the boat.

An analysis of the polar diagrams can be carried out, no matter whether rig characteristics are given in terms of actual forces or their coefficients. The horizontal components, F_X and F_Y, of the total aerodynamic force, acting parallel and perpendicular respectively to the hull centreline, can be calculated from equations similar to Eq 12a given earlier, ie:

$$\left. \begin{aligned} F_X &= L \sin(ß - \lambda) - D \cos(ß - \lambda) \\ F_Y &= L \cos(ß - \lambda) + D \sin(ß - \lambda) \end{aligned} \right\} \qquad \text{Eq 19}$$

C_X and C_Y which are coefficients of F_X and F_Y forces can be established in a similar manner to the C_L and C_D coefficients (Eq 11), ie:

$$C_X, C_Y = \frac{F_X, F_Y}{0.00119 \, V_A^2 \, S_A} \qquad \text{Eq 20}$$

Hence: F_X or $F_Y = 0.00119 \times V_A^2 \times S_A \times C_X$ or C_Y Eq 21

As an example, let us calculate how much driving force, F_X', will be developed on those two lateen sails, different in planform but of the same area, say, 100 ft^2 and at the same wind speed V_A = 20 knots (33.8 ft/sec).

The driving force generated by sail 1 will be:

$$F_X = 0.00119 \times V_A^2 \times S_A \times C_X = 0.00119 \times 33.8^2 \times 100 \times 0.47 = 63.8 \text{ lb}$$

while the driving force developed by sail 3 will be:

$$F_X = 0.00119 \times 33.8^2 \times 100 \times 0.31 = 42.1 \text{ lb}$$

ie 21.7 lb less than that developed by sail 1. In other words, area for area, sail 1 is potentially about 50 per cent more efficient than sail 3 – a surprising result!

Figure 137 presents two polar diagrams, one for the dipping lug and one for the sprit rig 1. Here again, one polar curve is shifted bodily towards lower drag relative to the other. However, at the same selected heading angle of 32.8 degrees, these two rigs produce different lift coefficients but at the same drag angle, ε_A. The dipping lug generates about 27 per cent more driving force, but its heeling force component is also higher by exactly the same amount.

Is the dipping lug thus more efficient than sprit 1? One may argue that this question cannot be answered without performance calculations, taking into account the hydrodynamic characteristics of the hull. According to such speed performance predictions, in true wind speed V_T = 12 knots, the dipping lug is faster close–hauled than the sprit 1 with V_{mg} = 3.5 and 3.4 knots respectively.

This numerical result corroborates our earlier criterion of sail efficiency discussed in Chapter 10 (Fig 132), namely: the higher the ratio of driving force to heeling moment, the more efficient the rig.

Reaching   When a boat begins to bear away from close-hauled, the windward criteria become gradually less stringent. Sails generate less and less heeling force off the wind, hence the ratio of C_X/C_Y increases. In the beam-reaching attitude shown in Fig 138, the relatively small heeling force component C_Y is a

Fig 137 Polar diagrams of the dipping lug and sprit no 1. The graph demonstrates the problem in applying the windward performance criteria when, at the same heading (ß – λ) and ε_A, one rig produces a higher driving force, C_X, but also a higher heeling force, C_Y, by the same percentage. Performance calculations in which the hydrodynamic characteristics of the hull are included, indicate that in wind $V_T = 12$ knots the dipping lug is faster close-hauled. Anyone would have come to the same conclusion (in a qualitative sense) by analysing the polar diagram data fully. At the same heeling force marked CYs, relevant to the sprit rig, the dipping lug rig delivers a *higher* driving component C_X, at *lower*, more favourable heading angle.

Fig 138 Depending on the course sailed, the sail (s) must be trimmed to operate over a particular part of the polar diagram. In reaching conditions, sails should be set at the incidence angle α which gives maximum lift coefficient C_L (about the same as the driving component C_X).

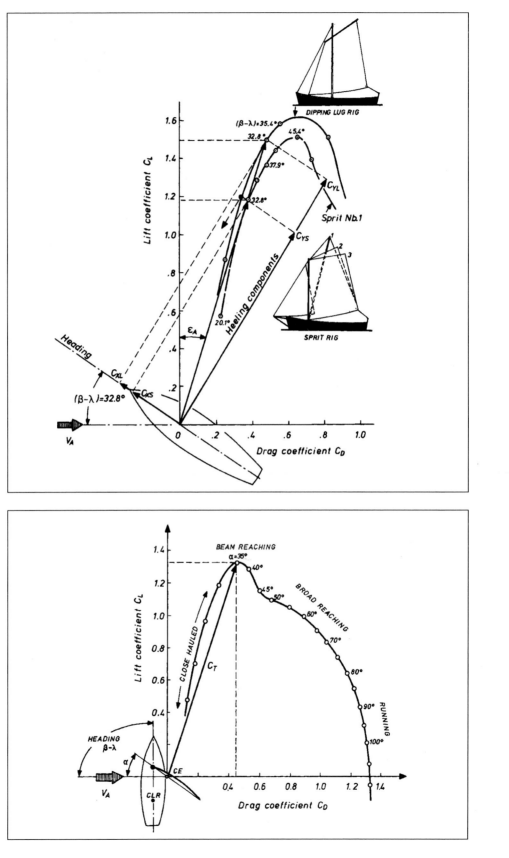

somewhat irrelevant factor; instead, the driving component C_X dominates – the higher the better. And since $C_L \simeq C_X$, the higher the lift the sail develops, the more powerful the rig.

Referring to Figs 135 and 137 again, it will be seen that the polar curves for lateen rig 1 and the dipping lug are bodily shifted upwards towards higher lift. One should therefore expect that these sails will be more efficient in reaching conditions than the lateen rig 3 and sprit 1, in relation to which lateen rig 1 and the dipping lug are compared.

Running On downwind courses, sails are usually set at an angle of incidence of about 90 degrees relative to the apparent wind; with the mast supported by normal rigging, this can sometimes be restricted by the fouling of the sail and boom with the shrouds. In such circumstances, the only criterion for sail efficiency is maximum drag of the rig, because the driving force is equivalent to drag. In practical terms, this means that the maximum possible sail area should be exposed to the action of the wind. Since drag is largely independent of the sail planform, all sails (except spinnakers) should produce roughly the same drag coefficient at an angle of incidence of 90 degrees – provided that their area is not distorted by twist or other deformations which reduce the projected sail area and hence the drag coefficient, C_D.

Summary of the sail criteria Bearing in mind the sail criteria discussed above, different rigs depicted in Fig 133 may be roughly ranked in merit for three basic courses; close–hauled, reaching and running, by comparing their ability to produce the highest driving component, C_X, with smaller possible hydrodynamic penalties incurred by heeling force component, C_Y.

Table 9 Sail criteria for different headings	
HEADING	GOALS FOR OPTIMUM PERFORMANCE
Close-hauled	Higher L/D ratio, ie, smaller drag angle, ε_A, Lower drag for the same lift at the same heading angle $(\beta - \lambda)$
	Higher C_R (C_X) component at the same C_X/C_y ratio
Reaching	Higher C_{Lmax}
Running	Higher C_D
	Largest possible sail area exposed to the wind

THE OVERALL POTENTIAL DRIVING POWER OF RIGS TESTED

Subject to the restrictions presented in Table 9, a plot of driving force component C_X against heading angle – ranging from close-hauled $(\beta - \lambda) = 30°$ to running $(\beta - \lambda) = 180°$ – may be used as a quick measure of potential performance of different sails. This concept is shown in Fig 139, in which, for example, the Bermudan rig (mainsail and large jib) is compared with the crab claw rig (Figs 140 and 141). The point of intersection of one curve by the other, marked O in Fig 139, indicates that at a certain heading angle one rig is losing its superiority; in this particular case, the Bermudan rig becomes inferior to the crab claw at $(\beta - \lambda)$ about 40 degrees.

Fig 139 The potential power of the crab claw compared with the Bermudan rig. The hatched area represents the margin of superiority of the former over the latter at heading angles ranging from 40 to 180 degrees.

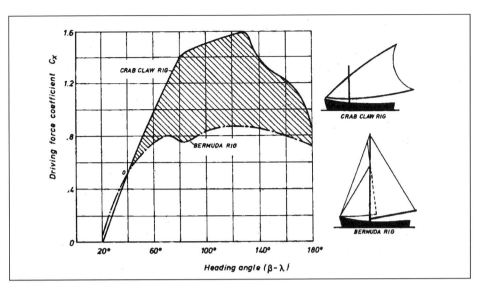

Fig 140 The Bermudan rig. The photograph shows the model with a modified (cut down) mainsail and small jib, tested in reaching conditions.

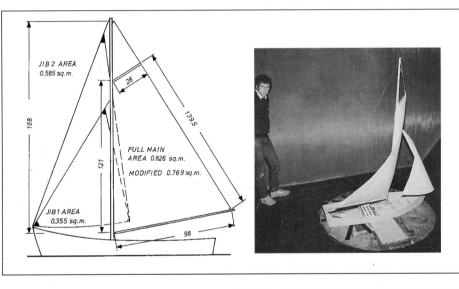

Fig 141 The crab claw rig. The photograph shows the model close-hauled.

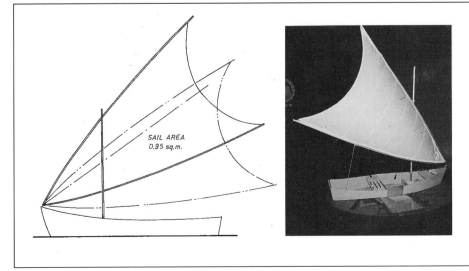

The whole area under the C_X curve, when considered over the entire range of heading angles, may be used as a yardstick of potential power of a given rig.

Even more startling is the extraordinary performance of the crab claw sail as presented in Fig 142, which demonstrates its superiority to a Bermuda mainsail right from the close-hauled condition. Its superiority increases when the boat bears away, and on reaching, with the heading angle 90 degrees, the driving force coefficient of the crab claw rig is about 1.7, whereas that of the Bermuda rig is about 0.9. That is, the crab claw rig delivers about 90 per cent more driving power than the Bermuda rig.

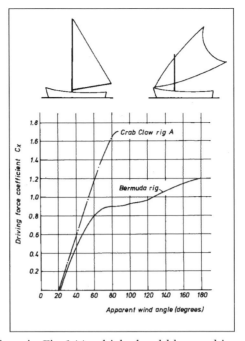

Fig 142 The driving force coefficients C_X of a crab claw rig and a Bermuda rig (mainsail only).

The comparison of all rigs tested is given in Fig 144, which should be read in association with the key below it. It will be seen, for example, that the crab claw rig has a marked overall superiority, with a value twice that of the poorest lateen rig (number 3) and about 25 per cent better than most of the others. The

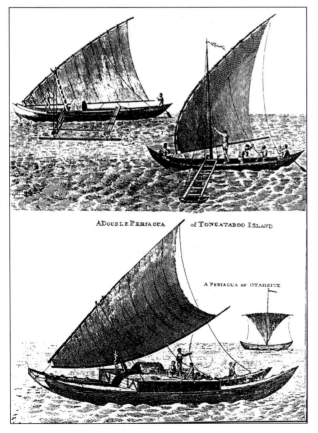

Fig 143 Crab claw rigs were characteristic of western Polynesia when Tasman and Schouten were exploring in the Tonga area in the 17th c. How and when the peculiar crab claw rig originated is lost in the mists of antiquity. These early crab claw rigs were classified by some prominent maritime historians as 'proto-lateen' or 'primitive oceanic lateen' sails. A similarity in planform (see Fig 135, rig no 3, and Figs 139 and 141) may account for such a guess. However, those two rigs are very dissimilar in their performance, the lateen form no 3 in Fig 135 being exceptionally poor. And the crab claw type of rig is by no means *primitive* when studied from an aerodynamic point of view.

Fig 144 A compari-
son of the overall
potential driving
power of the rigs
tested, obtained by
measuring the areas
under the C_X curves
plotted against the
heading angle, as
shown in Fig 139.
Rigs are compared
relative to the crab
claw, with its potential
power taken as 1.

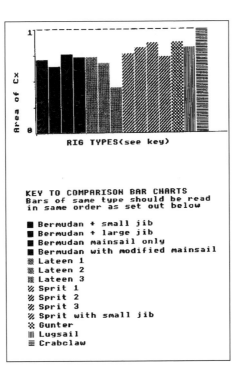

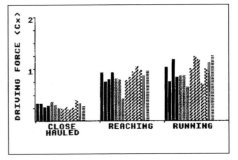

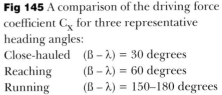

Fig 145 A comparison of the driving force
coefficient C_X for three representative
heading angles:
Close-hauled $(\beta - \lambda) = 30$ degrees
Reaching $(\beta - \lambda) = 60$ degrees
Running $(\beta - \lambda) = 150{-}180$ degrees
The key to these comparison bar charts is
given in Fig 144.

Bermudan rig, which appears to the majority of racing yachtsmen to be the
epitome of progress towards speed performance, is by no means the best rig
tested; the lateen rigs 2 and 3, the gunter and the lugsail (and, of course,
the crab claw), all come out of the tests as more powerful on some headings
(Fig 145).

In the light of these results, it appears that we have no reason to attribute
commendable performances to the Bermuda triangular sail. The practically
extinct crab claw type of sail – once used by Polynesian seafarers (Fig 143) – is
superior to the fiercely guarded product of racing and rating rules. The
Bermudan planform is so much protected that yacht designers are free to
experiment with any form of fin-keel (which, after all, operates like a sail upside
down, the leeway angle being analogous to the incidence angle of sail), but they
are not allowed to do the same with the rig. For some strange, incomprehensible reason, this sail planform is considered by the rule-makers as sacrosanct.

HOW DOES THE CRAB CLAW WORK?

'All men, by virtue, desire to know.'

Aristotle (384–322 BC)

The potential sail power of two types of rigs, Bermuda and crab claw was compared in the rather surprising graph (Fig 142) which casts doubt on the widely
assumed superiority of the Bermuda type of sail.

This raises an obvious question: why is the driving force of the crab claw rig
substantially higher than that of the triangular Bermuda alternative? The plot
of lift coefficients C_L in Fig 146 shows that the crab claw produces a greater C_L
at similar heading angles, and its superiority is particularly impressive in terms
of *maximum* C_L. Thus, beyond the heading angle of about 40 degrees, the lift

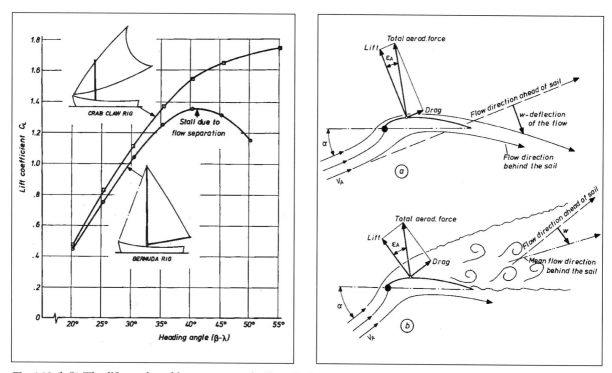

Fig 146 (left) The lift produced by two types of sail: crab claw and Bermuda, in the presence of the same hull. Note that, when bearing away, the lift produced by the Bermuda sail gradually increases to a maximum value of 1.35, at a heading angle of approximately 40 degrees. At this angle the sail is said to stall, and the flow round is considerably modified (see Fig 147).

Fig 147 (right)
a) Relatively high lift and low drag are characteristic of the so-called attached flow, ie, before stall occurs.
b) Total separation of the flow. At this moment, lift decreases and the drag increases. This is reflected in an unfavourable increase of the drag angle, ε_A.

generated by the Bermuda sail gradually decreases, while the lift produced by the crab claw continues to go up. I was so startled by this when the initial test data were recorded, that the wind tunnel was switched off for a time so that the balance system which measures the aerodynamic forces could be checked. But everything was in order.

The only sensible conclusion to draw from the experimental evidence is that the mechanism whereby the lift is generated by these two types of sails must be radically different. To assist the understanding and interpretation of the test results relevant to radically different sail configurations shown in Fig 146 (and other types of rigs too) it is worth while reminding ourselves of some principles of lift generation by the Bermuda sail, or any sail with its leading edge roughly normal to the wind direction. As demonstrated earlier in Figs 52–55, the lift generation can easily be explained in qualitative terms, although the quantitative estimate of lift is by no means an easy task without wind tunnel measurements.

It is seen in Fig 146 that there is a certain maximum lift (C_{Lmax}) that a Bermuda sail can produce, which is limited by the growth of the separation bubble shown in Figs 53a and 54. As the incidence angle, α, increases, so does the separation bubble, until its streamwise extension reaches the trailing edge.

At that moment, lift suddenly decreases and drag increases (Fig 147b). The reason for the growth of the bubble size with the incidence angle is that more and more boundary layer material, peeling off from the front part of the sail, accumulates inside the bubble.

It might be added that the stall observed during tests was usually so violent that, coincident with it, a sudden drop in the wind tunnel speed was recorded: evidence of wind energy being wasted. Most yachtsmen will be well aware of a similar effect which can be experienced in the region of the 'wind shadow' left behind the boat – a situation carefully avoided by racing helmsmen (Fig 147b).

Referring to Fig 147b, one may plausibly assume that the flow separation – a sort of 'unhealthy' flow – with its consequences of premature stall and rapid decrease in lift, could be prevented if the retarded air accumulating inside the separation bubble were continually removed. Consequently, the bubble would not grow, and the lift might continue to increase with the increasing incidence angle. Unfortunately, in the case of sail or foils of higher aspect ratio (that is, above 2), operating with their leading edge more or less normal to the oncoming airstream, there is no such natural mechanism available to remove this 'dead air'. That could only be done by artificial means which, so far, are not practical from the viewpoint of the ordinary sailor, though extractor pumps have been used experimentally in aeroplanes.

However, there is another type of flow, associated with a different planform, and with other types of lift-generating foil, where the continuous removal of the boundary layer which tends to stagnate inside the separation bubble can practically be accomplished. This type of flow, which is an efficient means of generating lift, and capable of persisting in stable form over a large range of incidence angles, can be developed around so–called *slender* foils. The Polynesian crab claw sail (Figs 143 and 148), the winglets attached to the keel of the American

Fig 148 A crab claw sail driving a fishing canoe under trial in Sierra Leone, Africa. Similar tests of other rigs shown in Fig 133 were conducted in three different countries – Sudan, Brazil and Tanzania. The aim of the project was to establish the correlation between the wind tunnel results and what could be achieved and measured in actual conditions (Ref 2.37).

challenger *Stars and Stripes* (which won the 1987 America's Cup series – Fig 149) and the delta-wing of *Concorde* – invented by different people living in different times to achieve different objectives – all belong to this category of slender foils.

This other type of flow, presented schematically and photographically in Figs 150–153, is so dissimilar to that shown in Fig 147 that it may seem a trifle odd to most sailors.

There are two different mechanisms for lift generation on the delta foils. One type of lift, called the *potential lift*, is produced in conventional manner described earlier (see for example Fig 147a); that is, at sufficiently small angles of incidence, the flow remains attached to the low pressure (leeward) surface of the foil. This is shown in sketch a of Fig 150 – there is no separation and streamlines leave the trailing edge smoothly (Ref 2.38–2.40).

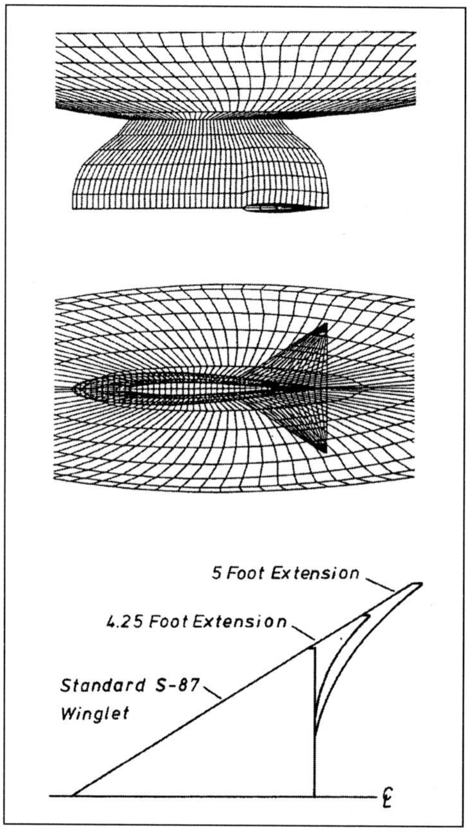

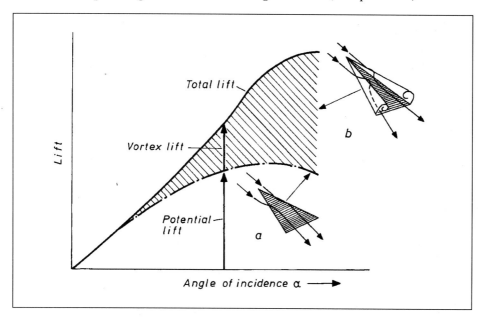

Fig 149 Computational model of the winged keel of the American 12 Metre *Stars and Stripes*, which won back the America's Cup in 1987. Note the slender winglets mounted on the inversed taper keel. They are capable of operating effectively at the large angles of incidence induced by the hull motion in heavy seas – that is when the boat is heaving, rolling and pitching (Ref 2.4). It has been found that the swallow-tailed foot extension improves the performance of winglets. The same effect was observed by the author when testing various planforms of crab claw sails in the wind tunnel.

Another type of lift, called *vortex lift*, is produced by two vortices which separate along the entire length of the side edges, as shown in sketch b, Fig 150. These two vortices, imperceptible at low angles of incidence, roll up rapidly into two nearly conical, spiral-shaped coils above the leeward surface, and grow in size with increasing angle of incidence.

Such fast spiralling vortices induce large suction (low pressure) over the

Fig 150 The contribution of two different mechanisms of lift generation to the total lift produced by the delta wing or crab claw sail.

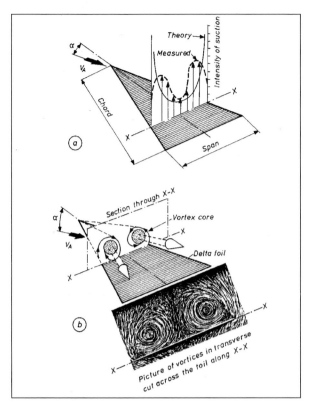

Fig 151

a) The theoretical and measured spanwise distribution of suction on the leeward side of a delta foil. The air flow accelerates rapidly round the leading edge (LE) – see photograph below. High velocity at the LE means low pressure (suction) there. *Suction* is just a quick way of designating the *pressure difference* which tends to move the foil from the higher pressure region (windward side) towards the lower pressure developed on the leeward side.

b) Air particles spinning inside the two coiled vortices. A vortex may rotate with a very high circumferential velocity, thus inducing a large suction over the adjacent surface of the foil. The entire flow over the leeward part of the slender foil, be it delta wing or crab claw sail, is dominated by these spiralling, conical-type vortices.

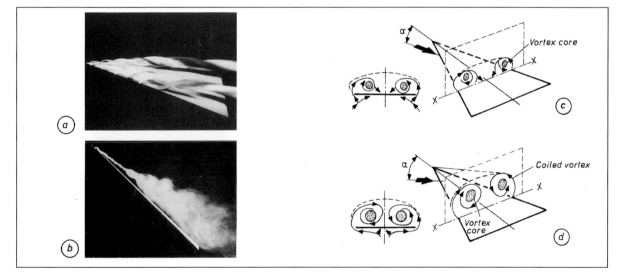

Fig 152 Flow over a delta wing at two different incidence angles:

a) coiled vortices are attached to the upper surface of the foil (small angle of incidence)

b) at a large angle of incidence, some distance from the apex, the vortices fail to reattach to the foil surface. From this point downstream, the vortex disintegrates. This is because as the incidence angle and lift increase, the vortex core spreads in volume and ultimately begins to decay from within.

c) and d)   When the incidence angle increases, the spiral vortices grow in size, and so do the cores within them. At a moderate incidence angle (sketch c), there is a certain space between the right and left coiled vortex and the vortices do not touch each other. But when the angle of incidence is increased (sketch d) the vortices become larger in diameter and finally touch each other. Vortex cores contain air circulating at low velocity as compared with that enveloping vortex sheet. This is why, at some point, with an expanding core, the vortex begins to disintegrate, as shown in b.

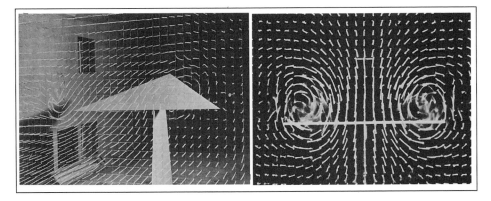

Fig 153a (far left) The general arrangement of a tuft grid set up to investigate the character of the flow pattern behind the triangular (delta) foil.

Fig 153b (left) A tuft grid survey of spiral vortices, developing round the leading edges of the foil shown in a, and left behind the trailing edge.

leeward surface of the foil (Fig 151a). The reason is that the vortex cores (Fig 150b) rotate like a wheel with high speed – and high speed implies a low pressure.

Incidentally, in a physical sense, although on a small scale, the character of these vortices is similar to the waterspout (tornado), an intense vortex system in which air may rotate with circumferential speed, ranging from 150 to 450 ft/sec. The visible funnel (vortex core), consisting of cloud droplets condensed due to expansional cooling, results from *markedly lower pressure* within the vortex compared with that in the surrounding atmosphere (see Ref 2.41). In the case of large transport aircraft, the centre of the trailing vortex core may revolve at over 18,000 rpm.

It will be seen in Fig 150 that the contribution of the vortex lift to the total lift gradually increases with the angle of incidence. Those stable coiled vortices, and so the lift, can be maintained over an incredibly wide range of incidence angles. It could be large enough to eliminate the need for high lift devices. The supersonic transport aircraft, *Concorde*, is safely controlled in landing attitude at an incidence angle of about 40 degrees, without use of any lift-augmenting devices such as the trailing edge flaps of conventional aeroplanes.

Because the coiled vortices are spiralling downstream, the boundary layer material (retarded by friction and tending to accumulate within the vortex cores) is dragged streamwise. As a result, the retarded 'lazy' mass of air is rejected downstream and left behind the trailing edge of the foil where it can do no harm. Such a mechanism which operates non-stop, as a sort of pump, limits the growth in the size of the vortex cores – a tendency which, if not tempered effectively, may lead to the breakdown of the vortex structure and consequently to a rapid drop in lift. This breakdown of an initially healthy pattern is demonstrated in Fig 152b.

One may interpret this event as a result of the drastically reduced pumping efficiency of a coiled vortex, no longer effective in quickly removing enough of the stagnating material accumulating within its core. It will be seen that downstream from the foil apex, the coiled vortex is attached to the front part of the leading edge, but that over the remaining part, a dead-air disordered flow predominates. Such an 'unhealthy' flow cannot and does not contribute to lift generation. The extent of each type of flow, varying with incidence angle, determines the degree of efficiency of the foil as a lift-producing device.

FACTORS AFFECTING THE CRAB CLAW'S EFFICIENCY

'The human mind is often so awkward and ill regulated in the career of invention that it is at first diffident, and then despises itself. For it appears at first incredible that any such discovery should be made, and when it has been made, it appears incredible that it should so long have escaped men's research.'

Francis Bacon

Since the flow over the crab craw sail is different to that over familiar Bermuda type of sail, and commonly used tell-tales are of no help in tuning the crab claw sail, a number of factors was investigated to find out their effects on the performance of this type of rig. As already mentioned, no tuning gadgets were included in the wind tunnel tests of rigs shown in Fig 133. So it would not be safe to assume that if gadgets were included, the result would be a uniform improvement for all rigs. A great deal of effort and ingenuity went into the development of the Bermuda type of rig, but very little attention, if any, has been paid to other types of rigs. This is the reason why it is difficult to predict which rig in Fig 133 would be favoured if enough imagination and skill was directed into their development as reliable and practical devices for extracting power from the wind.

Leading edge The tests on a crab claw sail with round spar edges, and then one with a sharp leading edge, although not entirely conclusive, indicated that the sail with sharp leading edge appeared to produce higher lift.

Some light has been thrown on the effect of leading edge shape on lift by a number of tests on pressure distribution over delta wings (Refs 2.39, 2.40, 2.42–2.44). It was found that the shape of the leading edges has an effect on distribution of suction developing over the leeward side of the foil. As in conventional planforms, most of the lift on delta planforms is generated by the suction forces, that is the static pressure below that of the main stream ahead of the foil. Theoretically, in the case of sharp leading edges, the suction peak at the edge of the foil, as presented in Fig 151a, should be very high, as symptotically increasing to infinity. However, when comparing the experimentally measured suction with the theoretical predicted distribution, it was established that such a high suction peak near the edge did not materialize; instead, relatively higher suction was measured over a greater portion of the foil inside. As a consequence, the loss in suction right over the leading edges was compensated for by the broadening of the suction region over the central part of the foil.

In more precise terms, this trend can be observed on a delta type of foil presented in Fig 154, which gives the suction distribution on the leeward side of two foils with different shapes of the leading edge. Measurements were taken at the forward station $\frac{x}{c} = 0.25$, as indicated in the figure. Shapes of the leading edges investigated are also shown; one of the foils had a thicker, round edge, the other had a thinner, elliptical edge. By comparing the

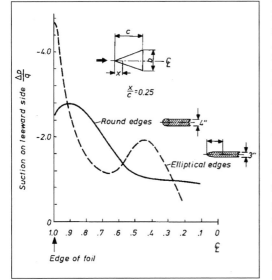

Fig 154 The distribution of suction over the leeward side of two delta foils of AR $= \frac{b^2}{\text{Area}} = 1.5$ with different shaped leading edges. Note that the suction due to vortex action is mainly generated along the foil area close to the leading edge; the middle area close to the centreline contributes less to the total lift.

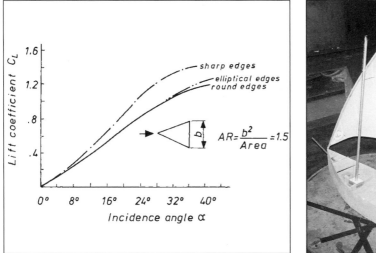

Fig 155 (far left) The lift developed on a delta wing with three different leading edges. Due to the sharp leading edge on one of these foils, higher suction develops over the leeward side of the foil and, as a consequence, the overall lift is larger than that produced by the two other foils, which have the same aspect ratio but somewhat blunter edges.
Fig 156 (left) Yards or spars which do not match wind loading and bend excessively may cause uncontrollable distortions in the sail shape and hence deterioration in sail performance (see for comparison Fig 134).

areas under the pressure distribution curves, one may infer that there is not much difference between the effects of different leading edges on lift.

This inference is confirmed in Fig 155, which shows the effect of the edge shape on lift for the same delta foil as in Fig 154. There is practically no difference between thicker, round and thinner, elliptic edge in terms of lift generated within the range of incidence angles up to about 40 degrees. However, when compared with yet another foil which had *sharp bevelled* edges, both round and elliptic edges gave inferior performance within the whole investigated range of incidence angles.

What is the practical conclusion one may derive from those tests? *First*; sharp leading edges produce higher lift per given area than any other tested edges. However, such efficient yards with sharp edges cannot easily be applied in the case of rigs used for fishing vessels in developing countries in which bamboo or other round sticks are used as spars or yards. Besides, it would be rather difficult to maintain sufficiently sharp edges on spars made of wood. *Second*; little, if anything, can be gained by using thinner spars for the crab claw type of sail. Moreover, if too thin yards are used to support canvas, it may result in a flimsy, uncontrollable and inefficient sail shape, as shown in Fig 156, no matter if the rig in question is a lateen or crab claw configuration. As a rule, the stiffness of the spars should be such that the shape of the sail does not distort with increasing wind strength. Figures 141 and 148 illustrate the crab claw type of sail, in which the stiffness of the yards appears to match the wind loading reasonably well.

Camber effect The basic function of the leading edges of a slender foil – and the crab claw type of sail belongs to this category – is to fix the separation line from which strong, conical-type vortices roll up. Sharp leading edges ensure regular, intense growth of these vortices and, in turn, create large lift. A sort of blunt round edge behind the yards, due to the presence of sail bulge, will preclude the generation of strong and efficient vortices (Ref 2.40).

In Fig 157a are shown three different types of camber (see sections 1, 2 and 3). Sections 2 and 3, with a moderate, conical-type of camber, are acceptable

Fig 157a (top) Cross-sections of the crab claw sail. Section 1 is inefficient, section 3 is preferable.

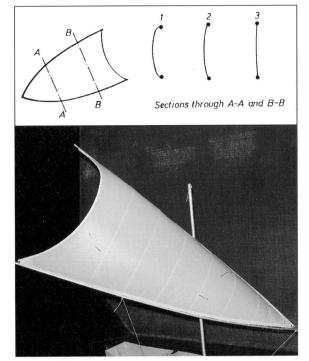

Sections through A-A and B-B

Fig 157b (below) By allowing the lower yard to move up, as shown in photograph b, the sail camber will increase and the sail area will decrease (compare with that in Fig 141). As a result, the sail will produce less driving power. Such a reduction in aerodynamic forces may be necessary in strong winds.

(the less the camber, the higher the lift), but section 1, with bulges right behind the yards, will reduce the sail effectiveness in producing the vortex lift.

In strong winds it may become necessary to put a limit on forces developed by the sail. This could be achieved by allowing the lower yard to move up, as indicated in Fig 157b by the black arrow (see Fig 141 for comparison). Such a deliberately introduced increase of the sail camber is similar to reefing in its effect.

To illustrate this point from yet another view, Fig 158 shows the same sail with different camber; photograph (a) demonstrates reasonably good trim and camber, while photograph (b) depicts a rather badly trimmed sail, with large camber and twist. Evidently the sail shape (camber and twist), and ultimately its efficiency, will depend on the way the sail is attached to the mast and hull, and also its sheeting arrangements – an unexplored field for future developments.

Fig 158 These two different sets of the same crab claw sail will result in different performance characteristics:

a) illustrates a reasonably correct setting for high lift

b) has large camber and twist and will result in lower lift

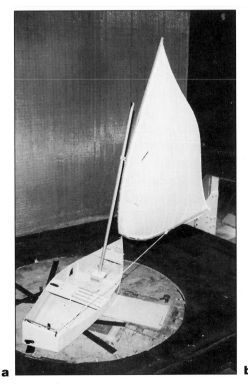

a   b

Rigging To illustrate this point quantitatively, two different ways of rigging were investigated in order to establish their effect on the driving force developed by the same sail. Figure 158a shows one rigging method (case 1), in which the upper spar and the tack were firmly attached to the mast and bow respectively. In case 2, the tack and halyard were eased so that the sail assumed a position some distance to leeward from the mast. The aerodynamic forces were measured for heading angles $(\beta - \lambda)$ from 20 to 55 degrees, and the relevant polar diagrams of lift and drag coefficients, C_L and C_D, are presented in Fig 159a.

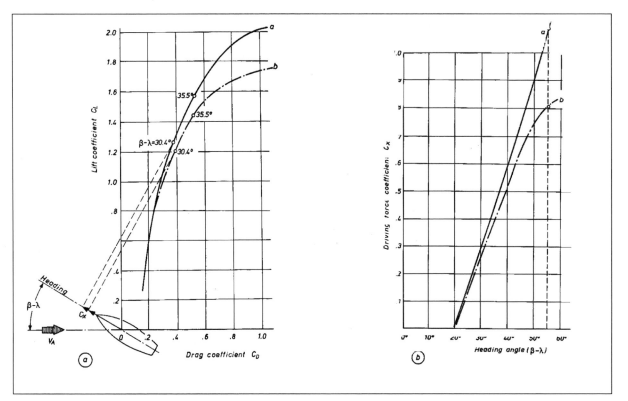

For example, at the heading angle 30.4 degrees, the sail which was firmly attached to the mast and to the bow (case 1) develops about 16 per cent more driving force than the sail loosely controlled at its tack and mast (case 2). The differences in sail performance, initially negligible at small angles of heading, increase gradually when the boat bears away from the wind. The superiority of rigging 1 over rigging 2 in terms of driving force coefficient C_x is reflected in Fig 159b, which presents the variation of C_x coefficient at different heading angles relative to the apparent wind within the range from 20 to 55 degrees. Thus, other things being equal, the boat driven by sail rigged in manner 1 of Fig 158a would, at the heading angle of 55 degrees, develop about 35 per cent more driving force than the sail rigged in manner 2. And these differences appear to increase still further when the heading angles become larger.

The reason for the deterioration of the sail performance in case 2 can be attributed to the difficulty in controlling the sail camber and twist. As mentioned earlier, the conditions for high efficiency of the crab claw sail operating on the delta wing principle, are: small camber, particularly near the spars, and

Fig 159a Polar diagrams of the same crab claw sail but set differently relative to the mast and hull (see Fig 158a for case 1). In case 2 the tack and halyard were eased.

Fig 159b Variation of the driving force component C_x for the same crab claw sail set in two different ways.

Fig 160 Crab claw rigs tested in natural conditions. Sails are planar and appear to be correctly set, except in case a where the spars at the sail apex are definitely too thick to encourage development of healthy vortices right from the beginning.

no twist. In other words, the sail should be planar, ie lying in a plane which is orientated at the same angle of incidence relative to the wind direction. What is meant by a 'non-planar' sail, with its unsymmetrical and appreciable curvatures, can be understood by analysing Figs 158b and 160.

Planform and the position of the sail relative to the vertical The high potential power of the crab claw sail, as demonstrated so far, gave rise to the practical question: how does the planform modification and the sweep angle affect its aerodynamic performance in terms of C_{Lmax}, ε_A and C_x?

Four additional sail models with varying leading and trailing edge profiles, together with model A tested earlier, were investigated. These are shown in Fig 161. Some models were tested in three different positions marked in Fig 162 as low (large sweep angle), high (small sweep angle) and medium. Tests were

Fig 161 (right) Crab claw sails tested. All previous results discussed so far are relevant to sail planform A.

Fig 162 (far right) Test positions of the sail at three different sweep angles.

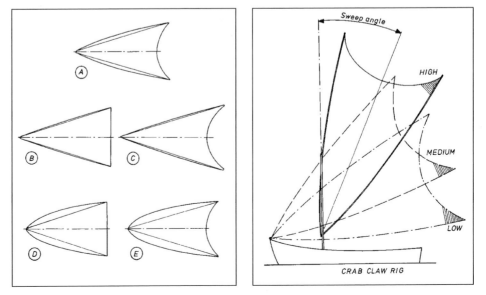

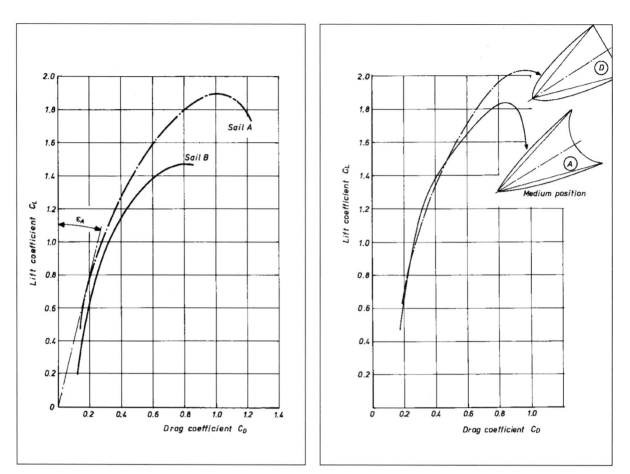

restricted to the range of heading from close-hauled to reaching conditions only, bearing in mind the fact already established that in downwind sailing the planform and aspect ratio become irrelevant as speed factors; what matters is the exposed sail area only. In this respect, all sails tested were virtually the same.

Figure 163 presents the results of tests on sails A and B set in similar low position (large sweep angle). Recorded characteristics in terms of ε_A (relevant to close-hauled performance), as well as C_{Lmax} (relevant to reaching performance), of sail B are much inferior to that of sail A. The drag angle, ε_A, of sail B is at least 2 degrees higher than that of sail A. Thus, other things being equal, the boat driven by sail A would perform 2 degrees closer to the wind than that driven by sail B. Available driving power of sail B in reaching, as reflected by its C_{Lmax}, is 1.48, while that of sail A is 1.90; therefore sail A generates about 28 per cent more power than sail B.

The order of merit of sails tested with respect to maximum power available (C_{Lmax} or C_{xmax}) is: sail D, A and E. For example, the superiority margin of sail D over sail A is demonstrated in Fig 164; C_{Lmax} developed by sail D is about 10 per cent higher than that of sail A. However, this gain is attained at a small expense in terms of L/D ratio (which might be due to some departure from optimum trim of sail D).

Sails B and C, with their sharp apex angle (Fig 161) are definitely inferior, particularly sail B. It appears that the rounded apex in the form incorporated

Fig 163 (far left) Polar diagrams of two crab claw sails, A and B, tested at a similar sweep angle (low position in Fig 162).

Fig 164 (left) Polar diagrams of two crab claw sails, A and D tested in a medium position.

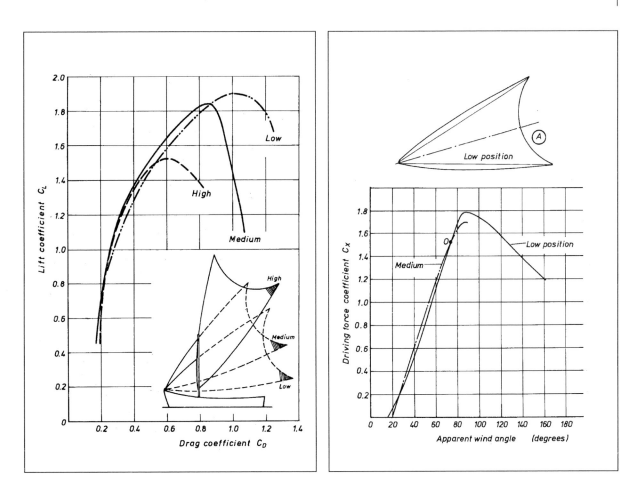

Fig 165 (above right) Polar diagrams of crab claw sail A tested in three different positions relative to the mast and hull. The sail set in a high position is inferior to other two configurations, regardless of the sailing heading angle.

Fig 166 (far right) The driving force coefficient of crab claw sail A developed in two positions: low and medium.

into sails D and E and to a lesser extent into sail A (which might be called a 'Gothic' planform) is superior to the 'Delta' planforms of sails B and C.

It is seen from Fig 165 relevant to sail A that, as the sweepback angle becomes larger, ie, the sail position is moved from high to low, the C_{Lmax} coefficient increases quite substantially from 1.52 to 1.9 – about 25 per cent. A high sail position (small sweepback angle) offers no advantage in either large C_{Lmax} nor high L/D ratio. To achieve the best performance to windward, the sail should be set in a *medium* position, but for reaching, the best efficiency is obtained in a *low* position.

As shown in Fig 166, which gives the driving coefficient C_x developed in two positions, the sail set in a medium position is losing its superiority beginning from the heading angle, about 70 degrees (close-reaching). This is indicated by the intersection point O, thereafter the sail set in a low position becomes gradually more efficient. The same trend was observed when testing other planforms depicted in Fig 161.

According to both theory and from numerous tests on delta wings, the crab claw sail should produce the best performance with its symmetry axis close to horizontal. However, according to Fig 165, this is not borne out experimentally. As demonstrated earlier, the delta or crab claw sail will eventually reach an angle of incidence where the flow breaks. The core of the coiled leading edge vortex depicted in Figs 152c and d experiences an abrupt expansion at some point, usually first in the wake downstream of the trailing edge, and as the

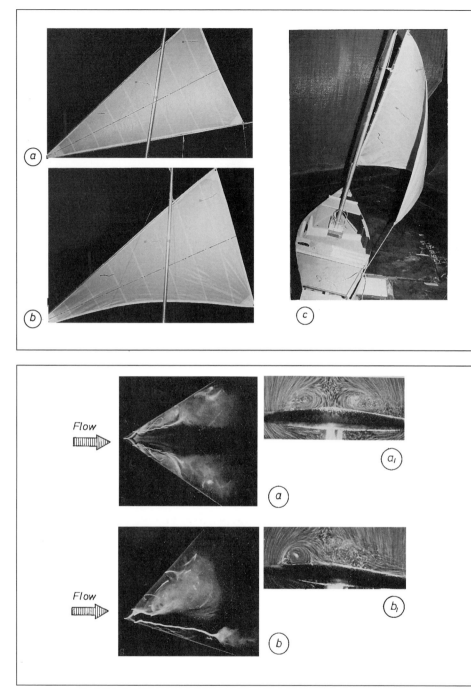

Fig 167a The crab claw sail B (see Fig 161); axisymmetric configuration, close-hauled. Note that the upper and lower leading edges supported by yards are straight.

Fig 167b and c Crab claw sail tested in close-hauled condition with the lower yard removed. The sail is no longer axisymmetric under wind pressure. When bearing away, the curvature of the lower leading edge of the sail increases, as seen when looking at the sail from behind (photo c). The sail departs further from the crab claw's geometrical configuration to the detriment of its driving performance.

Fig 168 Flow over the leeward side of a delta foil set at incidence angle $\alpha = 24$ degrees. In case a, the foil is aligned relative to the oncoming flow. Leading edge vortices are symmetrically placed on either side of the centreline of the foil. Both vortices (left and right side) contribute to the lift force. These are shown in Photo (a), as seen from behind the foil some distance from the foil apex. In case (b), the foil is not aligned relative to the flow direction. As a result, only one leading edge vortex is effectively developed (on the upper side of the foil). Such a lack of symmetry, clearly visible in photo b_1, is apparently responsible for the reduced lift generated under unsymmetrical flow conditions (pictures taken from Ref 2.45).

incidence angle continues to increase, so the *breakdown point* moves forward and will eventually reach the apex of the foil. Then the overall flow pattern changes radically, and is followed by decrease in lift. Such a breakdown of the flow is presented in photograph a of Fig 152.

It has been found that *premature* inception of the flow breakdown may occur if:

- The foil is not axisymmetric, ie, its area and camber are not uniformly distributed relative to the symmetry axis shown in Fig 167b by a broken line.
- The foil is not aligned relative to the oncoming flow, ie, the foil centreline is not parallel to the flow direction ahead of the foil apex (see Fig 168a and b).
- The foil does not operate in uniform flow, ie, the flow direction and/or its velocity are not uniform across the foil height.

If the leading edge vortices are to be generated efficiently, the foil area and camber distribution should be axisymmetric, and the aligned foil should operate in uniform flow velocity. As we shall see in the next chapter, the latter condition cannot be practically satisfied, either in the wind tunnel or in natural sailing conditions, even if the sail itself is axisymmetric geometrically as shown in Fig 167a. This is due to the effect of the wind gradient and also the hull interference to which all sails are subjected, usually to the detriment of their efficiency.

COMPARISON OF THE CRAB CLAW'S PERFORMANCE WITH THAT OF THE LATEEN SAIL

The lateen sail (Fig 167b) is not axisymmetric when under wind pressure; this appears to be the main reason why this sail with greater sweepback is so poor in terms of aerodynamic efficiency. Such a non-axisymmetric planform cannot possibly produce a large component of vortex lift. When compared area for area, the lateen sail (particularly number 3 in Fig 133) is much inferior to the crab claw sail (Fig 144). In order to find out why there is such a drastic difference in sail performance, two tests were done on one of the crab claw sails

Fig 169 (below) Polar diagrams of the sail of the same area and planform; the only difference is that in one case (Fig 167b), the lower yard of the crab claw sail shown in Fig 167a was removed, thus simulating a typical lateen configuration.

Fig 170 (far right) The driving force coefficient C_X (based on data given in Fig 169) relevant to two sail configurations: crab claw and lateen, tested at different apparent wind angles.

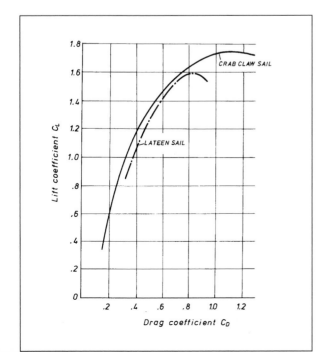

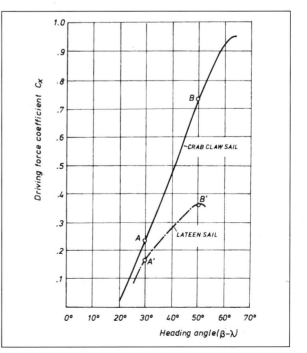

(type B in Fig 167a). It is seen that this sail closely resembles in its planform the strikingly poor lateen sail number 3.

In one series of tests, the aerodynamic characteristics of the crab claw sail were established in terms of C_L versus C_D, within the range of apparent wind angles from 20 to 60 degrees. Subsequently, the lower yard was removed, so the sail took the shape depicted in photograph b of Fig 167 – a typical lateen sail shape. The tests were then repeated for the same range of apparent wind angles. The results are presented in Figs 169 and 170. Figure 169 reveals that the polar curve of the lateen sail is bodily shifted towards higher drag, ie, the same lift on the crab claw sail can be obtained at lower drag – a desirable feature. Figure 170 is even more revealing. It shows the variation of the driving component coefficient C_x with apparent wind angle. Thus, at the heading angle 30 degrees, ie, in close-hauled attitude (see points A and A' marked on the curves), the crab claw sail (supported by two yards) develops about 45 per cent more thrust than the same sail supported by one yard only, ie, the lateen configuration. In close-reaching conditions, at heading angle 50 degrees (see points B and B'), the crab claw rig develops about twice as much thrust as the lateen type of sail – an enormous difference bearing in mind that, at first sight, all other geometrical factors appear to be similar. What matters is whether the lower edge of the sail is supported by a yard and is therefore straight, or is unsupported and hence flexible. To really understand what happens when the lower spar is removed would require detailed, expensive and time-consuming wind tunnel studies of the flow character associated with the two different shapes of the lower leading edge, and also some measurements of pressure on the leeward side of the two sails shown in Fig 167. Such research, although interesting, was beyond the scope of our investigations.

12 • WIND GRADIENT EFFECT AND SAIL–HULL INTERFERENCE

'...knowledge does not mean all the things we happen to know, but only those we have thought about enough to know how they hang together and how they can be applied usefully.'

George C Lichtenberg

As shown in Fig 165, depending on the sweepback angle, the aerodynamic characteristics of the crab claw sail may change substantially. To discover the factors which might be responsible for reducing the efficiency of the sail set in a low position (Fig 166), some measurements of local wind velocities in the proximity of the hull and mast were taken. Details of these measurements are given in Figs 171 and 170. It will be seen that these velocities, which in turn determine the forces developed on the sail, are by no means uniform. Beginning from the wind tunnel floor (flat water surface) upwards, there was a definite wind gradient; for example, close to the wind tunnel floor the local wind velocity was 9.2 ft/sec, while at the height of the lower yard of the sail, the recorded wind velocity was 27.2 ft/sec. The free wind velocity, measured further downstream at the height of about half the mast length (approximately 0.5 m) was 30.5 ft/sec. Figure 172 illustrates graphically how the local velocities are distributed close to the hull and mast.

Fig 172 (below right) The wind velocity distribution in the vicinity of the hull and mast of the model in the close-hauled attitude shown in Figs 158a and Fig 171.

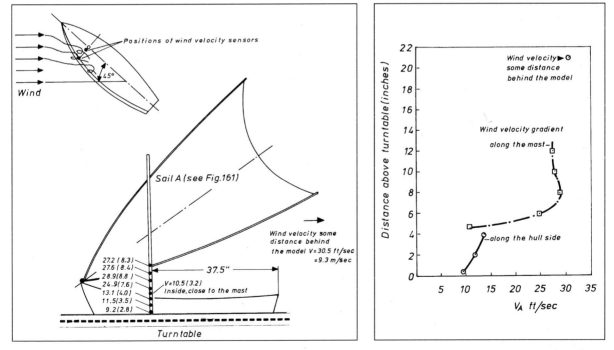

Fig 171 (above left) Measurements showing the local wind velocity of the hull and mast in the presence of a sail; heading angle = 45 degrees (Fig 141). The wind velocity sensor was kept about 1 in (2.5 cm) from the windward side of the hull and at the same distance from the mast. Measurements were taken at about 2 in (5.0 cm) intervals, beginning from the wind tunnel floor (turntable). Wind velocities are given in ft/sec and m/sec.

It was also observed that, apart from the recorded wind gradient, the wind flow just above the windward side of the hull separates in a sort of vortex, rolling up and along the hull. The small sketch in Fig 171 (top left corner) shows schematically the flow separation. Such a circulatory motion in the region in which the lower part of the sail operates is bound to affect its working conditions and so its efficiency. Thus, the high lift capabilities of the crab claw sail appear to be restricted not only because of the lack of flow symmetry in relation to the centreline of the sail, ie, the non-uniform velocity field; but also by the wind gradient and hull–sail interference effects.

This ties up with one more factor related to the aerodynamic forces or pressures developed on any kind of sail. Assuming that the lower part of the sail presented in Fig 171 is affected by a wind velocity of 27.2 ft/sec, and the upper part by a wind velocity of 30 ft/sec, the differences in sail forces developed over higher and lower parts of the sail will be proportional to the relevant ratio of wind velocities squared, ie, $(\frac{30.5}{27.2})^2 = 1.12^2 = 1.25$. Therefore, the forces or pressures per unit area developed on the lower part of the sail will be smaller than those acting on the upper part. The above example should only be regarded as a rough indication of just one consequence of the wind gradient effect. There are also other side effects such as, for example, the *crossflow*, in which case the streamlines over the foil surface (indicating the local flow) are not parallel to the flow direction ahead of the foil, but may be curved towards one or other end of the foil. We note in passing that the crossflow closely associated with separation of the flow will be discussed later.

The wind gradient actually measured in the wind tunnel may not be truly representative of the wind gradient experienced in nature; nevertheless its effect on sail performance will be similar. Meteorological investigations have revealed that the wind gradient, definable as the rate at which the wind gradually increases with height above the water, varies according to the cloudiness of the sky, prevailing wind speed and direction, wind turbulence, water temperature, etc (see Fig 290).

SAIL PERFORMANCE AT DIFFERENT HEADING ANGLES

The combined influence of the hull/sail interaction and wind gradient on the driving performance of any kind of sail depends on the heading angle relative to the wind. It was found that, when bearing away, the sail loses its potential power somewhat as compared with that measured in close-hauled conditions. These losses may be assessed from Fig 173, which gives the aerodynamic characteristics of the Bermuda type of mainsail. On the left is a plot of driving force coefficient, C_x, recorded at different heading angles from close-hauled to running with the wind astern. On the right is a polar diagram (C_L versus C_D) for the same sail, recorded in the close-hauled attitude.

In most methods of calculation of a sailing boat's performance (based on Davidson's concept, Ref 2.46), it has been tacitly assumed that if by application of an effective vang the sail twist and camber in reaching conditions were the same as when close-hauled, then the driving force coefficients on reaching could be derived from the polar diagram similar to that presented in Fig 173b. In other words, the sail driving power in reaching attitude could be determined

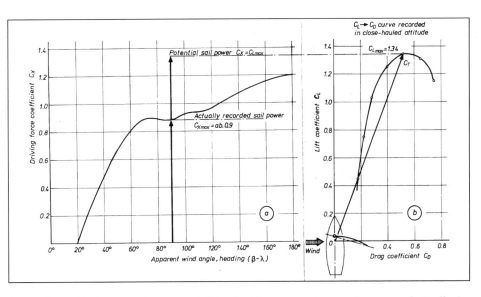

Fig 173 The aerodynamic characteristics of a Bermuda type of mainsail, expressed in terms of driving force coefficient C_X versus heading angle (a), and a polar diagram of the same sail recorded in close-hauled conditions (b). Due to the high sheet tension, the sail twist was relatively small. The position of the sail relative to the hull determines to a large extent its potential driving power.

from the sail characteristics established either experimentally or analytically in close–hauled attitude.

Thus, for example, one might expect that the driving force coefficient C_X of the Bermuda sail (shown in Fig 173b) in reaching conditions would be equal to C_{Lmax}, which is 1.34. In fact, the mainsail tested in reaching attitude delivered a C_X equal to only about 0.9, ie, about one third of the sail's potential power was lost. It was suggested that such a substantial power loss could be attributed mainly to the excessive twist and different camber distribution.

The other factors, not fully investigated, which might contribute to the deterioration of sail performance when bearing away, were those associated with air flow interaction between the hull and sail. It was anticipated that such a mutual interaction might be either beneficial or detrimental, depending on the position of the sail relative to the hull, the gap between the boom and deck, and other hull superstructure details (such as the presence of a deckhouse, etc).

To eliminate the effects of twist and camber variation on the aerodynamic characteristics of the sail when bearing away, a rigid foil was used. By testing a foil with constant camber and no twist, the effect of one factor only could be examined, namely the interaction between the flow over the foil and over the hull. The geometric and other data about the foil are given in Fig 174.

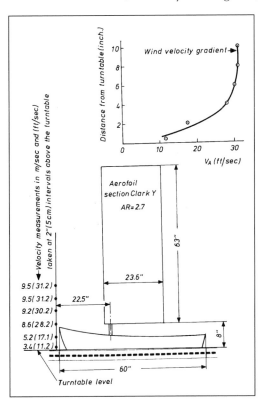

Fig 174 Configuration of an unsymmetrical rigid aerofoil Clark Y tested in the presence of the hull, at Reynolds Number Re = 330,000. Measurements of the wind velocities ahead of the hull were done with the foil removed. A graphical picture of the velocity distribution above the wind tunnel floor is given over the foil. The geometric aspect ratio of the foil was AR = 2.67. The free stream velocity measured some distance behind the foil was 29.2 ft/sec (8.9 m/sec).

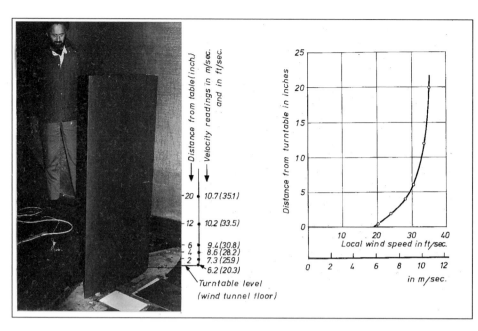

Fig 175 The wind velocity gradient measured along the leading edge of the rigid foil attached closely to the turntable (ie, with no gap between the lower tip of the foil and the turntable).

At first, the foil was tested without a hull and with no gap between its lower edge and the turntable (wind tunnel floor). Thereafter, the foil was lifted 8 inches (20 cm) above the floor, and the measurements of lift and drag were taken as before, within the incidence angles from 0 degrees to 25–30 degrees, ie, beyond the stall angle. A similar test was repeated, with the gap increased to 18 inches (45 cm).

With the foil set at an angle of incidence about 10 degrees, wind velocities were measured over the leeward (suction) side of the foil. Measurements were taken about 2 inches (5 cm) behind the leading edge, and about 1 inch (2.5 cm) above the foil surface. The results are presented in Fig 175.

As in earlier tests (see Fig 172), the wind velocities recorded vary, much as they do in nature. Such a wind gradient, a sort of large scale boundary layer, must necessarily affect pressure distribution and hence overall performance of the foil, no matter whether tests are done on a model or on its full scale replica operating in natural wind conditions.

Figure 176 shows the polar diagrams of the foil relevant to its three different positions relative to the turntable. Consider first the test results on the foil which had no gap between its lower tip and the wind tunnel floor. To facilitate analysis of the influence of the water surface, or any other surface for that matter, on the flow round any foil, a convenient and logical way is to apply a concept used in physics, the 'mirror-image method' (Ref 2.4). By this means, the effect of the sea's presence can be obtained by replacing the water surface by an

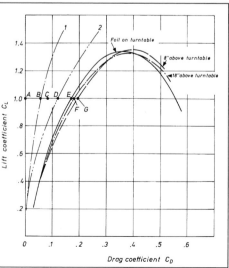

Fig 176 Polar diagrams of rigid, unsymmetrical foil Clark Y tested in three different positions relative to the turntable without hull. Curve 1 illustrates the variation of the induced drag component C_{Di}, assuming that the effective aspect ratio $AR_{ef} = 2 \times 2.67 = 5.34$. Curve 2 is relevant to the induced drag variation with lift for the actual geometric aspect ratio $AR = 2.67$. The results clearly indicate that the commonly accepted assumption that by closing the gap between the foil (be it sail or keel) and the hull, the effective aspect ratio of the foil can be increased twofold – with the ensuing advantages of reduced induced drag and a higher L/D ratio – is wrong.

inverted mirror- image of the foil with a *frictionless* dividing plane marked X–X in Fig 69b discussed earlier. Let us assume that the part of the foil shown above the dividing plane X–X is the real foil under investigation, and its aspect ratio AR = span/chord = $\frac{b}{c}$. That part which is below the dividing plane may be referred to as an *image* of the real one, ie, its image in a mirror at the position of the water plane. If the mirror-like plane X–X were really frictionless, and so the flow velocities were uniform (without any wind gradient) all along the foil span, then the pattern of the flow at the bottom of the foil along the border line plane X–X would look like that shown in Fig 69a. This physical picture leads to the concept of 'effective' aspect ratio.

EFFECTIVE ASPECT RATIO

If there is no gap between the real and imaginary foil, so that flow over the bottom of the foil (across the X–X line) is prevented, the tip vortex cannot develop there. In such conditions, the lift-producing foil will develop one tip vortex only. As a result, less flow energy will be dissipated and left behind in the form of the streaming tip vortices demonstrated in Fig 69a, b, c and d. Induced drag can be regarded as a sort of measure of this energy loss. The effect of the presence of the mirror-image foil (ie a flat, frictionless surface) on drag is equivalent to an increase in aspect ratio (AR) of the real foil. Consequently, the *effective aspect ratio*, AR_{ef}, should be twice that of the actual, geometric aspect ratio, AR, of the real part of the mirror-image combination.

$$AR_{ef} = 2\,AR = 2\,b/c \qquad \text{Eq 22}$$

Hence, according to the classic theory and relevant formula, the induced drag of the real foil should be reduced by half, ie:

$$D_i = \frac{L^2}{2\,\pi\,AR} = \frac{L^2}{\pi\,AR_{ef}} \qquad \begin{array}{l}\text{Eq 23}\\ \text{(see Eq 13)}\end{array}$$

which is applicable to foils of elliptical planform commonly considered as the ideal planform.

For most other planforms, the induced drag is greater. For example, according to Glauert's theory (2.47), for a rectangular planform of aspect ratio 3.0, the increase in induced drag should be about 3 per cent. Planform corrections are therefore needed, and formula 23 can be rewritten to accommodate the correction factor k:

$$D_i = k\,\frac{L^2}{\pi\,AR_{ef}} \qquad \text{Eq 24}$$

This k factor is different depending on the planform, and for a rectangular planform of AR = 3 it would theoretically be 1.03. As we shall see later, when discussing keels, experimentally established k factors depart from the theoretical ones – the drag increase is smaller than that predicted by theory.

It should be emphasized that equation 24 holds on *two conditions*:

1 there is no gap between the lower end of the foil and the dividing plate, X–X (the deck in the case of a sail, or the bottom of the hull to which the rudder is attached).

2 the dividing plate X–X is *frictionless*. That is, there is no flow velocity gradient of any kind developing along the leading edge of the foil.

The first condition can be satisfied, but the second one cannot be realized in practical design work. There are no such things as frictionless surfaces, along which the boundary layer, always characterized by the velocity gradient, will miraculously not occur.

Let us return now to Fig 176 and analyse the results of tests in the light of what has been just discussed. The total drag of any foil consists of two components:

$$\text{Total drag} = \text{profile drag} + \text{induced drag}$$

This can be rewritten in mathematical form in terms of coefficients:

$$C_D = C_{Dp} + k \;\frac{C_L{}^2}{\pi\, AR_{ef}} \qquad\qquad\qquad \text{Eq 25}$$

It is customary to distinguish the *profile drag* C_{Dp} as that part of the total drag which arises due to the action of viscosity and unavoidable friction whenever a foil is moving through any fluid, be it air or water, and no lift is produced. The magnitude of this component can be established experimentally, and in our tests (Fig 176) its value at $C_L = 0$ is about 0.03. This includes the small friction drag of the turntable and support wires. Within a large range of incidence angles, or lift coefficients below the stalling angle, the profile drag does not increase much, and may be considered as constant.

The second component of the total drag, the induced drag, depends primarily on the lift squared, and for that reason it is sometimes called *drag due to lift*. Assuming, for the sake of argument, that the conditions 1 and 2 (given earlier) are satisfied, we can calculate variation of the induced drag from formula 25:

$$C_{Di} = k \;\frac{CL^2}{\pi\, AR_{ef}}$$

Introducing known quantities, ie $AR_{ef} = 2 \times AR = 2 \times 2.67 = 5.34$, $\pi = 3.14$ and $k = 1.03$, we have:

$$C_{Di} = 1.03 \;\frac{C_L{}^2}{3.14 \times 5.34}$$

$$C_{Di} = 0.0614\, C_L{}^2$$

Curve 1 in Fig 176 illustrates the variation in the induced drag with lift based on the above premises, ie, by closing the gap between the turntable, the effective aspect ratio, AR_{ef}, increases twofold. Unfortunately, the test results are against these theoretical expectations which, incidentally, are quite commonly shared by many authors of books on naval architecture and aerodynamics, and also by boat designers.

What can be learned from the experimental results presented in Fig 176? Consider the total drag, C_D, of the foil, when the lift coefficient C_L equals, say, 1.0. The induced drag component $C_{Di} = 0.0614\, C_L{}^2 = 0.0614 \times 1^2 = 0.0614$, and this value is indicated by distance A–B in Fig 176. The other component of the total drag, C_{Dp}, which is about 0.03, is indicated by B–C. Thus, the total drag should be:

$$C_D = C_{Dp} + k \frac{C_L^2}{\pi \ AR_{ef}} = 0.03 + 0.0614 = 0.0914$$

as given by distance AC.

As a matter of fact, the actual measured total drag, C_D, was 0.17, ie, almost twice as big as expected. This is shown by the point which lies on the polar curve marked 'Foil on turntable'. For comparison, curve 2 in Fig 176 presents the variation in the induced drag component relevant to a foil of geometric ratio AR = 2.67, ie, the actual aspect ratio of the foil tested. This curve fits pretty realistically the experimentally established polar curve of the particular rigid foil.

One more point deserves to be mentioned; namely, the difference between the experimentally measured and the expected lift over drag ratio that can be regarded as an important criterion of foil efficiency. At $C_L = 1.0$, the total drag coefficient actually measured is about 0.17 (point E in Fig 176), so the relevant $L/D = \frac{1.0}{0.17} = 5.9$. If the theory were correct, the L/D ratio would be $\frac{1.0}{0.0914} = 10.94$, almost twice as high as that actually achieved.

These tests therefore invalidate the common belief that just by closing the gap between the tip of the foil (be it sail or rudder) and hull, the aspect ratio can roughly be doubled, with a resultant advantage of a higher L/D ratio. The detrimental effect of a large scale boundary layer, created along a hull body in motion, on the flow round any foil closely attached to it, cannot henceforth be ignored.

One more glance at Fig 176 will reveal that losses in terms of drag are not as large as might be expected, when the foil is lifted above the turntable and a gap opens below the lower tip of the foil. The fact that the additional drag (indicated by E–F) is reduced when the gap was larger (18 inches above as compared with 8 inches above the turntable) can be explained by taking into account the wind gradient effect shown in Fig 175. When the gap was 8 inches, the lower part of the foil was still affected by the non-uniform wind speed, but when the gap was increased to 18 inches, the whole foil operated in almost uniform flow.

THE EFFECT OF THE HULL ON SAIL FORCES

Past experiments on a Dragon class rig (Fig 63b and c) indicated that the hull interacting with the sails might contribute advantageously towards the aerodynamic forces, and that the magnitude of this contribution depends upon the heading angle, position of sails, shape of the hull, etc.

The following example, taken from the author's earlier work (2.4, 2.48), may illustrate the point. As might be expected, the part of the hull without rig which projects above the water contributes to the aerodynamic drag and side force that together result in a negative driving force when close-hauled. However, when the rig is added, the driving force of the whole model becomes larger than that produced by the sails alone. This mutual hull–sails interaction is demonstrated in Fig 177, which shows the driving force component, F_x, generated, with and without the hull, for a range of close-hauled heading angles.

To assess the hull–sail interference effect, with reference to fishing boats

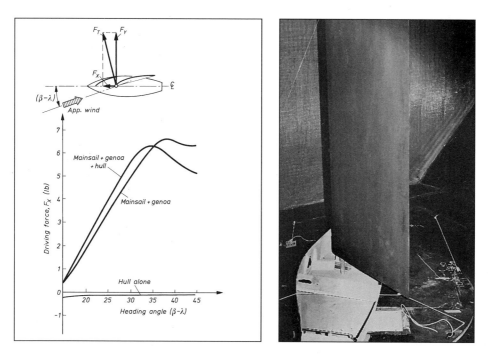

Fig 177 (far left) The effect of hull–sail interaction on the driving force in close-hauled conditions. Results are relevant to the Dragon model.

Fig 178 (left) The rigid unsymmetrical foil Clark Y tested together with hull (no deck) in close-hauled attitude.

without a deck, some tests were made with the rigid foil demonstrated in Fig 178. Results of these tests given in Fig 179 do not indicate similar advantages to those revealed in the case of the Dragon yacht test. Nevertheless, in close-reaching conditions, the presence of the hull becomes beneficial on account of the higher C_L; about 11 per cent higher as compared with $C_{L_{max}}$ of the foil alone.

To understand why in some conditions the presence of the hull improves the driving power of the rig, one should consider the interplay between the interfering wind gradient effect, and interaction between the flow underneath the lower edge of the sail and that above the hull deck. A contraction of the airflow above the deck due to the presence of the hull, and induced acceleration of the wind speed there – which is supposed to produce a more uniform flow – does not appear to be a dominating, beneficial factor. The test results and flow visualization do not support such an explanation. What then are the other factors which might explain the beneficial influence of the hull on sail forces?

In Fig 179 are two small sketches, a and b, which illustrate schematically the flow patterns round the upper edge of the windward side of the hull in close–hauled attitude, and also round the lower tip of the foil. The air impinging upon the hull, set at an oblique angle relative to the wind direction, will curl around the

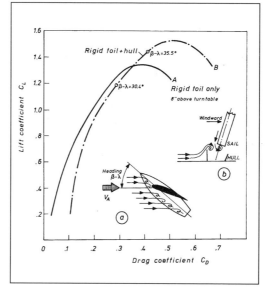

Fig 179 Polar diagrams of rigid foil tested with and without a hull (see also Photo in Fig 178). As shown in sketches a and b, two vortices develop; one over the windward side of the hull, and another beneath the lower tip of the sail. These contra-rotating vortices interact with each other, and their mutual action influences the total aerodynamic forces.

edge giving rise to a vortex similar in nature to that developing round the leading edges of a delta wing or crab claw sail. As shown in sketch b, which presents a view of the hull and foil as seen from behind, the flow must accelerate rapidly to get round the upper edge of the hull, thus initiating a conical vortex. The size and extent of this vortex, rolling up there and then streaming astern, will almost certainly depend on whether the hull has a deck or not, and on the height of the hull projecting above the water level.

Apart from the vortex developing over the windward side of the hull, there is another vortex – the tip vortex – also streaming astern from the lower tip of the foil. The cores of these two vortices are more or less *parallel* to each other when the boat is sailing close to the wind. In common with other velocity fields, the field created by each of these two vortices must interact with each other and this exerts a controlling influence upon the flow over the lower part of the sail. Although the nature of this influence may, for the time being, be obscure, the overall effect is such that the potential sail power can be improved, as demonstrated in Fig 177. However, this rather strong and beneficial sail–hull interaction gradually diminishes when the heading angle increases, and ultimately becomes detrimental.

Figure 180 illustrates just such a deterioration of foil performance when the boat changes her heading angle from close-hauled to reaching. Here it can be seen that the curve relevant to reaching (ß = 90 degrees) is shifted bodily towards higher drag and, at the same time, the maximum lift coefficient, C_{Lmax}, is reduced from 1.53 to 1.36, ie, by about 11 per cent.

Fig 180 Polar diagrams of the rigid unsymmetrical foil Clark Y, tested together with a hull in close-hauled and reaching conditions. The lower edge of the foil was 8 inches above the turntable. For details see Fig 174.

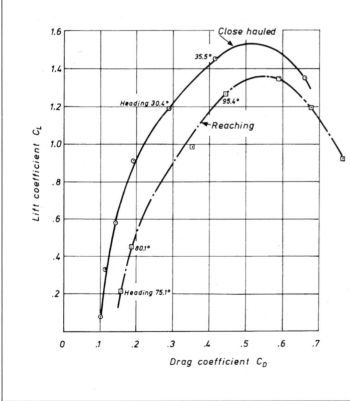

Similar (and even more drastic) reduction in sail power was observed in earlier tests on soft sails shown in Fig 173. This was initially attributed to the excessive twist and undesirable camber variation due to the lack of a kicking strap. This time, however, the possible influence of these two factors was eliminated. The rigid foil had no twist and its camber was constant. Therefore, the only factor that could be blamed was the flow pattern developing along and over the upper part of the hull, apparently different when close-hauled to that when reaching. Three photographs in Fig 181 give a clue as to what is happening. It becomes evident from photograph (a) that, although there is a sort of small scale turbulence visible in the airflow over the leeward side of the foil operating in close-hauled conditions, the airstream is attached to the foil contour and follows the camber up to the trailing edge. In photograph (b) the situation is quite different. The hull here, set at about 90 degrees to the wind, induces a large scale random turbulence or eddying in the airflow and, as a result, the flow over the leeward side of the sail does not appear to be attached. In such a condition, the lower part of the foil cannot be as effective in producing lift as the upper parts of sail depicted in photo (c). Consequently, C_{Lmax} must be reduced. This is reflected in Fig 180, and the results of tests confirm once again that the high lift capabilities of any foil are restricted by random, large scale turbulence, existing in the oncoming flow (Ref 2.49).

Test results given in Figs 177–181 demonstrate that, apart from the effect of wind gradient (to be expected in natural conditions), the interaction of the tip vortex developed at the lower edge of the sail, and independently over the windward side of the hull, is an important sail performance factor. Due to this interaction, the lift/drag ratio, ie, ε_A (which largely controls the close-hauled performance), and maximum attainable lift (which determines speed performance in reaching conditions) are affected. The presence of deck, cockpit openings, crew position and parasitic drag (Fig 94) also have an effect on boat performance.

Fig 181 The flow over the leeward side of the rigid foil when the hull is attached.

a) In the close-hauled attitude the flow is steady and follows the sail shape closely up to the trailing edge. Any irregularities in the smoke flow are due to the disturbances caused by the tube probe which injects the smoke. The tube probes are liable to cause flow disturbances. Nevertheless, they play an important part in flow surveying, and so in the solution of many problems in aerodynamics and hydrodynamics.

b) Large scale turbulence in the air flow caused by the hull. It is similar to the 'dirty' wind which appears in the wake of houses and trees. The lower part of the sail, which operates in this unsteady, eddying flow, continually changing in speed and direction, becomes less efficient aerodynamically.

c) The effect of the turbulence is to decrease the lift below that produced by the upper parts of the sail which will not be affected by the hull's influence (Ref 2.49).

THE EFFECT OF ASPECT RATIO ON THE PERFORMANCE OF RECTANGULAR SAILS

Figure 182 presents the results of tests on four different rectangular sails of aspect ratio 1.0, 1.3, 1.6 and 1.9, with the same camber of about 12 per cent of the chord. The attached picture shows one of the sails (of AR = 1.0), and the supporting wires which kept the leading and trailing edges under high tension so that the sail camber was reasonably constant along the sail height.

It is seen that, depending on the aspect ratio, the maximum values of lift vary considerably. As indicated in the plot, C_{Lmax} increased from 1.67 for AR = 1.9, to 2.13 for AR = 1.0, ie by about 28 per cent. Such a substantial increment of C_L is due to the dominating influence of the tip vortices developing round the upper and lower edges of the sail shown in Fig 69a, and similar to those observed round the crab claw sail. Their increasing importance as the AR is reduced should not be surprising: with decreasing AR the tip vortices are brought closer together. For lower aspect ratios – in the order of 1.0 – the concentration of vortex energy per unit length of the foil (span) becomes so intense that the boundary layer which tends to accumulate over the front or rear part of the foil section (Fig 53b) is swept away, and the flow continues without breakdown to high angles of incidence. This is evidenced by the data in Fig 182. Tip vortices so beneficial in one respect must, however, be paid for in other respects; the price is higher drag and hence lower L/D ratio as compared with L/D relevant to foils of higher AR.

Unlike the high aspect ratio sail, where the flow breaks down at a relatively small incidence angle, the low aspect ratio planform is much less sensitive to an increase in incidence angle, because the tip vortex flow does not break down until a much higher incidence angle is reached. This explains why low aspect

Fig 182 The results of tests on sails of four different AR = 1.0, 1.3, 1.6 and 1.9, set without the disturbing influence of a mast. The photograph shows the sail of AR = 1.0 supported by wires (luff and leech) which were kept under high tension in order to maintain a uniform camber (about 12 per cent) over the sail height.

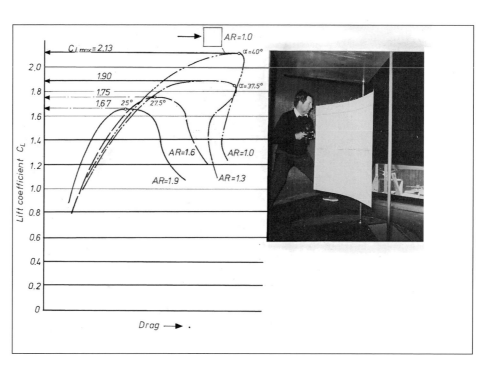

ratio gaff rigs (Figs 127 and 131) can deliver greater driving force in close-reaching and reaching conditions than the high aspect ratio Bermuda type of rig.

In conclusion, the lift produced by sails largely depends on which type of mixed flow actually dominates: either the type of flow in which the airstream is basically attached to the sail surface (classic aerofoil theory assumes such a flow, as shown in Figs 42, 53a and 54a), or else the spiral, trailing vortex type of flow (Fig 69). Higher L/D ratio is associated with the former: larger C_{Lmax} with the latter. One cannot have the best of both worlds at the same time. But variable geometry of the foil, ie the planform variation, could do that particular trick.

Figure 183 illustrates the performance of a soft, rectangular sail of AR = 1.0 tested in two

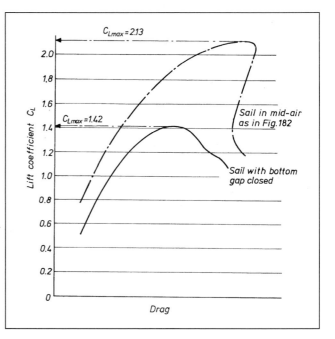

different positions: first in a free airstream in which the flow is symmetrical in relation to the upper and lower edges (see photo in Fig 182), and secondly, with its lower tip gap closed. In the second case, the flow could not possibly be symmetrical in relation to the top and bottom edges of the sail. The upper part of the sail was, as before, affected by the action of the trailing vortex, but the lower part was immersed in the boundary layer of the wind tunnel floor. As already argued earlier, such a boundary layer of greater or lesser thickness always exists in close proximity to the hull deck where a sail is concerned, or near the bottom of the hull in the case of a rudder.

It will be seen that the reduction in maximum lift for the sail with the bottom gap closed was large indeed – from 2.13 to 1.42, ie, about 33 per cent – followed by an increase in drag and hence an undesirable drop in L/D ratio. This test corroborates earlier tests on rigid foils, and thus invalidates the common view expressed in most textbooks on yacht design which is that if a sail is a so-called 'deck scraper', its AR will be doubled by the end–plate effect of the deck.

Fig 183 The results of tests on a mastless sail of AR = 1.0 operating in mid-air (so that the flow round the upper and lower edges was free). Subsequently, the sail was lowered to the wind tunnel floor, thereby closing the gap between its lower edge and the floor.

THE EFFECT OF DRYING SAILCLOTH ON C_L AND C_D (POROSITY)

A lift force originates primarily in the form of pressure distributed over the sail surface. Lift is generated as a result of a pressure difference between the windward and leeward sides of the sail surface. For that reason, the air porosity of sail fabric is another important parameter in rig performance. Porosity can be tested by a variety of methods (Ref 2.4) which usually involve timing the passage of a known quantity of air through the fabric, under a given pressure.

In the series of tests on artisanal rigs, the rig of sprit 3 (sketch 3, Fig 133) was made of fairly porous cotton as well as Terylene. The cotton sail was assessed in its dry condition (with the weave open) and then after being sprayed with water to tighten the weave through shrinkage, thereby reducing porosity. It was then compared with the Terylene sail of the same configuration.

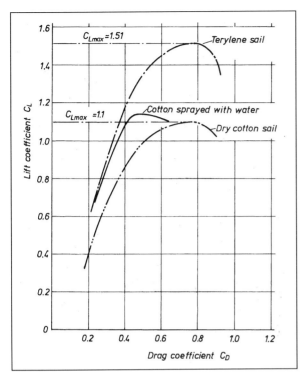

Fig 184 The effect of porosity on sail efficiency (sprit rig). Porous sailcloth allows pressure to equalize on either side of a sail; this reduces lift.

Figure 184 presents the results plotted in the form of three polar curves, C_L versus C_D. As might be expected, the sail made of Terylene is superior to both the dry and wet cotton sail. Of course, a more porous cloth allows greater transfer of air through the fabric into the boundary layer developing along the leeward side of the sail, thus accelerating separation and reducing the pressure difference between the leeward and windward sides of the sail.

We can see that the maximum lift coefficient of the Terylene sail was $C_{Lmax} = 1.5$, while in the same conditions, the C_{Lmax} of the dry cloth was about 1.1. The Terylene sail was therefore capable of producing about 37 per cent more power in reaching conditions. The windward ability of the Terylene sail was about 7 degrees higher than that of the dry cotton sail, but only about 2 degrees higher as compared with the same sail when freshly sprayed with water. These tests show the importance of porosity for windward sailing. If nothing but a cotton sail can be used (as is often the case in many developing countries), its pointing ability to windward can be improved by about 5 degrees if the sail pores are sealed with water, a trick which is often performed by fishermen of all countries. Water evaporates quite quickly under the drying influence of air currents, however, and so the sail efficiency deteriorates to that pertaining when the fabric is dry.

Table 10 illustrates this effect as recorded at one-minute intervals. The sail was set in the close-hauled attitude with the sheeting fixed, and a constant wind of 26.46 ft/sec (8 m/sec).

Table 10	Effect of drying sailcloth on CL and CD (porosity)	
TIME IN MINUTES	CL	CD
0	0.76	0.267
1	0.75	0.267
2	0.73	0.266
3	0.71	0.260
4	0.63	0.263
5	0.59	0.263
6	0.55	0.262
7	0.55	0.257

13 • WING SAILS AND OTHER UNCONVENTIONAL RIGS

'Human beings find it difficult in all spheres to base their opinions upon evidence rather than upon their hopes.'

Bertrand Russell, The Scientific Outlook

It may be that soft, conventional sails of the Bermuda and other types are destined to be displaced, as a propulsion system for fast sailing craft and in commercial maritime sailing, by rigid or semi-rigid wing sails. It is therefore desirable to estimate possible advantages offered by some already tested wing sails, and other unconventional lift-producing devices, in terms of their basic aerodynamic characteristics such as lift, drag, pressure distribution etc.

SINGLE ELEMENT WING SAILS

The purpose of the restricted experiments carried out in the wind tunnel by the author was to develop a viable *single element* rig which would produce maximum driving force per unit area for a given leading edge height. A number of rigs shown in Figs 185–187 were modified in the course of tests to provide 5 different configurations. All the rigs were supported by cantilever masts.

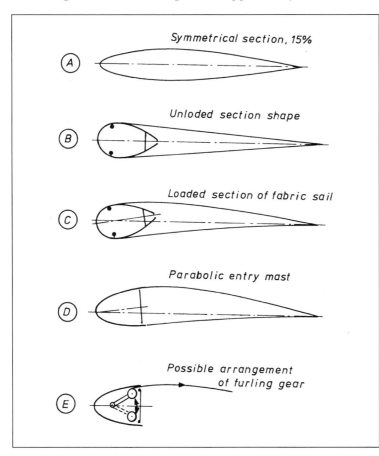

Fig 185 Cross-sections of the rigs tested.

A) A 15 per cent thick symmetrical section of rig A shown in Fig 186.

B) An 8.5 per cent thick, unloaded section shape of rig C.

C) The approximate shape of a double-skin section B for rig C, assumed under wind pressure. The thickness ratio of the section is about 8.5 per cent.

D) The approximate shape of a double-skin section of rig D, shown in Fig 187, assumed under wind pressure. Its thickness ratio is about 13.5 per cent. The rig is supported by a specially made mast of parabolic entry shape which could accommodate furling gear.

E) A vertical roller reefing system mounted inside the mast. This particular rig, with its roller-reefing system sited within the mast section, is patent pending (W M Symons, 8538B 12th Way No St Petersburg, FI, 33702, USA).

Fig 186 (right) Rig A of an elliptical planform and symmetrical section shown in Fig 185A.

Fig 187 (far right) Rig D of a rectangular planform with end-plates. Its double-skin section is shown in Fig 185D. This rig, and also rig C (of identical planform and end-plates), were tested with single and double-skin sections.

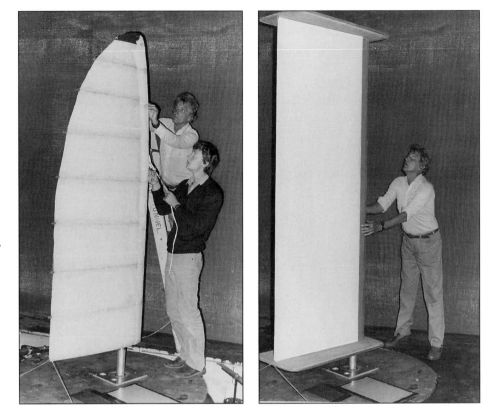

Details of three basic sections are presented in Fig 185: symmetrical section A, used for a wing sail of a roughly elliptical planform shown in Fig 186, and two non-symmetrical sections, C and D, which assumed that shape (originally B) under wind pressure. Wing sail C was supported by a commercially available streamline section mast, but sail D by a specially-made mast with parabolic entry shape. Both wing sails C and D were of rectangular planform and equipped with endplates as shown in Fig 187. Sails C and D were tested with a double and single skin made of Terylene sailcloth. Their basic dimensions, ie, height and width along the foot, were the same: 7.5 ft (2.28 m) and 3.0 ft (0.92 m) respectively. Tests were carried out at wind speed V = 24.0 ft/sec (c. 14.5 knots), ie the Reynolds Number was about 0.46×10^6.

The relative merits of the rigs can be assessed from Fig 188, which presents the relevant C_L versus C_D curves, interpreted in terms of driving component C_x delivered in close-hauled conditions at the heading angle 30 degrees. Thus, rig D, with the parabolic entry mast, produces about twice as much driving power as rig A with the symmetrical section, and about 30 per cent more driving force than rig C supported by a streamline, conventional mast. Also included for comparison is the polar curve of a triangular sail of the international Finn class, the geometry of which is given in Fig 64. This sail was supported by a cantilevered, rotating mast, and its height was the same as that of other rigs tested. We can see that the potential driving component, C_x, of the Finn sail is about the same as that produced by rig A with the symmetrical section, but half of that produced by rig D with the parabolic entry mast. The order of merits of all rigs discussed in Fig 188 should, more or less, be maintained while bearing

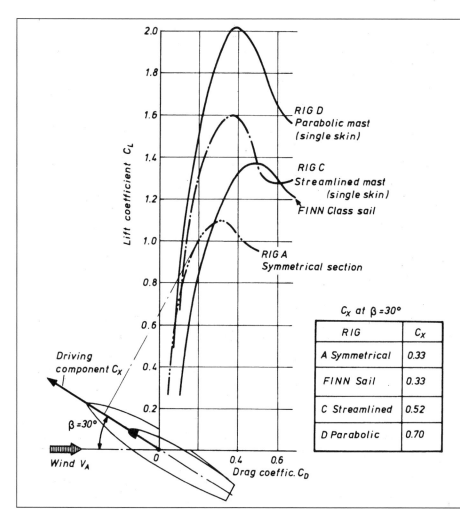

Fig 188 (left) Polar diagrams C_L versus C_D of three wing sails A, C and D, shown in Figs 185–187. For comparison, the characteristics of a Finn sail are also included (see Fig 65).

Fig 189 (opposite: top right) Polar diagrams of wing sail D (Fig 187) tested with single and double skin.

Fig 190 (opposite: bottom right) Upwind sailing. Effect of boat speed V_S on the apparent wind speed V_A and course sailed ß relative to V_A. When the boat speed increases, the apparent wind becomes stronger and is drawn more ahead (smaller angle). The harder the wind blows, the faster the boat will go to windward. Her speed performance will largely depend on the sail lift which can be attained, and on the aerodynamic drag angle ε_A which accompanies it. However, the lift which can be used is limited by the power of the hull to resist heeling. Thus, under these conditions, the driving force that can be obtained from the sail depends only on the ε_A, ie, L/D ratio (see Figs 109 and 110).

away up to close-reaching conditions. Within these points of sailing, sails operate at a relatively small angle of incidence to the apparent wind, ie, below the angle of stall.

DOUBLE SKIN VERSUS SINGLE SKIN SAILS

Figure 189 shows the rather intriguing results of the test on rig D (parabolic entry mast) with single and double skin. Leaving only the single, leeward skin, the maximum lift coefficient is increased by about 16 per cent, at relatively small cost in terms of increased drag in the range of the lower values of C_L applicable to strong winds in close-hauled conditions only.

On other courses, particularly in light and moderate winds, the single skin rig is superior to the double skin one, and for other practical and technological reasons (reefing inside the mast) preferable. By means of furling gear, such a reefing system allows the sail area to be quickly trimmed to match wind and sea conditions. Besides, it also allows almost instant stowage of the sail, without the use of sail ties.

Tests on a conventional mast with single and double skin demonstrated similar trends. With a single skin sail, attached to the centreline of the conventional

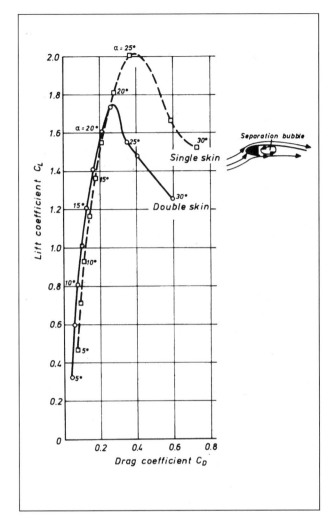

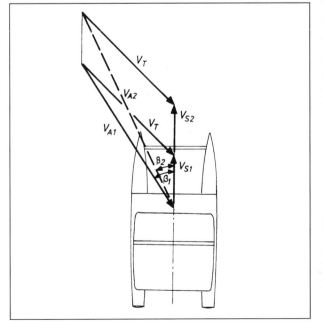

spar, a small drag penalty was paid relative to the same spar with single skin attached to the leeside; but no significant differences in the maximum lift were observed.

In conclusion, solution D in Fig 185 appears to be the most promising as a single element propulsive system, and deserving of further development.

Returning to Fig 188, we can see why the wing sails of type C or D are likely to be of greater advantage in fast boats such as multihulls. The superiority of wing sails over a conventional, soft sail rig like that of a Finn, lies in the smallness of their drag angle, ε_A, over a large range of lift coefficients, C_L. The drag coefficient of a soft sail, even if the sail is not flapping, is considerably higher than that of any of wing sail discussed in Fig 188. At a low lift coefficient which involves flapping, the comparison of relevant drag angles, ε_A, is even more in favour of the wing sail.

When the boat speed increases from V_{s1} (Fig 190), the apparent wind, initially V_{A1}, will be drawn more ahead, as indicated by the vector V_{A2}, so that the β_2 angle becomes smaller. Hence, according to the course theorem (Eq 17):

$$\beta = \varepsilon_A + \varepsilon_H$$

The benefit of a reduction in the sail angle, ε_A, becomes evident. Considering in turn the merits of the sails in windward work, and reaching in light and moderate winds, the unsymmetrical sails of type C and D maintain their superiority; they have much higher lift coefficients as compared with those produced by the soft sail Finn rigs or symmetrical wing sails of type A (Fig 186), though under these conditions, the normal soft sail rig will be superior to a symmetrical wing sail A of the same area.

The rigs discussed so far are not directly comparable for a number of reasons: the differences in their aspect ratio and the endplate effect to mention just two. Nevertheless, Fig 189 gives a rough exposition of some important aerodynamic characteristics of these diverse rigs, and trends that might guide the design of a propulsion system for high speed craft.

MULTI-FOIL (MULTI-SLOTTED) WING SAILS

There is no question that accumulated and available knowledge about multi-slotted airfoils, already developed for aircraft applications, may advantageously be used to design propulsion systems for high speed craft or wind assisted ships. Such rigid, multi-slotted airfoils are capable of producing significantly higher lift coefficients than conventional soft sails. Figure 191, based on tests made by Weick and Shortal (Ref 2.50) is a case in point. We can see in Fig 191a that multiple slots are relatively ineffective on the plain airfoil unless they include a slot near the leading edge – an effective headsail–mainsail combination already known to most sailors. For the two–slotted combination without slat, configuration number 6 (Fig 191a) produces the highest lift coefficient. A similar two-slotted section, but with deflected flap – number 4 in Fig 191b – generates $C_L = 2.442$, ie, about 45 per cent more lift than combination 6, and 90 per cent more lift than parent section number 1 in Fig 191a. No soft, thin sail combination comes close to this lift value.

It should be noted that the increment in lift coefficient of airfoils with multiple slots varies greatly, depending on the arrangement of slots and flaps, on the effective camber of the whole combination, and on the aspect ratio of the wing sail; but the importance of slot geometry cannot be overemphasized. In order to establish the exact form of the flap and/or slat to obtain the highest lift with a reasonably low drag angle, ε_A, a good deal of research into published data will be required. Experimentation will also be necessary, because the research such as that presented in Fig 191 has concentrated principally on its aeronautical implications, and not on its relevance in maritime terms.

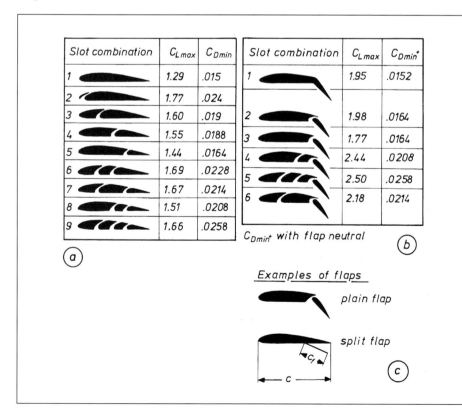

Fig 191 Effect of slots and flaps on the aerodynamic characteristics of a Clark Y wing of AR = 6. Minimum drag coefficient C_{Dmin} in table b refers to wing with flap neutral (Ref 2.50). Trailing edge flaps, whether plane or split, are evidently camber-increasing devices. Many and varied flap forms and configurations have been developed, some employing slats and slots, in order to delay separation and so to increase lift.

Fig 192a (below left) Variation of lift coefficient with angle of incidence for two different cambers of a double-slotted flap section of the *Patient Lady* wing shown in Fig 193 (Ref 2.51). The rapid drop in lift is characteristic of thick foils operating at low Reynolds Number (see Appendix 2, Fig A11–A13).

Figure 192 will serve to illustrate the influence of the effective camber of the two–slotted, flapped section, on the aerodynamic performance of a wing sail relevant to a C-class catamaran of the *Patient Lady* family depicted in Fig 193. This particular IYRU class is the ultimate development class, with rules which allow for almost unlimited variations on sail and hull designs. Their advanced wing sails are in the forefront of sailing boat rig technology, and on overall performance – in terms of available lift and L/D maximum – they are far superior to any conventional soft cloth rig. As a result, the wing-sailed catamarans may become the fastest course racing boats, provided the weather conditions are right. The results of the 1976 Little America's Cup Challenge are an excellent illustration of the merits and demerits of a modern wing sail versus a soft sail demonstrated at different wind speeds.

The American *Aquarius V*'s boomless, fully battened, soft sail rig of essentially elliptic planform (see sketch to the left of Fig 192b) permits twist and sail

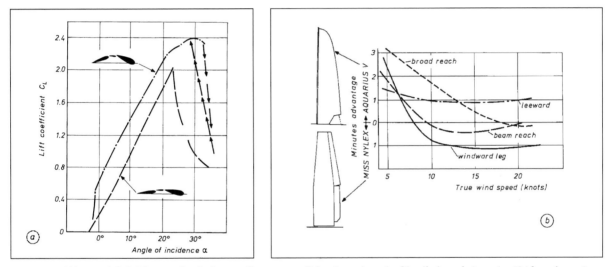

Fig 192b (Above right) Observed relative performance of the American 'soft' sail rigged *Aquarius V* (the winner) versus the winged *Miss Nylex* of Australia recorded during the Little America's Cup Challenge of 1976. The relative superiority and weaknesses of these two configurations for four different courses sailed relative to the true wind of increasing speed are given in minutes. The table below gives some of the geometry and weight characteristics of these two contrasting C-class rigs.

	Aquarius V	*Miss Nylex*
Mast height	36.5 ft	36 ft
Sail AR	4.4	4.3
Sail area	300 sq ft	300 sq ft
Rig weight	98 lb	210 lb
Crew weight	315 lb	355 lb
Sailing weight	790 lb	1035 lb

The C-class catamaran is an international development class with basic limits only on boat length (25 feet), maximum width (14 ft), maximum sail area (300 square feet), and the boat's crew of two. Beyond that, imagination and the sponsor's bank account are the only limits.

The figure is based on a paper 'Wing Sail Versus Soft Rig: An Analysis of the Successful Little America's Cup Challenge of 1976' by W S Bradfield and Suresh Madhavan, Chesapeake Sailing Symposium, Annapolis, 1977.

Designers of the *Patient Lady* C-class family of catamarans first pioneered and then proved the virtue of multi-element foil against the single element rigid or semi-rigid rigs. These are, however, too heavy and cumbersome for reliable open-water work.

camber control up to 20 per cent by means of a lightweight, bendy and rotating mast of a parabolic section.

The Australian *Miss Nylex* wing sail (also shown in Fig 192b) is more than double the weight of the *Aquarius V*'s. Its twist and camber control (from zero to about 16 per cent) are provided by the 25 per cent chord, full-span flap system. The wing has a symmetrical NACA 0015 section with maximum flap deflection up to 40 degrees. It was expected that winged *Miss Nylex* should win; but she did not.

The observed relative performance comparison for these two competing C-class catamarans shown in Fig 192b was obtained by plotting the recorded time differences on each leg – to windward, beam reach, broad reach and leeward – versus the corresponding true wind speed. The relevant curves, based on smoothed racing data taken from the reference given in the caption, indicate that: (1) *Aquarius V* is better than *Miss Nylex* on all points of sailing below 8 knots of the true wind velocity, V_T. (2) *Aquarius V* shows a better performance to leeward and on the broad reach over a large range of V_T. (3) *Miss Nylex* demonstrates better performance to windward in V_T over 8 knots and better reaching performance in V_T over 9.5 knots.

The authors of the 'post mortem' on these racing results came to the conclusion that: 'the *Miss Nylex* wing sail rig has the advantage both in magnitude of thrust available and ratio of thrust to heeling force for all low range (strong wind) and high range (light wind) values of aerodynamic force attainable by either rig, especially the large values. However, as events proved, the aerodynamic advantage by itself is not good enough. The total rig performance must be evaluated in terms of weight penalty inherent in the wing structure.'

This difference in all-up weight between the two boats was taken as 245 lbs (111.2 kg) and the resulting lower hull resistance of the lighter *Aquarius V* was assumed to be the dominant, race winning, factor, despite her aerodynamic disadvantage. On the other hand, in stronger winds, *Miss Nylex* gains the advantage because the greater heeling stability due to all-up weight permits her to extract proportionately more power from her wing sail. In the final analysis, the authors argued that 'if it were possible to build a wing of as little weight as that of the soft sail rig, *Aquarius V*, would never have won at all.'

Without denying that the displacement differences played their roles, there is one factor that was ignored altogether in examination of the race results, and that is the Reynolds Number effect. Figures A11–A13 in Appendix 2 vividly demonstrate significant anomalies in lift and drag produced by thick foils operating at *small* Reynolds Numbers, and to the detriment of their efficiency as thrust-producing devices. Their lift can be substantially lower and drag higher than those produced by the same foils at *larger* Reynolds Numbers (see Eq 12a).

Referring again to Fig 192b, it will be seen that *Aquarius V* enjoyed the greatest advantage on a broad reach in light winds – about 3 minutes at V_T equals 5 knots. For this superiority, consider the reason in the light of Figs A11–A13 of Appendix 2. Since the apparent wind on which the aerodynamic forces directly depend gradually decreases as the boat comes more and more off the wind (Fig 95), it can be estimated that at the true wind speed, $V_T = 5$ knots, the apparent wind V_A was 3 knots or less. Taking the average sail chord of *Miss Nylex* as 8 feet (2.44 m), the relevant Re number, calculated from Eq 3 given in Appendix 2, is about 250,000 or less, ie, in the region in which unusual performance characteristics of thick foils should be expected. Unfortunately, little reliable data exists in the range of Re numbers between 200,000 and 300,000, but it is known that 'the design of airfoils operating at Re below 300,000 is still a black art'.

Thus it might have been credible to attribute the superiority of *Aquarius V* in winds below 8 knots entirely to her lesser displacement if the Reynolds Number effect had not been involved. Certainly the *Miss Nylex*'s greater hydrodynamic drag, because of her larger displacement, might be compensated for, provided her aerodynamic drag (the drag angle, ε_A) was sufficiently lower than that of *Aquarius V* (see Eqs 17 and 26). Apparently, *Miss Nylex*'s greater weight proved to be too much of a disadvantage for her wing sail, operating in a low wind speed regime, to overcome.

As the winds pick up, the advantage shifts to the heavier boat for two reasons: she can fly a-hull, and the performance of her wing sail improves in terms of the aerodynamic drag angle, ε_A.

To sum up, when considering performance problems like this, one should assume that a number of factors, some not perceptible at first, may be involved; otherwise we may easily delude ourselves into believing that we are objective.

How does a multi-element wing sail produce so much drive? As suggested in another of the author's books (Ref 2.4) the multi-slotted foil can be regarded as a further development of the single-slotted foil. Thus, the action of the more complicated multiple system of airfoils, such as that shown in Fig 193 or Fig 194a, can be disentangled by considering the effect of the front foil on the following one. In principle, they interact like the jib–mainsail combination discussed earlier (Figs 43–46). In that combination of foils, each foil is subject not only to its own effects but also to those of the other foil or foils. In a favourable

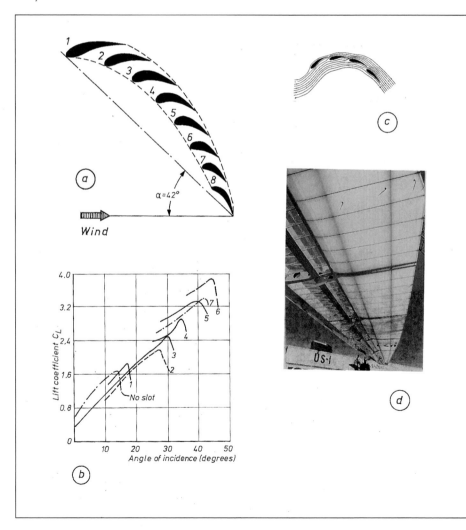

Fig 194

a) An RAF (Royal Aircraft Factory) eight-slat section with seven slots set at incidence angle $\alpha = 42°$ for maximum lift.

b) The recorded lift coefficient at this angle was about 3.9 – a three-fold increase over that of a single parent section.

c) Multi-slotted foil similar in principle to that shown in sketch (a).

d) A picture of the *Stars and Stripes* wing sail with wool tufts attached to the third panel (flap). These help to identify areas of flow separation and stall.

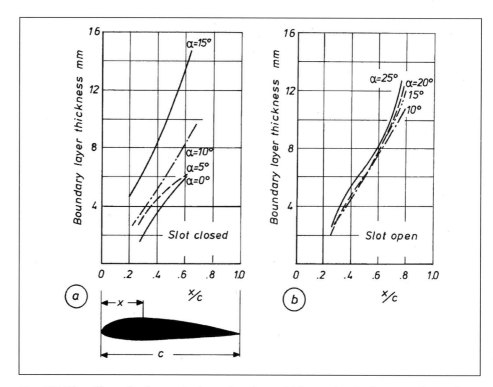

Fig 195 The effect of a slot on the boundary layer thickness developing over the suction side of the main wing (based on Ref 2.52).

a)   With the slot closed, the boundary layer thickens rapidly as the incidence angle is increased and tends towards separation.

b)   With the slot open, the boundary layer thickness changes little with increasing incidence angle; the stall is prevented until much higher lift is reached. As in the case of a single airfoil, the high lift capabilities of multi-slotted airfoil are restricted by the BL accumulation and finally its separation on the suction surface.

arrangement, the boundary layer thickness at any point along the multi-slotted section changes little with the increasing incidence angle (Fig 195). So the flow may remain attached, even to the trailing edge of the low pressure surface of the whole system of airfoils. In these type of flows, shown in Fig 194b, separation and stall are prevented. This accounts, firstly, for an incredible increase in the lift coefficient, C_L, approaching 4 for the six-slot combination (Fig 194c); and secondly, for an increase of the usable range of incidence angles relevant to reaching (tacking downwind) conditions.

It is thus seen that a multi-slotted wing sail, *when properly designed and set*, has enormous lift-producing capabilities. But what do I mean by 'properly designed and set'? As far as the available data permit any straightforward conclusions to be formulated, it is that the obtainable increment in maximum lift coefficient is sensitive to the foil-slot geometry. For any slot arrangement there is a rather unique condition, depending largely on the position of interacting foils relative to each other, and on the incidence angle, when the flow leaves the trailing edge of the upstream foil *tangentially*. Under this condition, the boundary layer developing over the entire system may remain attached. Otherwise, a breakdown of the flow over the suction surface of the next downstream foil, or both, is likely to occur. Consequently, the full aerodynamic potential of the multi-component airfoil cannot be obtained. Such a misshapen configuration, leading to separation and stall, can be detected by means of wool tufts attached to the flap, as demonstrated in Figs 194d and 198b.

The beneficial influence of the leading (upstream) foil on the pressure distribution and the boundary layer behaviour over the downstream foil, is only possible if the gap between them is sufficiently small. With increasing distance, the effect diminishes rapidly. That is, there is a certain optimum gap and overlap between interacting foils which prevents separation before the flow reaches the trailing edge of the flap. This is schematically illustrated in Fig 196.

Consider the flow around the main foil in Fig 196a, interacting with the leading edge. Boundary layers (BL^S) are formed on the upper and lower surfaces of the slat, and are subsequently shed at its trailing edge as a wake. This wake may or may not mix with the BL developing over the upper surface of the main foil. Similar flow situation can be observed between the main foil and the slotted flap, shown in Fig 196b, with enlarged BL thickness. Experiments have demonstrated that for positions of the flap (and slat too), for which the multi-component airfoil combination yields optimum aerodynamic performance, the

Fig 196a Typical development of healthy, attached boundary layer on a two-slotted foil which yields optimum aero-dynamic perfor-mance.

Fig 196b Schematic picture of the BL developing around the deployed flap. Both pictures, with greatly enlarged BL thickness, are based on Ref 2.53 and 2.54. The above method of BL control (without artificial blowing or suction), whereby separation and lift loss can be prevented or delayed is called *passive Bl control*.

It is perhaps interesting to mention that in the early days of aircraft development it was assumed that lift and drag were predestined characteristics of every airfoil, with which no man could or should tamper. Devices like slots, slats and flaps were often derisively termed 'slattery and flappery'.

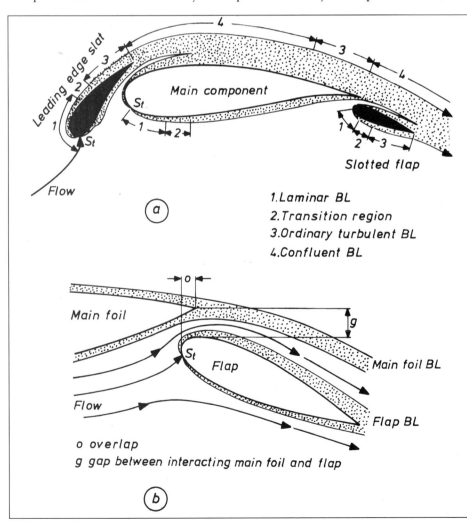

1. Laminar BL
2. Transition region
3. Ordinary turbulent BL
4. Confluent BL

o overlap
g gap between interacting main foil and flap

BLs developing over the main foil and over the slat or flap retain their separate identities. The meaning of *separate identities* is explained in Fig 196b. The main foil sheds its BL in the form of a wake leaving the trailing edge tangentially. Dotted stripes labelled 'Main foil BL' show the upper and lower BL. Beginning from the stagnation point S_T on the flap, two other BL^S gradually develop, as indicated by the dotted stripes. The blank narrow stripe between the main foil, BL, and the flap BL indicates that along this stripe the air flows undisturbed in a frictionless manner. That is, the confluent BL^S from the main foil and from the flap *do not mix* in this area. The confluent BL^S therefore retain their separate identities.

The airflow between the slat and the main foil can be analysed and interpreted likewise. If mixing of the two different BL^S does occur within the slot area, the BL of the main airfoil will be thickened, and so the propensity to separation towards the trailing edge will increase.

TUNING PROBLEMS OF MULTI-SLOTTED WING SAILS

'Not all wisdom is new, nor is all folly out of date.'

Bertrand Russell

Like many other human inventions, the multi-slotted wing sails, which are good in one respect as a means of developing driving force, are not so good in other respects. Tests on multi-slotted foils have indicated that, with multiple slot arrangements such as those shown in Figs 194a or 196a, the increase in the maximum lift which can be obtained is two to three times the usual C_{Lmax} of a slotless foil of AR = 6. However, the attainable lift/drag ratio, L/D, drops from about 20 for a slotless foil to about 6 for seven slots. This dramatic decrease in L/D ratio, which negates the benefit of any high lift capability, should be viewed primarily as the result of the quadratic increase of induced drag with lift, as reflected in formula 24. Another reason is that, due to presence of slots (surface irregularities), the foil surface is not aerodynamically smooth and this inflicts a drag penalty.

Attempts have been made to maintain low drag with slots open by locating the slots in such a position that there would be no flow through them in the low lift condition in order to gain high speed. Such combinations have however failed to improve the L/D ratio over that of the plain (*slotless*) wing section. Figure 191b reveals that any combination of slots investigated causes a substantial increase in the minimum profile drag, C_{Dmin}. And this drag penalty increases with the number of slots. Thus, for example, the minimum drag C_{Dmin} of combination 5 is about 70 per cent higher than that of the plain wing with section 1 (flap neutral).

The Little America's Cup course is 50 per cent upwind, for which the rig should be tuned to get a high L/D ratio (small εA). The other half – the downwind legs – require a rig with a high lift capability (see Table 9) to obtain a superior maximum driving force (for downwind tacking). To optimize the wing sail shape to meet these two different requirements is a formidable exercise. Wing sails are not as easy to adjust to changing course and wind conditions as soft sails.

Catamarans, like C-class or *Stars and Stripes* craft, have essentially three controls on the wing sail. Firstly, the mainsheet controls the angle of the whole rig in relation to the boat centreline. Secondly, the camber is controlled by changing the relative position of the three vertical panels (foils), which constitute the two-slotted wing. The third control is the twist control, whereby a number of flaps that make up the trailing edge of the wing can be adjusted to match the twist in the apparent wind.

It can be shown (Ref 2.4) that the speed made good to windward, Vmg, ie, the speed to the next mark but not the speed through the water can be estimated from the following formula:

$$\frac{V_{mg}}{V_T} = \frac{\cot \gamma}{\cot(\gamma - \beta) - \cot \gamma} \qquad \text{Eq 26}$$

but $\qquad \beta = \varepsilon_A + \varepsilon_H \qquad\qquad$ Eq 17 (repeat)

When sailing upwind the apparent wind angle, ß, of C-class catamarans is about 23 degrees. In such a condition the wing sail should operate at relatively small angle of incidence, α. close to the angle at which L/D maximum, ie, minimum drag angle, ε_A, is obtained. This requirement is clearly indicated in formula 26; both ε_A and ε_H are the denominator of the expression. Hence, in order to maximize the speed made good to windward, Vmg, for a given true wind speed, V_T, the aerodynamic drag angle, ε_A, should be minimized. Therefore all slots should be closed, so the leeward side of the wing sail along its entire height is smooth, resembling that of the parent section I in Fig 191a. Any opened up slot in flow condition when stall is not to be expected incurs drag penalty.

Formula 26 also implies that the speed performance to windward can be improved by reducing the hydrodynamic drag angle, ε_H. By keeping the windward hull at its optimal height – just clear of the water, with less wetted surface (Fig 193) – ε_H is substantially reduced and so the boat sails faster. When both hulls are immersed in waves the motion can be quite jerky, inflicting both aerodynamic and hydrodynamic losses. Relatively heavy wing sails, with a high centre of gravity and hence large inertia, are bound to encourage pitching and jerky motion, especially in rough seas.

In light winds it may not be possible to develop a large enough aerodynamic heeling force to keep the windward hull flying and, at the same time, maintain the ε_A optimum. Both ε_A and ε_H are *interdependent variables*, and it must be accepted as an *axiom* that, as such, these two variables cannot be minimized at the same time – mathematically this is an impossible operation. Thus, for a given ß angle, an increase in, say, ε_A, must necessarily be accompanied by decrease in ε_H and vice-versa. To keep the hull flying it may be necessary to increase the camber of the wing sail and trim the wing in order to generate maximum lift. In addition, the crew may be shifted to the leeward hull, as demonstrated in Fig 193; eventually a soft cloth jib may be hoisted if the wing alone is not capable of heeling the catamaran to the desired angle.

The driving power generated must be correlated with the wind strength, and the crew must constantly adjust the sail camber and its incidence to follow changes in the apparent wind. For gusty winds it is highly recommended that there should be some sort of panic button for emergency situations, when a sudden puff of wind hits and the windward hull comes out of the water rapidly. For example, the mainsheet of the *Stars and Stripes* is controlled by a hydraulic system with a quick release valve that lets the helmsman ease the sail instantly. To quote John Marshall, the design team coordinator of *Stars and Stripes* (2.56): 'We wanted the helmsman to have ultimate control of the boat because cats are so reactive and skittish that we didn't want to get into a situation where the helmsman was yelling at someone to let the sheet out. There is no way you can really have an effective panic button if you have a block-and-tackle mainsheet system. The valve lets the trimmer ease the sheet a fraction of an inch or dump it all at once... You never get a chance to relax, not even going downwind because you're still flying a hull... Capsizing is always a possibility, and it's still in the back of everyone's mind... the boat may go over in a minute – even in eight knots of wind.'

When sailing on a beam reach, the apparent wind on winged catamarans is about 35 degrees, increasing to 80 degrees when tacking downwind. In these modes of sailing, the main requirement is to obtain the greatest possible driving force by maximizing lift with almost complete disregard to the drag component (see Table 9). To generate maximum power, the crew must constantly adjust not only the wing camber but also its twist, to allow for the difference in apparent wind below and aloft (Fig 197). It has been found that an accurately matched amount of twist in the wing may be devastatingly effective in the downwind condition which is traditionally the Achilles' heel of wing sail boats.

Fig 197 The complex system of foils, slats and flaps of one of the *Patient Lady* family of wing sails (*PL IV*) permits control of camber, twist and flow of air through slots (see Fig 196). Camber – the effective curvature of the multi-slotted wing sail – may constantly be adjusted to match the driving force (and heeling force too) to the apparent wind strength and the course sailed. The wing sail of *Stars and Stripes* shown in Fig 92 and 193 was controlled in a similar manner.

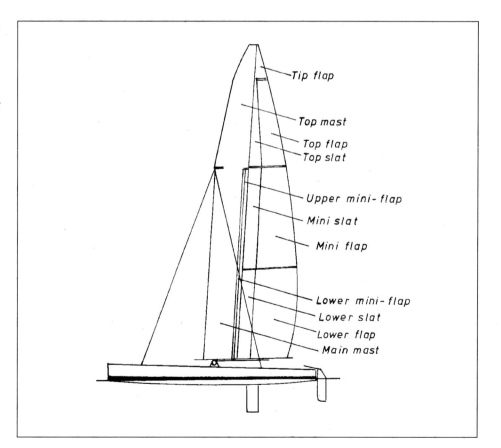

Alternative wing sail solutions Another auxiliary device (apart from the slotted flap) that permits a change in the geometric and aerodynamic characteristics of the wing sail is the split flap. Such a wing section, shown in Fig 198a is the key to the design of the British C-class cat *Hinge,* which competed (unsuccessfully) against the Australian defender *The Edge* in the 1987 Little America's Cup.

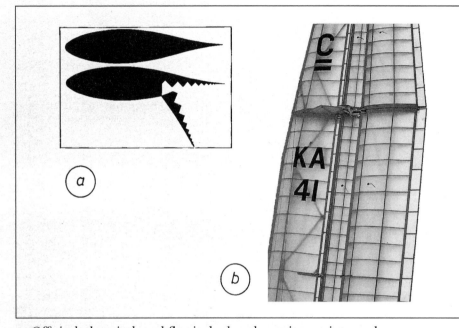

Fig 198a Split flap. Upwind (upper picture) and downwind configuration of the *Hinge* wing sail (British C-Class catamaran) competing in 1987 against the Australian defender the *Edge III.*

Fig 198b The successful Australian defender the *Edge III* also had a narrow split flap. This two-slotted wing, whose foils move relative to each other, allows it to produce the optimum lifting section for each leg of the course and wind strength.

Offwind, the windward flap is deployed, causing an intense low pressure area to develop between the flaps. This serves to accelerate the flow over the leeward, low pressure surface of the wing, thus increasing the stall angle and the maximum lift coefficient up to 2.8. Closed for upwind work, this configuration produces a higher L/D ratio than the multi-slotted wing sail with its less even surface.

At chord lengths (c_f/c ratio, Fig 191c) and deflections corresponding to the optimum values for a plain flap, the split flap will produce a slightly larger increment in C_{Lmax} (Refs 2.57, 2.58). The reason is that the leeward surface contour of the wing sail is undisturbed by the deflection of a split flap. As a result, the region of separated flow which occurs at the hinge of the plain flap, where the curvature of the wing surface changes abruptly is, in the case of a split flap, avoided. It will be seen from Fig 199a that both split and plain flaps appear to function most efficiently on a wing section with fairly thick leading edge. Definition of the thickness ratio y_5/c is given in Fig 199b, where y_5 is the section thickness at 0.05 of the chord c aft of the nose. With y_5/c in the order 0.1, both types of flaps produce the highest C_{Lmax}. Because the flow over the flapped part of the wing section has no tendency to stall up to relatively high deflections, by increasing both the flap deflection and its chord ratio c_f/c, appreciably larger C_{Lmax} increments may be achieved. This is shown in Fig 199c; the maximum lift coefficient of a foil with a split flap is increased by extending the flap chord, c_f, to some 40 per cent of the wing's total chord, c. The optimum split flap chord ratio, c_f/c, is approximately 0.3 for a 12 per cent thick foil, increasing to 0.4 or higher for thicker foils. The optimum thickness

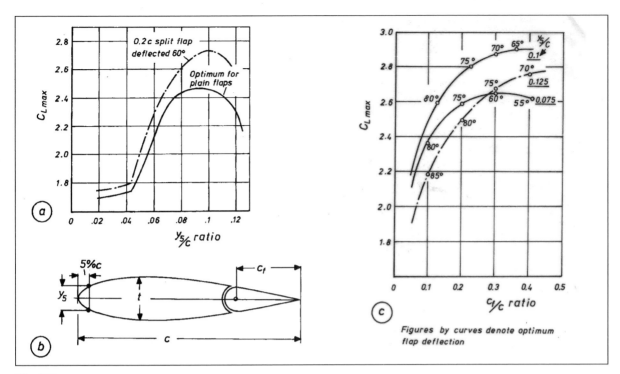

Fig 199

a)   A comparison of the sectional maximum lift coefficient obtainable on symmetrical airfoils with split and plain flaps.

b)   Definition of the leading edge thickness.

c)   The sectional maximum lift coefficients obtained by optimum deflexion of split flaps with various ratios of c_f/c and different leading edge thickness. Numbers by curves denote the optimum flap deflections. All results refer to wings with smooth surface conditions and operating at Re = 6 000 000.

ratio, t/c, of the foil is approximately 18 per cent and the maximum achievable lift increment, $\triangle C_{Lmax}$, is about 0.9 (Ref 2.59).

For plain flaps the optimum chord, c_f, is approximately 0.25c with a flap deflection of about 60 degrees. Leakage through the gap at the hinge (flap nose) may decrease the C_{Lmax} by about 0.4.

The lift characteristics of the flapped wing section presented in Fig 199 refer to wings with smooth surface conditions and operating at Re = 6 million. These data are dependent on the thickness/chord, t/c, ratio of the section (Fig 199b) and on the Reynolds Number, ie, the apparent wind speed at which the wing sail operates (see Appendix 2). It is shown in Fig 200a that for symmetrical sections without flap with thickness ratio, t/c, greater than 6 per cent, there is a significant drop in C_{Lmax} with a decreasing Reynolds Number below 6 million.

The effect of Re upon the maximum lift is associated with the different causes of stall. Instead of being due to the progressive growth of separation of the turbulent BL, beginning from the rear part of the suction side of the foil – as observed in Fig 201 on a thicker section – the stall on thin foils is caused by the growth of a local 'bubble' behind the nose, as discussed earlier and depicted in Figs 42 and 53. This type of stall is associated with the relatively poor lifting capabilities of thin foils, particularly noticeable on sharp nosed sections and due to the flattened suction peak near the leading edge, as shown in Figs 55–57.

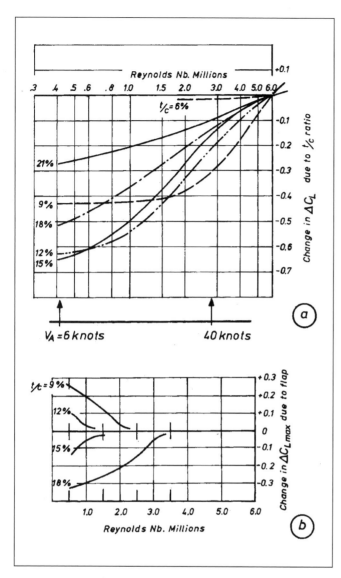

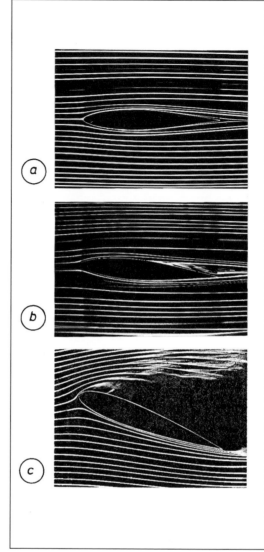

Fig 200a The effects of the Reynolds Number on the sectional maximum lift coefficient $C_{L max}$ for airfoils with smooth surfaces and leading edge thickness y_5/t of about 0.6. The range of apparent wind speeds V_A at which a 2 m (6.6 ft) wing operates (and equivalent to an Re ranging from 0.4 million to nearly 3 million) is given along the horizontal line at the bottom of the graph.

Fig 200b The change in $\triangle C_{L max}$ for foils with a split flap due to the Reynolds Number effect. These data, applicable to wings in smooth condition, indicate, for example, a significant loss in flap effectiveness $\triangle C_{L max}$ approximately – 0.35 for an 18 per cent thick wing operating at Re about half a million (equivalent to the apparent wind speed V_A about 6.5 knots); the chord of the wing is assumed to be 2 m (6.6 ft).

Fig 201 Flow past a relatively thick symmetrical section set at angles of incidence $\alpha = 0°$ (a) and 5° (b). At zero incidence angle, the streamlines follow the profile of the foil up to the trailing edge, and are evidently firmly attached to both the upper and lower surfaces of the foil. When the incidence angle is increased to 5 degrees, the boundary layer begins to separate from the rear half of the foil. With further increase of the incidence angle (photo c), separation moves to the leading edge, covering the entire suction surface with separated, highly disordered turbulent flow; the foil is said to be stalled. *Photos (a) and (b) Onera, Werle 1974; photo c, National Committee for Fluid Mechanics, USA.*

Returning to Fig 200, it will be seen in graph (b) that, according to some methodically compiled data (Ref 2.57), there are changes in maximum lift due to the split flap depending on the foil thickness. These changes – increments or decrements marked $\pm \triangle C_{Lmax}$ along the vertical axis – are *additional* to the changes due to the Reynolds Number effect given in graph (a) of Fig 200. Thus, for example, the 18 per cent thick section suffers a significant loss in split flap effectiveness, $\triangle C_{Lmax}$ about -0.35 at Re = 0.4 million (relevant to a wing sail with chord, c = 2m, operating in apparent wind speed V_A about 6 knots). In the same sailing conditions we can find in graph a that a loss in C_{Lmax} for an 18 per cent thick foil is $\triangle CL$ about -0.5, so the total loss in terms of C_{Lmax} efficiency of this particular wing sail with split flap would be:

$$\triangle C_{Lmax} = -0.35 + (-0.5) = -0.85.$$

As compared with split and plain flaps, the slotted flap is undoubtedly a more efficient high lift device. But there is little point here in attempting to predict accurately the performance of a slotted flap, as so much depends on the detailed design of the slot entry and in particular the vane, called mini-flap in Fig 197 (see also Figs 92 and 198). To function properly, the vane must be carefully located with respect to the flap and, in turn, so must the vane-flap with respect to the trailing edge of the foil ahead; the performance of the complete wing being sensitive to the location of the vane leading edge with respect to the trailing edge of the foil. This sensitivity appears to increase as the flap deflection becomes larger.

At best, the maximum lift performance of a slotted flap is a little better than the split flap, and certainly the drag is less. At worst, the slotted flap is merely an inefficient plain flap, with the slot acting as an unwanted gap. However, this gap, allowing air to leak through from the higher pressure to the lower pressure region, incurs a severe loss in flap effectiveness. Tests have shown that even so minute a gap as 1/300th of the chord may result in a loss of 0.35 in C_{Lmax}.

Bearing in mind the structural complications, possible pitfalls in the design, building, and the correct adjusting of the multi-slotted wing to ever changing sailing conditions, it is understandable that a much simpler split flap wing sail (Fig 198a) with less weight aloft may be competitive, at least in some conditions. It is a matter of gambling on the assumption that, as in the Little America's Cup, the racing course is 50 per cent upwind. A boat driven by a single element wing sail with higher L/D ratio – achieved on the account of better fairing on the suction side of the wing – may gain more time sailing upwind than she loses downwind. Here we have a trade-off case, in which the single element wing sail with a split flap is optimized for a higher L/D ratio (smaller ε_A) at the expense of the high C_{Lmax} produced by multi-slotted wing.

When not sailing in strong winds, wing sails are no longer superior to soft sail rigs. And, indeed, in light winds the soft sail boats have proved themselves and won races against high technology wings (2.4). This comes back to the Reynolds Number effect: wing sails are sensitive to it, whereas soft, thin sails are not. Depending on the size of the sailing craft, there is a certain critical wind speed below which a winged craft can only win racing matches by dint of superior strategy tactics, sailing skill and luck, rather than by superior boat speed.

High speed is in essence always a sort of gamble – the speed advantage can only be obtained at the expense of something else. And the price paid is usually in the longevity and reliability of the craft, expenses, seaworthiness, seakindliness, etc. It is impossible to find an uncontroversial measure for the value of speed in human life. The appreciation of speed is different for different people, and depends upon one's philosophy of life, that is, on rather irrational factors far beyond the scope of good engineering practices and economy.

To illustrate the point, let us look at two extracts: The first is from an article by RORC Commodore Don Parr (Ref 2.61). 'Offshore racing was always the sport likened to tearing up money under a cold shower; the only change has been the size of the denomination of the notes. It is, however, the sport which still has the challenge, the satisfaction of achievement, and the meeting of like 'madmen' who find it difficult to explain why they take part at such expense in such conditions. Long may it continue.'

The second extract is from a book published some 120 years earlier (Ref 2.62): 'Notwithstanding the numerous and melancholy accidents that occur year after year, through the mismanagement and upsetting of sailing boats, there are persons who will not take warning there from, but persist in rushing headlong into danger which, with ordinary prudence they might certainly avoid.'

EFFICIENCY OF FOILS WITH CURVED PLANFORMS (CRESCENT-SHAPED FOILS)

One more peculiar planform of lift-producing foils employed in the *Stars and Stripes* rig (Fig 202) deserves mentioning. Due to the action of selective evolution operating in Nature, many aquatic animals that cruise fast and sometimes for long distances, such as dolphins, tunnyfish, swordfish, mackerel-shark, whale (Fig 203) have developed caudal fins (foils) of the crescent-moon shape. Also, wings of certain efficiently soaring birds such as the albatross and swallow – feeding on the wing and spending most of their life in flight – display the characteristic backward curvature of leading and trailing edges, particularly near the tip.

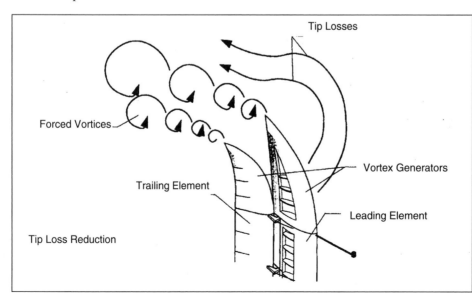

Fig 202 The unusual wing tip configuration applied to the *Stars and Stripes* rig (see also Fig 92). Interpretation of its action as 'tip loss reduction' – given in an article published in *Seahorse* magazine (Ref 2.61) from which this drawing is taken – is not the correct one. The peculiar tips of the *Stars and Stripes* rig do not operate as conventional vortex generators.

Fig 203 Nature seems to favour crescent-like shaped fins (foils). One cannot doubt that the caudal (tail) fin plays the most important part in generating the thrust that fishes exhibit. Any study of fish locomotion must consider how a fish can produce the thrust needed to overcome water resistance and maintain the speed observed. It has been found that a tunnyfish about the size of a man can swim *ten times* as fast as the Olympic champion! And certain fishes may produce an acceleration of 4 g in their lethal lunging attacks.

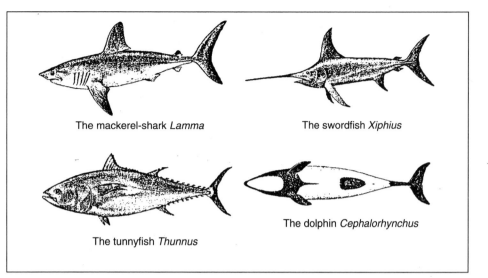

The mackerel-shark *Lamma*

The swordfish *Xiphius*

The tunnyfish *Thunnus*

The dolphin *Cephalorhynchus*

As indicated earlier, when discussing the implications of formula 24, one of the claims of classic, low speed aerodynamics and hydrodynamics is that the minimum induced drag of any lift-generating foil is obtained on an untwisted elliptical planform. One may ask why, after millions of years of evolution, Nature should produce peculiar, crescent-moon-shaped foils (Fig 203) when it is generally known since M Munk and L Prandtl proved it mathematically (Ref 2.63) that the elliptical planform is the most efficient single lifting surface in terms of induced drag?

Apparently, Nature knows the subject better than the most able mathematicians. Any quality that even slightly increases a fish's or bird's chances of survival is likely to be present in greater numbers in the next generation, greater still in the next, and so on. Swimming or flying efficiency is increased if the rate at which the energy of a fish or bird is dissipated in making a turbulent eddying wake (induced drag) becomes a smaller fraction of the rate at which useful thrust is produced. In this sense, better *propulsive efficiency* and hence *speed* might be regarded as a 'survival value', helping either to capture and eat other organisms, or to escape from a predator. Evidently, even small improvements in speed can reduce the chance of premature death through either of these causes (Ref 2.64). Nature also seems to know what *design criteria* should be applied to achieve its ultimate aim – the survival of the species. It selects the 'fittest' and operates in this way without mercy. For instance, speed is not always the factor giving the greatest chance of survival: sometimes, for example, body camouflage, precise manoeuvrability or defensive armour may be of key importance and give a net advantage to an animal even at the cost of reduced speed (2.64). Consequently, these 'survival values' get progressively more and more incorporated into the characteristics of a species. That is how Nature operates.

In another book (Ref 2.65), the author expressed a view that seaworthy fishing vessels with a high survival value, and the cruising yachts which descended from them, evolved in the past in a similar manner, through trial and error, when 'survive or perish' was the order of the day. These craft were expected to be capable of undertaking any planned voyage without loss and injury, and of making port *without outside assistance* after experiencing *unexpected* conditions.

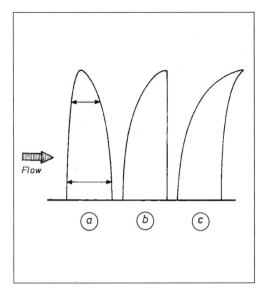

Flow

ⓐ   ⓑ   ⓒ

Fig 204 Planforms b and c with leading edges curved backwards have better efficiency in terms of induced drag than planform a, the K coefficients in formula 24 repeated below being about 0.96 for form b, and 0.92 for c.

$$\text{Induced drag } D_i = K \frac{L^2}{\pi \, AR_{ef}}$$

Backward sweep produces an increase in aerodynamic loading outboard towards the tip (a decrease inboard towards the root). Vortex phenomena prevail in the airflow in the region near the foil tip, be it soft sail or rigid wing sail. The tip vortex, similar in nature and action to the type found at the leading edge of the delta wing, shown in Figs 151–153, tends to greatly reduce the pressure (ie, increase suction) in its vicinity. Its contribution to overall lift and drag is relatively small for high aspect ratio wings, but becomes much greater with increasing sweep and decreasing aspect ratio, and largely depends on the detail of the shape of the wing tip.

Unfortunately – to use modern biological language – genetic engineering came along in the guise of rating rules. Cruising boats have not since been perfected by 'Nature', but 'designed' by unforeseen quirks of mathematical fancy incorporated into the measurements rules; and to the increasing detriment of the boat's survival value (see Fig 59). As a result, more and more misguided people necessarily rely upon rescue services to get them out of trouble.

After this brief digression, let's return to Fig 203. More recently, scientists have demonstrated, through the use of powerful computers and the application of computational fluid dynamic techniques, that crescent-shaped foils (Fig 204c) are more efficient: they produce less drag for a given lift than the elliptical planforms considered best in classical foil theory (Refs 2.66, 2.67). And the reason is that the classical wing theory does not account properly for the effect of the trailing vortex on the lift distribution in the tip region. Once the trailing vortex has left the aft edge of the foil, it is assumed that it is no longer responsible for what is going on with the lift developing on the foil. As a matter of fact, the tip vortex may advantageously affect the aerodynamic loading of the foil; and it has been found that, as compared with foil a in Fig 204, foil b (with a backward-curved leading edge and straight trailing edge) produces about 4.5 per cent less induced drag. Foil 3, with both leading and trailing edge curved backward, produces about 8.8 per cent less induced drag than foil 1. The above results were obtained at a constant $\alpha = 4°$. The spanwise chord distribution and the resulting aerodynamic load distribution have not been considered to be optimal. And the problem of determining the optimal load distribution for crescent-shaped foils is still being studied (Ref 2.66).

It is interesting to note that an efficient planform such as the one shown in Fig 205, closely approaching planform c in Fig 204, was developed by 'uneducated' people some 400 years or so ago, apparently by trial and error and probably inspired by clever observation of the forms 'designed' by Nature. The *jungadieros* (fishermen) from the north-eastern coast of Brazil, who almost certainly could not read, invented one of the most efficient sail planforms (many years before modern computers run by well educated mathematicians proved that

Fig 205a (Above) A print from an old drawing (1619) of a balsa raft, driven by the jungada type of sail.

Fig 205b (Right) The contemporary jungada sail is virtually identical to those which were developed in the 16th century along the north-eastern cost of Brazil.

they were on the right track). This ties up with the remark expressed by Sir d'Arcy Thompson (1860–1948) in his book, *Growth of Form*. 'There is never a discovery made in the theory of aerodynamics (and hydrodynamics too), but we find it adopted already in Nature.'

Interestingly perhaps, the crab claw type of rig, shown in Figs 141 and 146, although of lower aspect ratio than that of the caudal fins shown in Fig 203, belongs to the same category of crescent-moon-shaped foils. One might add that the winglets (Fig 149) attached to the keel of the 12 Metre *Stars and Stripes* – the victorious American challenger in the 1987 America's Cup contest – also had a notched delta shape, ie, a crescent-moon-like planform.

ROTATING TWO-SAIL RIGS

'Fools say that they learn by experience. I prefer to profit by others' experiences.'
Prince Otto von Bismarck (1815–98)

The lesson to be learned from the results of experiments presented in Figs 173 and 179 is that a realistic study of sail aerodynamics should take account of the air flow over the hull, as well as of the interacting sails, mast and rigging. It must also consider the wind gradient effect, modified to a greater or lesser extent by the presence of the hull, and depending on the course sailed relative to the apparent wind. Moreover, it requires little intuitive reasoning to deduce that the gap between foresail and mainsail, hardly ever optimum when sailing to windward, will be even further from the optimum if the boat bears away, and the crew can no longer control the camber and twist of the headsail precisely enough.

Another glance at Fig 173 will reveal that for all the reasons listed above, the

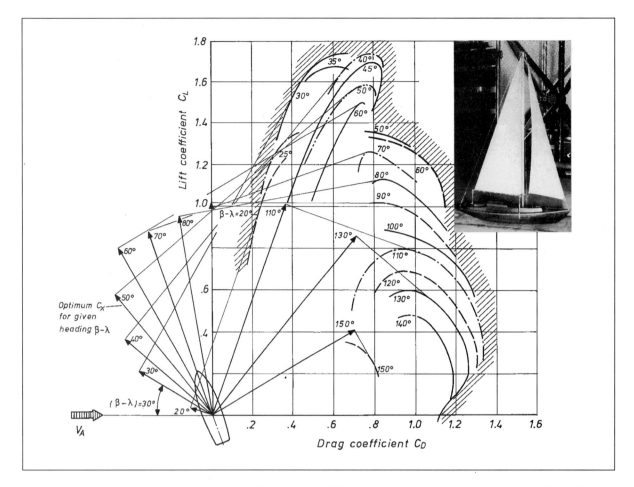

potential sail power, ultimately measured in terms of C_{Lmax}, of a sloop rigged boat and obtainable in close-hauled attitude, decreases when bearing away. For example, in reaching conditions when, say, the wind comes from an angle 90 degrees from the bow, the actually recorded driving force coefficient is only about 0.9. In other words, about one third of the potential driving force that a given rig is capable of producing is lost.

Figure 206 illustrates in the form of a series of polar diagrams the lift and drag coefficients of a model of a sloop rigged yacht, tested in the wind tunnel of Hamburg University (Ref 2.68). Aerodynamic forces were measured for a number of constant heading angles (ß – λ), from 20 to 150 degrees, and the driving force components, C_x, for each course sailed are indicated by the thick, continuous line arrows. It will be seen that although the maximum C_{Lmax} of the model is 1.74, the maximum driving component attainable at the heading angle (ß – λ) = 130° is only 1.12, ie, about 36 per cent less.

This evident deterioration of the aerodynamic performance of the rig – believed to be caused only by the difficulty in correctly trimming the headsail when bearing away – inspired some inventors to develop a rig whereby the trim deficiency could be radically removed. Merits of such a rig, shown in Fig 207a and invented by Carl Böss, were discussed in a German magazine *Yacht* in 1974 (Ref 2.69). As indicated in sketch b, the whole rig, with tightly trimmed headsail, can be rotated relative to the hull, and so the optimum gap between the

Fig 206 Polar diagrams of C_L and C_D coefficients for various heading angles ß – λ from 20 to 150 degrees in ten degree intervals, established in the wind tunnel for the sloop rigged model shown in the photograph. Thick arrows show the magnitude of the driving force coefficients C_x for the course sailed as indicated next to the arrow head.

Fig 207 A rotating rig suggested in 1974. Original drawings taken from *Yacht* magazine (Ref 2.69).

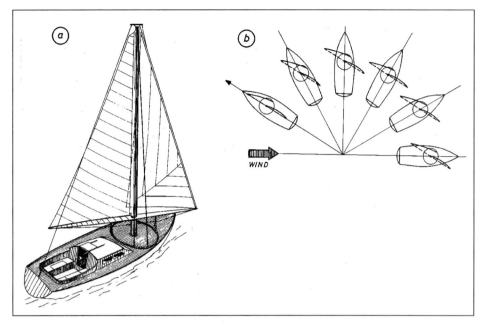

two interacting sails can be maintained, regardless of the heading angle. This concept follows, in a way, the assumption on which the *Gimcrack* sail coefficients are based, namely that sail trim can be varied in a manner 'which is equivalent to rotating the rig in the boat; and the direction of the wind vector and total force then change by an equal amount, keeping the total force coefficient and ε_A constant.' (Refs 2.28 and 2.70).

A photograph (Fig 208) taken in 1984 illustrates just such a rotating rig applied to the famous, flat-out racing catamaran *Elf Aquitaine*. This type of rig has not been accepted as a breakthrough invention, however, but it appeared again in 1991 on the pages of *Seahorse* magazine; this time as a patent pending, 'The Aero Rig', shown in Fig 209 (Ref 2.71).

Fig 208 A rotating rig applied to the French racing catamaran *Elf Aquitaine*. So far this type of rig has not caught on.

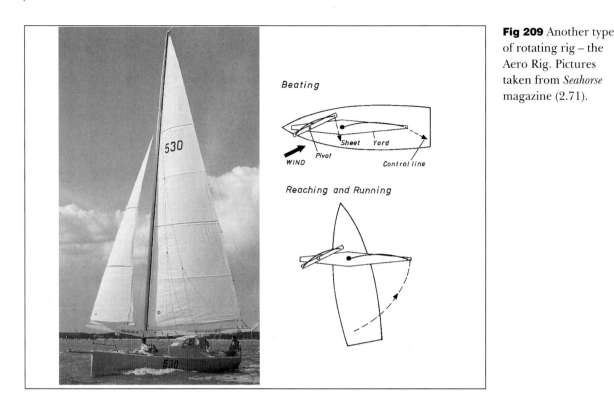

Fig 209 Another type of rotating rig – the Aero Rig. Pictures taken from *Seahorse* magazine (2.71).

According to the inventor the proposed new free-standing rig should offer:
- Simplicity and ease of handling
- Safety, ability to de-power quickly in an emergency
- Good performance, especially off the wind

In addition, the rig has fewer components (such as winches) to purchase and maintain, a single sheet control to just one sheet winch, and self-tacking capability.

At the time of writing, no wind tunnel tests have been done on rotating rigs, so it is impossible to pass proper judgement on their aerodynamic efficiency as compared with conventional fore-and-aft rigs. However, some preliminary tests have indicated that at the heading angle of about 25 degrees (close-hauled), a shift of the jib tack to leeward of the centreline of the hull improves slightly the L/D ratio (smaller ε_A) of the rig. At the same apparent wind angle, it was impossible to make the sail set with the jib tack shifted by the same amount to windward. At the heading angle of 45 degrees (close-reaching), a shift of the jib tack to windward (similar in effect to the rotating rig) does not increase the driving force but it does slightly reduce the heeling force.

These results tally in general with the biplane theory in its most essential aspect; that the ratio of the gap between two wings to their chord (width) affects both the lift and drag. In this respect, an interacting headsail and mainsail are similar to interacting biplane wings. Figure 210, relevant to a biplane wing of AR = 6, gives some idea of to what extent the gap/chord ratio determines the minimum drag and maximum lift coefficients (Refs 2.72 and 2.73). Converted into sailing terms, it means that by increasing the gap between sails, ie, across the wind direction, the maximum lift is increased and the induced drag is reduced. Why?

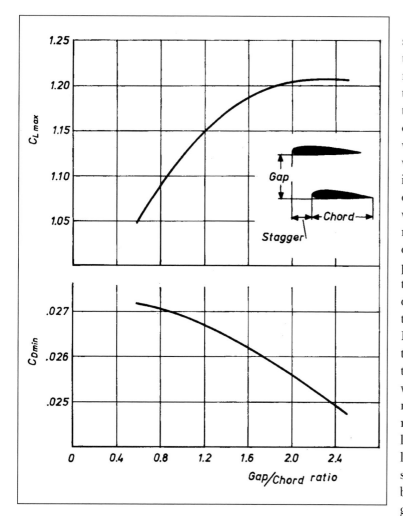

Fig 210 The effect of the gap between the wings of a biplane. Where two or more lift-producing foils are working in close proximity, there is an interaction between them, and their combination cannot therefore be treated simply as the sum of two single foils.

Earlier we looked at interacting sails (Figs 43 and 46), and saw that the flow round the headsail and the mainsail is modified both in direction and velocity as compared with the wind speed and direction ahead of them. With this fact in mind, it will be appreciated that each of the wings of a biplane operates in an inclined air stream (downwash), part of the inclination being due to the wing's own vortex system, and the reminder due to that induced by the other wing (Ref 2.4). Given this premise, we can deduce the general trend in the variation of induced downwash and induced drag with the gap of the biplane configuration. If the gap is very large, it is obvious that the additional induced velocities are negligible, and that the wings of the biplane behave as monoplanes. When the gap is reduced to zero, the two wings coalesce to form a monoplane with a loading (lift) of *twice* that corresponding to each wing of the biplane. Consequently, when the gap is very large, the induced drag of the biplane is one-half that of the monoplane producing the same lift (see Eq 23). The induced drag of the biplane of zero gap is, of course, equal to that of the monoplane. Thus, the most important feature of the biplane theory is that, in general, *we may expect a reduction of the induced drag for a given lift if a monoplane is replaced by a biplane (or multiplane) having the same span.*

As to the effect of gap on lift, the following explanation may suffice. When two or more wings are situated one above the other, so as to form a biplane arrangement, the low pressure region (suction) over the top of the lower wing is closely adjacent to the high pressure area below the upper wing, with the obvious result that some readjustment of pressure intensity must take place; and this reduces the effectiveness of both wings. Since the suction developed over the top surface of the wing is of greater importance than the pressure over the under surface, the lower wing of a biplane – as in the case of a mainsail interacting with a jib – suffers to a greater degree than the upper wing.

Bearing in mind the implication of Fig 210, one may argue that if the headsail could be made to set *well to leeward* of the mainsail with a very slack luff, the efficiency of the rig would increase. This is where the flat-cut reaching spinnaker becomes so effective (Ref 2.74). However, for years racing crews have been fighting to get tighter and tighter forestays, and hulls have been getting stiffer and stiffer in order to withstand the loads imposed upon them. Obviously, from the sailmaker's point of view, it is much simpler to produce a headsail with a nearly straight luff rather than one with a curvature which should fit a variable sag in the forestay. Usually it is assumed that the sag is constant, and preferably reduced in strong winds to flatten the sail.

Another practical objection to a slack forestay is that it would be difficult to steady the mast in a seaway, and any movement of the mast may drastically alter the flow around both sails to the detriment of their efficiency.

One significant effect of the gap between the interacting lift-producing foils shown in Fig 210 might be exploited in the rotating rigs depicted in Figs 207–209. All that is needed is to introduce a movable tack for the headsail, which should automatically shift the luff of the jib possibly far apart from the mainsail. A wider sheeting base for the headsail would also be advantageous.

14 · SAIL INTERACTION

'The gods did not reveal all things to men at the start; but as time goes on, by searching, they discover more and more.'

Xenophon, Greek historian, (c. 430–c. 355 BC)

Interaction between sails, particularly between the main and headsail, is certainly a highly controversial subject amongst sailing people. Broadly there are two camps. There are those who maintain that the foresail accelerates the air past the leeward side of the mainsail, thus increasing the suction; consequently the mainsail bears the burden of the overall lift increase. And there are those who argue that the headsail – like the leading edge slot of the airplane wing – should be regarded as a means of increasing the maximum lift, by postponing the stalling angle of the mainsail. They argue that it is the headsail which largely bears the burden of the increase in total lift. This is due to the fact that the headsail, located near the front of the mainsail, is subjected to local velocities set up by the main which are known to be large, as is the suction developed on the front sail (Figs 44 and 46). Proponents of the first of these theories frequently refer to the Venturi effect, arguing that the foresail as a sail in its own right is very efficient.

Depending on which idea one believes, the best position for the foresail relative to the main and its trim angle δ_F (Fig 211), is different, and one can usually quote an example to prove it. At various times, the correct close-hauled angle of trim of the foresail has been recommended as being anything from $\delta_F = 7°$ to $\delta_F = 20°$.

Who is right? Unquestionably a foresail can be an efficient sail. This was confirmed in chapter 3: 'Distribution of Pressure over Sails'. At the same time it can greatly improve the air flow over the leeward side of the mainsail. To obtain the maximum advantage from both conditions simultaneously (regardless of the course sailed relative to the wind) is difficult, if not impossible. Not infrequently, the most efficient configuration cannot be employed, and this is the reason why

Fig 211 The definition of sheeting and incidence angles for a sloop rig in close-hauled attitude.

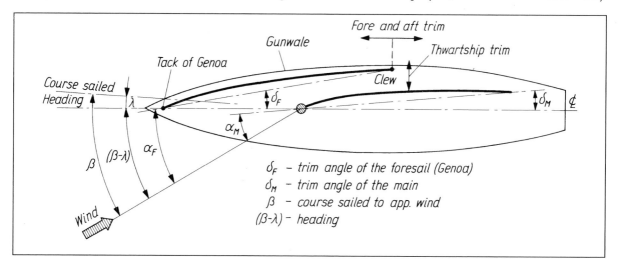

δ_F – trim angle of the foresail (Genoa)
δ_M – trim angle of the main
β – course sailed to app. wind
$(\beta-\lambda)$ – heading

an attempt was made to alleviate this difficulty by adopting the concept of a rotating rig.

On one point we can be quite definite. The question of sail interaction and, in particular, the problem of the 'backwinding' of a mainsail by a foresail is rather complicated and has not yet been fully explored.

INFLUENCE OF THE FORESAIL ON THE MAINSAIL

As an example of sail interaction, consider the commonly encountered case of a Bermudan sloop with a large overlapping genoa. Figure 212 presents some observations (made in the wind tunnel at Southampton University) on air flow over the leeward side of some model sails. The positions of the sails are given with reference to Fig 211. Trim angle δ_F for the foresail was 10°, and that for

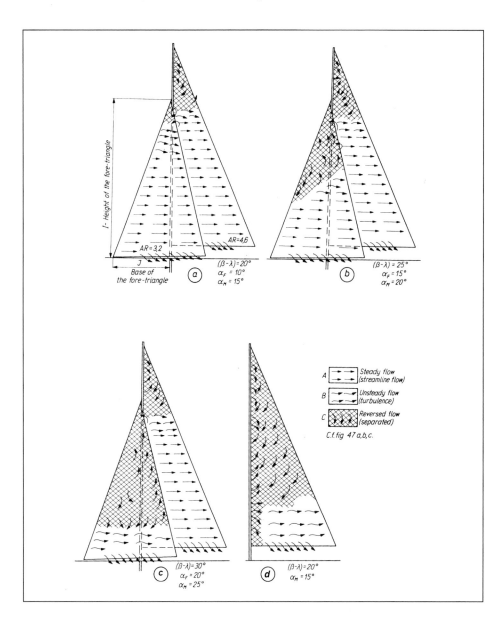

Fig 212 Visualization of the airflow over the leeward (suction) side of a sloop model in close-hauled attitude (Ref 2.33).

the mainsail δ_M was 5°. Both sails had a camber of 1/25 (4 per cent) and were almost without twist, so that at all heights above the 'deck', the trim angles, δ_F and δ_M, and the incidence angles, α_F and α_M, were the same. The four sketches in Fig 212 show the character of the airflow at various apparent heading angles (ß – λ). Thus, although the angles of incidence α_F and α_M were varied together, the relative position between the two sails remained constant.

Three basic types of air flow are mapped on the sails, and explained in the accompanying key. Type A – steady, attached flow – represents the condition when all the air particles are moving in the same direction in an orderly manner (Fig 81a). The unsteady flow B indicates the presence of random movement of the flow in addition to its main velocity (Fig 81b). The reversed flow, C, occurs when the flow separates from the sail and corresponds to the mechanism of stalling (Fig 53b). All these types of flow are often encountered in water. Type A is seen in a deep, slowly flowing river; type B in a fast, often shallow river; and type C behind a headland or on the inside bend of a river, where a local current in opposition to the main stream can be found.

In interpreting Fig 212, we must bear in mind that to obtain a high aerodynamic efficiency, the flow on the leeward side of the sail must be attached and steady. Fig 212a demonstrates that at the small heading ß – λ = 20°, when α_F = 10° and α_M = 15°, attached flow occupies the major part of both sails. Only in the regions at the head of the genoa and above this point on the mainsail is the flow turbulent B or separated C.

If the angle ß – λ is now increased to 25°, the disturbance on the mainsail progresses downward slightly. The upper parts of this sail are most affected, because the influence of the genoa is least, and the ratio of mast diameter to sail chord is greatest. The area of the genoa, on the other hand, which is now stalled, is considerably greater. A further increase of ß – λ to 30° leads the stalling on the foresail to spread almost to the foot, but the flow over the mainsail is still attached. This condition is maintained until at least ß – λ = 40°.

Fig 212d shows the flow over mainsail only, at the same heading as that of (a), and clearly demonstrates to what extent the foresail stabilizes the flow over the leeward side of the mainsail against unwanted separated flow, particularly just abaft the mast. It does this by reducing the flow speed over the forward-lee part of the mainsail. This in turn delays or prevents flow separation which usually commences from the mast.

Figure 213 depicts the air flow over a mainsail set at an angle of attack α = 35°. Case (a), for the mainsail only, shows definite separation of the flow on the leeward side, whilst the added foresail in case (b) eliminates this separation. Case (c) demonstrates 'backwinding', and subsequent deformation of the mainsail caused by a badly trimmed foresail. It is thus evident that the desired aerodynamic effect will be obtained only when the slot between the foresail and the mainsail is of a proper shape; in the case (c) the jib curling to windward is manifestly harmful.

According to Arvel Gentry's finding, which I also discuss fairly extensively in *Aero-hydrodynamics of Sailing*, the slot does not act as a giant Venturi with the airflow speeding up in the region of sail overlap. Instead, as shown in Figs 43 and 46, the airflow first slows down and then is speeded back up in the slot. Since less air goes between the leading edge of the headsail and the mast, Bernoulli's theorem tells us that the flow velocity at the leading edge of the mainsail is reduced, and so is the suction peak. As a result, the air particles, forced to make sharp turn around the mast to the leeside, have less difficulty in following the mast–sail contour, and thus flow separation is less likely to occur. The situation at the mast is, in a way, similar to that experienced by every car driver: he can safely negotiate a corner of small radius without skidding (separation), provided the car's speed is sufficiently reduced.

The sail area right behind the mast is a particularly sensitive place on the mainsail; this is where a helmsman sees the first warning signs that he is pinching the sail. When the suction at this point is reduced to such an extent that the pressure difference between the windward and leeward sides is nearly zero, the sail will flutter.

Once a sail starts to flutter near the luff, its smooth contour is destroyed, and with it the streamlined flow over the rest of the sail. In the course of experiments carried out on sail pressure distributions, Warner and Ober concluded that, if sufficient rigidity was supplied to a sail near the luff, to prevent shaking occurring at that point, the sail as a whole would be able to point higher. This idea was fully confirmed in practice. Sails equipped with full-length battens can be set closer to the wind, without fluttering, in spite of them being partly backwinded. The sail stiffness can be increased by using battens of suitable thickness and fixing them under longitudinal compression in their pockets, so that they have a natural curve, even in no wind.

The correct shape for the slot between two sails should be maintained at all heights. One frequently finds that the ineffectiveness of a foresail can be attributed to its having the correct camber near the foot but an excessive camber higher up, causing backwinding of the mainsail (Fig 213c). Photo 214 illustrates that this can be caused by sag in the forestay. The mainsail is backwinded in the region of the third batten, while lower down, where the foresail is relatively flat, this does not occur. This state of affairs is common; the mid-height of the foresail, where its camber is perhaps difficult to control, usually causes the trouble. The leech of the foresail may curl under the excessive tension put on it, and this too may cause backwinding of the mainsail.

The Analog Field Plotter tests done by Gentry (Ref 2.7), and the wind tunnel

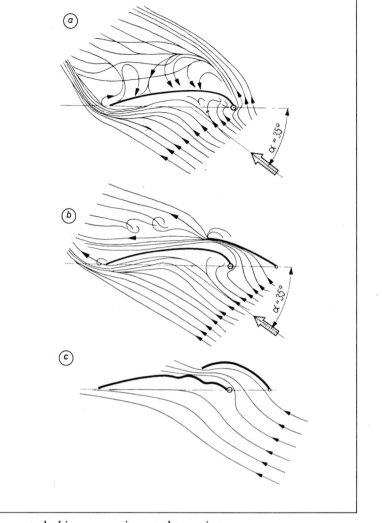

Fig 213 The pattern of flow round a single sail and the interaction of foresail with mainsail:

a) fully separated flow over the leeward side of single mainsail

b) at the same angle of incidence, the smooth flow over the mainsail is due to the effect of the foresail.

c) excessive camber of the foresail causes backwinding of the mainsail.

Fig 214 Backwinding is easy to see in a 'soft' main unsupported by battens. Full battens make the luff area more stable, so backwinding is more difficult to spot. But even with full battens you should be able to detect the soft area in the region of the third batten, caused by the increasing camber of the genoa towards its head. One of the advantages offered by full battens is better control of the mainsail shape in a light wind, ie, in conditions in which a soft sail is likely to be easily deformed to its aerodynamic detriment by choppy waves and a swinging boom.

measurements as well, clearly indicate that the amount of air that flows through the headsail-mainsail overlap – and thus the associated flow speed, together with the resulting pressure distribution developed on both sails – will vary depending on the relative sheeting angles, δ_F and δ_M. Figure 215 illustrates what happens to the flow within the slot as sail trim angles are changed. Sketch a shows the so-called 'stagnation streamlines' reaching the leading edges of the jib and mainsail. These are points at which the air particles stagnate (are brought to rest). The amount of flow which will go through the sail overlap is contained between these two stagnation streamlines. Configuration a is regarded as the basic sail setting.

If the jib is trimmed harder, say 5° closer to the mainsail, as shown in sketch b, this causes a 60 per cent reduction in the amount of flow passing through the slot. But of utmost importance is the fact that the stagnation streamline for the jib comes into contact with the sail on its windward surface, and the stagnation point for the mainsail is shifted to the leeward side. It is therefore likely that the flow over the headsail will separate. As for the mainsail, it is likely that there will be higher pressure on the leeward side than to windward and so the sail will luff (backwinding). Both effects are, of course, undesirable.

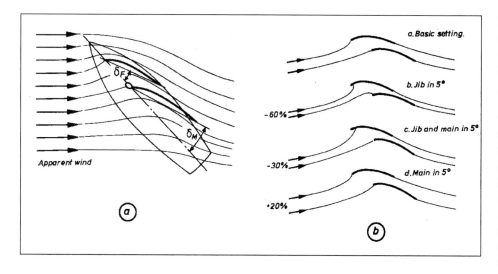

Fig 215 The amount of air that flows through the slot between the overlapping genoa and main varies depending upon the relative sheeting angles δ_F and δ_M of interacting sails. These angles have a direct influence over the way in which the stagnation streamlines shown come into contact with sail surfaces. The position of the stagnation points affect the pressure distribution, and determine whether or not the leeside boundary layer will separate and the sail will stall or whether backwinding (luffing) will take place (mainsail in sketch b). This figure is included by kind permission of Arvel Gentry.

SHEETING OF THE MAIN AND FORESAILS

There is another aspect of the interaction between main and foresails which favours reducing the convergence of the slot between them. This depends on the foresail, which we know to be a highly effective sail in its own right, if only it is allowed to be so. Compare b and c of Fig 212 with typical angles for close-hauled dinghy sailing, ie, the heading ß – λ in the range 25°–30°, angle of incidence of foresail α_F between 15° and 20°, and its angle of trim $\delta_F = 10°$. We can see that the foresail itself is not efficient, since although the flow over the mainsail is attached, that over the foresail is not. At the apparent heading ß – λ = 25°, about half the leeward surface of the foresail suffers from separated flow, and when ß – λ is increased to 30°, almost all its leeward side is affected. This means that the angle of incidence, α_F, is too large, and should be reduced by increasing its trim angle δ_F.

In racing circles it is well known how vitally important is the trim angle of the foresail when close-hauled. Sheeting the foresail too hard can reduce speed as no other factor can. Freeing the foresail sheet by only a small outboard shift of its fairleads may make a radical improvement in the performance of a boat. The effect of the sheeting base on sail efficiency was established in some numerical terms by measurements performed in the wind tunnel at Southampton University, and shown in Fig 216.

Tests were carried out on an accurate ⅓ scale rig model of the X-One-Design class yacht. Details of the sails made of Terylene of total area 20.5 sq ft (1.9m²) are shown in Figs 63b and 216. Lift L, drag D and heeling moment M_H were measured at a wind speed $V_A = 20$ ft/sec (12 knots); sketch a defines the relevant forces and angles. During this series of tests, the sheeting angle of the mainsail $\delta_M = 5°$ was constant, and measurements were taken for different sheeting angles of the foresail, δ_F, in the range from 7½° to 20° in increments of 2½°. These tests were subsequently repeated over ranges of heading angles ß – λ from 15° to 42½° to cover close-hauled conditions.

From the results shown in Figs 216b and c, we can clearly see that the sheeting angle of the foresail, δ_F, which determines the shape of the slot and thus the

Fig 216a Definition of angles and aerodynamic forces when sailing close-hauled; compare with Fig 136 and note that the driving force component F_R is parallel to the course sailed, whereas the F_x component, as measured in the wind tunnel, is parallel to the heading.

Fig 216b As the heading angle increases, so the foresail sheeting angle must also increase.

Fig 216c For headings larger than a beat – say a close reach – the driving force depends largely on the optimum lead angle, δ_F, which may actually be outside the hull. Under the racing rules it is at present illegal to use an outrigger, but it is legal to use your arm to hold the clew outboard. This can be done, provided the sail area is not too large, wind not too strong, and your stamina up to the task.

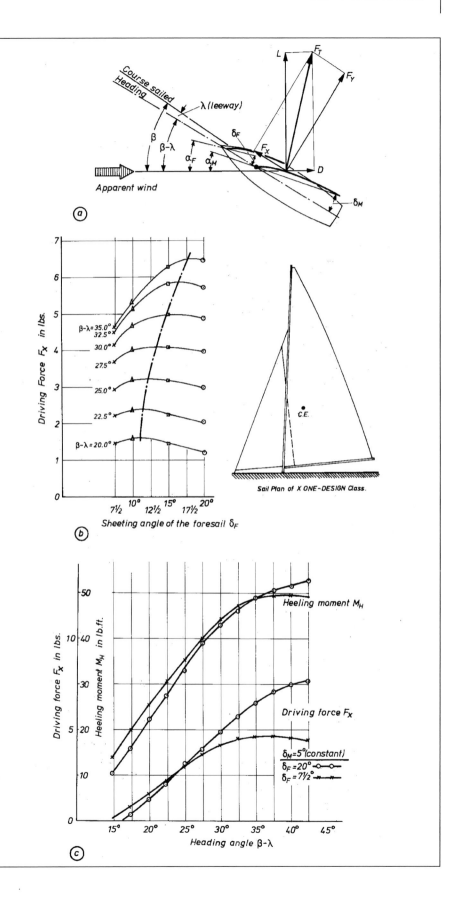

interaction between the two sails, does indeed have quite a big effect on the attainable value of the driving force, F_x. To take an example: for the heading angle $\beta - \lambda = 30°$, the driving force F_x increases by about 20 per cent if the sheeting angle δ_F is increased from $7\frac{1}{2}°$ to $15°$ (diagram b); at the same time the corresponding heeling moment, M_H (Fig 216c), remains practically unchanged.

The significance of the sheeting base becomes more and more important when bearing away off the wind and approaching close-reaching conditions. Thus, as shown in diagram c, for the heading angles $\beta - \lambda = 35°$ and $40°$, the corresponding increments of driving force F_x are about 40 and 65 per cent respectively, assuming that the sheeting angle δ_F can be increased from $7\frac{1}{2}°$ to $20°$.

It is evident from Fig 216b that there is a certain optimum in sheeting angle δ_F, for given heading $\beta - \lambda$ and, of course, for a given sheeting angle of the mainsail δ_M, which, in this particular case is $5°$. For a typical scope of heading angles in the close-hauled condition $\beta - \lambda = 25°–35°$ (Fig 216b), the optimum sheeting angle δ_F varies from about $12°$ to $18°$. As might be expected for the other sheeting angles of the mainsail, the optimum sheeting angle for the headsail will be different to maintain the optimum slot shape.

Since the curves in Fig 216b tend to have a steeper hump at the larger heading angles, the optimum sheeting angle of the foresail is more critical on a fine reach than on a beat. Experiments on other rig models of different aspect ratio and overlap extent indicated the same trend; that is, the crucial dependence of rig efficiency on foresail trim angle, δ_F.

For a given wind, there is an optimum heading which a particular yacht must sail in order to achieve the best speed made good to windward, V_{mg}. For a yacht such as a 12 Metre this optimum heading is about $20°$ or even less; larger optimum headings in the order of $25°–30°$ apply to ocean cruisers and centreboard dinghies respectively. Considering the V_{mg} *requirements only*, it seems that most sailing boats have a wide enough sheeting base to allow the optimum trim in close-hauled conditions. However, any sailing journey to a given destination may involve close-hauled, reaching and downwind sailing. It is obvious that inadequate sheeting arrangements severely limit the effectiveness of most common sail combinations (Ref 2.76).

Returning briefly to Fig 211, it should be noted that the available sheeting base for a headsail is not entirely determined by the distance of gunwale from the centreline of the hull, but also by the overlap, ie, the length of the headsail foot. Thus, as indicated, for a large genoa the maximum sheeting angle δ_F is $9\frac{1}{2}°$, but for a short footed jib without overlap, the maximum δ_F is $15°$.

Some interesting facts about the relationship between sail efficiency and overlap ratio have been brought to light through wind tunnel experiments on a two headsail rig (Ref 2.77). The rig tested is shown in Fig 217a. The mainsail and the *yankee jib topsail* were not changed throughout the experiments. *Three separate staysails* 1, 2 and 3, with increasing overlap were tested. Their overlap is given as the percentage increase of the length of the foot to the length J over the normal number 1 working staysail with zero overlap. The two staysails 2 and 3 had overlaps of 25 and 40 per cent respectively. The range of heading angles covered by the tests was from close-hauled to square reach, and for each heading angle the sheets were trimmed for best rig efficiency. The apparent wind speed was constant.

Fig 217 The influence of overlap on the performance of three staysails in a double head rig.

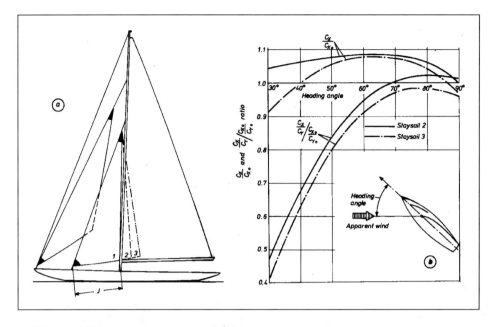

Figure 217b presents the results in comparative form. Measurements were taken at four headings: 30°, 50°, 70°, 90°. The rig efficiency is expressed in terms of driving force coefficient C_x/C_y. For the staysail 1, with zero overlap, its C_{xo} coefficient and C_{xo}/C_{yo} ratio were regarded as the yardstick, and therefore represented by 1.0 along the vertical axis of Fig 217b throughout the heading angle range. The effect of staysail overlap was evaluated by considering the driving and heeling forces produced per square foot of *actual sail area* exposed, and *not the rated area* of the fore triangle.

For staysail 2 (with 25 per cent overlap), an increase of about 4 per cent in driving efficiency (as given by the ratio of C_x/C_{xo}) at the heading angle 30° is seen to rise steadily to 8 per cent when the apparent wind is about 65° from the bow. Driving/heeling ratios $\frac{C_x}{C_y} / \frac{C_{xo}}{C_{yo}}$ follow a similar form of variation but are seen to fall below the yardstick at the heading angles under 70 degrees. Staysail 3 (with 40 per cent overlap) gave results (in terms of driving force coefficient) above the yardstick except for heading angles below 40 degrees and above 86 degrees. Again, the driving/heeling force ratio curve follows the form of the driving force coefficient curve but results are inferior to the yardstick over the whole range of heading angles. The overlap is thus shown to be useful for reaching, but it incurs a penalty in terms of rig efficiency in close-hauled conditions – a fact which is, perhaps, not fully appreciated. The heeling forces call for no special comment here, beyond noting a clear tendency to progressively higher values per square foot of sail area. Hence larger leeway angle should be expected as the staysail overlap increases. Thus, for the range of overlap considered, a staysail overlap of about 25 per cent was found to give the most advantage. As overlap increases towards 40 per cent, the benefit falls off fairly rapidly and is still falling at 40 per cent overlap.

15 • SOME REMARKS ABOUT SAIL TRIM

'So easie is the passage from one extreme to another; and so hard it is, to stop in that little point, wherein the right does consist.'

Thomas Sprat (1667)

The fundamental aims in trimming and tuning mast interacting sails (except some unconventional sails such as crab claw) are indicated in Table 11:

Table 11
Aims in trimming and tuning interacting sails
• To maintain high efficiency of the foresail, be it genoa or working jib, by preventing its partial and total stall
• To avoid or reduce extensive backwinding of mainsail except in stronger winds, when deliberately induced backwinding (by easing the mainsheet) may serve as a means to temporarily lessen excessive heeling force
• To adjust and maintain the optimum shape of sails and slots between them, ie, an even rate of opening between the foresail and the main from foot to head. This includes the correct twist, and correct vertical and horizontal camber distribution on both sails to match the apparent wind strength and gradient (*shear*, discussed in Chapter 7, and see Figs 96 and 97), and the course sailed relative to wind.

Two terms used in Table 11 – *backwinding* and *sail camber* – require some explanation. As rightly pointed out by Arvel Gentry, the term *backwinding*, frequently used in sailor's parlance, seems to imply that the headsail is throwing air against the lee side of the main. This is not the case. The reason backwinding occurs is due to an over-trimmed foresail, too much camber, or a hook in the genoa leech. As a result, the local air flow within the overlap *slows down* so much that the resulting pressure on the leeward side of the main may become greater than that on the windward side. If this is happening, the mainsail's fabric in the region affected by the backwinding will react accordingly, bulging to windward instead of to leeward (Figs 213c and 218).

The term *sail camber*, defined in Fig 60a as the ratio of maximum depth of sail curvature, f, to the sail chord, c, is not precise enough for trimming purpose. The proper amount of camber, ie, fullness or flatness of a sail, is important. It determines the driving power of the rig and heeling angle of the boat. But what is equally if not more important is the sail curvature right behind its leading edge, LE, which might be called the sail entry (or entrance), defined by the angle En between the tangent line to the sail curvature at the LE and the sail chord, c, as indicated in Fig 219.

For each value of foresail camber there is a small range of sail incidence angles, α, and an even smaller range of entry angles, En, at which there is negligible separation at the leading edge. These two angles are strictly interrelated in the sense that, if the entry angle is not matched to the sail camber and to the incidence angle at which the foresail actually operates, an extensive separation along LE will certainly take place. There must be as little opportunity as

Fig 218 The 12 Metre *Norsaga* which the author sailed in 1960 to get firsthand experience in studying backwinding problems. Backwinding is still a controversial issue, even amongst experts in the field of sailmaking and trimming. One of the leading sail magazines asked: 'Is backwinding fast?', and replied to its question, 'The simple answer is Yes, but then there is a host of considerations, conditions and techniques to apply' (Ref 2.79). It will be shown that backwinding, by itself, is not a device which makes the boat fast.

BACKWINDING

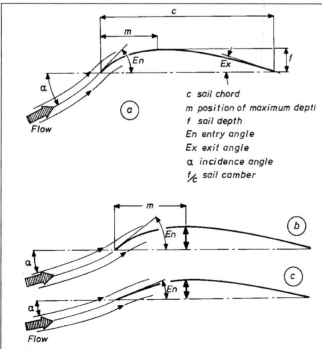

c sail chord
m position of maximum depth
f sail depth
En entry angle
Ex exit angle
α incidence angle
f/c sail camber

Fig 219 In order to avoid or delay premature separation at the leading edge of a headsail, which may greatly reduce the suction along its most important part, the entry angle En must correspond to the incidence angle α and sail depth (f/c ratio). The entry angle should be different depending on wind speed and heading. In general, when sailing upwind, the incidence angle α and sail depth should be larger for lighter winds and this requires *round entry* (sketch b); except in a very light wind, in which a flat sail set at small incidence angle and with *fine entry* (sketch c) is more resistant to premature leading edge separation (look again at Fig 42). The exit angle Ex is also an important shape factor; hooking to windward should be avoided.

possible for the creation of flow disturbances near the LE, because this is the place where the greatest pressure differences (large suction) across the sail occur. And these pressure differences contribute most to the driving force. Thus the shape of the sail entry, and hence what we may call the entrance efficiency, becomes the factor which primarily determines sail driving power. If a sail is to be employed successfully, it is necessary to have a means whereby the entrance shape can be adjusted in a controlled manner, according to what the wind strength and heading angle demand.

While a boat has one hull of known and fixed geometry, it is likely to have a wardrobe of sails which can be set in various combinations. It is impossible to give precise instructions on how every rig should be trimmed and tuned to suit every sailing condition. Adjustable sails require the crew to know their stuff. As Agatha Christie's fictional character, master detective Hercule Poirot, says: 'Above all – the method! What I always say is... the method!... That is also my watchword; method, tidiness and... the little grey cells!'

'Oh yes, of course, we all use them, I think.' 'Some to a larger and some to a smaller extent, and there are also differences in quality!'

What follows is by no means a comprehensive account of trimming practices, but here are a few examples:

Table 12 Adjustment factors affecting sail and slot shapes

- Trim (tension) of mainsail and foresail sheets
- Trim angles of foresail and mainsail (fore-and-aft, and thwartship, see Fig 211)
- Sag in the forestay
- Mast bend (fore-and-aft, and sideways)
- Cunningham holes (luff tension)
- Halyard tensions (in foresail and main)
- Outhaul tension
- Kicking–strap tension (boom vang)
- Shape of headsails (eg high-cut jib, low-cut genoa with large overlap)

Note: Above factors are not listed in order of importance; Each adjustment is likely to have an influence on every other adjustment.

There are numerous articles and books on this subject, and some entirely orientated towards the trimming and tuning problems encountered in particular classes of boats. It can be helpful to draw upon this ready-made knowledge (Ref 2.78) but the suggestions should be read with the open mind and inquiring spirit of Monsieur Poirot.

Depending on the type of boat, her size and her rig arrangement, the crew have a number of courses and adjustment factors – the most important of which are listed in Table 12 – under their control. Using these, the sails and rig can be trimmed and tuned to achieve the objectives given in Table 11.

LESSONS LEARNED FROM THE WIND TUNNEL TESTS

'Allow me to express now, once and for all, my deep respect for the work of the experimenter and for his fight to wring significant facts from an inflexible Nature who says so indistinctly "No" and so indistinctly "Yes" to our theories.'

H Weyl, physicist (1885–1955)

As already noted in Fig 44, the headsail interacting with the mainsail provides most of a boat's driving force, and trimming it should receive top priority. There are good reasons to follow a sailmaker's advice – *trim the front of the jib first and then the back of the main*, ie the exit angle (Fig 219).

Three factors regarding the headsail should be noted. Firstly, it operates in the upwash induced by the mainsail (Fig 43), which tends to shift the stagnation point around towards the windward side of the headsail. In other words, the headsail is set in a continually lifting wind. As a result, the boat can be pointed closer to the wind without the headsail luffing.

Secondly, the headsail works in a higher speed flow created by the interacting mainsail, as depicted earlier in Fig 46. Thus, the pressure distribution over the whole headsail is more favourable in terms of driving force as compared with that developed without mainsail.

Fig 220 A 1/4 scale Dragon class model in the wind tunnel. Horizontal camber stripes, added to both sails and photographed from above the mast top, helped to record and analyse the effect of sail camber, its streamwise and vertical distribution, sail twist, sail trim, etc, on the aerodynamic efficiency of the rig.

Note that in photo (b) the genoa halyard is not tightened enough and this causes the leading edge to scallop between hanks. When properly set, the sail should have its leading edge straight for better efficiency.

Thirdly, the headsail has no mast along its leading edge; the mast is usually blamed for making the mainsail less efficient. This factor is less influential than the first two factors, however.

Wind tunnel tests on a model of Dragon rig (Fig 220) revealed that in close-hauled conditions, with a heading angle from 25 to 30 degrees, a change in the mainsail sheeting angle δ_M over the range 0 to 10 degrees has little effect on the driving force F_x (Fig 221), but considerable influence on the heeling force, F_y, regardless of the heading angle (Fig 222), both forces progressively decreasing as δ_M is increased (Ref 2.48). The trim angle of the main significantly affects the pointing ability of the boat, for it directly determines the upwash and local flow velocities at the leading edge of the

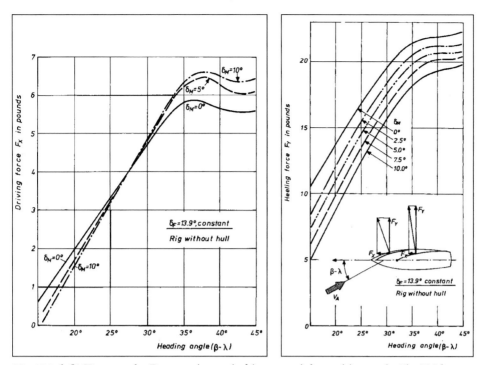

Fig 221 (left) Tests on the Dragon rig upwind in an upright position, as in Fig 220 but without the hull, at wind speed 25 ft/sec (14.8 knots, moderate breeze). The effects of the mainsail sheeting angle δ_M on the driving force F_x is shown. Optimum heading angle (best V_{mg}) for a Dragon class is around 22–25 degrees, depending on the wind speed.

Fig 222 (right) Tests on the Dragon rig in conditions as in Fig 221. The graph shows the effect of the mainsail sheeting angle δ_M on the heeling force F_H. The main contributes little to driving the boat, but affects the heeling force (side force) appreciably. This suggests that careful attention should be paid to trimming the main when upwind, even to the extent of allowing a certain amount of backwinding in order to reduce the heeling force. Although the primary object of trimming sails is to obtain the largest driving force from a given area, the reduction of heeling force is only slightly less important. A large heeling force is detrimental as it leads to increase in leeway, excessive heel and associated extra drag.

headsail. As a result, the headsail can be sheeted several degrees further off the centreline than the main without tending to luff. However, as shown in the small sketch of Fig 222, the mainsail 'pays' a penalty for the services rendered. Area for area, the main contributes substantially more to the heeling force, F_y, and less to the driving force, F_x, than the headsail. This is due to the downwash (the header effect) and also to diminished local flow velocities along the forward leeside of the main caused by the headsail.

The results presented in Fig 223 show that a significant difference in the driving force F_x can be achieved by making adjustments to the position of the genoa clew. This is particularly true of the foresail sheeting angles if the limitations imposed by the class rules are ignored. The sheeting angles $\delta_F = 13.9°$ and $\delta_M = 5°$ were used in this particular test, since they represent most closely what was 'normal' in a *Dragon* class boat sailing close-hauled in average wind conditions.

Fig 223 Tests on the Dragon rig in conditions as in Fig 221 but with the hull. This shows the effect of altering the position of genoa clew on the driving force.

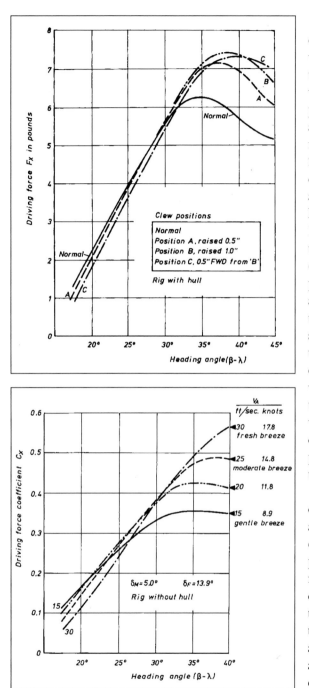

Fig 224 Tests on the Dragon rig without hull. The effect of the apparent wind speed on the driving force coefficient C_X is shown on the graph. The sailcloth is elastic so that, under aerodynamic loading, which largely depends on the apparent wind speed, the whole rig is subject to elastic deformations that affect the sail shape and therefore the sail forces.

The positions of the clews of both mainsail and genoa were initially adjusted so that the sail assumed a shape, with the wind on, that to the practised eye seemed reasonable. These positions are referred to as 'normal' in Fig 223, which was intended to demonstrate the effects of altering the tensions in the leech and foot of the genoa. For position A, the clew of the genoa was raised $\frac{1}{2}$ inch (1.3 cm) above the 'normal' position, and for position B, a further $\frac{1}{2}$ inch (equivalent to 2 inches or 5 cm in full scale). This adjustment had the effect of progressively decreasing the leech tension without seriously altering the foot tension. Position C was obtained by shifting the clew $\frac{1}{2}$ inch forward from position B, thus decreasing the foot tension.

Variations in the apparent wind velocity, V_A, have a conspicuous effect on the driving force coefficient, C_X, presented in Fig 224. The reason for the large differences in rig performance is that the depth and shape of the cambers of both interacting sails (including twist and entry shape) all vary depending on V_A; and these geometry factors are *time dependent* and due to recoverable and non-recoverable stretches in the sail fabric. It is evident that the internal stresses in a sail, although partly due to the way it is set, are also affected by the strength and direction of the wind, so that the sail 'suffers' an elastic deformation which contributes appreciably to its shape and therefore affects the forces which it will develop.

Figure 225 depicts the results of seven tests all plotted on the same graph. Each short full line represents the plot of L versus D for a constant heading (ß – λ) and constant trim angle of the main, but with eight different trim angles of the foresail δ_F from 7.5 to 22.5 degrees as indicated. The thick line indicates an envelope and illustrates once again but in a different way a previously discussed point, namely, the effect of a small alteration in trim angles on a given rig performance. It is quite surprising how different the rig sensitivity (in terms of L/D ratio to alterations in the δ_F angle) is at different headings. We can see that for heading angles of less than 27.5 degrees, a large number of the short L–D lines lie close to the envelope in spite of the variations in genoa trim. In other words, alterations in δ_F affect primarily the lift and the drag relatively little.

On the other hand, as the heading angle increases, the rig performance becomes gradually more sensitive to the trim

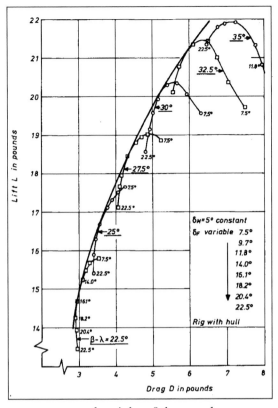

Fig 225 Tests on the Dragon rig with the hull as in Fig 220. Here we see a polar diagram L–D of two interacting sails. Each short full line represents the plot of lift and drag for a constant heading (ß – λ) and δ_M, but with eight different trim angles δ_F from 7.5 to 22.5 degrees. Wind speed is 25 ft/sec (14.8 knots). Probably due to differences between the model and real life, these angles are larger than those used in practice.

angles, and it is only too easy to move across to the right of the envelope curve (by sheeting the genoa too close), to drastically increase drag, and so to reduce the L/D ratio. For heading angles 35 and 37.5, the mainsail trim angle δ_M = 5 degrees seems to be too small. Another conclusion is that large increases in lift may be obtained by widening the slot between sails in the region near maximum lift, ie, by increasing the genoa trim angle. The optimum difference between the sheeting angles of main and genoa within the range of headings tested seems to be about 10 degrees further off the centreline than the main.

As already mentioned, there is a limitation on the available sheeting angle, δ_F, assuming furthest outboard fairlead position allowed by the class rules.

Table 13 indicates these maximum δ_F for a number of known keel boats and dinghy classes.

Table 13
Available sheeting angles for some known boats

CLASS	MAXIMUM δ_F	NOTE
12 Metre	8–9 degrees	The reason why dinghies have a larger sheeting
6 Metre	9–10	base than racing keelboats will be explained in a later
Star	11	chapter.
Dragon	14	
5.5 Metre	15	
Flying Dutchman	18	
5.05	20	

It is evident from Fig 225 and also Fig 216b that when bearing away from the optimum heading angles for the best V_{mg} – which varies between 20 and 27.5 degrees depending on the type of boat and the wind speed – that *large* dividends in terms of driving force could be obtained provided the sheeting angle of headsail is increased. This is particularly relevant to keel boats. In dinghy classes the wide sheeting base is nearly always used to advantage.

The cruising yachtsmen and cruising yacht designers are in a better position in this respect than their racing counterparts; they are not restricted by the class rules. Thus it is possible to arrange the sheeting of the genoa clew firmly outside the deck. A possible means of doing so might be, for example, a small boom pivoted at the mast, to which the genoa clew is attached. A preventer travelling in the track along the gunnel would allow fore-and-aft movement of the clew while preventing the sail rising and causing an uncontrolled increase in sail camber and twist. The sheets could be fastened and led in the usual manner.

In conditions when V_{mg} is not the dominant race winning factor, as it is on the triangular racing course, faster passages would result.

The amount and distribution of camber and the amount of twist, all of which contribute to the sail forces, depend upon the separate skills of the sailmaker and the sail setter. However, the crew is still the most important component, and the many adjustments to sail shape which go to make up what is described as 'tuning' can be more important than having the *best* sail design. The crew of a boat has a number of courses available, described in Table 12, and so a compromise between the various effects can be found whereby the sails are tuned to the requirements in Table 11.

Such devices as telltales, telltale windows, camber stripes, trim lines, still camera shots of the sail shape and ultimately a sort of sail scanner (which continually monitors the 'flying shape' of sails) may assist the tuning process.

Headsail trim

'Show us not the aim without the way.
For ends and means on earth are so entangled
That changing one, you change the other too;
Each different path brings other ends in view.'

Ferdinand Lassalle (1825–1864)

In the invisible medium of air flow the telltales, tufts, woollies, or ticklers, made of 4–6 inch long strips of yarn or any brightly coloured light material, are attached to the sail surface in some sensitive places to tell the crew whether the flow around the sails is 'healthy' or not. In other words, the telltales can detect the character of the flow immediately adjacent to the sail surface – but *nothing else*. They do not tell the crew whether the sail camber is correctly matched to the actual sailing conditions, nor can they indicate whether the sails are set at such an incidence angle that the boat is actually attaining her best performance. Although the telltales can aid the crew in finding the optimum groove (2.80) for maximum sail performance, they were invented – it has been said – in two forms: the ones you swear by and the ones you swear at.

What telltales tell The most important function of telltales is to warn the sail trimmer that flow separation has occurred, either along the luff (Fig 54a) or along the leech area (Fig 54b), and eventually remedial action may be necessary. Interpretation of the telltales' behaviour may appear rather simple: they follow and display the direction of air flow. It is therefore believed that when sailing to windward the crew should sheet the headsail and steer a course so that all telltales attached to both sides of the luff lie smoothly against the fabric of the sail, ie, without showing any agitation (Fig 226b). In this way, the leading edge separation on both sides of the luff is avoided and the sail operates near or at the *ideal angle of incidence*.

If the telltales on the leeward side begin to twirl in a manner shown in Figs 54a and 226c, this shows that they are in the region of separation flow caused either by sailing too freely or with the sheets too hard in. The identical behaviour of the telltales in these two very different circumstances clearly suggests that they *should not be used exclusively* as indicators of optimum sail setting to achieve the best speed made good to windward, V_{mg}.

If the sail incidence is made smaller than the ideal angle, the stagnation point S_t will shift to the leeward side of the sail and will cause reversal of sail curvature (luffing) with separated flow on the windward side as shown in Fig 226d.

In sailing literature one can find some firmly established advice about how to read the telltales. Let us quote some: 1) 'The leeward tickler is the most sensitive indicator of a stalled sail or that the boat is being sailed too low.' 2) 'The windward tickler can be carried effectively with a slight flutter.' 3) 'It is far better to have the windward tickler flutter (pointing high) than the leeward (stalling, sailing too low).' 4)'Optimum lift is achieved when the air flow around the sail maintains a smooth flow on both surfaces and when the lift/drag ratio is maximum. Both woollies stream evenly, and when they do, the sail is said to be in the groove.'

These precepts should not be blindly accepted: nothing in life is absolutely certain, alas, except death and taxes. To start with point 1: the telltale attached to the lee side luff should not be regarded as 'the most sensitive indicator of a stalled sail'. If any of those ticklers begins to twirl, the sail is not stalled, but an agitated tickler does indicate the presence of a relatively small separation bubble, as shown by yarns 1 and 2 in Fig 54b. Behind the bubble the airflow remains attached, as disclosed by yarns 3–7, Fig 54b, which are lying flat against the sail. The effect of the bubble can be likened to an increase in sail camber, and so the lift can be effectively generated. As the separation bubble expands further downstream, with an increasing angle of incidence, a growth of lift may and usually follows; a larger suction area for greater incidence in Fig 56b demonstrates this trend. Finally, the stall is reached, and with it the lift fails to keep going. Such a total separation cannot unmistakably be revealed by the leading edge telltale alone, but by the leech yarn number 8 in Fig 54b, which curls behind the leech being drawn into a reversed flow (back eddy area) shown in Fig 53b, and covering the whole leeward side of the sail.

Quotes 2 and 3 are only partially correct. A deliberate attempt to avoid leading edge separation by sailing on the verge of luffing is only justified in a strong wind and close-hauled conditions. Figures 115 and 117, applicable to a single

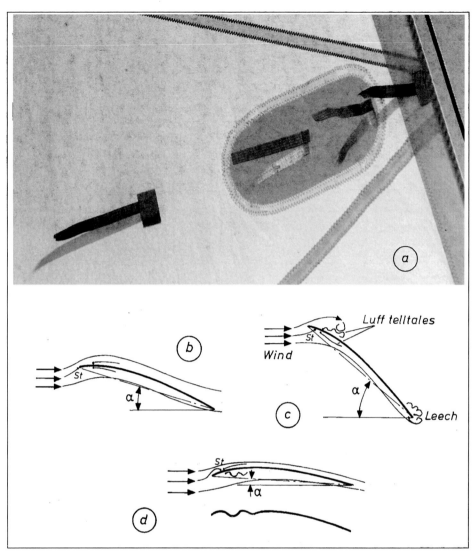

Fig 226

a)   The telltale window makes it possible to look through the sail and see easily the image of the tuft on the opposite side. The windows are sometimes unnecessary because modern sail materials may be sufficiently translucent to see dark woollies on the other side *Photo by A Gentry*.

b)   The sail is set at an ideal angle of incidence with the sail entry properly adjusted. The stagnation point S_t is situated right on the leading edge. Both windward and leeward telltales align smoothly with the local flow without fluttering.

c)   If the sail incidence is made greater than that in b, the stagnation point S_t travels to the windward side, with a separation bubble on the other. The luff telltale detects the bubble but not the stall. The stall can only be indicated by the leech telltale, as shown.

d)   The windward telltale flutters just before sail luffs. The stagnation point in this case forms on the leeward side, causing a reversal of sail curvature which ultimately may even cause sail flogging.

Note: There are only a few degrees' difference in heading between conditions (c) and (d). To be effective, the telltale should be attached in such a place that it can rotate 360 degrees and not foul on hank, forestay or seam.

sail rig, but relevant in a qualitative sense to interacting sails, demonstrate that the sail incidence (the trim angle) must vary depending on wind speed in order to achieve best speed to windward. Consequently, in medium and lighter winds, in close-hauled and close-reaching conditions, it does pay to increase the sail incidence to develop greater lift; even with two leeward telltales fluttering (Fig 54b).

Finally, precept number 4 is too dogmatic to be followed blindly; a glance at Fig 115 should be sufficient to understand its fallacy. In a variety of wind speeds and headings experienced in practice, the optimum lift that can be effectively exploited is different depending on the circumstances. The C_L/C_D maximum, indicated in Fig 115 by the tangential thin line touching the polar curve at the incidence angle of about 10 degrees, may only be regarded as an optimum for one particular wind, V_A. In other words, L/D_{max} ratio – a meaningful criterion for aircraft performance – is of limited importance from the sailing point of view.

It may be clear from this brief discussion that a reasonable use of telltales must necessarily be based on experimentation. Reasoning is essential, and by

Fig 227 An International One-Design sailing to windward. Even a narrow headsail without overlap may cause backwinding if its camber tends to increase too much towards the sailhead, and/or if the gap between two interacting sails is rapidly converging in the region of overlap. It seems that backwinding is less likely to occur when the overlapping portion of the headsail is approximately parallel to the adjacent part of the main.

trial and error each helmsman will ultimately find the *right position* for telltales, their number and their flutter behaviour for each wind and heading conditions, and all depending on the type of boat and rig.

One particular point deserves to be briefly touched on: what happens when sailing in unstable, gusty winds, ie in winds which veer and back from the mean direction. A sudden header can be spotted instantly; the sails flutter at the luff giving warning to helmsman that he must bear off to keep the boat well. Lifts do not produce such an instant warning. At first, nothing obvious happens and watching the leeward less visible telltales to spot lift requires attention.

Adjusting headsails by recutting Figure 227 illustrates a common headsail problem. Here we can see that the mainsail is badly backwinded in the region of upper half of the jib, in spite of the angle of incidence of the jib being less there than at the foot, due to the sail twist.

Sailing on *Norsaga* (Fig 218) the author found that up to around 20 per cent of the mainsail area suffered from backwinding, no matter how the genoa and main were trimmed; and as usual the area affected was near the luff, where the suction contributes most to the driving force.

The cause of such persistent backwinding in some parts of the mainsail is explained in Fig 228. In principle, headsails are three-sided sails supported relatively loosely by the forestay only. In effect, all edges are free to sag sideways, as well as in the plane of the sail, by different amounts for each edge, depending on a variety of factors. Sag in the forestay can be one factor which makes the problem of designing and cutting any headsail to a predetermined camber more difficult than creating a mainsail. If the sails were initially cut with a straight luff, the sag of the forestay would produce camber in the sail, even if the foot and leech sag contribution is assumed to be negligible. Forestay sag should be regarded like mast bend in reverse. Its contribution to the sail camber would, of course, depend on wind strength – the more sag the greater the sail camber. And in strong winds heavy backwinding may occur, even though the same sail, at the same trim, might not offend in lighter winds.

Fig 228a Camber distribution over the headsail height depends primarily on: 1. the luff curve introduced by the sailmaker, ie, the curvature of the luff of the sail when laid flat on the floor and 2. the amount of forestay sag. An s-shaped luff allows for forestay sag (c).

In diagram (c) a convex luff makes a sail fuller while a concave (hollow) curve flattens a sail. There is also an interaction between the forestay sag and the luff curvature – a convex luff curve tends to reduce the forestay sag, while a concave curve will increase the sag. The effect of these two factors on the sail camber may be greatly modified depending on the property and quality of the cloth used by the sailmaker (78c). There is now such a wide range of different construction materials available that sails that are identically designed but cut from different fabrics can perform in very different ways.

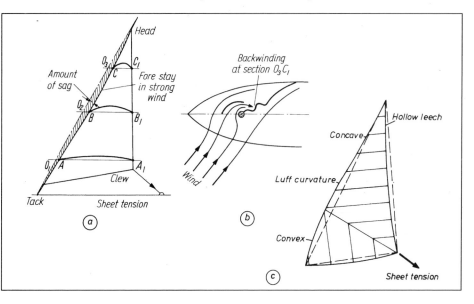

The camber of various sections O_1, O_2, O_3 in Fig 228a will be different depending on the amount of sailcloth pulled aft by the wind pressure. The biggest camber will occur somewhere close to section O_1, where the amount of sag O_3C in relation to the sailchord $C\,C_1$ is the greatest. As indicated, the camber of a sail cut in this fashion tends to increase towards the head: if this is overdone it becomes an undesirable but frequently encountered trait in headsails. Such a headsail cannot possibly be trimmed correctly for close-hauled work. If the lower, relatively flat, part of the sail is set at a proper sheeting angle so there is no backwinding of the mainsail, the upper part of the headsail with large camber will almost certainly cause backwinding. This is shown in Fig 228b and photographs in Figs 227 and 229. If the sheet is eased in order to alleviate backwinding, the upper part of the sail will probably flutter and so will not be fully effective.

In an attempt to counteract the effect of forestay sag, sailors frequently follow the old salt's advice: 'keep the jib stay bar taut'. Although, like most such sayings, there is some sense in it, it cannot be applied equally in all cases since, particularly in some boats, excessive forestay tension effected by tightening the backstay may only bend the hull and possibly the mast too, and may still not reduce the forestay sag! Even in strongly built, heavy displacement yachts, where this dictum might be applied to the limit, it is impossible to eliminate sag completely. It is necessary therefore to introduce some correction when establishing the luff rounding curve, and to have excess material near the foot but a

Fig 229 Battens with incorrect stiffness may ruin even the best sail. This photograph shows the fully battened mainsail of a Thai Mk 4 catamaran on which an undesirable tendency of the leech to curl to windward is apparent. This could be cured by increasing the batten thickness (stiffness) at the outer edge.

Fig 230 Since the leech of the genoa is unsupported, it will sag. As a result, sail camber will tend to increase above that which would occur if the luff round (surplus of cloth given by the sailmaker) alone contributed to the sail fullness. To counteract this tendency, a sail for close-hauled work may be cut with a hollow leech as shown. Under the sheet tension, such a leech will tend to assume a straight line, thus flattening the adjacent part of the sail; and this serves as a remedy to alleviate or eliminate the tendency for the main to luff or backwind (which is more likely to occur with a big overlapping genoa). Another factor that affects the sail camber is the backstay tension; it pulls against the forestay. Any increase in backstay tension tends to reduce the forestay sag and results in less camber in the headsail. The correct amount of backstay tension depends on the sail shape appropriate for a given heading, wind speed and sea conditions.

WELL
HALLOWED
LEECH

SAG IN
FORESTAY

'deficit' near the head, as shown in Fig 228. In effect one is subtracting the sag of the forestay from the basic allowance of cloth in a similar, though opposite, way to the method used when compensating for mast bending on the mainsail (Fig 279). The basic purpose of making such adjustment in the luff round is to produce a sail camber which is less likely to produce uncontrollable backwinding.

Another way of correcting a headsail cut in order to redistribute its camber is to create a hollow leech, as shown in Figs 228c and 230. This measure will produce horizontal forces, *indicated by the arrows in Fig 230*, which will tend to flatten the sail more in one place than another, depending on the cumulative effects of hollows in the leech and the luff. The amount of hollow in the leech of the genoa will be dictated by its proposed application. For example, a heavy genoa for strong winds should be well hollowed, while only slight hollowing – or none at all – may be required for the light genoa. This is because forestay sag is less in light winds, and also more camber can be desired in these conditions. Sails for reaching will have straight leeches, since more camber is appropriate in that context.

The length of the leech also has an effect on the amount of twist in the sail (ie, longer leech, greater twist); therefore a compromise must be found between the required flattening of the sail and the amount of twist required, consistent with minimum backwinding of the mainsail and the limitations of the foresail sheeting base.

Fairlead position The fairlead position can be altered in two different ways: 1) athwartship, which directly controls the trim angle δ_F at the foot of the headsail, and 2) fore-and-aft, which controls the tension applied along the foot and leech – in effect it determines the amount of twist, ie variation of the trim angle upward from the sail foot, and also to some degree the distribution of camber along the sail height. Because a number of interacting variables are involved expert opinion differs as to the best position of fairleads for sailing close-hauled. Thus, referring to the fore-and-aft trim, some say that the line of the sheet should be along the mitre line of the clew, sometimes called the trim line and marked by sailmakers on the clew of sail. Others maintain that it should lie above or below it.

The value of these conflicting prescriptions lies less in the actual advice given than in their recognizing that fairlead positions are important. Correct setting of the fairleads is important in order to attain the proper sail twist and also the right distribution of camber. In Fig 231a the tension force N in the sheet can be resolved into two components, N_1 and N_2, acting respectively along the leech and foot of the sail. The tension in the foot will be greater than that in the leech, and consequently the foot of the sail will be flat, but the upper parts will be twisted and will flutter first if the sail is pinched. In case b the leech tension is increased at the expense of the tension in the foot, and hence the sail will twist less but will be more cambered, and the leech may have a tendency to curl over.

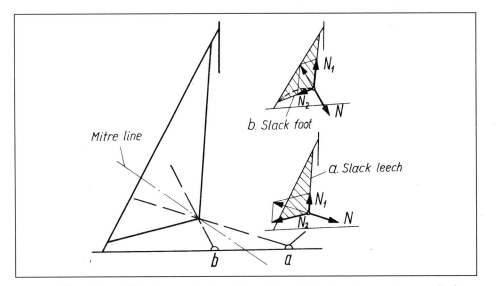

Fig 231 The effects of the fore-and-aft position of the fairlead on the tensions applied to the foot and leech of a jib. Apart from the influence of tensions N_1 and N_2 on sail twist and camber, there is an interaction between the position of the lead and sheet tension. The general rule is that, whenever the headsail sheet is significantly eased, the clew moves forward, and the fairlead should also be moved forward.

Fig 232 Yet another important tuning factor is the relative position of the sail plan to the hull and standing rigging. Often an alteration to the mast rake may reap dividends in higher performance. Until the headsail sheeting angle and twist are correct, there is not much use doing anything else. In the case shown, the mast rake primarily serves to tune the headsail.

A tentative compromise in fairlead positioning can be found by using the same method as is employed in setting the mainsail. Without changing the setting of the sheets, the boat is gently luffed. If the fairleads are positioned correctly, the whole of the luff of the foresail should start to flutter almost at one moment. Such behaviour indicates that the sail twist matches wind twist. If the upper parts flutter first it indicates either that the sail is too full there because of its cut, or else its twist is too large. This corresponds to case a in Fig 231, and the remedy is to move the fairlead forward. If the lower parts flutter first, the fairlead should be moved aft.

The evenly breaking luff, although logically an indicator of proper sail setting, should not actually be considered as a reliable yardstick but only as a first approximation. The shape of the slot, helm balance, trim angle at the jib sail foot, wind speed, angle of heel, heading angle, etc, are all performance factors which may, in effect and some conditions, be more important than having telltales swirling in accord along the luff. For example, in heavy air it may pay to have the upper part of the sail flutter first, ie, the top of the sail 'is spilled' to decrease the heeling moment. This can be achieved by moving the fairlead aft.

An interesting method of tuning the foresail has been evolved in one of the Olympic classes for sailing to windward. The weakness of the design of this light boat lies in the relatively low rigidity of the hull. Too large a tension in the forestay can deform or even damage the hull structure. In light winds, correctly tuning the genoa is comparatively simple. Difficulties arise, however, in strong winds, when the forestay sag becomes excessive and the camber of the upper parts of the genoa increases. By raking the mast aft (Fig 232), it is possible to maintain a tight foot to the sail and at the same time to slacken the leech. This follows, since the clew C, of a low-cut genoa is virtually fixed on the deck and the distance B_1C becomes less than BC; as a result the genoa sags to leeward, increasing the slot between the sails (opening the head). When this method proves insufficient, the genoa is changed for one of lower aspect ratio, AB_2C. This not only reduces the sail area, but also increases the clearance between the sails in the most important region near the jib halyard sheave. Thus the technique for tuning the genoa can be summarized as follows:

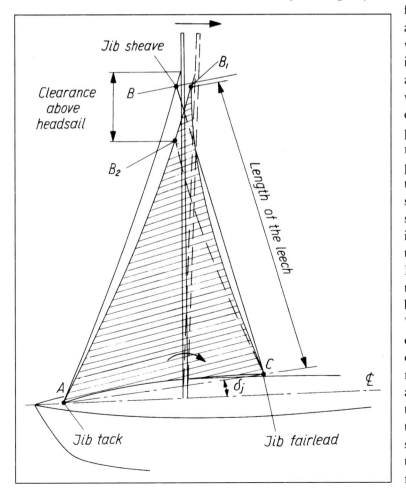

light winds: mast upright
foot relatively slack (controlled by sheets)
leech tight

strong winds: mast raked aft
foot tight
leech slack

very strong winds: low headsail to increase clearance above the head of the sail

Siting the fairleads should be considered in relation to the course sailed and the type of foresail being used, ie, the current weather conditions. A fairlead correctly set for a close-hauled course will not be as satisfactory on a close reach. Figure 233 shows one example of a system giving wide scope for the positioning of the fairlead. Even on boats where the deck width offers no restrictions, one frequently finds the fairleads set too far inboard. Catamarans have an exceptionally wide sheeting base (Fig 234) giving almost unlimited scope in the positioning of the foresail fairleads and the mainsheet horse for maximum efficiency. Yet Fig 235 shows that these advantages are often ignored. Figure 236, on the other hand, is a good illustration of how the sails can be trimmed if proper use is made of the available deck width and control devices. We can see that there is much less twist in the mainsail, and that the foresail fairlead is positioned correctly to produce adequate camber and efficient interaction between the sails without backwinding.

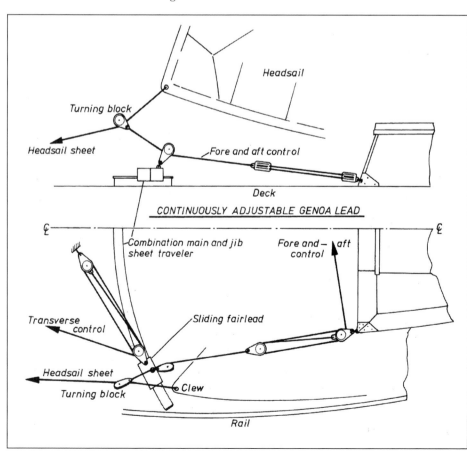

Fig 233 A continuously adjustable headsail lead allows an instant adjustment of the shape and trim of this most important sail on the boat to suit the ever-changing wind and sea conditions. The lead can be placed quickly anywhere within a large area of the deck, which is a particularly useful feature for short-handed cruising sailors.

Fig 234 In view of experimental evidence, as presented in Figs 216 and 225, the importance of continuous transverse trim of any headsail, including spinnakers, cannot be overemphasized. Athwartship trimming is the key to the slot and thus overall rig efficiency. In this respect, multihulls with a wide sheeting base can use the potential power of the rig more effectively than monohulls, particularly on headings away from close-hauled.

Fig 235 The photograph shows badly and unnecessarily twisted sails on the most difficult point of sailing, close-reaching in a fresh breeze. As soon as the tension on the mainsheet is eased, the sail twists, and keeping afloat and dry may become a struggle. The remedy is to have a wide mainsheet horse and an efficient kicking strap to enable a relatively twist-free sail to be let out far enough from the centreline. The penalty for excessive twist in terms of sail efficiency can be large, as is demonstrated in Fig 102.

Fig 236 An example of well tuned and trimmed sails. Only after seeing a sail set in operating conditions can the perfect battens be appreciated. It is important to get the right flexibility so that the battens curve in such a way that the 'natural' efficient flow round the sail is encouraged. To achieve this aim is something of an art, particularly with sails carrying a large amount of roach which tends to push the battens into the body of the sail.

OVERLAP

'There is, on the whole, nothing more important in life than to discover the right point of view from which things should be looked at and judged, and then to keep to that point.'
General Carl von Clausewitz, On War, 1832

Due to the combined influence of rating rules, scientific research, developments in rig technology, and design beliefs and practices, the sail plan of cruiser/racers, dominated at one time by large, low aspect ratio mainsails and comparatively small headsails, has changed radically. In the sixties and seventies, the most successful sail configurations were dominated by huge headsails with an actual area exceeding the mainsail area by a factor of about two (Fig 237). At the same time, the aspect ratio of shrinking mainsails increased so much that those in charge of the International Rating Rule (IOR), apparently thinking that mainsails had already become too small and might eventually degenerate into a vestige form, decided in one stroke to limit both its minimum area and maximum aspect ratio. Nonetheless, the trend towards high aspect ratio mains and a bewildering variety of headsails (Fig 237b) – high cut and low cut genoas, reachers, staysails, sneakers, windseekers, tall boys, and whatever new types and names were added to the description of a spread of canvas that could be set in the fore-triangle – has continued.

Fig 237a Under the IOR and IMS rules, penalty-free headsails can be set in the foretriangle and tacked down anywhere within it, but their clews must not go aft of the 'LP line'. LP is the perpendicular distance of the 'LP line' from the foremost headstay. Its minimum length is 1.5 J, where J is the length of fore-triangle base. As compared with the previous RORC rule, the IOR headsails are measured on the 'LP' instead of the foot. This encourages genoas with a large overlap. Note that in this case the rated area of the fore–triangle is almost twice that of the mainsail.

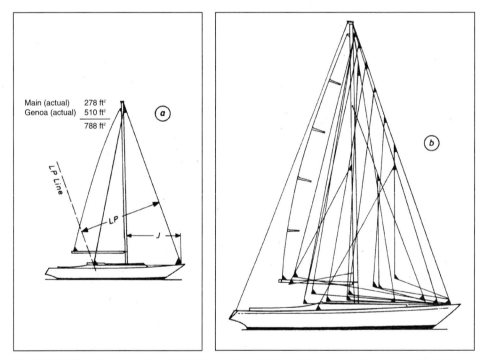

Fig 237b The sail plan of an old IOR masthead sloop. The rule-makers argue that it is wrong to say: 'The rule encourages huge fore-triangles. Fore-triangles may be huge, but this is because designers believe that they will improve boat performance' (Ref 2.81). In reply to that sort of reasoning, one may point out that apparently the underrated area of huge genoas does not reflect their much larger driving efficiency as compared with that of the rated mainsail area. And it should not be surprising that enlightened yachtsmen and designers have found good reason to maximize the effectiveness of the rated area, just because of measurement bias (Ref 2.82).

The discovery of the highly efficient genoa, with a large overlap on the mainsail, encouraged designers to exploit the low tax on foresail area. One of the first and famous examples of this new trend was the English cutter *Myth of Malham*, built to the RORC rule (Figs 238a and b). The mast is set nearly amidships and carries a small mainsail, but there is a wide selection of headsails. The sail list in Table 14 gives their areas.

No of Sail	Sail	Area (in sq ft)	No of Sail	Sail	Area (in sq ft)
0	mainsail	305	8	second heavy staysail	141
1	large genoa	637	9	baby staysail	72
2	light genoa	516	10	large RORC spinnaker	875
3	large yankee	300	11	small spinnaker	600
4	second jib	185	12	small yankee	250
5	third jib	100	13	second light staysail	143
6	genoa staysail	250	14	trysail	120
7	first staysail	216			

Table 14
Wardrobe of sails for Myth of Malham

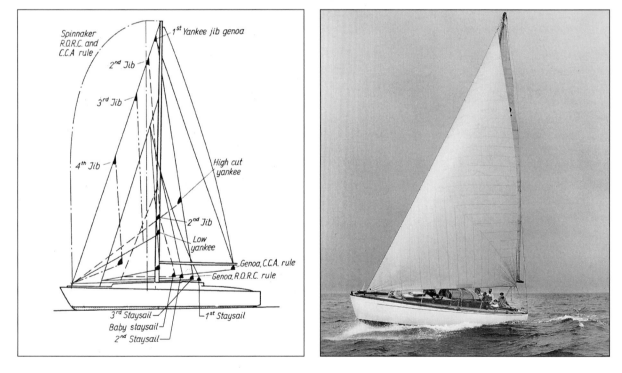

Fig 238a (left) The sail plan of the *Myth of Malham* (designed by Laurent Giles & Partners) as modified in 1950. When this boat first appeared she was seen as hideous, but as someone said, 'She carried more men more quickly across more sea with less sail area than any previous yacht, although she looked like a log which someone had kicked out of the way into the water.'

We should avoid – D Phillips–Birt believed – being misled by the sentimental misconceptions which find expression in such remarks as 'A pretty yacht is a good yacht' or 'A yacht which looks right is right'. An ugly one can be, and often is, efficient.

Fig 238b (right) The straight luff on the *Myth of Malham*, racing in US waters in 1948, demonstrates the merits of well designed staying.

When tuning the sails, the dual role of the foresail should be borne in mind, as a sail itself, and as one which has a profound effect on the mainsail. A change in the foresails is felt more strongly than a change in the mainsail setting. One should therefore give it priority when tuning the sails, and if any compromise is required, this should be made on the mainsail rather than the foresail.

According to the (IOR) rule, any number of headsails, together or one at a time could be set, so long as their clews were inside the 'LP line' marked in Fig 237a. However, practically only one mainsail can be carried throughout off-shore racing. And if a second main is carried, this must be as a *bona fide* spare for emergency replacement (materially smaller than a normal close-reefed mainsail and of strength consistent with use in extremely severe weather); but not in the expectation of use for improved performance in varying weather conditions (Ref 2.81).

The area of genoa within the headstay and LP (Fig 237) is rated by the IOR as less than its actual area. For a low cut genoa this restriction usually means that the overlap at the sail foot (without penalty) is up to 165 per cent of the J measurement. The rated area of the mainsail, and that of the genoa, is assessed by a roundabout and rather unintelligible mathematical formula, and is less than its actual size. The rule-makers apparently believed that introducing corrections to the actual areas of both types of sails for rating purpose justly compensated for the lesser efficiency of the mainsail as compared with the interacting genoa (2.82). But evidently they failed in this respect, and the foretriangle became a premium area, as demonstrated in Fig 237b. If, as would have been infinitely more sensible, headsails had been assessed on their actual size, possibly including their aerodynamic efficiency, the properly named *main sail* would have remained much larger.

The tests on a full scale yacht in real sailing conditions presented in Fig 44 clearly suggest that the efficiency of an interacting headsail in terms of its driving force is at least twice as high as that of a Bermuda type mainsail. Another interesting test on the Bembridge Redwing-class keel boat, reported by Uffa Fox (2.83) as early as 1939, should give much food for thought. The hull was One-Design, and the only limit on its rig has been that it should not have more than 200 square feet (18.6 m^2) of actual sail area. The owners have been free to put on whatever rig they wished. Over the years every conceivable type of rig has been tested, including Chinese batten sails, and even a free-turning, horizontal-axis turbine (like an autogiro) developed by Lord Brabazon. In the end it was found that all rigs were inferior to a Bermudan sloop (Fig 239). The best light–air boat had a mainsail of AR = 3.6, but the overall winner carried a main of AR = 3.0. The two consistent leaders had a mainsail area twice the *non-overlapping jib* area. One surprising thing had been found: the boat with a big overlapping genoa, in the proportion normal to a 6 Metre yacht, was the slowest.

This lengthy experiment, carried out in a variety of real sailing conditions, corroborates earlier wind tunnel tests presented in Fig 217, namely: the overlap, particularly in close-hauled attitude, *is of no advantage* if the total area of headsail is rated. From another lengthy experiment with the Australian 18 foot skiffs, a similar conclusion was reached. The sail area on these skiffs is effectively unlimited and they use three different rigs depending on forecast conditions.

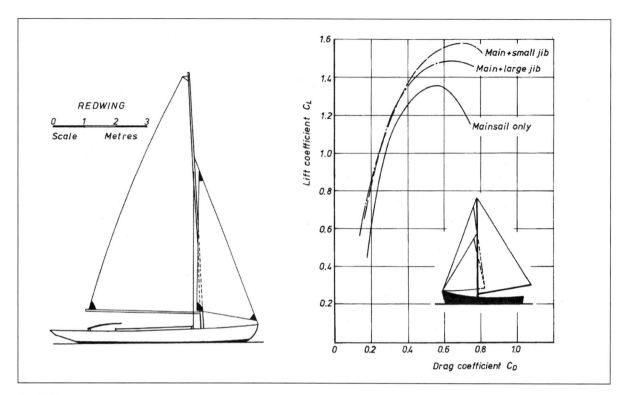

Fig 239

a)   Bembridge Redwing keelboat, one of the oldest One-Design boats (22 ft 1 in, 6.73 m LOA). The boat was redesigned in 1937 according to the same 200 ft^2 limit of S_A. Those popular Redwings had been a familiar sight in the Solent.

b)   Results of wind tunnel tests on a Bermudan rig with two jibs – a small one and a large one – seem to corroborate full scale tests on the Bembridge Redwing. Wind tunnel tests suggest that the overall efficiency of a masthead jib in terms of the driving force (see Fig 144) is inferior to that of a smaller jib. Note that the area of small jib in proportion to the mainsail area is similar to that of the Bembridge rig depicted in sketch (a).

All have fully battened mainsails and *non-overlapping* jibs (AYRS, Newsletter, April 1995).

   Any sail with increased area that goes unmeasured by the rule, ie, does not increase a boat's rating, is the most efficient sail from the viewpoint both of those racing and of yacht designers too. As a result, the headsail has become the truly *main* sail of the contemporary rig – with an almost infinite number of shapes that can be set within the fore-triangle boundaries. Consequently, the mainsail of decreasing area and unavoidably increasing aspect ratio gradually evolved into a slotted flap, to use the aircraft wing analogy; and as we know the flap does not need to be large to greatly increase the lift-producing capability of the wing. So the new sailplans became higher, with shorter booms and larger fore-triangle bases. Since the racing boats frequently set the fashion, overlapping genoas were soon seen on cruising boats too.

   Although the wind blows for nothing, to catch its energy by means of canvas costs money. And unfortunately for cruising folk, sailmakers do not charge customers for the rated sail area, but for the actual areas, regardless of *sail efficiency*. It is in the interest of cruising people to have sails which give them good value for money, ie, to maximize the effectiveness of the *actual* sail area.

But in sailing, like in anything else, there is always the possibility that a fad may overrule common sense.

It has been argued that if you are looking for ease of handling and aiming to save expense, stowage, valuable living space below and general wear and tear, genoas offer very little. As the famous American designer, Francis Herreshoff (Ref 2.84), once remarked: 'Perhaps, gentle reader, you can think of something more ridiculous to go to sea with than a parachute spinnaker and a genoa lashed on to a washtub. They require a large and specially trained crew... composed mostly of gigolo yacht jockeys... to handle their rule cheating sails... Certainly actual sail area should be the principal basis for rating, for sail area determines the number of crew... the only thing that a lapping jib cheats is the owner, or rather all the owners in the class, for they no longer have an easily handled yacht... I can't help but think rating eventually will be drived from actual sail area alone...'

Another famous British designer, Charles Nicholson, also recommended measuring the total area of sails, and in the first new rating rule after the Second World War (the 5.5 Metre-class rule), this principle was incorporated. The 5.5 Metre-class participated in five Olympic Games (between 1952 and 1968) and interestingly enough a genoa could be used if the crew wanted to, but nobody did because it had to be paid for in the rating for the mainsail area.

Self-tacking jib The aim of any sailing rig is to produce the greatest driving force for the least heeling moment per given area. It must be structurally and mechanically reliable, and it must be possible to set, reef and furl the sails as easily as possible.

Once the genoa becomes bigger than the mainsail (see Fig 237b), it will need frequent changing. Changing headsails is much more demanding, time consuming, even dangerous in rough weather for short handed or less experienced crew when compared with the latest ways of reefing mainsails. On cruising boats, where ease of handling is a desirable attribute, a return to bigger mainsails and smaller fore-tringles, eventually the self-tacking jib system, is quite a sensible labour – and expense-saving solution. A system, such as the one shown in Fig 240, affords the possibility of the total elimination of all sheet winches, and one person can handle the headsail. Sketches a and b demonstrate the self-tacking jib of the Soling-class boat. The Soling is not a boat where ease of handling has a high priority. Speed matters most. However, the Soling, like the Tornado-cat and the Star are three high performance Olympic sailing boats and they all manage well without genoas.

Fig 240c demonstrates another solution to the self–tacking jib, the clew of which, supported by a short auxiliary jib boom, runs on the track; it is therefore unnecessary to tend the jib sheet when tacking. However, to sail the optimum windward course, the jib sheet may need to be checked occasionally and eventually retensioned.

Apart from being less hard on the bank balance than large genoas, the self-tacking system offers another advantage: it may improve the tacking efficiency of any boat. It is well known that contemporary offshore boats with large overlapping genoas are rather slow in stays (in irons, Fig 241a). And it has been reported that an average half-tonner, in anything like a breeze, takes thirty sec-

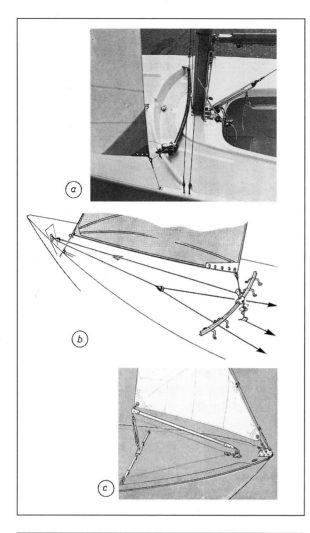

Fig 240 Three different solutions to the self-tacking jib arrangement.

a)   View of mounting details for self-tacking jib employed in the Soling class. The barber-hauler is used with the jib sheet which is a wire leading forward to a through-deck sheave, then aft to a 6 to 1 block and tackle controlled at the mast console.

b)   Another variation on the self-tacking jib arrangement in the Soling class. The trimming principle is simple. The single jib sheet and the single traveller adjuster control do nearly all functions of the conventional twin sheet system and also the adjustable jib fairleads shown earlier in Fig 233.

c)   Yet another way of installing the self-tacking jib. Since jibs are used for reaching as well as beating, the self-tacker track – which should be radiused approximately around the jib tack, as in (a) and (b) – needs to be as long as possible, ie, stretching from the port to starboard stanchion.

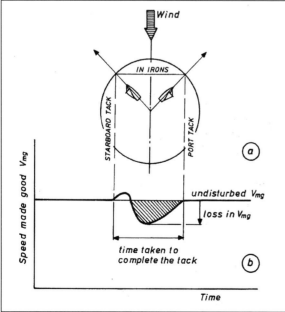

Fig 241 Ease of handling the headsails is one of the factors which may greatly improve the tacking efficiency by reducing the time the boat remains unpowered. On-board instruments and a computer make it possible to quickly calculate and even display the actual V_{mg} relative to the 'undisturbed' V_{mg}, that is the V_{mg} value just before and after the tacking manoeuvre. Figure (b) shows such a record (Ref 2.85). The hump at the beginning of the manoeuvre, ie, temporary increase in V_{mg} is caused by the boat shooting into the wind. The valley afterwards corresponds to the loss in V_{mg} as the boat heads off and loses speed. After a time, the apparent wind angle ß, the boat speed, V_s, and subsequently the V_{mg} return to their pre-tack values. The crossed area between the 'undisturbed' V_{mg} line and the actual V_{mg} recorded while going through the wind can be regarded as a meaningful measure of the distance lost to a mark. Such a plot informs the crew whether the tacking efficiency is satisfactory; if not it is up to them – and not to the instruments and computer – to correct what is wrong.

onds from the time she begins to tack until her genoa is properly sheeted and she regains her speed on a new, close-hauled tack. During this period, her speed made good to windward, V_{mg}, may be drastically reduced (Fig 241b). Heavy fluttering of the genoa before the sail is filled on the new tack inflicts a heavy drag penalty on the rig. And by the time the genoa is beginning to develop driving force, the boat may be sailing (not pointing) twenty degrees or more below her optimum course, depending on the crew's expertise, the water roughness and wind strength; with the rig developing large heeling force but little driving component. This in turn puts heavy loading on the keel or centreboard, which may stall due to large drift (incidence angle).

The hydrodynamic side force needed to balance the aerodynamic heeling force depends primarily on the yacht's speed, V_s, as the square of speed appears in the formula for calculating hydrodynamic reaction. The greater the speed of the boat, the smaller the drift (leeway) needed to achieve sufficiently large side force with lower resistance; in other words, the better the lift/drag ratio.

Figure 242 illustrates the relationship between the speed, V_d, at which the boat is drifting sideways, her forward speed, V_f, along the centreline of the hull, and the angle of drift, λ, all changing during the period in which the boat accelerates from a standstill, say, after unsuccessful tacking, to full speed. This acceleration time is usually longer for a ballast-keel yacht, with its greater displacement (inertia), than for a light dinghy. However, it always takes some time to reach full speed, and this is connected with loss of 'weather gauge' when, at the windward mark before the start of a race, a helmsman, trying to keep his position to weather, loses speed. The period of acceleration can be unconsciously prolonged by a helmsman who hauls in the sheets too much; a common habit of inexperienced crews starting to windward in a tight pack of boats.

Fig 242 A certain delay in the attainment of the optimum speed (V_{mg}) after a tacking manoeuvre is due to the combined effect of two trends causally intertwined. The first one is the decreased efficiency of the sails and resulting large heeling force, and is borne by the hull appendages. The second one, the reduced hydrodynamic efficiency of the underwater part of the hull forced to counteract a large heeling force at low speed, is burdensome to a keel or centreboard operating at an excessive leeway angle and results in a substantial increase in induced drag (Fig 106 and Eq 23).

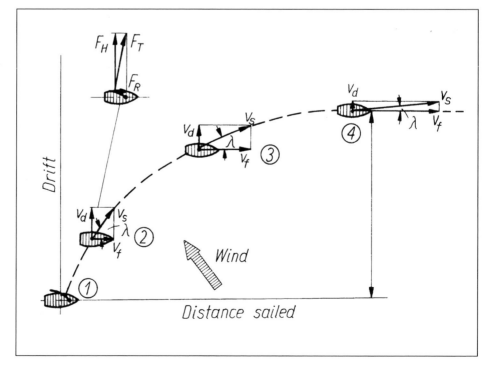

For the boat whose speed, V_s, is low (Fig 242 cases 1 and 2), the apparent wind will be relatively full. Excessive hauling in on the mainsheet will produce a large amount of F_H, which causes excessive drift, with simultaneously a small amount of driving force F_R. A yacht with its sails sheeted like this would go on drifting until, with the slow increase of boat speed, V_s, and a consequent change in the direction of the apparent wind, the general hydro-aerodynamic efficiency of the yacht gradually improves and finally the boat attains her optimum V_{mg}.

A jib on its own self-tacking track will be particularly effective in confined waters, where the ability to tack smoothly, accelerate quickly, and point high in strong winds is most important.

When considering the relative merits of the genoa and the self-tacking jib, it might be appropriate to say that it does no harm to re-examine from time to time our firmest convictions, for these are most likely to be suspect.

Fore-and-aft distribution of camber

'When it is not in our power to determine what is true, we ought to act in accordance with what is most probable.'

René Descartes, French philosopher (1596–1650)

However headsails are taxed, the question of how they should overlap the mainsail will always remain. Some light is thrown on the subject from results obtained at Southampton University of force measurements on a model sloop with rigid sails. The proportions of the sails are shown in Fig 243, and the 4 per cent camber profile in Fig 211. Various models A_i, A_{ii} and A_{iii}, were investigated, which had different positions of maximum camber of the sails, at 15 per cent, 25 per cent and 50 per cent respectively, of the local chord. A general conclusion was reached that the position of maximum camber of the mainsail should be, for maximum advantage, forward of the leech of the foresail. Figure 243 shows some of the results, giving curves of driving force coefficient C_x in the practical range of conditions for sailing to windward, ie heading $\beta - \lambda = 20°$–$30°$, trim angle of genoa $\delta_F = 12\frac{1}{2}°$, trim angle of mainsail $\delta_M = 5°$. Model A_i was shown to be superior over model A_{iii} by virtue of its higher driving force (up to 7 per cent higher), and also because its heeling moment was about 20 per cent to 25 per cent lower. The results for model A_{ii} were between those of A_i and A_{iii}. This pattern was largely repeated for different sail trims.

In the light of more recent wind tunnel results, the maximum camber position for 'soft' sails should be between $\frac{1}{3}$ and $\frac{1}{2}$ of the sail chord from the leading edge (luff). The shape of the camber should be essentially parabolic forward with a flat run aft: such a cross-section provides the highest value of driving force with the least heeling force. The effect of headsail shape (and its deformation due to wind strength variation) on the mainsail is far more pronounced than the effect of mainsail shape on the headsail.

While interpreting the wind tunnel results shown in Fig 243, one should bear in mind the fact that the sail models tested were rigid, therefore the full conclusions reached may not be applicable to soft sails. However, the results may be relevant to fully battened, semi-rigid sails. As already mentioned earlier, the problem of sail interaction is complicated and not fully explored as yet. It is therefore difficult to generalize about the optimum position of the mainsail's

Fig 243 A series of wind tunnel tests on a typical sloop configuration suggests that the position of maximum camber on the mainsail should be forward of the trailing edge of the foresail to obtain full advantage from the sloop rig.

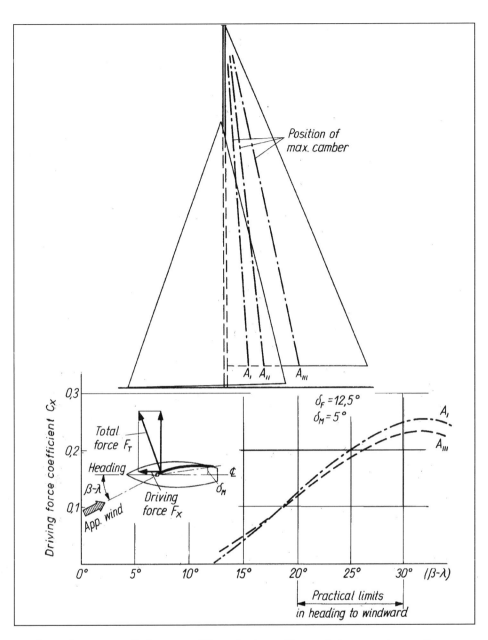

camber when two sails interact. The solution will certainly vary, depending on a number of factors such as the overlap ratio, shape of the genoa (its camber distribution) and the vertical extent of genoa overlap, whether the boat has a masthead or fractional rig, and so forth:

Sail shape is not fully described by the magnitude of maximum camber of a single sail, interacting sails overlapping each other, and fore-and-aft position of camber at each section of sail along its height. Although the maximum camber and its position are frequently considered as the main parameters, three further factors are important in defining three-dimensional sail shape. These are:

- entry angle
- exit angle (Fig 219a)
- sail twist (Fig 235)

Aspect ratio Another experiment in the same series concerned tests on models having different sail plans. Two of the models and some results are given in Fig 244. Model A_i has been previously described (Fig 243); model C had the same sail area and camber, but the ratio of fore-triangle area to mainsail area was 50 per cent as against 35 per cent for model A_i. Model A_i had the typical proportions of offshore racers, in which the ratio of mainsail luff to foot is, as a rule, between 2.7 and 3.2. Model C, with a masthead genoa, could be considered as a rather extreme example of a rig. Here, the high tax on aspect ratio means that the mainsail luff is more than twice the length of the foot. For both models, the values of driving force coefficient and the heeling moment coefficient were measured for heading $\beta - \lambda = 20-32\frac{1}{2}°$ covering close-hauled sailing. Both foresail and mainsail trim angles δ_F and δ_M were varied, but the curves of Fig 244 refer only to $\delta_F = 12\frac{1}{2}°$, $\delta_M = 10°$. Nevertheless these curves are typical of those obtained at other sail settings.

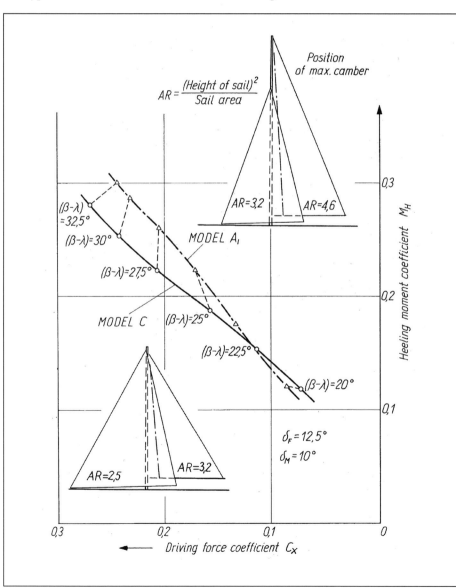

Fig 244 None of these two rigs of different aspect ratios is superior over the whole range of heading angles when close-hauled. Thus, at a heading angle of 20°, model A is better than model C, but at headings beyond 27.5°, model C becomes superior; particularly in a strong wind when the heeling moment becomes a dominating performance factor.

In cases where a model has, at the same heading $\beta - \lambda$, a larger driving force coefficient C_x and an equal or smaller heeling moment coefficient M_H than another model, then it can be considered superior. Some doubt as to relative merits will arise in cases where, say, C_x is greater, and M_H too. Then the question of wind strength will have to be considered, since in strong winds heeling moments become important, while in light airs the driving force is the predominant factor to be considered.

Thus, at a heading $\beta - \lambda = 20°$, model A_i is superior, since for the same heeling moment it has a higher driving force than model C.

At $\beta - \lambda = 22^{1}/_{2}°$ and $25°$, it is difficult to say which is the better model, since A_i has in both cases more driving force but also more heeling moment. It is likely, however, that model A_i would be the better in light winds and model C in strong winds. Above $\beta - \lambda = 25°$, model C is undoubtedly superior. Thus at $\beta - \lambda = 27^{1}/_{2}°$ it has the same driving force, but less heeling moment, and this improves as the heading increases.

It is clear therefore that no one rig is superior over the whole range of courses considered. Model Ai will certainly be better on extremely close-hauled courses, while model C will excel when close-reaching. On triangular courses round the buoys; when the windward leg usually decides a race, model A_i, of higher aspect ratio, should finish in front of model C. In ocean races, where good all-round performance is required, model C may be superior.

It is encouraging for us to note that the conclusion we derived in Chapter 10 when dealing with single sails of different aspect ratio are fully confirmed by these later experiments on sloop rigs with overlapping sails.

A question hotly debated in Britain some years ago was the rather shattering success in offshore races of beamy, shallow-draft American centre-boarders built under the CCA rules. Both on rating and handicaps these have virtually eliminated the competition of the narrow, deep-keeled yachts. This rather unexpected result had been attributed to the differences between the hull types, particularly to the supposed high efficiency of fins having a large centreboard. Even the hastily introduced changes in the CCA formula supported this view by taxing, more heavily than before, broad-beam, shallow-draft centreboarders. Without denying the advantages to be gained from these hull conceptions, it would be worthwhile considering also their effects on the sails. It has been conclusively shown that for ocean racing, where close-hauled performance is not usually of predominant importance, a low aspect ratio sail rig on a wide sheeting base may be superior to the usual rig found on the traditional narrow-hulled English yachts.

SPINNAKER

Taking, for instance, the sail wardrobe of *Myth of Malham* shown in Fig 238a, we may recognize that the area of her spinnaker of 875 sq ft is almost three times that of the mainsail. In the 12 Metre-class, the spinnaker is 4.4 times the area of the mainsail (5570 sq ft). Although not all spinnakers are so enormous, nevertheless they are much larger than mainsails. This fact alone underlines their importance as sails providing a powerful driving force. Their position in the sail list has improved considerably as their mode of operation has become under-

stood. Initially treated as a sort of bag to catch the wind, and exclusively used dead downwind (Fig 245), the spinnaker was promoted into the role of a head-sail, and has now usurped the large genoa on courses from a run to a close reach.

The evolution of modern spinnaker can best be understood by considering how it is cut and the influence of its cut on its shape and properties at different angles of incidence. The 'spherical' shape of old spinnakers was obtained by cutting the panels as in Fig 246a. These spinnakers suffered from radial creases, tending to reduce the lateral spread of the shoulders and so the sail driving power. The creases were due to the differences in fabric strength and stretch along the warp A–A and along the seams, which over most of their length ran at an angle (diagonal) to the warp and weft.

The fewer the panels in the spinnaker, the larger the distortion of its surface. This method of cutting was subsequently replaced by a system of panels, laid diagonally as shown in Fig 246b. The diagonally laid spinnaker has less tendency to form folds, due to the better disposition of fabric strength. Hence the amounts of stretch along the largely diagonal line B–B and on the middle seam, also diagonal, are simimlar. The amount of camber is controlled by the number of panels and the broad seams joining them. Figure 247 shows a splendid Herbulot balloon spinnaker cut on the above principle and used by the English yacht *Sceptre* in the 1958 America's Cup Races.

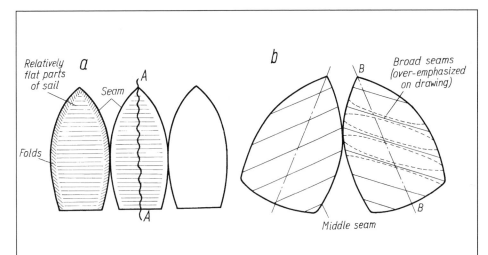

Fig 246 When stresses within the fabric due to wind action – particularly stresses radiating from the spinnaker head, clews and along the seams – are not aligned with the threadlines of the woven fabric, the sail surface will deform. Numerous knobs and hollows will appear and spoil the smooth airflow, ie, wind will be tripped into eddies at each bulge and wrinkle over the sail surface to the detriment of the total driving force developed on other courses than dead running.

Note: the least stretch in any woven fabric is in the direction of the threadlines running at right angles in the warp and weft (fill). The greatest stretch will be in the bias direction, ie, the direction running at an angle of 45 degrees to the warp and weft. The largest deformation in the fabric will occur along the bias.

Fig 247 A balloon spinnaker. Its enormous shoulder and depth (camber) makes such a spinnaker hard to trim on courses other than running and broad reach.

When running, the sail is set at a large angle of incidence and is totally stalled, resulting in a broad eddying wake developing on the leeward side (Figs 248 and 249). The air stream separates periodically right behind the edges of the sail, and the quality of the curved sail surface is not of importance except on aesthetic grounds. Any irregularities such as may occur at the seams have little aerodynamic significance. In any case, the roughly uniform distribution of pressures and suctions on the sail surfaces favours equal tensions throughout the fabric, producing few wrinkles.

The ductile, lightweight Nylon or other fabrics used for the sails will stretch enough to accommodate errors in cutting which might result in excessive local tensions. Handling and trimming the spinnaker when running presents few problems, because the leeches have no tendency to collapse. However, under certain circumstances, the fluctuating wake from the leeward side of the sail may induce violent rolling.

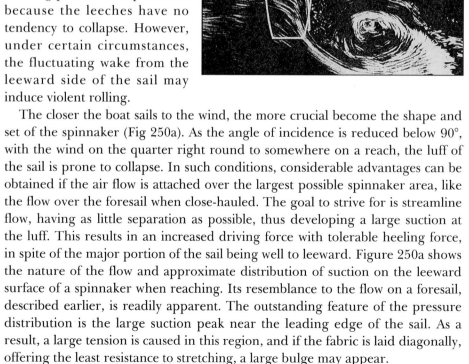

Fig 248 The essential features of the airflow are illustrated schematically. At the edges of the spinnaker, bands of vortex are generated which separate the freely moving air outside the spinnaker from the 'dead water' region at the back of the sail. At some distance behind, these vortex bands roll up to form what is now known as a *vortex street*.

Fig 249 A photographic representation of the vortex street, consisting of vortices shed at each side of the sail in regular intervals. It is known that the periodic detachment of vortices behind a sail produces periodic alternating cross-forces on the sail, tending to make it oscillate across the airstream. This causes the boat to roll (see Part 3, chapter 7). The mainsail is deliberately over-sheeted to demonstrate the vortices developing periodically behind the leeward side of the sail. These vortices, alternately shed from the edges of the sail, are responsible for fluctuating lift and drag.

The closer the boat sails to the wind, the more crucial become the shape and set of the spinnaker (Fig 250a). As the angle of incidence is reduced below 90°, with the wind on the quarter right round to somewhere on a reach, the luff of the sail is prone to collapse. In such conditions, considerable advantages can be obtained if the air flow is attached over the largest possible spinnaker area, like the flow over the foresail when close-hauled. The goal to strive for is streamline flow, having as little separation as possible, thus developing a large suction at the luff. This results in an increased driving force with tolerable heeling force, in spite of the major portion of the sail being well to leeward. Figure 250a shows the nature of the flow and approximate distribution of suction on the leeward surface of a spinnaker when reaching. Its resemblance to the flow on a foresail, described earlier, is readily apparent. The outstanding feature of the pressure distribution is the large suction peak near the leading edge of the sail. As a result, a large tension is caused in this region, and if the fabric is laid diagonally, offering the least resistance to stretching, a large bulge may appear.

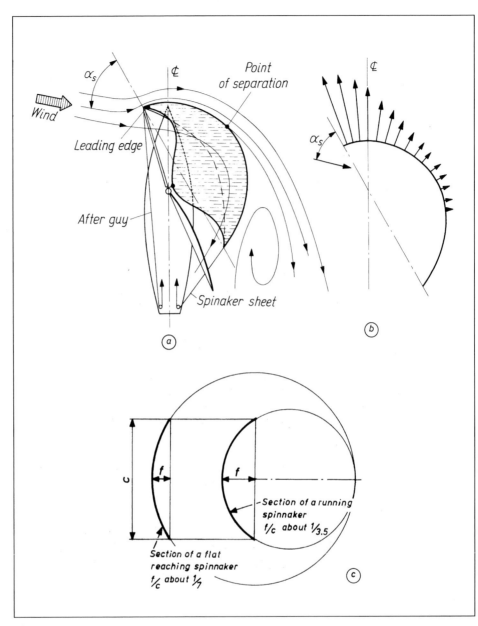

Fig 250

a) Approximate flow around the section of the spinnaker when reaching.

b) The magnitude and direction of the thrust developed on a spinnaker depends on the pressure distribution, which in turn is primarily controlled by the sail set, its camber (f/c ratio) and the shape of the leeches which should be flat and smooth. If we consider a spinnaker, shaped so that the weather leech is shorter than the leeward and the point of maximum fullness is nearer the weather leech, then it is possible to produce a thrust line closer to the direction of the course steered. The sail, of course, must be of a much flatter cut than usual.

c) This diagram shows sections of a flat and a running spinnaker. The curvatures of the arc sections are circular. The problem of selecting the optimum shape of the section is a controversial one. Some sailmakers recommend an elliptical section. The argument against is that, for a given chord-camber ratio (f/c) and given arc length, a circular arc yields the greatest projected width of all possible curvatures.

Figure 251 illustrates *Sceptre*'s Herbulot spinnaker developing a large bulge running the length of the luff as a result of the sail fabric stretching considerably more than the reinforced leading edge. It is not difficult to visualize the detrimental effect of this on the flow over the sail. It could be likened to an enormous mast creating turbulent flow behind it. In other words, if the leech were to stretch excessively, the entire shape of the spinnaker will be distorted.

Fig 251 Herbulot's balloon. If leeches have a tendency to curl in as shown, the spinnaker may suddenly collapse like a pricked balloon.

Coming still more on the wind, the testing of the spinnaker's cut, its cross–section (profile) and trim becomes more severe. Then, the critical angle of iincidence at which the luff collapses imposes a limit for sailing to windward using a spinnaker. It is logical to suggest that the limitations, in this respect, of the diagonally cut spinnaker could be improved by altering the cut so that the greatest tensions at the edges are along the line of greatest resistance of the cloth, ie, along the weft. This led to the idea of the cross-cut spinnaker in which the panels are laid horizontally in the lower part and perpendicular to the leeches toward the head. With this it is easier to achieve relatively flat and smooth edges, favouring streamline attached flow, and hence a lower minimum setting angle. Figure 252 shows *Columbia*'s spinnaker 'Little Harry' on close-reaching. Comparing this sail with that of *Sceptre* (Fig 251), on a similar point of sailing, one cannot but be struck by its flat, clean edges and smooth shape as against the latter's baggy, crinkled 'Herbulot'.

Undoubtedly in light winds, dead aft, when the criterion for a good spinnaker is frontal area, the diagonally cut balloon spinnaker is at least as good as any other. Under these conditions its large depth and broad shoulders make it easy to fly, and keep setting. With the wind abeam, however, when the spinnaker begins to function partly as a headsail, its area is increasingly of less importance than its shape and depth. Under these conditions, the cross-cut spinnaker with relatively small chord and low f/c ratio (in the order of 15 per cent or less) becomes superior (Fig 250c). On balance, it is a better all-round sail, particularly in strong winds. Because of its smaller chord and lower depth

Fig 252 The cross-cut spinnaker carried by the victorious *Columbia* on a shy spinnaker leg during 1958 America's Cup race.

(f/c ratio), it can be set flatter, and hence at a smaller angle of incidence, α_s, before it collapses. It can be used effectively up to a close reach, when it is then acting as a genoa. The genoa, on the other hand, begins to lose its efficiency when close-reaching because of its limited sheeting base. Easing the sheets as one comes off the wind from close-hauled does not produce the expected and desired interaction of genoa with the mainsail because of the increased sail twist and camber. In the case of a spinnaker under similar conditions, its wider sheeting base allows a better trim than a genoa.

As predicted in the first edition of this book, the spinnaker will evolve with the genoa into the 'spinoa', a word coined for the author by an officer of the Royal Navy. And indeed, such a new sail, variously called a spanker or a genniker, was introduced some years ago to bridge the gap between genoa and spinnaker. Technically it is spinnaker, yet with its flat cut and spinnaker pole carried down to the stemhead to give a straight luff, it handles like a genoa; it may be said to have been an ancestor of the cruising chute.

Recently, significant progress has been made in the development of reaching and close-reaching spinnakers. The object aimed at was the elimination of adverse effects of spinnaker distortions on its performance, ie, distortion of its surface in conditions when the right shape of the sail (operating under unsymmetrical, occasionally tremendous loadings) matters most (Figs 250b and 254).

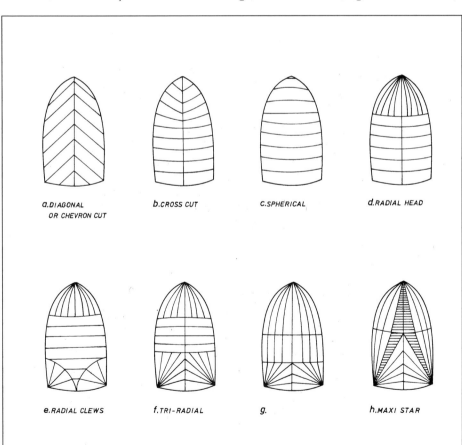

a. DIAGONAL OR CHEVRON CUT b. CROSS CUT c. SPHERICAL d. RADIAL HEAD

e. RADIAL CLEWS f. TRI-RADIAL g. h. MAXI STAR

Fig 253 The evolution of spinnaker design leading us to the maxi star. Nowadays, modern spinnakers are designed with the aid of a computer whose objective is to plot the panels that, when assembled, allow the spinnaker to retain its shape regardless of the wind speed.

Fig 254 Observation of the flow around a spinnaker in the Southampton University wind tunnel.

The greatest emphasis has been put on shaping the panels and on their arrangement in such a way that *panels carry the loads* from corner to corner along the actual *load path*. The arrangement of radiating panels from the head (radial head) shown in Fig 253d – keeping each individual panel at right angles to the strain – appeared to be a logical step. Such a shape stabilizing solution, applied to the sail head only, did not, however, prevent distortions originating from the clews and spreading over the lower cross-cut part of the sail as depicted in Fig 254.

The next evolutionary step was therefore pretty obvious: since stresses radiate from the clews and head, so should the cloth panels. Thus, the ultimate star-cut spinnaker was born. A number of evolutionary variations leading to the maxi-star spinnaker which was developed on the above principle are presented in Fig 2533d–g. Some of the spinnaker patterns demonstrated are advertised under all sorts of fancy names and, as admitted, 'much of the terminology has been created by marketing wizards looking for ways to sell more sails'.

The key to understanding the variations in cutting patterns and their evolution lies in studying the underlying concept and reasoning that go into the design of a particular type of sail.

An essential consideration when making a spinnaker is selecting the correct fabric weight, strength and stretch characteristics. If the material is too heavy, it will not set properly in light winds and will collapse in every lull, while if too light it may be damaged in stronger winds. The universal sail for all conditions does not exist, and it is true to say that the more universal it becomes, the less fitted it is for a specific use. Nowadays the spinnaker is not only a fair weather sail: storm spinnakers, for heavy weather, are smaller and made of heavier fabric.

In this context, let's consider the alleged merit of a light, 0.5 ounce spinnaker – a so-called *floater*. It has been argued that the main reason why lighter spinnakers outperform heavy ones in light weather conditions is, quote: 'the flow of air over the top of the sail and down the front side which makes lift such an important characteristic of the spinnaker. If the sail is more or less drooping straight down from the masthead, there will be no such flow, and consequently less thrust. If, on the other hand, the sail is lifting well, with the upper portion of his head almost parallel to the water, the necessary flow will take place... thus reducing the portion of the total area which is stalled and increasing the resulting thrust.'

Well, there is a less complicated explanation as to why a light floater does outperform a heavier spinnaker. This is the effect of wind shear (wind velocity gradient), which determines the driving forces developed on two different sails. This effect is illustrated in Fig 255 (see also Part 3, Chapter 2). As shown, the wind velocity increases with height above the water quite rapidly up to about 15 feet, and less rapidly thereafter. A heavier, drooping spinnaker, operating in lower wind strata, experiences weaker winds than the lifted up, lighter floater. Assume, for example, that the difference in average wind strength affecting both spinnakers is 5 per cent, say 5 knots and 5.25 knots. Since the wind force is proportional to the square of the wind velocity, the boat driven by the floater will develop roughly 10 per cent more aerodynamic drive.

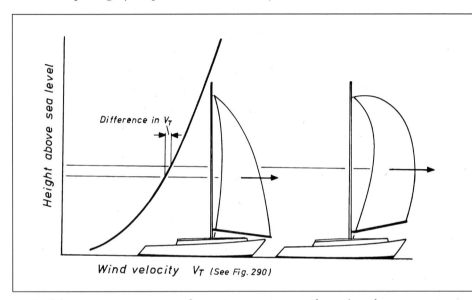

Fig 255 The effect of wind velocity gradient on forces developed on two spinnakers of different cut sailing downwind.

Cruising crews are, as a rule, not eager to use the spinnaker, except on a dead run in light weather. The reason is easy to find. The main and foresails, being suspended on the mast and forestay respectively, are easily controlled by a single sheet. On the other hand, the spinnaker, being freely suspended, is more difficult to control, particularly when reaching. It is enough to look at Fig 256 (showing the system for rigging a spinnaker) to appreciate the difference between handling it and a Bermudan mainsail. More than other sails, it demands rapid and skilful cooperation between its operator and the helmsman. In strong winds, when the sail can develop enormous forces, its handling may become a nightmare for an inexperienced crew. Working the spinnaker on the foredeck will be considerably simplified by having reliable, light and easily handled fittings, enabling the boom to be handled with the minimum of fuss.

Trimming the spinnaker is effected by adjusting the positions of its head, tack and clew (the latter two swap names when jibing). The allowable clearance between the head of the spinnaker and the mast depends on the yacht's course, the cut of the sail, and the rolling characteristics of the yacht. When running, it is desirable to ease the halyard so that the sail can be set well forward to reduce the blanketing from the mainsail. The amount by which the halyard is eased is dictated by the lower parts of the sail, which should set roughly vertical. Excessive forward or backward slope is generally harmful.

Fig 256 The terminology of a sheeting system for spinnakers. Trimming sheet leads correctly is most difficult when the heading angle is between about 90 and 120 degrees.

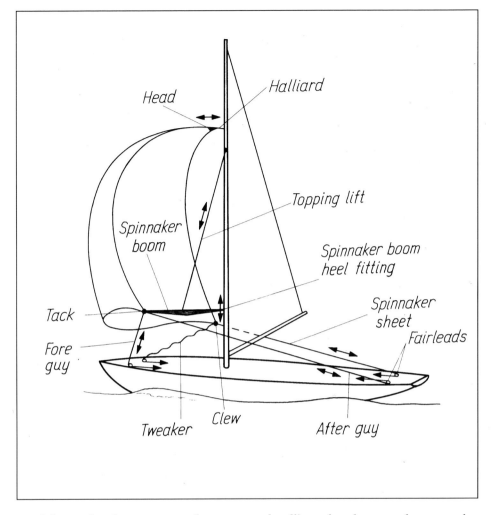

If the yacht shows any tendency toward rolling, the clearance between the head of the sail and the mast may become important. It controls the way in which the sail swings relative to the mast. A critical distance can often be found, at which the swinging of the spinnaker magnifies the rolling of the yacht, and this, in turn, leads to the collapse of the edges of the sail. In these circumstances one should depart from the critical condition by setting the sail either higher or lower.

The distance between the head of the spinnaker and the halyard sheave should be progressively reduced as one comes on the wind. The boom should be kept more or less parallel to the water so that its full length is exploited. The slide fitting on the mast should be of ample length to allow the sail to be set high, improving its efficiency, since then the blanketing of the mainsail becomes less, the wind strength is greater, and the sneaker, or spinnaker staysail works more effectively. In light winds, lowering or dipping the boom will tauten the luff and may prevent its collapsing. The fore and after-guys and the topping lift together keep the boom steady and control its position in relation to the wind. It is usually set parallel to, or a little forward of, the line of the main boom (Fig 250). The best position for the tack of the spinnaker depends to a large extent on the way the sheets are arranged, which in turn fix the position of the clew.

The position of the tack and clew control the angle of incidence and, to some extent, the shape of the lower parts of the sail. Figure 257 shows some different ways of leading the sheets. A particularly effective way is to run the sheet through a block on the after end of the main boom, a method allowed for instance under the old RORC Special Regulations. This arrangement gives the most effective combination of sail forces arising from the sail shape produced. A comparatively large driving force, F_R, is produced, with a small heeling force, F_H.

Jibing a large spinnaker in a fresh breeze can be a dangerous undertaking. In extreme cases it is necessary to use the blanketing effect of a headsail or the mainsail. To obtain this, one may have to bear away for a moment, taking care not to prematurely jibe the mainsail. Figure 258 shows how this might be done on a cutter or a small yacht, using interchangeable guys and sheets. The spinnaker boom is double-ended, so that either end can be fitted to the sail or the mast slider.

On larger yachts, where the loading on the spinnaker boom and therefore its weight are considerable, it is better to use a single-ended boom. In this case the topping lift is run to the end of the boom rather than to the middle. When jibing, the boom is disconnected from the sail, passed under the forestay, and attached to the sail again, while the heel of the boom is secured all the time to the mast. This method can be applied to any yacht on which there is a sufficient distance between the mast and the forestay.

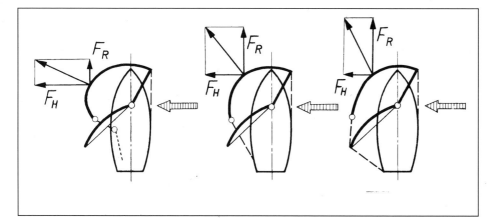

Fig 257 Three different sheetings and their approximate effect on the driving force component F_R.

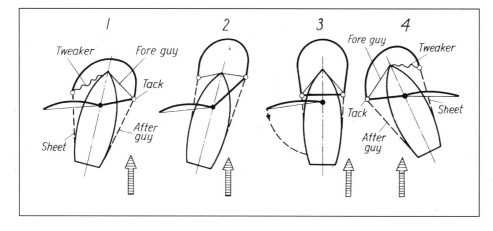

Fig 258 Various stages, 1–4, of a simplified single-pole jibing method. There are a number of other jibing methods, using, for example, twin spinnaker poles and modifications of single or twin pole systems.

Fig 259 The dark stripes painted on the mainsail and genoas (see also Figs 63c, 116, 182, 220) photographed from above, with the camera mounted at the masthead, allow the sail shape to be established, ie, the magnitude of camber at any given section, fore-and-aft distribution of camber, sail twist, forestay sag, the entry and exit angles etc. Microcameras may produce video images of the sail geometry which can subsequently be compared instantly with the target sail shapes, stored in the memory of the on-board computer, and relevant for each particular sailing condition. Comparison of the actual sail shapes with reference (target) shapes for similar conditions allows the crew to adjust the trim of sails to match the desired target quickly.

In passing it could be mentioned that, although a number of published data on fore-and-aft sail coefficients is available, no such information exists on spinnakers. There are two reasons: first, the spinnaker geometry factors, such as incidence angle, camber, twist, mutual geometric relationship between the spinnaker and interacting main and foresails, etc, are extremely difficult, if not impossible, to keep under control. It is also very difficult to relate measured coefficients to those factors. In the case of conventional, fore-and-aft sails tested in wind tunnels, conversely, all relevant geometric factors are relatively easy to establish, control and record photographically or otherwise (eg, Figs 259, 63c, 116 and 65).

Secondly, there are difficulties in establishing reliably the 'wind tunnel wall corrections' when spinnakers occupy a large area in relation to the area of cross– section of the wind tunnel (Ref 2.86). The presence of a large model in the test section reduces the area through which the air can flow and inevitably, therefore, there is an increase in the velocity of air as it flows past the model. And this increase in velocity will greatly depend upon the sail configurations and the angular position of the rig relative to the flow direction. As shown in Fig 254, the author did carry out tests on spinnakers but the investigation was limited to establishing flow patterns around the sail at various attitudes relative to the wind direction.

16 • CENTRE OF EFFORT

'In fact, everything we know is only some kind of approximation, because we know that we do not know all the laws as yet. Therefore, things must be learned only to be unlearned again or, more likely, to be corrected.'

R P Feynman, Lectures on Physics (1966)

When discussing the suctions and pressures which are distributed in quite a complicated fashion over the leeward and windward sides of a sail, we found it convenient to assume that their effect could be represented by a single total aerodynamic force, F_T, acting along a particular line. In Fig 35b this line of action of the force, F_T, cuts the sail at a point termed the 'centre of pressure'. In sailing terminology this point is known as the 'centre of effort', CE, and most books, when discussing this subject, assume that the CE remains stationary and lies at the geometrical centre of the area of the sailplan (centroid).

A traditional method for determining the position of the CE is given in Fig 260a and b. One first determines the geometric centres of area of the individual sails (CE_F and CE_M respectively for the foresail and mainsail, Fig 260a). Then the line joining these two points is divided into two parts, by a simple geometrical construction, in proportion to the areas of each sail. Thus the common CE is found, being nearer the larger sail. In Fig 260b, the lengths CE_F–A and CE_M–B were drawn to scale, representing the mainsail and foresail areas respectively. The line A–B then cut CE_F–CE_M at CE.

Fig 260 Traditional method of establishing the position of the centre of effort, CE, for a sloop.

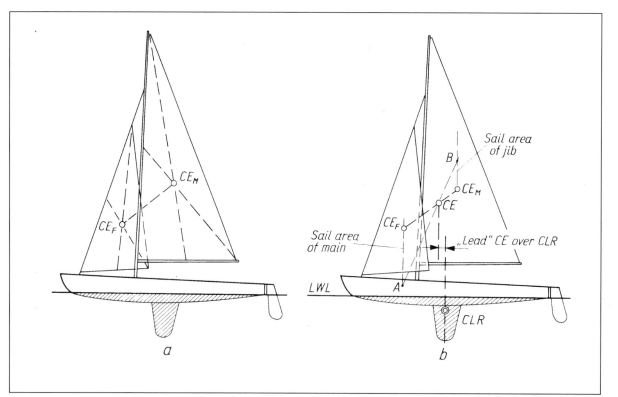

a

b

THE CENTRE OF EFFORT AND ITS RELATION TO DIRECTIONAL BALANCE OF A YACHT

This traditional method of finding the geometrical CE gives a point which does not, in fact, correspond with the true position of the 'centre of pressure'. Nevertheless, it has a certain practical value for yacht designers in helping them to evaluate the directional balance of a design. In reality the true CE changes its position within wide limits, and for the majority of courses is in front of the geometrical CE.

The effects due to errors in fixing the CE of the aerodynamic forces are partly compensated for by similar errors arising from the determination of the 'centre of lateral resistance', CLR. This point is taken as the geometrical centre of area of the submerged hull and fin when viewed from the side, and sometimes does and sometimes does not include the rudder area (Fig 260b). Once again, the CLR is not in reality a fixed point, but moves about as the hull changes its attitude, heel, leeway, speed, heading angle. The true CLR is forward of the geometrical CLR when close-hauled, and shifts aft as one bears away.

The method of finding the CE and the CLR (shown in Fig 260) allows an approximate evaluation of the close-hauled directional balance of a yacht to be made. A balance is found when the total aerodynamic force, F_T, and the total hydrodynamic force, R_T, act along the same line. If they do not act in the same line, but are separated by some distance 'a' known as the 'unbalance arm' (Fig 58) then some compensation using the rudder will be necessary to keep a steady course. In other words, if F_T is aft of R_T by the distance 'a', weather helm must be applied to react against the luffing moment $F_T \times a$ (equal to $R_T \times a$). The magnitude of the unbalance arm 'a' determines whether the yacht is balanced and, to some extent, whether it is well tempered or hard mouthed. A yacht which is not well balanced is likely to be slow, since it requires constant rudder, with its resulting resistance, to keep on course, and is difficult to steer as every wind change causes it to luff or bear away. In broad terms, the balance is that complex of qualities that makes a boat *always* docile and under the complete control of the helm.

As a rule, designers' calculations of CE and CLR are made treating the wind and water forces as acting on the unheeled centreline plane. Figure 58a demonstrates how, due to heel, the originally balanced yacht, when upright, does produce an unbalance arm 'a' (F_T given by the broken line). (The yacht is viewed from above.) Designers compensate for this tendency in a rule-of-thumb manner, by shifting the CE in front of the CLR by an amount termed the 'lead' (Fig 260b, the boat is upright). Books on naval architecture express this 'lead' as a proportion of the waterline length of the hull, but opinions among authors vary, the 'lead' being given variously as anything from 0 per cent to 12 per cent of the waterline length. The success or otherwise of this somewhat arbitrary correction can be gauged by the number of badly balanced boats one encounters.

Due to the shortcomings of the above philosophy concerning CE and CLR, it is often necessary to tune a yacht's balance. In practice it is not usually feasible to change the shape of hull or keel, and so tuning becomes a matter of adjusting the position of the sailplan, or the sailplan itself, in relation to the hull. Shifting the mast in the appropriate direction, or reapportioning the total sail area between main and foresails can work wonders for directional balance.

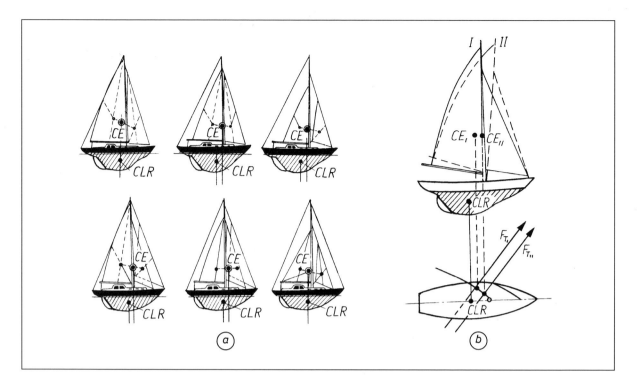

Figure 261a illustrates how the geometrical CE shifts on a sloop and a cutter for different arrangements. When reefing or changing sails for different weather conditions, some attention should be paid to the effect on the yacht's balance. Selecting sails thoughtlessly can ruin the balance, which in bad weather can lead to getting in irons or broaching-to.

The effect of mast rake on the helm is shown in Fig 261b. A yacht which originally carried weather helm can, after raking the mast forward, end up carrying lee helm. It should be emphasized, however, that when making any changes of this sort, one must also ensure the correct trim of the sails, since these can have a profound effect on the balance. As in most things, a compromise must be found. It is of little use balancing the boat perfectly if by so doing one seriously impairs the efficiency of the sails.

Fig 261 The effect of variations in sail plan (reefing) and mast rake on the position of CE in relation to CLR.

MOVEMENT OF THE TRUE CENTRE OF EFFORT

With the help of experiments on aerofoils of different aspect ratio and camber made by G Eiffel and also at Göttingen (Ref 2.87) it was confirmed that the true CE varies its position as the angle of incidence, α, is altered. For small angles of α, the true CE lies near the leading edge, and as α is increased to 90°, it shifts toward the centre of area, ie, towards the geometrical CE.

Figure 262 demonstrates this phenomenon for an airfoil of aspect ratio AR = 5 and 1/10 camber. For convenience, the position of the true CE is given as a percentage of the chord length c measured from the leading edge. It is easy to understand why this must occur. At the smaller angles of incidence, the pressure distribution on the sail (see Figs 35, 39, 41, 51) is characterized by a large suction near the luff, on the leeward side, and hence the resultant total force F_T is well forward. As the incidence increases and the sail stalls, the distribution of

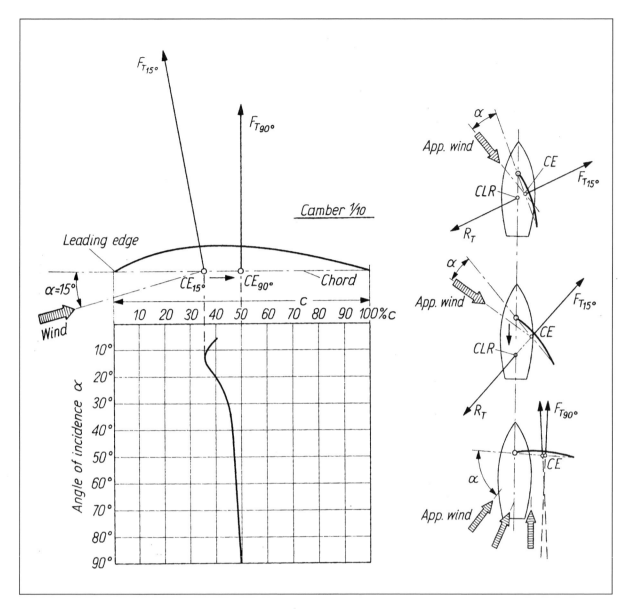

Fig 262 Movement of the CE along the chord of a sail section with camber 1/10 depending on the incidence angle.

pressures and suctions becomes more uniform (Fig 51b) and the resultant total force tends to act nearer the centre of area. On the graph of Fig 262 are shown two specific cases, forces F_{T15} and F_{T90} for angles of incidence of 15° and 90°. The former would be appropriate for courses from close-hauled to a reach, and the latter represents a dead run. The three sketches on Fig 262 demonstrate how widely travelled is the intersection point of F_T along the yacht's centreline. When close-hauled, the true CE is about 35 per cent of the sail chord and the intersection point is a little aft on the centreline. As one comes off the wind, however, the intersection point moves aft rapidly until, on a run, F_T does not intersect the hull centreline. Since the yacht, under the action of sail, hull and rudder forces, must be in balance, it follows that the weather helm due to sail action must be exactly balanced by the rudder action.

The position of the CE will also depend on the camber of the sail. This has some practical significance, since a yacht will tend to have lee helm when a flat

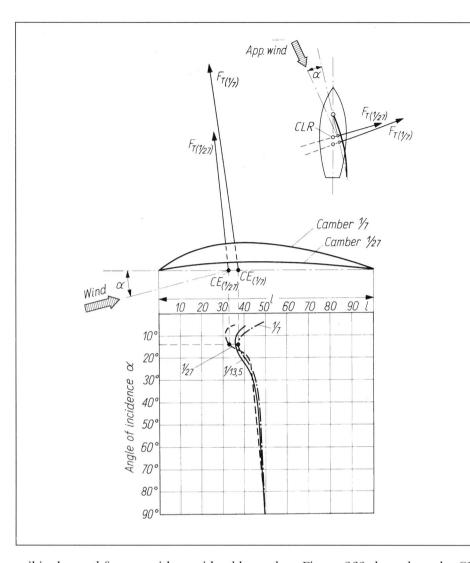

Fig 263 Movement of the CE along the sail chord for three sail sections with camber 1/7, 1/13.5 and 1/27, depending on the incidence angle.

sail is changed for one with considerable camber. Figure 263 shows how the CE shifts for three aerofoils, all of aspect ratio AR = 5 but having cambers of 1/7 (14.3 per cent) 1/13.5 (7.4 per cent) and 1/27 (3.7 per cent). We can see that the resultant aerodynamic force F_T in the case of a fairly flat (camber 1/27) sail, at a representative angle of incidence α = 14° is about 4 per cent of the sail chord forward of those with greater camber. The small inset to the figure shows how this must influence the position of the CLR, the shift in practice being accomplished by use of the rudder. Once again, on a run, when the sail incidence is near 90°, the CE tends toward the centre of area.

The general pattern shown in Figs 262 and 263 for an aspect ratio AR = 5 is also true for sails of other aspect ratios. Since, however, the shifts were expressed as a percentage of the sail chord, it follows that sails with a low aspect ratio, and therefore a relatively large chord, will experience a larger shift in CE than those of high aspect ratio. In other words, shift in CE for a gaff-rigged yacht will be greater than for a Bermudan yacht. In the design stage, when one is assessing directional balance, this fact must be borne in mind. If the yacht is not to be hopelessly off balance as one comes off the wind, one should give more lead for a sail rig of low aspect ratio, even though this may entail it being slightly unbalanced when close-hauled.

THE CENTRE OF EFFORT FOR THE COMBINATION OF MAIN, MIZZEN AND FORESAIL

When considering the CE for the combination of several interacting sails, it is necessary to bear in mind their relative aerodynamic efficiencies. From the analysis of the pressure distributions on the main and foresails, we learned that the mean pressure on the latter can be twice that on the mainsail, if the sheeting permits. The efficiency of the mainsail, because of the influence of the mast and possible backwinding, is generally lower than that of headsails. It would be incorrect therefore to assume that the resultant CE for these two sails is related directly to their separate areas, as was done in Fig 260b. It is difficult to say what one can assume, but it would certainly be an unjustifiable simplification to assume a twofold efficiency for headsails.

A reasonable assumption is adopted by the Davidson Laboratory of the Stevens Institute of Technology, when balancing fore, main and mizzen sails. Firstly they find the geometrical CE for each sail as in Fig 264a. The mainsail is then rated at 100 per cent of its area and the foresail as $2 \times 0.85 \times (I \times J)/2$, ie, as double the area $0.85 \times (I \times J)/2$ used in some rating rules.

Figure 264b shows how these two 'effective areas' are combined, at the true centres of area, to give the CE_{F+M} for fore and mainsails.

When the yacht has a mizzen, it is assessed at 50 per cent of its area, and this is again applied at its centre of area. Its efficiency is assessed so low because of interference from the mainsail (downwash) as well as its own mast. The final $CE_{Resultant}$ for all the sails is then determined as in Fig 264c.

The prediction of directional balance, using these arbitrary simplifications, has been found in practice to be quite successful.

The dependence of the position of the CE on the aerodynamic efficiency of the separate sails is often confirmed when tuning racing yachts. Merely by altering the trim of the sails one can make, or mar, the directional balance. At the risk

Fig 264 Method of establishing resultant position of the CE for a ketch used by the Davidson Laboratory, USA.

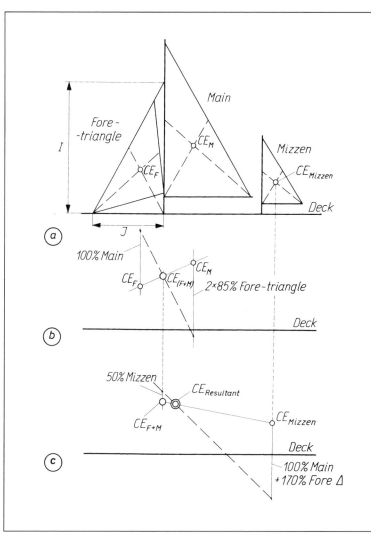

of stating the obvious, it must be emphasized that before making radical changes to the sailplan or its position on the hull, one should ensure that the sails are properly trimmed. While performance and not balance should be the primary objective, yet at the same time, optimum performance will rarely be achieved where the balance is bad.

Wind tunnel experiments carried out by the author on an X One-Design class model confirmed in principle the designer's assumption about the vertical position of the CE, which is usually established by means of geometry as shown in Fig 264. However, the actual position of the CE varies to some extent with wind speed. Thus, when close-hauled the true CE has a tendency to go down, below the geometrical CE, as wind speed increases; this is caused by increasing twist of the sails. At greater wind speeds, the upper part of the sail, operating close to the flutter point, contributes less to generation of the aerodynamic force than the lower part of the sail. When a yacht bears away, the true vertical position of the CE approaches the geometrical CE. Depending on the changes in the CE position, the values of the heeling moment vary in a similar manner.

The enigmatic nature of the real positions of CE and CLR has prompted some research establishments to develop yet another method of estimating the CE position of sailplans (2.88). Thus, the CE of the fore-triangle is taken to act

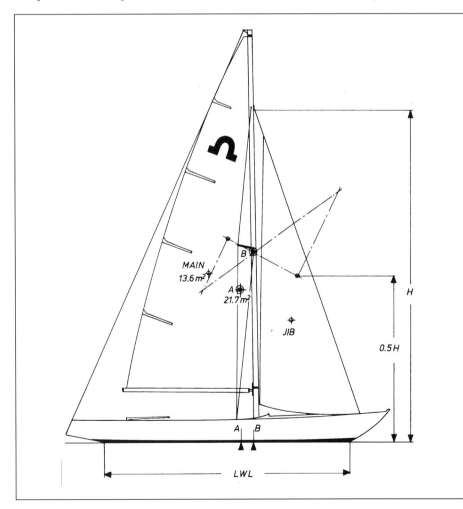

Fig 265 Two positions of CE established for the Soling class by different methods: a) the traditional, and b), a new method used by the Industrial Research and Development Unit, Southampton University. The second method is applied to assess the balance of boats, the CLR of which was found by model tests in the towing tank. As might be expected, the real position of CLR for a model tested is closer to the leading edge of the keel, ie, it is ahead of the CLR assessed as a centroid of lateral area of the hull. Similarly, the real CE of a rig should also be situated closer to the leading edge of sails, ie, ahead of the geometrically established CE. After all, most lift comes from near the leading edge, no matter whether we are dealing with a sail or a keel.

at the local $^1/_4$ chord, half the height above the waterline. A similarly defined location is taken for the mainsail and mizzen if present. Moments are then taken in the manner shown in Fig 260 to find the resultant CE, counting the full area of the fore-triangle (ie no overlap) and of the main and mizzen for the purpose. Admittedly this yields a location which is in surprisingly close agreement with that obtained from wind tunnel tests on a wide range of rigs, including sloops and ketches with multi-sailed fore-triangles. This method seems also to take account of the contribution of the hull and superstructure to the aerodynamics of the vessel, which is larger than is sometimes realized. With the CE obtained this way, it has been found in practice that acceptable balance is achieved with an uncorrected juxtaposition of model test CLR and calculated CE.

Figure 265 shows the sailplan of the Olympic class *Soling* with two CE calculated in two different ways: A) by a traditional method and B) on the principle described just above. It is seen that the B centre of effort is in front of the A centre of effort by a distance of about 5 per cent of LWL length.

17 • SOME REMARKS ABOUT THE CUT, SET AND DEFECTS OF SAILS

This quiet sail is as a noiseless wing
To waft me from distraction'

Lord Byron, Childe Harold's Pilgrimage

Irrespective of what fabric the sail is made of – Nylon, Dacron/Terylene, Mylar/Melinex, Kevlar or a combination in the form of a plastic film laminated on to a lightly woven substrata made of polyester or other material – its shape, predetermined by the cut, will inevitably undergo some changes in use.

Even ordering a sail from a reputable sailmaker does not always ensure a perfect fit. Sail design is still largely a craft and, as one sailmaker complained, 'The paucity of available literature that clearly explains the working of sails in terms other than mathematical hieroglyphics' makes it possible that fresh generations of sailmakers will perpetuate the mistakes of their predecessors in the name of tradition. Only recently has science been allowed to help improve the state of the art.

The best way to learn the importance of cut on sail performance is by making one's own sail. Although this is indeed within the scope of sailing dinghy enthusiasts, most people prefer to rely on the help of professionals. There must, inevitably, be some lack of rapport between the helmsman, who may know the boat and sails intimately (ie, how they behave in varied weather conditions), and the sailmaker who may even speak a different 'language', (unless he or she is in the crew). Some knowledge of the properties of the different fabrics, of sail technology, of the fundamentals of sail cutting, and of sail setting or tuning appears to be an indispensable aid for those who race and cruise. Without such knowledge it is difficult to specify one's requirements when ordering new sails, or to correct evident faults in sail shape (or to know whether they are caused by improper sail cut or were inflicted by the crew while sailing).

When discussing sails and their problems, we may perhaps assume that the Admiral's Cup or America's Cup sailor belongs to a race apart. The average person engaged in cruising or weekend racing at club level cannot afford the expense of exotic sails which last for only half a season. Therefore, while developments are constantly taking place, new materials are arriving, and ever more sophisticated techniques are being evolved, it is with the basics of practical use that we should be primarily concerned. So let us look first at conventional sailplans using conventional materials, and then devote a little time to considering modern trends.

THE PROPERTIES OF SAIL FABRICS

What are the important properties which distinguish a good sailcloth from a bad one? Why do sails distort? How big are the stress forces acting within a sail? Why are some fabrics more suited to one type of sail than another? Has the perfect or ideal sailcloth already been invented – as some sailmakers claim? These

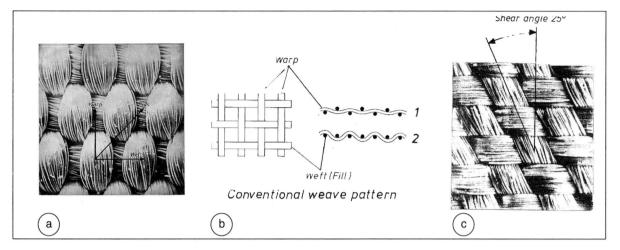

Fig 266

a) A conventional sailcloth as seen through the lens of the microscope.

b) The shape-retaining ability of a sail made from conventionally woven fabric largely depends on the tightness of the weave.

c) A loosely woven fabric (not sailcloth) in the sheared state. Threads become jammed at large shear angles.

are among the important questions which sailing people have been discussing for a long time.

A sail, during its lifetime, is subject to variable and often very strong forces from the wind, sheets, halyards and tuning devices. These forces produce a state of stress in the woven fabric, under which the sail shape may distort, usually to the detriment of its performance, if no measures to prevent this are taken by means of control devices. To understand the role of fabric in determining sail shape, the modes of deformation and stretch behaviour of the sailcloth must be considered in some detail.

In conventional Terylene or Dacron sail fabric woven to a plain weave (Fig 266), the threads of warp and weft (also called fill) go under and over each other alternately. The warp threads (ends) are those which run along the cloth while weft threads (picks) run across the cloth. When warp and weft yarns cross over one another the yarns are curved (crimped) in the manner shown in sketches 1 and 2 of Fig 266b. It is possible to adjust the weave in such a way that the warp and weft go up and down an equal amount (sketch 1) and, if the ends and picks are of equal size, a square weave is produced. Sketch 2 demonstrates another weave pattern, where the warp crimp is greater with the weft pulled tight and lying almost straight. Between these two combinations any weave variant is possible, by changing the thread spacing, yarn twist, or using yarns of different denier in warp and weft (denier is the weight in grammes of 9000 metres of yarn; it indicates the size of thickness of yarn).

Depending on the degree of initial crimp in warp and weft, deliberately introduced while weaving, the fabric will have different stretch characteristics to suit different kinds of sails. Crimp increases the tendency to stretch (as the yarn straightens under load) unless a counteracting load is applied in the other direction. When the sailcloth is under load there occurs a crimp interchange between the warp and weft yarns. That is to say, stretching the cloth in the weft direction will tend to straighten the yarns and bring the warp yarns closer together; this induces greater crimp in the warp, so tightening it. Conversely, stretching the cloth in the direction of the warp will tend to tighten the weft. For example, stretching a sailcloth in the weft direction, say by 5 per cent, can result in a shrinkage of 2 per cent in the warp direction. However, with the crimped warp and almost straight weft yarns (as shown in sketch 2 of Fig 266b),

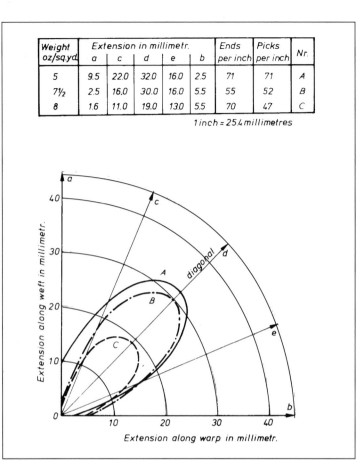

Weight oz/sq.yd	Extension in millimetr.					Ends per inch	Picks per inch	Nr.
	a	c	d	e	b			
5	9.5	22.0	32.0	16.0	2.5	71	71	A
7½	2.5	16.0	30.0	16.0	5.5	55	52	B
8	1.6	11.0	19.0	13.0	5.5	70	47	C

1 inch = 25.4 millimetres

Fig 267 The stretch characteristics of some conventionally woven sailcloth. The essential feature of these fabrics is that they are directionally unbalanced, ie, under the same load they elongate much more along the bias than along the warp or weft. It has been argued (and rightly so) that it is erroneous to use the term bias stretch instead of bias elongation. This is because conventionally woven fabrics stretch little along the threadline, and any measured extension along the warp or weft is due to a genuine stretch of the fibres under load, and to some flattening of the crimp. In the case of the loadings on the bias, the measured elongation in the cloth is almost entirely caused by shear deformation in the weave pattern, as shown in Fig 266c, and the threads which are sheared (displaced) may not stretch in themselves at all. To illustrate the point, take for example a square wire net. If it is pulled in any bias direction, the net will elongate easily, although the individual wires will not stretch; the original square pattern of the net will be transformed into a rhombus pattern.

stretching the weft has very little effect on the warp since the weft yarns are already almost straight.

Because of the way conventional fabrics are woven, they do not stretch (or elongate) equally in all directions under equal loadings. Figure 267 demonstrates, in the form of a polar plot, the stretch-behaviour pattern of three different Terylene sailcloths under the same load. Tests were done on 15 inch long and 1 inch wide strips with sealed selvedges cut from the fabric in the 5 directions marked a–e in Fig 267; a loading of 6 kg was applied and extensions were recorded in millimetres. These results were obtained from tests on single samples of the cloth concerned.

Two observations are of particular importance:

1 In the case of sailcloth C the extension on the warp exceeds the extension on the weft, while in A the reverse appears. In seeking a reason for this, it was concluded that the relatively greater number of ends in the warp of cloth C was causing the weft to lie flat, ie, with little uptake; whereas in the case of A (an almost square cloth with equal ends and picks) the smaller weft permitted more crimp and therefore relatively more uptake on the weft.

2 The sailcloth extensibility on the bias angles 22½°, 45° and 67½° (marked by arrows c, d, e, respectively) is much greater than that along the warp or weft. Since stresses actually occurring in the sail need not be confined to warp and weft directions, more extensibility along the diagonal will tend to produce what might be called 'stretch-fold'. A simple experiment with any conventionally woven fabric, be it a sailcloth or a tablecloth, will show that when uniform loading is applied along the warp or weft direction, the fabric's surface remains smooth, while a bias load, particularly along the diagonal, will produce stretch-folds (wrinkles). Evident bias instability is an inherent characteristic of any cloth produced on conventional looms where the warp and weft threads intersect each other on right angles and hence have little initial shear resistance. The reason is obvious – glossy synthetic fibres are too smooth to bind well, instead they slip easily at the intersections until the yarns are jammed against one another. This shear behaviour is shown in Fig 266c, which illustrates a loosely woven fabric sheared through 25°.

Referring to test results in Fig 267, one may find widely different stretch characteristics from one bolt of the fabric to the next, even if the weight of cloth is the same or differs little. This stretch variation due to the way the fabric is woven may differ further depending on the kind of finishing treatment (such as heat-setting, calendering, resination, etc) that is used on it. Substantial advances made in sailcloth technology during the last two decades were largely aimed at improving the bias stability of the fabric, to ensure consistent shear performance throughout a long service life. Apart from improvements in weave structure, most of the significant developments have been made in the finishing processes. These are the most influential in determining not only the stretch characteristics of the sailcloth, but also its other important features such as *wear and tear strength, recovery, fatigue and porosity*.

Perhaps the most important finishing treatment of woven sailcloth is the heat- setting of the fabric by controlled shrinkage under heat; during this process a resin such as melamine may be added. If a fabric is to be resinated, it first passes through a container of the resin solution and then through a pair of rollers, which squeeze the resin into the weave. The melamine resin is not chemically bonded until the fabric has been heat-set at a temperature rising slowly to about 200°C. The yarns swell at first, allowing the resin molecules to penetrate deeper into the material. Subsequently the cloth is allowed to shrink, thus tightening the weave to a state which would be impossible to achieve on the loom. The result is an extra-tight, densely impregnated fabric. However, if it is not precisely controlled, this heat shrinkage tends to increase the crimp in warp and weft threads, which in turn would decrease resistance to stretch, particularly if the cloth is not resinated. If low extensibility in the weft (fill) direction is of primary importance (and as we shall see soon, it is indeed significant for high aspect ratio mainsails), then a special machine is used to hold the weft threads to their initial length as the fabric cools from the heat-setting temperature. This allows the warp threads to shrink and crimp while retaining the weft threads virtually without crimp.

Two other important finishing operations are *yarn-tempered finish* and *calendering*. In the first the fabric undergoes an additional resin treatment, in the second the cloth is passed through heated steel rollers under very high pressure. The fibres are then compressed on to one another at intersections, thus the weave is further tightened and the fabric is given smoothness; at the same time

directional stability is improved and porosity reduced. There are also other finishing processes which can be used in various combinations to achieve specifically desired results ranging between two extremes – from a tightly woven, resin-
free, soft fabric to a hard finish sailcloth sometimes known as 'tinplate' or 'yarn
tempered'.

Not so long ago the weight per running yard or square yard was practically
the only measure in deciding what fabric was suitable for the sail of given area.
Today, within one weight range, a number of weave finishes and hence a variety of stretch characteristics are available, all of which can be used for different
applications. With so much variety, how can we make a decision on which fabric
is best? How are the type of sail, its geometry, range of wind speed, specific
requirements (cruising or racing, etc) relevant to the properties of various sailcloths?

There is no doubt that distortions of the designed sail shape under stress
results from stretch in the fabric and is bound to affect the aerodynamic efficiency of the sail. By 'designed sail shape' we mean a desirable shape intended
by the sailmaker, crew – and perhaps the theoreticians too! By straightforward
deduction one may expect that, if the stretch characteristics of a cloth do not
match the stresses in the sail inflicted by the aerodynamic and other loadings
(sheet, halyards etc), the designed sail shape is likely to distort in an unpredictable manner. To put the problem another way, on the one hand the airflow
around the sail depends upon its shape and, on the other hand, the pressure
distribution resulting from the flow largely determines the sail shape; ie its camber, camber distribution, twist etc.

Some good attempts to determine quantitatively the amount of sail deformation, and the functional relationships between the observed distortion and fabric properties, were carried out by ICI Fibres in England (1967) (Figs 268 and
269). The purpose was to gain information not only about the magnitude of
stresses in a full scale sail in natural wind conditions, but also about the pattern
of stresses and subsequently the fabric's rate of recovery. The rig was designed
to examine sails of many different types, cloth-weights and weave construction.
Photographs taken on a pair of high-precision cameras were analysed on a
stereo-autographic plotter, using a technique similar to that for preparing maps
from aerial photographs. A big advantage of this 'photogrammetry' method is
that there is no direct contact between the measuring devices and the sail, and
therefore no distortion of the air flow. Some initial results presented in Fig 269
indicate in which direction stretch occurs in each part of the sail. Such a picture
may suggest what steps in fabric design and finishing processes need to be taken
to reduce and balance the overall extension. In other words, a rational attempt
can be made to weave and finish the fabric with reduced stretch in the direction
of *greatest importance*.

The observation that appreciable weft (fill) yarn extension had occurred even
in a good quality sailcloth highlights the important effect of weave pattern and
the conditions under which sailcloth fabrics are finished. Thus, the practice of
allowing fabrics to shrink (and unfortunately crimp) to a great extent during
heat-setting (in order to consolidate the weave structure and thereby reduce
bias extensibility) inevitably increases extensibility of the weft and warp yarns,
unless deliberate precautions are taken to reduce crimp and so the stretch in

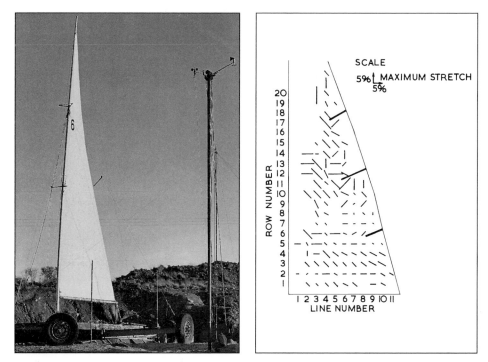

Fig 268 (left) The ICI test rig. This 60 ft yacht mast, rigged on the Yorkshire moors, provided scientists with more information on the stresses and strains imposed upon a sail. They wanted to know not only the severity of the stresses in the full scale sail, but the pattern of stress and subsequently the fabric's rate of recovery. The purpose of these tests was the development of a more convenient laboratory rig – one which would *simulate the stress pattern a yacht imposes*. This rig comprised a metal mast mounted on a wooden platform so that the mast could be rotated about its own axis. It was designed to test sails of different types, weights and designs.

Fig 269 (right) A technique developed by ICI Fibres makes it possible to measure accurately the distortion which occurs in a sail while actually under stress. The diagram shows the magnitude and direction of maximum stretch at various points in the sail, recorded at a wind speed of 27 mph. Further details of stretch distribution in the sail can be found in *Aero-Hydrodynamics of Sailing* (Ref 2.4).

the direction of greatest importance (for instance, along the lee). Ultimately, further sails can be made using corrected fabric and their performance studied in detail by the same photogrammetric technique. As expected by ICI, this will either confirm or refute the initial conclusions which have been drawn, and may uncover other factors which are of importance in determining the interdependence between measured sail shape, fabric deformation and sail efficiency.

Figure 270 demonstrates the effect of resination on the aerodynamic forces developed on two sails. The forces were measured indirectly by recording load on the mainsheet. Although the sail with half-resin finish showed a similar stretch pattern to its equivalent with a soft finish, at low wind speeds the soft finish sail generated a higher aerodynamic force, as indicated on the load dynamometer in the mainsheet. Seeking an explanation for this, one must take into account the fact that the sail made of soft cloth takes up its shape more readily and assumes a smooth contour even when wind forces are relatively

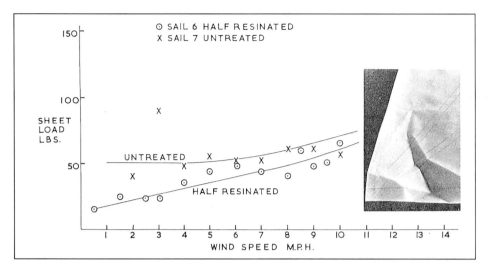

Fig 270 The effect of cloth resination on mainsheet load (ICI tests). The graph compares the load recorded on the mainsheet of two sails of similar fabric construction – one relatively hard with a half resin finish, and the other soft (untreated).

small. Assymetrical loadings applied to the edges of such a sail by sheet, halyard and downhaul are easily redistributed within the soft finish cloth to a roughly symmetrical loading pattern. On the other hand, resinated hard finish cloth is too stiff to behave that way. Its inherent rigidity, perhaps aggravated by already existing creases all over its surface, makes the sail resist assuming the desired smooth shape; the small photo to the right in Fig 270 illustrates the point. Wind forces must be strong enough to smooth out irregularities in shape before the sail will resume aerodynamic efficiency. For this reason, sails made of hard finish and particularly of yarn-tempered cloth should never be tightly furled or stuffed into their bags.

The photogrammetric technique can also be used to answer many other questions related to sailcloth and sailmaking technology. For instance, let us hypothetically assume that the sailmaker knows what the optimum sail configuration is, ie, sail camber, its horizontal and vertical distribution, the leech twist, mutual position between genoa and mainsail, etc, for a given boat and given range of wind speed. Let us further assume that the sailmaker designed the sail, ie, curvature of panels (broadseam) round to the luff and foot, lay of cloth, etc. (see Fig 275c) to reproduce the chosen shape from a deliberately selected weave of known stretch characteristics. Can he be sure that the sail he produces will correspond to the desired shape? Unfortunately, so far there is no method or scientific theory whereby the three dimensional shape of new sail design may be predicted accurately. Stretch of the fabric itself contributes to the shape in an unpredictable manner. And even if exact knowledge of the stretch characteristics of the cloth obtained in laboratory conditions were available, this would not answer the question of what happens in actual sailing conditions. Pictures of the sail shape, be it based on the photogrammetric technique or shots taken (with a wide-lens camera) from directly under the middle of the foot of the main or headsail, and from different angles and under different conditions, can be extremely useful. The basic sail shape parameters (camber to chord ratio, position of maximum draft, leading edge angle, twist, mast bend, forestay sag, evident faults in cut, etc) can be identified, thus helping the sailmaker to decide whether the sail design is correct or needs rethinking, and whether the fabric used meets expectations.

Fig 271 Sail shape as recorded by photogrammetry of one of the most successful 470-class dinghies in France (1977), at a wind speed of 10.8 knots.

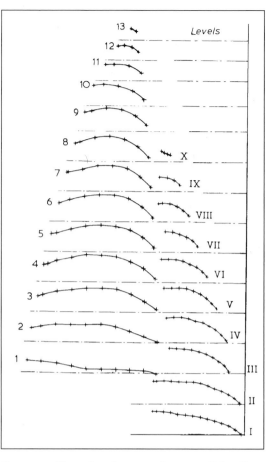

Figure 271 illustrates, for example, photogrammetric sail pictures of one of the most successful 470 class boats in France (1977). According to comments made by the French sailmaker, B Cheret, evident distortions in the sails were mainly due to hard finish cloth (weight 4.75 oz per sq yard) and relatively low wind speed (10.8 knots) which apparently was not sufficient to fill the sails properly. Tables 15 and 16 give more details about some shape characteristics of the main and headsail, according to their trim angles in relation to the boat centreline, δ, and incidence angle, α.

Race winning sails are rarely produced at the first attempt and, for example, to make competitive America's Cup sails, the sailmaker may have to produce up to 50 sails before he can deliver a suit near to perfection.

By recording the shapes of successful sail configurations, new ideas in cutting and new fabrics can, with some traditional justification, be incorporated into new concepts of sail design. Then, by controlled performance testing while sailing two well-matched boats of the same class, the sailmaker can reasonably judge how inspired his designs were.

Figures 272a, b and c depict another way of presenting stereo–photographs

Table 15	470 class mainsail camber/chord ratio			
SECTION	MAXIMUM CAMBER %	POSITION OF MAX CAMBER FROM LE %	TRIM ANGLE δ (DEGREES) RELATIVE TO CL	INCIDENCE ANGLE α (DEGREES)
12	15.4	45.0	17.0	18.0
11	12.8	41.0	13.0	22.0
10	14.3	46.4	15.0	20.0
9	16.7	46.3	12.0	23.0
8	19.2	49.3	11.0	24.0
7	15.4	38.8	9.7	25.3
6	17.5	40.3	8.8	26.2
5	15.9	39.1	7.2	27.8
4	15.4	39.7	6.7	28.3
3	13.1	37.2	6.0	29.0
2	8.9	42.0	5.4	29.6
LE = Leading edge of the sail CL = Centreline of the hull				

SECTION	MAXIMUM CAMBER %	POSITION OF MAX CAMBER FROM LE %	TRIM ANGLE δ (DEGREES) RELATIVE TO CL	INCIDENCE ANGLE α (DEGREES)
X	10.0	–	23.7	11.3
IX	13.7	41.0	21.8	13.2
VIII	13.7	52.0	21.4	13.6
VII	13.0	47.0	19.0	16.0
VI	13.2	50.0	17.5	17.5
V	15.9	46.0	16.6	18.4
IV	15.2	53.0	13.4	21.6
III	13.9	54.0	14.8	20.2
II	10.6	49.0	14.5	20.5
I	7.1	38.0	14.3	20.7

Table 16   470 class headsail camber/chord ratio

of sails while under actual sailing conditions. These are the contour maps of an International 14 ft class mainsail recorded at a wind speed of 7, 10, and 12 knots. From such three-dimensional contours, other shape data can be obtained at arbitrary sail sections. Some results, as given in Table 17, for three different levels above the sail foot, illustrate how much the sail shape changes with a relatively small variation in wind speed. Once out of the loft and aboard the racing boat, it is up to the helmsman and crew to learn how to control sail shape by changing the amount of stretch on the luff and foot and, where possible, by altering the curvature of the sail through bending the mast and/or boom.

Yet another way of recording sail shape is presented in Fig 273. The final measure of how well the various allowances on luff, roach, foot and sail panels

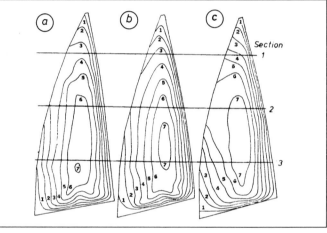

Fig 272 Contour map of an International 14 ft class mainsail under different wind loadings (Ref 2.89).

WIND SPEED	7 knots (A)			10 knots (B)			12 knots (C)		
SECTION	1	2	3	1	2	3	1	2	3
TWIST (DEGREES)	13.0	6.0	2.0	13.0	7.0	3.0	25.0	15.0	6.0
MAXIMUM CAMBER %	15.4	18.9	19.3	13.3	17.3	16.5	13.5	16.0	16.2
POSITION OF MAXIMUM CAMBER	40.5	40.5	40.5	35.0	35.0	35.0	34.0	39.0	38.5

Table 17   International 14 ft class mainsail

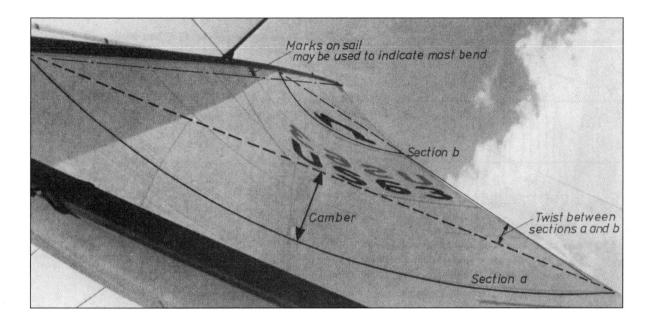

Fig 273 One way to record some features of sail shape in the form given in Table 17 is to take shots with a wide-angle lens from directly under the foot of the sail.

have been calculated and built into the sail can only be taken when the sails are properly set. Some years ago the quality of sails was judged by the eye; however, it is sometimes said that pretty sails don't win races. The 12 Metre *Vim* was probably the first racing boat whose sails were given some quantitative assessment (Fig 274). Her sails were separately hoisted (to avoid backwinding) and the profiles at various sections measured: Table 18 gives the magnitudes of cambers at a number of sections, expressed as a percentage of the appropriate chord length, so that the figures can be directly compared.

On both sails the camber is considerably more at mid–height than near the foot, and it decreases towards the head. In particular, the mainsail undergoes a striking deformation as it progresses from the boom to section 3; even more surprising is the large amount of twist, over 40° from foot to head. Although it is not easy to say just what the ideal sail shape should look like, we can be quite certain that here we have a rather poor suit of sails, almost certainly set on a reach without a kicking strap. The amount of draft in sections III and IV of the jib appears to be excessive. If the boat is not reaching, this could be due to headstay sag being greater than the sailmaker compensated for, in which case the jib would cause backwinding, unless a large twist is allowed to open the slot: not a particularly good remedy on the windward leg. The mainsail's twist, in the

	Table 18	12 Metre Vim camber/chord ratio		
SECTION	MAXIMUM CAMBER %	SECTION		MAXIMUM CAMBER %
6	10.7			
5	13.5	V		16.0
4	12.7	IV		18.0
3	11.4	III		17.0
2	9.4	II		11.8
1	1.2	I		5.9

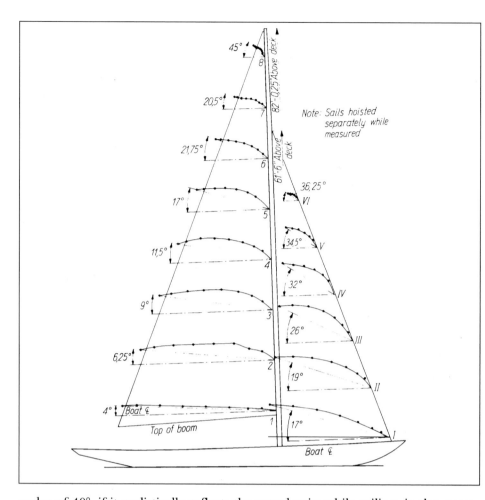

Fig 274 Distribution of a camber and twist on the mainsail and jib of the 12 Metre class yacht *Vim*.

order of 40°, if it realistically reflects the actual twist while sailing, is also excessive. Allowing for the twist in apparent wind direction due to wind gradient, a twist of about 7° over the height of the sail is justified. In addition a few degrees more twist should be allowed to alleviate any tendency to premature stalling of the upper part of the sail, to which every triangular aerofoil is readily susceptible (Fig 212). More detailed information about sail shape and sail efficiency factors are given in Part 2 of *Aero-Hydrodynamics of Sailing*.

THE PRINCIPLES OF CUTTING MAINSAILS

From old paintings we are quite familiar with the simple square sail (Fig 275a). Under the action of the wind, the sail attains a certain camber f and, in so doing, the free edges are pulled inward by an amount X. The original width AB is reduced by 2X, and if we wished to retain more or less straight sides to the sail when set, it would be necessary to add some excess width to the sail as shown in Fig 275b. The amount of extra material required for this camber could be found by measuring the curved profile between the points 1 and 2 (equal to A–B) and subtracting the straight distance 1–2. The above example gives the general idea behind what might be called excess of cloth (or rounding along the foot and luff), a method which is still used as the basis for cutting sails

Fig 275 Excess of cloth in the form of luff and foot round is particularly suited to soft finish cloth, and is the traditional method of sail-shaping used over many years. Shaped panels must also be used, particularly with hard finish cloth. The calculation of the correct taper of the sail panels (or broad seaming) is a matter of pure geometry; however, fabric stretch itself contributes substantially to the sail shape, although not in an entirely predictable manner.

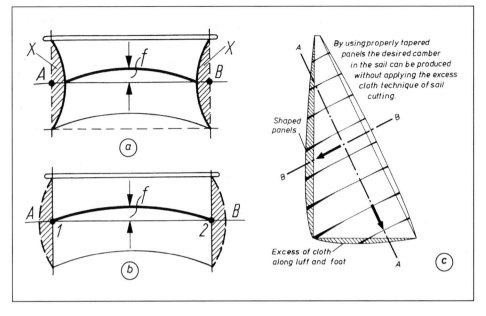

of small or medium camber from a conventionally woven fabric.

Let us now consider a Bermudan sail set on a straight, rigid mast and boom and cut according to this simple and old method (Fig 275c). To obtain some camber, certain excess cloth both along the luff and foot must be added. This is because the sail surface curves three-dimensionally, ie in all directions, and thus excess length is required along both A–A and B–B to allow the point of intersection of these two lines to move out of the flat original plane of the sail to create camber. If these excess lengths, ie luff and foot roundings, are not in correct proportion to each other, creases may appear in the sail. If, say, no or insufficient allowance were made on the foot, the creases would occur along lines approximately parallel to A–A, due to uneven loading along the A–A and B–B directions. The appearance of such creases suggests either faulty hoisting (too much halyard tension) or faulty cutting, including wrongly selected sailcloth. In the second case, the deformation can only satisfactorily be removed by recutting the sail so that the stresses within the sailcloth are more evenly distributed. This is the most important aim of the sailmaker, and one which is not easy to fulfil, especially when catering for a variety of weather conditions. Indeed, it is almost axiomatic that a sail has only a limited range of wind speed in which it will set well; above or below this range its performance may not be wholly satisfactory. Understanding what options the sailmaker has when facing this age-old problem of avoiding cutting faulty or badly shaped sails may help the crew in setting the sail correctly. Those who are interested in practical aspects of fault-finding in sails are recommended to read Jeremy Howard-Williams's book *Sails* published by Adlard Coles Nautical.

The sail design problem is primarily an aerodynamic one, similar to those encountered when designing a rigid aerofoil (wing) for an aircraft, or a turbine blade, but even more complex. A rigid aerofoil is deliberately shaped; the airflow must adapt itself to that predetermined shape. By contrast, the shape assumed by a soft sail *depends* on the airflow; there must therefore be a complicated compromise reached between the air pressure exerted and the flexibility of the sailcloth, which deforms in a rather unpredictable manner depending on a number of factors, some of which are beyond the sailmaker's control.

No matter what technological means are used to produce a sail, there are five essential ways whereby the camber shape (flow Fig 212) can be designed or controlled:

- Rounding the luff and foot
- Tapering the panels of the cloth (broad seam)
- Lay of the cloth
- Tension on the cloth (Cunningham hole)
- Tension on the rope, tape or wire (halyard)

The first three ways are used by the sailmaker, the remaining two depend on the skill of the crew.

Technological means includes both computer aided design and manufacture (ie laser cutters, plotters, etc) and traditional methods. The difference between them is that the computer driven equipment enhances the sailmaker's skill, improves manufacturing accuracy and makes the sail panels ready for instant assembly. Otherwise, the basic principles of the sail camber design (1–3 above) are the same.

The principal difficulty which arises in mainsail cutting according to the traditional excess cloth method (Fig 275c) is that the effect on sail camber (its magnitude and location) of round along the luff and foot cannot be predicted accurately – although it can be guided by the careful use of broad seams in tapering the panels. The stretch properties of the cloth play an important role here, they also determine how the cloth should be laid so as best to resist loadings due to wind action and sheet tension.

Since the mainsail is supported along the luff by the mast and usually along the foot by the boom, the adjacent areas do not suffer concentrated loads and stresses. However, the totally unsupported leech bears a heavy load. To counteract the forces which tend to lift the boom and increase twist, high mainsheet tension is required. This implies little curvature in the leech, particularly important in strong winds and when close-hauled. If the leech were to elongate excessively, the entire sail shape would be distorted because, in general, the sail camber tends to move towards the area of greatest stretch: in this case towards the leech. It is imperative therefore to have the cloth orientated with its greatest resistance to stretch running up and down the leech. Usually, for design purposes, this direction is along the fill, and so the panels of the mainsail are laid at approximately a right angle to the leech (Fig 276a).

The relationship between aerodynamic loading, leech curvature and mainsheet tension is shown in Fig 276b. The aerodynamic force, F, tending to increase the leech curvature, must be balanced by an equal and opposite reaction, R. This can only be obtained from the sheet tension, S, which in turn inflicts large tensile stresses in the fabric in the leech area, and the force T represents these stresses. Relative magnitudes of R, T and S forces can be found by plotting a parallelogram of forces as shown. It is clear that the tensile forces (stresses), T, in the fabric are considerably greater than the aerodynamic force, F, causing them. To set the leech with a small curvature (expressed by f in Fig 276b), great sheet tension S is required and, no matter how large this tension

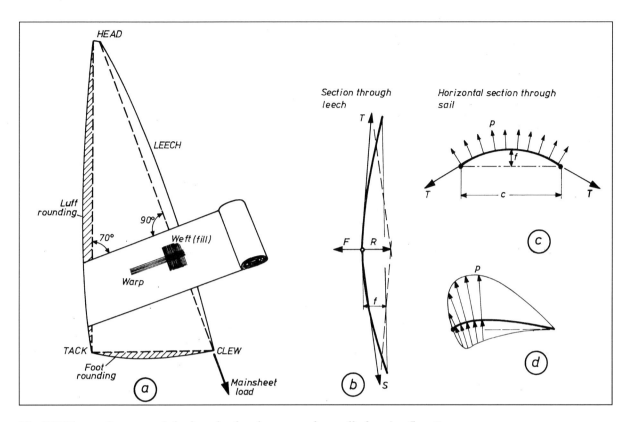

Fig 276 The performance of a sail depends on its shape, which in turn depends on the overall stretch resistance, particularly in the off-threadline (diagonal) direction. Whatever the pundits may say, the sailmaker's most valuable aid is the 'seat of his pants'. There is no substitute for experience, nor for trial and error with its empirical results.

might be, the leech cannot be pulled quite flat. Some curvature must occur to prevent enormous stresses.

The most desirable conventionally woven mainsail fabric then would be the one in which the weft yarns stretch as little as possible, so that the leech would have negligible elongation. By implication it means that the weft yarns should have no crimp, and so the warp yarns only must be crimped, and bias extensibility must somewhat be sacrificed. Although different sailmakers may have different stretch requirements for the mainsail fabric, they do not object to higher bias stretch, assuming that in high aspect ratio mainsails the Cunningham adjustment will take care of the effect of bias stretch.

When Dupont's Kevlar (Fibre B) was introduced some years ago, it appeared to be an ideal fibre to construct a weave that would complement the huge strains experienced in the leech. Kevlar fibres are reputed to be stronger than steel per unit weight; thus, if woven into a sailcloth as weft yarns, they might easily withstand the tensile stresses that tend to distort the design shape of a sail. And indeed, when the first sail made of Kevlar/Dacron hybrid was used in the Admiral's Cup series in 1973 it lived up to expectations. Its performance was good; it held its design shape well throughout the wind range, and required significantly fewer adjustments to adapt to varying wind and sea conditions. Another advantage of Kevlar is that, by being much stronger per unit weight than Terylene/Dacron, it allows lower weight fabric to be used. It was claimed that the weight saving, particularly aloft where it matters most, might be as much as 30 per cent.

Unfortunately, although the hybrid Kevlar/Dacron cloth has superior characteristics in some respects, it also has severe drawbacks. Kevlar is expensive, brittle, highly subject to tear and, more than Nylon, is affected by ultraviolet light. Because of that, its strength degrades quickly, particularly if the sail is allowed to flutter. As resported, before the Admiral's Cup series was over, the Kevlar hybrid sail which had performed well as the racing sail, blew out along one of the horizontal seams, starting at the leech. It is unlikely that the Kevlar-reinforced hybrid sailcloth might – to quote a contemporary expert opinion – 'be considered as a viable material which can be used with confidence in sails which must perform in long ocean races with no backup.'

When the sail is set on a straight mast and boom or spars that bend less than the luff and foot curvatures (round as given in Fig 276a), the wind pressure will push the excess material into the middle of the sail and a camber will appear. It is instructive to consider now the shape assumed by a horizontal narrow strip of sail loaded by air pressure as shown in Fig 276c. If such a strip of length 1 and unit width is held at both ends and subject to a uniform wind pressure, p, it will assume the shape of a circular arc of camber c = f/l, and the tension in the strip will be p × l/8c where p × l is the total load on the strip and c is the camber. The term 'wind pressure' refers to the difference in pressure on the two sides of sailcloth, ie, the sum of the suction or negative pressure on the leeward side and the positive pressure on the windward side (Figs 41 and 51).

If the pressure varies along the strip as shown in Fig 276d, which roughly depicts the pressure distribution relevant to the close-hauled condition, the position of maximum camber will move towards the mast. The tension in the strip will be different and so the shape of the strip will also change, from circular to roughly parabolic. Of course, if ends of the strip, ie, the edges of the sail are allowed to move inward under tension, or the sailcloth elongates, this would contribute to the sail shape and hence the number of interrelated variables would increase. Consequently, predicting the sail shape, on the basis that the luff and foot roundings together with roach are known, becomes impossible. In practice, the sailmaker must rely heavily on the trial-and-error or cut-and-try method, as well as accumulated experience, in order to produce a sail that 'looks good' and will hopefully perform as desired, or whether it is one that must be returned to the loft for recutting. The major disadvantage of this method is that *why* certain factors contribute to successful sail design can remain somewhat obscure, and thus consistent results can hardly be achieved.

During the last three decades or so, a number of solutions to the problem have been suggested. As opposed to the empirical method (particularly suitable to soft finish sailcloth where the sailmaker's art is to use stretch as one of the ways of creating the shape of the sail), the new, analytical methods are based on aerodynamic theories used to design airframe wings. The advent of high speed digital computers have made this approach economically practical.

The anlalytical design of a sail, as suggested by J Milgram, for example, is similar to the method used in Prandtl's lifting theory, on which I expand in *Aero– Hydrodynamics of Sailing*. Three steps are taken in designing a suit of sails.

1 Determination of the *desired distribution of pressure on the sails*. This pressure (which can be measured by a small pressure gauge embedded in the surface of the sail in a manner shown in Figs 37–39) varies from point to point on the sail. For any assumed set of conditions, such as:

a) sail plan

b) relative wind direction

c) range of wind speeds

d) sea state

e) hydrodynamic characteristics of the hull

There is a unique pressure distribution which gives the optimum performance. The primary effects determined by the pressure distribution are the driving force, the heeling force, and the heeling moment. Obviously, these effects are related to each other and, for instance, the sail designer may seek a pressure distribution which gives maximum driving force at minimum heeling force or, say, maximum lift force at minimum induced drag, tantamount to maximum driving force when close-hauled in light and moderate winds when the heeling moment is of secondary importance. This first step is relatively easy.

2 The next step – designing the shape which the sails should attain under wind action in order to achieve the desired pressure distribution – is much more difficult. By sail shape we mean the three-dimensional shape, in which case the cross-sectional profile at any one level of the sail (ie maximum camber and its location: Fig 277) may not, and usually is not, the same at any other level. In addition, the cross-sections are twisted in relation to the boom. As a matter of fact, depending on conditions (a)–(e) of stage 1, both twist and cross-section shape must vary from the foot to the head of the sail to make any performance gain possible.

Fig 277a Mainsail control devices which control the sail shape.

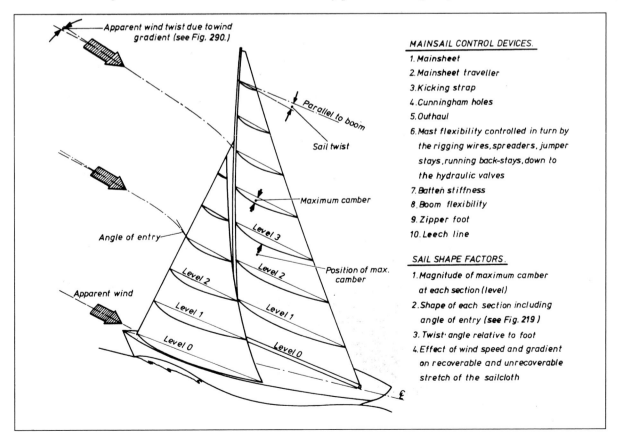

MAINSAIL CONTROL DEVICES.

1. Mainsheet
2. Mainsheet traveller
3. Kicking strap
4. Cunningham holes
5. Outhaul
6. Mast flexibility controlled in turn by the rigging wires, spreaders, jumper stays, running back-stays, down to the hydraulic valves
7. Batten stiffness
8. Boom flexibility
9. Zipper foot
10. Leech line

SAIL SHAPE FACTORS.

1. Magnitude of maximum camber at each section (level)
2. Shape of each section including angle of entry (see Fig. 219)
3. Twist· angle relative to foot
4. Effect of wind speed and gradient on recoverable and unrecoverable stretch of the sailcloth

To illustrate the point, take one sail section, on an arbitrary level, with 10 per cent camber. Obviously, there is an unlimited number of different shapes within this 10 per cent camber restriction. The location of maximum camber may vary somewhat between practical limits, say 20 per cent chord point and the mid-chord. The cross-section may take up a parabolic shape forward with a flat run aft, can be circular, or may have a hooked leech configuration.

The gist of the sail design problem is to find the best sail section shapes to achieve the desired pressure distribution. One thing is certain, there is no best sail shape (or best combinations of sail shape factors listed in Fig 277) which could satisfactorily work in conditions (a)–(e) of stage 1. For example, if stablity requirements are not prohibitive, the main objective in shaping the vertical (spanwise) distribution of pressure is to minimize induced drag at high lift coefficients and so to obtain the largest possible driving force. While in shaping the cross-sections of the sail in order to achieve desired chordwise pressure distribution, the overriding concern is to prevent or delay flow separation at high lift coefficients. The angle of entry at the leading edge (the luff) and the

Fig 277b Sail trim and tuning is as good as the crew is in pulling and easing all those strings shown.

mast shape may play a role here, in the sense that they may determine whether or not flow separation will occur. If it does, and as a result a large area of the sail plan is affected by eddies caused by separated flow (as is shown in Fig 212), there is so far no method whereby the chordwise pressure distribution could analytically be related to the cross-section of the sail. In other words, if the airflow does not remain attached over the entire sail, there is no known way of calculating what the cross-section of the sail should be to produce the desired chordwise pressure distribution. Of course, if only a small percentage of the sail area is affected by the separated flow, the errors are small but, as the size of this area increases, the errors may become too large, thus making the calculation meaningless. This is the weak point of the concept of analytical sail design; but not the only one.

3 The third and final step in analytical sail design is to calculate the correct combination of tapered panels as shown in Fig 275c, and eventually luff and foot round, necessary to create the chosen sail shape established in step 2. As shown, the panels are cut wider in the middle to have the maximum camber where it is wanted. With the shape built in by means of properly designed panels, and some small degree of stretch in the fabric, the sail readily assumes the desired shape even with little wind.

A description of the results of the computer aided sail design hailed as a marvel in one of the letters issued by the Amateur Yacht Research Society, may serve as an illustration of another aspect of analytical sail design. 'The most outstanding of these sailmaking softwares was a suite of programs... alas costing many thousands of dollars [which] allowed a complete sail development program to be undertaken using inputs of fabric characteristics, panel shape and orientation as well as taking into account the effects of batten position and stiffness, mast behaviour, sheet tension and wind loading. All these combined to give the full three dimensional (3D) shape, with the stresses in the sail at any point. Similarly the 3D shape could be altered and the attendant effect on all the other parameters could be used to suggest where reinforcement should be placed.'

Taken at its face value, all that sounds impressive. But, bearing in mind the time-dependent imponderable qualities of sailcloth alone, one may wonder whether it is just another expensive computer game? Only time will tell.

For a number of reasons, the stretching properties of the fabric amongst them, there is no assurance that the desired sail shape and thus the assumed pressure distribution can be realized in practice. The theoretically promising sail shape could, of course, be achieved if the sails were made of metal sheets, possibly using a mould layout-system for sheet forming. Such an ideal shape, however, could work efficiently only in a narrow range of wind and sea conditions. Since sailing vessels operate in a variety of conditions, it is necessary to have sails responsive to adjustments which can deliberately be used to modify their shape to match optimally the ever-changing requirements.

Adjustments such as downhauls and outhauls or spar bend have less effect on sails whose shape was created by the use of tapered panels (Fig 275c) – the sail cutting technique particularly suitable for hard finish cloth. Some sailmakers prefer this method of panel cutting because the camber tends to stay where it was designed to be. Whereas the sail shape created by the luff and foot roundings – a technique suitable rather to soft finish cloth – is less predictable, although more controllable by varying the edge tensions (Cunningham Holes) or spar bend. The main disadvantage of the second method of sail cutting is that certain minimum wind pressure is required to produce camber by forcing the excess cloth from the sail edges towards the centre. Besides, the maximum camber tends to shift back and forth from mast to leech, as the wind speed changes.

No matter which sail shaping method is used (or a proper blend of these two) some degree of stretch in the fabric must be accepted as a factor of great importance to the racing sailor. On the other hand, uncontrolled fabric stretch constitutes a severe drawback – the sail may simply be stretched out of its intended shape. The importance of stretch varies greatly with wind speed. According to equation $q = 0.00119 \times V_A{}^2$, the wind dynamic pressure q acting on the sail fabric is proportional to the apparent wind squared (V_A^2). Thus, if the sail operates in the wind range, say, from $V_A = 3$ knots to $V_A = 15$ knots, the strain in the sail at higher wind speed will increase in proportion $15^2/3^2 = 225/9$ ie, 25 times! Inevitably, if too lightweight a fabric is used and it suffers a significant amount of stretch, the sail may change its shape drastically to the point where the sail distortion can no longer be compensated for by luff and foot adjustments. If, for high apparent winds, these adjustments are not adequate, the sail camber may increaswe well beyond the design fullness at the time when less fullness would be beneficial. Thus, the claims occasionally made that one sail made of one fabric (currently available) could efficiently be used over a wide range of winds, does not appear to be realistic: fabric too must be used appropriately and to its optimum advantage.

THE PROBLEM OF FLEXIBLE SPARS

The method of mainsail cutting shown in Figs 275c and 276 can only be applied as it stands to sails supported by rigid spars. When the mast bends appreciably, as for instance in the Star or Finn classes or even ocean racers, the effect of fore-and-aft curvature of the mast bend on sail shape must be taken into account. No matter whether the mast bends uniformly along its whole length, or extensively at the top only (as the *Lionheart*'s does), it allows deliberate adjustment to be made in order to change the pressure distribution developed on the sails to suit optimally the prevailing sailing condition. Such adjustments can be made provided, of course, the mast bend is fully controllable and the sail cut is well matched with luff round to suit the curvature of the flexed mast. This is not easy to achieve.

Figure 278 shows a typical bent Finn mast when sailing to windward. The cross-hatched area of the sail forward of the line A–B represents the material which was partly drawn forward from the belly of the sail and partly from the leech area by pulling the roach inward. As a result, parts of the sail immediately adjacent to the luff are flattened and the sail fullness tends to move towards the leech. As the wind speed increases, if no further adjustments are made, this fullness settles at the aft end of the sail, tightening the leech. In an extreme case this may lead to the 'hooked-leech' configuration, the worst possible sail shape for close-hauled work. Such a tendency is shown in three sketches in Fig 278. This undesirable change in sail shape may be aggravated if the mast is too limber. The appearance of small stretch folds (wrinkles) along the luff radiating towards the clew is a first warning that the downhaul tension along the luff is not sufficient to compensate for the mast bend effect. Figure 278 shows such a deadly combination of overbend in the middle of the mast with too little downhaul tension. Due to excessive mast flexibility, the distance from the clew to the point of maximum mast bend has increased so much that the sailcloth is stressed almost into a straight line, thus a conspicuous stretch-fold marked F in Fig 278 must appear. Evidently, the mast bend is too much for the cut of the sail, ie, the luff round is not sufficient for the curvature of the mast bend, and no matter how much the downhaul tension is increased, it will not remedy this defect in sail shape.

To avoid such a distortion in the sail, either the flexibility of a rig must be

Fig 278 The shape of the cross-sections of the Finn sail depends on the combined effects of wind strength, sheet tension and bending characteristics of the mast.

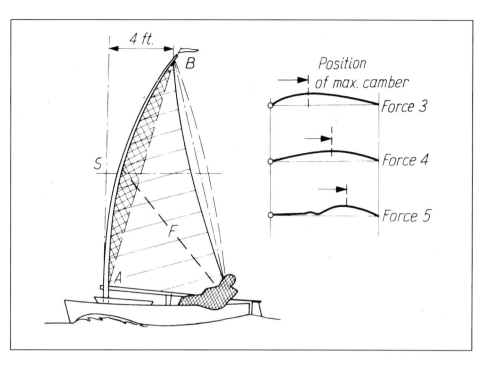

Fig 278 The shape of the cross-sections of the Finn sail depends on the combined effects of wind strength, sheet tension and bending characteristics of the mast.

reduced or the sailmaker must allow proper luff round (material surplus) for the mast bend. As shown in Fig 279, this can be achieved by adding to the luff rounding curve A (for a straight mast), the curve B representing the shape of the bent mast at given sheet tension. Thus, the final curve C obtained by adding together the offsets of curves A and B, represents more realistically the luff round necessary to achieve the desired sail camber when sailing close-hauled in a particular range of wind strength. On other courses, when the mast does not bend to any great extent, the sail camber will tend to increase.

As might be expected, a given mast/sail combination has a fairly limited range

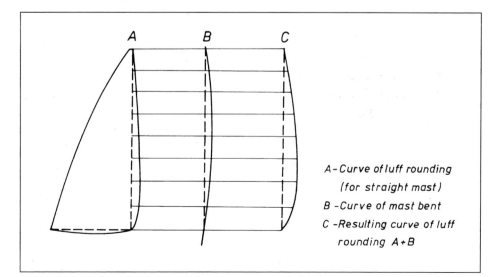

A - Curve of luff rounding
(for straight mast)

B - Curve of mast bent

C - Resulting curve of luff
rounding A + B

Fig 279 The fullness of the sail camber largely depends on the excess of sailcloth along the mast height, determined by the combined luff curve, which is a sum of the luff rounding for a straight mast, plus the curve due to mast bend.

of wind speeds (and thus sheet tensions) over which the mast bend curve is well tuned to the sail-cut and consequently the sail shape is as desired. Not infrequently, the mast is too soft. As a result, the sail leech, particularly at the top, cannot be set properly – it is too free – no matter how hard the sheet is trimmed.

The performance advantages offered by the widely accepted bendy mast became apparent in the early thirties. The method of controlling sail shape by changing mast bend was applied for the first time by W Hutchler in the Star class, and with great success. Since then, it quickly revolutionized racing technique in the smaller classes, well before it was adopted by large, offshore racers. An interesting point is that the flexible Star rig was not developed deliberately to bend. W Hütchler told the author that initially his intention was to make the mast thinner in order to reduce windage and weight aloft. When the thinner mast began to bend under sheet tension, the evident performance advantages due to mast flexibility were immediately recognized.

Today it is rare for any Olympic class boat to be reefed. The aerodynamic forces on the sail are controlled not by reducing the sail area, but by changing the sail shape and thus the aerodynamic sail coefficients. In turn, this approach has increased the importance of correctly tuning the sail shape by means of flexible spars and other devices – an art in itself. Modern masts can be designed in such a way that both fore-and-aft and athwartships bend can be controlled hydraulically through kicking straps, adjustable backstays, jumper strut wires and diamonds. The amount of aft bend can be limited by the fixed jumper wires. The port and starboard wires may also be independently adjustable by hydraulic or other means. Their function is to prevent sideways bend whilst sailing to windward, and to induce the mast bend sideways to leeward whilst running, as in the *Lionheart*'s mast configuration (Fig 77). In light winds the topmast is pulled aft by the backstay, but in stronger winds mainsail leech tension alone is sufficient.

Often neglected but important is the way the sheet is attached to the boom.

Fig 280 The bending characteristics of a mast depend partially on the direction of the sheet tension.

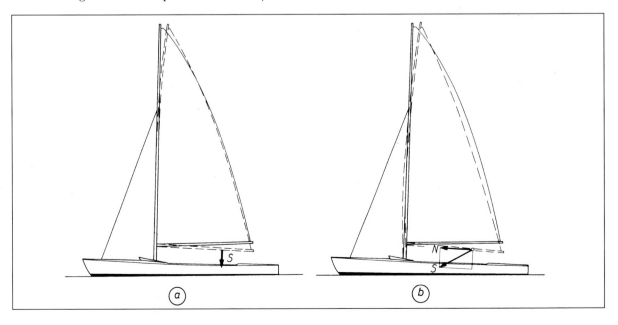

In case (a) in Fig 280 the sheet tension S is normal to the boom and the mast bending will be mostly above the forestay. In case b the sheet tension has a component N along the boom which pushes the lower part of the mast forward. For maximum effect the mast should be restricted athwartships at the deck, but is free to move fore-and-aft. It follows that the curvature of the masts in (a) and (b) will be different.

Bending of the boom also has a considerable effect on the shape and set of the sail. As in the case of the mast, it can either be controlled by the crew or be accidental. The degree of bending will depend on the construction of the boom, its cross-sections and the way the mainsheet is attached.

CUTTING HEADSAILS

Fig 281 Tensile stresses within a conventional mitre-cut genoa.

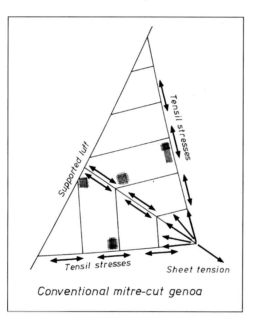

Conventional mitre-cut genoa

It has been mentioned when referring to Fig 228 that the sag in the forestay, like the bend of the mast, is one uncertainty which complicates sail design. Another problem may arise from the fabric itself and the way the sail panels are orientated in relation to stresses imposed by wind pressure and sheet. Let us consider, for example, a conventional mitre-cut genoa as shown in Fig 281. There are concentrated loads on the cloth radiating out from the clew in all directions between the leech and foot. As in a mainsail, the panels are aligned so that the weft (fill) runs in the direction of greatest importance (free edges), ie, up and down the leech and along the foot. However, unlike the load distribution in the mainsail there is an area under bias loading along the mitre. Due to the sheet pulling directly against the bias, the adjacent sail area will suffer much more elongation than other parts of the sail. This causes excess fullness in the sail's centre, which will tend to increase the harder the wind blows – a tendency exactly opposite to high performance requirements.

The fabric with stretch characteristics as shown in Fig 267, with a large imbalance between the stretch on the bias and the other two directions, warp and weft, is obviously, therefore, not an ideal choice of sailcloth for genoas. What is needed is a cloth with more uniform stretch characteristics, ie, one which has as even a stretch as possible in all directions. Sails made of such a fabric are apt to grow in size with wind and strength, the degree of growth depending on the ultimate resistance of the cloth to stretch, but its shape (camber) would not change. Conventionally woven fabric can hardly satisfy such an equal stretch requirement which is essential to sail performance.

In an attempt to accomplish directionally more stable cloth, a triaxial weave

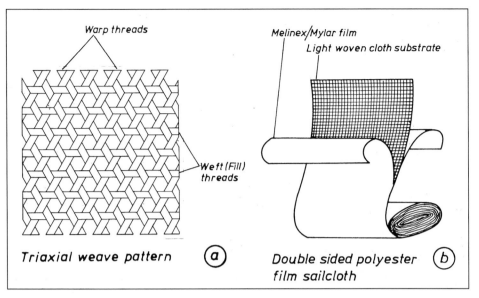

Fig 282

a) Triaxial weave pattern. Advantages claimed include a more uniform strength ie less bias stretch than conventional bi-axial weave, and good tear and overall shear resistance.

b) An example of a 3 ply laminate. Since their introduction as a fabric for racing sails, where expense and durability are of secondary importance, laminates have undergone some developments to become more durable and, as a result, more affordable. This type of fabric is being seen in some cruising applications, where performance is measured in terms of years of use, not races won.

was developed. In the pattern of weave shown in Fig 282a, two sets of warp threads are employed, and the weft (fill) threads interlace them at 60° angles. Triaxial fabric has one basic, alleged advantage over conventional weave: the bias stretch is reduced, and so the cloth has relatively uniform stretch characteristics in all directions. Thus a genoa made of triaxial cloth should retain its design shape over a wider range of wind speeds, at least theoretically. Triaxial cloth is still subject to a number of conflicting claims. It has been argued, for instance, that the stretch of currently available triaxial cloth, both in its soft and hard finish state, is still too great as compared with tightly woven conventional cloth. Besides, it is several times more expensive. In addition, the weave has been somewhat overtaken by the introduction of plastic film, usually in conjunction with woven substrate as shown in Fig 282b. It is made of Melinex/Mylar, laminated on one or both sides by conventionally woven Terylene/Dacron or some other suitable material. Because film does not suffer elongation due to crimp, it has the same stretch characteristics in all directions and is more stretch resistant, weight for weight, than any conventionally woven fabric. For these reasons, a sail made of plastic fabric has good shape-retention properties through a wide range of wind strengths.

Although this type of sailcloth is free from some variables that have plagued sailmakers using conventionally woven fabrics, it has a drawback too – this is lower durability. Plastic films are susceptible to relatively rapid degradation in sunlight (ultraviolet) and are fragile in the sense that, if locally overloaded (sensitive areas are the clew and head), lamination, rips, broken seams, separated clew patches and incurable overstretch may occur. Another aspect of durability is resistance to tear and chafe. In this respect Melinex/Mylar films are not as good as conventional cloths. Yet another drawback is the price: laminated fabrics are expensive. Unfortunately, too often an improvement in one characteristic can only be achieved by sacrifices in others. So far, it appears that laminated fabric is best suited for high performance rigs on boats of America's Cup or Admiral's Cup type, and for racing round the cans. As in the case of Kevlar hybrid cloth, the laminated fabric cannot yet be regarded with confidence as a viable material which can be applied to sails which are intended to be used in long ocean races or just by people cruising.

Tightly woven cloth of a traditional pattern will certainly remain a more universally used fabric. Any deficiency associated with unbalanced stretch can partly be compensated for by selecting heavier cloth, and partly by laying up the panels to allow the sail to stretch more evenly. Some of these compensating configurations are shown in Fig 283. Thus, for example, the spider-web arrangement shown in sketch c, and also the radial cut of configuration b, are aimed at maintaining the loads radiating from the clew on the same thread direction. In the spider–web cut the weft is parallel to the leech and foot, while in the radial cut the warp is roughly parallel to the load direction. In both cases the cloth at the leading edge intersects the luff at varying bias angles, and this may cause some distortion of the designed sail shape. Even though sailmakers continually experiment with different arrangements of sail panels, so far no easy answer has been found to the problem of sail distortion inherently associated with imperfect stretch characteristics of the woven cloth itself.

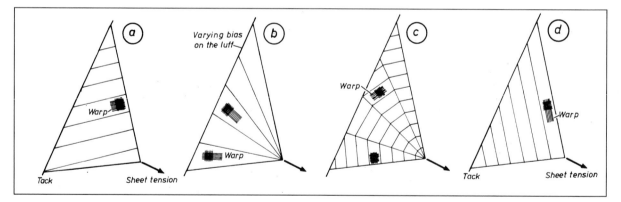

Fig 283

a) Horizontal or cross-cut. b) Radial or sunray cut. c) Spiderweb or multi-mitre cut. d) Vertical cut. Some of the various cuts of headsails; similar patterns can be applied to mainsails. There is no easy answer to the problem of how to equalize stretch (or elongation) in various loading directions, in order to maintain and/or control within reasonable limits sail shape in variable wind strengths. Each pattern a–d has certain advantages, but drawbacks too. For example, the horizontal cut with more or less horizontally running seams allows a continuous, smooth aerofoil section across the sail. The vertical cut tends to produce discontinuous sections, with a flat part between each seam; however, it has been claimed (not fully justifiably) that such a configuration is more stretch-resistant under heavy loads occurring along the leech than the horizontally cut pattern. It has been argued that the bewildering array of fabrics already available, and the other exotic sailcloths being currently developed, are bound to encourage a breed of sailmakers ready to return to basic principles and orientated towards mathematics and engineering rather than to a questionable 'art' form.

ADJUSTING THE RIGGING

The function of standing and running rigging is to support the mast and control the spars. There is nothing mysterious about the influence of rigging, both standing and running, on a boat's performance, no matter what type the rig. *The only way* the rigging can affect performance is if, through applied tensions and use of control devices, the shape and position of the sails change – either in relation to each other or along the hull centreline. These days it has become almost axiomatic that flexible and adjustable spars are inherently better for windward work than rigid ones. Flexible rigs which can be instantly adjusted for varying sailing conditions are immensely superior to the old and rigid rigs. The possibility of modifying sail shape at the helmsman's will offers enormous advantage in terms of boat performance. And the scope for improvement in sail efficiency (or the scope for mistakes!) increases with the number of control devices available.

Since every woven sailcloth stretches or elongates, sails have a live nature and change their shape continuously under wind and sheet loading. Moreover, the shape of a sail changes with time; that is to say, if a sail shape is optimum when new, it may not be optimum when old, or vice-versa. The cause of this time-dependent change is the non-recoverable stretch of the fabric and possibly the seams. It was reported that gluing the seams prior to stretching may reduce the non-recoverable seam stretch by a factor as large as ten in some cases; for instance, when some stretching has been chafed away by the shrouds. It is unlikely that an ideal fabric for sailmaking will be discovered that could radically change the current state of the art in this field. Sails operate like elastic membranes, and should stretch (possibly in a recoverable manner) within reasonable limits. A sail fabric which does not stretch at all – an ideal material some unaware enthusiasts are dreaming and writing about – would be of no value to sailing people.

Wind speed, sea conditions, points of sailing and even wind gradient (see Fig 290) vary continually as the boat sails round the course and from race to race; and each sea condition, each wind speed and each course sailed requires a different and particular sail shape. Thus an ideal sail would be capable of automatically changing its relevant shape parameters, such as the magnitude of camber, its horizontal and vertical distribution, the amount of twist, etc, to suit the ever changing requirements during the race. Obviously, such an ideal cannot be realized. Given these uncertainties, it seems academic to pursue a high degree of accuracy in purely analytical sail design. The crew must rely heavily upon their own experience and judgement in determining the correct sail trim and shape-control settings in order to obtain the best performance from the rig. What instant shape-control is necessary, and which resulting adjustment is the best to obtain the optimum driving efficiency from the sails is the essence of the problem. To talk meaningfully about the optimum sail shape tuned to the best boat performance, the following group of shape factors should be considered:

Sail camber – largely determines the driving force, the ratio of driving force to heeling force, and also tolerable heeling moment.

Position of maximum camber – together with camber curvature determines the flow round sail, pressure distribution, separation and flow reattachment.

Trim angle – controls the geometric incidence angle at which the sail sections are set. Due to wind gradient the incidence angle tends to increase with height above the foot of the sail.

Sail twist – ie, variation of incidence angles (trim angles) with height above the sail foot. Stall of the upper part of the sail and vertical pressure distribution critically depend on the amount of sail twist.

Leading edge entrance angle – ie, the sail curvature at the very leading edge determines whether or not the air flow enters the leading edge smoothly, thus avoiding or delaying premature flow separation.

Slot shape – determines the pressure distribution between headsail and mainsail, and so controls backwinding and also the upwash in front of the headsail.

The effect of these factors can be altered by deliberately designed control devices, or by indirect control means which, in the case of the mainsail alone, are registered in the table of Fig 277. Tuning and control gadgetry has now reached such a level of complexity that very few people can boast of understanding precisely enough what those devices can really do. The whole problem of boat tuning is further complicated by the fact that the sail inventory increases in number, and ultimately there are too many sails to allow a sensible decision to be made. (Sails accumulate fast simply in the irresistible hope that the next one might be a little better.) The multitude of variables involved, and the reciprocal causal feedback effects, makes the tuning of a boat near to perfection an elusive goal.

Without a monitoring system which records the tuning action taken and immediately evaluates results, say in terms of boat speed V_{mg} or/and V_s, and then compares those with a previously established yardstick, the crew that is burdened with the task of sailing a boat consistently near to perfection is bound to fail. Anyone who, for example, has logically analysed the failures in America's Cup races, must come to the conclusion that racing helmsmen cannot resolve the many and variable performance equations by the seat of their pants alone. It was reported that Denis Conner, the helmsman of the victorious American defender *Freedom* (1980) spent about 1600 hours evaluating sails – with the help of an on-board monitoring and computer system.

PART 3

STEADY AND UNSTEADY WIND

1 • The Significance of Barometric Depressions

'There is no part of the world of coast, continents, oceans, seas, straits, capes and inlands which is not under the sway of a reigning wind, the sovereign of its typical weather. The wind rules the aspects of the sky and the action of the sea. But no wind rules unchallenged his realm of land and water.'

Joseph Conrad, The Mirror of the Sea

Every sailor, no matter whether he be racing or cruising, tries to get a forecast of the wind's direction and strength before setting the sails. Before a long off-shore race, most attention will be given to getting a synoptic picture of the weather over a broad area, while for racing in sheltered waters an intimate knowledge of local wind conditions will be more useful.

Weather conditions, and therefore winds, over large areas come under the influence of 'lows', ie depressions, and 'highs' (anticyclones), moving generally from west to east (Figs 284 and 285). The mean speed of depressions across the British Isles is between 10 to 30 miles an hour. This refers to the movement of the depression centre and not the winds of the system. The winds within a depression, moving inward in a spiral, may reach speeds of 135 knots (250 km/hour). Although this occurs very seldom, strong winds are a characteristic of these swiftly moving and violent atmospheric disturbances.

Fig 284a Typical pressure and wind distribution in the North Atlantic (Summer).

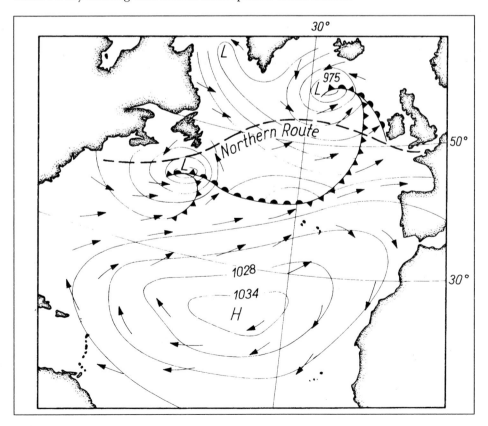

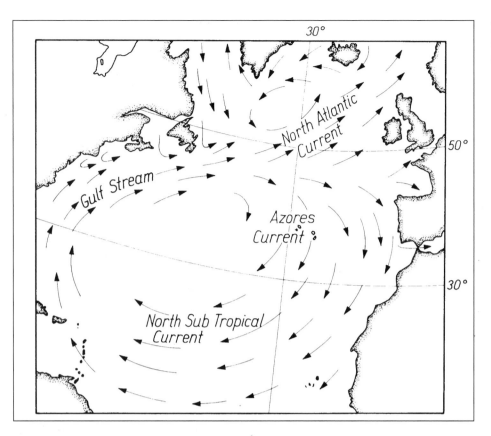

Fig 284b Ocean currents linked to the wind pattern.

Fig 285 A photograph of two tropical depressions (large air vortices) *Bonnie* and *Charley* to the west of Africa, taken by satellite Meteosat 4, on 23 September 1992. With reported wind speeds 165 and 175 km/h respectively, these two cyclones belonged to class 2 on the Saffir-Simpson scale.

Cyclone is the name given to a rotary wind system in the southern Indian Ocean. Cyclones occur most frequently between December and April, but they can and do occur every month of the year. The American term 'extra-tropical cyclone' relates to a depression.

Hurricanes or typhoons are terms given to a low pressure area and strong winds, depending on whether you are sailing in the Atlantic, the Pacific or the China Seas. Hurricanes occur most frequently between July and October. These strong cyclonic winds over 64 miles an hour ie; above 12 on the Beaufort scale are divided into five classes as given in Table 19.

Fig 286 Wind changes within a depression (Low) in the northern hemisphere. According to the so-called Buys Ballot's Law: 'If you stand with your *back* to the wind in the northern hemisphere, the *Low* centre is on your left.' This law, formulated by Professor Buys Ballot of Utrecht, is applicable also to the southern hemisphere, provided one *faces* the wind, when the *Low* centre will again be on the left.

Table 19
Classification of cyclonic winds according to Saffir-Simpson

CLASS	RANGE OF WIND SPEED			
1	64– 82.5	mph	119–153	Km/h
2	82.5– 95.5	"	154–177	"
3	95.5–112.7	"	178–209	"
4	112.7–134.5	"	210–249	"
5	over 134.5	"	over 250	"

The aim of ocean racers, as well as cargo ships propelled by sails, is to move across large expanses of water at maximum speed. For many years, sailing ships were weather-routed by 'Masters', who used a combination of published data on prevailing winds and currents, local knowledge, practical experience and, to some degree, guesswork. At the beginning of the nineteenth century, a voyage from Europe to Australia lasted about 130 days. Half a century later, Lieutenant M F Maury, author of the famous *Sailing Directions* (Ref 3.1), plotted the quickest route, taking into consideration the most advantageous wind and current systems of the world's oceans, and the same voyage was shortened to about 100 days.

In the northern hemisphere, winds rotate anticlockwise round the 'lows'. As Fig 286 demonstrates, the winds in a cyclone may aid or hinder the progress of a sailing craft, depending on the position of the yacht in a particular quadrant. For example, if a yacht follows the course AB which cuts through the depression system, then in position 1 she will be reaching on the port tack. In position 2 she is forced to sail close-hauled, still on the port tack. When the yacht passes to quadrant II, however, she is forced to go on to a starboard tack. Clearly, therefore, the art of offshore sailing involves not only a skilful use of the possibilities offered by the

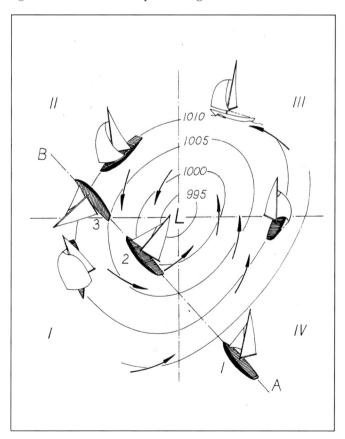

yacht's aerodynamic and hydrodynamic efficiency, but also a knowledge of how to take advantage of the weather conditions. Route planning is therefore of paramount importance to ensure that the boat is in the right place at the right time.

As an example of this, let us consider the transatlantic race, which is run along the northern route (Fig 284) in the region of the track followed by lows. The results of these races, as a rule, are decided by eastward moving depressions, which the racing fraternity have nicknamed 'expresses'. A boat which catches a cyclone and keeps within its sphere of influence may pass the finishing post at Marstrand (Sweden) as much as 5 days earlier than rivals who 'missed the express'.

Heavy displacement yachts, in the most favourable weather conditions, can attain a maximum relative speed, $V_{max} \simeq 1.4\sqrt{LWL}$. Clearly, then, a yacht with a longer waterline length, and so with a higher relative speed, will have a better chance of keeping in contact with a low for a longer time. Thus in the same weather conditions a 40 ft yacht could sail 8.8 knots, while a 30 ft yacht could only reach 7.7 knots:

$$V_{smax} = 1.4\sqrt{40} = 8.8 \text{ knots}$$
$$V_{smax} = 1.4\sqrt{30} = 7.7 \text{ knots}$$

The handicap supplementing the rating formula does not compensate for this, as the influence of a low is not a factor considered in working out a yacht's rating. Naturally, a more efficient crew, better navigation, sailing a yacht to her best advantage, especially at night, and so on, may give the victory to a yacht of shorter waterline length. More recently, new handicap systems have been operating in which it is assumed that winds may not be uniformly distributed over the racing area. Thus different size yachts will not experience the same wind and sea conditions in the same race.

In the example described, the depressions were moving in approximately the same direction as the race. Figure 287, however, shows what happens when the centre of a depression moves at an angle across the course. The track of the low is shown by the broad arrow, and the course of the voyage across the Baltic from Hel (A) to Hoburgen (B). Now, if the actual wind blowing near Hel at the beginning of voyage were all that could be known, the shortest course AB would be assumed to be the most advantageous. But as the depression will be moving eastwards somewhere near point O, a boat would find herself compelled to tack close-hauled against a rising wind and rougher sea.

Fig 287 An optimum route should be based on the weather forecast; in other words, the choice of course from the departure point A to the destination B depends upon the expected track of dominating depressions.

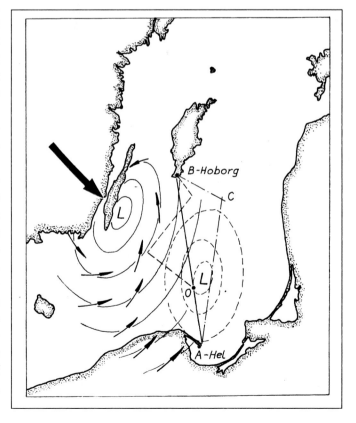

In fact, during the voyage, what started as a south wind will change to a westerly, then to a northwesterly, and finally to a northerly wind. A more advantageous plan, therefore, would be to anticipate these changes and follow the course ACB. This will ensure a favourable wind for the whole passage and higher boat speeds will be reached.

In this context it is perhaps worthwhile quoting an excerpt from a story published in *SAIL* magazine (3.2): 'A Frenchman I met once in the tiny south Atlantic island of St Helena, asked me what a pilot chart was. I showed him. For an hour we pored over the chart, planning the next leg of his voyage. But finally he shook his head sceptically, "You say that to go to Cape Town, which is 1700 miles direct, it is better to go west first, a distance of 2700 miles? But, *mon ami*, my boat is more than 50 feet in length. It goes well to windward." In the end he sailed directly to Cape Town. It took him over 50 days of merciless pounding to windward to do that 1700 miles. My proposed longer route, using 100 miles a day made good as a rule of thumb, could be expected to take half that time, and would probably have been more comfortable.'

This admittedly somewhat extreme (but nonetheless true) example illustrates the value of pilot and routing charts in planning an ocean passage.

As distinct from cyclones, anticyclones, ie, areas of high pressure, generally move slowly, and the winds rotate around them in a clockwise direction, the opposite way to the cyclonic winds. Because the air mobility of anticyclones is much slighter, the possibility of utilizing the associated winds are much less than with cyclones. These lazy and widely spread anticyclones can, however, exert a powerful effect upon the sea. For example, the Gulf Stream, which makes about 5 knots off the eastern coast of North America, is driven by the winds flowing around the more or less stationary high which extends from the Azores towards the Caribbean Sea (Fig 284b).

To take full advantage of variable weather, the synoptic weather chart of the area must be studied before and during a longer race. The meteorological service may supply weather maps via weather-fax recorder or telex and similar forecast charts can be prepared from broadcast weather forecasts. Above all, one needs to have the plot of isobars on a map of the region involved; then during the race, by noting variations in pressure and wind direction, it is possible to deduce in which quadrant of the depression (or anticyclone) the boat is sailing. This makes it possible to determine the direction in which the weather formation is moving, its speed, and any forthcoming variations in wind. A quick change in wind direction would indicate that the isobars are concentrated in a small area; one may assume from this that the focus of low or high pressure is small and that the boat is at its centre.

From experience it is known that, for safety reasons, the storm centre and the 'dangerous semicircle' should be avoided. The *dangerous semicircle* is that part of the depression which is on the right when facing the direction towards which the Low is moving; the *navigable semicircle* is on the left of the storm track. A yacht sailing in the dangerous semicircle would tend to be pushed by wind and ocean currents into the path of the depression.

The forecasting process is simplified because cyclones do not travel along irregular paths but follow definite tracks. For example, the cyclonic tracks for the North Sea and the Baltic are shown in Fig 288. It must be emphasized that

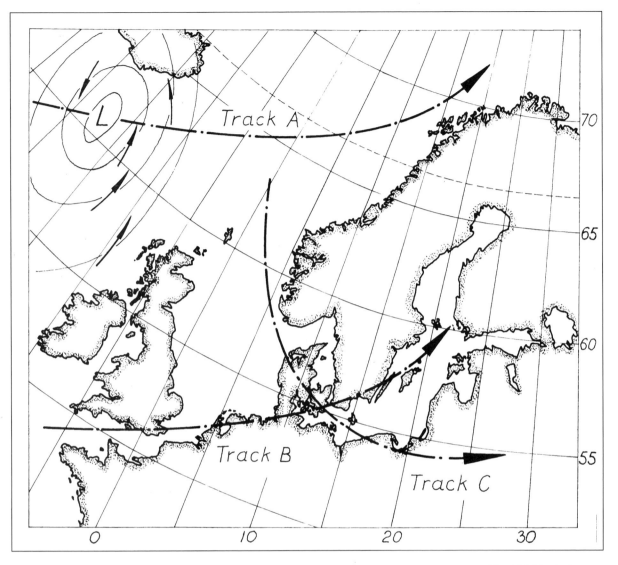

Fig 288 Typical tracks of depressions over the North Sea and Baltic.

the character of the winds in a cyclone depends to a large extent on the track it is following. Details of these for the oceans and lesser seas are published in various aids to navigation.

The conclusions reached by observing changes in wind direction and barometric pressure can be tested by watching for such other signs of approaching changes in the weather as nature offers. The colour of the sky at sunrise and sunset, the concentration, shape and movement of the clouds, different light phenomena in the atmosphere, the behaviour of birds, and so on; all these can greatly assist in the correct assessment of the weather situation and in forecasting changes.

The language of many maritime nations contains pithy, rhyming proverbs for predicting weather changes, which embody the experience of generations of sailors:

When the wind shifts against the sun,
Trust it not, for back it will run.

The clouds look black, and the glass is low;
Last night the sun went pale to bed;
The halved moon now hides her head.

Look out, my lads! A wicked gale
With heavy rain will soon prevail.

First rise after low
Foretells stronger blow.

Evening red and morning gray,
Two sure signs of one fine day.

The purpose of all these proverbs is to help sailors forecast the wind changes in the immediate future, for to them 'the weather' means, above all, the wind.

Referring briefly to Fig 24a, it should be noted that the cruising routes in the North Atlantic can be subdivided depending on prevailing winds and whether the crossing is made in high or low latitudes. Passages in high latitudes are greatly influenced by the predominantly westerly winds and are therefore suitable for eastbound yachts, whereas westbound passages are best undertaken along the southern routes, with the help of the NE trade winds and favourable ocean currents. Routing charts give the sailor essential wind and current information to plan a voyage in other stretches of water.

Winds are driven by the forces caused by horizontal variation in the atmospheric pressure, so it is appropriate to consider the general trend in wind distribution by way of the distribution of lows and highs at sea level. In most areas a systematic variation of winds according to season can be observed. Figure 289a and b depicts the pattern of average pressure distribution in terms of highs, H,

Fig 289a Average sea level pressures, July.

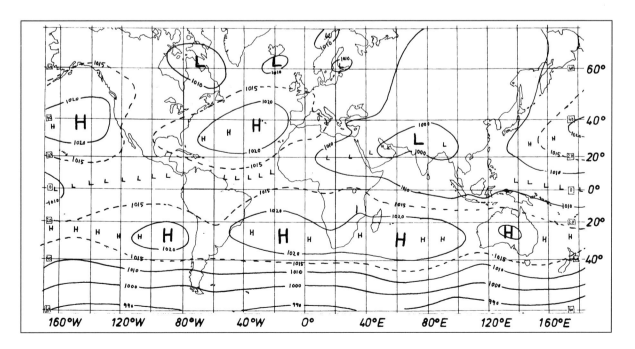

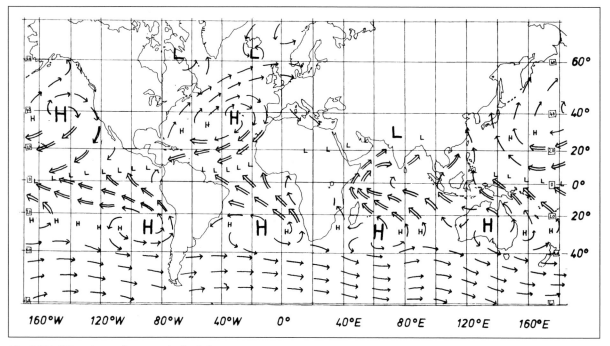

Fig 289b Directions of mean winds, July.

and lows, L, for July, and relevant wind distribution for the same period of mid-summer (Ref 3.3). There is a certain corrolation between these two phenomena which demonstrates the major tendency and does not pretend to show the complexity that seasonal variations may have.

2 • TRUE WIND STRUCTURE

The surface wind (the actual wind from 0 to 100 ft) differs considerably from the wind aloft, whose direction and speed can be observed from the movements of the clouds. The factors which determine the quality of the surface wind are:

1 The atmospheric pressure gradient, ie, the pressure difference between a neighbouring low and high
2 The sun's heat input
3 The height above water level
4 The thermal differentiation of the area
5 Wind barriers, such as local obstructions, etc.

Factors 2–5 deform the basic wind structure and are the principal causes behind local winds. Because of them, the wind which actually can be of use to the sailor is never constant in direction and strength.

In the discussion earlier of Figs 96 and 97 it was mentioned that there is a definite wind velocity gradient produced by air friction against the water surface. The gradient is definable as the rate at which the wind gradually increases with height above the water level. This affects the direction of the apparent wind, and therefore the efficiency of the sail. Meteorological investigations have revealed that this velocity gradient varies according to the extent the sky is covered by cloud, the wind speed, wind turbulence, etc. From Fig 290 it can be seen that in a light wind, a smooth sea and an overcast sky, the wind velocity changes are relatively great. In such conditions, therefore, the desirable twist in the sail from the boom to the top of the mast can be greater because of the twist in the apparent wind.

Figure 290 shows the conspicuous difference between curves representing wind velocity gradient for light winds, and those for average or gusty ones. This is distinguished by two vectors plotted at approximately the height of the centre of effort of the Dragon class rig. It can be explained as follows. In the case of light winds and overcast sky, there is probably no significant activity of vertical thermal currents which could mix the successive air layers and thus transmit wind energy from one layer to another. In such conditions, laminar flow prevails inside the whole mass of air in motion and, due to viscous forces, the friction (being greatest at the sea surface) is gradually transferred upwards through successive air layers in the boundary layer manner shown earlier in Fig 80b.

In the case of gusty winds, when turbulent flow prevails, a certain exchange of wind energy between the higher and the lower layers of the mass of air takes place. As a result, the air flow (wind) nearer to the surface is accelerated and this energy exchange is reflected in the shape of the wind gradient curve.

The presence of the yacht's hull between the water surface and the sail affects the velocity gradient comparative to that shown in Fig 290. The presence of the hull induces a contraction of the air flow above the deck, and this accelerates the wind speed here, reducing the effect of the true wind vertical gradient on the apparent wind speed. An interesting observation of this phenomenon is given in Fig 291a, b and c, reproduced here from the film *Airflow* by Austin

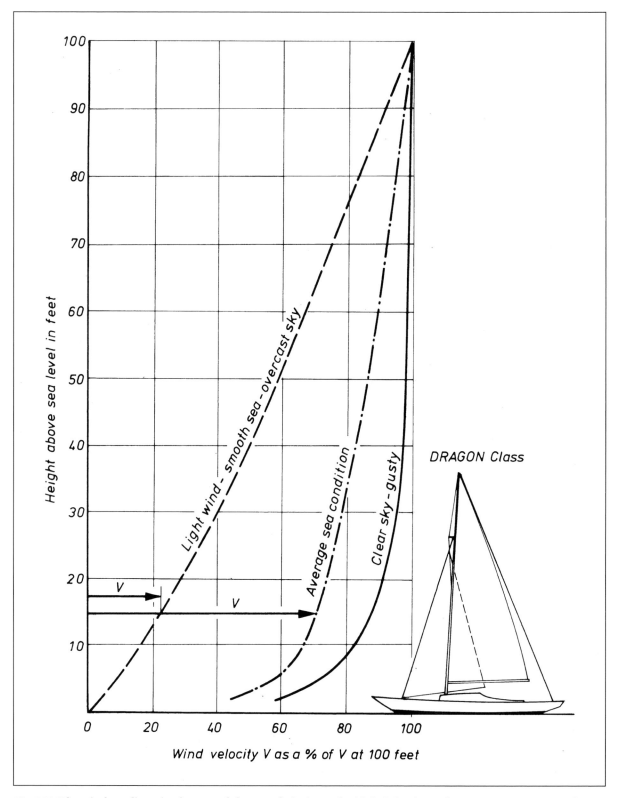

Fig 290 The wind gradient, ie, the rate of change of wind speed with height above the water, may vary greatly depending on the type of weather and the state of the sea. Thus, the apparent wind 'felt' by sails varies in strength and direction over the mast height, even if the true wind is steady.

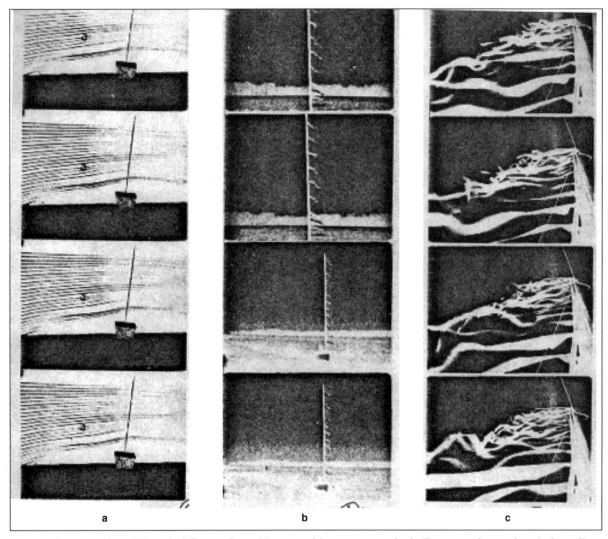

a   b   c

Fig 291 A contraction of the wind flow and resulting speed increase over the hull may moderate the wind gradient. The extent of the wind gradient determines how much sail twist should be applied to achieve better sailing performance.

Farrar and General J Parham. Pieces of tape were tied to the dinghy mast and then the dinghy was towed at a fixed angle to the true wind. Figure 291c does not reveal any twist in the apparent wind V_A, as all the tapes, whatever their height, have remained in the same plane. When interpreting the above experiment, one should clearly distinguish between the amount of sail twist intended to compensate for the wind gradient alone (with possible modification of its effect by the presence of the hull), and sail twist deliberately used as a dodge against premature stall of the upper part of the Bermudan sail.

It is known from practical experience and measurements that winds blowing across a coastline undergo changes both in direction and speed. This is mainly due to the different thermal properties of the land and sea surface, but abrupt changes in the roughness characteristics of the surface over which the wind is blowing also play their role. The influence of the coastline on the wind direction is especially noticeable near the shore.

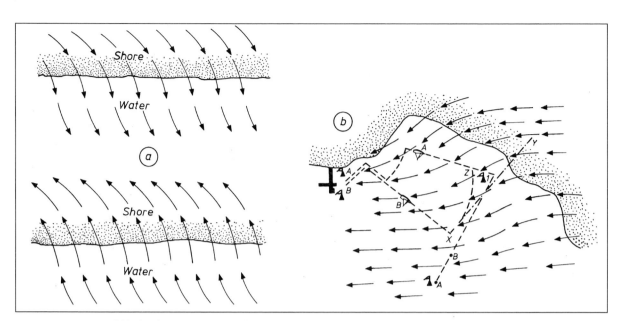

Fig 292 a and b Shifts in the surface wind direction over the shoreline. In coastal waters the surface wind is much influenced by the contours and nature of the adjacent land.

a) Wind blowing from the land to the sea leaving the coast tends to be refracted to a direction more perpendicular to the shoreline. This phenomenon, which occurs due to different frictions experienced by the airflow over the land and the sea, is termed by professional meteorologists, *shoreside refraction*.

b) Wind blowing from the sea towards the coast will also tend to bend in a similar manner, ie, toward the shoreline. The amount of refraction depends on the height and steepness of the shore and wind (air) stability. In stable airflow, indicated by extensive low clouds, the wind bends more than in turbulent airflow, associated, say, with cumulus clouds and showers. For more details consult the book *Wind and Sailing Boats* by Alan Watts.

There is a widespread belief amongst sailing people that no matter whether the wind is blowing onshore or offshore, its direction varies so that it tends to bend out at right angles to the coastline before it resumes its original direction (Fig 292a). If winds really behave in that way, the importance of this to sailors planning tactics in a race where the course lies near the shore would be considerable.

Figure 292b demonstrates how one can take advantage of a directional change of wind. Assuming that yachts A and B crossed the starting line at the same time, one may rightly expect that the helmsman of A, having chosen the course closer to the shore, would round buoy number 1 before yacht B. When yacht B reaches point X and tacks toward buoy number 1, it becomes evident from the direction of the wind at that point that by sailing along the course X–Y the buoy will be reached on the starboard tack. However, as the boat approaches the coast, the wind may change its direction enough to force her to bear away along the course X–Z and consequently to incur a loss of time.

According to Brettle from the Meteorological Office Research Unit (see reference given in caption to Fig 292c), winds do not stubbornly obey the rule demonstrated in Fig 292a. Instead, as shown in Fig 292c, winds change direction depending on the difference between the land and sea temperature. This difference is of critical importance. The argument goes as follows: if the sea temperature is sufficiently low, then an inversion will form and prevent mixing (exchange of wind energy) between the surface and upper layers of air. Usually,

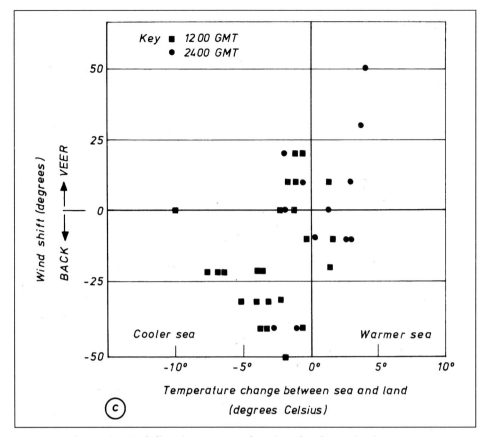

Fig 292c Change in wind direction measured against the change in air temperature. This figure is based on measurements given by M J Brettle in an article 'Sea Temperatures and Coastal Winds', *Weather* magazine, June 1989.

air temperature decreases with height at an average rate of about 3° Fahrenheit per 1000 feet of ascent. However, occasionally air temperature increases with height. Layers of air in which this happens are called *inversions*. An effect of an inversion is to separate the surface wind from above. As a result the effects of air friction are confined to a shallow boundary layer and consequently the surface wind speed will be reduced, followed by backing in direction further offshore. On the other hand, if the sea is warmer than the air, the surface wind will tend to increase, followed by a veering offshore. This could occur much closer to the coast, possibly within a few kilometres. Measurements (Fig 292c) taken from two coastal stations reveal what can happen in practice.

It is believed that a remarkable spread in changes of direction is partly due to the rather coarse measurements of wind direction (reported to the nearest 10 degrees). There is, however, a distinct tendency for a rise in temperature over the sea to result in a veering of direction, and a drop in temperature to result in backing. Since the land is likely to be warmer than the sea at midday, at this time therefore backing is more likely to occur, and Fig 292c confirms this. Contrary to the advice usually given in weather guides to yachtsmen, an off-shore wind can back out to sea, predominantly when the sea produces a cooling of the surface air.

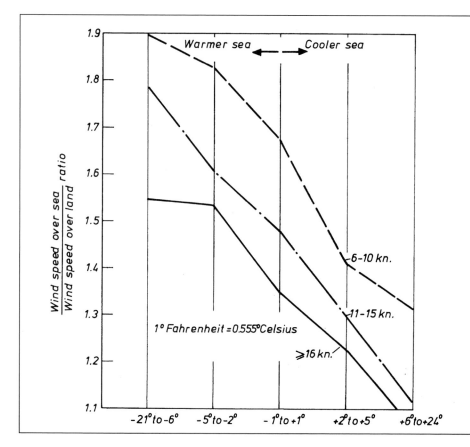

Fig 292d
Variations of wind
speed over sea in
comparison with that
over land, versus
temperature differ-
ences between land
and sea. This figure
is based on test
results given by P E
Francis in an article
'The Effect of
Changes of
Atmospheric Stability
and Surface
Roughness on Off-
shore Winds over the
East Coast of Britain',
Meteorological maga-
zine 99, 1970.

Differences in temperature between land and sea, together with the change in the surface roughness, also influence the wind speed over the sea. As shown in Fig 292d, the wind over the sea is always stronger than the wind actually blowing over the land; the ratio of wind speed over the sea to that over the land is greater than one and tends to increase quite rapidly when the temperature of the sea increases, ie, the temperature, T, difference (T over land – T over sea) becomes greater.

The temperature change marked along the horizontal axis in Fig 292d can be regarded as a measure of the stability of the surface layers of atmosphere. The cool sea water seems to have a stabilizing effect on winds in a sense that the ratio between wind speed over the sea and over land for offshore winds decreases as the sea becomes cooler. Such a decrease in ratio is most conspicu-ous for light land winds, as indicated by the upper line in Fig 292d.

For strong gusty winds, the vertical velocity gradient (wind sheer in Fig 290) is dominated by the mechanical turbulence (turbulent boundary layer) and hence the effect of changes in air stability becomes relatively small, as shown by the lower continuous line in Fig 292d labelled 16 knots. The final conclusion in the study (see caption to Fig 292d), which corroborates the data in Fig 292c, is that: when air conditions over the sea are stable (cool sea), the wind backs; when air conditions are unstable (warmer sea), the wind veers.

The influence of the surface over which the air is moving is also responsible for the wind's turbulent character. Air, like water, only maintains a steady lami-nar flow at low speeds and over a smooth surface. Unevenness in the ground,

Fig 293 It has been found that there are, horizontally and vertically distributed in the wind mass, sets of 'eddies', within which both the wind speed and its direction changes. The contour lines drawn represent a particular wind velocity (iso-velocity contours), and their spacing indicates the rapidity with which the velocity is changing. Each number is the average wind velocity in miles per hour for the half-second interval in which it is shown. Below is an artist's intuitive view of wind unsteadiness, recorded scientifically above, and in Fig 294a.

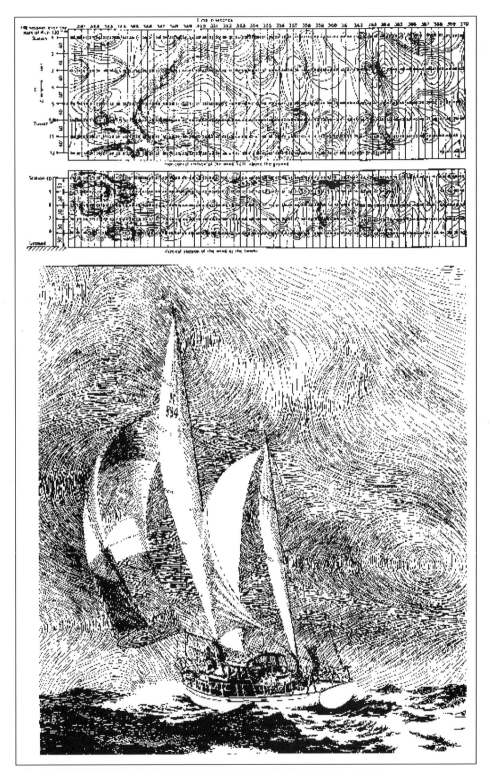

and the vertical air movements caused by thermal differences, create wind turbulence, which manifests itself in fluctuations in speed and direction.

Interesting conclusions can be derived from the measurements made by Sherlock and Stout (Ref 3.4) which were presented in the form shown in Fig 293.

These measurements were made with quick response anemometers, which recorded electrically. Some of these were mounted 50 ft above the surface, 60 ft apart, in a line at right angles to the wind direction, while others were placed at 50 ft intervals on a 250 ft tower. Lines of constant wind speed were plotted for both the horizontal and vertical sections, and these show the character of the wind turbulence. The numbers marking the lines give the average wind velocity in miles per hour for the half-second interval in which it is shown. The prevailing wind was westerly. An interesting but unexplained phenomenon is that the wind tends to rise rapidly to its maximum in a gust, but falls away more slowly.

The temperature of the surface has a marked effect on wind turbulence and gusts. If the surface is cooler than the moving air masses, it tends to stabilize the wind and slow it down. A warm surface, on the other hand, causes a rapid increase in speed in cool, fresh air masses. It is the cooling of the land in the evening which is the main reason why winds tend to drop later in the day. Sailors are also aware that in the spring, while the sea's temperature is still low, the wind is usually steady and not gusty. In spite of strong winds, the sea's surface will remain relatively smooth, for the character of the wave formation depends on the character of the wind. A squally wind will induce very much greater waves than a steady wind. Far offshore, a wind of force of 6 produces waves similar to those which may develop close to land in winds of force 4. As a rule, the further from shore, the steadier the wind.

However, even supposedly steady winds are never really steady from the viewpoint of racing sailors, but are more or less disturbed by variation in direction and velocity. These may throw a racing crew into confusion, with particularly acute consequences on the windward leg. Indeed, as John Masefield says:

A very queer thing is the wind
I don't know how it beginned
And nobody knows where it goes.
It is wind, it beginned and it blows.

Wind is an invisible, capricious motive power, and this fact alone makes it difficult to time one's tack correctly. There are many helmsmen who are able to do their windward work consistently well in a steady breeze; but there are few who can fully exploit the opportunities offered by unsteady by unsteady winds: this can often be the deciding factor which wins a series.

Meteorological records indicate that winds rarely shift less than ± 5° of the mean direction, and usually the periodical shifts are larger. Figure 294a demonstrates, as an example, some actual short-time wind variations registered by instruments. The wind from the north was of nearly gale force, but the correlation between the direction and wind speed oscillation in time is the same in a typical sailing wind. The following conclusions can be derived:

1 Usually a veer accompanies a gust (in the northern hemisphere).
2 The veer is sharp at the gust front, but quickly reverts to a direction backed from the mean wind direction.
3 The wind has a tendency to back before it gusts. In cases where the veer and speed increase do not noticeably coincide, the wind usually veers as it gusts and backs as it lulls, although there may be a time lag between these events.

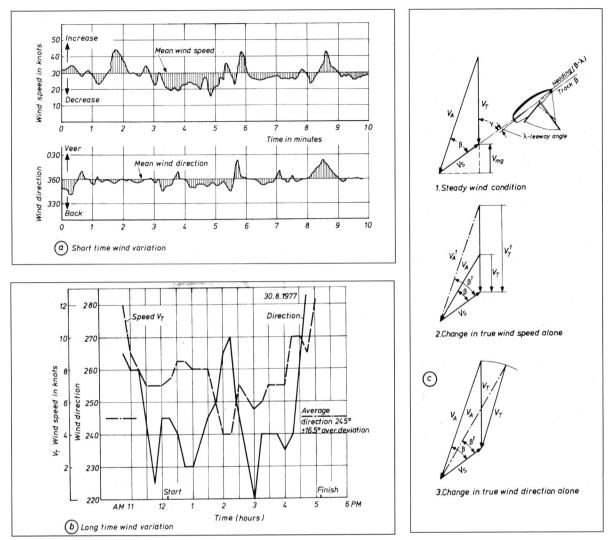

Fig 294 a) and b) Recorded short and long time variations in true wind speed and direction.

c) Effect of changes in true wind speed and its direction on the apparent wind.

Apparent winds V_A are veered and backed relative to the mean V_A, although the true wind V_T may not change its direction, only its speed. Thus in sketch c2 it is shown that an increase in V_T alone is 'felt' by the helmsman as a lifting wind, ie, a swing of the apparent wind from V_A to V_A^1, although the direction of V_T did not change. If in such circumstances the boats were on the starboard tack, the apparent wind V_A^1 would be regarded as a header, in which case the 'tack when headed' rule should not be blindly followed. When the wind heads the boat, it seems an advantage to tack on impulse, provided one is capable of distinguishing between an ephemeral header when the V_T direction does not change, and a real one when the *true wind direction* V_T *changes* as shown in sketch c3. Usually, the wind V_T veers from the mean direction as it gusts, and will back from that direction when it lulls. So, do not make hasty tack when the luff of the jib gives you early warning of a heading shift in V_A, but wait for a while to find out if the V_T really has shifted.

Note: *veering* is a change in wind direction clockwise

backing is a change in wind direction anticlockwise

a gust is a period when the wind speed is increased substantially above the mean speed

a lull is a period when the wind speed is substantially below the mean

Figure 294b illustrates a typical record of long term variations in wind speed and direction over the Newport America's Cup course. As shown, the average deviation in wind direction is in the order of $16\frac{1}{2}°$, and the recorded variations in wind speed, V_T, are large. The effect of these short term and long term variations is illustrated in Fig 294c where sketch 1, as a reference, depicts the usual assumption of steady wind condition for the V_{mg} calculations, while sketches 2 and 3 demonstrate reality.

The helmsman guided by conventional instruments will use the readout of the apparent wind angle ß as an indicator of the windshift, to which he will tend to respond accordingly. However, as demonstrated in sketches 2 and 3, care is recommended, since a sudden gust, ie, change in true wind speed alone from V_T to V_{T1} (sketch 2), would cause a change in both the apparent wind speed V_A and the apparent course ß; whilst a shift in the true wind direction, without alteration in its speed, V_T (sketch 3), may have a hardly detectable effect on the apparent wind speed, V_A, instrument. But in both cases the apparent wind instrument measuring the ß angle will behave as if a true wind shift had occurred. Of course, one should only tack for a genuine change in the true wind direction, not necessarily in the apparent wind direction. Let us illustrate this point in two examples:

If a boat is sailing close-hauled (as in Fig 295), then in position I the mainsail is trimmed to suit the apparent wind OB at an angle α. The vector AB gives the speed of the yacht, and OA the speed of the true wind. If at position II the speed of the true wind increases to a value of O_1A, the yacht due to her inertia will not change her speed immediately. However, the direction and magnitude of the apparent wind will change from OB to O_1B, thus increasing the angle of the sail α by $\triangle α$. If the sails had previously been trimmed to the optimum angle α, the angle at which the most advantageous aerodynamic force was developed, then to maintain the same angle (or even to reduce it for the sake of stability) either:

1 The sheets must be eased, as in position II, or
2 The boat must luff, as in position IIa.

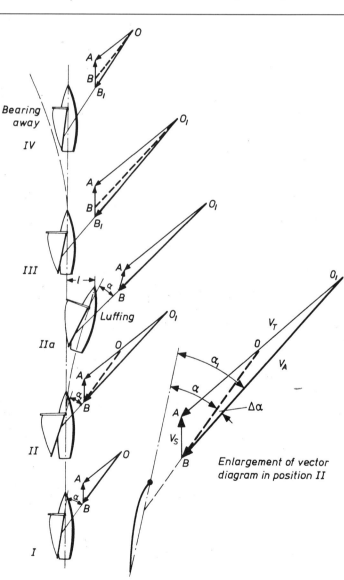

Fig 295 The sequence of course changes when sailing on the starboard tack in a lifting gust. Note that the true wind V_T did not change its direction but its speed only.

Enlargement of vector diagram in position II

During the gust, the yacht will accelerate as in position III, and this will cause another shift in the direction of the apparent wind from O_1B to O_1B_1. To prevent the sails fluttering, the sheets must now be hauled in to preserve the desirable trim angle α. Those who luffed to position IIa will not get further benefit from tightening the sheets, and will have to bear away on to their original course.

A squall lasting one or two minutes, then, can help a yacht in two ways. She can either continue on her original course and increase her speed or, by luffing, work up a little to windward, nearer the next marker buoy by distance l. The actual situation in a given race will determine which is the more profitable move, and the strength of the gust and the type of yacht have to be borne in mind as well. Another example is given in Fig 296a. It shows two yachts which have turned at the marker buoy I and are now beating towards buoy II. The watchful helmsman of yacht B, sailing on the port tack, notices the wind shift

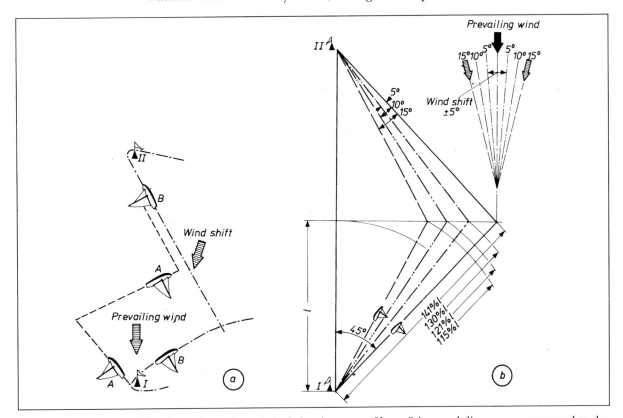

Fig 296 The cost of making the tack may be relatively low in terms of loss of time and distance, as compared to the cost of being on the wrong tack; one should not ignore detectable headers. The distance/time lost when tacking on a header largely depends on the displacement of boat and degree of genoa overlap. The only way to radically improve the tacking efficiency of an offshore boat (sailing round the buoys) is to shorten the genoa foot and reduce the length of the sheet that has to be handled. It is rather rare for the wind to be shifting by less than about 5 degrees each side of the mean direction. Usually the shifts are greater. The theoretically possible gain with a wind which shifts evenly 5 degrees either side of the mean direction can be about 120 yards per mile to windward, provided the helmsman tacks on every wind shift. Most sailors do not tack as readily as they should for three reasons:
1) either they fail to appreciate how much is gained or lost by sailing in shifting winds,
2) or they do not notice the wind shift,
3) or they are simply too lazy to bother to do so.

when it occurs, and quickly tacks on to starboard. These tactics allow him to lay buoy II without further tacking. The less observant helmsman of yacht A, choosing his tack without any proper consideration of possible wind shifts, finds himself behind his opponent.

When beating to windward, at an angle of 45° to the true wind, the distance covered will be 141 per cent of the distance in a straight line between buoys I and II in Fig 296b. The geometrical constructions of this figure show that, by making skilful use of wind shifts of no more than 5°, the distance to be covered by tacking will be reduced to 130 per cent of the shortest distance. If the wind shifts are as much as 10°–15°, the distance gained by exploiting them will give an observant helmsman a big margin over one too careless to pay attention to variations in the wind. If the distance between the buoys I and II is one nautical mile, the helmsman who makes use of wind shifts ± 5° (other things being equal) may theoretically gain about 120 yards made good to windward over his rival who ignores the shifts and sails an average course 45° off the wind. If the wind shifts are in the order of ± 10°, the possible gain might be about 225 yards per every nautical mile sailed. How often one should go about depends mainly on the type of yacht being sailed. Modern centreboard boats will turn in a few seconds, and the loss on each turn is so small that it pays to tack at almost every shift of the true wind. Heavy keel boats with their greater inertia may lose a great deal of speed while tacking (particularly if they carry huge overlapping genoas), and only gain speed slowly on a new course. For such boats a change of tack in shifting winds may be hazardous.

Yet it is difficult for a helmsman to react correctly to changes in wind direction, since his attention is usually distracted by so many other factors. To get proper benefit from wind shifts, nothing is more helpful than keeping a constant check on the course by observing objects in the distance, including marker buoys and rival yachts, or by watching the compass. If it is allowed by the class rules, a special computerized instrument which continually calculates and graphically monitors the true wind behaviour in the form shown in Fig 294a or b can be of great help. Otherwise the helmsman or afterguards are short of feedback as to what is happening. The victorious helmsman of the 1980 America's Cup races, Dennis Conner, admitted that such a true wind indicator had helped him to pick the shifts in situations when the wind was too variable for mindless boat covering.

Because of these continually occurring variations in the apparent wind, V_A, and the course sailed, ß, not to mention the problems associated with tuning and trimming the sails to suit constantly variable winds, it is difficult for the helmsman to sail a racing boat at her optimum speed made good to windward (except momentarily and by chance), even if an experienced crew makes every attempt to achieve the best performance.

The prospects for making further, genuine improvements in the hull or rig design of racing boats are strictly limited, and in all probability any feasible gain will numerically be smaller in terms of V_{mg} than the measured loss in yacht performance incurred by inefficient sailing. Thus one is bound to come to the conclusion that the only promising development which can lead to consistently better racing results is through proper instrumentation.

The accuracy of air and water flow measuring devices has had a rather profound effect on the performance actually achieved. For instance, measurements of boat speed on the two American 12 Metre contenders sailing side-by-side indicated that their speedometers were accurate to within 0.15 knots at any given instant, at a V_s of about 8 knots; this represents about 2 per cent discrepancy, which might be regarded as small or even negligible. However, even with this small difference in precision, it is difficult if not impossible to compare merits of two sails or rigs on one boat.

Wind measuring sensors are, for many reasons, even less reliable and precise than water sensors. No doubt there will be further progress in this field, and more precise instruments will sooner or later be developed. And if the resulting accuracy in, say, Vs measurements, can be improved from 2 per cent to 1 per cent, this improvement alone might result in about 90 seconds less in terms of elapsed time when sailing along the 24.3 mile America's Cup course in average winds. In other words, precision of that order may decide whether the race is won or lost.

3 • LOCAL WINDS

The fact that different parts of the globe warm up at different rates is the principal cause of the various circulatory movements of the earth's atmosphere; winds are the horizontal movements of these displaced air masses. A sea breeze is undoubtedly the best-known example of this phenomenon of atmospheric circulation.

To keep the circulation going, a constant supply of thermal energy is needed. In fact the supply of this energy increases in the afternoon, so the rate of circulation rises; the intensity of the thermal wind derives directly from the amount of thermal energy absorbed by the air and converted into air's kinetic energy – wind.

Numerous measurements have proved that the thermal wind increases with the rise of the temperature gradient. The strongest wind of this type can therefore be expected in the vicinity of the coastline, since it is there that the greatest differences in the gradient of temperature of neighbouring air masses are found.

The range of a sea breeze, like its speed, will be greater for a greater thermal capacity of the surface below. Surfaces, therefore, which can be warmed quickly when the sun shines on them, like sand near a cold sea, favour the development of a strong steady sea breeze, while, on the other hand, if adjacent surface areas are of high thermal capacity as well, like woodland, this will not favour the formation of a strong onshore breeze. The sea or onshore breeze begins about 9 to 12 am and ends at sunset. The strength of the wind increases gradually, reaching a maximum, possibly about force 4, during early afternoon.

Sea breezes do not cause high waves, because their range is limited. Their effect seldom extends more than a few miles out to sea, and so in certain circumstances, since the waves are negligible, the stronger sea breezes allow yachts to achieve higher sailing speeds.

Vertical thermal currents in the atmosphere are revealed by clouds of the cumulus type (Cu). They can be observed during sunny weather over the land (even though the skies over the sea may remain clear), and usually foretell the development of a sea breeze.

Naturally, sea breezes can be observed most clearly when there are no strong winds caused by the barometric weather system, which can deform the strength and direction of the sea breeze. In certain latitudes, where cyclones or depressions rarely penetrate and the weather system depends on anticyclones, as in Italy for instance, the sea breezes are very fierce and appear with the regularity of clockwork.

A similar cycle of local winds of daily occurrence can be encountered over the larger lakes; these are called lake breezes. They are weaker than sea breezes, but can still be of great assistance, especially on days when the gradient wind is very light or nonexistent. Like the sea breeze, a lake breeze blows at right angles to the coastline, and its range and strength will depend on the land's thermal topography.

An example of a lake breeze is given in Fig 297. If the day is sunny and windless, the range of the breeze may be revealed by small ripples (capillary waves)

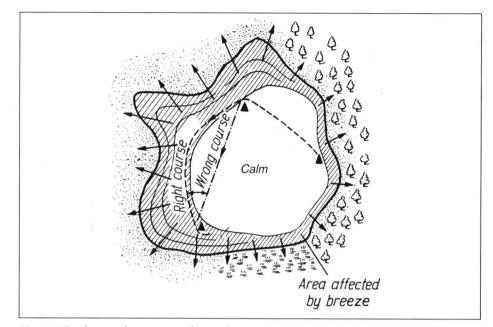

Fig 297 During a calm summer day, a characteristic lake breeze may develop. It's 'unusual' feature is that the wind emerges from the lake's centre and spreads like the spokes of a wheel in all directions towards the shoreline. The lake breeze becomes stronger the closer it comes to the shore. Paradoxically, given a large enough, roughly circular lake, it seems possible that one could sail completely around the lake without ever touching a sheet or tacking or jibing. If there is a wind of another origin blowing over the lake, it will of course interfere with the lake breeze, modifying its direction and speed.

which cover the surface adjacent to the beach, while frequently the centre of the lake lies glittering in the sun, as motionless as a mirror.

In very light winds, the race may become a 'drifting match', when the wind varies from flat calm to delicate puffs, shifting direction continually. Under these conditions one must watch for local coastal winds like those described above. It can be seen from Fig 297 that it would pay to sail the long way round, and keep closer to the coast, rather than to take the shorter, straight course between buoys. By keeping within the range of the breeze, it will be possible to cover the longer distance faster, perhaps without even touching the sheets or tacking or jibing, and thus to sail round the lake while calm reigns in the middle. In a case like this, as racing yachtsmen well know, there is no reason to be afraid of bearing well away from the shortest course in search of a better wind. Finding one's own path does not always lead to loss of ground.

Similarly, on a big river, there is frequently some breeze near the bank during hot weather. In the evening after sunset, the best chance of picking up a land breeze is found near a dry coast free from afforestation. Local thermal winds are most apparent during the summer. In spring and autumn, when the difference in temperature between sea and land is small, the thermal winds die out.

Gusts and puffs of wind are frequently caused by rising and falling thermal currents disturbing the air currents which move parallel to the surface of the earth, and this type of thermal circulation can affect techniques in yacht racing.

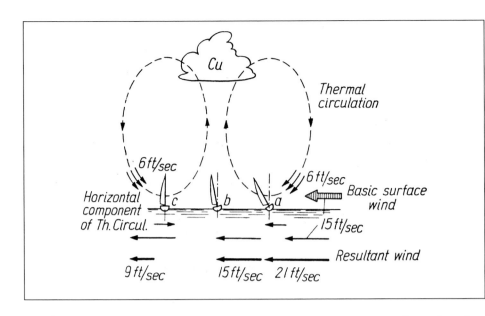

Fig 298 The effect of thermal circulation on the speed of a surface wind. Depending on the position of boats relative to the system of thermal circulation, they will experience gusts and lulls.

The so-called *fine weather cumulus* not only indicates the type of weather, but also demonstrates the existence of the vertical currents responsible for this kind of cloud formation. The effect of air circulation on the speed of the surface wind is shown in Fig 298. Near the surface, the thermal current changes direction through 180°. If we assume that the speed of the thermal circulation is 6 ft/sec and the speed of the prevailing surface wind is 15 ft/sec, then clearly the resultant wind affecting sailing boats will vary between 9 and 21 ft/sec. In 'drifting match' conditions, when there is little or no wind, a thermal circulation which reveals itself through unexpected gusts and puffs may upset the calculations of the competing yachts. Even if the boats are close together, the puffs may affect them quite differently. In Fig 298, yacht a is benefiting from a wind blowing at 21 ft/sec, whereas yacht (c) will lose ground through feeling only a breeze at 9 ft/sec.

Figure 299 illustrates the effect of rising and falling thermal currents near the water surface. When the descending currents (downstreams) 1 and 3 strike the water surface, they will tend to spread sideways, and the resultant wind will be variable in both direction and speed.

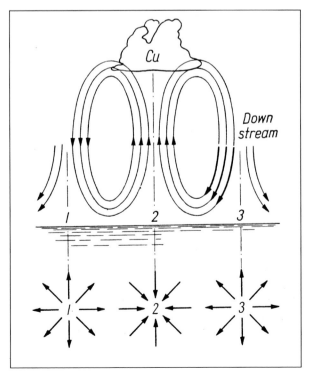

Fig 299 Another schematic view of thermal circulation. It will be seen that the downstream (cold down-draft) tends to spread in all directions as it approaches the water surface, and then, warmed up, rises back aloft as an up-current towards a capping cumulus cloud, which reveals the presence of the thermal circulation.

Fig 300 As the down-stream (descending current of cool air) hits the water, it spreads across its surface in the form of a fanning puff (gust front). Depending on the position of boat relative to the gust, the helmsman will experience rapid changes in wind direction – first a header followed by a lifting wind.

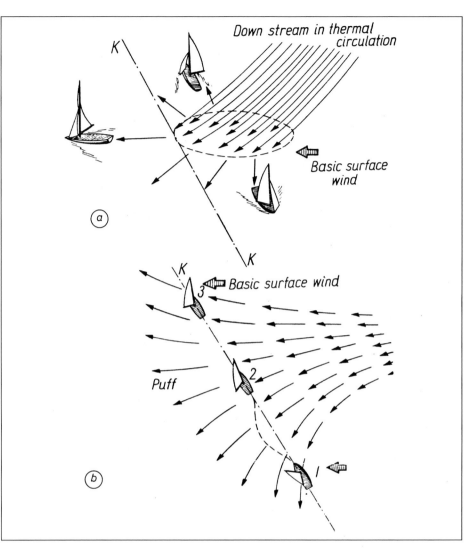

From Fig 300 it can be seen that the combined effect of a light surface wind and thermal currents can leave two yachts sailing before the wind in opposite directions. Gusts of this kind are encountered, as a rule, in areas covered by a high pressure system, where conditions are suitable for the development of strong thermal circulations, whose presence will be indicated by fine weather cumulus. Puffs of wind are revealed when they mark the surface with a faint ripple. They can appear suddenly amongst a group of sailing boats, selecting one, or perhaps a few lucky ones, and pushing them forward, sometimes for several minutes, to the envy of those left becalmed. A yacht sailing straight toward a gust that is visible on the water (Fig 300) must expect a change in the direction of the wind. At first (position 1), the wind will suddenly increase in force and will be ahead. Sails previously trimmed correctly will stop pulling and flutter. It will be necessary to haul in the sheets, and even to bear away from the proper course K–K. At position 2 the wind appears to come from abeam, so that sheets can be eased and speed increased. Around position 3 a following wind may be felt, until the light, prevailing wind takes over again and the sheets are trimmed as before.

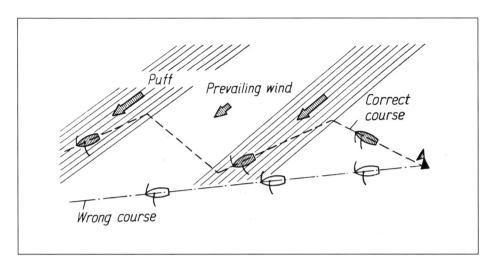

Fig 301 It is possible to benefit from a series of puffs (gust fronts), likely to be found under the groups of cumulus clouds. In order to exploit puffs successfully, a course must be chosen that keeps the boat within the gust that is much stronger than the prevailing wind. Puffs can be seen by an experienced eye well ahead on the water. Different wind velocities ripple the water in different ways and this may give some indication as to where the gust fronts actually operate, in relation to flat spots dominated by a much weaker prevailing wind.

Racing in light winds with occasional puffs demands special tactics. There is no point in sticking stubbornly to the shortest route to the next marker buoy. It is far better, if there is any chance of doing so, to sail toward a puff, and when that has been reached, to keep it capricious company as long as possible on the approximately correct course. An example of right and wrong tactics for two yachts in this kind of situation is given in Fig 301.

Winds, it must be remembered, tend to increase in strength at midday. Solar radiation is the main cause of wind, so on sunny, cloudless days one would expect the greatest exchange of thermal energy into the kinetic energy of wind at noon. It has been found that for the speed of the wind to increase during the day, there must be a suitable vertical distribution of temperature in the atmosphere – vertical gradient. Observations show that the greater the gradient of temperature, the greater the increase in the wind speed. The relationship is shown in Fig 302. The figures near each curve indicate the magnitude of the vertical gradient, the change (in this case a fall) being given in degrees centigrade for each 100 m (328 ft) of height above the specified level. The gradient curve of 0.7°–1.0°/100m is characteristic for cold, polar air moving over a warmed terrain. The lowest of the gradient curves, 0.2°/100 m, is typical of the dry, warmed air masses found in stationary high-pressure systems.

A practical problem arises when competitors, due to start a race in the morning, wonder whether to use a flat sail or a full one, and whether the wind will increase and by how much. It is fairly certain that there will be some increase in wind strength in the afternoon if the area is one where the incoming air masses are fresh and cool. However, if the area has been affected by an anticyclone for some time, even if the day is sunny and cloudless, the chances of the wind strengthening are small.

Figure 302 shows that the strongest winds blow between 10 am and 4 pm. Therefore, if a race is started before noon, the possibility of a rise in the strength of the wind must be considered and flat sails chosen, to be reefed perhaps. Races that start in the afternoon are not likely to meet with stronger winds, and competitors can more easily decide to set a more cambered sail, anticipating a drop in the wind later. This rule applies, of course, only in settled weather, and not when, say, a cold front is expected.

Together with the increase in wind strength in the afternoon, there will usually be a change in wind direction, by as much as 60°, perhaps, clockwise, following the sun. Later in the afternoon a failing wind will tend to back, changing again to the opposite direction.

Fig 302 The influence of the vertical temperature gradient on expected wind speed. Ultimately, wind is the consequence of a variation in air temperature, ie, heating energy received from the sun which peaks in early afternoon.

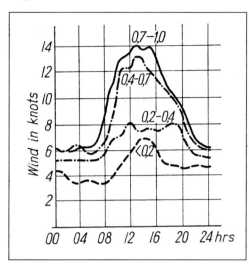

4 • THE WIND OVER A REGATTA COURSE

The wind blowing over an area where racing is taking place has already been shown to be unsettled, either in direction or speed. It is affected in addition by two other factors:

1 Obstructions, or wind barriers
2 The presence of the competing yachts

Although the prevailing surface wind is affected by the thermal conditions of the atmosphere in the unpredictible manner described, obstructions and wind barriers act on the wind according to fixed rules, so that it is possible to forecast the way in which they will disturb it. For example, in a lake or bay surrounded by hills (as in Fig 303), even though the prevailing wind is blowing from the west, wind A (which is close to the land) is actually blowing almost at right angles to wind C, and while the wind blows steadily enough in some places, there will also be areas of turbulence and of calm. In this example the air masses are being guided over passes which control their direction and velocity.

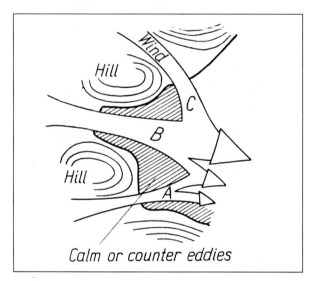

Calm or counter eddies

Fig 303 Due to the effect of surface friction and the presence of terrain features such as hills in the wind's path, the wind is altered by slowing, accelerating and diverting from its basic direction.

Yachtsmen who know their local waters are usually well aware of certain wind effects, varying according to the direction of the prevailing wind. For this reason they usually prove superior to visiting yachtsmen who are racing over a course they do not know, who are having to resolve the mysteries of the local topography by trial and error. If unfamiliar with local conditions a good plan is to study the ways of the wind by observing the ripples on the water from well above it; say from a nearby hill, or, even better, to get experience by making reconnaissance trips on the water. In the earlier races it might also be advisable to keep near a helmsman familiar with local conditions, rather than to strike off on a lone course, even if it looks advantageous.

A very irregular coastline affects the winds in the same way as the passes just described.

Fig 304 A narrowing (converging) gap between a barrier of fully grown trees may induce large local acceleration of the surface wind.

Although obstructions can cause complicated deformations of the wind, their effects can be reduced to two basic types:

1 Contraction of the air flow (Venturi effect). This will increase, sometimes considerably, the speed of the wind for a relatively small change in direction.

2 Large scale turbulence. This may considerably change the direction of the prevailing surface wind, and may reduce its speed.

The first type is illustrated in Fig 304. While a yacht is sailing on the sheltered water below a high cliff (position a), she feels only a light wind, mainly on the upper part of her sails, but as soon as she approaches an open gap (position b), she is struck by a strong wind, whose force is the greater, the narrower the passage for the air stream between sections f and f_1. The formation of the coast in certain cases may produce a contraction of the flow that will double the wind speed; and, remember, if the speed of the wind is increased twofold, the effect of the wind on the sails increases fourfold. Since a sudden gust is more dangerous than the pressure of a steady wind, it is hardly surprising that many helmsmen at such times fail to free the sheets in time and their boats unexpectedly capsize. For this reason, anyone sailing near a coast full of sharp bends, valleys and open spaces should be ready to take immediate action to prevent sudden changes in the lateral stability of their yacht.

Figure 305a, b and c demonstrates the second type of wind change caused by obstructions. In a the disturbance is due to trees growing on the coast. The influence of this barrier can be felt up to a distance of 4 to 20 times its height, depending on its density (a single tree will have less effect than a dense clump). The reaction of the wind to the barrier varies remarkably at different distances from it, causing apparently incomprehensible behaviour on the part of the sails. Wind eddies are to be expected not only to leeward of a barrier, but also on its windward side if the distance from the barrier is small; for example, below a steep, tall cliff (as in Fig 305b, c). Again, the range of turbulence depends on the height of the barrier.

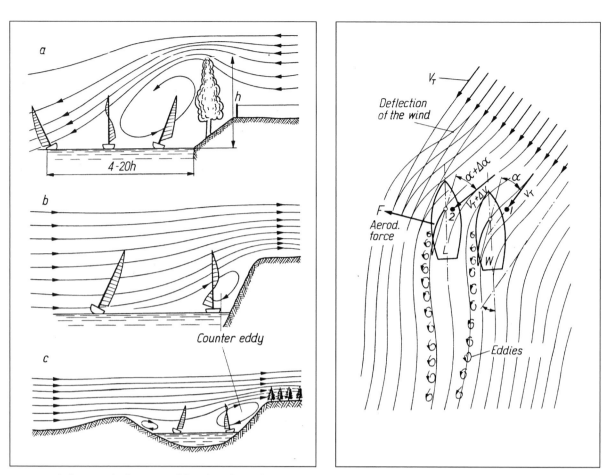

Fig 305 (left) Terrain features of the shoreline – be it trees, buildings or cliffs – modify the wind, inducing large scale eddies, regardless of whether the wind is blowing offshore (a) or inshore (b and c). The presence of eddies explains the abnormal behaviour of sails depending on the boat's position relative to the shoreline. The full force of the wind will not appear at the water surface until it has passed 4 to 20 times the height of the obstruction protruding above the shoreline, sketch (a).

Fig 306 (right) The spectrum of wind affecting two boats sailing in proximity. The leeward boat L, affected by the upwash produced by the windward boat, W, finds herself in the 'safe leeward position'. The advantages of sailing in that position are twofold: the wind is favourably deflected by the amount, $\triangle\alpha$, which is 'felt' as a sort of lifting shift; besides, the wind speed is increased by the amount $\triangle V$.

When racing, another factor affecting the wind that has to be kept in mind is the presence of rival yachts. Both experience and aerodynamic measurements have shown that the interaction between two sails is such that they will be working in rather different flow conditions. The sails of yachts sailing close together create a specific wind distribution, even though they appear to be affected by the same true wind. In Fig 306 the sail of windward yacht W is causing a slight deflection of the wind to the left in front of her bow. If the wind velocities were measured at points 1 and 2 in the vicinity of windward yacht, W, it would be noticed that the speed would be greater by $\triangle v$ on the leeward side of yacht W. The direction of the wind to the leeward of yacht W, being deflected to some degree, benefits yacht L by angle $\triangle\alpha$ (upwash) in as much as the wind striking yacht L will be stronger and more on the beam, giving the helmsman the chance of developing a greater driving force.

In fact, it could be said that yacht W is helping the helmsman of yacht L to sail faster. Experienced yachtsmen know this quite well, and it is not difficult for anyone who has already studied sail aerodynamics to follow. Yacht L is in what is called the 'safe leeward position' (Fig 307) and can overtake yacht W, and then luff. This is one of the classic yacht racing manoeuvres.

The safe leeward position can undoubtedly be very advantageous, especially when sailing to windward in winds that are not too strong, so that it is possible to maintain the desirable lateral stability, that is, to keep the boat nearly upright. If the wind is so strong that the crew has difficulty in ballasting the boat, the safe leeward position will magnify these difficulties by increasing the tendency to heel. The helmsman would then have to either ease the mainsheet and spill some of the wind, or sail at a greater angle of heel than the windward yacht. In such circumstances the safe leeward position may bring little benefit, for the aerodynamic and hydrodynamic losses suffered by a yacht which heels at an excessive angle limit any advantage that might be derived from the leeward position.

Fig 307 Boat number 25 is sailing in the 'safe leeward position'. Her greater angle of heel suggests that she is affected by a stronger wind than her windward neighbour. Because the invisible fuel driving her is of a higher grade, she enjoys a commanding position over her rival.

Fig 308 Boat number 11 is in the so-called 'hopeless position'. The physical reasons for her predicament are shown in Fig 309.

Assuming, then, that the helmsman of the yacht in the safe leeward position does not make mistakes in sailing her, and that both yachts are of one design and similar in performance, she could overtake the windward yacht, which is said to be then in the 'hopeless position' (Fig 308).

Figure 309 may explain the difficulties of a helmsman who has found himself in the 'hopeless position'. One may fairly accurately reckon that the aerodynamic effect, F, received on a sail for each unit of time, is equivalent to the increase in the momentum of the air thrown by this sail in the opposite direction to F. If the mass of air thrown off to windward by the sail is denoted by, m, and the speed with which the mass m is thrown aside by V, then F = mV. From this formula it follows that the deflection of the windstreams to the side of the centre-line will be intensified as force F is increased. Adding the speed V to the speed of the wind in front of the sail, V_1, confirms that the windstreams behind the sail are deflected in such a way as to give any boat sailing in them a closer wind, V_2, which will force her either to bear away or change her tack. Now, if the yacht in the hopeless position bears away, she has to cross the turbulent wake of air and water which follows the leading yacht, and this will increase her losses.

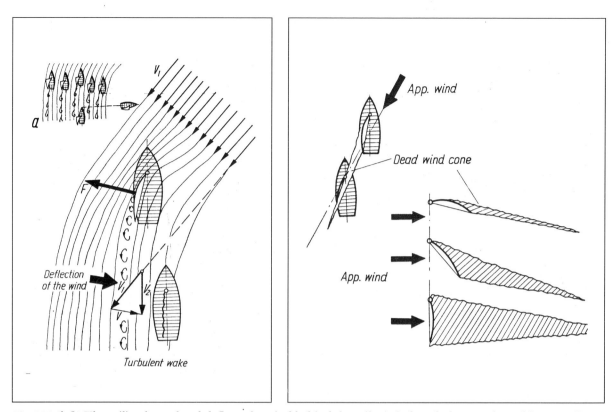

Fig 309 (left) The sailing boat ahead deflects the wind behind the sail to windward (downwash) and leaves a disturbed area of used up (dirty) wind. For these two reasons, the following boat cannot extract as much energy from the wind as does the leading boat. The best solution for the boat in the hopeless position is to alter course to pass quickly through the zone of dirty wind and find clear wind unimpeded by the proximity of other boats or obstacles of any kind.

Fig 310 (right) The size of the dead wind shadow produced by the leading boat depends on the incidence angle at which her sails are set.

The direction of the turbulent wake behind the sail when sailing close-hauled is deflected away from the line of the apparent wind toward the stern (Fig 310). The span of this disturbance, or 'dead wind cone', depends on the angle of sail incidence. It is not excessive for courses ranging from close-hauled to close-reaching, but increases when sailing before the wind.

The influence of the wind deflection and turbulence behind a yacht can be felt for a distance of up to ten boat lengths. This depends on the speed of the wind, the course, and the number of yachts causing a wind disturbance over the course. A particularly bad position is one behind a number of yachts sailing on a close-hauled course (as in Fig 309a). The helmsman of a following yacht will find himself facing a strongly deflected wind and eddies which absorb a considerable portion of the wind's energy. As one would expect, these disadvantages are increased if the yachts ahead are sailing close together.

Some interesting quantitative information on the interaction between two similar yachts can be found in Fig 311. This experiment on the effect of interference by one yacht on another was carried out by M S Hooper on models of J-class yachts in Fairey's wind tunnel (Fig 63a). The position of the 'interfering' yacht was fixed, while the 'interfered with' yacht was moved about in relation to

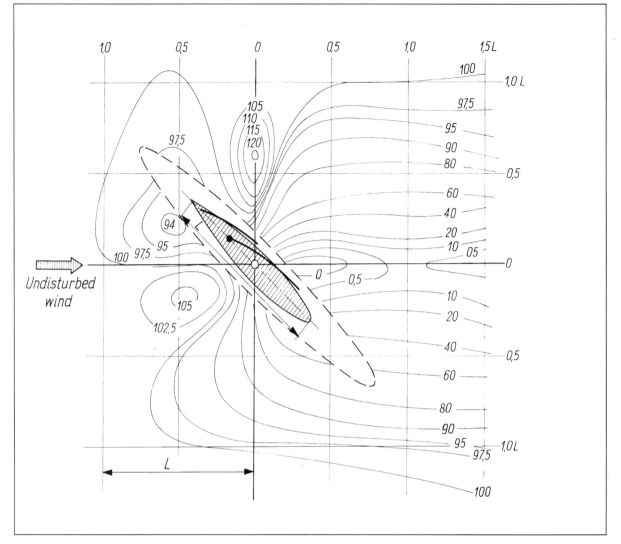

Fig 311 The distribution of available wind energy, modified by the presence of a boat sailing close-hauled. Note the substantial increase in available wind energy recorded on the leeward side of the boat, which can be exploited by another boat. Also, note the large loss in wind energy behind the boat and left by her in the wake.

the fixed yacht. The origin of the coordinates was chosen similarly for each yacht, and the apparent course for both yachts was 40° and the angle of heel 15°. The graph (Fig 311) shows the contours of available driving force around the 'interfering' yacht, which were measured on the 'interfered with' yacht as percentages of the driving force which would be available in an undisturbed wind. The horizontal and vertical units of the graph correspond to the deck length (L) of the yacht. The silhouette of the 'interfering' yacht only is drawn, and the broken line outside shows the limit of approach for the 'interfered with' yacht, on the same tack and pointing the same course. Easily spotted is the area of extra driving force stretching to leeward of the 'interfering' yacht, where the 'interfered with' yacht can gain up to 20 per cent extra. This is the 'safe leeward position'. Losses in driving force, on the other hand, can amount to about 95 per cent in certain areas downwind from the 'interfering' yacht.

The 'hopeless' and 'safe leeward' positions are well known in yacht racing tactics, and are commonly used in sailing to windward. On other courses, the comparable tactics involve blanketing an opponent's sail. While a detailed discussion of these tactical procedures can be left to books devoted to the technique of yacht racing, the question of blanketing when running is worth consideration.

Some interesting experiments were carried out by Eiffel to measure the aerodynamic forces which appeared on similarly shaped plates blanketing each other axially, at different distances apart. The results are presented in Fig 312. On the vertical axis the force is given in kg, and on the horizontal the distance between the plates as a multiple of the plate's width. These results can be adapted to the situation met with when sailing before the wind.

The magnitude of the force F (Fig 312a) on a sail without interference amounted to 6.8 kg. If sail 1 is 1.5 sail widths from sail 2, then the force that acts on sail 2 is equal to 30 per cent of F and opposite to the yacht's motion. Case b

Fig 312 The blanketing effect which influences sail forces developed on sails of two boats sailing downwind and covering each other.

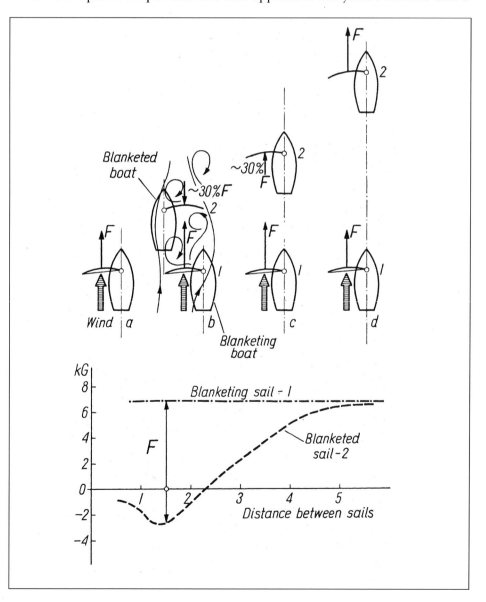

therefore shows the greatest negative blanketing effect for yacht 2 in the aerodynamic shadow of yacht 1. As the distance between them increases, the blanketing effect on yacht 2 decreases in importance and practically disappears when the distance is increased to seven times the sail chord. Figure 313 demonstrates this blanketing effect used practically in a racing duel.

Fig 313 Blanketing in a crafty luffing match. Here the leeward FD, PZ8, strives to keep her wind clear, but superior work by PZ1 kills her opponent stone dead.

5 • MICROBURSTS

The anatomy of the so called *microburst* or *white squall*, is similar to that shown in Fig 300a. A microburst can best be defined as an intense, short-lived downburst – a column of rapidly descending air – which is deflected outward radially, like the spokes of a wheel, when the column nears the surface of the sea. This meteorological phenomenon is receiving publicity because of some tragic airline and maritime casualties attributed to microburst (Ref 3.5).

Vessels in the path of the microburst may experience wind velocities as high as 150 knots; and because microbursts occur rapidly, and the wind may hit the vessel from unexpected direction regardless of the prevailing wind, the crew may be caught off guard. Survivors of such incidents reported that 'the high winds suddenly came from a completely different direction without any warning'. Research to date has not provided a definite set of signs of approaching microburst (such as exist for an approaching thunderstorm), which would enable a crew to prepare for it. 'The real danger for a sailor occurs when the microburst is encountered while the prevailing weather appears to be simply unsettled'; for example, overcast skies with moderate wind, or possibly occasional light rain with some turbulence. 'It would be an ordinary, ill-defined, dirty-looking day that gets a crew thinking that later they might have to put on oilies and Wellingtons. The boat is at risk in an encounter because of the surprise and shock of the crew, for they do not understand what is happening. Thus, they react slowly and possibly inappropriately to a situation which requires quick action.' (Ref 3.5).

What is needed is an alert attitude towards probable rapid wind change: 'If the skipper sees her shaking and the breeze is in the making; then O Johnny, O Johnny, – then *look out for squalls*!'

There has been a belief among sailors of the old school that many a good ship met with disaster through being struck by such 'a raging tempest with hardly a cloud in sight.' The white squall, then, is a traditional blast that gives warning of its approach only by a turbulence arising on the water surface, while frequently accompanied by a clear sky.

Some maritime accidents attributed to microburst include the 117-foot British bark *Marques,* which sank during the Tall Ship Race of 1984 with the loss of 19 lives. According to survivors, just before the squall hit the vessel, the sea suddenly turned milky white. 'The *Marques* was violently driven forward, buried the bow into sea and was driven over the starboard.' In less than one minute, the *Marques* sank, approximately 80 miles north of Bermuda. The sailing vessel the *Pride of Baltimore* sank in 1986 in similar circumstances, with the loss of 4 lives.

One likely hint of approaching microburst may be a rapid increase and possible shift in the prevailing wind, as occurs with a strong gust. But instead of lasting 3 or 4 seconds like a gust, the wind would rapidly and steadily increase over 30 seconds or more, and may be considerably colder than the ambient air.

An encounter with a microburst is not a likely event, but microburst are probably much more common than tornadoes and severe storms. Meteorologists estimate that the number of microbursts capable of inducing surface winds stronger than 70 knots can reasonably be as many as 13000 per year over the United States; and they are as destructive over water as over land. Their peak season is from June to August (Ref 3.5).

6 • PUMPING – A LEGITIMATE SAILING TECHNIQUE?

'On the whole, the difficult thing about persuading others is not that one lacks the knowledge to state his case nor the audacity to exercise his abilities to the full. The difficult thing about persuasion is to know the mind of the person one is trying to persuade and to be able to fit one's words to it'.

Han Fei Tzu, Chinese philosopher

Pumping, which in sailing parlance simply means a regularly repeated process of trimming the sails, in which they are first sheeted-in abrubtly, and then eased rather slowly, had become a pretty subject to debate during many meetings of the International Yacht Racing Union (IYRU). Pumping has been recognized '...to be a problem in all centreboard classes' and attempts were made to find '*...ways of stopping this practice.*' Why?

On the one hand, the influence of pumping on increasing the boat's speed has been demonstrated conclusively, and it has been found particularly effective in planing or surfing conditions, in which planing has been achieved earlier and prolonged after the wind strength has lessened.

On the other hand, an observer can get the impression that the helmsman is helping to propel the boat by dint of the muscular effort put into alternately hardening and easing the sheets. Whether this impression is justified is questionable, but it is certain that this view lies at the root of the unshakeable, uniform opinion of the authority about this practice. Accordingly, pumping, or frequent, quickly repeated trimming and releasing of the mainsail to increase propulsion has not been regarded as 'the natural action of the wind on the sail'. Although, it must be admitted, the IYRU jury has recognized that, 'for some *aerodynamic reason which is not fully understood*, abrupt changes in the angle of incidence of the mainsail can impart additional speed to a boat' [the italics are mine].

Under the heading, *Actions That Are Permitted*, the IYRU rule relevant to pumping reads: 'The following actions are permitted for the sole purpose of accelerating a yacht down the face of a wave (surfing) or, when planing conditions exist, responding to an increase in the velocity of the wind.

a) Not more than three rapidly-repeated trims and releases of any sail (pumping).
b) Sudden movement of the body forward or aft (ooching).

There shall be no further pumping or ooching with respect to the wave or increase of wind.'

As reported and complained about on many occasions, in spite of the rule and its interpretation, leaders in the Olympic classes in particular used to manifest more or less openly their great skill in pumping, some of them even became famous as 'the worlds's lustiest pumpers'.

One is bound to wonder whether something is wrong if so many good sailors have been breaking the rule. After all, why are 'not more than three' pumpings permitted? Does this rule imply that while pumping three times the helmsman is using decent aerodynamic forces in agreement with 'the natural action of the wind'? And, by pumping for the fourth time, does something radically-change, so from this moment muscular effort is used to propel the boat? How had the magic borderline number 'three' been derived?

There are good reasons to believe that the confusion and dissatisfaction related to the IYRU rule simply stems from a misunderstanding of the physical facts underlying the pumping effect. Making the aerodynamic aspects generally known would certainly be useful, and should help to resolve the key problem of whether or not pumping can be included with the natural action of the wind on the sails. To answer this question we must first discuss the mechanism of forces generated on the aerofoil 1) in the steady flow condition and 2) in the unsteady one.

GRADUAL CHANGES OF INCIDENCE ANGLE

Consider in some detail the changes in the aerodynamic forces when the incidence α of an aerofoil is slowly increasing and then decreasing. The reaching case shown in Fig 314, when the apparent wind is at 90° to the hull centreline, allows us to simplify the discussion, since in this case the driving force F_R corresponds to the lift force L measured in the wind tunnel. It is seen that the lift rises pretty regularly as the angle of incidence is increasing (thick curve), until it reaches a maximum at point A. This is the stalling angle. Beyond this point sudden drop in lift force takes place – from A to B shown by the broken line. This

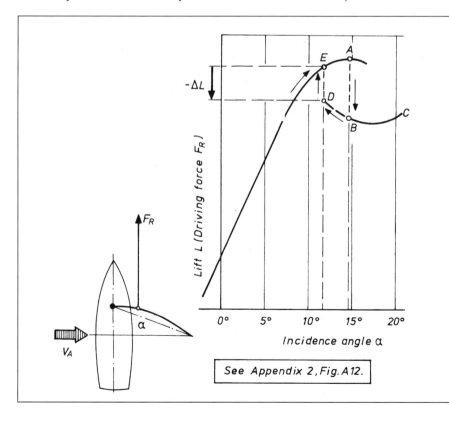

See Appendix 2, Fig. A12.

Fig 314 Variation of lift with incidence angle for one of the NACA aerofoils in *steady* flow conditions. Actual measured lift for a given incidence depends on the past history of the flow; that is, once the flow separation has taken place, it is necessary to reduce the incidence angle well below the stalling angle to have an attached flow again with a corresponding lift value. In this respect the sail, in a qualitative sense, appears to be no different from any other aerofoil.

sudden fall in lift indicates radical change in the nature of the flow over the leeward side of the aerofoil, caused by the boundary layer separation right from
the leading edge.

As the incidence increases still further, the lift will follow the thick curve BC.
If now, after stall has been reached (point B), the incidence is reduced, the lift
will not be recovered on the instant but will follow the broken curve BDE as
indicated by the arrows. Thus, when the incidence angle is decreased to about
10 degrees (point D), the lift will be reduced by an amount $-\triangle L$ as compared
with its pre-stall value (point E). This *delay* in lift recovery is reflected by so
called 'hysteresis loop', ie, a closed curve EABDE. The term hysteresis in this
context means: lagging of lift behind the incidence angle. This is the result of
the crucial role played by the boundary layer, in the sense that the BL, once
separated, requires time and certain conditions to become attached to the leeward surface of the foil again.

RAPID AND REPEATED CHANGES OF INCIDENCE (PUMPING)

In the preceding example, the incidence was increased slowly and smoothly.
This is the 'steady condition'. It has been established, however, first in laboratory tests on aerofoils and subsequently on full scale aeroplanes, that if instead the
incidence is increased quickly well beyond the angle of stall for steady conditions, the leeward flow does not manifest separation tendencies. For a short
while after the incidence is increased to a value which in the steady condition
would have separated flow and developed a full stall, the boundary layer
adheres smoothly to the sail. Because of
this temporary suspension of separation,
the lift force can greatly exceed the maximum lift corresponding to the steady condition. This phenomenon is recorded in
Fig 315, where the full line represents the
lift change obtained by slow increases in
incidence, and the upper broken line,
ABC, the values obtained by rapid change
in incidence, ie, in unsteady or dynamic
conditions.

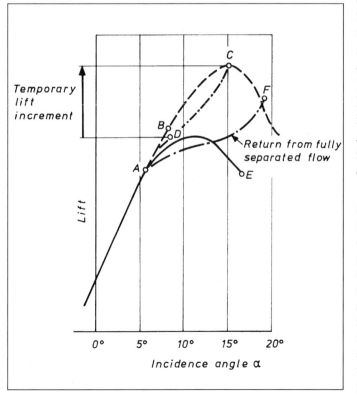

Fig 315 Variation of lift with incidence angle
in unsteady flow condition. It was demonstrated first by Kramer (3.8) that C_{Lmax} can be
greatly, albeit temporarily, increased over the
C_{Lmax} relevant to the steady flow condition, if
the angle of incidence is increased rapidly
above the angle at which stall occurs in steady
flow. The influence of pumping on increasing
the boat's speed has been found particularly
advantageous in planing or surfing conditions,
when planing has been achieved earlier and
prolonged after the wind strength has lessened.

The upper line represents only a temporary increment, and if the incidence is held after the rapid increase, the separation will progress forward to the leading edge followed by sudden drop in lift. Thus, referring to Fig 315, having managed to traverse the portion of the graph ABC by a single 'pump', if the sail (or any foil) is now held steady for a sufficiently long time, then lift would fall to F or to an even lower value, which is clearly undesirable. If instead the sheet were eased gradually in the right moment, it would be possible to return to A along CDA, giving a substantial increase in time-average lift over the maximum lift relevant to steady conditions. Thus, if all else remains the same, the rapid increase in lift will give an additional boost to the boat.

On the other hand, if return from point C is delayed and the full separation on the leeward side has already developed, the lift recovery may follow line FA, labelled 'return from fully separated flow condition'. In such case, the time-average value of lift may decrease well below that which can be obtained in steady conditions. So, pumping is working two ways: it may or may not be advantageous.

Figure 316 illustrates perhaps better than words the flow character over the upper surface of the foil, when the foil recovers from the fully separated flow in dynamic conditions (upper and lower left hand pictures). In spite of the fact that the angle of incidence is reduced to zero, as depicted in the lower picture to the right (and therefore one might expect to have an attached flow), the separation still persists and will so for a certain time.

It is possible by means of pumping to get temporary increases of lift, even up to about 80 per cent, as shown in Fig 317, which demonstrates the lift

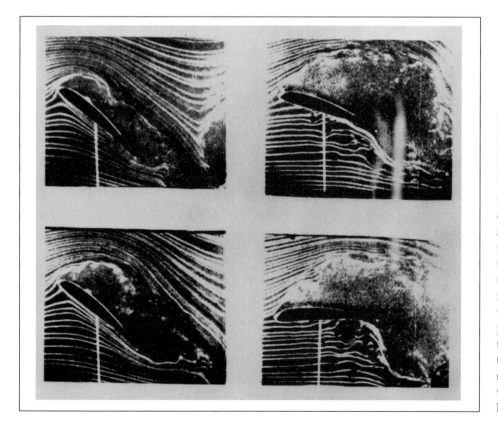

Fig 316 Photographs illustrate vividly the physical meaning of the 'hysteresis' or 'memory effect' on the flow pattern developed around an aerofoil. Although the foil attitude relative to the flow direction is altered, the fluid (be it air or water) *remembers* the previous flow pattern; and it takes time to achieve a steady attached flow with corresponding lift.

developed on one of the Göttingen aerofoils set in a flow the angle of which increases with time (Ref 3.7).

It has been established that the aerodynamic reaction depends on the rate of change of incidence α with time $\frac{\triangle\alpha}{\triangle t}$; in other words, an increase of the incidence (measured in radians) per one second (1 radian = 57.3 degrees). The rate of change of incidence, $\frac{\triangle\alpha}{\triangle t}$, is made nondimensional by multiplying with the foil chord c and dividing by the speed of flow V. Hence, the nondimensional rate of incidence change, K, can be expressed as:

$$K = \frac{\triangle\alpha}{\triangle t} \times \frac{c}{V} \qquad\qquad Eq\ 27$$

In Fig 317 there are plotted lift coefficients for several values of rate of incidence change K, and they are directly compared with lift characteristics obtained in the steady condition when K = 0.

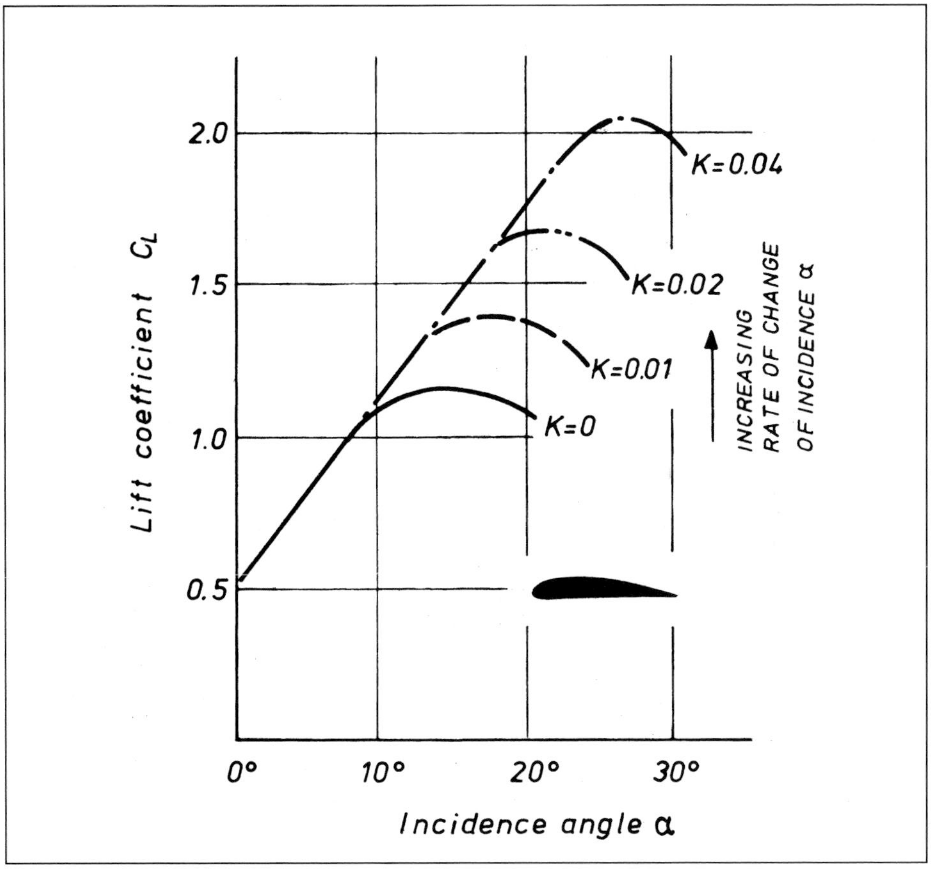

Fig 317 The effect of the rate of change in the incidence angle on the maximum lift coefficient. It is seen that the stall angle in dynamic flow condition increases if the rate of change in the incidence angle increases. Temporary increments of maximum lift (dynamic stall) over its stationary value, K = 0, can be quite substantial.

The practical implications of Figs 315 and 317 are that if helmsmen wish to obtain the maximum advantage from pumping, they must be fully aware of what the airflow is doing on the leeward side, and must adjust *the frequency and amplitude of its action, as well as the mean angle of incidence* to suit the wind speed and sailing conditions. Pumping should be started from a point when the sail has no separated flow, ie, close to the angle of incidence at which maximum lift occurs, and the sheet eased before the separation tends to develop. Pumping should be particularly effective when the sail has little twist, when all sections are working at about the same effective incidence. No doubt effective pumping can be mastered by conscious training.

The 'pumping effect' was not discovered by sailors but by a German scientist, Kramer, in 1932, and since then has been named by some other scientists, 'Kramer's effect' (Ref 3.8). Because of an obsessive discoverer's complex which plagues humanity, the same phenomenon has been recognized by others as a 'hysteresis effect', meaning a lag in establishing the flow corresponding to the conditions at any given instant angle of incidence. Quite recently, yet another term has been suggested: 'memory effect' (Ref 3.9). This means that, although the foil attitude relative to the flow may be altered instantaneously, the fluid flow and the resulting lift force 'remembers' the initial state, and it takes certain time to achieve both a steady character of the flow round the foil and corresponding lift value. Consequently, an allowance necessity for 'memory effects' has been recognized in modern ship-science when assessing the manoeuvring characteristics of seaborne craft.

Pumping, aerodynamic hesteresis, Kramer's effect, memory effect; all these terms describe the same dynamic stall phenomenon that lies at the root of some of the unpredictable, sometimes mischievous quirks of man-made machines and structures. Numerous aircraft have crashed because of so-called stall-flutter of wings, in which Kramer's effect plays a prominent role. Suspension bridges have collapsed in relatively weak winds, just because, amongst other factors, the aerodynamic hysteresis was in operation.

Not infrequently, certain phenomenae that are good in one respect, ie as the sole driving force, are likely to be disastrous in other respects.

The pumping effect is a strange but nevertheless legitimate physical phenomenon that has nothing to do with the muscular effort a helmsman may put into the sail system by hardening and easing sheets. It is 'the natural action of the wind on the sail' which makes a boat sail faster. As such, pumping should not be banned by the IYRU. That is of course, unless the authority can find another reason for doing so.

The pumping effect should not be confused with, for example, the flapping of the sail in calm or near-calm conditions, in which the sail is used in frequent tacks and jibes as a big fan. This is nothing but an attempt to convert the muscle power of the crew directly into forward motion of the boat, and as such it certainly contravenes the racing rule. Interpretation is straightforward, and all helmsmen who indulge in this practice know unmistakably what they are doing. Pumping when the wind blows is something entirely different.

Critics occasionally misunderstood the physical aspect of the pumping effect. To quote from a letter addressed to the author: 'In the first place, there is no doubt that the helmsman may be doing mechanical work (the sheet probably does require more force to harden than to ease). Also, there is no doubt that if there is any advantage in 'pumping', it will appear as increased lift coefficient. What *is* in doubt is how much of the increased work of the sail on the boat is due to more efficient use of the wind, and how much to the work put in by the helmsman. Proof that at least some of the advantages of pumping comes from more efficient use of the wind would require a showing that the additional power derived was more than the power supplied by the helmsman... how could one prove that the work supplied by the helmsman does not contribute to the propulsion?'

Fig 318 The amount of muscle effort required for the helmsman to change the incidence angle largely depends (sheet friction ignored) on the distance between the centre of pressure, CP, and the axis of sail rotation. This effort can be negligible and completely out of proportion compared to the large lift increases due to a rapid change in incidence angle. In a way, the helmsman's effort can be compared with the stick force required from the pilot to hold the aeroplane in a rapid pull-up. Certainly, the pilot does not physically contribute to the extra lift.

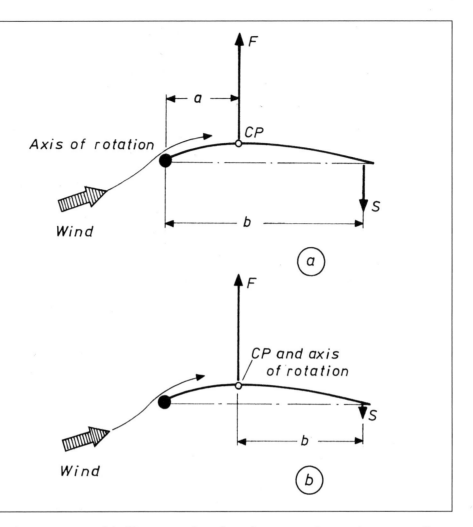

Figure 318a and b illustrates that the advantage of pumping comes from more efficient use of the wind, and not from the effort that the helmsman puts into alternately hardening and easing the sheet.

It is apparent from Fig 318a that the physical effort a helmsman puts into maintaining the balance of forces F (aerodynamic), and S (sheeting), is essentially a function of distance a from the mast (axis of sail rotation) to the centre of pressure CP (assuming for simplicity a Finn rig) and distance b between the axis of sail rotation and the point where the sheets are attached to the boom. The sail incidence α relative to the wind will be constant if respective moments are in equilibrium, ie,

$$F \times a = S \times b$$

Now, let us imagine (an experiment can easily be devised along these lines) that the axis of rotation is gradually shifted towards the CP (Fig 318b). Force S on the sheets becomes gradually smaller and finally vanishingly small when the axis of rotation coincides with CP. In such a case the helmsman's effort in changing the incidence angle α becomes negligible, but the lift hysteresis or Kramer's effect will be the same regardless of the relative position of CP and axis of rotation; so the effect is independent of the physical effort of the helmsman.

It is quite possible to devise an oscillating system which will utilize the Kramer effect by extracting energy from the wind without any additional force. The spectacular vibrations which resulted in the collapse of the Tacoma Washington bridge under the action of a relatively low wind speed were in part generated by the lift hysteresis effect.

As already mentioned earlier, the dynamic lift overshoot ie conspicuous increase of lift maximum above that relevant to steady flow condition, is primarily the result of a delay of the boundary layer separation. In other words, since a certain amount of time is required for the BL to build up, separation may be temporarily postponed, and the aerofoil responds to the dynamic increase in the incidence angle without stall.

In most textbooks on aerodynamics, the unsteady flow effects have often, for simplicity, been ignored. Science is largely determined by commonly adopted methods of translating the dynamic into the static, mainly because of the motionless pictures in books (presentation of forces are static, and hence in most cases divorced from reality). However, the motion of a sailing boat is essentially unsteady dynamic motion, mainly due to wind unsteadiness and wave action; therefore the role of unsteady flow effects cannot be ignored. By taking into account these challenging flows, important advances can be made toward understanding the peculiar behaviour of sailing craft in some conditions. In the following chapters, two more unsteady phenomena are discussed.

Readers with enquiring minds who might obstinately hesitate to recognize the significance of the dynamic lift stall as applied to the sail are recommended to consult reference 3.10. Criticism is certainly the precondition for better understanding, but it is not in itself creative.

7 · SAILING DOWNWIND (ROLLING)

'...one must learn by doing the thing; for though you think you know it, you have no certainty until you try.'

Sophocles (495–406 BC)

When running, the apparent wind speed and the forces on the sail at given true wind are at their minimum. In addition they appear to act along the line of maximum hull stability. It would seem that sailing a yacht on a run should not present any difficulty, yet in practice it is frequently very unpleasant and difficult, because of rolling.

Nicknamed by experienced dinghy sailors *'the death roll'* (Fig 319) – ie, the progressively wilder oscillation of rig over boat on the square run, that if allowed to continue ends in capsize – remains probably the biggest problem of sailing single-handed dinghies like Lasers, OK's and Finns downwind (Ref 3.11). Neither is the keel boat immune from rolling (Fig 320).

When running before a fresh wind, rhythmic rolling – usually coupled with a more or less uncomfortable, if not dangerous, tendency to broach-to – becomes an almost inevitable characteristic of all monohull sailing craft. There is evidence that this coupling effect between rolling and yawing, subsequently leading to a serious broaching, was partly responsible for some of the incidents during the 1979 Admiral's Cup series. A few excerpts from the Fastnet race reports might well illustrate the point.

Fig 319 A 'death roll'. 'All of a sudden she began to roll and roll and roll.' Once triggered, the rolling is self-perpetuating.

Fig 320 Offshore cruisers can roll as easily as small dinghies.

'The wind was very square so naturally the yachts began to roll. Setting bloopers did not appear to counter this tendency... As soon as crewmen went forward to handle guys and poles the really vicious broaching began... *Evergreen*, the only drop-keel boat in the series, broached as flat as any; only her exceptionally wide beam preventing the mast from hitting the water... Suddenly the broaches were no longer hilarious – they were damnable. They damned a rule that produced boats that, in spite of *being handled by the best in the world*, run amok in sheltered waters off-wind. *Something was seriously wrong with the state of art.*'

What is wrong, why does it happen and what can we do to stop it? These questions of immediate practical importance have been answered in various ways: recipes given occasionally in various magazines are frequently conflicting and therefore cannot be applied with confidence. The only helpful way forward is to resort to strictly controlled experiments in which the relevant factors can be investigated one by one. Since the main danger when running downwind in heavy air comes from rolling, one must become conversant with the mechanics of the rhythmic roll first. No doubt, the crew who understand the nature of forces operating on the boat in critical situations can take the necessary action to lessen the severity of rolling, knowing full well that if nothing is done in the early stages, the yacht may become unmanageable so that broaching-to or a capsize is inevitable.

Whilst the interaction of aerodynamic and hydrodynamic forces is important, the many problems of heavy weather sailing can be tackled more easily by separating the one from the other. Let us first consider the aerodynamic forces.

Experimental work carried out by the author in the wind tunnel of Southampton University on two different rigs (Finn and Dragon) throws some light on this grey area of sail action or contribution towards rolling. The turbulent air flow behind a sail set at a large angle of incidence, as shown in Fig 321a and b, is not quite as irregular as it might appear. There is some kind of order in this apparent disorder of large eddies shed alternately from each edge of the sail and travelling downwind, in the form of the so-called *Karman vortex trail*. With the vortex swirling in the direction indicated in Fig 321a, there is instantaneously a velocity differential between the opposite edges of the sail, ie, velocity V_1 at the upper edge of the sail is higher than velocity V_2 at the lower edge.

Fig 321

a) The wake behind a cambered plate or sail. The periodic detachment of vortices produces a periodic alternating force ± F on the plate, tending to make it oscillate across the stream.

b) Large scale turbulent wake caused by sails of a boat sailing on a dead run. Photo by The Fluid Mech. Lab. Imperial College, UK.

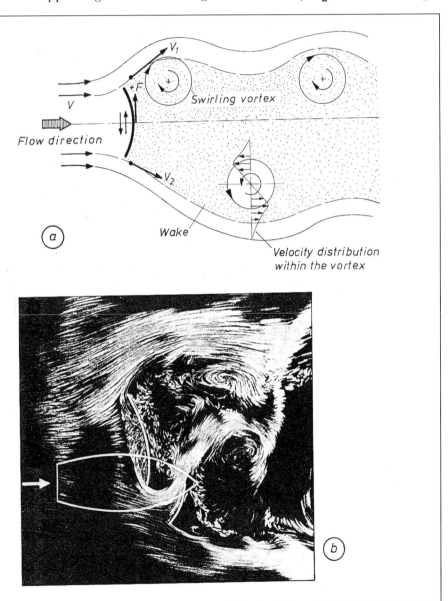

This is because in the particular instance illustrated, the flow velocity close to the upper edge of the sail is accelerated due to the presence of the swirling vortex. This difference in flow velocity produces a differential static pressure component, resulting in a lateral force + F pushing the sail in the direction shown. A short interval of time later, with the succeeding vortex forming close to the opposite edge, a similar interaction between the vortex and flow develops. This gives rise to a lateral force –F, acting in the opposite direction as before. Thus, with the formation of alternating vortices, there appears an alternating transverse force which tends to oscillate the sail in a plane perpendicular to the flow direction.

If any initial disturbance in roll is introduced from the Karman vortex or by waves, or even from the wash of a motor boat for that matter, such initial rolling motion of the boat induces further changes in the aerodynamic sail forces. As the sail swings, say, to port (Fig 322a), thus acquiring an angular velocity, the resultant wind, its incidence and aerodynamic force, change both in magnitude and direction. The apparent wind V_A is modified by the velocity induced by the sail swing. The resultant wind V_R, which is at any instant the sum of the two wind vectors V_A and V, will increase in magnitude, and the instantaneous angle of incidence relative to the sail will be less than 90°. As a result, the flow pattern round the sail changes radically from that when there is no rolling. This modified flow pattern, marked by the line of arrows, determines in turn the instantaneous aerodynamic force F in such a way that its magnitude increases and the force is inclined towards the direction of sail motion. The total aerodynamic force F can now be resolved into two components:

1 A driving force F_R, acting along the direction of the course
2 A heeling force F_H, acting perpendicular to both the course and the mast, which will tend to increase the angle of roll

Fig 322 Forces developed on a rolling sail. Note that the roll-inducing force F_H acts towards the direction of actual swing, thus magnifying the angle of roll.

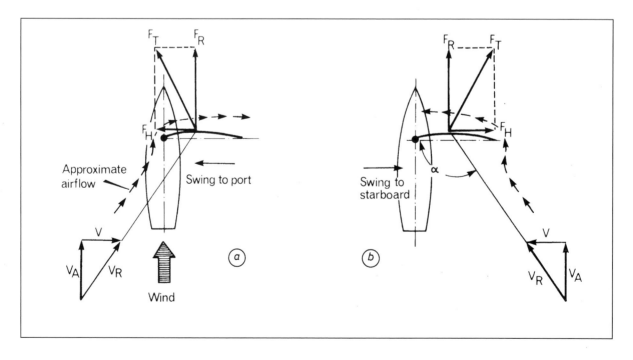

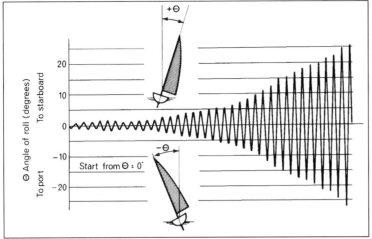

Fig 323 Record of self-excited rolling caused entirely by aerodynamic forces beginning from zero angle of roll.

When the sail swing is reversed – to starboard – the flow pattern is also reversed, as shown in Fig 322b. The airflow is opposite to that in the previous swing, and so the aerodynamic force component F_H is again directed towards the motion pushing the sail to starboard. Figure 323 which presents a record of the behaviour of a model yacht simulating downwind condition (ß = 180°) and sail trim (δ_m = 85°) illustrates the point. The rig, initially in equilibrium, begins to oscillate, being forced to do so by the Karman vortex trail which produces an unbalanced force across the flow direction. It is seen from it that wild rolling can be induced by a sail for an aerodynamic reason, and the rolling angle ± θ increases in the absence of any obvious external disturbance such as wave action. Once triggered, the aerodynamic roll is self-perpetuating.

The alternating forces that initiate rolling might be regarded as an *ignition*, which is responsible for starting the oscillatory motion. Once the rig is set in motion, the forces that amplify and sustain the oscillation are created and controlled by the oscillating rig itself. Hence we can distinguish this kind of rolling as self-excited and different in its very nature from the rolling caused by wave action. The character of aerodynamic excitation is such that one may say: *the more a boat rolls, the more she wants to roll.* The sail can rightly be regarded as a *rolling engine* extracting energy from the wind in a self-excited manner; and rolling may grow to the point where the crew loses control over subsequent events.

The modern masthead spinnaker has been cited as the villain responsible for wild rolling. However, wind tunnel tests have proved beyond any doubt that such a motion can be induced, for aerodynamic reasons, by almost any sail, and the boat can capsize or broach-to even *in a completely flat sea* (Fig 324).

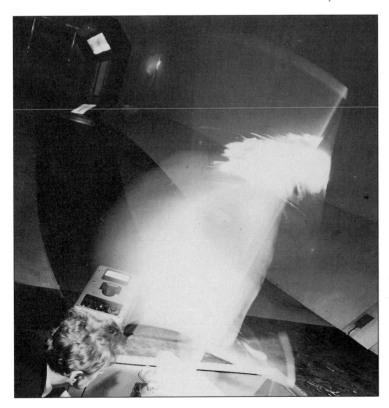

Fig 324 The Dragon rig, consisting of mainsail, genoa and spinnaker, tested in the wind tunnel. When set for downwind sailing, the rig develops unstable rolling with rapidly increasing roll angles. The blurred picture of the sails is due to rolling agitation.

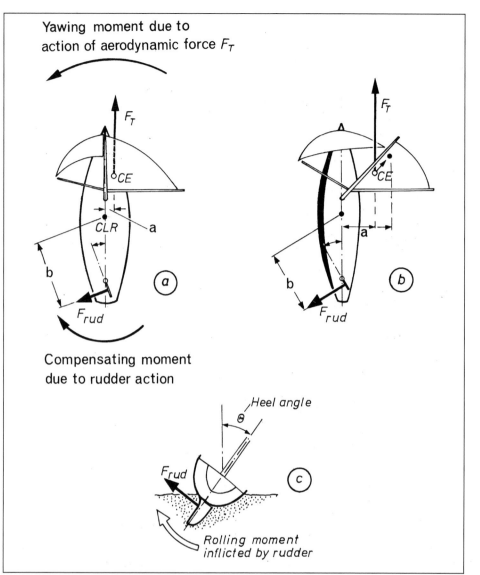

Fig 325 Rolling inflicted by rudder action applied in order to control the yawing motion of the hull.

The helmsman can, by inappropriate steering, aggravate already developed rolling due to aerodynamic excitation. Consider first Fig 325a which depicts an equilibrium of yawing moments when the yacht sails downwind and upright. The yawing moment due to the action of the aerodynamic force, F_T shifted by distance a, relative to the centre of lateral resistance CLR, is balanced by the rudder action. The boat will maintain her straight course as long as there is an equilibrium of moments $F_T \times a = F_{rud} \times b$.

When the boat begins to roll heavily, large variations in the yawing moments will also occur. Measurements taken in the wind tunnel indicate that – depending on the distribution of the total sail areas between the mainsail, headsail and possibly spinnaker – an increase in the yawing moment due to rolling can be several times greater than that when there is no rolling. The yawing moment is usually at its maximum when the yacht is heeling towards the side on which the boom is rigged, as shown in Fig 325b. For evident reasons, the yawing moment may greatly increase at large rolling angles.

To correct unwanted deviation from the course sailed, the helmsman must increase the rudder force F_{rud}, as shown in Figs 324b and c, by pulling the tiller to port. However, an application of helm to correct the yaw inevitably aggravates the roll angle. In unsteady motion conditions, characterized by simultaneous rolling and yawing, delayed effects on the sail as well as on the hull forces are to be expected. That is to say, the behaviour of the boat, since it has a certain inertia, will to some extent be unpredictable in the sense that there will be a time lag between the rudder's action and the boat's response. In other words, to maintain the desired heading in following or quartering seas, rudder control is indispensable to stop large yawing motions. However, the rudder is neither capable of immediately checking the yawing, nor of producing the corrective moment at the same time as destabilizing yawing occurs. Besides, a lag in boat response implies also a lag in sensing the imminent deviation from the course by the helmsman; this is of incalculable consequence if there is a backlash in the steering system and the helmsman is losing control over the rudder blade movement and action through its centreline position. The unpredictable time-lag relationship between the yawing moment and the rudder-produced corrective moment, and their effects on the boat motion, is a complicated game.

Observations made by practical sailors give some indication that the timing of the helm action is as important as the amount of rudder applied. By improper timing of the rudder movement to fight the yawing motion, one may amplify the rolling, as in a vicious circle. It has been suggested that by deliberately delaying the application of the rudder, in an attempt to fight the rolling instead of the yawing motion, some degree of success at stabilizing the boat can be achieved without using too much helm. Of course, the optimum timing of the corrective rudder action in order to cope successfully with effects of rolling and yawing will be different for different types of boats, depending on their inertia, the actual sail area and configuration used in any given condition, and on the shape of the underwater parts of the hull including keel and rudder.

A number of preventive measures to eliminate or alleviate the rolling induced by aerodynamic forces were investigated in the wind tunnel and have been discussed in the author's *Aero-Hydrodynamics of Sailing*. They are effective according to both theory and practice, if put into operation soon enough. The influence of the heading angle ß on rolling described below may serve as an example.

Figure 326a and b shows a number of graphs of recorded rolling oscillations for various heading angles ß from 145° to 200°. The angle of trim of the mainsail δm was 85° and constant. At the beginning of each run for the selected ß the rig was given an initial heel angle and then released. We can see that within the range of ß from 145° to 180° (Fig 326a), the angle of roll grows more or less rapidly with time, so the boat clearly manifests instability in rolling.

However, we may also notice that the rate at which the rolling angle increases with time depends on the course sailed, ß. Thus, for instance, when ß = 145°, the roll angle 25° is reached after eight swings to starboard. But at ß = 180°, the attained angle of roll is only 15°, after the same number of swings. The heading angle ß has therefore considerable effect on rollilng. The degree of instability (given by the curve in Fig 326) being a maximum at ß = 165°, decreases when ß increases, and when ß is about 190° (ie the boat is sailing by the lee), rolling

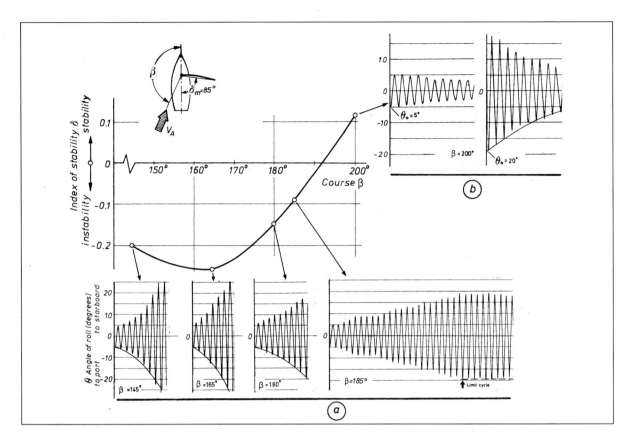

oscillation is no longer generated by the sail. From now on, when the heading angle ß is further increased, the sail does not work as a rolling engine but, on the contrary, as a *rolling preventer* or damping device (Fig 326b). This general trend in sail behaviour is well reflected by the stability index curve in Fig 326. Positive stability index (+ SI) indicates, in relative units, how quickly the rolling motion will be damped out by the action of aerodynamic forces. Negative stability index (–SI) indicates the degree of rolling instability.

Sailing by the lee has been always considered to be a cardinal sin on the part of the helmsman. Yet, according to wind tunnel findings, it may eliminate rolling. The danger of an unintentional jibe can be avoided by using a combination of fore-guy and preventer, or kicking strap, to lock the main boom effectively.

The most frequently committed error in the Finn class when rolling occurs is to ease the sheets. This is a natural reaction, learned from spilling the wind when close-hauled, but in this case it usually ends in an early bath. What happens to the sail if the mainsheet is eased when sailing nearly before the wind? Figure 327 explains that the total force F_T is rotated, whereby the driving force F_R is reduced, and the heeling force F_H acts now to windward. Yachtsmen not accustomed to capsizing to windward are taken by surprise by such a turn of events. In the Finn class it is usually not even necessary to ease the sheets to capsize, merely doing nothing can suffice.

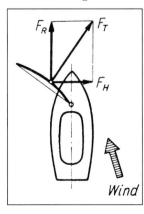

Fig 326 Rolling intensity (rate of growth or decay) recorded at different heading angles. Note that the most vigorous rolling occurs when the heading angle is about 165 degrees. Thereafter, when bearing away, the intensity of the rolling diminishes; and, when sailing by the lee, the sail operates as a roll-damping device.

Fig 327 Easing sheets when the boat rolls may cause a capsize to windward due to the action of the heeling force, F_H, directed to windward.

The most commonly encountered hydrodynamic force of a rhythmic or periodic nature is that due to the action of waves on hull. Thus, rolling can also be induced by waves. The forced, synchronous rolling caused by a number of successive waves is similar in its nature to what children experience when using a swing: they quickly learn that by 'pumping' at proper time intervals, ie, in synchronism with the swing motion, they can move with ever increasing amplitude.

When a boat meets several regular waves in succession which are 'tuned' to the natural rolling period of the boat, the roll-exciting energy of each wave adds to the rolling energy of the boat acquired in the previous roll; the successive roll increments being proportional to the wave slope (steepness). Thus the boat will tend to roll with increasing angular velocity and to an ever increasing angle of roll. If the damping effectiveness of the hull, together with its keel and rudder, is small, and the energy added by the wave train continues to exceed the energy removed by damping, the boat will roll more and more deeply and will inevitably head for disaster. Perhaps it might be added that such a resonant condition is not frequently met in practice. Fortunately, most waves encountered at sea are irregular, and often a series of waves travelling in different directions spread simultaneously. In such a confused sea, the boat rolls with an irregular period and amplitude. The rolling may build up to a maximum over a period of several rolls, when the boat motion is tuned to the wave train, and then detuning takes over and rolling diminishes. The successive maxima attained in rolling are not equal, nor are the number of rolls the same in the successive cycles from maximum to maximum. However, one should never ignore the possibility that fairly uniform trains of waves can be met and so the resonant conditions may occur. Then, if the waves are high and steep, containing a great deal of energy, and aerodynamic rolling forces also contribute, large roll amplitudes can build up in a few cycles, giving little warning that matters are past remedy. Synchronous or nearly synchronous conditions may arise at any time, waiting to catch the unwary. This explains the old rule of seamanship: *keep your eye on synchronism*. Accordingly, the practical way to ease wave induced rolling is to change course, and radically. The next remedy is to reduce speed, thereby changing the period of encounter with roll-producing waves.

One more factor must be considered when studying the whys and wherefores of excessive rolling – broaching tendencies and casualties amongst modern yachts in rough seas. There is growing evidence that contemporary boats, including modern fishing boats, are not as seaworthy as their predecessors. There are good reasons, both theoretical and practical, to believe that the trend in yacht design towards:

• Greater beam
• Reduced area of the hull underbody
• Lighter displacement
• Higher centre of gravity
• Increased freeboard

directed towards higher speed for a given rating, is likely to be incompatible with seaworthiness requirements. Thus, for example, the fashion of reducing the fin area shown in Fig 328 (*Prospect of Whitby*), may have originated from the assumption that most of the hydrodynamic lateral resistance to combat leeway is

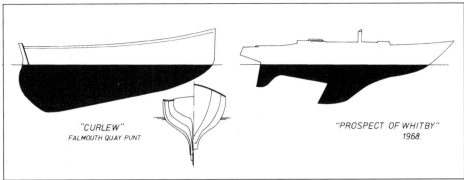

"CURLEW"
FALMOUTH QUAY PUNT

"PROSPECT OF WHITBY"
1968.

Fig 328 The long keels of old fishing and pilot boats provided good directional stability and were also efficient roll-damping devices. In these two respects, modern boats with separated fin-rudders are deficient.

generated near the leading edge, and that the area aft of the section of greatest draft contributes only skin friction. There is some evidence that this may be justified in light to moderate winds, when fin-keel action as a roll-damping device is of no significance. Under such conditions, the boat's speed, V_S, is nearly proportional to the true wind speed, V_T, so that the hydrodynamic side force balances the aerodynamic side force with little change in the leeway angle. However, in severe wind and sea conditions, the shape and area of the hull underbody (keel shape) become the seaworthiness factor of paramount importance. A glance at the hull form of an old fishing boat *Curlew* in Fig 328, an ancestor of cruising yachts before speed fever descended on sailing people, should suffice to show how much contemporary hull forms have departed from the older but sounder forms of sailing craft. These seaworthy fishing and pilot boats, capable of standing up to the severe gales of the western approaches to Britain, were built some hundred years ago without much mathematics, and they were sailed by men without any relieving hope that hovering helicopters or lifeboats might pick them from the sea if anything went wrong.

For this and other practical reasons their builders had to satisfy a number of requirements. To mention just a few: the vessels were expected to keep the sea and work on it all year round and in all weathers, and to have an easy motion which provided a stable working deck in reasonably rough water over a range of speeds when fishing or carrying pilots. These boats were not designed in the modern sense of the word. They evolved, like sea animals, by natural selection of the fittest to the environmental demands of the sea, through a long but reliable process of trial-and-error which creates more advanced forms and mercilessly eliminates the unsuitable. In yacht design, as in biology, the evolutionary process rewards faithful representation of reality (pitiless sea) with high degree of survival probability; unfaithful images of reality have a low survival value. It has been correctly observed that 'the intellectual exercise of selecting a boat is largely a self-deluding justification for an emotional decision.' Viewed from this point, the hull of the better fishing or pilot boat of the past can be regarded as a genuinely seaworthy form. And it should perhaps be remembered that the *Jolie Brise*, converted to a cruising yacht, became one of the most famous ocean racers of her day; in 1925 she won the first Fastnet Race.

Despite what we would like to believe, there is no such thing as higher performance or higher speed without penalty. A convincing example of this point might be the Australian entry for the America's Cup (Spring 1995) folding in half in weather conditions far from severe.

8 • THE KATZMAYR EFFECT

'What do you imagine that it means?' remarked Watson. 'I have no data yet. It is a capital mistake to theorize before one has data. Insensibly one begins to twist facts to suit theories, instead of theories to suit facts.'

Sir Arthur Conan Doyle, Sherlock Holmes

There exists a certain lack of correlation between the sail efficiency in terms of L/D ratio and drag measured in the course of wind tunnel tests or in full-scale trails, and in those established from a theoretical basis. We should not be surprised by these inconsistencies: similar differences are observed in aeronautics, despite the conspicuous development of computational techniques and testing facilities.

The question arises as to whether this discrepancy might be due to the wind unsteadiness which occurs in real sailing conditions. Without doubt, of all the natural energy sources, the wind is the most variable; it is known that the true wind, V_T, which determines the apparent wind, V_A, is seldom steady either in direction or velocity. Figure 329 illustrates a record of short-time variation in wind direction. And an earlier Fig 294c demonstrates the changes in the apparent wind V_A due to variation in the true wind *speed* alone and also due to variation in the true wind *direction* alone. Measured variations of V_T are frequently in the order of ± 20 degrees in direction and ± 3 knots in velocity at approximately rhythmic intervals.

Fig 329 A record of short-time variation in wind direction.

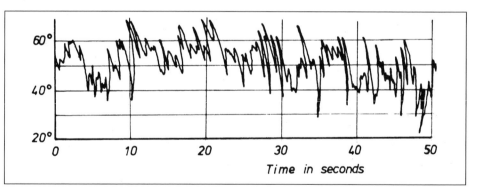

This kind of incidence variation experienced by sails in natural conditions is similar to the periodic changes in direction of air flow investigated by Katzmayr over 70 years ago (3.12). In the course of wind tunnel tests, he showed that the average drag of an aerofoil could be drastically reduced, or even made negative (propulsion), by altering the direction of the wind periodically with a sufficiently large amplitude. Figure 330 gives typical results of his tests performed on a thin aerofoil of aspect ratio 6. Depending on the amplitude of wind oscillation, the C_L versus C_D curves obtained in unsteady wind conditions are bodily shifted towards a lower drag relative to the curve representing steady wind conditions, over the range of C_L and C_D values appropriate to close-hauled sailing. A shift of such magnitude signifies a marked improvement in aerofoil efficiency.

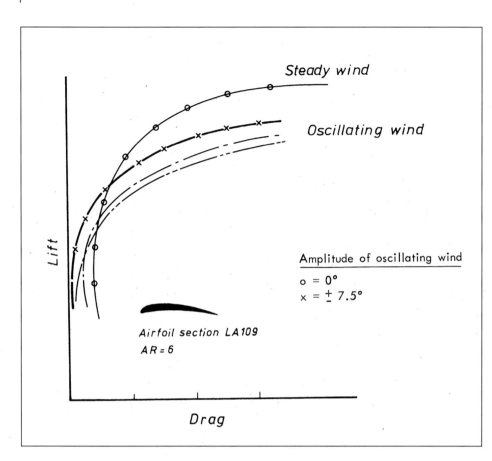

Lift

Steady wind

Oscillating wind

Amplitude of oscillating wind

o = 0°
x = ± 7.5°

Airfoil section LA109
AR = 6

Drag

Fig 330 Katzmayr's experimental results. The effect of periodically varying wind direction on lift and drag.

An interesting point is that, as reported by Karman (3.13), Otto Liliental, a 19th century glider pioneer, observed that a natural, unsteady, undulating wind is more favourable for soaring flight than a steady, uniform one. In his gliding experiments (which ended fatally) he found that a non-uniform wind facilitates soaring even in the absence of upward thermal components.

As a matter of fact, some soaring birds, notably the albatross, are capable of extracting energy from a wind with velocity variation of the sort which generally prevails in the natural wind, particularly in the lower layer of the atmosphere.

Thus, the dynamic soaring flight of birds clearly proves that unpowered flight without permanent loss of altitude is possible. And moreover that a non-uniform wind has more extractable kinetic energy than a uniform wind with the same average velocity.

Experiments made by Toussaint, Kerneis and Girault (3.14, 3.15) corroborated Katzmayr's discovery. They found that indeed the drag can largely be reduced and even *negative drag* can be obtained, so effortless soaring has a good experimental foundation. As in Katzmayr's tests, the airstream in the wind tunnel was made to change its direction periodically by means of deflecting blades mechanically activated and situated ahead of the foil tested. Some of the results taken from reference 103 and shown in Fig 331 demonstrate considerable improvement in the polar curves C_L versus C_D with increasing amplitude of oscillations; and negative values for the average drag were obtained in some cases for relatively large values of the average lift. Various rates of oscillation were tried, but without any appreciable difference in the results.

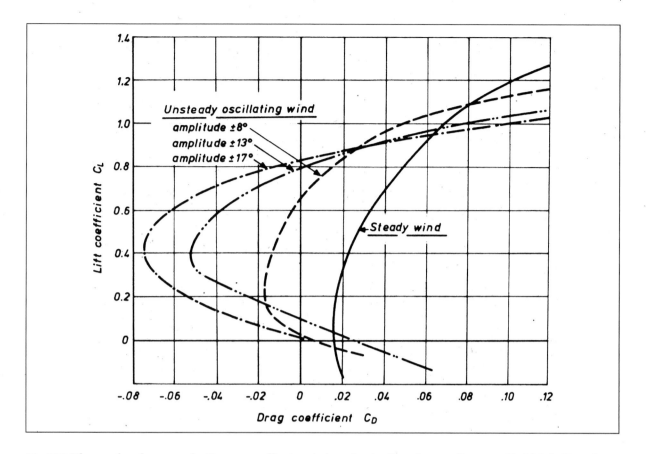

Fig 331 The results of tests on the Katzmayr effect carried out by the French experimenters (Ref 3.14). Note that large values of negative drag were obtained. It was found that the rate of variation in wind direction did not materially affect the results. What matters is the amplitude of oscillation (compare the drag recorded when the amplitude of oscillation was ± 17° with that when the amplitude was ± 8°). For the sake of clarity the drag scale is enlarged.

With a little consideration we can see that it is possible to combine two kinds of motions: 1) when the angle of incidence of the airfoil varies in a harmonic manner in a steady wind (as in the case of pumping); 2) when the airfoil is fixed, but the wind changes its direction periodically relative to the foil, thus varying the effective incidence angle too. It was found that by a judicious combination of these two motions, a very large improvement in airfoil efficiency could be achieved (3.15).

It appears surprising at first that a negative average drag can be obtained when a wind blows as often and as strongly in one and then in the other direction relative to the average direction. Why should an oscillating wind reduce the airfoil drag?

There is nothing mysterious about the Katzmayr effect. A simplified explanation is presented in Fig 332a and b in which, for the sake of simplicity, the air inertia forces such as are usually involved in oscillatory motion, are not considered. L_b and D_b denote the basic lift and drag, which are measured in relation to the average wind direction at which the aerofoil operates (at incidence angle α). As the wind direction changes and the incidence angle increases by $+ \triangle\alpha$, a component of instantaneous lift L_i on the average wind direction, marked $-D_i$

in Fig 332a, is substracted from the *basic* drag, D_b. When the wind direction changes by $-\triangle\,\alpha$ in the opposite direction as shown in Fig 332b, the instantaneous lift component D_i on the average wind direction is *added* to the basic drag.

Within the usual working range of angles of incidence, however, the lift components to be substracted from the basic drag are larger than those to be added, simply because lift at the larger angles of incidence ($\alpha + \triangle\alpha$) is much greater than that at the smaller incidence ($\alpha - \triangle\alpha$). The mean component of lift, parallel to the average wind direction, will therefore reduce the drag which would otherwise be experienced in steady wind conditions.

Whether or not, in fact, the Katzmayr effect is really responsible for the difference between the results of full scale sail tests and the results of laboratory experiments, is an open question which will perhaps one day provide some lucky investigator with the opportunity for some fascinating research into the dynamic aspects of sailing in the natural sea and wind.

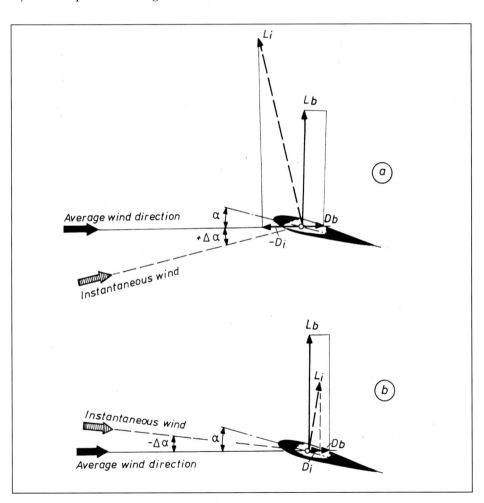

Fig 332
An explanation of why an oscillating wind causes drastic reduction of drag. This figure shows clearly that the effect found by Katzmayr is rational and readily explicable.

APPENDICES

APPENDIX 1 • ABOUT FORCES AND VECTORS

The Singular Incident of the Vectorial Tribe

It is rumored that there was once a tribe of Indians who believed that arrows were vectors. To shoot a deer due northeast, they did not aim an arrow in the northeasterly direction; they sent two arrows simultaneously, one due north and the other due east, relying on the powerful resultant of the two arrows to kill the deer.

Skeptical scientists have doubted the truth of this rumor, pointing out that not the slightest trace of the tribe has ever been found. But the complete disappearance of the tribe through starvation is precisely what one would expect under the circumstances; and since the theory that the tribe existed confirms two such diverse things as the nonvectorial behaviour of arrows and the Darwinian principle of natural selection, it is surely not a theory to be dismissed lightly.

B Hoffmann, About Vectors

CHARACTERISTICS OF FORCE AND MOTION

It can easily be proved that if a body is moving at a given speed and in a given direction, its motion is the result of certain forces applied to it. Of course, in ordinary life we are all aware of forces weak and strong, but to predict the effect of a force its special characteristics must be known, so it is customary to treat it as a measurable quantity.

A force can be represented graphically as in Fig A1. Here the line AB represents a force of about 5 lb, the length of the line showing its magnitude and the arrow at B its direction, while A at the other end of the line is the point at which the force is applied.

Fig A1 The everyday concept of a force is a push or a pull which can be of different origins. These pushes and pulls, ie forces, can be exerted by our muscles or be a result of wind pressure exerted on sails or water pressure acting on hulls. For convenience, the force can be graphically represented by a *vector*, that is by an arrow which has three characteristics: magnitude, direction and point of application. Once the forces acting on a boat are known, her behaviour (acceleration, velocity, angle of heel) can be predicted.

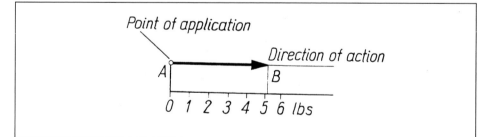

A force then has three characteristics:

1 Magnitude
2 Direction
3 Point of application

These are also characteristics of such quantities as velocity, acceleration, and pressure; any quantity which fulfils the requirements a, b and c above is known as a *vector*, and can be represented graphically in a similar way to the force in Fig A1. The weight of a body, for example, although actually distributed with its mass, can be drawn as a single vector, applied at the point which is called the centre of gravity (CG). With a simple geometrical shape such as a ball, the CG is at its centre, but the CG of a yacht is more difficult to find.

A very important characteristic of the CG is that a body suspended or supported at the CG will remain in equilibrium; in other words, if a body is turned about its CG to a new position, it will remain there. An iron ball again is the classic example of this rule. A vector representing graphically forces due to gravity will have its point of application at the CG of a body.

The action of a force may set a body in motion, or may change the velocity or direction of motion of a body already moving. It is difficult to find an example in which only one force is applied, since normally at least two forces act simultaneously. Even in such a simple case as a stone falling through the air under the force of gravity, there is also a force of air resistance which acts upward, reducing the velocity.

The elementary mechanics of motion were formulated by Sir Isaac Newton (1643–1727) in three laws, but for our purpose it is sufficient to consider two only:

1 *The Principle of Inertia*. Every body remains at rest or in uniform motion in a straight line when acted on by a system of forces whose resultant force is zero.

2 *The Independence of Forces*. Every external force acting on a body produces acceleration of that body in the direction of the acting force. This acceleration is directly proportional to the magnitude of the force and inversely proportional to the mass of the body:

$$a = \frac{F}{m}$$

where   a = acceleration ft/sec^2

F = force in lb

m = mass in slugs

$$(1 \text{ slug} = \frac{1 \text{ lb/sec}^2}{32.2 \text{ ft}})$$

A floating boat being hauled along by a rope as in Fig A2 provides an illustration of the relations between forces and motion. For the boat to move at a uniform velocity the water resistance R must be equal to force F, but acting in opposite directions. If the pulling force F is suddenly stopped, the boat will continue to move ahead (due to inertia), but at a gradually lessening speed (retardation) until she comes to rest due to water resistance.

There are still other forces acting which do not contribute to the motion of the boat: her weight, W, and the vertical upward buoyancy force acting on the immersed hull, $\triangle$, the two again being equal and opposite.

While the boat is in steady motion the distance covered increases in proportion to the time elapsed. This may be stated symbolically

$$S = V \times T$$

where   S = distance in feet

V = velocity in ft/sec

T = time in seconds

Fig A2 When the boat is acted upon by a number of forces of different origins which are in equilibrium (balance) she will move steadily (with uniform velocity). Note that the weight W of the boat is a force (the pull of the Earth) just like any other force except for two peculiarities: it is vertical and unavoidable.

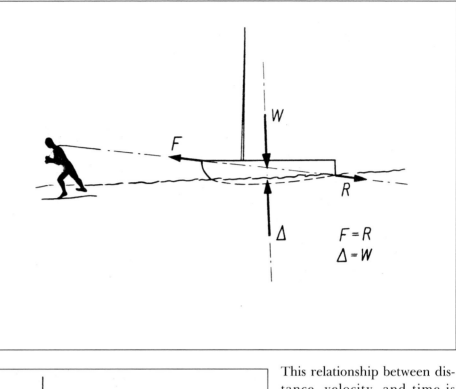

Fig A3 Time/distance graph for a boat sailing with uniform (constant) velocity. In such a case, as illustrated in Fig A2, the forces acting on the boat are in equilibrium.

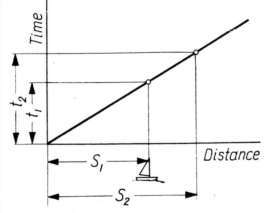

This relationship between distance, velocity, and time is expressed graphically as a straight line in Fig A3.

When the boat of Fig A2 is on the point of being hauled from her position at rest, the velocity is zero. When the force F is first applied, the velocity will not be uniform, but will be increasing to a point; the distance covered by the boat can be calculated from the equation:

$$S = \tfrac{1}{2} at^2$$

where
S = distance in feet
a = acceleration in ft/sec^2
t = time in seconds

After a certain time, t, when the applied force F has become equal to the resistance of the water, R, the velocity will be constant, and the equation for uniform velocity ($S = V \times t$) will apply. The acceleration of the boat in the initial stage is greater the greater the force F.

The equation $a = F/m$ implies that the magnitude of the acceleration depends on the boat's mass. If the force F is the same, the acceleration will be greater for the lighter boat. Figure A4 shows the distance sailed by two yachts with similar rigging but of different displacement (mass) during a short squall.

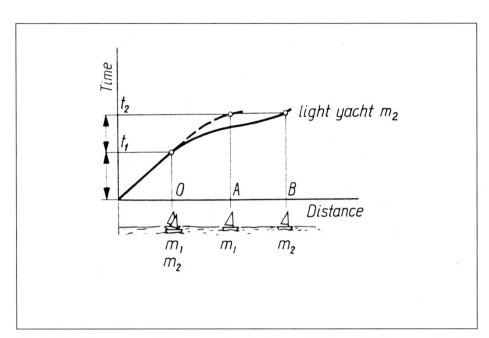

Fig A4 Time/distance graph for two accelerating boats of different displacement (mass). If a boat begins to accelerate, ie increases her speed, some agency is at work. In our case this agency is an increased driving force due to squall. The same net driving force will produce different accelerations depending on the boat's displacement. If mass m_2 of a lighter boat is half the mass m_1 of a heavier boat then under the action of the same net driving force, the acceleration of the lighter boat will be double of that of the heavier boat.

Acceleration is defined as the time rate of change of velocity, ie how much velocity changes, say, per second. The displacement (mass) of a boat is a measure of her inertia, ie her reluctance to change in speed. The acceleration caused by the force propelling a boat is proportional in magnitude to this force and is inversely proportional to the mass of the boat.

It might be added that ordinarily we think of speed and velocity as being the same, but in scientific parlance these two terms have slightly different meanings.

Assume that at the time they encountered the squall both were at the same position O and sailing at the same velocity; the mass (m_1) of yacht 1 is larger than the mass (m_2) of yacht 2. If we also assume that during a squall lasting $t_2 - t_1$ seconds, both yachts were sailing under the same increased sail force, F, then the acceleration of the lighter yacht $a_2 = F/m_2$ will be greater than the acceleration of the heavier one, $a_1 = F/m_1$, and so yacht 2 will cover a longer distance (OB) than yacht 1 (OA).

The product of mass and velocity, $m \times V$, is called momentum. A heavy yacht must drop her sails some distance before reaching her mooring, so that her momentum can be dissipated by the resistance of the water, R, during a period of time t, ie, $m \times V = R \times t$. The graph in Fig A5 illustrates the braking time for two yachts of different displacements entering a port at the same speed. It is evident that for the heavier yacht it is not only more difficult to gather speed, but also to stop. For this reason, the heavier yacht is less sensitive to the wave action.

Fig A5 Time/distance graph for two decelerating (breaking) boats of different displacements.

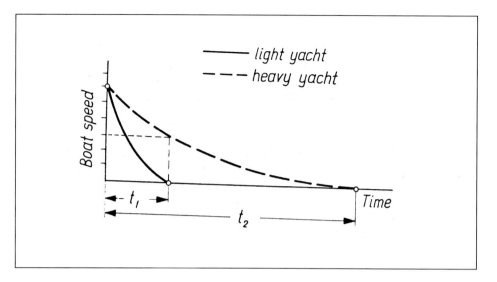

THE PARALLELOGRAM OF FORCES AND VELOCITIES

Newton's second law states that each force acting on a body produces acceleration in the direction of its action. If a body receives several accelerations simultaneously, an observer will detect only their combined effect, that is, that the body is affected in one direction only.

Figure A6 shows a boat hauled by two ropes, spaced symmetrically, the force acting on each rope being F. Under the action of these two forces, the boat will move in the direction midway between the ropes, as though instead of two forces there were only the one resultant force F_T. The direction and the magnitude of this F_T can be found graphically by constructing the so called '*parallelogram of forces*'. Two adjacent sides represent the direction and size of the two forces F, and the diagonal drawn across the complete parallelogram from the point at which the forces are applied gives the direction and magnitude of the resultant force. Moreover, the construction of the parallelogram, which makes it possible to replace two forces by one force, also works the other way, so that one force can be replaced by two forces, a process which is known as the *resolution of a force*.

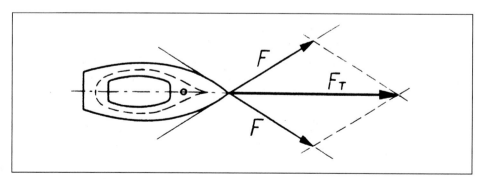

Fig A6 An example of geometrical addition of two vectors F into the single resultant (total) vector F_T. This resultant vector has the same physical effect as the original component vectors taken together. The term vector comes from the Latin verb meaning *convey*.

This method is useful in practice, for when studying the motion of a yacht it is often easier to treat the action of the force by resolving it into convenient directions. In this case the vector representing a total force must be treated as the diagonal of a chosen parallelogram. For instance, it is sometimes convenient to resolve the aerodynamic force F_T on the sail (Fig A7)

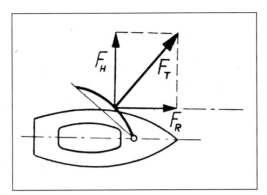

Fig A7 An example of resolution of a total vector F_T into two components F_H and F_R. The advantage of such a method of breaking up a single vector into components is that the analysis of a boat behaviour is thereby simplified. Splitting of a single vector into components is the reversed process of the geometrical addition demonstrated in Fig A6.

into forces acting in two directions: the driving force F_R along the direction of the boat motion, and the heeling force F_H perpendicular to it. Velocities, and indeed vectors of any kind, can be treated in the same way, adding and resolving them by using the parallelogram of forces.

Suppose a yacht (as in Fig A8) is sailing at a velocity V_S heading toward a marker buoy M which the helmsman wishes to round to port. At the point A she meets a strong current of velocity V_C. Obviously the yacht will tend to drift to starboard, since the resultant velocity V_R and course sailed are not in the direction of the buoy (Fig A8a). Now, by resolving V_R into its forward-motion

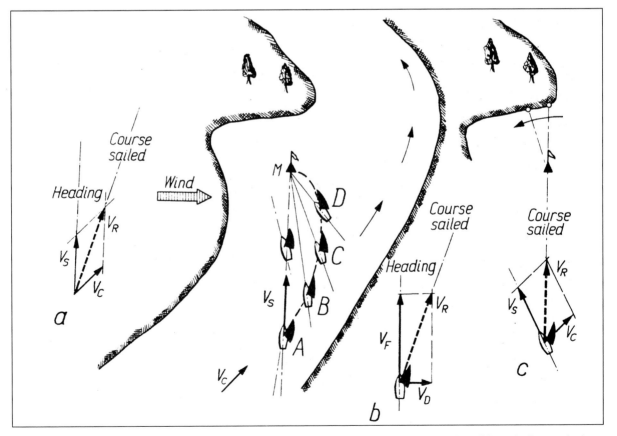

Fig A8 The motion of a boat affected by the river current can be analysed more easily by adding the boat velocity V_S and the current velocity V_C as vectors and considering the effect of the resultant velocity on the actual course in relation to the destination buoy.

component V_F, and its drift component V_D (as in Fig A8b), the basic velocity in the direction of the buoy and the drift velocity can be obtained. If an inexperienced helmsman keeps his boat always heading toward the buoy, the boat will follow the course shown by the curve ABCD. Eventually he might even be compelled to tack before he can round the buoy. To avoid this and reach the buoy by the shortest course in the shortest time, the helmsman should choose his course so that the boat velocity V_s combined with the current velocity V_c will produce a resultant velocity V_R in the direction of the buoy (Fig A8c). In practice this means selecting some object, such as a tree on the horizon, behind the buoy and steering so that it remains fixed relative to the buoy.

Appendix 2 • Reynolds Number and 'Scale Effect'

Total drag of a foil, or any object immersed in the moving air (or water) can be calculated from the formula:

$$D = C_D \times \frac{\rho V^2}{2} \times S$$

$$D = C_D \times q \times S \qquad\qquad\qquad\qquad \text{Eq 1}$$

This means that the drag, D, apart from being proportional to the flow dynamic pressure $q = \frac{\rho V^2}{2}$ and projected area of the object S is also proportional to the total drag coefficient C_D. In turn C_D depends on the shape of the object and on the flow pattern accompanying the given form. One might presume that, say, the flow past a circular mast would always follow the same pattern, hence the drag coefficient of mast C_D would be fairly constant. But as we shall see, this is not entirely true.

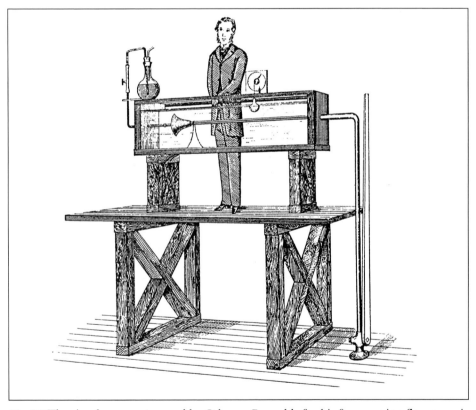

Fig A9 The simple apparatus used by Osborne Reynolds for his famous pipe-flow experiments which led to the concept of the Reynolds Number, Re, and its seminal and lasting implications in aeronautics, ship science and yacht design. The figure is taken from Reynolds's original paper 'An Experimental Investigation of the Circumstances Which Determine Whether the Motion of Water in Parallel Channels Shall Be Direct or Sinuous and the Law of Resistance in Parallel Channels', published in the Philos. Trans. of the Royal Society in 1883, London (174, pp 935–982).

Experiments carried out by Osborne Reynolds (Fig A9), in which he studied the transition from laminar to turbulent flow, led him to the conclusion that the critical velocity above which the flow will be laminar, and at which transition occurs, depends upon the *ratio of inertia forces to the friction forces* involved.

Inertia forces can be defined as the reluctance of air (or water) to move out of the way of the object subjected to the flow and then to close in behind.

Friction forces can be understood as a result of viscous shear stress operating over a given 'wetted' surface area (see Ref 2.9).

It can be proved that in mathematical form the ratio of inertia to friction forces can be nondimensionally expressed as follows:

$$\frac{\text{inertia force}}{\text{friction force}} = \frac{VL}{\nu} \qquad\qquad \text{Eq 2}$$

where: V = flow velocity (in ft/sec)

L = length of the object, usually measured along the flow direction (in ft)

ν = coefficient of kinematic viscosity (in ft^2/sec) of air (or water)

Reynolds himself did not give his name to the above parameter (2); it was Arnold Sommerfeld – a German physicist involved in quantum theory – who named the parameter in honour of Reynolds in 1908.

Since at a 'normal' temperature of 15 degrees (69°F), the kinematic viscosity of *air* at sea level is $\nu_A = 1.57/10^4$ ft^2/sec, the Reynolds Number can be written:

$$Re = \frac{V \times L}{1.57/10^4} = 6370 \times V \times L \ (V \text{ in ft/sec, L in ft}) \qquad \text{Eq 3}$$

or $Re = 68500 \times V \times L$, if V is in m/sec and L is in m.

The kinematic viscosity of *water* is $\nu_w = 1.23/10^5$ ft^2/sec, hence the Reynolds Number may be written:

$$Re = \frac{V \times L}{1.23/10^5} = 81300 \times V \times L \qquad\qquad \text{Eq 4}$$

or $Re = 877200 \times V \times L$, if V is in m/sec and L is in m.

Tables 1 and 2 give the Reynolds Numbers for various velocities of air and water flow calculated on the assumption that the characteristic streamwise length of the object L = 1 ft. The corresponding values of speed in four different units – ft/sec, m/sec, knots and Beaufort scale – are given in Table 3 at the end of this appendix.

What makes the Reynolds Number so important is that it is related to what we may call *dynamic similarity* or *scale effect*, a problem of enormous practical significance when comparing the flow patterns and associated forces developed at different speeds on objects of varying size.

If the Reynolds Number remains the same, the flow patterns will be geometrically similar. With geometrically similar flows round, say, two foils or hulls of different size, the corresponding streamlines will be geometrically similar, the relevant pressure distribution will be similar too, and hence the force coefficients will also be the same.

Table 1		
Reynolds Numbers (Re) for various velocities of air flow (Length L = 1 ft)		
Velocity V (FT/SEC)	V (KNOTS)	Re
5	2.96	$3.19 \times 1 \times 10^4$
10	5.92	6.37
15	8.88	9.55
20	11.85	$1.27 \times 1 \times 10^5$
25	14.80	1.59
30	17.75	1.91
35	20.70	2.23
40	23.65	2.55
45	26.60	2.87
50	29.60	3.19
55	32.50	3.50
60	35.50	3.82

Table 2		
Reynolds Numbers (Re) for various velocities of air flow (Length L = 1 f)t		
Velocity V (FT/SEC)	V (KNOTS)	Re
1	0.59	$0.81 \times 1 \times 10^5$
2	1.18	1.63
3	1.77	2.44
4	2.37	3.25
5	2.96	4.06
6	3.55	4.88
7	4.15	5.70
8	4.74	6.51
9	5.33	7.32
10	5.92	8.13
11	6.51	8.95
12	7.10	9.76
13	7.70	$1.06 \times 1 \times 10^6$
14	8.28	1.14
15	8.88	1.22
16	9.47	1.30
17	10.05	1.38
18	10.65	1.46
19	11.25	1.55
20	11.85	1.63

Different combinations of model scale, flow velocity and fluid density give the same coefficients if the relevant Reynolds Numbers are the same. Thus, smaller scale can be compensated for by a larger velocity; for example, if the diameter of, say, a mast is reduced by half, then the flow speed should increase twofold to be sure that the same drag coefficient C_D is applicable in both cases (Eq 1). Since the kinematic viscosity of water is roughly eight times smaller than that of air, the flow velocity of water must be also by eight times lower than that of air, in order for the flow patterns developed round two identical foils – one operating in water and another in air – to be similar.

The phenomenon of transition from laminar to turbulent flow within BL is fundamental when considering aero or hydrodynamic properties and merits of various forms of foils to be used in yacht design as sails, keels or rudders. The problem of flow separation, and hence the problem of calculating drag as well as lift, is governed by this transition. Analysis of Fig A10 should clarify the issue. It shows the variation of the total drag of a circular cylinder (mast) as a function of Reynolds Number. It can be noticed that in a narrow range of Reynolds Number from 2.0×10^5 to 2.5×10^5 ie, from Re = 200,000 to Re = 250,000 the drag coefficient can drop drastically, from about 1.2 to about 0.4.

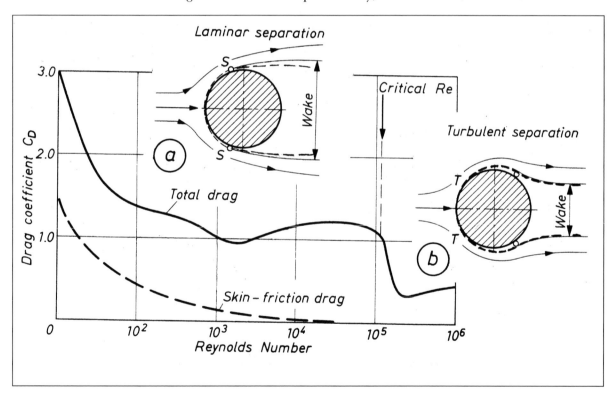

Fig A10 Dependence of the total drag coefficient of a circular cylinder on Reynolds Number Re. At Re from 1×10^5 to about 4×10^5, transition takes place in the BL forward of the separation points, accompanied by a sudden rearward shift of the separation points and attendant abrupt reduction in the size of the wake and drag coefficient to $^1/_3$ its value at lower Re!

In other words, when the Reynolds Number is small (sketch a), the transition point is downstream of the separation point S, and early separation of laminar BL occurs. An increase in the Reynolds Number causes the transition point T to be shifted upstream (sketch b), the BL at the separation points is already turbulent and so clings to the surface longer.

The drag coefficient is ordinarily found to be a slowly varying function of Reynolds Number, but in some instances, as shown in Fig A10, rather sharp changes may occur depending on the position of the separation point. In the case of laminar separation, the separation points, distinguished in the sketch in Fig A10 by small circles, are located in front part of the cylinder. The stream-lines are diverted and encompass a wide wake behind the cylinder. At a certain critical Reynolds Number, rapid transition to turbulent flow takes place, accompanied by a sudden rearward shift of separation points, and an attendant abrupt reduction in the wake size and associated decrease in the drag coefficient.

It should perhaps be stressed that the nondimensional lift and drag coefficients for geometrically similar foils which are set at the same angle to the incoming flow direction are function of one variable only, namely the Reynolds Number:

$$C_L = f(Re) \text{ and } C_D = f(Re) \qquad\qquad Eq\ 5$$

where $f(Re)$ designates – is a function of Re.

The actual value of Re at which transition occurs depends markedly on the disturbances in the free stream ahead of the object in the sense that the intensity of turbulence in the free stream exerts a decisive influence on the process of transition, accelerating its inception.

Experimental results published since Reynolds have vindicated his initial hypothesis that the process of transition from laminar to turbulent flow is the consequence of an instability in the laminar flow, ie, the breakdown of laminar flow and, hence, commencement of turbulence.

Lift and drag produced by thick foils operating in air (wing sails), or in water (keels, rudders) depend profoundly upon their size and the flow velocity, be it apparent wind or boat speed. This dependence, likewise that exhibited by the circular cylinder in Fig A10, is called the *scale effect*.

To avoid the pitfalls into which many yacht designers have fallen, it is necessary to have some appreciation of the possible anomalous if not downright bizarre behaviour of foils operating at Reynolds Numbers below 500,000. It appears that the most significant lift and drag anomalies arising from laminar separation occur below Re = 300,000; and then the thickness of the foil (particularly its nose radius) and its camber become the most prominent factors affecting foil efficiency in producing lift and associated lift/drag ratio.

Readily available data given in the NACA or NASA publications are relevant to high Re numbers, well above one million, which are not always applicable to sailing craft operating in light winds, and may be misleading.

The aerodynamic properties of thin foils and soft sails, whose stall is due to a leading edge separation, have been found to be relatively insensitive to changes due to the scale effect (Ref 2.4). For this reason, thin wings used in early, slow flying aircrafts such as World War I fighters, were proper and best. On the other hand, thick foils (including most 'modern' airfoils), yield embarrassingly poor results at low Reynolds Numbers. This is demonstrated in Figs A11–13.

A comprehensive discussion of many engineering problems associated with low Reynolds Numbers can be found in the proceedings of the International Conference: 'Aerodynamics at Low Reynolds Numbers $10^4 < Re < 10^6$', London 1986.

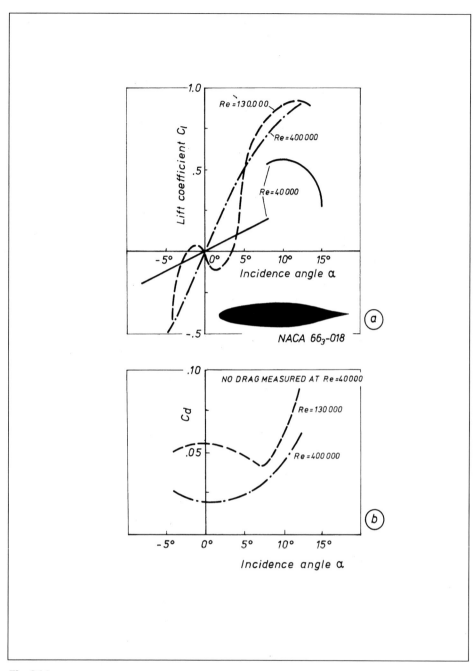

Fig A11

a) Lift curves for a smooth modern NACA symmetrical airfoil of 18 per cent thickness ratio at three low Reynolds Numbers. The unusual properties of the airfoil at Re = 130 000 are particularly evident in the angle of incidence range from – 4 to + 4 degrees, as evidenced by a wiggly lift curve.

b) Drag curves for the same airfoil at two low Reynolds Numbers. The drag curve relevant to Re = 130 000 shows less drag at 5 degrees angle of incidence than at zero – an almost incredible state of affairs.

The figure is based on an article by T J Mueller and S M Batill, 'Experimental Studies of Separation on a Two-Dimensional Airfoil at Low Reynolds Numbers' *AIAA Journal*, Vol 20, No 4, April 1982.

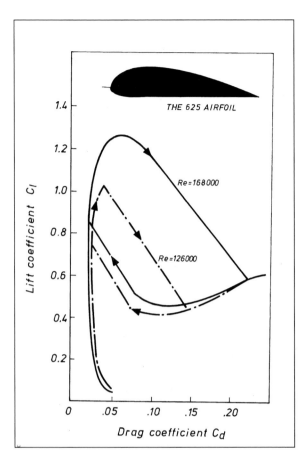

THE 625 AIRFOIL

Re=168000

Re=126000

Lift coefficient C_l

Drag coefficient C_d

Fig A12 The effect of two different low Reynolds Numbers on the polar diagrams for the Göttingen airfoil shown above the curves. Complicated flow phenomena such as separation, transition and reattachment (described elsewhere in the book) take place within the boundary layer and affect both lift and drag. The surface curvature of the foil, its roughness and vibration, and the free stream turbulence all play a part. As seen, the foil performance deteriorates rapidly when the Reynolds Number is reduced.

Another important property of any thick foil operating at low Reynolds Numbers is the so called *hysteresis loop*, occurring when the incidence angle α is first increased up to the value beyond the stall and then decreased. Once the flow over the suction side becomes separated, the process is irreversible in the sense that reducing α will not immediately result in reattachment. Typically, as α is increased, say to 14 degrees or beyond (see curve relevant to Re = 168,000) and complete separation over the suction side occurs, the incidence angle must then be reduced to around 6 degrees before the flow will again reattach. In other words, the polar curve will not retrace the upper portion of the loop, but will follow the lower part of the loop, with full reattachment not returning until incidence α is reduced to 6 degrees. In the meantime, the lift-producing capability of the foil is drastically reduced.

Fig A13 The Reynolds Number effect on lift and drag of an airfoil No 60R. As compared with properties of the foil as reflected by the polar diagram relevant to Re = 8 000 000 (8.0 × 10⁶), the properties of the same foil operating at a lower Re are much worst. For thick foils there is a certain Reynolds Number at which the foil will be efficient, below it the foil will be increasingly less efficient. Note for example that the lift coefficient produced at Re = 8 000 000 which is 1.4, drops to a value of about 1.0, ie, by nearly 30 per cent for the same foil operating at Re = 126 000. In this respect, the thin foil results are nearly independent of Re, since the separation point at the leading edge is well defined. A search of the literature will show little airfoil data available in low range Reynolds Numbers.

This figure and Fig A12 are based on 'Aerodynamics of Model Aircraft' by Schmitz F W, RTP translation No 2460, issued by Ministry of Aircraft Production.

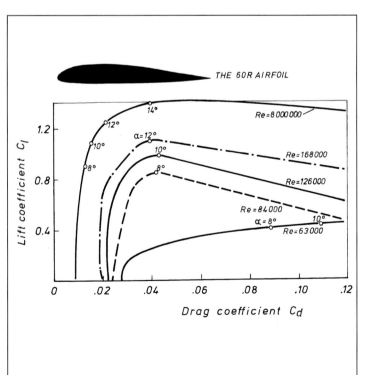

THE 60R AIRFOIL

Re=8 000 000

Re=168 000

Re=126 000

Re=84 000

Re=63 000

Lift coefficient C_l

Drag coefficient C_d

Table 3
Corresponding values of speed, in four different units

FT/SEC	M/SEC	KNOTS	BEAUFORT SCALE	FT/SEC	M/SEC	KNOTS	BEAUFORT SCALE
1.69	0.52	1		81.07	24.71	48	
3.38	1.03	2	1	82.76	25.22	49	
5.07	1.55	3		84.45	25.74	50	
				86.14	26.25	51	
6.76	2.06	4		87.83	26.77	52	10
8.44	2.57	5	2	89.52	27.28	53	
10.13	3.09	6		91.21	27.80	54	
				92.90	28.31	55	
11.82	3.60	7		94.58	28.83	56	
13.51	4.12	8		96.27	29.34	57	
15.20	4.63	9	3	97.96	29.86	58	
16.89	5.15	10		99.65	30.37	59	
18.58	5.66	11		101.34	30.89	60	
20.27	6.18	12		103.03	31.40	61	11
21.96	6.69	13		104.72	31.92	62	
23.65	7.21	14	4	106.41	32.43	63	
25.34	7.72	15		108.10	32.95	64	
27.02	8.24	16		109.78	33.46	65	
28.71	8.75	17		111.47	33.97	66	
30.40	9.27	18		113.16	34.49	67	
32.09	9.78	19	5	114.85	35.00	68	
33.78	10.30	20		116.54	35.52	69	
35.47	10.81	21		118.23	36.03	70	
37.16	11.33	22		119.92	36.55	71	
38.85	11.84	23		121.61	37.06	72	
40.54	12.36	24	6	123.30	37.58	73	
42.22	12.87	25		124.99	38.10	74	
43.91	13.38	26		126.68	38.61	75	
45.60	13.90	27		128.36	39.12	76	
47.29	14.41	28		130.05	39.64	77	
48.98	14.93	29		131.74	40.15	78	
50.67	15.44	30		133.43	40.67	79	
52.36	15.96	31	7	135.12	41.18	80	
54.05	16.47	32		136.81	41.70	81	
55.74	16.99	33		138.50	42.21	82	12
57.43	17.50	34		140.19	42.73	83	
59.12	18.02	35		141.88	43.24	84	
60.80	18.53	36		143.56	43.75	85	
62.49	19.05	37	8	145.25	44.27	86	
64.18	19.56	38		146.94	44.79	87	
65.87	20.08	39		148.63	45.30	88	
67.56	20.59	40		150.32	45.82	89	
69.25	21.11	41		152.01	46.33	90	
70.94	21.62	42		153.70	46.85	91	
72.63	22.14	43	9	155.39	47.36	92	
74.32	22.65	44		157.08	47.88	93	
76.00	23.16	45		158.77	48.39	94	
77.69	23.68	46		160.46	48.91	95	
79.38	24.19	47		162.14	49.42	96	
				163.83	49.93	97	
				165.52	50.45	98	
				167.21	50.96	99	
				168.90	51.48	100	

BEAUFORT SCALE OF WIND SPEED

BEAUFORT No	SEAMAN'S DESCRIPTION OF WIND	TERMS USED IN US WEATHER BUREAU FORECASTS	WIND SPEED		APPROXIMATE PRESSURE IN POUNDS PER FT2
			IN KNOTS	IN M/SEC	
0	Calm		Less than 1	Less than 0.3	Less than 0.01
1	Light air	Light	1–3	0.3–1.5	0.01–0.06
2	Light breeze		4–6	1.6–3.3	0.06–0.2
3	Gentle breeze	Gentle	7–10	3.4–5.4	0.2–0.4
4	Moderate breeze	Moderate	11–16	5.5–8.0	0.4–1.0
5	Fresh breeze	Fresh	17–21	8.1–10.7	1.0–2.0
6	Strong breeze		22–27	10.8–13.8	2.0–3.0
7	Moderate gale (high wind)	Strong	28–33	13.9–17.1	3.0–4.0
8	Fresh gale		34–40	17.2–20.7	4.0–6.0
9	Strong gale	Gale	41–47	20.8–24.4	6.0–9.0
10	Whole gale (heavy gale)		48–55	24.5–28.3	9.0–12.0
11	Storm	Whole gale	56–65	28.4–33.5	12.0–16.0
12	Hurricane	Hurricane	Above 65	Above 33.6	Above 16.0

BEAUFORT SCALE OF WIND SPEED

DESCRIPTION OF SEA	APPROXIMATE EFFECT ON RACING DINGHY	PSYCHOLOGICAL SCALE
Sea like a mirror		
Ripples, no foam crests	Crew sit on leeward side of boat or on centreline.	Boredom
Small wavelets, crests have a glassy appearance and do not break	Crew sit on windward side of boat	Mild pleasure
Large wavelets, crests begin to break. Perhaps scattered white caps	Crew ballasting on weather gunwale. Racers like 5–0–5, FD may plane	Pleasure
Small waves becoming longer. Fairly frequent white caps	Crew ballasting out hard over weather gunwale. Most dinghies will plane	Great pleasure
Moderate waves, taking a more pronounced long form. Many white caps, some spray	Light dinghies have to ease sheets in heavier gusts	delight
Large waves begin to form. Extensive white caps everywhere, some spray		Delight tinged with anxiety
Sea heaps up and white foam from breaking waves begins to be blown in well-marked streaks along the direction of the wind	Start reefing main sails small jibs	Anxiety tinged with fear
Moderately high waves of greater length. Edges of crests break into spindrift. The foam is blown in well-marked streaks along the direction of the wind.	Very difficult to sail, even under jib only	Fear tinged with terror
High waves. Dense streaks of foam along the direction fo the wind. Spray may affect visibility. Sea begins to roll		Great terror
Very high waves with long overhanging crests. The surface of the sea takes on a white appearance. The rolling of the sea becomes heavy and shocklike. Visibility is affected		Panic
Exceptionally high waves. The sea is completely covered with long white patches of foam. Visibility is affected. Small- and medium-sized ships are lost to view for long periods.		I want my mummy
The air is filled with foam and spray. Sea completely white with driving spray. Visibility very seriously affected.		Yes, Mr Jones

APPENDIX 4

CONVERSION FACTORS

	MULTIPLY	BY	TO OBTAIN
LENGTH	inches	2.54	centimetres
	feet	0.3048	metres
	miles	5280	feet
	miles	1.609	kilometres
	miles	0.8684	nautical miles
	nautical miles	6080	feet
AREA	sq inches	6.45	sq centimetres
	sq feet	0.093	sq metres
	sq feet	144	sq inches
VOLUME	cubic feet	0.0283	cubic metres
	cubic feet	1728	cubic inches
VELOCITY (SPEED)	ft/sec	0.592	knots
	ft/sec	0.682	miles
	ft/sec	1.097	kilometres/hour
	ft/sec	0.305	metres/sec
	knot	1.69	ft/sec
	metre/sec.	3.28	ft/sec
	metre/sec.	3.6	kilometre
	kilometre/hour	0.911	ft/sec
	kilometre/hour	0.539	knots
	kilometre/hour	0.278	metres/sec
WEIGHT	tons (short)	2000	pounds
	tons (short)	907.18	kilograms
	tons (short)	0.907	tons (metric)
	tons (long)	2240	pounds
	tons (long)	1016	kilograms
	tons (metric)	1000	kilograms
	tons (metric)	2205	pounds
	kilogram	2.205	pounds
	pounds	0.454	kilogram
PRESSURE	Atmospheres	76.0	centimetres of mercury
	Atmospheres	29.92	inches of mercury
	Atmospheres	1.033	kilograms/sq centimetres
	Atmospheres	14.7	pounds/sq inch
	Atmospheres	2116.2	pounds/sq foot
	inches of water	5.198	pounds/sq foot
	inches of water	25.38	kilograms/sq metre
	kilogram/sq metre	0.2048	pounds/sq foot

REFERENCES AND NOTES

REFERENCES AND NOTES (PART I)

1.1 Boehmer R, 'West–east Transatlantic Sailing Records: Speed Analysis', Ancient Interface Symposium, November 1984.

1.2 Davidson K S M, 'The Mechanics of Sailing Ships and Yachts', Davidson Lab. Techn. Mem. No 135, 1956.

1.3 Marchaj C A, *Seaworthiness – the Forgotten Factor*, Adlard Coles Nautical UK and International Marine USA, 1986.

1.4 Waddington C H, *Tools for Thought*, Granada Publishing, 1977.

1.5 Heckstall-Smith B, *The* Britannia *and Her Contemporaries*, Methuen & Co Ltd, London, 1929.

1.6 Phillips-Birt D, *British Ocean Racing*, Adlard Coles Nautical UK, 1960.

1.7 Reynolds Brown A E, 'How the Sail Plans Changed', *Yachts and Yachting* Aug.5, 1955.

1.8 Barkla H M, 'Allometric Scaling of the Sailing Yacht', AIAA/SNAME Symp. Ancient Interface XVI Los Angeles, October 1986.

1.9 Marchaj C A, *Aero-Hydrodynamics of Sailing*, Adlard Coles Nautical, UK and International Marine, USA, 1979.

1.10 Boehmer R, '*Transat En Double*: An Analysis of On-Wind and Off-Wind Sailing Performance', Ancient Interface XV Proceed., 1985.

1.11 The Argos system is the result of a cooperative project between the French Centre National d'Études Spatiales (NES) and two branches of the USA Government – NASA and NOAA. The system utilizes the Tiros-N satellites to locate fixed and moving platforms emitting environmental data by use of a platform transmitter terminal (PTT). Argos is solely used for environmental application. PTTs placed on yachts provide an opportunity to collect some meteorological data. The tracking of yachts just gives the added, welcome benefits of safety and publicity for a race. Since 1979, the ARGOS has been used for a number of long distance ocean races.

1.12 Bernot I Y, 'Electronic Charts and Computer Aid for Navigation MACSEA', *Seahorse* Magazine, May/June 1986.

1.13 For instance, in *The Architectural Interpretation of History* by John Gloag (published in 1975 by Adam & Charles Black, London) we read following remark on page 246: 'The Corinthian, is a Columne lasciviously decked like a courtesan, and therein much participating (as all Inventions do) of the place where they were first born: Corinth having been (without controversie) one of the wantonest Towns in the World...'

REFERENCES AND NOTES (PART 2)

2.1 Newton's premise was as follows: assuming that the area of the plate is A, its projection normal to the air stream is A sin α, as indicated in Fig 29a. Therefore, the mass flow per unit time on this surface will be:

$$\rho_A \, (A \sin \alpha) \, V$$

The component of the stream speed V normal to the surface of the plate is V sin α. Since, according to Newton's *second law*, force equals mass flow times speed, we can write that the force F_N normal to the plate will be:

$$F_N = \rho_A \, (A \sin \alpha) V \, (V \sin \alpha) = \rho_A \, V^2 A \sin^2 \alpha$$

In Newton's time, the sine-squared law was incompatible with what could be observed in the case of flying or, in particular, soaring birds. Assuming, for example, that the only thing which holds an albatross moving at the speed of 15 miles an hour is the pressure acting upon the underside of its wing, then in order to develop a lift force equal to the bird's weight, its wing incidence should be in the order of 60 degrees. No bird could possibly soar or glide as they do with wings tilted to that degree, to say nothing about the drag factor.

As we shall learn soon, the magnitude of this lifting force is a function of the wing (or sail) shape, and can in some cases be fifty times greater than that calculated from Newton's sine-squared law.

2.2 This instrument takes its name from M Pitot, the French scientist who published in 1732 his 'Description of a Machine for the Measurement of the Velocity of Flowing Water'.

2.3 Clayton B R, Massey B S, 'Flow Visualisation in Water: a Review of Techniques', *Journal of Scient. Instr*; 44, 2–11 (1967).

2.4 Marchaj C A, *Aero-Hydrodynamics of Sailing*, Second edition, Adlard Coles Nautical UK and International Marine USA, 1988.

2.5 Williams A and Liljeberg H, 'Revival of the Flettner Rotor' SNAME Transactions, Vol 91, 1983.

2.6 Warner E P, Ober S, 'The Aerodynamics of Yacht Sails', SNAME Transactions, November 1925.

2.7 Gentry Arvel wrote a series of articles on sail interaction published during 1973 in *Sail* magazine. The distribution of streamlines about sails, such as those shown (for example) in Fig 46, was obtained by application of a device called an 'analog field plotter'. This equipment and a method of using it is described in:

1) *Journal of Royal Aer. Soc*, Vol 51, 1947: 'The use of Rheo-Electr. Analog in Certain Aer. Probl', by L Malavard.

2) Reports & Memor. Vol 28, Apr, 1924, 'An Electr. Method of Tracing Streamlines for the Two-Dimensional Motion of a Perfect Fluid', by E F Relf.

2.8 The experimental result obtained by means of pressure distribution measurements on a full scale Bristol fighter with unslotted and slotted wings (see Reports & Memor. No 1477 by A Ormerod, 1932) demonstrated that 'the lift coefficient of the main wing alone, operating behind the slot, never exceeds the maximum lift coefficient of the unslotted section', and that the slot bears the burden of the increase in lift.

2.9 Viscosity is a measure of the ease with which a fluid will flow. It can be also regarded as the 'stickiness' or internal friction of a fluid (be it air or water) which resists the sliding of one layer of fluid past another. Because of viscosity, a friction force occurs whenever air flows over the sail or mast surface. Although viscosity may appear very small in comparison with other forces acting on fluids in motion, it plays a vital role in the flow of air or water, the flow of blood, the lubrication of engine parts and many other areas of practical importance.

2.10 Marchaj C A, 'Wind Tunnel Tests in Support of !2 M Rig Designs', Southampton University, Rep. N 183, December 1973.

2.11 Theodorsen T, 'On the Theory of Wing Sections', NACA Rep No 383, 1930.

2.12 Gault D, 'An Experimental Investigation of Regions of Separated Laminar Flow', NACA, Tech. Note No 3505, 1955.

2.13 Kraemer K, '*Flugelprofile in Kritishen Reynoldszahl-Bereich*', Forschung a.d. Geb.d.Ing. 27, 1961.

2.14 Wilkinson S, 'Static Pressure Distributions over 2 D Mast/Sail Geometries', *Marine Technology*, Vol 26, No 4, October 1989.

2.15 Davies P O, Dyke R W, Marchaj C A, 'The Wind Tunnel Balances in the Large Low Speed Tunnel at Southampton University', AASU Rep. No 208, December 1962.

2.16 Marchaj C A, 'The Aerodynamic Characteristics of a 2/5 scale Finn Sail and Its Efficiency When Sailing to Windward', SUYR Rep. No 13, 1964.

2.17 '*Ergebnisse der Aerodynamischen Versuchanstalt*', Göttingen, 1922, Germany.

2.18 Marchaj C A, 'Rig Development', a series of articles published in *Yachts and Yachting*, January–February, 1981.

2.19 Crosseck H, '*Beiträge zur Theorie des Segelns*', Berlin, 1925.

2.20 Gentry A E, 'The Application of Computational Fluid Dynamics to Sails', Proceedings of the Symp. on Hydrod. Perform. Enhancement for Marine Applications. Newport, Rhode Island, Nov 1988.

2.21 Ljungström F, 'Elements of Scientific Sailing', *Segel och Motor*, No 8, 1937.

2.22 The Paul Cayard Column, *Seahorse* magazine, January 1992.

2.23 Marchaj C A (in collaboration with J Howard-Williams), 'Design Factors Affecting Sail Power Based on Wind Tunnel Research into Rigs Used for Fishing Vessels, Part I', publ. MacAlister Elliot & Partners Ltd, Lymington, England, 1985.

2.24 Marchaj C A, 'The Comparison of Potential Driving Force of Various Rig Types Used for Fishing Vessels', Proceedings of the Eighth Chesapeake Sailing Yacht Symposium, US Naval Academy, Annapolis, 1987.

2.25 Ata Nutku, 'Model Tests with Sailboat Hulls II', Turkish Shipbuilding Research Institute, Istanbul, 1953.

2.26 Lanchester W F, 'Aerodynamics', London 1907.

In Appendix VIII, Propulsion by sails, we read: 'We may look upon the sailing boat, and especially the racing craft with its fin or deep keel, as an aerofoil combination in which the underwater and above-water reactions balance one another... Under these conditions, the problem resolves itself into an aerofoil combination in which the aerofoil acting in the air (the sail spread) and that acting underwater (the keel, fin, or dagger plate) mutually supply each other's reaction.

The result of this supposition is evidently that the minimum angle at which the boat can shape its course relative to the wind is the sum of the under- and above–water gliding angles.' Lanchester's 'gliding angles' are, in our terminology, the hydrodynamic and aerodynamic drag angles ε_H and ε_A respectively.

2.27 Marchaj C A, 'A Critical Review of Methods of Establishing Sail Coefficients', Proceedings of the Symposium; 'Tests on Sailing Boats', Napoli, Italy, June 1986.

2.28 Davidson K S M, 'Some Experimental Studies of the Sailing Yacht', Trans. SNAME, 1936.

2.29 Kerwin J E, Oppenheim B W, Mays I H, 'A Procedure for Sailing Performance Analysis based on Full Scale Log Entries and Towing Tank Data', MIT Dept of Ocean Eng. Rep. N 74–17, 1974.

Widespread discontent with the International Offshore Rule resulted in the launching of a new MIT project. Its aim was, 'To remove entirely the non-scientific basis for rating rules and time allowance handicaps that have always plagued the sport.' In principle. This new project is a combination of previous attempts to relate the speed potential to the measurable aero and hydrodynamic characteristics of each boat, and that of Davidson's technique of predicting the boat performance if the sail and hull forces are known or can reliably be assessed. A set of the *Baybee* sail coefficients is a part of the project.

2.30 Eiffel G, *The Resistance of the Air and Aviation*, Constable & Co Ltd, London, 1913.

2.31 Although the use of sail area as a factor in yacht measurement was suggested in 1836 by Philip Maret, an English yachtsman who was far in advance of his day, the idea was rejected. It was only after years of fruitless agitation in the London magazine *Field* – under the editorship of the outstanding British naval architect Dixon Kemp – that sail area was reluctantly recognized as a factor which should be incorporated into the rating rule. Dixon Kemp's proposal was not, however, taken up in his own country, but in the USA first. In 1882 the Seawanhaka Corinthian Yacht Club of New York decided to adopt Kemp's suggestion in the form:

$$\frac{L \times S_A}{4000} = \text{Sail tons}$$

After one season of trials, this rating formula was changed to what has since been known as the 'Seawanhaka Rule':

$$\frac{L \times \sqrt{S_A}}{2} = \text{Racing length}$$

Until that time, and for some years after, the privilege of crowding unlimited sails on a restricted hull waterline had been cherished as 'an inalienable right' by the majority of British and American yachtsmen. The introduction of sail area as a rating factor was bitterly opposed: the slogan of the opposition being *a tax on sail is a tax on skill* (the skill in this context being that of 'the professional boat-handler who could keep a sand-bag boat on her keel and bring her in ahead').

Needless to say any rating rule based on hull geometry only (length and/or displacement) is bound to develop a yacht form of unwholesomely excessive sail-carrying power in relation to the hull size. Such a form, shown in the picture of *Suzanne* (Fig 116), and described in early yachting parlance as a 'brute', dominated the racing scene at the end of the 19th century.

2.32 Marchaj C A, Chapleo A Q, 'A Preliminary Note on the Results of Rigid Sail Tests in the Unheeled Position', Southampton University ACYR, February 1961.

2.33 Marchaj C A, Chapleo A Q, 'Visual Observation of the Flow around the Sails of a Model 12 Metre Yacht', SUYR No 4, September 1960.

2.34 The quotation taken from *Wooden Boat*, No 7, November 1986.

2.35 Marchaj C A, 'Planform Effect of a Number of Rigs on Sail Power', Proceedings of Regional Conference on Sail-Motor Propulsion, Manila, November 1985. The paper presented was the result of a research programme founded by the Overseas Development Administration of the British Government. The programme carried out by MacAlister Elliot and Partners Ltd, was aimed at improving the performance and the fuel economy of sailing fishing craft in the developing world.

2.36 The test envelope shown in the Fig A, ie, the driving force coefficient C_x versus heading angle $(\beta - \lambda)$, that encloses the complete family data, gives the best attainable driving force coefficients of a given rig. All measurement points which do not lie along the envelope curve represent C_x coefficients relevant to those sheeting

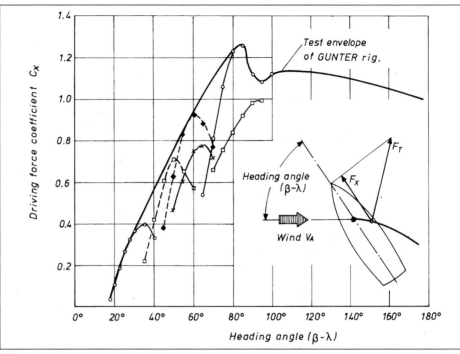

Fig A

angles which were not optimally adjusted to the heading angle variation. In other words, these should be taken as indicating the sort of mistake a crew may make when adjusting sails to the course sailed.

2.37 Field tests shown in Fig 148 – part of a project of the Overseas Development Administration of the British Government – were managed by MacAlister Elliot and Partners Ltd, Lymington, UK.

2.38 Polhamus E C, 'Prediction of Vortex-Lift Characteristics by a Leading Edge Suction Analogy', *Journal of Aircraft*, April 1971.

2.39 Küchenmann D, 'Types of Flow on Swept Wings', *Journal of the Royal Aeronautical Society*, October 1953.

2.40 Polhamus E C, 'Concept of Vortex Lift of Sharp Delta Wings based on a Leading Edge – Suction Analogy' – NASA TND – 3767.

2.41 The difference in static pressure recorded inside the tornado core and outside may easily reach 34 millimetres or 44 millibars. Such a difference in pressure over short distances may be comparable with the dynamic pressure of the wind. Thus, a pressure of eight millibars is, for example, the mean pressure of the wind hurricane force (75 mph) on a disc of one square foot normal to the wind direction. Much of the damage done by tornadoes is due to the bursting outwards of closed structures such as buildings, when the static pressure outside falls suddenly (2.4).

2.42 Bartlett G E and Vidal R J, 'Experimental Investigation of Influence of Edge Shape on the Aerodynamic Characteristics of Low Aspect Ratio Wings', *Journal of the Aeronautical Sciences*, August 1955.

2.43 Pappas C E and Kunen A E, 'An Investigation of the Aerodynamics of Sharp Leading Edge Swept Wings at Low Speeds', *Journal of the Aeronautical Sciences*, October 1951.

2.44 Marchaj CA, 'Design Factors Affecting Sail Power Based on Wind Tunnel Research into Rigs Used for Fishing Vessels, Part 2', 1987.

2.45 Werle H, '*Structures Décollements Ailes en Flèche*', Rech. Aèrosp. No 1980–2, *Mars–Avril*.

2.46 Davidson K S M, 'Some Experimental Studies of the Sailing Yacht', Stevens Inst. of Techn, T.M. No 130, 1930.

2.47 Glauert H, *The Elements of Aerofoil and Airscrew Theory*, Cambridge Univ. Press, 1942.

2.48 Marchaj C A, Tanner T A, 'Wind Tunnel Test on a ¼ Scale Dragon Rig', Southampton University, Rep No 14, 1964.

2.49 The word *turbulence* is used in technical literature in a rather vague sense to mean any departure from the condition of uniform and steady flow. The same word is used for a number of distinct flow concepts such as, for example, the turbulence within the boundary layer, ie, small scale, hardly visible to the naked eye variations in the flow direction and speed, and also large scale turbulent flow or, preferably, eddying flow with random fluctuations in direction and speed, observed and easily felt in the wake of houses, behind the sails set in running attitude, or behind high trees and other obstacles to the wind flow.

2.50 Weick F E, Shortal J A, 'The Effect of Multiple Fixed Slots and Trailing– Edge Flap on the Lift and Drag of a Clark Y Airfoil', NACA Report No 427, 1932 (NACA – National Advisory Committee for Aeronautics, now NASA – National Aeronautics and Space Administration).

2.51 Scherer I O, 'Aerodynamics of High-Performance Wing Sails', *Marine Technology*, July 1974.

2.52 Lachmann G V, '*Neuere Versuchsergebnisse mit Spaltflugeln*', Z. Flugtech. 15 (1924).

2.53 Goradia S H, Colwell G T, 'Analysis of High-Lift Wing Systems', *Aeronautical Quarterly* 26, (2), 1975.

2.54 Horton H P, 'Fundamental Aspects of Flow Separation under High-Lift Conditions', AGARD paper Vol 43, 1970.

2.55 Robinson R, 'Little America's Cup, US Wins War of Wings', *Sail* magazine, December 1978.

2.56 Interview, America's Cup News, *Seahorse* magazine, Sept/Oct, 1988.

2.57 Nonweiler T, 'Maximum Lift Data for Symmetrical Wings', *Aircraft Eng.* January 1955.

2.58 Abbot I H, Von Doenhoff A E, *Theory of Wing Sections*, Dover Publ, 1959.

2.59 Cahill I F, 'Summary of Section Data on Trailing-Edge High-Lift Devices', NACA Rep. 938, 1949.

2.60 'Oh For the Wings of a Cat', *Seahorse* magazine, December 1988.

2.61 'The Future of Offshore Racing', *Seahorse* magazine – No 52 May/June 1979.

2.62 Folkard HC, 'The Sailing Boat', 1870.

2.63 Prandtl L, 'Application of Modern Hydrodynamics to Aeronautics', NACA Rep 116, 1921.

Munk M, 'The Minimum Induced Drag of Airfoils', NACA Rep 121, 1921.

The expression 'induced drag' was suggested first by Munk, a leading German aerodynamicist, in the year 1917 in a note '*Spannweite und Luftwiderstand*' (Span and Resistance), *Technische Berichte*, Vol I p 199. This new term replaced the older one 'edge drag', initially introduced on account of the fact that 'if the span increases more and more and the influence of the two edges becomes less and less, so does the edge drag become less and less and finally will quite disappear. In an actual airplane the span, in comparison with the wing chord, is never very large and therefore there is always an edge drag'. This note was one of several classified German wartime reports on airplane aerodynamics.

Later, Max Munk, emigrated to the USA to become a professor holding a chair of aerodynamics in one of the American Universities.

2.64 Lighthill J, 'Aquatic Animal Locomotion', Trans. NECIES, Vol 93, 1977.

2.65 Marchaj C A, *Seaworthiness: The Forgotten Factor*, Adlard Coles Nautical UK and International Marine USA, 1986.

2.66 Van Dam C P, 'Efficiency Characteristics of Crescent-Shaped Wings and Caudal Fins', *Nature*, 29 January 1987.

2.67 Ashenberg I and Weihs D, 'Minimum Induced Drag of Wings with Curved Planform', *Journal of Aircraft*, January 1984.

2.68 Wagner B and Boese P, '*Windkanaluntersuchungen einer Segelyacht mit verschiedenen Segelführungen*', Int. für Schiffbau der Univ Hamburg, Bericht No 207, 1968.

2.69 Nissen G, '*Der neue Dreh: Halben Winds mit dichten Schoten*', *Yacht* mag. 4, 1974.

2.70 Spens P G, 'Sailboat Test Technique together with Note on 'Preliminary Estimation of Sail Coefficients from *Yeoman* Sailing Trials', Note No 509, 1960 Stevens Institute of Technology, USA.

2.71 'The Aero Rig', *Seahorse* mag, July 1991. For further information contact: Carbospars, Hamble Point Quay, School Lane, Hamble, Hants.

2.72 Pannel I R, and others, 'Experiments on Models of Biplane Wings', Rep. & Memor No 196, also Nos 648, 774, 857.

2.73 Stinton D, *The Design of the Aeroplane*, Granda Publishing, 1983.

2.74 Hannay I, Private correspondence, December 1984.

2.75 Marchaj C A, 'Wind Tunnel Tests of a ⅓ Scale Model of an X-One-Design Yacht's Sails', ACYR Rep No 52, 1962.

2.76 Most readers will probably be acquainted with *Sod's Law* which suggests that: when sailing, 90 per cent of your journey will be made to destinations which are upwind of your departure. But some have experienced passages which have been made on just one heading, without a single tack or jibe.

2.77 Some unpublished reports on J-Class development; 'Yacht Wind Tunnel', by M S Hooper (see Figs 62 and 63a).

2.78 a)*The Best of Sail Trim*, Adlard Coles Nautical, 1975.
b) *More Sail Trim*, edited by A Madden, Adlard Coles Nautical, London, 1979.
c) *Sails*, Howard-Williams J, Sixth edition, Adlard Coles Nautical, 1988.
d) *Sail Power*, Ross W, Adlard Coles Nautical, 1975.

2.79 'The Race Course', 'Mainsail Trim', *Yachting World*, March 1984.

2.80 The *groove* can be defined as the optimal combination of sail trim, boat speed and pointing ability at which the boat comes alive. Helmsmen are always searching for the groove when sailing upwind.

2.81 Johnson P, and others, *Yachtsman's Guide to the Rating Rule*, Nautical Publishing Co, 1971.

2.82 The large overlapping foresail made its début at the Genoa Week regatta in 1927 on the 6 Metre class *Lilian*. The owner of the boat, Sven Salen, was first to spot the advantage of carrying free unmeasured sail area; the rule was, for the Metre boats, that only the foretriangle and not the actual area of the jib was measured. Strangely enough, the Metre class rules were never altered to prevent exploitation of this loophole. There is no doubt that *unmeasured* sail area makes a boat go faster than it will with a non-overlapping jib. Understandably, overlapping sails (named by the Americans *genoas*) proliferated and were soon used by cruising people – a rather silly imitation, since *unmeasured sail area* does not offer the advantages enjoyed by racing people due to the measurement fault.

The big genoas have been also encouraged by a similar feature of all rating rules; that is, that spinnaker size is linked to headsail size, and both are related to the size of the fore-triangle. Bearing in mind the racing advantages, it is rather surprising that fore-triangles, genoas and spinnakers did not grow bigger at the expense of mainsails more quickly, but this is probably because there is an inevitable reluctance to change the established ways of doing things and try something different.

2.83 Fox Uffa, *Thoughts on Yachts and Yachting*, Charles Scribners Sons, 1939.

2.84 Herreshoff Francis, *The Common Sense of Yacht Design, Vol. II*, Maritime Books, NY, 1973.

After the revision in 1956 of the RORC and IYRU formulas, it was agreed to take the area of the headsails as (I × J), in other words, the total area of the fore-triangle. The overlap was limited to 0.5J.

In the American CCA Rule, the foresail area was taken as 1.2 × fore-triangle area, and there was no limit or tax on overlap. Figure 238a shows the genoa according to both RORC and CCA Rules.

Figure 238b shows *Myth of Malham* carrying her enormous masthead CCA genoa.

Because of the greater proportion of headsail area to total sail area, there had to be a large number of headsails so that the correct combination could be selected for any weather condition and course. This is expensive and demands considerable skill from the crew when changing and trimming the sails for each course and wind strength.

2.85 Pedrick D R, McCurdy R, 'Yacht Performance Analysis with Computers', Chesapeake Sailing Yacht Symposium, Annapolis 1981.

2.86 Marchaj C A, 'Wind Tunnel Blockage Effects on a Soft Sail at Incidence Angles Beyond Stalled Flow', SUYR Report No 35, August 1973.

2.87 Eiffel G, *The Resistance of the Air and Aviation*, Constable & Co Ltd, London, 1913. also: Göttingen Aerodynamic Inst, *'Ergebnisse der Aerodynamische Versuchanstalt'*, 1922.

2.88 Written contribution of J Flewitt to the RINA paper, 1980: 'Methods to Determine the Hydrodynamic Centre of Lateral Resistance and Directional Stability of Yacht Forms' by C H Williamson.

2.89 Fourney M E, and Baker D B, 'Contour Mapping of Sailboat Sail', 5 Interfac Symposium, California, 1974.

REFERENCES AND NOTES (PART 3)

3.1 Maury M F, *Maury's Sailing Directions*, 4th Edition, 1852.

3.2 Saunders M, 'Pilot and Routing Charts', *Sail* magazine, 1975.

3.3 Atkins J E, and Painting D J, 'Wind Propulsion of Ships – Climatological Factors', Symposium on Wind Propulsion of Commercial Ships, RINA Nov 1980.

3.4 Sherlock R H, and Stout M B, 'Wind Structure in Winter Storms', *Journal of the Aeronautic Sciences 5*, 1971.

3.5 Frey A H, 'Handling Heavy Weather – the Microburst', and Chatterton H A, and Maxham J C, 'Sailing Vessel Stability', New England Sailing Yacht Symposium, March 1988.

3.6 Thwaites B (editor), 'Incompressible Aerodynamics' – Oxford University Press, 1960.

3.7 Wieselberger C, 'Electric Measurement of Forces by Varying an Inductivity' Forsch. Ber. 266, 1935.

3.8 Kramer M, '*Die Zunahme des Maximalauftriebes von Tragflugeln bei plotzlicher Anstellwinkelvergrosserung*' Z. Flugtechn. Motorluft 23, 1932.
Farren W S, 'The Reaction on a Wing whose Angle of Incidence is Changing Rapidly, Br. Aeron. Res. Com., R.M. No 1648, 1935.

3.9 Bishop R, Burcher R, and Price W, 'On the Linear Representation of Fluid Forces in Unsteady Flow', *Journal of Sound and Vibration*, Vol. 29, 1973.

3.10 Fung Y C, 'An Introduction to the Theory of Aeroelasticity', Dover Publication Inc, NY, 1969.

3.11 Newsletter of the Finn Association of Victoria, Australia, and Finnfare, Fall 1982, by Shimon-Craig Van Collie.

3.12 Katzmayr R, '*Zeitschrift für Flugtechnik und Motorluftschifffahrt*', March 31 and April 15, 1922. ('Effect of Periodic Changes of Angle of Attack on the Behaviour of an Airfoil').

3.13 Karman von T, *Aerodynamics*, McGraw-Hill, NY, 1963.

3.14 Toussaint, Kerneis and Girault, 'Experimental Investigation of the Effect of an Oscillating Airstream (Katzmayr Effect) on the Characteristics of Airfoils', NACA Techn. Note No 202.

3.15 Cowley W L, 'A Note on the Katzmayr Effect, that is, the Effect on the Characteristics of an Aerofoil Produced by an Oscillating Airstream', Rep. and Mem. No 969, March 1925, British ARC.

INDEX